THE BLACK WORKER

Vol. I

The Black Worker to 1869

Other volumes in this series:

The Black Worker

A Documentary History from Colonial
Times to the Present

Volume I

The Black Worker
to 1869

Edited by
Philip S. Foner and Ronald L. Lewis

Temple University Press, Philadelphia

Temple University Press, Philadelphia 19122
© by Temple University. All rights reserved
Published 1978
Printed in the United States of America

Library of Congress Cataloging in Publication Data
  Main entry under title:

The Black worker.

    Includes index.
    CONTENTS: v. 1. The Black worker to 1869.
    1. Afro-Americans--Employment. 2. Afro-Americans
    --Economic conditions. 3. United States--Race rela-
    tions. I. Foner, Philip Sheldon, 1910-
    II. Lewis, Ronald L., 1940-
    E185.B59   331.6'3'96073   78-2875
    ISBN 0-87722-136-7 (v. 1)

To Roslyn and Susan

TABLE OF CONTENTS

PART I

BLACK LABOR IN THE OLD SOUTH

PART II

RACE RELATIONS IN OLD SOUTHERN INDUSTRIES

PART III

FREE BLACK LABOR IN THE NORTH

PART IV

LIVING CONDITIONS AND RACE RELATIONS IN THE NORTH

PART V

BLACK WORKERS IN SPECIFIC TRADES

PART VIII

CONDITION OF THE WORKER DURING EARLY RECONSTRUCTION

ACKNOWLEDGEMENTS

The compilation of this volume and other volumes in this series would
have been impossible without the cooperation of the staffs of many historical societies, state libraries, college and university libraries, and public and private libraries. We wish to take this opportunity, in connection
with the present volume, to express our gratitude to the staffs of the Historical Society of Pennsylvania, New York Historical Society, Rhode Island
Historical Society, Connecticut Historical Society, New Jersey Historical
Society, Maryland Historical Society, Historical Society of Delaware,
Charleston (South Carolina) Library Society, Library of Congress, New York
State Historical Association, New York Public Library, Boston Public Libra-
ry, Virginia State Library, Harvard University Library, New York University
Library, Columbia University Library, Library Company of Philadelphia,
Brown University Library, Schomburg Library, New York Public Library System,
Howard University Library, and the National Archives. We owe a special debt
to the library staff of Lincoln University library, especially the inter-
library loan department, for assistance in obtaining materials from libraries and historical societies.
    We wish to thank Mrs. Roslyn Foner, who designed these volumes and gave
us the benefit of her considerable experience in production. Also, we are
indebted to the Black American Studies Program at the University of Delaware, under the direction of professor James E. Newton, which has been generous with its material assistance and the use of its facilities. Most im-
portantly, we owe our appreciation to Mrs. Gail Brittingham, whose efforts
at the typewriter transformed a garbled manuscript into a readable book.

                                                    Philip S. Foner
                                                    Ronald L. Lewis

PREFACE

There are several documentary histories of Black America, but *The Black Worker: A Documentary History From Colonial Times to the Present* represents the first compilation of original materials which encompasses the entire history of Afro-American labor. Since the vast majority of Afro-Americans are, and always have been, "workers," this series fills a crucial gap in our understanding of a hitherto neglected, but highly significant, aspect of the black experience. Consequently, it is hoped that this collection will do for the black working class what John R. Commons, most particularly, did for the white working class in his famous *Documentary History of American Industry*.

Volume I, *The Black Worker to 1869,* launches a four-volume series on the nineteenth century. Since there are numerous documentary histories relating to the experience of slaves in agriculture, including two recent studies by Willie Rose Lee and John Blassingame, this volume deals only with "the other slaves," the mechanics, artisans, and craftsmen. The major importance of this volume, however, is that it presents the first detailed picture of free black workers during the slave era, both in the North and the South. In the participants' own words, it chronicles the daily conditions of life and work among black people during the Civil War, and concludes with a portrait of the entire black working class during the early years of Reconstruction and the formation of the Colored National Labor Union, the first federation of black labor unions.

Volume II, *The Era of the National Labor Union* (1870s), documents the economic and organizational activities of black workers, and race relations between black and white workers during this turbulent period of labor unrest.

Other volumes in the series on the nineteenth century include Volume III, *The Era of the Knights of Labor* (1880s), and Volume IV, *The Era of the American Federation of Labor and the Railway Brotherhoods* (1890s).

A second series of four volumes examining the twentieth century, presents documents relating to the black worker during the period from World War I to the present, and will follow publication of the volumes in the present series.

The documents are accompanied by introductions and notes which are intended to provide background information essential to understanding the documents themselves. In order to maintain authenticity, as well as the "flavor" of the period, we have retained the original spellings, except where they were obvious typographical errors, or where they obscured the meaning of the text. Even though there are obvious mechanical limitations inherent in this effort, nevertheless, we have attempted to preserve these documents in their original form.

We hope these volumes will stimulate an interest in black labor history among laymen and students, while at the same time provide scholars with a wealth of little-known primary source materials, and suggest new lines of inquiry for future research.

Philip S. Foner
Lincoln University,
Pennsylvania

Ronald L. Lewis
University of Delaware

PART I

BLACK LABOR IN THE OLD SOUTH

Part I

BLACK LABOR IN THE OLD SOUTH

Until the end of the Civil War, slaves constituted the backbone of the southern labor force. While picking cotton and other agricultural employments are commonly associated with black bondsmen, it is not so widely known that they also predominated in craft and industrial labor as well. The Documents in Part I reveal the use and extent of slave labor in the Old South, and some of the unique occupational patterns which developed under the "peculiar institution."

An overview of the Afro-American prevalence in southern crafts is presented in Documents 1-3, with W. E. B. Du Bois and A. G. Dill suggesting that this propensity could be attributed to African ancestry (Doc. 1). Whether or not their assertion is true, slaves were found in all the crafts, from the most skilled to the least skilled. Documents 4-23 clearly show the variety of skills practiced by slave craftsmen. Equally striking is the significance of slave labor in virtually all of the important southern industries. In fact, it is difficult to see how most industries could have operated without bonded labor. Documents 24-37 indicate the extent of this omnipresence. According to the famous southern novelist Thomas Nelson Page, in 1865 blacks held "without a rival the entire field of industrial labor throughout the South." Indeed, Page claimed that "ninety-five per cent of all the industrial work of the southern states" was performed by black labor (Doc. 24). While this was an exaggeration, slaves were heavily concentrated in the industries.

The skills these slaves learned naturally increased their economic value. Because the slave artisan or mechanic could not be regulated as easily as the farm hand, especially in urban areas, he usually enjoyed more mobility than his more regimented brother in the field. While owners frequently hired, or leased, the services of their slaves to industrial employers, for example, bondsmen sometimes were permitted to hire their own time. As long as their earnings were turned over to the master, these slave mechanics experienced a relative freedom. This was not entirely enviable for frequently the hired mechanic encountered physical and psychological difficulties with his work which were as unique as the status itself (Doc. 38-40). Because slave artisans and mechanics were in great demand, they frequently used their free time to perform extra work for money which they kept for themselves. Sometimes they were able to accumulate enough money to purchase freedom for themselves or for loved ones, several cases of which are indicated in Documents 41-45.

Nevertheless, like other slaves, black artisans and mechanics yearned for freedom. In fact, that degree of liberty which they did enjoy only highlighted the inability to control their own destinies, which represented the most disillusioning aspect of bondage. When it became too unbearable, these "privileged" bondsmen often fled to freedom in the North. Frederick Douglass' own escape from a Baltimore shipyard is a pointed example (Doc. 46).

By the 1850s, perhaps as many as ten per cent of the black population of the South consisted of free people of color. Even though their status is best described as "quasi-free," being grossly restricted by malevolent laws designed to keep them under white control, free blacks also labored in every occupation requiring all degrees of skill to be found in the region. Documents 47-58 describe the range of free black occupations in the Old South and some of the discrimination black workers experienced.

BLACKS IN THE CRAFTS AND INDUSTRIES OF THE OLD SOUTH

1. AN OVERVIEW: AFRICA

Is there any evidence of mechanical skill among the African natives? A glimpse into African life may help us to answer . . . ; for among the Pygmies, the Hottentots, the Bushmen, the Ashantis and in practically all parts of the continent of Africa, we find concrete evidences of that ability which makes for artisanship.

While the Pygmies, still living in the age of wood, make no iron or stone implements, they seem to know how to make bark cloth and fibre baskets and simple outfits for hunting and fishing. Among the Bushmen the art of making weapons and working in hides is quite common. The Hottentots are further advanced in the industrial arts, being well versed in the manufacture of clothing, weapons and utensils. In the dressing of skins and furs as well as in the plaiting of cords and the weaving of mats we find evidences of their workmanship. In addition, they are good workers in iron and copper, using the skeepskin bellows for this purpose. The Ashantis of the "Gold Coast" know how to make "cotton fabrics, turn and glaze earthenware, forge iron, fabricate instruments and arms, embroider rugs and carpets, and set gold and precious stones." Among the people of the banana zone we find rough basket work, coarse pottery, grass cloth, and spoons made of wood and ivory. The people of the millet zone, because of uncertain agricultural resources, quite generally turn to manufacturing. Charcoal is prepared by the smiths, iron is smelted and numerous implements are manufactured. Among them we find axes, hatchets, hoes, knives, nails, scythes and other hardware. Cloaks, shoes, sandals, shields and water and oil vessels are made from leather which the natives have dressed. Soap is manufactured in the Bautschi district, glass is melted, formed and colored by the people of Nupeland, and in almost every city cotton is spun and woven and dyed. Barth tells us that the weaving of cotton was known in the Sudan as early as the eleventh century. There is also extensive manufacture of wooden ware, tools, implements and utensils.

Leo Africanus writing of Timbuctu in the sixteenth century said: "It is a woonder to see what plentie of Merchandize is dayly brought hither and how costly and sumptuous all things be. . . . Here are many shops of artificiers and merchants and especially of such as weave linnen and cloth." [1]

Kuka, on the west shore of Lake Tchad, and Sokoto, in the northwestern part of the empire of the same name, are the principal manufacturing centers of this district. Here cotton is spun and woven into cloth; skins are tanned and manufactured into boots, shoes and saddles; and implements, ornaments and tools are wrot of iron.

Thruout the continent of Africa we find evidences of the industrial ability of the natives. Anthropologist and geologist, scientist and man of letters alike record the achievements of the African people along this line.

W. E. B. Du Bois and Augustus Granville Dill (eds.), "The Negro-American Artisan," Atlanta University Publications, No. 17 (Atlanta 1912), pp. 25-26.

2. AN OVERVIEW: THE AMERICAN SOUTH

During the days of slavery the Negro mechanic was a man of importance. He was a most valuable slave to his master. He would always sell for from two to three times as much in the market as the unskilled slaveman. When a fine Negro mechanic was to be sold at public auction, or private sale, the wealthy slave owners would vie with each other for the prize and run the bidding often up into high figures.

The slave owners early saw the aptitude of the Negro to learn handicraft, and fully appreciating what vast importance and value this would be to
them (the masters) selected their brightest young slavemen and had them
taught in the different kinds of trades. Hence on every large plantation you
could find the Negro carpenter, blacksmith, brick and stone mason. These
trades comprehended and included much more in their scope in those days than
they do now. Carpentry was in its glory then. What is done now by varied
and complicated machinery was wrot then by hand. The invention of the
planing machine is an event within the knowledge of many persons living
today. Most of our wood-working machinery has come into use long since the
days of slavery. The same work done now with the machine, was done then by
hand. The carpenter's chest of tools in slavery times was a very elaborate
and expensive outfit. His "kit" not only included all the tools that the
average carpenter carries now, but also the tools for performing all the work
done by the various kinds of "wood-working" machines. There is little opportunity for the carpenter of today to acquire, or display, genuis and skill in
his trade as could the artisan of old.

One only needs to go down South and examine hundreds of old southern
mansions, and splendid old church edifices, still intact, to be convinced of
the fact of the cleverness of the Negro artisan, who constructed nine-tenths
of them, and many of them still provoke the admiration of all who see them,
and are not to be despised by the men of our day.

There are few, if any, of the carpenters of today who, if they had the
hand tools, could get out the "stuff" and make one of those old style mas-
sive panel doors,--who could work out by hand the mouldings, the stiles, the
mullions, etc., and build one of those windows, which are to be found today
in many of the churches and public buildings of the South; all of which testify to the cleverness of the Negro's skill as artisan in the broadest sense
of the term. For the carpenter in those days was also the "cabinet maker,"
the wood turner, coffin maker, generally the pattern maker, and the maker of
most things made of wood. The Negro blacksmith held almost absolute sway in
his line, which included the many branches of forgery, and other trades which
are now classified under different heads from that of the regular blacksmith.
The blacksmith in the days of slavery was expected to make any and everything
wrot of iron.. He was to all intents and purposes the "machine blacksmith,"
"horseshoer," "carriage and wagon ironer and trimmer," "gunsmith," "wheelwright;" and often whittled out and ironed the hames, the plowstocks, and the
"single-tree" for the farmers, and did a hundred other things too numerous to
mention. They were experts at tempering edge tools, by what is generally
known as the water process. But many of them had secret processes of their
own for tempering tools which they guarded with zealous care.

It was a good fortune of your humble servant to have served his time as
an apprentice in a general blacksmithing shop, or shop of all work, presided
over by an ex-slave genius known thruout the state as a "master mechanic."
In slavery time this man hired his own time,--paying his master a certain
stipulated amount of money each year, and all he made over and above that
amount was his own.

The Negro machinists were also becoming numerous before the downfall of
slavery. The slave owners were generally the owners of all the factories,
machine shops, flour-mills, saw-mills, gin-houses and threshing machines.
They owned all the railroads and the shops connected with them. In all of
these the white laborer and mechanic had been supplanted almost entirely by
the slave mechanics at the time of the breaking out of the Civil War. Many
of the railroads in the South had their entire train crews, except the conductors, made up of the slaves--including engineers and firemen. The "Georgia Central" had inaugurated just such a movement, and had many Negro engineers on its locomotives and Negro machinists in its shops. . . .

From a letter of J. D. Smith, stationary engineer, Chicago, Ill., quoted in
W. E. B. Du Bois and Augustus Granville Dill (eds.), "The Negro American
Artisan," Atlanta University Publications, No. 17 (Atlanta, 1912), pp. 34-36.

3. THE SLAVE MECHANIC

An ex-governor of Mississippi says:
"Prior to the war there were a large number of Negro mechanics in the
Southern States; many of them were expert blacksmiths, wheelwrights, wagon-
makers, brick-masons, carpenters, plasterers, painters and shoemakers. They
became masters of their respective trades by reason of sufficiently long service under the control and direction of expert white mechanics. During the
existence of slavery the contract for qualifying the Negro as a mechanic was
made between his owner and the master workman."
Such slaves were especially valuable and formed usually a privileged
class, with a large degree of freedom. They were very often hired out by
their masters and sometimes hired their own time although this latter practice was frowned upon as giving slaves too much freedom and nearly all states
forbade it by law; although some, like Georgia, permitted the custom in certain cities. In all cases the slave mechanic was encouraged to do good work
by extra wages which went into his own pocket. For instance, in the semi-
skilled work of the Tobacco factories, the Virginia master received from $150
-$200 annually for his slave and the employer fed him; but the slave, by
extra work, could earn for himself $5 or more a month. So carpenters some-
times received as much as $2 a day for their masters, and then were given the
chance to earn more for themselves. In Texas nine slaves, some of them carpenters, were leased at an average of $280.22 a year and probably earned
something over this. If the mechanic was a good workman and honest the master was tempted to allow him to do as he pleased so long as he paid the master a certain yearly income. In this way there arose in nearly all Southern
cities a class of Negro clients free in everything but name; they owned property, reared families and often lived in comfort. In earlier times such
mechanics often bought themselves and families and became free, but as the
laws began to bear hard on free Negroes they preferred to remain under the
patronage and nominal ownership of their white masters. In other cases they
migrated North and there worked out their freedom, sending back stipulated
sums. Many if not most of the noted leaders of the Negro in earlier times
belonged to this slave mechanic class, such as Vesey, Nat Turner, Richard
Allen and Absalom Jones. They were exposed neither to the corrupting privileges of the house servants nor to the blighting tyranny of field work and
had large opportunity for self development. [2]
Usually the laws did not hinder the slaves from learning trades. On the
other hand the laws against teaching slaves really hindered the mechanics
from attaining very great efficiency save in rare cases--they must work by
rule of thumb usually. North Carolina allowed slaves to learn mathematical
calculations, but not reading and writing; Georgia in 1833 decreed that no
one should permit a Negro "to transact business for him in writing." Gradually such laws became more severe: Mississippi in 1830 debarred slaves from
printing offices and Georgia in 1845 declared that slaves and free Negroes
could not take contracts for building and repairing houses as mechanics or
masons. Restrictions, however, were not always enforced, especially in the
building trades, and the slave mechanic flourished.
There were, no doubt, many very efficient slave mechanics. One who
learned his trade from a slave writes us an interesting and enthusiastic account of the work of these men:
"During the days of slavery the Negro mechanic was a man of importance.
He was a most valuable slave to his master. He would always sell for from
two to three times as much in the market as the unskilled slaveman. When a
fine Negro mechanic was to be sold at public auction, or private sale, the
wealthy slave owners would vie each other for the prize and run the bidding
up into high figures.
"The slave owners each saw the aptitude of the Negro to learn handicraft,
and fully appreciated what vast importance and value this would be to them
(the masters) selected their brightest young slavemen and had them taught in
the different kinds of trades. Hence on every large plantation you could
find the Negro carpenter, blacksmith, brick and stone mason. These trades
comprehended and included much more in their scope in those days than they do
now. Carpentry was in its glory then. What is done now by varied and

complicated machinery was wrought then by hand. The invention of the planing
machine is an event within the knowledge of many persons living today. Most
of our 'wood working' machinery has come into use long since the days of
slavery. The same work done now with the machine, was done then by hand.
The carpenter's chest of tools in slavery times was a very elaborate and expensive outfit. His 'kit' not only included all the tools that the average
carpenter carries now, but also the tools for performing all the work done by
the various kinds of 'wood-working' machines. There is little opportunity
for the carpenter of to-day to acquire, or display, genius and skill in his
trade as could the artisan of old.

     "One only needs to go down South and examine hundreds of old Southern
mansions, and splendid old church edifices, still intact, to be convinced of
the fact of the cleverness of the Negro artisan, who constructed nine-tenths
of them, and many of them still provoke the admiration of all who see them,
and are not to be despised by the men of our day.

W. E. B. Du Bois, The Negro Artisan (Atlanta, 1902), pp. 15-16.

SLAVE CRAFTSMEN IN AMERICA

4. PLANTATION CRAFTSMEN

     My father had among his slaves carpenters, coopers, sawyers, black-
smiths, tanners, curriers, shoemakers, spinners, weavers and knitters, and
even a distiller. His woods furnish timber and plank for the carpenters and
coopers, and charcoal for the blacksmith; his cattle killed for his own consumption and for sale supplied skins for the tanners, curriers, and shoemakers, and his sheep gave wool and his fields produced cotton and flax for
the weavers and spinners, and his orchards fruit for the distiller. His
carpenters and sawyers built and kept in repair all the dwelling-houses,
barns, stables, ploughs, barrows, gates &c., on the plantations and the out-
houses at the home house. His coopers made the hogsheads the tobacco was
prised in and the tight casks to hold the cider and other liquors. The tanners and curriers with the proper vats &c., tanned and dressed the skins as
well for upper as for lowere leather to the full amount of the consumption of
the estate, and the shoemakers made them into shoes for the negroes. . . .
The blacksmiths did all the iron work required by the establishment, as making and repairing ploughs, harrow, teeth chains, bolts &c., &c. The spinners, weavers and knitters made all the coarse cloths and stockings used by
the negroes, and some of finer texture worn by the white family, nearly all
worn by the children of it. The distiller made every fall a good deal of
apple, peach and persimmon brandy. . . . All these operations were carried
on at the home house, and their results distributed as occasion required to
the different plantations. Moreover all the beeves and hogs for consumption
or sale were driven up and slaughtered there at the proper seasons, and whatever was to be preserved was salted and packed away for after distribution.

*Edmund S. Morgan, Virginians at Home: Family Life in the Eighteenth Century
(Charlottesville, Va., 1963), pp. 53-54.*

5. FUGITIVE SKILLS

Approximately 1,500 notices in newspapers published from 1736 to 1801 in Williamsburg, Richmond, and Fredericksburg were analyzed, including all notices in all of the various editions of the *Virginia Gazette* that are extant. These described 1,138 men and 142 women. . . .

Thirty-two percent (359 of the 1,138) fugitives were listed as skilled. Almost 50 per cent of this group (168) were tradesmen; one in four (89) were house servants, nearly the same proportion (85) were slaves who "went by water," and 17 slightly less than 5 per cent, worked in small-scale extractive and craft industries (forges, mines, ropewalks, etc.).

N.B. Among the 30-odd artisans skilled in more than one trade (usually in combination with carpentry or shoemaking) were 19 not listed below, among whom were: a butcher, scytheman, coarse carpenter, a currier, a whiskey distiller, and a flax spinner.

Artisans ("Tradesmen")
blacksmiths; one also a carpenter (20)
shoemakers (47)
    shoe- and harness-maker (1)
    shoemakers who were also skilled as carpenters, blacksmiths, house
    servants or watermen (18)
woodworkers; about one-sixth of all skilled fugitives (60)
    carpenters (18)
    sawyers (14)
    carpenters and coopers (12)
    coopers (9)
    carpenters and sawyers (4)
    ship's-carpenter (1)
    carpenter and joiner (1)
    sawyer and clapboarder (1)
wheelwrights; all skilled in other crafts (3)
    wheelwright, house-carpenter, joiner, and carpenter (1)
    wheelwright, carpenter, glazier, and painter (1)
    wheelwright, house-carpenter, and sawyer (1)
wagonmakers and wheelwrights; one also a blacksmith (2)
bricklayers (2)
miller (1)
millwrights (2)
tailors (5)
weaver (1)
pressman (1)
painter and carpenter (1)
house-carpenter, cooper, bricklayer, plasterer, whitewasher, and gardener (1)

Slaves who Worked on the Water
watermen (55), 14 per cent of all skilled slave runaways, including those
designated:
    flatboatman (1)
    skippers of flats (2)
    pilots (2)
    ferrymen (3)
    sailors (30)

House Servants
waitingmen (37), 10 per cent of all skilled fugitives
hostlers (11)
jockeys (4)
brabers (3)
cooks (2)
gardeners (3)
hostler and jockey (1)
servants in inns and taverns (2)

coachmen (2)
unspecfied house servants (24)

Fugitives from Small-scale Extractive and Craft Industries
ironworkers (6)
    Hunter's Iron forge (1)
    Jerdone and Holt's Providence Forge, New Kent County (1)
    John Tayloe's Neabasco Furnace, Maryland; also a runaway, listed as
    an artisan, from his Prince William, Occoquan Iron Furnace (2)
    Mossy Creek Ironworks, Augusta County (1)
    Isaac Zane's Marlborough Furnace, Frederick County (1)
laborers, public Armory, Westham, Henrico County (3)
miners (3)
    Moses Austin and Co., lead mine, Augusta County (2)
    William Kennan's Mine, Buckingham County (1)
ropemakers (3)
    Chatham Rope Walk, New Kent County (1)
    Campbell Rope Walk, Norfolk (2)
saltmakers (2)
laborer, Dismal Swamp Land Company (1)
canal worker, Richmond City, J. Ballendine and T. Southall, managers (1)
warehouseman (1)

*Gerald W. Mullin, Flight and Rebellion: Slave Resistance in Eighteenth-
Century Virginia (New York, 1972), pp. 57, 94-96.*

6. CARPENTERS, CAULKERS, BRICKLAYERS

This is to forewarn all Manner of Persons whatsoever, not to employ two
Negro Carpenters, . . . Mingo and Norwich, belonging to Lawrence Dennis of
Charles town, without first agreeing with the said Dennis, or his Spouse for
the same.

This is to give Notice to all Persons, that they do not hire or employ
these following Negroes . . . Cuffee and Beavour, two Caulkers, and Anselm a
Bricklayer, without first agreeing with . . . Nicholas Trott, or Sarah his
Wife.

John Vaughan and Ralph Rodda Bricklayer[s] having two Negro Boys brought
up to their Trade, which are employed by Persons without their Master's
Leave or Licence, they hereby forwarn all and every Person from doing so in
the future.

South Carolina Gazette, January 20, 1733; March 10, 1733; July 31, 1736.

7. SAWYERS

Run away near two Years, two Negro Men (being Sawyers) . . . , by Names
Quamino and Quacco short, but very well Set, they both speak English very
well, and are so crafty, that they would almost deceive any Body, and if

taken, will frame a very Plausible Story that they are not runaways: The
said Quacco is mark'd in the Forehead with Gunpowder thus RS.

South Carolina Gazette, August 4, 1733.

8. WHITE WASHER

Whereas a Negro-Man named Lancaster, commonly known about the Two for a
White washer, and Fisherman, has of late imposed upon his Employers, and defrauded me of his Wages; I do therefore advertise all Persons not to employ
the said Lancaster, without first agreeing with me, or his producing a proper Ticket, unless they are willing to pay the Fine prescribed by Law; and
all Negroes who shall carry the said Lancaster a Fishing, shall be rigorously
prosecuted by Elizabeth Smith.

Whereas I have formerly advertis'd all Persons not to employ my Negro-
Man Lancaster in white washing or any other kind of Work whatever, but to
little Purpose; since he constantly earns Money (which he loses either by
Gaming or spends among the little Punch-Houses.) altho' he has been run away
for this Month past: I do therefore once more peremptorily forbid all Persons from employing the said Lancaster in any Manner whatever, unless they
first agree with, and have a Ticket from Dr. Dale, and pay unto him whatever
Money the said Lancaster shall earn, otherwise they will assuredly be prosecuted according to Law.

                                                        Elizabeth Smith

South Carolina Gazette, December 25, 1740; October 17, 1741.

9. BRICKLAYERS

To be Let, to work in Charles Town, at five shillings a Day each, Four
able Negro Men, who have been used to labour for Brick layers.

South Carolina Gazette, December 7, 1747.

10. COOPER [3]

A Negro Man to be sold by Samuel Dunnscomb in New-Street, he is about
32 years of Age, understands most of the Cooper's Business: Price 90₤. he
has been some Voyages to Sea.

New York Gazette or Weekly Post-Boy, August 28, 1763.

11.   JACK-OF-ALL-TRADES

He is an indifferent shoemaker, a good butcher, ploughman, and carterer; an excellent sawyer, and waterman, understands breaking oxen well, and is one of the best sythemen, in *America;* in short, he is so ingenious a fellow, that he can turn his hand to any thing.

Virginia Gazette, October 27, 1768.

12.   WATCHMAKER

At Mr. *M'Lean's,* Watch-Maker near the Town-House, is a Negro Man whose extraordinary Genius has been assisted by one of the best Masters on *London;* he takes Faces at the lowest Rates. Specimens of his Performances may be seen at said Place.

Massachusetts Gazette, January 7, 1773.

13.   PAINTERS

The SUBSCRIBER,

Intending to leave the Province in April next,
            WILL DISPOSE OF
    His NEGRO FELLOWS, *Painters,*
      On Wednesday the Seventh of *April* next,
    At *his Yard in Queen-Street, directly opposite* Mr. CANNON'S
            AS to their Abilities, he thinks them evident, they having
transacted the Whole of his Business, without any hired Assistance;
and he has taken no little Pains in initiating them in the true Principles
of their Profession.
            LIKEWISE,
        A good HOUSE-WENCH,
Who can wash and iron exceeding well, and is a tolerable Cook.

                                JOHN ALLWOOD.

South Carolina Gazette, March 8, 1773.

14. GOLDSMITH

Philadelphia, April 27.

Eight Dollars Reward.

RAN-AWAY from the subscriber, a negro man, named JOHN FRANCES, but commonly called JACK: he is about 40 years of age, five feet ten inches high, ender [sic] built, speaks good English, by trade a goldsmith; he generally affects to be very polite, and it's more than probable he may pass for a freeman. Said negro was carried to New York and left in charge of Mr. Ephraim Brasher, goldsmith, from whom he absconded, and returned to me after skulking about this city for a considerable time: had on when he went away, an old gree coat, fustian waistcoat and breeches, a pair of half-boots, but may probably change his dress. All mates of vessels and others are forbid to harbour or carry him off at their peril. Whoever takes up said negro and delivers him to John Le Telier, goldsmith in Market street, or to the subscriber in New York, shall have the above reward, and all reasonable charges paid.

BENJAMIN HALSTED.

Pennsylvania Packet, May 1, 1784.

15. A SLAVE LOT

FIFTY PRIME NEGROES FOR SALE. To be sold on Tuesday, the 15th March Instant by the Subscribers, before their office near the Exchange.

About fifty prime orderly Negroes; consisting of Fellows, Wenches, Boys and Girls. This gang taken together, is perhaps as prime, complete and valuable for the numbers as were ever offered for sale; they are generally country born, young, able and very likely; two of them capable of acting as drivers, and one of them a good jobbing carpenter. The wenches are young, and improving; the boys, girls and children are remarkably smart, active and sensible; several of the wenches are fitted either for the house or plantation work; the boys and girls are trades or waiting servants. The age, descriptions and qualifications of these negroes, may be seen at the office of the Subscribers, and of Brian Cape and Son, or of Treasdale or Kiddell, merchants in Queen-street, who can give directions to those who desire it where the negroes may be seen. . . .

Charleston City Gazette, March 10, 1796.

16. BLACKSMITH'S APPRENTICE

WANTED IMMEDIATELY.--As an apprentice to the blacksmith's business, a smart, active boy, of from twelve to fifteen years of age, who can come well recommended. A black boy of this description will be taken. Wanted also, a

Journeyman who understands his business and has good recommendations for honesty, industry and sobriety. A black man would not be rejected.

ELLIS MADDOX, Nashville.

Tennessee Gazette and Mero District Advertiser, Nashville, October 24, 1804.

17. SHOEMAKER

GUY is a shoemaker by trade, and may probably endeavor to get employment--he carried off with him his tools of every description.

Richmond Enquirer, June 6, 1806.

18. BLACKSMITH'S APPRENTICE

APPRENTICES WANTED.--The subscriber carrying on the blacksmith's business in all its branches on Reynold street, near Calffrey and Bustin's hotel, would willingly receive three Negro fellows as apprentices. The owners may confidently rely that every necessary attention will be given to their instruction. J. J. PERIN.

Augusta (Ga.) Chronicle, March 2, 1811.

19. SEAMSTRESS

To be hired immediately, a very complete Seamstress; a complete worker of muslin, sober, and no runaway; she is a young colored Woman in her eighteenth year; she is very fond of children, can make their clothes and dress them with taste.

Charleston Courier, October 11, 1813.

20. CARPENTER

Twenty Dollars Reward. Ran away on the 9th instant, from the plantation of David Aiken, Winnsborough, Fairfield District, a Negro Man named March, a Carpenter by trade, well known in this city as formerly the property of John Duncan, Esq. having worked at his Mills, for years. . . . March is about 5 feet 8 inches high; very black, with large whiskers, and a scar on the upper

lip. He had a forged pass, to pass him on to Charleston, where he no doubt
is now or in the neighborhood of this city.

Charleston Courier, December 12, 1826.

21. A SLAVE LOT

More negroes! Received from this day's steamer from Mobile, 42 likely
negroes, from Georgia and Virginia. Buyers are requested to call and see
for themselves. All descriptions: Field-hands, mechanics, cooks, washers
and ironers, and body servants. . . . Among them I have a No. 1 Blacksmith,
two seamstresses, two No. 1 Body-servants, and a Barber.

Louisiana Gazette, April 16, 1857.

22. ARTICLE OF APPRENTICESHIP

This Indenture witnesseth that Ignatius Digges of Prince George County
and Province of maryland gentlemen doth bind his Slave mulatto Jack to
William Nicols of said county carpenter to learn his Art or Mistery as a
carpenter and Joyner, and with him the said William Nicols after the manner
of an apprentice to serve from the day of the date hereof for and During the
Term of four years next running During which term the Said apprentice his
said master shall faithfully Serve and all his Lawfull Commands obey, and
further the Said Ignatius Digges covenanteth that in Case the said apprentice should be Sick that he will take him at his own expence, and the Said
William Nicols Shall procure and provide for him the Said Jack sufficient
meat Drink Appearil Lodging, and all Necessary Tools for Learning his Trade,
the Said William Nicols is also to pay his Levy and permitt the Said apprentice to go on Sundays and Hollydas to Church, when the Said Ignatius Digges
shall Direct, the said Nicols further agrees that he will not During the
Term aforesaid, Carry or permitt the said Apprentice to go out of the Province, in witness whereoff the parties have hereunto felt their hands and
Sealt this the thirty first day of July Anno Dom. 1771

    Witness
                                              Ign. Digges
        David Crawford
                                              Wm Nicolls

Maryland Historical Society, Ms. 446

23. APPRENTICE IRONWORKER

On Sept. 23, 1798 John Jones took Negro Jack into the forge to learn
him the trade of half-bloomer. To work nine months without pay and then
three years at 10/ per ton.

Joseph E. Walker, "Negro Labor in the Charcoal Iron Industry of Southeastern
Pennsylvania," Pennsylvania Magazine of History and Biography 93 (October,
1969):474.

INDUSTRIAL SLAVERY

24. A SOUTHERNER'S VIEW

In 1865, when the Negro was set free, he held without a rival the entire field of industrial labor throughout the South. Ninety-five per cent
of all the industrial work of the Southern States was in his hand. And he
was fully competent to do it. Every adult was either a skilled laborer or a
trained mechanic.

Thomas Nelson Page, The Southerner's Problem (New York, 1904), p. 127.

25. IRONWORKERS

Oxford Iron Works, Bedford County, October 16, 1777

I will give ready money for likely young Negroes from 15 to 20 Years of
Age. I would also hire between this and the first of January 50 or 60 Negro
Men for one, two, or three Years. One half the first Year's Hire will be
paid down, if required. The Situation of the Works is very healthy, the
Labour of the Slaves moderate, and they shall have a plentiful Diet. I will
allow an advanced Price for Carpenters and Wheelwrights, but will not be concerned with any that are noted Runaways. . . .

David Ross

Virginia Gazette, November 7, 1777.

26. COTTON FACTORY SLAVES

MANUFACTURES IN THE SOUTH. The capacity of the Southern States for
manufacturing their great staple, is no longer a matter of speculation.
Practical experiment has demonstrated, not only their capacity to manufacture, but to manufacture their own staple at a cheaper rate than any part of
the Union! Last February a year, I accompanied a most intelligent planter
from Pittsburgh to Nashville, a Mr. Nightingale, formerly of R. Island. He
was then taking with him a "foreman" from Providence, Rhode Island, to superintend his cotton factory.--The factory is located in Maury county, Tennessee. The machinery is propelled by a never failing, and never freezing
stream. The entire labour is performed by slaves. Mr. Nightingale now

supplies a large portion of Tennessee and North Alabama with coarse cotton cloths.

(Augusta), Georgia Courier, April 24, 1828, reprinted in Ulrich B. Phillips (ed.), A Documentary History of the American Industrial Society, Vol. II (Cleveland, 1910), p. 358.

27. STEVEDORES

It is quite astounding to see the legions of steamers from the upper country which are congregated here [New Orleans]; for miles and miles the levee forms one unbroken line of them, all lying with their noses on shore -- no room for broadsides. On arriving, piled up with goods mountain high, scarce does a bow touch the levee, when swarms of Irish and niggars rush down, and the mountainous pile is landed, and then dragged off by sturdy mules to its destination. Scarce is she cleared, when the same hardy sons of toil build another mountainous pile on board; the bell rings, passengers run, and she is facing the current and the dangers of the snaggy Mississippi. The labour of loading and unloading steamers is, as you may suppose, very severe, and is done for the most part by niggers and Irishmen. The average wages are from Ŀ7 to Ŀ8 per month; but, in times of great pressure from sudden demand, etc., they rise as high as from Ŀ12 to Ŀ14 per month, which was the case just before my arrival. The same wages are paid to those who embark in the steamers to load and unload at the different stations on the river. Every day is a working day, and as by law, the slave has his Sunday to himself to earn what he can, the master who hires him out on the river is suppose to give him one-seventh of the wages earned; but, I believe, they only receive one-seventh of the ordinary wages -- i.e., Ŀ1 per month.

H. A. Murray, Lands of the Slave and the Free, or Cuba, the U. S. and Canada, Vol. II (London: 1855), p. 25.

28. COAL MINERS

The Mid-Lothian Coal Mining Company wish to hire for the year 1846, able-bodied, healthy, well disposed Negro MEN: . . . The Company have been liberal in the expenditure of money and labour, to put their Mines in good working condition, and they are under the superintendence of skillful Mining Agents. . . . There is no service in which Slaves are better treated, fed, clothed, and attended in sickness, or enjoy better health. A well conducted Hospital, under the care of a careful steward, and daily attended by three Physicians, is provided at the Mines, and owners of slaves may have them secured from all Medical and Surgical charges, by the payment of three dollars each per annum.

No slaves are hired who are not willing to enter the Company's service, and it is desired that none of bad character should be offered, as the Company are using every effort to improve the moral character of their own slaves and hirelings, to which end, they have the present year sold three disorderly men. The slaves have a Church of their own at the Pits, and divine service is regularly performed on the Sabbath by white Ministers. At least one half of those now in the Company's service are temperance men, and the use of spirituous liquors discountenanced. The Company feel gratified in being able to say, that their slaves and hirelings are as orderly, well-behaved, and moral, generally, as a like number of labouring men any where

to be found. There is no work in which slaves are better satisfied and contented than coal-mining; and there is no service in which they have an equal
chance of making money for themselves. There have been fewer deaths amongst
the Company's hands from disease or casualties, since its organization some
12 years ago, than will be found in a like number of men any where. The
Company have in their employment several free coloured men, who hire themselves annually upon the same terms and conditions as slaves, and are subject to the same discipline, and have been so employed for years. They have
also in their Mines many white labourers.

There has been but one instance of any slave in the Company's service
being committed for felony, and that one was discharged at the instance of
the Commonwealth's Attorney, who states that the proof did not sustain the
charge. . . .

The lives of Slaves hired to the Midlothian Company can be insured at a
reasonable premium, if desired by the owners.

Richmond Whig and Public Advertiser, January 2, 1846.

29. COTTON FACTORY HANDS

On the banks of the Oconee river--one fork of which runs close by the
town of Athens, in a deep valley, the town itself being on a hill, and the
other forks at a distance for a few miles only--are three cotton factories,
all worked by water-power, and used for spinning yarn, and weaving cloth of
coarse qualities for local consumption only. I visited one of these, and
ascertained that the other two were very similar to it in size and operations. In each of them there are employed from 80 to 100 persons, and about
an equal number of white and black. In one of them, the blacks are the property of the mill-owner, but in the other two they are the slaves of planters,
hired out at monthly wages to work in the factory. There is no difficulty
among them on account of colour, the white girls working in the same room
and at the same loom with the black girls; and boys of each colour, as well
as men and women, working together without apparent repugnance or objection.
This is only one among the many proofs I had witnessed of the fact, that the
prejudice of colour is not nearly so strong in the South as in the North.
Here, it is not at all uncommon to see the black slaves of both sexes, shake
hands with white people when they meet, and interchange friendly personal
inquiries; but at the North I do not remember to have witnessed this once;
and neither in Boston, New York, or Philadelphia would white persons generally like to be seen shaking hands and talking familiarly with blacks in the
streets.

The negroes here are found to be quite as easily taught to perform all
the required duties of spinners and weavers as the whites, and are just as
tractable when taught; for their labour is dearer than that of the whites,
for whilst the free boys and girls employed receive about 700 dollars per
month, out of which they find themselves, the slaves are paid the same wages
(which is handed over to their owners,) and the mill-owner has to feed them
all in addition; so that the free labour is much cheaper to him than the
slave; and the hope expressed by the proprietor to me was, that the progressive increase of white population by immigration, would enable him to employ
wholly their free labour, which, to him would be more advantageous. The
white families engaged in these factories, live in loghuts clustered about
the establishment on the river's bank, and the negroes repair to the huts
allowed them by their owners when they are near, or stay at the mill, when
their master's plantation is far off.

*J. S. Buckingham, Slave States of America, Vol. II (New York, 1842), pp. 111-
13.*

30. SLAVE LABOR UPON PUBLIC WORKS AT THE SOUTH

The Cheapness of Slave Labor Belonging to Companies in Constructing
Improvements, Compared to the System of Contracts.

The Commonwealth of Virginia having at this time many improvements in
progress of construction, it becomes a question of serious importance, as to
the cheapest mode of making these improvements. The system of making contracts with individuals is universally adopted in the free, and generally in
the slave States. There can be no question but it is the better plan in the
Northern States, and can be done cheaper than if companies were to hire labor; but in slave States, where the labor can be owned by the companies, we
are decidedly of the opinion, that the grading, masonry, and mechanical work
on railroads, and the entire construction of canals, will be less than half
the cost it would be under the system of contracts. To sustain this view of
the subject, is the object of our essay, for we are deeply interested not
only as a large tax payer, but as a stockholder in two of the most important
improvements in the State--the James River and Kanawha Company, and the Virginia and Tennessee Railroad Company. [5]
As a lover of our native State, we should delight to see not only those
two important improvements completed, but also the other great lines commenced, and some that are contemplated carried on to consummation. Then, we
should expect to see all our geographical divisions healed, and our good old
Commonwealth take the position in the confederacy to which she is entitled
by the extent of her territory, the productiveness of her soil, and her
mineral resources. . . .
The plan proposed, we are convinced, will have this effect, and ought to
be embraced by all the improvement companies in the slaveholding States.
To sustain the position assumed, it is necessary to compare the cost of
labor to a company owning the slaves, and a contractor who hires them, for
it is generally known that but a small portion of the laborers can possibly
belong to the contractors--that they principally rely upon hirelings--and
that they have found slaves the most profitable laborers. As proof of this
fact, more than three-fourths of the laborers on the James River and Kanawha
Canal the last year were slaves.
The average hire the present year of negro men to work on public improvements is about $120. If a railroad or canal company were to purchase
at the present price, say $600, the annual cost to the company compared with
the hirelings, will be nearly as follows:

Interest on $600................................... $36
Insurance of life,................................   10

        Total,................................ $46

less than half for a hand to be employed in grading or excavating earth, besides the profit to the contractor; but upon mechanical work, a still greater difference exists. Take masonry, for example, and upon all these improvements a vast amount of masonry has to be done. A sprightly negro man will,
in six months, make a tolerable mason, and in twelve months an excellent one,
for it is a simple trade, easily learned. Yet masons are scarce, and demand
a high price, and a contractor offering for work bases his calculations upon
paying these high prices. The cost to a company owning slaves who are masons, and to contractors who hire them, will approximate to the following
calculation:

Interest on $600................................... $36
Insurance on life,................................   10
Clothing, &c.,....................................   10
200 lbs. bacon per year,..........................   15
3 barrels corn   do............................   7 50
Vegetables,.......................................   2 50

                                                    $81 00

Eighty-one dollars per annum, allowing 250 working days, are equal to 32½ cents per day; whereas the hired mason will cost the contractor $2 50 per day, more than seven times as much as the mason costs the company who owns him. In this estimate there is no allowance made for tools and over-seering, as both use the former; and the hired mason, though white, requires as much overseeing as the slave. Other mechanical work will show a considerable difference, but perhaps not as much as masonry.

Again, let us make an estimate of what excavation of earth and masonry will cost a company if owning slaves, and the price that is usually paid to contractors. We will base this estimate also upon the cost of negro men at $600:

Interest per annum,...............................	$36 00
Insurance,...	10 00
Clothing,..	10 00
Feeding,...	25 00
Overseeing,..	15 00
Tools, including blacksmith's work,................	10 00
Entire cost of a man in one year,.................	$106 00

In excavating earth, &c., ten cubic yards are considered an average day's work for a man--allowing 250 working days to a year, a man will excavate 2,500 yards; then divide $106 by 2,500, and excavation will cost the company about four cents per cubic yard. The usual price for excavation of earth paid to contractors is about twelve cents per cubic yard, for eight cents is the lowest price we have ever known to be paid to a contractor, and frequently fifteen cents. The calculation of excavating rock is attended with more difficulty; but still we can approximate sufficiently near to show that the difference of cost, if performed by labor belonging to a company and by contractors, will be greater than in the excavation of earth; for instance, by the calculation we have made, the entire cost to a company owning slaves, for a man, is $106 per annum, allowing 250 working days to the year, and the cost per day is 42 cents; and as the excavation of three cubic yards of rock is considered a fair average day's work per man, by dividing the 42 by 3, we have the cost per cubic yard fourteen cents, whereas the usual contract price is sixty cents. As a proof that this calculation is nearly correct, the writer made in the year 1839, when employed on the James River and Kanawha Company's canal, about $600 to each hand in excavating rock; and a friend told him that last year his hands, similarly employed, made from $600 to $700 each.

From the above calculations, we have these results, that slaves belonging to a company can excavate earth for less than half--can excavate rock for about one-fourth--and can construct culverts, bridges, abutments, locks, dams, &c. at about one-seventh that the same kind of work will cost contractors. With these facts, ought companies to hesitate as to the mode of constructing their improvements? and ought not the Legislature to require the State proxies to vote for the adoption of the system, here proved to be so decidedly superior to one almost in universal use, particularly as the State has so large an interest in all the improvements?

Let us test the two systems in the tobacco crop. Suppose a planter were to cultivate tobacco by contract; advertise that proposals would be received to repair ___miles of fence; plough, re-plough, and manure ___ acres of land; put up ____ thousand tobacco hills, and plant, work, worm, and sucker this tobacco; cut, hang, house, fire, strip, bulk and prize the crop--at what price could he afford to sell this tobacco? We will answer at not less than twenty dollars per hundred; yet, by owning slaves, he can realize a small profit at five dollars. It may, however, be answered that greater skill is required to make canals or railroads, than is necessary in the cultivation of tobacco; but we beg leave to rejoin and say, that having had much experience in making tobacco and canals, we believe that more sound judgment is necessary in the former, than is required in the latter operation.

We have frequently heard the objection urged against companies making their improvements with slaves belonging to them--that contractors feel a

greater interest, and with fewer hands to superintend, will have more work
done by their laborers than companies can have performed by their slaves.
It is admitted that this might be the case to some inconsiderable extent;
but with a good system, and with a man of good common sense to manage the
affairs of a company, we feel satisfied that this difference would be inconsiderable. For proof that this opinion is well formed, we refer to a contractor now at work, both on the canal and railroad, (Mr. Chas. Scott,) who
has from three to five hundred men employed, (principally slaves,) and yet,
from the best information that could obtained, he makes a larger profit in
proportion to numbers than the contractors who work, comparatively speaking,
but few hands—he has to rely upon a good system and upon overseers, and so
would the president of a company. It is readily admitted that, with inefficient officers—with a president, whose only qualification is the ability to
write long reports, with beautiful figures of speech and handsomely rounded
periods; and who believes it is his only duty to preside at the meeting of
the directors—or one whose time is almost entirely occupied with his own
concerns—or one who knows nothing of the management of works of this character, nor of the governing and controlling of men, that such presidents might
progress with more ease to themselves, and other officers; but with a good
system and good officers, we contend that it is not much more difficult to
manage one thousand than ten men.

We would recommend the following system for the government of a large
number of slaves upon a work of internal improvement. The slaves, we think,
ought to be divided into companies of about thirty men, including boys for
the driving carts, if this be required—each company should have an overseer,
a cook, and a blacksmith, with all necessary carts, horses and tools—the
companies should be located as nearly to each other as the work, with accompanying circumstances, would justify—for about every ten companies an assistant engineer would be necessary, and for about one thousand men, a commissary, to purchase provisions, carts, horses, tools, &c. It should be the
duty of the assistant engineer, aided by two sprightly slaves, (for rodmen)
to designate particularly by metes and bounds the work to be executed by the
overseers—pass along the work intrusted to his supervision as often as possible, noting in a book, or check roll kept for the purpose, the number of
hands at work on each section, and at the end of the month make an accurate
estimate of the quantity of work done by each overseer.

It should be the duty of every overseer to keep an account of all tools,
provisions, &c., received from the commissary, and a check roll of the number of hands at work each day, with the causes of the absence of any hand.

At the end of the month, the quantity of work done by each overseer
would indicate to the president his value, and notwithstanding there is great
difference in the quality of earth and rock, yet a man of good common sense
would soon form a pretty correct judgment of what could be excavated and removed, and also of the value of the overseer, and should any of the overseers
prove unworthy, dismiss them and employ others. With such a system as this,
well carried into effect, there is no doubt that the work would not only be
well executed, but as much done to the hand as is usually obtained by contractors. . . .

The canal from Richmond to Lynchburg cost nearly $6,000,000; with that
sum it is contended that the canal could have been constructed in Ohio,
(whether a sufficient feeder could have been obtained on the Alleghany, we
shall not now attempt to discuss,) and much the larger portion, if not the
whole of that amount, returned to the State and stockholders.

When the canal was commenced, negro men were worth about $400, but we
are willing to make our calculations upon their present selling price, $600.
At the commencement of the work we would have bought one thousand negro men,
which would have cost $600,000; and used the first year, $400,000 to purchase the necessary carts, horses, and tools, to pay land damages, engineers'
salaries, and all other necessary expenditures, which would have been an
ample allowance; and the remaining $5,000,000, at interest, would yield
$300,000 annually, which would be sufficient for each succeeding year's ex-
penditure, and to purchase as many slaves as would be probably necessary to
keep up their number. When the canal was completed to Lynchburg, the income
derived from tolls would be increased from $150,000 to $200,000. This sum,
after defraying the necessary expenses of the unfinished canal, might have

been made a sinking fund, and as the canal progressed, this sinking fund
would be increased, until the completion of this great work; when it would,
together with the slaves, have been sufficient to pay back the $1,000,000,
together with the greater part of the interest annually drawn to carry on
the work. . . .

The same system might be applied to railroads, with the exception of
the cost of the rails. Take, for example, the Virginia and Tennessee Railroad, the grading of which, we are satisfied, might be done for less than
half it will cost under the system of contracts with private owners for
hired slaves. If negro men were purchased as fast as the funds of the company would justify the expenditure, and the first two hundred of the negroes
so purchased (except such as might be required for other particular services) put into companies with a skillful and prudent mason to superintend
and instruct them, in one year they would be good masons, and whilst learning the trade, effect a large saving over the system of contracts; and at
the expiration of that time, their value would be doubled to the company.
The same system might be pursued as to carpenters and blacksmiths; and when
the company had sufficient funds for the purpose, negroes might be purchased
to do part of the excavation of rock and earth, until the road was completed, when a large number will be always required to keep it in repair, to
work at the depots in loading and unloading the cars, and in cutting wood
and locating it where it may be wanted for the use of the steam-engine.

Unsigned article in DeBow's Review 17 (July 1854):76-82.

31. SLAVE FISHERMEN

The shad and herring fisheries upon the sounds and inlets of the North
Carolina coast are an important branch of industry, and a source of considerable wealth. The men employed in them are mainly negroes, slave and
free; and the manner in which they are conducted is interesting, and in
some respects novel.

The largest sweep seines in the world are used. The gentleman to whom
I am indebted for the most of my information, was the proprietor of a seine
over two miles in length. It was manned by a force of forty negroes, most
of whom were hired at a dollar a day, for the fishing season, which usually
commences between the tenth and fifteenth of March, and lasts fifty days.
In favorable years the profits are very great. In extremely unfavorable
years, many of the proprietors are made bankrupt.

Cleaning, curing and packing-houses are erected on the shore, as near
as they conveniently may be to a point on the beach suitable for drawing
the seine. Six or eight windlasses, worked by horses, are fixed along the
shore, on each side of this point. There are two large seine-boats, in each
of which there is one captain, two seine-tenders, and eight or ten oarsmen.
In making a cast of the net, one-half of it is arranged on the stern of
each of the boats, which, having previously been placed in a suitable posi-
tion--perhaps a mile off shore, in front of the buildings--are rowed from
each other, the captains steering, and the seine-tenders throwing off, until
the seine is all cast between them. This is usually done in such a way that
it describes the arc of a circle, the chord of which is diagonal with the
shore. The hawsers attached to the ends of the seine are brought first to
the outer windlasses, and are wound in by the horses. As the operation of
gathering in the seine occupies several hours, the boat-hands, as soon as
they have brought the hawsers to the shore, draw their boats up, and go to
sleep.

As the wings approach the shore, the hawsers are from time to time carried to the other windlasses, to contract the sweep of the seine. After the
gaff of the net reaches the shore, lines attached toward the bunt are

carried to the windlasses, and the boats' crews are awakened, and arrange
the wing of the seine, as fast as it comes in, upon the boat again. Of
course, as the east was made diagonally with the shore, one wing is beached
before the other. By the time the fish in the bunt have been secured, both
boats are ready for another cast, and the boatmen proceed to make it, while
the shore-gang is engaged in sorting and gutting the "take."

My informant, who had $50,000 invested in his fishing establishment,
among other items of expenditure, mentioned that he had used seventy kegs
of gunpowder the previous year, and amused himself for a few moments with
letting me try to conjecture in what way villainous saltpetre could be put
to use in taking fish.

There is evidence of a subsidence of this coast, in many places, at a
comparatively recent period; many stumps of trees, evidently standing where
they grew, being found some way below the present surface, in the swamps and
salt marshes. Where the formation of the shore and the surface, or the
strength of the currents of water, which have flowed over the sunken land,
has been such as to prevent a later deposit, the stumps of great cypress
trees, not in the least decayed, yet protrude from the bottom of the sounds.
These would obstruct the passage of a net, and must be removed from a fish-
ing-ground.

The operation of removing them is carried on during the summer, after
the close of the fishing season. The position of a stump having been ascertained by divers, two large seine-boats are moored over it, alongside each
other, and a log is laid across them, to which is attached, perpendicularly,
between the boats, a spar, fifteen feet long. The end of a chain is hooked
to the lóg, between the boats, the other end of which is fastened by divers
to the stump which it is wished to raise. A double-purchase tackle leads
from the end of the spar to a ring-bolt in the bows of one of the boats,
with the fall leading aft, to be bowsed upon by the crews. The mechanical
advantages of the windlass, the lever, and the pulley being thus combined,
the chain is would on to the log, until either the stump yields, and is
brought to the surface, or the boats' gunwales are brought to the water's
edge.

When the latter is the case, and the stump still remains firm, a new
power must be applied. A spile, pointed with iron, six inches in diameter,
and twenty feet long, is set upon the stump by a diver, who goes down with
it, and gives it that direction which, in his judgment, is best, and driven
into it by mauls and sledges, a scaffold being erected between the boats
for men to stand on while driving it. In very large stumps, the spile is
often driven till its top reaches the water; so that when it is drawn out, a
cavity is left in the stump, ten feet in depth. A tube is now used, which
is made by welding together three musket-barrels, with a breech at one end,
in which is the tube of a percussion breech, with the ordinary position of
the nipple reversed, so that when it is screwed on with a detonating cap,
the latter will protrude within the barrel. This breech is then inserted
within a cylindrical tin box, six inches in diameter, and varying in length,
according to the supposed strength of the stump; and soap or tallow is
smeared about the place of insertion, to make it water-tight. The box contains several pounds of gunpowder.

The long iron tube is elevated, and the diver goes down again, and
guides it into the hole in the stump, with the canister in his arms. It has
reached the bottom--the diver has come up, and is drawn into one of the
boats--an iron rod is inserted in the mouth of the tube--all hands crouch
low, and hold hard--the rod is let go--crack!--whoo--oosch! The sea swells,
boils, and breaks upward. If the boats do not rise with it, they must sink;
if they rise, and the chain does not break, the stump must rise with them.
At the same moment the heart of cypress is riven; its furthest rootlets quiver; the very earth trembles, and loses courage to hold it; "up comes the
stump, or down go the niggers!"

If I owned a yacht, I think I would make a trip to Currituck next summer, to witness this Titanic dentistry. Who could have invented it? Not a
Carolinian; it is too ingenious: not a Yankee; it is too reckless: not a
sailor; it is too hard upon the boats.

The success of the operation evidently depends mainly on the discretion
and skill of the diver. My informant, who thought that he removed last

summer over a thousand stumps, using for the purpose seventy kegs of gunpowder, employed several divers, all of them negroes. Some of them could remain under water, and work there to better advantage than others; but all
were admirably skillful, and this, much in proportion to the practice and
experience they had had. They wear, when diving, three or four pairs of
flannel drawers and shirts. Nothing is required of them when they are not
wanted to go to the bottom, and, while the other hands are at work, they
may lounge, or go to sleep in the boat, which they do, in their wet garments.
Whenever a diver displays unusual hardihood, skill, or perseverance, he is
rewarded with whisky; or, as they are commonly allowed, while diving, as
much whisky as they want, with money. Each of them would generally get
every day from quarter to half-a-dollar in this way, above the wages paid
for them, according to the skill and industry with which they had worked.
On this account, said my informant, "the harder the work you give them to
do, the better they like it." His divers very frequently had intermittent
fevers, but would very rarely let this keep them out of their boats. Even
in the midst of a severe "shake," they would generally insist that they were
"well enough to dive."

        What! slaves eager to work, and working cheerfully, earnestly and skill-
fully? Even so. Being for the time managed as freemen, their ambition
stimulated by wages, suddenly they, too, reveal sterling manhood, and honor
their Creator.

*Frederick Law Olmsted, A Journey in the Seaboard Slave States, With Remarks
on Their Economy (New York: Mason Brothers, 1859, originally 1856), pp.
351-55.*

32. WORKING AT A RICHMOND TOBACCO FACTORY

        I was much struck by a forcible illustration of the loss attending the
employment of slaves, by a visit to one of the largest tobacco factories in
Richmond. . . .
        Down the centre of a long room were twenty large presses, at each of
which some dozen slaves, stripped to the waist (it was very hot), were tug-
ging and heaving at long iron arms, which turned screws, accompanying each
push and pull by deep-drawn groans. Within a few yards of the factory runs,
or rather rushes, an illimitable supply of water, the merest fraction of
which would furnish power to turn the screws of all the tobacco pressed in
Richmond. On suggesting the desirableness of using this great natural
force, instead of numerous Negroes now employed, thus saving their labor,
the proprietor of the factory, who kindly acted as my guide, assured me the
slaves did the work far better than it could be done by machinery, as the
overseer could direct them to apply precisely as much pressure as the tobacco required.

*Charles Weld, A Vacation Tour of the United States and Canada (London,
1855), pp. 313-14.*

33. LUMBERMEN

        The "Great Dismal Swamp," together with the smaller "Dismals" (for so
the term is used here), of the same character, along the North Carolina
Coast, have hitherto been of considerable commercial importance as

furnishing a large amount of lumber, and especially of shingles for our Northern use as well as for exportation. The district from which this commerce proceeds is all a vast quagmire, the soil being entirely composed of decayed vegetable fibre, saturated and surcharged with water; yielding or *quaking* on the surface to the tread of a man, and a large part of it, during most of the year, half inundated with standing pools. It is divided by creeks and water-veins, and in the centre is a pond six miles long and three broad, the shores of which, strange to say, are at a higher elevation above the sea, than any other part of the swamp, and yet are of the same miry consistency.

The Great Dismal is about thirty miles long and ten miles wide on an average; its area about 200,000 acres. And the little Dismal, Aligator, Catfish, Green, and other smaller swamps, on the shores of Albemarle and Pamlico, contain over 2,000,000 acres. A considerable part of this is the property of the State of North Carolina, and the proceeds of sales from it form the chief income of the department of education of that Commonwealth.

An excellent canal, six feet in depth, passes for more than twenty miles through the swamp, giving passage not only to the lumber collected from it, but to a large fleet of coasting vessels engaged in the trade of The Albemarle and Pamlico Sounds, and making a safe outlet towards New York for all the corn, cotton, tar, turpentine, etc., produced in the greater part of the eastern section of North Carolina, which is thus brought to market without encountering the extremely hazardous passage outside, from Cape Hatteras to Cape Henry. This canal is fed by the water of the pond in the centre of the swamp, its summit-level being many feet below it.*

Of the main products of the country, the annual freightage on the Dismal Swamp Canal is about as follows:

Shingles	24,000,000
Staves	6,000,000
Plank and scantling, cubic feet.	125,000
Ship timber.	40,000
Cotton bales	4,500
Shad and herring, barrels.	50,000
Naval stores, barrels.	30,000

Much of the larger part of the "Great Dismal" was originally covered by a heavy forest growth. All the trees indigenous to the neighboring country I found still extensively growing, and of full size within its borders. But the main production, and that which has been of the greatest value, has been of cypress and juniper; (the latter commonly known as white cedar, at the North). From these two, immense quantities of shingles have been made. The cypress also affords ship-timber, now in great demand, and a great many rough poles of the juniper, under the name of "cedar-rails," are sent to New York and other ports, as fencing material, (generally selling at seven cents a rail,) for the farms of districts that have been deprived of their own natural wood by the extension of tillage required by the wants of neighboring towns or manufactories.

The swamp belongs to a great many proprietors. Most of them own only a few acres, but some possess large tracts and use a heavy capital in the business. One, whose acquaintance I made, employed more than a hundred hands in getting out shingles alone. The value of the swamp land varies with the wood upon it, and the facility with which it can be got off, from 12½ cents to $10 an acre. It is made passable in any desired direction in which trees grow by

Spirits turpentine, barrels.	700
Bacon, cwts.	5,000
Lard, kegs	1,300
Maize, bushels	2,000,000
Wheat, bushels	30,000
Peas, bushels.	25,000

The canal was made with the assistance of the National Government and the State of Virginia, who are still the largest owners. It is admirably constructed, repairs are light, and it is a good six per cent stock.

laying logs, cut in lengths of eight or ten feet, parallel and against each
other on the surface of the soil, or "sponge," as it is called. Mules and
oxen are used to some extent upon these roads, but transportation is mainly
by hand to the creeks, or to ditches communicating with them or the canal.

Except by those log-roads, the swamp is scarcely passable in many
parts, owing not only to the softness of the sponge, but to the obstruction
caused by innumerable shrubs, vines, creepers and briars, which often take
entire possession of the surface, forming a dense brake or jungle. This,
however, is sometimes removed by fires, which of late years have been frequent and very destructive to the standing timber. The most common shrubs
are various smooth-leafed evergreens, and their dense, bright, glossy foli-
age, was exceedingly beautiful in the wintry season of my visit. There is a
good deal of game in the swamp--bears and wild cats are sometimes shot, rac-
coons and opossums are plentiful, and deer are found in the drier parts and
on the outskirts. The fishing, in the interior waters, is also said to be
excellent.

Nearly all the valuable trees have now been cut off from the swamp.
The whole ground has been frequently gone over, the best timber selected and
removed at each time, leaving the remainder standing thinly, so that the
wind has more effect upon it; and much of it, from the yielding of the soft
soil, is uprooted or broken off. The fires have also greatly injured it.
The principal stock, now worked into shingles, is obtained *from beneath the
surface*--old trunks that have been preserved by the wetness of the soil, and
that are found by "sounding" with poles, and raised with hooks or pikes by
the negroes.

The quarry is giving out, however, and except that lumber, and especially shingles, have been in great demand at high prices of late, the business
would be almost at an end. As it is, the principal men engaged in it are
turning their attention to other and more distant supplies. A very large
purchase had been made by one company in the Florida everglades, and a
schooner, with a gang of hands trained in the "Dismals," was about to sail
from Deep-creek, for this new field of operations.

Slave-Lumbermen.

The labor in the swamp is almost entirely done by slaves; and the way
in which they are managed is interesting and instructive. They are mostly
hired by their employers at a rent, perhaps of one hundred dollars a year
for each, paid to their owners. They spend one or two months of the winter
--when it is too wet to work in the swamp--at the residence of their master.
At this period little or no work is required of them; their time is their
own, and if they can get any employment, they will generally keep for themselves what they are paid for it. When it is sufficiently dry--usually early
in February--they go into the swamp in gangs, each gang under a white overseer. Before leaving, they are all examined and registered at the Court-
house, and "passes," good for a year, are given them, in which their features and the marks upon their persons are minutely described. Each man is
furnished with a quantity of provisions and clothing, of which, as well as
of all that he afterwards draws from the stock in the hands of the overseer,
an exact account is kept.

Life in the Swamp--Slaves Quasi Freemen.

Arrived at their destination, a rude camp is made, huts of logs, poles,
shingles, and boughs being built, usually upon some place where shingles
have been worked before, and in which the shavings have accumulated in small
hillocks upon the soft surface of the ground.

The slave lumberman then lives measurably as a free man; hunts, fishes,
eats, drinks, smokes and sleeps, plays and works, each when and as much as
he pleases. It is only required of him that he shall have made, after half
a year has passed, such a quantity of shingles as shall be worth to his master so much money as is paid to his owner for his services, and shall refund
the value of the clothing and provisions he has required.

No "driving" at his work is attempted or needed. . . . No force is used
to overcome the indolence peculiar to the negro. The overseer merely takes a

daily account of the number of shingles each man adds to the general stock,
and employs another set of hands, with mules, to draw them to a point from
which they can be shipped, and where they are, from time to time, called for
by a schooner.

At the end of five months the gang returns to dry-land, and a statement
of account from the overseer's book is drawn up, something like the following:

Sam Bo to John Doe, Dr.

Feb. 1.	To clothing (outfit)........................	$5 00
Mar. 10.	To clothing, as per overseer's account,.....	2 25
Feb. 1.	To bacon and meal (outfit)..................	19 00
July 1.	To stores drawn in swamp, as per overseer's	
	account,.................................	4 75
July 1.	To half-yearly hire, paid his owner.........	50 00

$81 00

Per Contra, Cr.

July 1. By 10,000 shingles, as per overseer's
         account, 10c............................. 100 00
         Balance due Sambo............................... $19 00

which is immediately paid him, and which, together with the proceeds of sale
of petry which he has got while in the swamp, he is always allowed to make
use of as his own. No liquor is sold or served to the negroes in the swamp,
and, as their first want when they come out of it is an excitement, most of
their money goes to the grog-shops.

After a short vacation, the whole gang is taken in the schooner to
spend another five months in the swamp as before. If they are good hands
and work steadily, they will commonly be hired again, and so continuing,
will spend most of their lives at it. They almost invariably have excellent
health, as do also the white men engaged in the business. They all consider
the water of "the Dismals" to have a medicinal virtue, and quite probably
it is a mild tonic. It is greenish in color, and I thought I detected a
slightly resinous taste upon first drinking it. Upon entering the swamp
also, an agreeable resinous odor, resembling that of a hemlock forest, was
perceptible.

The Effect of Paying Wages to Slaves.

The negroes working in the swamp were more sprightly and straight-forward in their manner and conversation than any field-hand plantation-negroes
that I saw at the South; two or three of their employers with whom I conversed spoke well of them, as compared with other slaves, and made no complaints of "rascality" or laziness.

One of those gentlemen told me of a remarkable case of providence and
good sense in a negro that he had employed in the swamp for many years. He
was so trust-worthy, that he had once let him go to New York as cook of a
lumber-schooner, when he could, if he had chosen to remain there, have
easily escaped from slavery.

Knowing that he must have accumulated considerable money, his employer
suggested to him that he might *buy* his freedom, and he immediately determined to do so. But when on applying to his owner, he was asked $500 for
himself, a price which, considering he was an elderly man, he thought too
much, he declined the bargain; shortly afterwards, however, he came to his
employer again, and said that although he thought his owner was mean to set
so high a price upon him, he had been thinking that if he was to be an old
man he would rather be his own master, and if he did not live long, his
money would not be of any use to him at any rate, and so he had concluded
he would make the purchase.

He did so, and upon collecting the various sums that he had loaned to
white people in the vicinity, he was found to have several hundred dollars
more than was necessary. With the surplus, he paid for his passage to Liberia, and bought a handsome outfit. When he was about to leave, my

informant had made him a present, and, in thanking him for it, the free man
had said that the first thing he should do, on reaching Liberia, would be to
learn to write, and, as soon as he could, he would write to him how he liked
the country: he had been gone yet scarce a year, and had not been heard
from.

*Frederick Law Olmsted, A Journey in the Seaboard Slave States, with Remarks
on Their Economy (New York: Mason Brothers, 1859, originally 1856), pp.
149-56.*

34. SLAVE IRONWORKERS

. . . I am employing in this establishment [the Tredegar works], as
well as at the Armory works adjoining, of which I am President, almost exclusively slave labor except as to Boss men. This enables me, of course, to
compete with other manufacturers and at the same time to put it in the power
of my men to do better for themselves. With this [in] view, I am now giving
my men, who are [as] steady and respectable as are to be found, each two
furnaces at puddling and furnish them three of my own hands who are blacks--
one of them [among each three negroes] capable of acting as Foreman of one
of the Furnaces, and I pay each Boss puddler two [dollars] pr. [ton] net on
the iron he makes in his furnaces. I am getting on very satisfactorily and
will eventually have enough of Puddlers here; but I am told you are a respectable man and one who can be relied on, and if you are anxious to make
money it is to your interest to come on here . . . as Mr. Morris tells me
you would like to have three furnaces I will add, that I shall have no objections to increase the number when I am satisfied you are capable of it.
With such iron as we work a puddler can easily make a ton at each furnace in
his time of twelve hours. [6]

*Reproduced in Kathleen Bruce, Virginia Iron Manufacture in the Slave Era
(New York, 1931), pp. 237-38.*

35. STRIKES AN ATTACK AGAINST SLAVE OWNERSHIP

To the Editors of the *Enquirer*. [7]
Gentlemen: It is mistake to suppose, as reported in your paper of this
morning, on the authority of a statement in the *Republican,* that an accommodation has been effected between the "employer & employees" at the Tredegar
works. The employer took the position which he chose to occupy deliberately
and it was one which, under no circumstances, would he change or depart from.
It was simply that those who enter into his employment must not expect to
prescribe to him whom he shall be at liberty to employ; and that he would not
consent to employ men who would unite and combine themselves into an association to exclude slaves from our factories. It was because the late workmen
asserted such a pretension that he determined that their employment should
cease; and because they were understood to have entered into a combination
to effect their purpose, that he thought they had committed an offence
against the laws, for which they deserved to be prosecuted. In that aspect,
he regarded it as a matter in which the whole community was concerned; it
must be evident that such combinations are a direct attack on slave property;
and if they do not originate in abolition, they are pregnant with its evils.

It is a rule of public law which has been recognized in states in which there are no slaves, that combinations against any interest, or to accomplish private ends are public offences, and as such are prohibited and punished. The rule exists in this commonwealth, and there can be no case which calls more loudly for its application than combination to prevent masters from employing their slaves as it may be their pleasure.

You will perceive then that the "employer" could enter into no compromise or arrangement with the "employees." This community, it is presumed, would not sanction or excuse a proceeding which yielded everything to the pretension in question. Nothing occurred, but that the prosecution was dismissed upon the workmen disclaiming any purpose or design to commit an offence, avowing that they had not pledged themselves one to another; and expressing their regret if their proceedings were against the laws; and the dismissal of the prosecution was the act of the Mayor.

Trusting that the facts of a case involving a principle so important to the whole community and the South, may now be full understood. I will conclude by asking the Editors of the *Republican* to copy this communication.

> Very respectfully,
> Your obedient servant,
> JOSEPH R. ANDERSON.

Reproduced in Kathleen Bruce, Virginia Iron Manufacture in the Slave Era (New York, 1931), pp. 237-38n.

36.   TREDEGAR ADVERTISEMENT FOR SLAVES

W A N T S.

WANTED--1,000 NEGROES.--We wish to hire for the year 1864, ONE THOUSAND NEGROES, to be employed at the Tredegar Iron Works, Richmond, and at our Blast Furnaces in the counties of Rockbridge, Botetourt and Alleghany, and Collieries in Goochland and Henrico, for which we are willing to pay the market prices.

Having made arrangements for a supply of provisions and clothing, we can safely promise that servants entrusted to us shall at all times be well fed and clothed.

Our furnaces and other works are located in healthy sections of the c country, remote from the enemy's line, offering unusual inducements to the owners of negroes to send them to us.

Parties having families of negroes, consisting of men, women and boys, may make arrangements with us for the whole, provided the classes are not disproportioned, as there are farms attached to some of the furnaces and collieries, on which the women and boys can be employed.

We would be glad to hear from those whose hands we have hired this year as early as possible, as to rehiring them another year, and whether they desire that the hands shall be sent home or retained under our protection at the end of the year.   J. R. ANDERSON & CO.
                                                      Tredegar Iron Works, Richmond Va.

The Augusta (Georgia) Constitutionalist, Atlanta (Georgia) Intelligencer, and Montgomery (Alabama) Mail will please copy semi-weekly till first of January, 1864, and forward their bills to us for payment.

                                                      J. R. ANDERSON & CO.
nov14--Stawlm   Tredegar Iron Works.

Richmond Examiner, November 14, 1863.

Railroad Hands

ONE HUNDRED ABLE-BODIED HANDS
        WANTED.--Forty dollars per month and board will be paid for able-
bodied hands to work on the repairs of the Virginia Central Railroad until
Christmas. Apply to either of the station agents along the line; to W. G.
Richardson, Frederick's Hall; or to the undersigned.
                                              H. D. WHITCOMB.
nov11-12t   General Superintendent

Richmond Examiner, November 14, 1863.

37. ANNUAL MAINTENANCE COST PER INDUSTRIAL SLAVE, 1820's-1861
                        (in dollars)

Location	Year	Food or Board	Clothing	Food Plus Clothing
1. Maramec Iron Works, Missouri	1829's-30's	36.50	29.20	
2. Colhoun's woolen mill, South Carolina	1830	23	5	
3. River snag boats	1829-39			120
4. Various sugar planta- tions, Louisiana	1830			50
5. Pine Forge, Virginia	1831-33	72		
6. Savannah River Improve- ment Project, Georgia	1835	54.75		
7. Robert Leslie's tobacco factory, Petersburg, Va.	1835	30		
8. William Clark's hemp factory, Kentucky	1838	72		
9. LaGrange and Memphis R.R., Tennessee	1839	96		
10. Nesbitt Iron Manufac- turing Company, S.C.	ca. 1839	73		
11. Cherokee Iron Works, South Carolina	1839-40	10	3	
12. Sugar plantations, Louisiana	1845	10 (pork)	15	30+
13. Graham cotton mill, Kentucky	1847-50	35 low 40 typical 50 high	7.50	
	1851	75		
14. Louisa R.R., Virginia	1848			33.25-34.25
15. Turpentine distillery, Alabama	1849			30
16. South Carolina R.R., South Carolina	1847		16	
17. A cotton mill, Missis- sippi	1849	73		
18. Public improvement projects, Virginia	1849	25		
19. Rocks Mill, Virginia	1838-50	120.45		
20. Vicksburg and Jackson R.R., Mississippi	1848-50	28 low 31.45 average 33.50 high		

21. Chesterfield R.R., Virginia	1851		25	
22. Virginia Central R.R., Virginia	1852	52		
23. James River and Kanawha Canal, Virginia	1854	43	14+	
	1858	42		
24. Gold Hill Mine, North Carolina	1855	42-48		
25. Nolensville Turnpike Company, Tennessee	1854	46.40	24.50	
	1855	29	11.65	
	1856	21	14.30	
	1858	15	6.87	
	1859	20.67	10.83	
26. Hardinsburg and Cloverport Turnpike Co., Kentucky	1859-60	125		
27. Charleston and Savannah R.R., South Carolina	1855		20	
28. Cape Fear and Deep River Navigation Co., N.C.	1859	109		
29. Blue Ridge R.R., South Carolina	1860	60		
30. Silver Hill Mine, North Carolina	1860	60		
31. Richmond, Fredericksburg and Potomac R.R., Va.	1860			60
32. J. H. Couper's rice plantation, Georgia	1859			22-25
33. Woodville mines, Virginia	ca. 1850's	23	15	
34. Evan's estimate		110		
35. Olmsted's estimate of a sugar plantation	1850's	24	15	
36. W. Dearmont, builder, Georgia	1850-61	91.25		
AVERAGES:	1820's-61	51.57	14.50	44.94

Robert S. Starobin, "The Economics of Industrial Slavery in the Old South,"
Business History Review 44 (Summer, 1970):172.

HIRING-OUT OF SLAVE MECHANICS

38. SLAVES HIRING THEMSELVES OUT

The slaveholders' ever watchful jealousy has discovered great danger to their "system," from the practice of allowing slaves to look for work wherever they can get it, and bring a fixed amount of wages to their masters weekly. Newspapers in various parts of the South are urging the subject on the attention of the slaveholders. At Jackson, in Mississippi, a public meeting has been held and Committees appointed to promote "measures of reform necessary to correct the evils and grievances occasioned by the present condition of the free black and slave population."

They propose to "expel all free negroes from the city; prohibit, under

severe penalties, the practice of permitting slaves to hire their own time;
prevent all slaves residing without the limits of the city from coming to
the place on Sunday, except on business of their own masters; establish an
efficient and strict patrol for the city; and prohibit preaching by the
slaves and free negroes."

A Norfolk paper says:--"Our laws in relation both to free negroes and
slaves have remained for years a dead letter on the statute book, while that
species of population have gone on acquiring privileges and immunities until
they have amounted to a grievance too intolerable to be endured, and which
the public voice calls in imperious tones for reform. The supposed clemency
of the owners of slaves, in permitting them, in open violation of law, to
hire their own time, so far from proving a kindness, often becomes an absolute wrong--productive only of positive injury to him who is the subject of
it. Its effects, too, upon those denied these privileges, (if privileges
they be deemed,) though the most servile and submissive, are often seen to
be injurious--inviting, inducing and impelling discontent and insubordination. The result in many cases is most disastrous and awful."

The Suffolk Intelligencer says:--"To allow slaves to go at large and
act as free persons, causes them to be restless under restraint, and if,
after being allowed such a privilege, they are restricted, they become sul-
len and less willing to do their duty--this is one step to insubordination,
and is apt to be followed by an attempt to go North. It begets in them a
desire to have money, to have a *chance* for themselves, as it is usually called, and renders them dissatisfied, unless they always have the same opportunities.

"It causes other negroes not so circumstanced to become dissatisfied because their owners do not allow them the same privileges, and tends to insolence and rebellion on their part, and consequently produces trouble to
the owner. It violates the letter and spirit of the law, and should not be
tolerated.

"Persons owning slaves should always make the contract for the hires of
their negroes, and collect the same when due.

"Let each owner of slaves whose interest it should be to make them valuable, put a stop to a practice which is so wrong in itself--one that is the
cause of difficulty and trouble, not only to themselves but to others."

By the following from the *Jackson Mississippian* it seems that the burdens and vexations of Slavery are accumulating.

"There is not a greater evil existing among our servile population, than
the privileges granted to negroes of allowing them to hire their own time.
No slave should be permitted to remain out of the personal control of his
master. It is the security which the State has given to us for the government of the slave population, and it should be the duty of every good citizen to see the laws on this subject faithfully carried out. The State as
far back as 1822, enacted laws against slaves hiring out their own labor.

"It is evident that the slave has been made discontented with his condition by this kind of unlawful privilege. He enjoys a license for all manner of rascality, which the slave who has not this privilege regards with
longing eyes, and is continually desiring to obtain himself. He sees, too,
that these negroes are impudent to the whites, and compete with white laborers in our towns; that they have fine clothes, coffee and tea, work when
they please, and lie in the shade when it suits their inclination; that they
can hold intercourse with whites or blacks in their houses, and there cover
up their plans for robbery, or crimes more dangerous. It is no wonder, then,
that the slave should wish to hire out his time. But we think that at the
present time, most especially, when abolition documents are circulating all
over our country, that all violations of the law like the present should be
summarily punished. In the absence of the restraining hand of the master;
in houses tenanted by slaves exclusively, and having the power to hold intercourse with whom they please, we do not know what conspiracy may yet be
hatched, and what sad disaster ensue, by allowing this law to be violated
with impunity. We think it the duty of every good citizen to see that it is
enforced. We know that the public press of our State is adorned by many
noble and disinterested advocates of the public weal, and we shall look to
them for a strong expression of opinion upon this interesting subject."

Another Southern paper uses this language in relation to slaves hiring their time:

"This important subject, we are pleased to find, is attracting more and more the attention of the public. The press, generally, at the South, is endeavoring to excite a more healthful tone of feeling and action in reference to this momentous interest--an interest which comes home to the business and fireside of every member of the community.

"The bad effects resulting from the practice of slaves hiring their time are too striking to require much proof. The evils produced by the residence of the *free* negroes amongst us are everywhere complained of; Gov. Smith's recommendation for *their* removal was hailed with a unanimity, proportionate to the extent with which those evils are felt. Yet our citizens blindly, thoughtlessly, permit the continuance of a practice by which those very evils are immeasurably increased, and others of a still more deplorable character created.

'All our experience has proven that the restraining hand of the master is essential to the slave's happiness, and to our safety. In Virginia the slave is worth, at best, little more than the cost of the chain that holds him in bondage; and at a time when so great an influence is at work tending to create excitement and insubordination amongst the population, it is hardly the part of prudence or of patriotism to continue that, the inevitable tendency of which is to aggravate those evils.

"The law of the land prohibits, with penalties, this practice, and the well being of the negro and the safety of the master alike demand that the law, to its fullest extent, should now be enforced."

There is probably no source more prolific of suffering to the slaves than that of being hired out by their masters. It would be difficult to ascertain the exact number thus hired, but they have been estimated at one third of the adult slave population. When we consider the cruel nature of slavery under the most favorable circumstances, we cannot doubt that this class must suffer fearfully from overwork, from insufficient clothing, food and shelter, and from various cruelties which may be inflicted upon them without incurring damages to the owner.

The Non-Slaveholder, 4 (1849):254-55.

39. FREDERICK DOUGLASS ENCOUNTERS RACIAL [8]
     VIOLENCE IN A BALTIMORE SHIPYARD

. . . Very soon after I went to Baltimore to live, Master Hugh succeeded in getting me hired to Mr. William Gardiner, an extensive shipbuilder on Fell's Point. I was placed there to learn to calk, a trade of which I already had some knowledge, gained while in Mr. Hugh Auld's shipyard. Gardiner's, however, proved a very unfavorable place for the accomplishment of the desired object. Mr. Gardiner was that season engaged in building two large man-of-war vessels, professedly for the Mexican government. These vessels were to be launched in the month of July of that year, and in failure thereof Mr. Gardiner would forfeit a very considerable sum of money. So, when I entered the shipyard, all was hurry and driving. There were in the yard about one hundred men; of these, seventy or eighty were regular carpenters-- privileged men. There was no time for a raw hand to learn anything. Every man had to do that which he knew how to do, and in entering the yard Mr. Gardiner had directed me to do whatever the carpenters told me to do. This was placing me at the beck and call of about seventy-five men. I was to regard all these as my masters. Their word was to be my law. My situation was a trying one. I was called a dozen ways in the space of a single minute. I needed a dozen pairs of hands. Three or four voices would strike my ear at the same moment. It was "Fred, come help to cant this timber here,"-- "Fred, come carry this timber yonder,"--"Fred, bring that roller here,"--

"Fred, go get a fresh can of water,"--"Fred, come help saw off the end of
this timber,"--"Fred, go quick and get the crow-bar,"--"Fred, hold on the
end of this fall,"--"Fred, go to the blacksmith's shop and get a new punch,"
--"Halloo, Fred! run and bring me a cold chisel,"--"I say, Fred, bear a hand,
and get up a fire under the steam box as quick as lightning,"--"Hullo, nigger! come turn this grindstone,"--"Come, come, move, move! and bowse this
timber forward,"--"I say, darkey, blast your eyes! why don't you heat up some
pitch?"--"Halloo! halloo! halloo! (three voices at the same time)"--"Come
here; go there; hold on where you are. D--n you, if you move I'll knock
your brains out!" Such, my dear reader, is a glance at the school which was
mine during the first eight months of my stay at Gardiner's shipyard.

At the end of eight months Master Hugh refused longer to allow me to remain with Gardiner. The circumstance which led to this refusal was the committing of an outrage upon me, by the white apprentices of the shipyard.
The fight was a desperate one, and I came out of it shockingly mangled. I
was cut and bruised in sundry places, and my left eye was nearly knocked out
of its socket. The facts which led to this brutal outrage upon me illustrate
a phase of slavery which was destined to become an important element in the
overthrow of the slave system, and I may therefore state them with some mi-
nuteness. That phase was this--the conflict of slavery with the interests
of white mechanics and laborers. In the country this conflict was not so
apparent, but in cities, such as Baltimore, Richmond, New Orleans, Mobile,
etc., it was seen pretty clearly. The slaveholders, with a craftiness peculiar to themselves, by encouraging the enmity of the poor laboring white
man against the blacks, succeeded in making the said white man almost as
much a slave as the black slave himself. The difference between the white
slave and the black slave was this: the latter belonged to one slaveholder,
while the former belonged to the slaveholders collectively. The white slave
had taken from him by indirection what the black slave had taken from him
directly and without ceremony. Both were plundered, and by the same plunderers. The slave was robbed by his master of all his earnings, above what
was required for his bare physical necessities, and the white laboring man
was robbed by the slave system of the just results of his labor, because he
was flung into competition with a class of laborers who worked without wages.
The slaveholders blinded them to this competition by keeping alive their
prejudice against the slaves as *men*--not against them as *slaves*. They appealed to their pride, often denouncing emancipation as tending to place the
white working man on an equality with negroes, and by this means they succeeded in drawing off the minds of the poor whites from the real fact, that
by the rich slave-master they were already regarded as but a single remove
from equality with the slave. The impression was cunningly made that slavery
was the only power that could prevent the laboring white man from falling to
the level of the slave's poverty and degradation. To make this enmity deep
and broad between the slave and the poor white man, the latter was allowed
to abuse and whip the former without hindrance. But, as I have said, this
state of affairs prevailed mostly in the country. In the City of Baltimore
there were not unfrequent murmurs that educating slaves to be mechanics
might, in the end, give slave-masters power to dispense altogether with the
services of the poor white man. But with characteristic dread of offending
the slaveholders, these poor white mechanics in Mr. Gardiner's shipyard, instead of applying the natural, honest remedy for the apprehended evil, and
objecting at once to work there by the side of the slaves, made a cowardly
attack upon the free colored mechanics, saying they were eating the bread
which should be eaten by American freeman, and aimed to prevent him from
serving himself, in the evening of life, with the trade with which he had
served his master, during the more vigorous portion of his days. Had they
succeeded in driving the black freemen out of the shipyard, they would have
determined also upon the removal of the black slaves. The feeling was, about
this time, very bitter toward all colored people in Baltimore (1836), and
they--free and slave--suffered all manner of insult and wrong.

Until a very little while before I went there, white and black carpenters worked side by side in the shipyards of Mr. Gardiner, Mr. Duncan, Mr.
Walter Price, and Mr. Robb. Nobody seemed to see any impropriety in it.
Some of the blacks were first-rate workmen and were given jobs requiring the
highest skill. All at once, however, the white carpenters swore that they

would no longer work on the same stage with Negroes. Taking advantage of
the heavy contract resting upon Mr. Gardiner to have the vessels for Mexico
ready to launch in July, and of the difficulty of getting other hands at
that season of the year, they swore that they would not strike another blow
for him unless he would discharge his free colored workmen. Now, although
this movement did not extend to me *in form,* it did reach me in *fact.* The
spirit which is awakened was one of malice and bitterness toward colored people generally, and I suffered with the rest, and suffered severely. My fel-
low-apprentices very soon began to feel it to be degrading to work with me.
They began to put on high looks and to talk contemptuously and maliciously
of "the niggers," saying that they would take the "country," and that they
"ought to be killed." Encouraged by workmen who, knowing me to be a slave,
made no issue with Mr. Gardiner about my being there, these young men did
their utmost to make it impossible for me to stay. They seldom called me to
do anything without coupling the call with a curse, and Edward North, the
biggest in everything, rascality included, ventured to strike me, whereupon
I picked him up and threw him into the dock. Whenever any of them struck me
I struck back again, regardless of consequences. I could manage any of them
singly, and so long as I could keep them from combining I got on very well.

In the conflict which ended my stay at Mr. Gardiner's I was beset by
four of them at once--Ned North, Ned Hayes, Bill Stewart, and Tom Humphreys.
Two of them were as large as myself, and they came near killing me, in broad
daylight. One came in front, armed with a brick; there was one at each side
and one behind, and they closed up all around me. I was struck on all
sides, and while I was attending to those in front I received a blow on my
head from behind, dealt with a heavy handspike. I was completely stunned by
the blow, and fell heavily on the ground among the timbers. Taking advantage of my fall they rushed upon me and began to pound me with their fists.
With a view of gaining strength, I let them lay on for awhile after I came
to myself. They had done me little damage, so far, but finally getting
tired of that sport I gave a sudden surge, and despite their weight I rose to
my hands and knees. Just as I did this one of their number planted a blow
with his boot in my left eye, which for a time seemed to have burst my eyeball. When they saw my eye completely closed, my face covered with blood,
and I staggering under the stunning blows they had given me, they left me.
As soon as I gathered strength I picked up the handspike and madly enough
attempted to pursue them but here the carpenters interfered and compelled me
to give up my pursuit. It was impossible to stand against so many.

Dear reader, you can hardly believe the statement, but it is true and
therefore I write it down--that no fewer than fifty white men stood by and
saw this brutal and shameful outrage committed, and not a man of them all interposed a single word of mercy. There were four against one, and that one's
face was beaten and battered most horribly, and no one said, "That is
enough," but some cried out, "Kill him! kill him! kill the d--n nigger! knock
his brains out! he struck a white person!" I mention this inhuman outcry to
show the character of the men and the spirit of the times at Gardiner's shipyard, and, indeed, in Baltimore generally, in 1836. As I look back to this
period I am almost amazed that I was not murdered outright, so murderous was
the spirit which prevailed there. On two other occasions while there I came
near losing my life. On one of these, I was driving bolts in the hold
through the keelson, with Hayes. In its course the bolt bent. Hayes cursed
me and said that it was my blow which bent the bolt. I denied this and
charged it upon him. In a fit of rage he seized an adze and darted toward
me. I met him with a maul and parried his blow, or I should have lost my
life.

After the united attack of North, Stewart, Hayes, and Humphreys, finding that the carpenters were as bitter toward me as the apprentices, and
that the latter were probably set on by the former, I found my only chance
for life was in flight. I succeeded in getting away without an additional
blow. To strike a white man was death by lynch law, in Gardiner's shipyard,
nor was there much of any other law toward the colored people at that time
in any other part of Maryland.

After making my escape from the shipyard I went straight home and related my story to Master Hugh, and to his credit I say it, that his conduct,
though he was not a religious man, was every way more humane than that of

of his brother Thomas, when I went to him in a somewhat similar plight, from
the hands of his "Brother Edward Covey." Master Hugh listened attentively
to my narration of the circumstances leading to the ruffianly assault, and
gave many evidences of his strong indignation at what was done. He was a
rough but manly-hearted fellow, and at this time his best nature showed itself.

The heart of my once kind mistress Sophia was again melted in pity towards me. My puffed-out eye and my scarred and blood-covered face moved the
dear lady to tears. She kindly drew a chair by me, and with friendly and
consoling words, she took water and washed the blood from my face. No
mother's hand could have been more tender than hers. She bound up my head
and covered my wounded eye with a lean piece of fresh beef. It was almost
compensation for all I suffered, that it occasioned the manifestation once
more of the originally characteristic kindness of my mistress. Her affec-
tionate heart was not yet dead, though much hardened by time and circumstances.

As for Master Hugh, he was furious, and gave expression to his feelings
in the forms of speech usual in that locality. He poured curses on the
whole of the shipyard company, and swore that he would have satisfaction.
His indignation was really strong and healthy, but unfortunately it resulted
from the thought that his rights of property, in my person, had not been respected, more than from any sense of the outrage perpetrated upon me *as a
man*. I had reason to think this from the fact that he could, himself, beat
and mangle when it suited him to do so.

Bent on having satisfaction, as he said, just as soon as I got a little
better of my bruises, Master Hugh took me to Esquire Watson's office on Bond
street, Fell's Point, with a view to procuring the arrest of those who had
assaulted me. He gave to the magistrate an account of the outrage as I had
related it to him, and seemed to expect that a warrant would at once be issued for the arrest of the lawless ruffians. Mr. Watson heard all that he
had to say, then coolly inquired, "Mr. Auld, who saw this assault of which
you speak?" "It was done, sir, in the presence of a shipyard full of hands."
"Sir," said Mr. Watson, "I am sorry, but I cannot move in this matter, except upon the oath of white witnesses." "But here's the boy; look at his
head and face," said the excited Master Hugh; "*they* show what has been done."
But Watson insisted that he was not authorized to do anything, unless white
witnesses of the transaction would come forward and testify to what had
taken place. He could issue no warrant, on my word, against white persons,
and if I had been killed in the presence of a *thousand blacks*, their testimony combined would have been insufficient to condemn a single murderer.
Master Hugh was compelled to say, for once, that this state of things was
too bad, and he left the office of the magistrate disgusted.

Of course it was impossible to get any white man to testify against my
assailants. The carpenters saw what was done, but the actors were but the
agents of their malice, and did only what the carpenters sanctioned. They
had cried with one accord, "Kill the nigger! kill the nigger!" Even those
who may have pitied me, if any such were among them, lacked the moral courage to volunteer their evidence. The slightest show of sympathy or justice
toward a person of color was denounced as abolitionism, and the name of abolitionist subjected its hearer to frightful liabilities. "D---n abolitionists," and "kill the niggers," were the watchwords of the foul-mouthed ruffians of those days. Nothing was done, and probably would not have been,
had I been killed in the affray. The laws and the morals of the Christian
city of Baltimore afforded no protection to the sable denizens of that city.

Master Hugh, on finding that he could get no redress for the cruel
wrong, withdrew me from the employment of Mr. Gardiner and took me into his
own family. Mrs. Auld kindly taking care of me and dressing my wounds until
they were healed and I was ready to go to work again.

While I was on the Eastern Shore, Master Hugh had met with reverses
which overthrew his business and had given up ship-building in his own yard,
on the City Block, and was now acting as foreman of Mr. Walter Price. The
best that he could do for me was to take me into Mr. Price's yard, and afford me the facilities there for completing the trade which I began to learn
at Gardiner's. Here I rapidly became expert in the use of calkers' tools,
and in the course of a single year, I was able to command the highest wages
paid to journeymen calkers in Baltimore.

The reader will observe that I was now of some pecuniary value to my master. During the busy season I was bringing six and seven dollars per week. I have sometimes brought him as much as nine dollars a week, for wages were a dollar and a half per day.

After learning to calk, I sought my own employment, made my own contracts, and collected my own earnings--giving Master Hugh no trouble in any part of the transactions to which I was a party.

Here, then, were better days for the Eastern Shore slave. I was free from the vexatious assaults of the apprentices at Gardiner's, free from the perils of plantation life, and once more in favorable condition to increase my little stock of education, which had been at a dead stand since my removal from Baltimore. I had on the Eastern Shore been only a teacher, when in company with other slaves, but now there were colored persons here who could instruct me. Many of the young calkers could read, write, and cipher. Some of them had high notions about mental improvement, and the free ones on Fell's Point organized what they called the "East Baltimore Mental Improvement Society." To this society, notwithstanding it was intended that only free persons should attach themselves, I was admitted, and was several times assigned a prominent part in its debates. I owe much to the society of these young men.

The reader already knows enough of the ill effects of good treatment on a slave to anticipate what was not the case in my improved condition. It was not long before I began to show signs of disquiet with slavery, and to look around for means to get out of it by the shortest route. I was living among freemen, and was in all respects equal to them by nature and attainments. Why should I be a slave? There was no reason why I should be the thrall of any man. Besides, I was not getting, as I have said, a dollar and fifty cents per day. I contracted for it, worked for it, collected it; it was paid to me, and it was rightfully my own; and yet upon every returning Saturday night, this money--my own hard earnings, every cent of it--was demanded of me and taken from me by Master Hugh. He did not earn it--he had no hand in earning it--why, then should he have it? I owed him nothing. He had given me no schooling, and I had received from him only my food and raiment, and for these, my services were supposed to pay from the first. The right to take my earnings was the right of the robber. He had the power to compel me to give him the fruits of my labor, and this *power* was his only right in the case. I became more and more dissatisfied with this state of things, and in so becoming I only gave proof of the same human nature which every reader of this chapter in my life--slaveholder, or non-slaveholder-- is conscious of possessing.

To make a contented slave, you must make a thoughtless one. It is necessary to darken his moral and mental vision, and, as far as possible, to annihilate his power of reason. He must be able to detect no inconsistencies in slavery. The man who takes his earnings must be able to convince him that he has a perfect right to do so. It must not depend upon mere force—the slave must know no higher law than his master's will. The whole relationship must not only demonstrate to his mind its necessity, but its absolute rightfulness. If there be one crevice through which a single drop can fall, it will certainly rust off the slave's chain.

My condition during the year of my escape (1838) was comparatively a free and easy one, so far, at least, as the wants of the physical man were concerned, but the reader will bear in mind that my troubles from the beginning had been less physical than mental, and he will thus be prepared to find that slave life was adding nothing to its charms for me as I grew older, and became more and more acquainted with it. The practice of openly robbing me, from week to week, of all my earnings, kept the nature and character of slavery constantly before me. I could be robbed by indirection, but this was too open and barefaced to be endured. I could see no reason why I should, at the end of each week, pour the reward of my honest toil into the purse of my master. My obligation to do this vexed me, and the manner in which Master Hugh received my wages vexed me yet more. Carefully counting the money, and rolling it out dollar by dollar, he would look me in the face, as if he would search my heart as well as my pocket, and reproachfully ask me, "Is that all?"--implying that I had perhaps kept back part of my wages, or, if not so, the demand was made possibly to make me feel that

after all, I was an "unprofitable servant." Draining me of the last cent of
my hard earnings, he would, however, occasionally, when I brought home an
extra large sum, dole out to me a sixpence or shilling, with a view, perhaps, of kindling my gratitude. But it had the opposite effect. It was an
admission of my right to the whole sum. The fact that he gave me any part
of my wages was proof that he suspected I had a right to the whole of them,
and I always felt uncomfortable after having received anything in this way,
lest his giving me a few cents might possibly ease his conscience, and make
him feel himself to be a pretty honorable robber after all. . . .

*Frederick Douglass, Life and Times of Frederick Douglass Written by Himself,
His Early Life as a Slave, His Escape From Bondage, and His Complete History
(London: Collier-Macmillan Ltd., 1962, originally 1892), pp. 178-93.*

40. ONE YEAR IN THE LIFE OF A HIRED-OUT SLAVE [9]

    Soon afterwards, my master removed to the city of St. Louis, and pur-
chased a farm four miles from there, which he placed under the charge of an
overseer by the name of Friend Haskell. He was a regular Yankee from New
England. The Yankees are noted for making the most cruel overseers.
    My mother was hired out in the city, and I was also hired out there to
Major Freeland, who kept a public house. He was formerly from Virginia,
and was a horse-racer, cock-fighter, gambler, and withal an inveterate drunkard. There were ten or twelve servants in the house, and when he was present, it was cut and slash-knock down and drag out. In his fits of anger,
he would take up a chair, and throw it at a servant; and in his more rational moments, when he wished to chastise one, he would tie them up in the
smokehouse, and whip them; after which, he would cause a fire to be made of
tobacco stems, and smoke them. This he called *"Virginia play."*
    I complained to my master of the treatment which I received from Major
Freeland; but it made no difference. He cared nothing about it, so long as
he received the money for my labor. After living with Major Freeland five
or six months, I ran away, and went into the woods back of the city; and
when night came on, I made my way to my master's farm, but was afraid to be
seen, knowing that if Mr. Haskell, the overseer, should discover me, I
should be again carried back to Major Freeland; so I kept in the woods. One
day, while in the woods, I heard the barking and howling of dogs, and in a
short time they came so near that I knew them to be the bloodhounds of Major
Benjamin O'Fallon. He kept five or six, to hunt runaway slaves with.
    As soon as I was convinced that it was them, I knew there was no chance
of escape. I took refuge in the top of a tree; and the hounds were soon at
its base, and there remained until the hunters came up in a half or three
quarters of an hour afterwards. There were two men with the dogs, who, as
soon as they came up, ordered me to descend. I came down, was tied, and
taken to St. Louis jail. Major Freeland soon made his appearance, and took
me out, and ordered me to follow him, which I did. After we returned home,
I was tied up in the smoke-house, and was very severely whipped. After the
major had flogged me to his satisfaction, he sent out his son Robert, a
young man eighteen or twenty years of age, to see that I was well smoked.
He made a fire of tobacco stems, which soon set me to coughing and sneezing.
This, Robert told me, was the way his father used to do to his slaves in
Virginia. After giving me what they conceived to be a decent smoking, I was
untied and again set to work.
    Robert Freeland was a "chip of the old block." Though quite young, it
was not unfrequently that he came home in a state of intoxication. He is
now, I believe, a popular commander of a steamboat on the Mississippi river.
Major Freeland soon after failed in business, and I was put on board the
steamboat Missouri, which plied between St. Louis and Galena. The commander
of the boat was William B. Culver. I remained on her during the sailing

season, which was the most pleasant time for me that I had ever experienced. At the close of navigation I was hired to Mr. John Colburn, keeper of the Missouri Hotel. He was from one of the free states; but a more inveterate hater of the negro I do not believe ever walked God's green earth. This hotel was at that time one of the largest in the city, and there were employed in it twenty or thirty servants, mostly slaves.

Mr. Colburn was very abusive, not only to the servants, but to his wife also, who was an excellent woman, and one from whom I never knew a servant to receive a harsh word; but never did I know a kind one to a servant from her husband. Among the slaves employed in the hotel was one by the name of Aaron, who belonged to Mr. John F. Darby, a lawyer. Aaron was the knife-cleaner. One day, one of the knives was put on the table, not as clean as it might have been. Mr. Colburn, for this offence, tied Aaron up in the wood-house, and gave him over fifty lashes on the bare back with a cow-hide, after which, he made me wash him down with rum. This seemed to put him into more agony than the whipping. After being untied he went home to his master, and complained of the treatment which he had received. Mr. Darby would hive no heed to anything he had to say, but sent him directly back. Colburn, learning that he had been to his master with complaints; tied him up again, and gave him a more severe whipping than before. The poor fellow's back was literally cut to pieces; so much so, that he was not able to work for ten to twelve days.

There was, also, among the servants, a girl whose master resided in the country. Her name was Patsey. Mr. Colburn tied her up one evening, and whipped her until several of the boarders came out and begged him to desist. The reason for whipping her was this. She was engaged to be married to a man belonging to Major William Christy, who resided four or five miles north of the city. Mr. Colburn had forbid her to see John Christy. The reason of this was said to be the regard which he himself had for Patsey. She went to meeting that evening, and John returned home with her. Mr. Colburn had intended to flog John, if he came within the inclosure; but John knew too well the temper of his rival, and kept at a safe distance:--so he took vengeance on the poor girl. If all the slave-drivers had been called together, I do not think a more cruel man than John Colburn--and he too a northern man--could have been found among them.

While living at the Missouri hotel, a circumstance occurred which caused me great unhappiness. My master sold my mother, and all her children, except myself. They were sold to different persons in the city of St. Louis. I was soon after taken from Mr. Colburn's, and hired to Elijah P. Lovejoy, who was at that time publisher and editor of the "St. Louis Times." My work, while with him, was mainly in the printing office, waiting on the hands, working the press, &c. Mr. Lovejoy was a very good man, and decidedly the best master that I had ever had. I am chiefly indebted to him, and to my employment in the printing office, for what little learning I obtained while in slavery. [10]

Though slavery is thought, by some, to be mild in Missouri, when compared with the cotton, sugar and rice growing states, yet no part of our slaveholding country is more noted for the barbarity of its inhabitants than St. Louis. It was here that Col. Harney, a United States officer, whipped a slave woman to death. It was here that Francis McIntosh, a free colored man from Pittsburg, was taken from the steamboat Flora and burned at the stake. During a residence of eight years in this city, numerous cases of extreme cruelty came under my own observation; to record them all would occupy more space than could possibly be allowed in this little volume. . . .

While living with Mr. Lovejoy, I was often sent on errands to the office of the "Missouri Republican," published by Mr. Edward Charles. Once, while returning to the office with type, I was attacked by several large boys, sons of slave-holders, who pelted me with snow-balls. Having the heavy form of type in my hands, I could not make my escape by running; so I laid down the type and gave them battle. They gathered around me, pelting me with stones and sticks, until they overpowered me, and would have captured me, if I had not resorted to my heels. Upon my retreat they took possession of the type; and what to do to regain it I could not devise. Knowing Mr. Lovejoy to be a very humane man, I went to the office and laid the case before him. He told me to remain in the office. He took one of the

apprentices with him and went after the type, and soon returned with it;
but on his return informed me that Samuel McKinney had told him he would
whip me, because I had hurt his boy. Soon after, McKinney was seen making
his way to the office by one of the printers, who informed me of the fact,
and I made my escape through the back door.

McKinney not being able to find me on his arrival, left the office in
a great rage, swearing that he would whip me to death. A few days after, as
I was walking along Main street, he seized me by the collar, and struck me
over the head five or six times with a large cane, which caused the blood to
gush from my nose and ears in such a manner that my clothes were completely
saturated with blood. After beating me to his satisfaction he let me go,
and I returned to the office so weak from the loss of blood that Mr. Lovejoy
sent me home to my master. It was five weeks before I was able to walk
again. During this time it was necessary to have some one to supply my
place at the office, and I lost the situation.

After my recovery, I was hired to Capt. Otis Reynolds, as a waiter on
board the steamboat Enterprise, owned by Messrs. John and Edward Walsh, commission merchants at St. Louis. The boat was then running on the upper Mississippi. My employment on board was to wait on gentlemen, and the captain
being a good man, the situation was a pleasant one to me;--but in passing
from place to place, and seeing new faces every day, and knowing that they
could go where they pleased, I soon became unhappy, and several times thought
of leaving the boat at some landing-place, and trying to make my escape to
Canada, which I had heard much about as a place where the slave might live,
be free, and be protected.

But whenever such thoughts would come into my mind, my resolution would
soon be shaken by the remembrance that my dear mother was a slave in St.
Louis, and I could not bear the idea of leaving her in that condition. She
had often taken me upon her knee, and told me how she had carried me upon her
back to the field when I was an infant--how often she had been whipped for
leaving her work to nurse me--and how happy I would appear when she would
take me into her arms. When these thoughts came over me, I would resolve
never to leave the land of slavery without my mother. I thought that to
leave her in slavery, after she had undergone and suffered so much for me,
would be proving recreant to the duty which I owed to her. Besides this, I
had three brothers and a sister there--two of my brothers having died.

My mother, my brothers Joseph and Millford, and my sister Elizabeth, belonged to Mr. Isaac Mansfield, formerly from one of the free states, (Massachusetts, I believe.) He was a tinner by trade, and carried on a large
manufacturing establishment. Of all my relatives, mother was first, and sister next. One evening, while visiting them, I made some allusion to a proposed journey to Canada, and sister took her seat by my side, and taking my
hand in hers, said, with tears in her eyes--

"Brother, you are not going to leave mother and your dear sister here
without a friend, are you?"

I looked into her face, as the tears coursed swiftly down her cheeks,
and bursting into tears myself, said--

"No, I will never desert you and mother!"

She clasped my hand in hers, and said--

"Brother, you have often declared that you would not end your days in
slavery. I see no possible way in which you can escape with us; and now,
brother, you are on a steamboat where there is some chance for you to escape
to a land of liberty. I beseech you not to let us hinder you. If we cannot
get our liberty, we do not wish to be the means of keeping you from a land
of freedom."

I could restrain my feelings no longer, and an outburst of my own feelings caused her to cease speaking upon that subject. In opposition to their
wishes, I pledged myself not to leave them in the hand of the oppressor. I
took leave of them, and returned to the boat, and laid down in my bunk; but
"sleep departed from mine eyes, and slumber from mine eyelids."

A few weeks after, on our downward passage, the boat took on board, at
Hannibal, a drove of slaves, bound for the New Olreans market. They numbered from fifty to sixty, consisting of men and women from eighteen to forty years of age. A drove of slaves on a southern steamboat, bound for the
cotton or sugar regions, is an occurrence so common, that no one, not even

the passengers, appear to notice it, though they clank their chains at every step. There was, however, one in this gang that attracted the attention of the passengers and crew. It was a beautiful girl, apparently about twenty years of age, perfectly white, with straight light hair and blue eyes. But it was not the whiteness of her skin that created such sensation among those who gazed upon her—it was her almost unparalleled beauty. She had been on the boat but a short time, before the attention of all the passengers, including the ladies, had been called to her, and the common topic of conversation was about the beautiful slave-girl. She was not in chains. The man who claimed this article of human merchandise was a Mr. Walker—a well known slave-trader, residing in St. Louis. There was a general anxiety among the passengers and crew to learn the history of the girl. Her master kept close by her side, and it would have been considered impudent for any of the passengers to have spoken to her, and the crew were not allowed to have any conversation with them. When we reached St. Louis, the slaves were removed to a boat bound for New Orleans, and the history of the beautiful slave-girl remained a mystery.

I remained on the boat during the season, and it was not an unfrequent occurrence to have on board gangs of slaves on their way to the cotton, sugar and rice plantations of the south.

Toward the latter part of the summer Captain Reynolds left the boat, and I was sent home. I was then placed on the farm, under Mr. Haskell, the overseer. As I had been some time out of the field, and not accustomed to work in the sun, it was very hard; but I was compelled to keep up with the best of the hands.

I found a great difference between the work in the steamboat cabin and that in a corn-field.

My master, who was then living in the city, soon after removed to the farm, when I was taken out of the field to work in the house as a waiter.

Soon after this, I was hired out to Mr. Walker, the same man whom I have mentioned as having carried a gang of slaves down the river on the steamboat Enterprise. Seeing me in the capacity of a steward on the boat, and thinking that I would make a good hand to take care of slaves, he determined to have me for that purpose; and finding that my master would not sell me, he hired me for a term of one year.

When I learned the fact of my having been hired to a negro speculator, or a "soul driver," as they are generally called among slaves, no one can tell my emotions. Mr. Walker had offered a high price for me, as I afterwards learned, but I suppose my master was restrained from selling me by the fact that I was a near relative of his. On entering the service of Mr. Walker, I found that my opportunity of getting to a land of liberty was gone, at least for the time being. He had a gang of slaves in readiness to start for New Orleans, and in a few days we were on our journey. I am at a loss for language to express my feelings on that occasion. Although my master had told me that he had not sold me, and Mr. Walker had told me that he had not purchased them, I did not believe them; and not until I had been to New Orleans, and was on my return, did I believe that I was not sold.

There was on the boat a large room on the lower deck, in which the slaves were kept, men and women, promiscuously—all chained two and two, and a strict watch kept that they did not get loose; for cases have occurred in which slaves have got off their chains, and made their escape at landing-places, while the boats were taking in wood;—and with all our care, we lost one woman who had been taken from her husband and children, and having no desire to live without them, in the agony of her soul jumped overboard, and drowned herself. She was not chained.

It was almost impossible to keep that part of the boat clean.

On landing at Natchez, the slaves were all carried to the slave-pen, and there kept one week, during which time several of them were sold. Mr. Walker fed his slaves well. We took on board at St. Louis several hundred pounds of bacon (smoked meat) and corn-meal, and his slaves were better fed than slaves generally were in Natchez, so far as my observation extended.

At the end of a week, we left for New Orleans, the place of our final destination, which we reached in two days. Here the slaves were placed in a negro-pen, where those who wished to purchase could call and examine them. The negro-pen is a small yard, surrounded by buildings, from fifteen to

twenty feet wide, with the exception of a large gate with iron bars. The
slaves are kept in the building during the night, and turned out into the
yard during the day. After the best of the stock was sold at private sale
at the pen, the balance were taken to the Exchange Coffee-House Auction
Rooms, kept by Isaac L. McCoy, and sold at public auction. After the sale
of this lot of slaves, we left New Orleans for St. Louis. On our arrival at
St. Louis I went to Dr. Young, and told him that I did not wish to live with
Mr. Walker any longer. I was heart-sick at seeing my fellow-creatures
bought and sold. But the Dr. had hired me for the year, and stay I must.
Mr. Walker again commenced purchasing another gang of slaves. He bought a
man of Colonel John O'Fallon, who resided in the suburbs of the city. This
man had a wife and three children. As soon as the purchase was made, he was
put in jail for safe keeping, until we should be ready to start for New Orleans. His wife visited him while there, several times, and several times
when she went for that purpose was refused admittance.

In the course of eight or nine weeks Mr. Walker had his cargo of human
flesh made up. There was in this lot a number of old men and women, some of
them with gray locks. We left St. Louis in the steamboat Carlton, Captain
Swan, bound for New Orleans. On our way down, and before we reached Rodney,
the place where we made our first stop, I had to prepare the old slaves for
market. I was ordered to have the old men's whiskers shaved off, and the
grey hairs plucked out where they were not too numerous, in which case he
had a preparation of blacking to color it, and with a blacking brush we
would put it on. This was new business to me, and was performed in a room
where the passengers could not see us. These slaves were also taught how
old they were by Mr. Walker, and after going through the blacking process
they looked ten or fifteen years younger; and I am sure that some of those
who purchased slaves of Mr. Walker were dreadfully cheated, especially in
the ages of the slaves which they bought.

We landed at Rodney, and the slaves were driven to the pen in the back
part of the village. Several were sold at this place, during our stay of
four or five days, when we proceeded to Natchez. There we landed at night,
and the gang were put in the warehouse until morning, when they were driven
to the pen. As soon as the slaves are put in these pens, swarms of planters
may be seen in and about them. They knew when Walker was expected, as he
always had the time advertised beforehand when he would be in Rodney, Natchez, and New Orleans. These were the principal places where he offered his
slaves for sale.

. . . we proceeded to New Orleans, and put the gang in the same negro-
pen which we occupied before. In a short time the planters came flocking
to the pen to purchase slaves. Before the slaves were exhibited for sale,
they were dressed and driven out into the yard. Some were set to dancing,
some to jumping, some to singing, and some to playing cards. This was done
to make them appear cheerful and happy. My business was to see that they
were placed in those situations before the arrival of the purchasers, and I
have often set them to dancing when their cheeks were wet with tears. As
slaves were in good demand at that time, they were all soon disposed of, and
we again set out for St. Louis. . . .

He soon commenced purchasing to make the third gang. We took steamboat,
and went to Jefferson City, a town on the Missouri river. Here we landed,
and took stage for the interior of the state. He bought a number of slaves
as he passed the different farms and villages. . . .

We finally arrived at Mr. Walker's farm. He had a house built during
our absence to put slaves in. It was a kind of domestic jail. The slaves
were put in the jail at night, and worked on the farm during the day. They
were kept here until the gang was completed, when we again started for New
Orleans, on board the steamboat North America, Capt. Alexander Scott. We
had a large number of slaves in this gang. One, by the name of Joe, Mr.
Walker was training up to take my place, as my time was nearly out, and glad
was I.

After selling out his cargo of human flesh, we returned to St. Louis,
and my time was up with Mr. Walker. I had served him one year, and it was
the longest year I ever lived.

*William Wells Brown, Narrative of William W. Brown; A Fugitive Slave (Bos-
ton: The Anti-Slavery Office, 1848), second edition, as reproduced in Robin
W. Winks, Larry Gara, Jane H. and William H. Pease, and Tilden G. Edelstein
(eds.), Four Fugitive Slave Narratives (Reading, Massachusetts: Addison-
Wesley Publishing Company, 1969), pp. 5-12, 14-18, 21, 26.*

SELF-PURCHASE BY SLAVE MECHANICS

41. FREE BLACKS PURCHASE FAMILY MEMBERS

I visited this week about 30 black families, and found that some members of more than half these families were still in bondage, and the father,
mother and children were struggling to lay up money enough to purchase their
freedom. I found one man who had just finished paying for his wife and five
children. Another man and wife had bought themselves some years ago, and
have been working night and day to purchase their children; they had just
redeemed the last and had paid for themselves and children 1,400 dollars!
Another woman had recently paid the last installment of the purchase money
for her husband. She had purchased him by taking in washing, and working
late at night, after going out and performing as help at hard labor. . . .

*Theodore D. Weld to Lewis Tappan, March 18, 1834, in Gilbert H. Barnes and
Dwight L. Dumond (eds.), Weld-Grimke Letters, Vol. I (New York, 1934), p.
134.*

42. A CALL FOR FINANCIAL HELP

We have just received a call from Mrs. E. B. WELLS, a slightly colored
lady, one who has experienced in her own person the evils inherent in slavery, a member of the Baptist Church in St. Louis, in good and regular standing, having any number of certificates of excellent character, and has given
proof of the good qualities of her head and heart by having purchased her own
freedom at the enormous price of sixteen hundred dollars, of which one thousand was raised by the citizens of St. Louis, and who had also purchased her
mother and sister by the payment of one thousand five hundred dollars. This
lady (for a lady she really is) is now in the city of Rochester for the purpose of raising money with which to purchase the freedom of her only remaining sister in slavery. This sister is owned by Mrs. BRENT, of Boonville,
Mo., and Mrs. BRENT is willing to take one thousand dollars for this Christian chattel, of which sum five hundred dollars have already been raised by
the indefatigable exertions of Mrs. WELLS.--Her case is commended to the
humane and benevolent portion of our citizens, and we cannot but hope that at
least a part of the five hundred dollars still remaining to be raised for
this ransom may be obtained in the city of Rochester.

Douglass' Monthly, April, 1859.

43. ANOTHER SLAVE FREED

We take pleasure in publishing the following letter, which contains an
account of the purchased freedom of a slave who seems to be a man of remarkable intellect:--

G. HALLOCK, Esq.,
   Dear Sir:--I am very happy to inform you that the freedom of the slave
Benjamin Bradley has been accomplished by the payment of $1,000, to which
you contributed the final $122 necessary to make it up.
   Some particulars of the case will perhaps be of interest to your readers.
   Bradley was owned by a master in Annapolis, Md. Eight years ago he was
employed in a printing office there. He was then about sixteen, and showed
great mechanical skill and ingenuity. With a piece of a gun-barrel, some
pewter, a couple of pieces of round steel, and some like materials, he constructed a *working model of a steam engine.*
   His master soon afterwards got him the place of helper in the department of Natural and Experimental Philosophy in the Naval Academy at Annapolis. He sold his first steam engine to a Midshipman. With the proceeds,
and what money he could lay up (his master allowing him five dollars a month
out of his wages), he built an engine large enough to drive the first cutter
of a sloop-of-war at the rate of sixteen knots an hour. He was assisted in
planning this engine, being told how to find the resistance of an immersed
floating body, and the size, &c., of his propeller.
   Professor Hopkins, of the Academy, says that he gets up the experiments
for the lecture-room very handsomely. Being shown once how to line up the
parabolic mirrors for concentrating heat, he always succeeded afterwards.
So with the chemical experiments. He makes all the gases, and works with
them, showing the Drummond light, &c. Prof. Hopkins remarks of him that "he
looks for *the law* by which things act."
   He has been taught to read and write, mainly by the Professor's children; has made very good progress in arithmetic, and will soon take hold of
algebra and geometry.
   Great interest was naturally felt in such a man, and his master expressing a willingness to take $1,000 for him, if paid by Oct. 6th, though
well worth $1,500, a subscription was set on foot privately for the purpose.
Two gentlemen in Annapolis agreed to lend Ben $500. He had his own savings,
$100. The friends of Ben devoted themselves to raising the money, and at
the time we called on you, the sum was completed with the exception of $122,
which you supplied. This was forwarded to Annapolis. Meantime Professor H.
H. Lockwood, with the utmost generosity, had himself borrowed the necessary
amount at the bank of his own note (namely, $900), and thus secured the
freedom of Ben beyond a contingency.
   In saying the sum is completed, I of course mean to include the money
which has been loaned to Ben, and which he is to repay.
   He is now free, and the question is, what is best for him to do? He is
a mere child as to worldly matters, and his only plan is, to remain at Annapolis and finish his education as far as he can. But it seems very desirable to furnish him employment of a nature suited to his abilities. The pro-
fessors consider him perfectly competent to take charge of the engine of a
steamship. It is possible that some of your readers may be able to suggest
employment for him; and, if so, a letter addressed to him at the Naval Academy, Annapolis, will be thankfully received.

                                        I am yours, &c.

The Anglo-African Magazine 1 (November, 1859):367-68.

44. A FOUNDER PURCHASES HIS FAMILY'S FREEDOM

A St. Louis paper of a recent date has the following paragraph:--

'In the foundry of Gaty, M'Cune & co., in this city, among its two hundred and seventy operatives are two negroes, who began life at the establishment, in 1849, as slaves. By dint of unlagging industry, in due course
of time one of them bought himself, wife and five children, paying for himself $1400, and on an average for his wife and children $800 each. The negro is now supposed to be worth, in his own right, more than $5000 in real
estate in that city. Another negro entered the factory about the same time,
amassed sufficient money by his attention to duty to purchase himself at the
price of $1500, his wife at $500, and four children at $400, and is now
worth $6000 in real estate. These negroes were bought from their masters by
Mr. Gray, with the understanding that they should work themselves free, and
out of his own pocket he gave two per cent. interest on the deferred payments.'

The Liberator, October 26, 1860.

45. THE LATE W. H. CROMWELL
A Biographical sketch

Died at his late residence in Philadelphia last Sunday afternoon, Willis
Hoges Cromwell, in the ninety-second year of his age.
The deceased was born near Shoulders' Hill in Nansemond Co., Va., May
25th, 1792. He belonged to what was known as "the free school estate" of
that county, the circumstances of the establishment of which adds another
page to the chapter of the many outrages perpetrated, under the system of
American Slavery on the rights of colored people. His maternal great grand
parents were Jack and Julia Cromwell. Julia belonged to one James Yates, a
Scotchman who as he had no children, gave by will Julia and her two daughters their freedom and two plantations and left seven plantations for the education of the poor. The land left to Julia and her family was taken, they
were cheated of their freedom, and they and their posterity were taken to
support the free schools under the name of "the free school Negroes." Up to
the time of the war there were some hundreds of these who were hired out
from year to year to the highest bidder.
Mr. Cromwell made his home in early manhood in the city of Portsmouth.
Up to the time of his leaving Virginia in '51 and since, the deceased was
looked up to as the general adviser of the large community above referred to,
as much because of his independent spirit, industry and pluck as for any
other reason. Because of his refusal to be dogged and driven about by hard
task masters or overseers, he was allowed to hire his own time and that of
his family.
He was a ship carpenter and wharf builder and he eventually ran a
freight ferry between the two cities of Norfolk and Portsmouth--a business
then monopolized by two colored men--the other being the late Charles Cooper
of Monrovia, West Africa, but since run by the captain of the noted Merrimac.
From the profits of this business he accumulated quite a sum, and at the age
of fifty-six he paid three hundred dollars for his time and more than three
thousand dollars for his wife and seven children, the youngest being then
two years of age. One of his children a daughter, had but recently been married. The "owner" of her husband, L. Bilisoly, the proprietor of a large
grocery, to whom Mr. Cromwell voluntarily gave his services on Saturday evening, put that husband in jail and threatened to send him to New Orleans, on
the pretext that as his wife had become under the law a free woman, her

husband would at the first opportunity escape from slavery. He did this
knowing that before he would be allowed to send him to New Orleans his father-in-law would secure his freedom, which the sequel proved to be true.

Besides this expenditure of nearly four thousand dollars for personal
freedom, he had in his possession receipts for $9000 paid at different times
for the *hire of his own family*.

According to the laws of Virginia persons obtaining their freedom could
not remain in the state except on humiliating conditions. So merchants and
preachers alike used their influence to have Willis, as they termed him, "go
to Liberia where he could be a free man indeed, and see his children grow up
to usefulness, if not to distinction." His views and theirs conflicted and
he rebuked them for the solicitude for his welfare--"they stood between him
and the sun and then blamed him for not seeing." In company with his wife he
made a tour of several northern cities, including New Haven, Brooklyn, New
York and Philadelphia, returned to Virginia and finally in 1851 settled in
the last named city.

Mr. Cromwell grew restive under the hardships and persecutions against
his race and gave support to all movements for their amelioration. He conducted a retail coal and wood business, and set a personal example of encouraging colored men in business. We have known him repeatedly to send his
orders for coal to Smith (Rev. Stephen) and Whipper (William) Smith and
Vidal (U.B.) colored merchants, four miles away, although he could have been
as well supplied by hundreds of others, nearer his place of business--simply
because the former were colored men.

On more than one occasion he was station agent of the underground railroad. He had no patience with pro-slavery arguments as they found expression in the Northern press. We have known him time and again to be overcome
because of his indignation against some time-serving policy or plea in the
interest of the slave owner. One day, in the darkest hour of the war, before colored people were allowed to ride in the street cars of Philadelphia,
he had occasion with a son and grandson to ride on one of these cars. He
had not gone far before espying an unoccupied seat within without asking
leave he left the platform, took the seat and then made room for those who
were with him, and made them come in. The conductor came up, told him to
get up and not violate the rules of the company, &c., but he insisted on his
right to ride and retained his seat. A white gentleman on leaving the car
handed Mr. Cromwell his card as "Attorney at law" and said, "You are in the
right, and should you need any assistance call on me."

The funeral services were held Wednesday afternoon at the Zion A. M. E.
Church of which the deceased was a member and his first wife a founder. Eu-
logistic remarks having been made by Revs. B. F. Combash (the pastor), Theo.
Gould, Dr. B. T. Tanner, F. P. Main and B. Siers, the paster said a gentleman had requested an opportunity to pay a tribute to the deceased, whereupon
a venerable looking white gentleman came forward, and said that he could
heartily indorse all that had been said, for he had known the deceased for
over sixty years in his home in Virginia where he was universally esteemed,
both in his business transactions and as a private citizen. He gave a few
reminiscences which illustrated how Mr. Cromwell stood as the business man of
his race in the community from which he came. This stranger was unknown to
the family of the deceased and he had only heard of the funeral by seeing it
announced in the daily papers. The venerable Rev. Thomas Jones paid a most
eloquent tribute saying the deceased was the man referred to in the 1st
Psalm. [11]

The remains were interred in the Lebanon Cemetery. Mr. Cromwell leaves
a widow, five children and sixteen grand children. His children are Mrs. M.
A. Armstead and Mrs. E. Nash, Levi Cromwell, the restaurateur, Willis H.
Cromwell, jr., Supt. of Bethel A. M. E. Sunday School of Philadelphia and J.
W. Cromwell of THE ADVOCATE of this city.

The People's Advocate, July 14, 1883.

A SLAVE MECHANIC'S ESCAPE TO FREEDOM

46. THE ESCAPE FROM SLAVERY OF FREDERICK DOUGLASS, BLACK SHIP-CAULKER

My condition during the year of my escape (1838) was comparatively a
free and easy one, so far, at least, as the wants of the physical man were
concerned; but the reader will bear in mind that my troubles from the beginning had been less physical than mental, and he will thus be prepared to
find that slave life was adding nothing to its charm for me as I grew older,
and became more and more acquainted with it. The practice of openly robbing
me, from week to week, of all my earnings, kept the nature and character of
slavery constantly before me. I could be robbed by indirection, but this
was too open and barefaced to be endured. I could see no reason why I
should, at the end of each week, pour the reward of my honest toil into the
purse of my master.

My obligation to do this vexed me, and the manner in which Master Hugh
received my wages vexed me yet more. Carefully counting the money, and
rolling it out dollar by dollar, he would look me in the face, as if he
would search my heart as well as my pocket, and reproachfully ask me, "Is
that all?"--implying that I had perhaps kept back part of my wages; or, if
not so, the demand was made possibly to make me feel that after all, I was
an "unprofitable servant." Draining me of the last cent of my hard earnings, he would, however, occasionally, when I brought home an extra large
sum, dole out to me a sixpence or shilling, with a view, perhaps, of kindling my gratitude. But it had the opposite effect. It was an admission of
my right to the whole sum. The fact that he gave me any part of my wages
was proof that he suspected I had a right to the whole of them; and I always
felt uncomfortable after having received anything in this way, lest his giving me a few cents might possibly ease his conscience, and make him feel
himself to be a pretty honorable robber after all.

Held to a strict account, and kept under a close watch,--the old suspicion of my running away not having been entirely removed,--to accomplish my
escape seemed a very difficult thing. The railroad from Baltimore to Philadelphia was under regulations so stringent that even *free* colored travelers
were almost excluded. They must have free papers; they must be measured and
carefully examined before they could enter the cars, and could go only in
the day time, even when so examined. The steamboats were under regulations
equally stringent. And still more, and worse than all, all the great turn-
pikes leading northward were beset with kidnappers; a class of men who watched the newspapers for advertisements for runaway slaves, thus making their
living by the accursed reward of slave-hunting.

My discontent grew upon me, and I was on a constant lookout for means
to get away. With money I could easily have managed the matter, and from
this consideration I hit upon the plan of soliciting the privilege of hiring
my time. It was quite common in Baltimore to allow slaves this privilege,
and was the practice also in New Orleans. A slave who was considered trust-
worthy could, by regularly paying his master a definite sum at the end of
each week, dispose of his time as he liked. It so happened that I was not in
very good odor, and was far from being a trustworthy slave. Nevertheless, I
watched my opportunity when Master Thomas came to Baltimore (for I was still
his property, Hugh only acting as his agent,) in the spring of 1838, to purchase his spring supply of goods, and applied to him directly for the much-
coveted privilege of hiring my time.

This request Master Thomas unhesitatingly refused to grant and charged
me, with some sternness, with inventing this stratagem to make my escape.
He told me I could go *nowhere* but he would catch me; and, in the event of my
running away, I might be assured that he should spare no pains in his efforts
to recapture me. He recounted, with a good deal of eloquence, the many kind
offices he had done me, and exhorted me to be contented and obedient. "Lay
out no plans for the future," said he. "If you behave yourself properly, I

will take care of you." Kind and considerate as this offer was, it failed
to soothe me into repose. In spite of all Master Thomas had said and in
spite of my own efforts to the contrary, the injustice and wickedness of
slavery were always uppermost in my thoughts and strengthening my purpose to
make my escape at the earliest moment possible.

About two months after applying to Master Thomas for the privilege of
hiring my time, I applied to Master Hugh for the same liberty, supposing him
to be unacquainted with the fact that I had made a similar application to
Master Thomas and had been refused. My boldness in making this request
fairly astounded him at first. He gazed at me in amazement. But I had many
good reasons for pressing the matter, and, after listening to them awhile,
he did not absolutely refuse but told me that he would think of it. There
was hope for me in this. Once master of my own time, I felt sure that I
could make, over and above my obligation to him, a dollar or two every week.
Some slaves had, in this way, made enough to purchase their freedom. It was
a sharp spur to their industry; and some of the most enterprising Negro men
in Baltimore hired themselves in that way.

After mature reflection, as I suppose it was, Master Hugh granted me
the privilege in question, on the following terms: I was to be allowed all
my time; to make all bargains for work, and to collect my own wages; and in
return for this liberty, I was required or obliged to pay him three dollars
at the end of each week, and to board and clothe myself, and buy my own calking tools. A failure in any of these particulars would put an end to the
privilege. This was a hard bargain. The wear and tear of clothing, the
losing and breaking of tools, and the expense of board, made it necessary
for me to earn at least six dollars per week to keep even with the world.
All who are acquainted with calking know how uncertain and irregular that employment is. It can be done to advantage only in dry weather, for it is useless to put wet oakum into a ship's seam. Rain or shine, however, work or
no work, at the end of each week the money must be forthcoming.

Master Hugh seemed, for a time, much pleased with this arrangement; and
well he might be, for it was decidedly in his favor. It relieved him of all
anxiety concerning me. His money was sure. He had armed my love of liberty
with a lash and a driver far more efficient than any I had before known; for,
while by this arrangement, he derived all the benefits of slaveholding without its evils, I endured all the evils of being a slave, and yet suffered
all the care and anxiety of a responsible freeman.

"Nevertheless," thought I, "it is a valuable privilege--another step in
my career toward freedom." It was something even to be permitted to stagger
under the disadvantages of liberty, and I was determined to hold on to the
newly gained footing by all proper industry. I was ready to work by night
as by day, and being in the possession of excellent health, I was not only
able to meet my current expenses, but also to lay by a small sum at the end
of each week. All went on thus from the month of May till August; then, for
reasons which will become apparent as I proceed, my much-valued liberty was
wrested from me.

During the week previous to this calamitous event, I had made arrangements with a few young friends to accompany them on Saturday night to a
camp-meeting, to be held about twelve miles from Baltimore. On the evening
of our intended start for the camp-ground, something occurred in the shipyard where I was at work which detained me unusually late, and compelled me
either to disappoint my friends, or to neglect carrying my weekly dues to
Master Hugh. Knowing that I had the money and could hand it to him on another day, I decided to go to camp-meeting and, on my return, to pay him the
three dollars for the past week.

Once on the camp-ground, I was induced to remain one day longer than I
had intended when I left home. But as soon as I returned I went directly to
his home on Fell street to hand him his (my) money. Unhappily the fatal mistake had been made. I found him exceedingly angry. He exhibited all the
signs of apprehension and wrath which a slaveholder might be surmised to exhibit on the supposed escape of a favorite slave. "You rascal! I have a
great mind to give you a sound whipping. How dare you go out of the city
without first asking and obtaining my permission?" "Sir," I said, "I hired
my time and paid you the price you asked for it. I did not know that it was
any part of the bargain that I should ask you when or where I should go."

"You do not know, you rascal! You are bound to show yourself here every Saturday night." After reflecting a few moments, he became somewhat cooled down, but, evidently greatly troubled, said: "Now, you scoundrel, you have done for yourself; you shall hire your time no longer. The next thing I shall hear of will be your running away. Bring home your tools at once. I'll teach you how to go off in this way."

Thus ended my partial freedom. I could hire my time no longer. I obeyed my master's orders at once. The little taste of liberty which I had had --although as it will be seen, that taste was far from being unalloyed,--by no means enhanced my contentment with slavery. Punished by Master Hugh, it was now my turn to punish him. "Since," thought I, "you *will* make a slave of me, I will await your order in all things." So, instead of going to look for work on Monday morning, as I had formerly done, I remained at home during the entire week, without the performance of a single stroke of work. Saturday night came, and he called upon me as usual for my wages. I, of course, told him I had done no work, and had no wages. Here we were at the point of coming to blows. His wrath had been accumulating during the whole week; for he evidently saw that I was making no effort to get work, but was most aggravatingly awaiting his orders in all things.

As I look back to this behavior of mine, I scarcely know what possessed me, thus to trifle with one who had such unlimited power to bless or blast me. Master Hugh raved, and swore he would "get hold of me," but wisely for *him,* and happily for *me,* his wrath employed only those harmless, impalpable missiles which roll from a limber tongue. In my desperation I had fully made up my mind to measure strength with him in case he should attempt to execute his threat. I am glad there was no occasion for this, for resistance to him could not have ended so happily for me as it did in the case of Covey. [12]

Master Hugh was not a man to be safely resisted by a slave; and I freely own that in my conduct toward him, in this instance, there was more folly than wisdom. He closed his reproofs by telling me that hereafter I need give myself no uneasiness about getting work; he "would himself see to getting work for me, and enough of it at that." This threat, I confess, had some terror in it, and on thinking the matter over during the Sunday, I resolved not only to save him the trouble of getting me work, but that on the third day of September I would attempt to make my escape. His refusal to allow me to hire my time therefore hastened the period of my flight. I had three weeks in which to prepare for my journey.

Once resolved, I felt a certain degree of repose, and on Monday morning, instead of waiting for Master Hugh to seek employment for me, I was up by break of day, and off to the ship-yard of Mr. Butler, on the City Block, near the draw-bridge. I was a favorite with Mr. Butler, and, young as I was, I had served as his foreman, on the floatstage, at calking. Of course I easily obtained work, and at the end of the week, which, by the way, was exceedingly fine, I brought Master Hugh nine dollars. The effect of this mark of returning good sense on my part was excellent. He was very much pleased; he took the money, commended me and told me that I might have done the same thing the week before.

It is a blessed thing that the tyrant may not always know the thoughts and purposes of his victim. Master Hugh little knew my plans. The going to camp-meeting without asking his permission; the insolent answers to his reproaches and the sulky deportment of the week after being deprived on the privilege of hiring my time, had awakened the suspicion that I might be cherishing disloyal purposes. My object, therefore, in working steadily was to remove suspicion; and in this I succeeded admirably. He probably thought that I was never better satisfied with my condition than at the very time I was planning my escape. The second week passed, and I again carried him my full week's wages--*nine dollars;* and so well pleased was he that he gave me *twenty-five cents!* and bade me "make good use of it." I told him I would do so, for one of the uses to which I intended to put it was to pay my fare on the "Underground Railroad."

Things without went on as usual; but I was passing through the same internal excitement and anxiety which I had experienced two years and a half before. The failure in that instance was not calculated to increase my confidence in the success of this, my second attempt; and I knew that a second failure could not leave me where my first did. I must either get to the *far North* or *be sent* to the far *South*. Besides the exercise of mind from this state of facts, I had the painful sensation of being about to separate from a circle of honest and warm-hearted friends. The thought of such a separa-tion, where the hope of ever meeting again was excluded, and where there could be no correspondence, was very painful.

It is my opinion that thousands more would have escaped from slavery but for the strong affection which bound them to their families, relatives, and friends. The daughter was hindered by the love she bore her mother and the father by the love he bore his wife and children, and so on to the end of the chapter. I had no relations in Baltimore, and I saw no probability of ever living in the neighborhood of sisters and brothers; but the thought of leaving my friends was the strongest obstacle to my running away. The last two days of the week, Friday and Saturday, were spent mostly in collect-ing my things together for my journey. Having worked four days that week for my master, I handed him six dollars on Saturday night. I seldom spent my Sundays at home, and for fear that something might be discovered in my conduct, I kept up my custom and absented myself all day. On Monday, the third day of September, 1838, in accordance with my resolution, I bade fare-well to the city of Baltimore, and to that slavery which had been my abhor-rence from childhood.

In the first narrative of my experience in slavery, written nearly for-ty years ago, and in various writings since, I have given the public what I considered very good reasons for withholding the manner of my escape. In substance these reasons were, first, that such publication at any time dur-ing the existence of slavery might be used by the master against the slave, and prevent the future escape of any who might adopt the same means that I did. The second reason was, if possible, still more binding to silence-- for publication of details would certainly have put in peril the persons and property of those who assisted.

Murder itself was not more sternly and certainly punished in the State of Maryland than was the aiding and abetting the escape of a slave. Many Negro men, for no other crime than that of giving aid to a fugitive slave, have, like Charles T. Torrey, perished in prison. The abolition of slavery in my native State and throughout the country, and the lapse of time, render the caution hitherto observed no longer necessary. But, even since the abo-lition of slavery, I have sometimes thought it well enough to battle curios-ity by saying that while slavery existed there were good reasons for not telling the manner of my escape, and since slavery had ceased to exist there was no reason for telling it. I shall now, however, cease to avail myself of this formula, and, as far as I can, endeavor to satisfy this very natural curiosity. I should perhaps have yielded to that feeling sooner, had there been anything very heroic or thrilling in the incidents connected with my escape, for I am sorry to say I have nothing of that sort to tell; and yet the courage that could risk betrayal and the bravery which was ready to en-counter death if need be, in pursuit of freedom, were essential features in the undertaking. My success was due to address rather than to courage; to good luck rather than to bravery. My means of escape were provided for me by the very men who were making laws to hold and bind me more securely in slav-ery. [13]

It was the custom in the State of Maryland to require of the free Negro people to have what were called free papers. This instrument they were re-quired to renew very often, and by charging a fee for this writing, consid-erable sums from time to time were collected by the State. In these papers the name, age, color, height and form of the free man were described, to-gether with any scars or other marks upon his person which could assist in his identification. This device of slaveholding ingenuity, like other de-vices of wickedness, in some measure defeated itself--since more than one man could be found to answer the same general description. Hence many slaves could escape by personating the owner of one set of papers; and this was of-ten done as follows: A slave nearly or sufficiently answering the descrip-tion set forth in the papers, would borrow or hire them till he could by their means escape to a free state, and then, by mail or otherwise, return them to the owner.

The operation was a hazardous one for the lender as well as for the borrower. A failure on the part of the fugitive to send back the papers would imperil his benefactor, and the discovery of the papers in possession of the wrong man would imperil both the fugitive and his friend. It was therefore an act of supreme trust on the part of a freeman of color thus to put in jeopardy his own liberty that another might be free. It was, however, not unfrequently bravely done, and was seldom discovered.

I was not so fortunate as to sufficiently resemble any of my free acquaintances as to answer the description of their papers. But I had one friend--a sailor--who owned a sailor's protection, which answered somewhat the purpose of free papers--describing his person and certifying to the fact that he was a free American sailor. The instrument had at its head the American eagle, which at once gave it the appearance of an authorized document. This protection did not, when in my hands, describe its bearer very accurately. Indeed, it called for a man much darker than myself, and close examination of it would have caused my arrest at the start. In order to avoid this fatal scrutiny on the part of the railroad official, I had arranged with Isaac Rolls, a hackman, to bring my baggage to the train just on the moment of starting, and jumped upon the car myself when the train was already in motion. Had I gone into the station and offered to purchase a ticket, I should have been instantly and carefully examined, and undoubtedly arrested. In choosing this plan upon which to act, I considered the jostle of the train, and the natural haste of the conductor in a train crowded with passengers, and relied upon my skill and address in playing the sailor as described in my protection, to do the rest.

One element in my favor was the kind feeling which prevailed in Baltimore and other seaports at the time, towards "those who go down to the sea in ships." "Free trade and sailor's rights" expressed the sentiment of the country just then. In my clothing I was rigged out in sailor style. I had on a red shirt and a tarpaulin hat and black cravat, tied in sailor fashion, carelessly and loosely about my neck. My knowledge of ships and sailor's talk came much to my assistance, for I knew a ship from stem to stern, and from keelson to cross-trees, and could talk sailor like an "old salt."

On sped the train, and I was well on the way to Havre de Grace before the conductor came into the Negro car to collect tickets and examine the papers of his black passengers. This was a critical moment in the drama. My whole future depended upon the decision of this conductor. Agitated I was while this ceremony was proceeding, but still, externally at least, I was apparently calm and self-possessed. He went on with his duty--examining several colored passengers before reaching me. He was somewhat harsh in tone and peremptory in manner until he reached me, when, strangely enough, and to my surprise and relief, his whole manner changed. Seeing that I did not readily produce my free papers, as the other colored persons in the car had done, he said to me in a friendly contrast with that observed toward the others: "I suppose you have free papers?" To which I answered: "No, sir; I never carry my free papers to sea with me." "But you have something to show that you are a free man, have you not?" "Yes, sir," I answered; "I have a paper with the American eagle on it, that will carry me round the world." With this I drew from my deep sailor's pocket my seaman's protection, as before described. The merest glance at the paper satisfied him, and he took my fare and went on about his business.

This moment of time was one of the most anxious I ever experienced. Had the conductor looked closely at the paper, he could not have failed to discover that it called for a very different looking person from myself, and in that case it would have been his duty to arrest me on the instant and send me back to Baltimore from the first station. When he left me with the assurance that I was all right, though much relieved, I realized that I was still in great danger: I was still in Maryland, and subject to arrest at any moment. I saw on the train several persons who would have known me in any other clothes, and I feared they might recognize me, even in my sailor "rig," and report me to the conductor, who would then subject me to a closer examination, which I knew well would be fatal to me.

Though I was not a murderer fleeing from justice, I felt, perhaps, quite as miserable as such a criminal. The train was moving at a very high rate of speed for that time of railroad travel, but to my anxious mind, it was moving

far too slowly. Minutes were hours, and hours were days during this part of
my flight. After Maryland I was to pass through Delaware--another slave
State, where slave-catchers generally awaited their prey, for it was not in
the interior of the State, but on its borders, that these human hounds were
most vigilant and active. The border lines between slavery and freedom were
the dangerous ones, for the fugitives. The heart of no fox or deer, with
hungry hounds on his trail, in full chase, could have beaten more anxiously
or noisily than did mine from the time I left Baltimore till I reached Philadelphia.

The passage of the Susquehanna river at Havre de Grace was at that time
made by ferry-boat, on board of which I met a young colored man by the name
of Nichols, who came very near betraying me. He was a "hand" on the boat,
but instead of minding his business, he insisted upon knowing me, and asking
me dangerous questions as to where I was going, and when I was coming back,
and so on. I got away from my old and inconvenient acquaintance as soon as
I could decently do so, and went to another part of the boat.

Once across the river I encountered a new danger. Only a few days before I had been at work on a revenue cutter, in Mr. Price's ship-yard, under
the care of Captain McGowan. On the meeting at this point of the two trains,
the one going south stopped on the track just opposite to the one going
north, and it so happened that this Captain McGowan sat at a window where he
could see me very distinctly, and would certainly have recognized me had he
looked at me but for a second. Fortunately, in the hurry of the moment, he
did not see me, and the trains soon passed each other on their respective
ways. But this was not the only hair-breadth escape. A German blacksmith,
whom I knew well, was on the train with me, and looked at me very intently,
as if he thought he had seen me somewhere before in his travels. I really
believe he knew me, but had no heart to betray me. At any rate he saw me
escaping and held his peace.

The last point of imminent danger, and the one I dreaded most, was Wilmington. Here we left the train and took the steamboat for Philadelphia. In
making the change I again apprehended arrest, but no one disturbed me, and I
was soon on the broad and beautiful Delaware, speeding away to the Quaker
City. On reaching Philadelphia in the afternoon I enquired of a colored man
how I could get on to New York? He directed me to the Willow Street Depot,
and thither I went, taking the train that night. I reached New York Tuesday
morning, having completed the journey in less than twenty-four hours. Such
is briefly the manner of my escape from slavery--and the end of my experience
as a slave.

*Life and Times of Frederick Douglass Written by Himself (New York, 1941),
pp. 210-23.*

OCCUPATIONS OF FREE BLACKS IN THE SOUTH

47. THE FREE NEGRO AND THE SOUTH

That class of politicians opposed to the President's proclamation, which
he proposes to issue on the 1st of January, for the general emancipation of
the negroes belonging to those in rebellion at that time, are trying to make
the people of the North believe, that as soon as these negroes are liberated,
there will be an influx of this entire population into the Northern States. [14]

The statistics of 1850 develop the following facts:
Virginia had 54,333 free negroes.
While Ohio had 25,279.

Maryland had 74,723 free colored persons, with only 90,368 slaves.
At this time, New York had only 49,069 free negroes.
At this time, the District of Columbia had 10,059 free negroes and 3,688 slaves.
Delaware had then 18,073 free negroes, and 2,290 slaves.
North Carolina had 27,463 free negroes.
Alabama had 2,265 free negroes.
Georgia had 2,981 free negroes.
Illinois had only 5,436 free negroes.
Indiana had only 11,262 free negroes.
While Louisiana had 17,662 free negroes.
The white population of Indiana was 977,943, while the white population of Louisiana was only 255,491; while Maryland, with a population of 417,943 whites, has a population of free colored persons of 74,728.
And New York, with a population of 3,048,325 whites, has only 49,069 free negroes.

The Liberator, November 7, 1862.

48. THE GAINFUL OCCUPATIONS OF FREE PERSONS OF COLOR

Georgia, Richmond County, Clerk's Office Inferior Court, 2nd March, 1819.
I certify that the following is a correct list of the names of persons of color registered in this office, in conformity to the act of the 19th December, 1818 supplementary to, and more effectually to enforce an act prescribing the mode of manumitting slaves in this state, etc. and all persons concerned or interested will take notice that certificates will issue to them on or before the first Monday in May next, if objections are not filed thereto, on or before the second Monday in April next, viz.

NAMES	AGE	PLACE OF NATIVITY	HOW LONG IN GEO.	OCCUPATION
Jack Harris	52	Maryland	40	Boating
Rachel Harris	12	Savannah	12	house servt
Harry Todd	53	Va.	35	Carpenter
Peggy Todd	40		17	Sew'g and Wash'g
Maria Todd	12	Savh	12	house servt
Sarah Todd	10	Augusta	10	House servt
Hanna Todd	8		8	"
Susannah Todd	5		5	
Matthew Todd	2		2	
Delia Todd	2 mos		2 mos	
Jenny Magnan	30	St. Domingo	24	house serv
Stephen Frost	58	Baltimore	30	boat corker
William Hill	42	Virginia	26	barber
Patsy Hill	39	Geo	39	sewing
Caesr Kennedy	43		43	boating
Hannah Kennedy	40		40	sewing
Jaria Kennedy	21		21	
John Kennedy	18		18	sadler
Mary Ann Kennedy	15		15	sewing
William Kennedy	11		11	
Caesar Kenedy	9		9	
Rosella Kennedy	5		5	
Thomas Kennedy	3		3	
Dickey Evans	30		30	pilot steam boat
Lindey Kennedy	25	Africa	11	house servant

John Coleman	35	Virginia	6	Carpenter
Molly Coleman	30	Augusta	30	Sewing
Mason Harris	50	Georgia	50	rafting
Nelly Harris	58	Africa	40	washing
Chas. Grant	50	N. Car	20	Carpenter
Peter Johnson	46	Savh	46	
Sally Johnson	16	Augusta	16	Sewing
John Johnson	14		14	carpenter
Caty Johnson	7		7	
Peter Johnson Jr.	9		9	
Betty Johnson	11		11	
Nancy Johnson	3		3	
Nancy Johnson	43	S. Car		washing
Nancy Fox	55	Augusta	55	washing
Junus Kelley	20		20	sawing
Betsy Kelley	22		22	washing
George Kelley	19		19	carpenter
Alfred Kelley	3 mos		3 mos	
Sam Kelley	5		5	
Richard Kelley	70	S. Car	25	common laborer
Josiah Kelley	1	Georgia	1	
Venice Mabre	55b	Guinea	30	washing
Vienna Kelley	22	Augusta	22	sewing
Henry Kelly	2			
Sally Langley	35	Maryland	22	washing
Isabell Wilson	20	Georgia	20	sewing
Sarah Carnes	35	N. Car	8	sewing
Jack Carns	22	S. Car	15	boating
Joe Carns	20		15	
Vienna Carns	15		14	sewing
Lucy Carns	20		15	sewing
Thomas Carter	26	Maryland	14	carpenter
Sarah Richards	30	S. Car	20	sewing
Junus Course	30	Augusta	30	
Juda Kelley	35	S. Car	25	washing
William Kelly	13	Augusta	13	carpenter
Madison Kelly	10		10	
Augustus Kelley	7		7	
Ann Kelly	5		5	
Emily Kelly	2		2	
Nancy Kelly	55	S. Car	30	Washing
Ann Kelly	33		25	sewing
Nanny Harris	50		30	washing
Venice Kelly	30		10	washing
Amy Dobbins	25		3	washing
Sylvester Dobbins	6		3	
Edin. Dobbins	5		3	
Sarah Fitch	35		22	
Sikey Fitch	4		4	
Matilda Fitch	3		3	
Andrew Fitch	6 days		6 days	
Deanna Caroline	33		22	sewing
Martricia Caroline	5	Augusta	5	
Alick Pope	38	Penn	20	drayman
Jenny Keating	35	Virginia	25	washing
Polly Keating	12	Augusta	12	sewing
Betsy Keating	11		11	
Martha Keating	8		8	
Thomas Keating	3		3	
Augustus Keating	11 mos		11 mos	
David Knight	22	S. Car	2	boating
Milly Sibbald	40	Maryland	12	washing
Eliza Estaerlin	45	St. Domingo	24	sewing
Babet Aesterlin	20	Georgia	20	sewing
Adella "	17		17	sewing

Name	Age	Place	Number	Occupation
Mariah Monroe	18	Augusta	18	sewing
Edy Sheitall	26	Savh	26	sewing
Charlotte Tubman	20	Augusta	20	sewing
Sarah Walton	25		25	washing
Chloe Walter	50	Savannah	50	washing
Martha Walton	5	Augusta	5	washing
Betsey Magnan	40	St. Domingo	25	washing
James Triplet	60	Va	10	waggoning
Marv Ann "	19		2	washg and cookg
Richard Triplet	13		10	
James " Jr	2	Augusta	2	
Sambo Campbell	70	S. Car	60	gardening
Thomas Kelly	25		20	boating
Mary Jenne Cloe	32	St. Domingo	25	washing
Jenny Ross	60	Georgia	60	washing
Thomas Bradley	79	Virginia	8 mo	carpenter
Amelia Brown	23		15	sewing
Elenor Knight	30	S. Car	7	sewing
Benj. Knight	2	Savh	2	
Peggy Haynes	24	Georgia	24	house servant
Bod Martin	23	Georgia	23	draying
Nelly Kelly	23	Augusta	23	washing
John Kelly	9		9	
Jane Scott	17		17	sewing
Elenor Harris	29	S. Carolina	12	sewing
Robert Kelly	12		1	house servant
G. M. Scott	7		3	
James Larry	51	Va	30	laborer
Katey Larry	20	Augusta	20	weaving
Eliza Larry	10		10	
James Larry Jr	8		8	
Nelly Jones	30	Va	16	washing
Robert Jones	14	Augusta	14	
Sary Ann Jones	1		1	
Augustus Larry	1		1	
Daniel Caroline	35	N. Car	8	carpenter
Rachel Shavers	30	S. Car	20	sewing, washing, etc.
Linda Lambert	50		22	market
Suckey Young	50	Va	15	washing
Nancy Kevan	27	Ga	27	washing
Ursele Poison	24	N. Car	18	sewing
Betsey Keating	27	S. Car	26	sewing
Caroline "	9	Ga	9	
Emily "	7		7	
Eliza "	5		5	
Jos. "	3		3	
Ceasar Tanner	76b	S. Car	2	sexton African Church
Sopha	78		25	sewing
Harriet Williams	36		9	weaving
Billy Collins	55		25	boating
Roderick Dent	23	Maryland	15	blacksmith
Kitty Shifton	13	Augusta	13	sewing
Louis Monroe	4 mos	Augusta	4 mos	
Willis Carter	26	Va	22	carpenter
Joseph Smith	22	Augusta	22	sadler
Joseph Lee	16	Savannah	16	farmer
David Russell	13	S. C.	2	
John Wright	30	Ga	30	planter
Polly Wright	32		32	spinning, weaving
Jane Coleman	14	S. Car	11 mos	spinning
Moses Jones	65		20	boating
J. T. Welch	27	Newark	4 mo.	harnessmaker

Isaac Harman	27	Ga	27	common laborer
Matthew Marham	25		25	"
James Harman	22		22	"
Abram Harman	20		20	"
Ailcey Hagland	50	Va	32	spinning
Martha Hulin	36	S. Car	12	"
John Evans	54	Va	35	millwright
James Evans	9	Richd county	9	
William Hulin	14	S. Car	12	farming
Navel Hulin	9		9	house servant
John Hulin	7		7	
Anna Hulin	5		5	
Betsey Bond	25	S. Car	24	washing
John Cousins	55	Va	5	ostler
Pricilla Bing	43	S. Car	23	spinning, weaving
Sally Rouse	22	Ga	22	
William Evans	20		20	common laborer
Henry Smith	35	Phila	12	waiting man
Peter Leigh	58	Va	38	farming
Stephen Coleman	60		40	boating--raftg
Caesar Johnson	51	N. Car	46	carpenter
Lucy Johnson	41	Va	28	sewing and weaving
Rebecca Johnson	11	Augusta	11	seamstress
Eliza Johnson	7		7	
Martha Johnson	4		4	
Susanna Frazier	32	S. Car	30	weaving, sewing
Eliz. Harman	21	Augusta	23	weaving
G. F. Harman	1 mo	Ga	1 mo	
Eliza Ann Collins	30	S. Car	23	"
William Frazier	5	Ga	5	
Tom Paris	50	Ga	50	boating
Sarah Rouse	30	S. Car	20	washing
Oliver Anthony	26	Ga	26	boating
Moses Hill	43	Va	19	boathand
Jacon Jones	23	S. Car	3	carpenter
Joseph Gowan	24	Ga	24	attending sawmill
Violet Sharper	56	Maryland	30	washing
Jeremiah Smith	55	N. Car	9 mos	waggoning
William Chaves	51		8	millwright
Sandy Hall	25	Ga	25	boating
Dick Taylor	60	S. C.	8	"

JOHN H. MANN, Clerk.

*Adapted from Augusta (Ga.) Chronicle, March 13, 1819, as reproduced in
Ulrich B. Phillips (ed.), A Documentary History of the American Industrial
Society, Vol. II (Cleveland, 1910), pp. 143-47.*

49. OCCUPATIONS OF SLAVES AND FREE BLACKS IN CHARLESTON, 1848

SLAVES

1--Contributing to Building
Bricklayers.................. 68
Carpenters...................110
Painters..................... 9
Plasterers.................. 16
Wharf Builders.............. 10

   Total...................213

FREE COLORED

1--Contributing to Building
Bricklayers.................. 10
Carpenters................... 27
Painters..................... 4

   Total................... 41

2--Contributing to Clothing

	Male	Female
Barbers	4	..
Bootmakers	4	..
Mantua Makers	0	4
Seamstresses	0	20
Shoemakers	2	..
Tailors	36	..
Washerwomen	0	33
Total	46	57

2--Contributing to Clothing

	Male	Female
Barbers	14	..
Bootmakers	3	..
Drygoods Dealers	1	..
Laundresses	0	45
Mantua Makers	0	128
Milliners	7	..
Seamstresses	0	68
Shoemakers	14	..
Tailors	42	6
Upholsterers	1	..
Total	82	247

3--Contributing to Food

	Male	Female
Bakers	39	..
Butchers	6	..
Confectioners	4	..
Cooks	3	11
Fishermen	15	..
Fruiterers	..	1
Hucksters	..	11
Market Dealers	..	6
Pastry Cooks	..	1
Cigarmakers	5	..
Gardeners	3	..
Total	75	30

3--Contributing to Food

	Male	Female
Bakers	1	..
Butchers	4	..
Confectioners	2	2
Cooks	16	..
Fishermen	14	..
Fruiterers	1	1
Hucksters	4	..
Market Dealers	1	4
Pastry Cooks	..	16
Cigarmakers	1	..
Hotel-Keepers	1	1
Housekeepers	..	4
Tavern-Keepers	1	..
Total	46	28

4--Contributing to Furniture

	Male	Female
Cabinetmakers	8	..
Tinners	3	..
Upholsterers	1	..
Total	12	..

4--Contributing to Furniture

	Male	Female
Tinners	1	..
Total	1	..

5--Contributing to Health

	Male	Female
Nurses	..	2
Sextons	1	..
Total	1	2

5--Contributing to Health

	Male	Female
Nurses	..	10
Sextons	4	..
Total	4	10

6--Contributing to Locomotion

	Male	Female
Coachmen	15	..
Coach Makers	3	..
Draymen	67	..
Saddlers	2	..
Total	87	..

6--Contributing to Locomotion

	Male	Female
Coachmen	4	..
Draymen	11	..
Livery Stable Keepers	3	..
Saddlers	1	..
Wheelwrights	1	..
Total	20	..

7--Contributing to Literature

	Male	Female
Bookbinders........	3	..
Printers...........	5	..
Total........	8	..

7--Contributing to Machinery

	Male	Female
Millwrights.......	5	..
Total.......	5	..

8--Contributing to Navigation

	Male	Female
Boatmen............	7	..
Sailors............	43	..
Ship Carpenters....	51	..
Total........	101	..

8--Contributing to Navigation

	Male	Female
Seamen............	1	..
Ship Carpenters...	6	..
Total.......	7	..

9--Unclassified Mechanics

	Male	Female
Blacksmiths........	40	..
Brassfounders......	1	..
Coopers............	61	..
Mechanics..........	45	..
Total........	147	..

9--Unclassified Mechanics

	Male	Female
Blacksmiths.......	4	..
Coopers...........	2	..
Coppersmiths......	1	..
Mechanics.........	2	..
Total	9	..

10--Unclassified Residue of Blacks

	Male	Female
Apprentices........	43	8
House Servants....	1,888	3,384
Laborers..........	838	378
Porters...........	35	..
Stevedores........	2	..
Total.......	2,806	3,770

10--Unclassified Residue of Blacks

	Male	Female
Apprentices.......	14	7
House Servants....	9	28
Janitors..........	1	..
Laborers..........	19	2
Millers...........	1	..
Porters...........	5	..
Stevedores........	1	..
Storekeepers......	5	..
Woodfactors.......	3	..
Total.......	58	37

11--Superannuated and Disabled

Male	Female
38	54

11--Superannuated and Disabled

Male	Female
1	4

Census of the City of Charleston for the year 1848, pp. 34-35, reprinted in Charles G. Wesley, Negro Labor in the United States (New York, 1927), pp. 34-36.

50.   OCCUPATIONS OF NEGROES IN CHARLESTON IN 1850

Occupations	(1,579 Males)
Artists...	0
Apothecaries...	0
Barbers..	17
Basketmakers...	0
Blacksmiths..	16

Boardinghouse Keepers..............................	0
Boatmen..	0
Bootmakers...	10
Brickmakers..	0
Bricklayers..	18
Butchers...	23
Bookbinders..	0
Bakers...	1
Bootblacks...	1
Cabinetmakers......................................	4
Capstone Workers...................................	0
Carters..	7
Carpenters...	122
Cigarmakers..	2
Clerks...	0
Clothiers..	0
Coachmen...	3
Confectioners......................................	2
Coopers..	11
Chimney-Sweeps.....................................	0
Coppersmiths.......................................	0
Cotton-gin Makers..................................	1
Cooks..	3
Daguerreotypers....................................	0
Doctors..	0
Draymen..	45
Domestics..	0
Drummers...	3
Engineers..	6
Fruiterers...	3
Farmers..	34
Fishermen..	23
Gardeners..	0
Gymnasts...	0
Glaziers...	1
Hairdressers.......................................	6
Hostlers...	7
Laundresses..	3
Jewelers...	0
Job Workers..	0
Laborers...	91
Locksmiths...	2
Lawyers..	0
Mariners...	1
Marketmen..	1
Mattress Makers....................................	3
Mantua Makers......................................	2
Mechanics (General)................................	2
Merchants..	0
Millwrights..	14
Ministers..	0
Millers..	1
Musicians..	0
Machinists...	0
Masons...	1
Painters...	11
Pasteboard Makers..................................	1
Planters...	9
Porters..	14
Pump Makers..	1
Printers...	1
Paperhangers.......................................	1
Pavers...	0
Riggers..	2

```
Saddlers................................................    1
Seamstresses............................................    2
Servants................................................    7
Sextons.................................................    1
Shopkeepers.............................................    5
Shoemakers..............................................   30
Stewards................................................    0
Seamen..................................................    0
Saloon-Keepers..........................................    0
Silversmiths............................................    0
Ship Carpenters.........................................    1
Stevedores..............................................    3
Tailors.................................................   87
Tinners.................................................    3
Tenders.................................................    0
Truckmen................................................    0
Traders.................................................    0
Traders.................................................    0
Traders.................................................    0
Tobacconists............................................    0
Tavern-Keepers..........................................    1
Trimmers................................................    2
Upholsterers............................................    2
Wheelwrights............................................   14
Waiters.................................................    2
Woodfactors.............................................    7
Whitewashers............................................    1
Curriers................................................    0
Hotel-Keepers...........................................    1
Teachers................................................    0
Restorators.............................................    0
Restaurateurs...........................................    0

Total occupations known.................................  700
```

Charles G. Wesley, Negro Labor in the United States (New York, 1927), pp. 43-44.

51. OCCUPATIONS OF NEGROES IN ST. LOUIS IN 1850

```
  Occupations                                      (780 Males)
Artists.................................................    0
Apothecaries............................................    0
Barbers.................................................   33
Basketmakers............................................    1
Blacksmiths.............................................    2
Boardinghouse Keepers...................................    0
Boatmen.................................................   56
Bootmakers..............................................    0
Brickmakers.............................................    0
Bricklayers.............................................    0
Butchers................................................    3
Bookbinders.............................................    0
Bakers..................................................    1
Bootblacks..............................................    2
Cabinetmakers...........................................    0
Capstone Workers........................................    0
Carters.................................................    0
Carpenters..............................................    5
```

Cigarmakers...	0
Clerks..	0
Clothiers...	0
Coachmen..	1
Confectioners...	0
Coopers...	0
Chimney-Sweeps..	0
Coppersmiths..	0
Cotton-gin Makers.....................................	0
Cooks...	36
Daguerreotypers.......................................	0
Doctors...	1
Draymen...	20
Domestics...	0
Drummers..	0
Engineers...	5
Fruiterers..	0
Farmers...	0
Fishermen...	0
Gardeners...	1
Gymnasts..	0
Glaziers..	0
Hairdressers..	0
Holstlers...	0
Laundresses...	0
Jewelers..	0
Job Workers...	0
Laborers..	46
Locksmiths..	0
Lawyers...	0
Mariners..	0
Marketmen...	0
Mattress Makers.......................................	0
Mantua Makers...	0
Mechanics (General)...................................	0
Merchants...	0
Millwrights...	0
Ministers...	2
Millers...	0
Musicians...	0
Machinists..	0
Masons..	0
Painters..	0
Pasteboard Makers.....................................	0
Planters..	0
Porters...	11
Pump Makers...	0
Printers..	0
Paperhangers..	0
Pavers..	0
Riggers...	0
Saddlers..	0
Seamstresses..	0
Servants..	3
Sextons...	1
Shopkeepers...	0
Shoemakers..	0
Stewards..	56
Seamen..	0
Saloon-Keepers..	0
Silversmiths..	0
Ship Carpenters.......................................	0
Stevedores..	8
Tailors...	0

Tinners..   2
Tenders..   0
Truckmen...   0
Traders................................. Mexican   1
Traders................................. California   3
Traders................................. Mountain   2
Tobacconists.......................................   2
Tavern-Keepers.....................................   0
Trimmers...   0
Upholsterers.......................................   0
Wheelwrights.......................................   0
Waiters..   16
Woodfactors..   0
Whitewashers.......................................   1
Curriers................................ Firemen   20
Teachers................................ Mountaineers   2
Restorators............................. Cabinboys   25
Restaurateurs........................... Deckhands   12
                                         Rivermen   4

Total occupations known.........................   384

Charles G. Wesley, Negro Labor in the United States (New York, 1927), pp. 43-44.

52. LEADING NEGRO OCCUPATIONS[a] IN BALTIMORE IN 1850 AND 1860*

	Occupation	1850	1860	Difference
1	Barbers	91	96	+ 5
2	Blacksmiths	31	27	− 4
3	Bricklayers	63	93	+ 30
4	Butchers	16	9	− 7
5	Carriage Drivers	33	34	+ 1
6	Carters, Draymen, etc.	385	331	− 54
7	Carpenters	26	13	− 13
8	Caulkers	75	63	− 13
9	Cooks	22	26	+ 4
10	Grain Measurers	27	17	− 10
11	Hod Carriers	14	10	− 4
12	Hucksters	19	28	+ 9
13	Laborers	799	571	−228
14	Ostlers	11	9	− 2
15	Oystermen	24	50	+ 26
16	Porters, Waiters, etc.	236	226	− 10
17	Rope Makers	12	1	− 11
18	Sawyers	146	47	− 99
19	Seamen	94	107	+ 13
20	Seamstresses	20	4	− 16
21	Shoe Makers	24	11	− 13
22	Shop Keepers	21	13	− 8
23	Stevedores	35	34	− 1
24	Washers	260	142	−118
24	White Washers	70	62	− 8
	TOTALS	2,754	2,044	−710

aTotal Negro labor decrease of 38.8 percent from 1850 to 1860.

*Matchett's *Baltimore Directory,* For 1849-50 (Baltimore: R. [Richard] J. Matchett, 1849, pp. 439-473; *Woods' Baltimore City Directory* (Baltimore: John W. Woods, [1860]), pp. 427-459.

M. Ray Della, Jr., "The Problems of Negro Labor in the 1850's," *Maryland Historical Magazine* 66 (Spring, 1871):28.

53. OCCUPATIONS OF FREE NEGROES OVER FIFTEEN YEARS OF AGE IN NEW ORLEANS, 1850

Occupations	Blacks	Mulattoes	Total
Apprentices	...	4	4
Architects	...	1	1
Bakers	...	1	1
Barkeepers	...	2	2
Barbers	6	35	41
Blacksmiths	4	11	15
Boardinghouse Keepers	1	17	18
Boatmen	5	32	37
Bookbinders	...	4	4
Brickmakers	...	2	2
Brokers	1	8	9
Butchers	1	17	18
Cabinetmakers	2	17	19
Capitalists	...	4	4
Carmen	19	20	39
Carpenters	56	299	355
Cigarmakers	13	143	156
Clerks	...	61	61
Collectors	...	2	2
Coachmen	4	6	10
Confectioners	...	...	...
Cooks	7	18	25
Coopers	17	26	43
Doctors	...	4	4
Druggists	...	...	...
Engineers	...	...	1
Farmers	...	...	...
Gardeners	4	5	9
Gunsmiths	...	4	4
Hatters	...	...	...
Hostlers	...	3	3
Hunters	4	3	7
Ink Makers	...	...	...
Jewelers	...	5	5
Laborers	71	108	179
Lawyers	...	...	...
Lithographers	...	1	1
Mariners	1	9	10
Marketmen	6	19	25
Masons	65	213	278
Mechanics (general)	6	46	52
Merchants	6	58	64
Ministers	...	1	1
Musicians	...	4	4
Music Teachers	...	1	1
Overseers	1	10	11

Painters.................	4	24	28
Pedlers..................	2	7	9
Pilots...................	...	2	2
Planters.................	...	2	2
Printers.................	...	...	...
Sailmakers...............	...	2	2
Servants.................	...	...	...
Sextons..................	...	1	1
Ship Carpenters..........	2	4	6
Shoemakers...............	16	76	92
Stevedores...............	1	6	7
Stewards.................	...	9	9
Students.................	...	7	7
Tailors..................	3	79	82
Teachers.................	...	12	12
Upholsterers.............	1	7	8
Other Occupations........	...	...	...
TOTAL	329	1,463	1,792

Statistical View, Compendium of the Census of 1850, pp. 80-81.

54. THE CASE OF HENRY BOYD, A FREED CARPENTER

Henry Boyd was born a slave in Kentucky. Of imposing stature, well-known muscles, and the countenance of one of Nature's noblemen, at the age of eighteen, he had so far won the confidence of his master, that he not only consented to sell him the right and title to his freedom, but gave him his own time to earn the money. With a general pass from his master, Henry made his way to the Kanawha salt works, celebrated as the place where Senator Ewing, of Ohio, chopped out his *education* with his axe! And there, too, with his axe, did Henry Boyd chop out his *liberty*. By performing double labor, he got double wages. In the daytime, he swung his axe upon the wood, and for half the night, he tended the boiling salt kettles, sleeping the other half by their side. After having accumulated a sufficient sum, he returned to his master, and paid it over for his freedom. He next applied himself to learn the trade of a carpenter and joiner. Such was his readiness to acquire the use of tools, that he soon qualified himself to receive the wages of a journeyman. In Kentucky, prejudice does not forbid master mechanics to teach colored men their trades.

He now resolved to quit the dominions of slavery, and try his fortunes in a free State, and accordingly directed his steps to the city of Cincinnati. The journey reduced his purse to the last *quarter of a dollar;* but, with his tools on his back, and a set of muscles that well knew how to use them, he entered the city with a light heart. Little did he dream of the reception he was to meet. There was work enough to be done in his line, but no master-workman would employ *"a nigger."* Day after day did Henry Boyd offer his services from shop to shop, but as often was he repelled, generally with insult, and once with a *kick*. At last, he found the shop of an Englishman, too recently arrived to understand the grand peculiarity of American feeling. This man put a plane into his hand, and asked him to make proof of his skill. "This is in bad order," said Boyd, and with that he gave the instrument certain nice professional knocks with the hammer till he brought it to suit his practised eye. "Enough," said the Englishman, "I see you can use tools." Boyd, however, proceeded to dress a board in a very able and workmanlike manner, while the journeymen from a long line of benches gathered round, with looks that bespoke a deep personal interest in the matter. "You may go to work," said the master of the shop, right glad to employ so good a workman. The words had no sooner left his mouth, than his American

journeymen, unbottoning their aprons, called, as one man, for the settlement of their wages.

"What, what," said the amazed Englishman, "what does this mean?"

"It means that we will not work with a *nigger*," replied the journeymen.

"But he is a first-rate workman."

"But we won't stay in the same shop with a *nigger*. We are not in the
habit of working with *niggers*."

"Then I will build a shanty outside, and he shall work in that."

"No, no; we won't work for a *boss* who employs *niggers*. Pay us up, and
we'll be off."

The poor master of the shop turned, with a despairing look, to Boyd--
"You see how it is, my friend, my workmen will all leave me. I am sorry for
it, but I can't hire you."

Even at this repulse, our adventurer did not despair. There might still
be mechanics, in the outskirts of the city, who had too few journeymen to be
bound by their prejudices. His quarter of a dollar had long since disappeared; but, by carrying a traveller's trunk or turning his hand to any chance
job, he contrived to exist till he had made application to every carpenter
and joiner in the city and its suburbs. *Not one would employ him.* By this
time, the iron of prejudice, more galling than any thing *he* had ever known
of slavery, had entered his soul. He walked down on the river's bank below
the city, and, throwing himself upon the ground, gave way to an agony of despair. He had found himself the object of universal contempt; his plans were
all frustrated, his hopes dashed, and his dear-bought freedom made no effect!

*William C. Nell, The Colored Patriots of the American Revolution (Boston,
1855), pp. 265-68.*

55. "AS HIGH AS A COLORED MAN COULD RISE"

My first call was on a Mr. Knowles, a first-class carpenter, to see if
he would take me as an apprentice. His excuse was that he had but little
work and that he was going to close up business. I next applied to a Mr.
Langley, a shoemaker, but he refused without giving me an excuse. I next
called on Mr. Ira B. Winsor, a grocery man. His promise to hire me as a
clerk encouraged me very much. He had first to consult his uncle, who was
his guardian. His uncle bitterly opposed hiring a black boy while there
were so many white boys he could get.

Other [white] boys of my acquaintance with little or no education, were
learning trades and getting employments, and I could get nothing. I found
it was on account of my color, for no colored men except barbers had trades.
I was now seventeen years old and was at a loss to know what steps to take
to get a living, for if I possessed the knowledge of a Demosthenes or Cicero,
it would not bring to me flattering prospects for the future. To drive carriage, carry a market basket after the boss, brush his boots, or saw wood
and run errands was as high as a colored man could rise.

The Life of William J. Brown (Providence, 1883), p. 56.

56. THE WASHERWOMAN

Saturday night! *Dunk!* goes the smoothing-iron, then a swift gliding
sound as it passes smoothly over starched bosom and collar of one of the

many dozen shirts that hang round the room on chairs, lines and every other
thing capable of being hanged on. *Dunk! Dunk!* and that small and delicately
formed hand and wrist swell up with knotted muscles and bursting veins!

The apartment is small, hot as an oven, the air in it thick and misty
with the steam rising from the ironing table. In the corners, under the tables, and in all out-of-the-way places are stowed tubs of various sizes, some
empty, some full of clothes soaking for next week's labor. On the walls hang
pictures of old Pappy Thompson, or Brother Paul, or Sammy Cornish; in one
corner of the room a newly varnished mahogany table is partly filled with
books--Bunyan's *Pilgrim's Progress,* Watts' *Hymns,* the *Life of Christ,* and a
nice "greasy novel" just in from the circulating library. Between the windows stand an old bureau, the big drawer of which is the larder, containing
sundry slices of cold meat, second-handed toast and carcass of a turkey, the
return cargo of a basket of clothes sent downtown that morning. *Dunk! Dunk!*
goes the smoothing-iron. The washerwoman bends again to her task. Her mind
is far away in the South, with her sisters and their children who toil as
hard but without any pay! And she fancies the smiles which will gladden
their faces when receiving the things she sent them in a box by the last
Georgetown packet. *Dunk! Dunk! Dunk!!!* goes the iron, this time right swift
and cheerily. Oh Freedom! Her tired muscles forget all weariness. The iron
flies as a weaver's shuttle, shirts appear and disappear with rapidity and at
a quarter to twelve, the groaning table is cleared, and the poor washerwoman
sinks upon her knees in prayer for them, that they also may soon partake of
that freedom which, however toilsome, is yet so sweet.

James McCune Smith, Heads of the Colored People -- No. 3.

57. OBSERVATIONS OF SAMUEL RINGGOLD WARD ON DISCRIMINATION [15]

I grew up in the city of New York as do the children of poor parents in
large cities too frequently. I was placed at a public school in Mulberry
Street, taught by Mr. C. C. Andrew, and subsequently by Mr. Adams, a Quaker
gentleman, from both of whom I received great kindness. Dr. A. Libolt, my
last preceptor in that school, placed me under lasting obligations. Poverty
compelled me to work, but inclination led me to study; hence I was enabled,
in spite of poverty, to make some progress in necessary learning. Added to
poverty, however, in the case of a black lad in that city, is the ever-pre-
sent, ever-crushing Negro-hate, which hedges up his path, discourages his efforts, damps his ardour, blasts his hopes, and embitters his spirits.

Some white persons wonder at and condemn the tone in which some of us
blacks speak of our oppressors. Such persons talk as if they knew but little
of human nature, and less of Negro character, else they would wonder rather
that, what with slavery and Negro-hate, the mass of us are not either depressed into idiocy or excited into demons. What class of whites, except the
Quakers, ever spoke of *their* oppressors or wrongdoers as mildly as we do?
This peculiarly American spirit (which Englishmen easily enough imbibe, after
they have resided a few days in the United States) was ever at my elbow. As
a servant, it denied me a seat at the table with my white fellow servants; in
sports of childhood and youth, it was ever disparagingly reminding me of my
colour and origin; along the streets it ever pursued, ever ridiculed, ever
abused me. If I sought redress, the very complexion I wore was pointed out
as the best reason for my seeking it in vain; if I desired to turn to account
a little learning, in the way of earning a living by it, the idea of employing a black clerk was preposterous--too absurd to be seriously entertained.
I never knew but one coloured clerk in a mercantile house. Mr. W. L. Jeffers
was lowest clerk in a house well known in Broad Street, New York; but he never was advanced a single grade, while numerous white lads have since passed
up by him, and over him, to be members of the firm. Poor Jeffers, till the
day of his death, was but one remove above the porter. So, if I sought a

trade, white apprentices would leave if I were admitted; and when I went to
the house of God, as it was called, I found all the Negro-hating usages and
sentiments of general society there encouraged and embodied in the Negro
pew, and in the disallowing Negroes to commune until *all the whites,* however
poor, low, and degraded, had done. I know of more than one coloured person
driven to the total denial of all religion, by the religious barbarism of
white New Yorkers and other Northern champions of the slaveholder.

However, at the age of sixteen I found a friend in George Atkinson Ward,
Esq., from whom I received encouragement to persevere, in spite of Negro-
hate. In 1833 I became a clerk of Thomas L. Jennings, Esq., one of the most
worthy of the coloured race; subsequently my brother and I served David Ruggles, Esq., then of New York, late of Northampton, Massachusetts, now no
more.[16]

*Samuel Ringgold Ward, Autobiography of a Fugitive Negro (London, 1855), pp.
28-29.*

58. WELL PUT.--THE COLOURED RACE AT THE NORTH

Major NOAH of the N. Y. *Sunday Messenger* makes the following truthful
remarks on a subject, which is more misrepresented and misunderstood at the
North, than all others put together:
"A FRIEND IN NEED.--The coloured race in this country never wanted
friends more than they do at the present time--not professing friends who
calculate how much political capital can be made by being clamarous in their
behalf, but true friends, who wish to see them comfortable, safe and happy.
When has Africa been happy? Labouring under divine displeasure, a marked and
differently created race from the white man, always at war with each other in
their own country, sold as slaves by our *Northern* ancestors, and purchased by
the South to till the land, the only comfort, protection, security and safety
which they have ever enjoyed since they left the land of Cush, is in what is
called the Slavery in the Southern States; and this comfort and safety they
are about to be robbed of by a host of sympathising politicians, calling
themselves Free Soil men and the friends of the coloured race.
Here, at the North, the poor blacks are not permitted to work alongside
of the white man. We reduce them to the lowest grades of civilization by
making them our servants, our waiters, and our dependants. Once they were
permitted to follow the humble employment of carrying up bricks and mortar,
but they were kicked from the ladder by our white fellow-citizens. They
clean boots, scour clothes but are not permitted to sweep streets--they do
not won or command a ship, they are only cooks and stewards--they are not
merchants, bankers, or brokers--they hold no public appointments, and are
rudely thrust from our cars and carriages--we do not eat with them or pray
with them, and in our places of amusement there are pens and divisions in
which they may sit by themselves. Is it any wonder that they are poor, vicious, and the inmates of our hospitals and prisons? And yet we, who persecute neglect and repudiate the free black man here, are filled with holy zeal
to make the slave free at the South, and deprive him of a home, of food and
clothing, and of a kind considerate master; and we struggle for that freedom
even at the expense of breaking down, dividing and destroying our glorious
republic! Well may the blacks say: "Save us from our friends!--Save us from
the pity and protection of the political Abolitionists!"
What is to become of the poor free blacks, when thrown upon the world
without protection, deprived of their happy home in the slave States, and of
kind and sympathising masters? The Governor of Virginia, in his last message
to the Legislature, proposes to direct by law that the free blacks shall
leave the State. True, they work but little, and idleness is the parent of
crime--true, they corrupt the honest and industrious slave, are useless to
themselves, and a burden and injury to the State. That freedom so essential

to the whites is to them an unbearable burden. What, however, is to become
of 100,000 poor, friendless, free blacks, driven from their own State to
take refuge in the North, where we allow them so few privileges? Suppose
all the slave States were to say to their free blacks--"My friends, we have
given you employment and bread, but your abolition friends in the North are
anxious that you should come forth from the iniquity that surrounds you--go
to them, and see if they will do as much for you as we have done!" What is
to become of more than half a million of freed blacks driven forth to seek
the cold charities of the North? *They will starve!* We of the North will
give them no succour, no employment, and yet we are even in favour of rending
our glorious constitution to pieces in order to give them liberty!--When will
the age of reason be revived? We cannot rebuke the slave States in ridding
themselves of their free blacks, which are a dead weight upon them; and yet
we dread the day when they shall be thrown upon the North for support and
protection. Wherever we turn, we see nothing in the agitation of the slave
question but ruin and distress to the coloured race.

A circumstance occurred here last week which has led to the foregoing
reflections. Passing down Nassau street, three or four persons were standing
inside of a store talking to a black man, and they invited us to come in.
"Here is a black man," said one of the gentlemen "who wishes to sell himself
as a slave for $150.

We entered the store, and saw a short stout fellow in rags, with a good
countenance, and no indication of vice.

"Where do you belong?"

"To New York; I was born there."

"Don't you know that you can't sell yourself as a slave in this State?"

"What am I to do? I can get no work; I have had no breakfast; I am almost naked; no one cares for me, and I have no friend. Is it not better to
have a good master whom I can work for, and who will care for me?"

Here was an illusion of the practical benevolence of domestic African
Slavery, while it exhibited the rank hypocrisy of the Abolitionists. They
could raise Ŀ2,000 to purchase the liberty of two mulatto girls, and yet allowed a poor black to offer to sell himself as a slave to save himself from
starving in a free Northern State!"

It has ever been the misfortune of very poor and ignorant people in all
christian and densely populated nations, to be the victims of untold privations and hardships. Somehow it always happens that the Benevolence of high
civilization cannot see the pressing wants--the cruel hunger and nakedness
at its own door; while it will labour day and night with untiring zeal, to
remove the purely imaginary distress of persons in some far off country.
Thus, English Humanity, which could tax itself Ŀ20,000,000, or one hundred
millions of dollars to emancipate the slaves in the West Indies, who were
in comparatively a comfortable condition, experienced little uneasiness in
permitting thousands of whites to die of starvation in Ireland.

Emancipate the three millions of slaves now in the Union, and distribute
them equally in every State, to compete with the Anglo-Saxon race for employment and bread, and instead of a blessing, the act would be an infliction,
from the blighting effects of which, both blacks and whites would suffer to
an incalculable degree. Of course the inferior race would suffer in the conflict, far more than the stronger one. The withdrawal of all guardianship
now extended over this class of servants, which is in truth so much needed,
would operate like a general law declaring all children to be of age, and
quite independent of parental care and government when twelve years old.
Every intelligent person can appreciate the supreme folly of such precocious
liberty. Why then, it may well be asked, cannot all intelligent men and women at the North discover the necessity of humane and legal guardianship
over the African race, imported into the planting States and sold by their
own merchants and slave dealers? Undoubtedly this guardianship, or relation
of master and slave, may be abused; but so may the relation of parent and
child, husband and wife, employers and employed. There are very few of us
who do not abuse some of the blessings of life, yet this abuse would hardly
justify the destruction of all life on that account.

All abuses, whether of servants, children, hirelings or neighbours,
should be corrected. But when this task of correction shall be undertaken
in good earnest, there will be found as many and as serious wrongs in

Northern as in Southern communities, which demand abatement. We have seen able-bodied men in Northern cities beg for employment at twenty-five cents a day, to command the means to purchase a little corn meal or a few potatoes, to keep a wife and small children from starving; and then often beg in vain. In Georgia every slave enjoys the legal right to transform his honest sweat into bread. In no State in the Union has a poor white man this right, provided no one sees fit to employ him and he owns no land. Take the case of the free man of colour seen by Mr. NOAH. If no one saw fit to purchase his labour and sell him bread or a shirt, how could he get either without stealing it? What is the labour of a white man worth in Ireland, New York or Georgia when he is in immediate want, and no human being will buy his labour or supply his wants?

To stimulate industrious habits, and cure the vices incident to improvidence and excess when poor free persons have employment, civilized communities regard it as wise to let all such understand distinctly, that they must lay up their surplus earnings, and provide in seasons of plenty for those of scarcity. To guaranty employment and food at all times and under all circumstances, as was strongly demanded by the poor in France, would be in effect to offer a bounty on general indulgence and improvidence, by saying to all that Government would never permit them to lack work, wages and bread. Three millions negroes would make a sorry showing in the way of providing against all contingencies of bad harvests, sickness, infancy and old age if left entirely at liberty to work or play as they might feel inclined.

The necessity for guardianship by persons better informed and more provident than slaves are, for their own good, is so apparent that a man with half an eye ought to see it. That the labour of this class of people is now generally employed to the best possible advantage, we are far from believing. It can be made vastly more productive than it now is, for the equal benefit of master and servant.

National Anti-Slavery Standard, April 26, 1849, quoting the Augusta (Ga.) Chronicle and Sentinel.

PART II

RACE RELATIONS IN OLD SOUTHERN INDUSTRIES

RACE RELATIONS IN OLD SOUTHERN INDUSTRIES

Even though slave labor was employed extensively throughout the crafts
and industries, the practice sparked a heated debate among southern leaders
during the Ante-Bellum Era. More than a simple controversy about who would
perform what types of labor, the argument represented a conflict over just
what kind of society would prevail in the South. The tension between rural-
agricultural and urban-industrial interests further complicated the debate.
Although planters favored an increase in manufactures, they viewed industrial-
ization as a threat to their way of life. Moreover, the relative loss of control over slaves in such a fluid setting caused planters to fear the social
consequences of industrial slavery. On the other hand, sporadic white labor
militancy, and white labor's anxieties over competition with slaves, caused
planters to fear any increase in the white working class as well.

Two influential arguments favoring the use of slave operatives by Thomas Jones (Doc. 1) and Charles Fisher (Doc. 2), published in 1827 and 1828 respectively, argued that blacks not only were capable of learning the "mechanical arts," they were more profitably employed as well. Proponents of free
white mechanics, on the other hand, such as James H. Hammond (Doc. 3), and
Christopher G. Memminger (Doc. 4), both prominent South Carolinians, usually
concerned themselves with maintenance of the social-political status quo.
They believed that the poor whites must be uplifted from poverty and squalor;
otherwise they constituted a danger to the slave regime. A letter from the
New York black activist William P. Powell (Doc. 5), living in England in 1851,
provides a corrective point of view.

The search for a consensus on a proper southern labor policy was not an
issue which concerned a small elite. Pressures were generated from white workers whose means of expression were much less genteel. Documents 6-11 provide
examples of free white southern mechanics, from South Carolina to Texas, who
banded together to petition legislative bodies for laws restricting the employment of black tradesmen as competitors who depressed wages.

As a result of these political pressures, numerous restrictive measures
were enacted throughout the South (Doc. 12-19). In some cases, these laws
were aimed directly at black mechanics (Doc. 20), and generally pressed blacks
into abject poverty (Doc. 21-23). Sometimes white mechanics struck when black
workers were introduced into a plant. The 1847 strike of white wokers at the
famous Tredegar Iron Works in Richmond, Virginia, was one such occurrences
When the white mechanics struck, however, they were fired and blacks filled
their positions. The legal authorities upheld Tredegar's right to employ
slaves as it saw fit (Doc. 32).

Where the arm of the law did not reach, white working class vigilantism
was sometimes directed against blacks or whites, usually foreigners, who dis-
obeyed local racial taboos (Doc. 24, 26). White hostility over competition
with slave and free blacks frequently erupted into violence (Doc. 25). But
the nature of race relations varies greatly in the region, from violent conflict to the integrated and seemingly cordial relations found in a few plants
(Doc. 27-34). Occasionally, well-intentioned whites attempted to improve the
lot of free blacks, such as the Baltimore Society for the Protection of Free
People of Colour, formed in 1827 (Doc. 35).

THE DEBATE OVER THE USE OF FREE OR SLAVE MECHANICS

1. "THE PROGRESS OF MANUFACTURES"

The great progress which has been made in the work of internal improvements, and more especially in the establishment of manufactures, has hitherto been principally confined to the eastern, the middle and western states.
There are, however, several works for the spinning of cotton to the south of
the Potomac, and others are on the eve of being established; and if I am not
greatly in error, another bond of union will, in the course of a very few
years, be added to the confederacy by a community of pursuit, in the extension of manufactures, over that important section of our country.
    I have, for some years, been convinced, that the plans in those states
might be advantageously employed in the manufacturing of some staple articles, and more particularly in that of cotton; this conviction I have long
foreborne to promulgate, because I have thought that the only result would
be to afix on myself the imputation of singularity, at least, if not of absurdity. I rejoice, however, to percieve that the question of the practicability, and the eligibility of the measure has lately become the subject of
discussion in the public papers, and that much has been said in its favour.
While expressing my own convictions and anticipations upon this point, I am
aware that they will appear sanguine, if not extravagant, even to those who,
to a certain extent, think favourably of the proposition: these opinions,
however, have been the result of much observation and reflection, under circumstances particularly favourable to the formation of correct judgment.
    It has formed no small portion of my occupation through life; to render
myself familiar with the structure of machines, and their application to
manufactures; and to estimate the portion of skill required in their management, in establishments upon a large scale, where the division of labour is
necessarily carried to the utmost extent. I have also resided for a considerable number of years in the southern states, and have in consequence,
acquired some share of knowledge, with regard to the habits, inclinations,
and capacities of negroes; the result of which is, that I am thoroughly convinced, not only that they may be profitably employed as manufacturers, but
that they are peculiarly suited to this purpose. It would be improper here,
to enter into a discussion of the question, whether the negroes are absolutely inferior to the whites in intellect; and indeed were we able to settle this question, it would scarcely affect that upon which I am speaking,
as only a small degree of intelligence is necessary to the acquisition of
the utmost skill in the performance of an individual operation, however delicate it may be. In all extensive manufactories, we meet with the veriest
dolts, who become, as it were, from habit, adepts in the business allotted
to them, with a degree of dexterity and precision which appears almost miraculous; and those which are adepts in other departments of the same business might essay in vain.
    The object proposed to be accomplished, is to teach the negroes to work
machines which have already been invented, and extensively used; their occupation would be those of mere routine, and for this they are peculiarly
fitted; their deficiency in imagination and inventive genius may fairly be
thrown into the scale of advantages, rather into that of objections. With
respect to the actual employment of slaves in manufacturing hempen bagging
in Kentucky I extract the following remarks upon the subject, which appear
in the Ariel, published at Natchez, Mississippi, and since in the American
Farmer, and some other papers.

        Strange as it may appear to those who have never observed
    for themselves, nor reflected on this matter, it is demonstrably
    true, that *slaves* are the most profitable of all *operatives,*
    in the business of manufacturing coarse fabricks, where inge-
    nuity has furnished them with suitable machinery. In Kentucky,
    for instance, by the assistance of trifling machines, slaves

manufacture vast quantities of *hempen bagging*. We, indeed,
scarcely see any other operatives in the great factories of
Lexington, Paris, Danville, Shelbyville, and other towns in
Kentucky. If we except a manager or two, and a machinist,
neither Englishmen, Scotchmen, nor even New Englandmen, are
to be seen in the profitable establishments. Why are slaves
employed? Simply because experiment has proved that they
are more *docile,* more constant, and *cheaper* than freemen,
who are often refractory and dissipated; who waste much time
by frequenting public places, attending musters, elections,
&c. which the *operative* slave is not permitted to frequent.
The habits of slaves, too, are more uniform, and the deficiency of inventive genius can seldom endure the monotonous
occupation of attending a spindle or a loom; whereas experience has amply proved that slaves are competent, not only
to these pursuits, but are capable of exercising many trades
where much more intelligence is required. It surely requires but little talent to draw out a thread with a mule,
to join it to a spindle, or apply the cotton to a carding
apparatus. England, in the plentitude of her power, imagined that two millions of people, in her colonies were incapable of making a hoe handle or a hobnail; and with a
spirit as blind, New England now seemed to imagine that the
cotton growing states, with a million or two of the best
operatives *in the world,* would continue incapable of using
these simple machines, which the very *children* of the white
slaves of Europe can learn to manage in a month. The *erad-
ication* of this gross and silly prejudice, in the north and
in the south, will produce a complete revolution in public
opinion with regard to manufactures, in every portion of our
country. To secure the cotton crop of the south in *cotton*
bagging and rope, will require 28,000 bales of cotton annually. This is no inconsiderable market; but it would be
prodigiously augmented by the use of our cotton in blankets,
and coarse negro clothing.

A proposition to encourage the employment of slaves in the manufacturing of cotton bagging, cotton cordage, cotton blankets, and coarse clothing,
was made at a public meeting convened for the purpose at Natchez, in July
last, and such preliminary measures adopted, as were thought to be necessary
for the attainment of the end. The resolutions passed were conceived in a
spirit of liberality, embracing the promotion of manufactures in every part
of the union. Their view, very properly, restricted to saying, in the first
instance, the coarser fabricks; it will be seen, however, in the course of
this address, that I am of opinion much more than this, can, and will be accomplished, as I believe the slave population to be peculiarly fitted to
learn, and to perform most of the operations required in a cotton mill.
     Early impressions, and habit, are alone sufficient to account for the
expectations, and even the desires, of the slaves being circumscribed, within very narrow limits; one of his most ardent wishes, however, is to learn
some mechanical business, and he who has a trade is, by common consent, considered as superior in situation to him who works upon the plantation, and
even to the house servant. Many, indeed the greatest part of them, are but
indifferent workmen; this, it is evident, does not arise from a want of capacity to become otherwise, but from defective instruction, indifferent
tools, and that slovenly habit of doing almost everything in makeshift, as
they are called, which is perhaps unavoidable under existing circumstances.
Indeed it is rather a matter of surprise, that so much skill exists as is
frequently manifested, where nearly every plantation has its blacksmith, and
its carpenter, whose operations are limited to the immediate wants of home;
were white men brought up under like circumstances, it may be fairly questioned whether they would exhibit any portion of that superiority which is so
generally ascribed to them.
     In all the larger towns, and in many of the smaller, there are negro
workmen, particularly blacksmiths, who execute with great cleverness, and

sometimes, with extraordinary skill. I have seen several well made screw
presses, for baling cotton, which were entirely the work of negroes; the
gins, which are almost as numerous as the larger plantations, are usually
tended exclusively by them, although they exact as much care and skill as
are generally required in the process of the manufacture of that article into yarn and cloth.

The negro possesses, in general, a degree of emulation, equal, at least
to that of the white labourers; I say at least equal, but, in my estimation
it is superior. I have been repeatedly struck with the avidity with which
they seek, and the gratitude with which they receive instruction on any
point relating to their business; and surprised to hear how anxiously the
wish has been expressed that they could visit the north, to see and to learn
new methods of working; a wish entirely unconnected, I am sure, with any
other idea than the simple one expressed. Although thus emulous, the emulation of the negro is limited to his own particular business, and if this be
one simple operation, requiring to be perpetually repeated, he is perfectly
satisfied to pursue it, and will be proud of any superior skill which he may
acquire.

Assuming these positions as facts, and such I know them to be, it will
readily be admitted, that better materials for making workmen, in any regular and ordinary manufacture, where labour saving machinery is employed, do
not exist anywhere. It is not merely in cotton bagging, and other fabrics
of the coarser kind, that the negro may be employed; although these will
necessarily come first in order, he, I am convinced, will be found equal to
the production of some of the finer articles furnished in the spinning factory, and by the loom; what valid reason can be urged to the contrary, I am
utterly at a loss to divine.

So little aware of this fact, or so adverse to its manifestations, have
been those persons which have conducted the establishments for cotton spinning to the south, that in mills which have been in operation for three or
four years, none but white persons are, or were lately, employed, except in
offices of mere labour. Some enterprising gentlemen are now establishing
cotton works in the vicinity of Petersburg, in Virginia. A gentleman who has
taken great interest in this subject, accidently met with the superintendent,
and inquired whether it was his intention to employ negroes in the manufactory; he replied that it was a thing of which he had never thought; and until very lately, all the owners of slaves appear to have been in the same
predicament; even now, there are but few of them prepared to give credit to
the doctrine which I have so confidently advanced. This, however, need not
excite surprise, as most of them are acquainted with the manufactured goods
in their finished state only, and cannot, therefore, estimate the moderate
portion of skill required by each individual employed in their formation.
This can be done only by those acquainted with the details of the workshop.

Should the truth of the doctrine which I have advocated be admitted, the
philanthropists, and the political economist will hail with equal pleasure,
the change which will be affected in the south, by the introduction of manufacturing establishments, as it will, at the same time, add greatly to the
comfort of the slave, and to the solid wealth of the community. For a considerable period the planters in many places have found it extremely difficult to pay their current expenses, and to feed and clothe their negroes,
from the annual produce of their lands; and thousands have removed to the
more fertile regions in the western states, not with the expectation of accumulating wealth, but merely for the purpose of obtaining a ready and abundant supply for their negro families. Thousands more of our southern fellow
citizens will be compelled to adopt the same expedient, unless some new re-
source be obtained.

Do not imagine I am a friend of slavery, or that I would willingly promote any measure which I believed to be in the slightest degree calculated
to extend and perpetrate this great moral evil. At the present day slavery
has but few advocates; and they are as rare among the intellectual slaveholders to the south, as they are with us. A long residence among them, enables me to make this declaration with the most undoubting confidence; and I
feel, therefore, that in making it I perform an act of simple justice only,
and should be much gratified if I were able to remove any portion of that
prejudice which tends to estrange one part of our country from the other.

When I first came to the South, I carried with me many of those prejudices which are common in the non-slave holding states; and although, for
the very nature of moral truth, it was impossible for me to see anything
which could lessen my abhorrance of slavery, in the abstract, I found that
much more had been done than I had apprehended, and that much is still in
progress, to lessen its attending evils; and was also thoroughly convinced,
that its removal is a problem of no easy solution. The work, however, is
making a sure, though slow, progress; the slaves are gradually acquiring information, and their owners generally both confess, and *feel* the iniquity of
the system. Examples of cruelty are very rare, and indelible disgrace af-
fixes itself to him who has the character of being a bad master. The friends
of emancipation must rejoice should one of the most serious obstacles to its
accomplishment be removed, by training the slave to habits of industry, in a
business which will tend to prepare him for a state of freedom, and thus
pave the way for the gradual removal of an entailed evil, which cannot be
directly or suddenly, touched, without committing monstrous injustice in the
case of both parties concerned.

At present, the occupation of the plantation slave is, in many instances, an alteration between absolute idleness and severe labour; but most
of the crops raised, demanding at one period, unremitted attention, and at
others, allowing long intervals of complete relaxation. The principal product of the plantation, which exacts regular attention and affords employment to the younger negroes, is the cotton crop; and this circumstance has
operated as a strong inducement to many planters to cultivate it; as every
intelligent man is aware that moderate, and regularly continued labour is
the most favorable to the physical and moral constitution of man. The period, however, has arrived, when, as I have already remarked, the cotton crop
will not, in many situations, pay for its culture, preparation, and carriage
to market; and it is absolutely necessary that other employment should be
found for the hands, there being no probability, and scarcely a possibility,
of an advance in the price; indeed, the very reverse of this may be anticipated. I have attempted to indicate that new employment, which is so much
needed, and to prove that it is not only necessary and desirable, but practicable.

In the introduction of every system, difficulties are to be encountered, and removed; but those which at first appear insuperable, yield readily, and rapidly to the energy of determined perseverance. In the present
instance, as in most others, prejudice and habit both stand in the way. The
south will not supply persons able to establish or superintend these new manufactories, and the proper management of the slave requires considerable
knowledge and experience; his usefulness, and even his happiness, demands
that the kind of familiarity which is admissable among white persons should
be avoided, and that the difference of situation should be constantly and
distinctly marked; and all this may be, and is done, without violating the
duties of kindness, or of humanity. Persons brought up to the north frequently err in this point; for though there are some whose understanding will
enable them at once to adopt the right course, the greater number are inclined to be at first too familiar, and subsequently too severe, and there is
constantly some well grounded prejudice against making them the managers of
negroes. This may limit the number of suitable managers, yet it is not an
insuperable objection to the system I am advocating; the practice of a few
years would enable the south to supply her own superintendents, and in many
respects with manifest advantage to herself.

There is another class of persons existing in the southern states, who
are in fact, though free, less happily situated than the slaves themselves,
and which by the extensive introduction of the manufacturing system, would
not only be redeemed from wretchedness, but become a mine of wealth to the
country, instead of remaining a degraded *case,* and a heavy burden; I allude
to the poorer portion of the white inhabitants. Among these there is a very
large number of widows, with families of children, who, with the utmost efforts of their industry, earn a miserable and precarious subsistence; of
these, all who are able, would soon be employed. That the number of widows
and orphans, in the situation represented, should be comparatively much
greater in the southern, than in the northern states, may, to some, appear
paradoxical and incredible, it is, however a fact, and one for which it

would not be difficult to assign a reason, were it necessary, or suitable to
the occasion.

It is a subject of increasing difficulty in the part of our country of
which I am speaking, that the occupations are so few, which are deemed respectable for the sons of those who are in good circumstances; and, in the
present state of things, this difficulty is a real one. The encouragement
to become planters is very small indeed, and the professions of medicine,
and of law, are overstocked. Manufactories do not exist on a scale sufficiently extensive to afford acceptable stations, and until they do, it would
argue but little knowledge of the state of affairs in the south, or of the
principles of human nature, to expect those who are considered as holding a
station in the higher walks of society, to devote their attention to the mechanic arts. A deficiency in the requisite talents will not be expected,
for although the opportunities of displaying it have been less numerous, the
same aptitude at invention and adaptation exist in the south, which is so
characteristic of the inhabitants of the northern states. The records of
the patent office, and numerous ingenius contrivances which have been divided, and are in use, might be adduced, were proof of this. . . .

Of the awakening attention of the south, to the diffusion of information on the important subject of the mechanic arts, many evidences might be
adduced; one only shall be mentioned. The board of visitors of the University of Virginia, have, by a recent resolution, made it the particular duty
of the professor of natural philosophy, to include in his course of lectures,
the application of this science to operative mechanics.

It may be thought by some, and perhaps correctly, that a subject might
have been chosen better suited to the purpose of an opening address to the
Franklin Institute, than that to which I have given a prominent place.

*Thomas P. Jones, "The Progress of Manufactures and Internal Improvements in
the United States, and Particularly on the Advantages to be Derived from the
Employment of Slaves in the Manufacturing of Cotton and Other Goods," The
American Farmer, 9 (November 30, 1827), 290-91, reproduced in The Textile
History Review, 3 (January, 1962), 155-61.*

2. "FISHER'S REPORT"

It has hitherto been urged against the establishment of manufactures in
North Carolina, and in the southern country generally, that the price of labour is too high to yield profits, or to enable us to compete with the northern states and England, where population is more dense. This is a great mistake. If it were so, when the price of cotton ranged from 15 to 20 cents per
lb. it is certainly not so now, since the great fall in price in that and
other staples.

We have two species of labour—*white* labour and *black* labour. As to
white labour, we hazard nothing in saying, that it is cheaper in North Carolina than it is either in England or at the north. The price of labour in
England is regulated by the price of provisions and the onerous taxes imposed
upon the people. When these are considered, it is clear that a common opera-
tor could not live in that country, unless he received nearly double what is
paid here. In England, veal is worth from 16 to 18 cts. per lb.; beef, from
14 to 16; mutton from 12 to 14 cents; while here, beef in plenty can be had
from 3 to 5 cents per lb. and other provisions in proportion.

Mr. Thomas Massey, a very intelligent manufacturer, who has been engaged
for eighteen years in the business, gives the following as the lowest prices
ever known in his neighbourhood, viz:

For boys and girls under 12 years, per week, $1 00
For do.   do.   15   do.   1 50
For do.   do.   18   do.   2 00

In the flannel factories at Amesbury, Massachusetts, the wages for females is 50 cents per day, and of males one dollar. The wages of girls at
14 years old, at Lowell, average more than one dollar a week and their board.

According to a statement, taken from the Paterson Intelligence, there
are employed at the Paterson factory, 381 men, 386 women, and 686 girls and
boys. The average wages of the whole is $152 per year, or nearly $3 per
week.

Now let any one compare these prices with similar labour in the interi-
or of North Carolina, and he will at once come to the conclusion that labour
is cheaper here than at the north. Indeed, labourers of the south can always afford to take lower wages, as they require less fuel and clothing than
in New England. The species of labour that has been high at the south, is
that of male adults; while that of females and children has always been low.

Mr. Donaldson, who owns a cotton factory at Fayetteville, and another
at the falls of Tar river--a gentleman who has visited the northern establishments and those of England, and who is well acquainted with the subject,
gives it to the committee as his decided opinion, that factory labour is
cheaper here than in either in Old or New England.

Black Labour.--But if this be the fact as to white labour, it is still
more so when black labour is employed.

We are aware, that the opinion is entertained at the north, and even by
some persons among ourselves, that our slaves cannot be advantageously employed in manufactories. 1st. Because, as is alleged, they are deficient in
intellectual qualifications; and 2d. Because they have no moral principle.
Now, that the northern manufacturers should hold out these ideas, is not to
be wondered at, when we consider that it is their interest to do so; but that
these notions should be entertained by any well informed persons acquainted
with our black population, is strange indeed. What branch of mechanics have
we in our country, in which we do not find negroes often distinguished for
their skill and ingenuity? In every place we see them equalling the best
white mechanics.

But if the evidence drawn from analogous pursuits be deemed insufficient, we offer proof in point. Mr. Donaldson, before mentioned, says, that
he has been for some time in the habit of working blacks in his factories,
and that he not only finds them equal to whites in aptness to learn and skill
to execute, but, all things considered, he actually prefers them. Mr. D.
further states, that he has had several superintendants from the north, and
all of them, with the exception of one, decidedly preferred black help, as
they term it, to white. With the blacks, there is no turning out for wages,
and no time lost in visiting musters and other public exhibitions.

But one of the great advantages of black labour is, that you can attach
it permanently to the establishment by purchase. The following calculations
will show the difference in cost between white and black labour.

We suppose a factory is erected in New England, to be carried on for
ten years, by white operatives.

Another is erected in North Carolina, to be carried on for the same
length of time by black operatives. Each of 1000 spindles, and both conducted by good managers.

1.   The one with white labour.

According to statements to be relied on, it requires 33
    hands, large and small, to carry on 1000 spindles.
    At the most moderate rates, and the hands will
    cost per week, ... $70
Or, if paid at the end of the year, ... $3,640

The fact is, however, that the $70 is always paid at the end of each
week, which, when the interest is carried forward, to the end of the year,
makes yearly, or altogether $109 more; but we will throw this aside, and
state the sum of $3,640.

From the time of paying the first $3,640 to the end of the term of ten
years, will be nine years; therefore count the interest on that sum for nine
years. On the payment of the wages for the second year, count interest for
eight years; on the wages of the third year, add interest for seven years;

and so on to the end of ten years. When it will be ascertained that the sum
paid out for *wages alone,* with simple interest thereon, will amount to more
than $46,000.

2. The establishment with black labour.

In place of hiring hands, we say let them be purchased, and we allow
enough, when we estimate that hands of the right description may be had for
200 dollars each, on an average.

Instead of taking 33 operatives, the number employed in the white establishment, add one in eleven, making 36. These supernumeraries are put in to
make up for any loss of time on account of sickness or other causes. Thirty-
six slaves, at $200 each, is $7,200.

The next inquiry is, what will it cost per annum to clothe and feed
these thirty-six blacks? Some very intelligent gentlemen, large owners of
slaves, give it as their opinion, that slaves of this description can be decently clothed and plentifully fed for 25 dollars each, which would make 850
dollars per year; but not to fall under the mark, the committee estimate
that the cost will be 1000 dollars per year. To these sums should be also
added, the wages of a superintendant--say 500 dollars per year. This being
the expenses of black labour, we wish now to compare it with the cost of
white labour of 33 hands.

The 33 whites, we have seen, will cost 3640 dollars per year; or, in
other words, their wages may be put down as worth 3640 dollars.

Now 36 blacks, and one white superintendant, can certainly do as much
work as 33 whites. We therefore put their labour down at the same price of
3,640 dollars.

Having thus ascertained the cost of black labour, and its value in
wages, we proceed to make the annual calculations during the term of ten
years.

At the end of the 1st year.

Dr.	To capital vested in the purchase of slaves, . . .	$7,200 00
	To interest thereon for 12 months, ...	432 00
	Clothing and feeding slaves, 1st year, ...	1,000 00
	Wages to a white superintendent, ...	500 00
		$9,132 00
Cr.	By what the same quantum of labour will cost, if performed by white operatives, ...	3,640 00
		5,492 00

At the end of the 2d year.

Dr.	To balance unpaid, as above, ...	5,492 00
	Interest thereon, ...	329 52
	Clothing and feeding blacks, and wages to superintendant, ...	1,500 00
		7,321 52
Cr.	By wages, as above, ...	3,640 00
		3,681 52

At the end of the 3d year.

Dr.	To balance as above, ...	3,681 52
	Interest for twelve months, ...	220 89
	Third item, as above, ...	1,500 00
		5,402 41
Cr.	As above, ...	3,640 00
		1,762 41

At the end of the 4th year.

Dr.	To balance as above, ...	$1,762 41
	Interest thereon, ...	157 44
	Third item, as above, ...	1,500 00
		3,419 85
Cr.	By wages, as above, ...	3,640 00
	Over-pays by	220 15

Thus, at the end of the fourth year, the capital invested in slaves, with interest regularly carried forward, will be paid off, and more than paid, by $220.15. Besides this, the slaves have been well fed and clothed, and 500 dollars annually allowed as wages to a white superintendant.

Now carry on this sum of $220.15, with interest, from the end of the 4th year, to the end of the term of ten years, is	$299 40
Nett wages of the 5th year, (after deducting 1000 dollars for clothing and feeding, and 500 dollars for superintendant, will be 2140 dollars, and interest to end of term, ...	2,740 00
Nett wages of 6th year, with interest, . . .	2,653 00
Do. of 7th year, ...	2,525 00
Do. of 8th year, ...	2,396 00
Do. of 9th year, ...	2,298 00
Do. of 10th year, ...	2,140 00
	$15,021 80

Thus, at the end of the term of ten years, the establishment carried on by white operatives, has cost for labour alone, $46,000.

While the one carried on by blacks has paid the purchase money with interest; has fed and clothed the hands; has paid a superintendant, and made a saving on the basis of white labour, of $15,021.80. In addition to this, the blacks are still on hand, and worth more than when first purchased. But, to be on the safe side, deduct for deaths and casualties 25 per cent. from first cost, leaves $5,400.

Then so far as regards wages of the operatives, if you employ white labour, at the end of ten years you pay about $46,000.

If blacks are employed, you have the same labour, and at the end of ten years, actually save $15,021.10.

The two sums added together, $61,021. shows the difference between black and white labour for ten years, in an establishment of only 1000 spindles. But there are many establishments of 5000; of course the difference would be in proportion--that is, $305,105.

To this add the item of transportation on the raw material for ten years, on 500 bales, at $7.50 per bale, that being the quantity of cotton annually consumed by such an establishment, equal to 5000, at $7.50, is $37,500.

Total difference in favour of black establishment is $342,605.

The committee have thus, at greater length than they could wish, presented their views on the policy of introducing the manufacturing system into North Carolina. They firmly believe that it is the only course that will relieve our people from the evils that now so heavily press on them. We have nearly reached the lowest point of depression, and it is time for the reaction to begin. Our habits and prejudices are against manufacturing; but we must yield to the force of things, and profit by the indications of nature. The policy that resists the change is unwise and suicidal. Nothing else can restore us.

Let the manufacturing system but take root among us, and it will soon flourish like a vigourous plant in its native soil: It will become our greatest means of wealth and prosperity; it will change the course of trade, and, in a great measure, make us independent of Europe and the north.

Nature has made us far more independent of them than they are of us. They can manufacture our raw material, but they cannot produce it. We can raise it and manufacture it too. Such are our superior advantages, that we may anticipate the time, when the manufactured articles of the south will be shipped to the north, and sold in their markets cheaper than their own fabrics, and when the course of trade and difference of exchange will turn in our favour. The committee, at this time, are not aware that it is within the power of this General Assembly, by any legislative act, to forward the introduction of the system into North Carolina. They, however, recommend the granting of acts of incorportion to companies for manufacturing purposes as often as suitable applications may be made.

All which is respectfully submitted,

CHARLES FISHER, *Chairman.*

Charles Fisher (Chairman), "A Report on the Establishment of Cotton and Wollen Manufactures, and on the growing of Wood; made to the House of Commons of North Carolina, by Mr. Fisher, from Rowan, on Tuesday, January 1, 1828," reprinted in The American Farmer, 9 (January 18, 25, 1828), 346-48, 353-54.

3. JAMES HAMMOND, "PROGRESS OF SOUTHERN INDUSTRY" [17]

The great item of cost in manufacturing, next to the raw material, is that of labor. And the final result of the great struggle, for the control and enjoyment of the most important industrial pursuit of the world, will probably depend on its comparative cheapness. We are forever told of the "pauper labor" of Europe, and for the reason I have just given, the North is, perhaps, excusable for never having been able to look with composure at this bug-bear. The cheapness of labor is undoubtedly much influenced by density of population, though labor is dearer in Massachusetts, with a population of one hundred, than it is in South Carolina with a population of twenty-two, to the square mile. Ultimately, however, the value of labor must depend on climate and soil. Wherever men can work the most, and under a just and secure government, live at least expense, there, in the long run, labor must be the cheapest. In England, factory labor is now limited by law to sixty hours a week. In our northern States, the average of available weekly labor is estimated at seventy-three and a half hours--in the middle States at seventy-five and a half hours, and, the further south we come, the more it is susceptible of increase. Cold, ice and snow, rarely present impediments to working in the cotton region, and the steady heat of our summers is not so prostrating as the short, but frequent and sudden, bursts of northern summers. If driven to that necessity, there is no doubt we can extend our hours of labor beyond any of our rivals. The necessary expenses of the southern laborer, are not near so great as are those of one, in Northern latitudes. He does not require as much, nor as costly clothing, nor as expensive lodgings, nor the same quantity of fuel, nor even an equal amount of food. All the fermented and distilled liquors which, in cold climates, are in some sort necessaries, are here uncalled for and injurious indulgences. Corn bread and bacon, as much as the epicure may sneer at them, with fresh meat only occasionally, and a moderate use of garden vegetables, will, in this region at least, give to the laborer greater strength of muscle and constitution, enable him to undergo more fatigue, and insure him longer life and more enjoyment of it, than any other diet. And these, indeed, with coffee, constitute the habitual food of the great body of the southern people. Thirteen bushels of corn, worth now, even in the Atlantic southern States only about $6 on the average, and one hundred and sixty pounds of bacon, or its equivalent, worth about $9, is an ample yearly allowance for a grown person. Garden vegetables bear no price except in cities. If sugar and coffee be added, $18 or at most $19, will cover the whole necessary annual cost of a full

supply of wholesome and palatable food, purchased in the market. . . . In
addition to sound theoretical reasoning we have strong practical proofs to
lead us to the conviction, that the cotton region is entirely competent to
convert the whole cotton crop into goods of all descriptions, at a cost so
low as to distance all competition. And the South has only to address herself earnestly to the great work to accomplish it, in a space of time that
no one, not intimately acquainted with our people, would deem credible, if
suggested now. . . .

The immense benefits the South would derive from such a result, are not
generally appreciated. Few have the remotest idea of them. Indeed they
would be so vast as to defy all previous calculation. . . . How would the
failing industry of South Carolina recuperate under an increased annual expenditure of $14,000,000 within her limits? How would her cities grow, and
new ones spring into existence? How would her marshes be drained, and her
river swamps be dyked in, until pestilence was driven from her land, and
virgin fields of exhaustless fertility, conquered for her agriculture? What
railroads would be built along her thoroughfares, and what steamships would
be launched upon her waters? How many colleges, and schools, and charities,
would be founded and endowed? How would her strength be consolidated at
home, and her influence abroad augmented and extended? I am not conjuring
up ideal visions to excite the imagination. All these things have been actually done. They have been, in our own times; and under our own eyes, carried out and made legible, living, self-multiplying and giant-growing FACTS
in Old England and New England; and they have been mainly accomplished by
the incalculable profits which their genius and enterprise have realized on
the products of OUR LABOR. But the question will naturally be asked, can
South Carolina manufacture 100,000,000 pounds of cotton? Has she, without
drawing from abroad, which is not desirable if it can be obviated--has she
capital, the motive powers of machinery, and the operatives, that will enable her to do it to advantage? The answer is yes! and the truth of it may
be demonstrated in a few words. To manufacture this amount of cotton, $40,
000,000 of capital would be an ample and liberal investment, that would
cover all contingencies, if made judiciously. Now, for the want of profitable investment, a much larger amount of South Carolina capital has, within
the last twenty years, actually left our State, and been lost to us forever.
And that, without diminishing our agricultural productions, or foreign exports, which have increased considerably in quantity, if not in value, since
1830. I have already shown, that from 1830 to 1840, upwards of 80,000 slaves
were carried from our State, and it may be assumed as certain, that full as
many have gone within these last ten years. These 160,000 slaves, at $400
each, were alone worth $64,000,000. But for each one of these slaves, at
the very least, $100 worth of land and other property must have been sold
here, and the cash proceeds transferred with them beyond our borders. This
would amount to $46,000,000 more. And if to this be added the $10,000,000
which, made here by mercantile and other pursuits, has been sent elsewhere
for investment, as has undoubtedly been done, we have, without computing
interest, the immense sum of $90,000,000, of which, within these last twenty
years, South Carolina has been drained, in currents which still flow, and
bid fair to flow deeper and broader every year. No one is to be blamed for
the transfer of this vast amount of capital. No one is under obligation to
make or keep unprofitable investments. It is not to be expected. It never
will be done to any great extent by enlightened and enterprising men. But if
we had embarked in manufactures twenty years ago, as successfully as others,
and afforded to capital here returns of thirty, or twenty, or even ten per
cent., not a dollar of that $90,000,000 would have left the State. The
slaves might have gone, and the lands they cultivated might have been sold--
but the enterprising owners would have remained here, and the full cash
equivalent of this property would have remained with them. In their hands,
it would not only have sufficed to erect all the factories requisite to spin
our entire crop, but the vast overplus of $50,000,000, would have constructed
and paid for thousands of miles of railroad, and built fleets of steamships
and merchant vessels, sufficient to carry our augmented commerce in direct
lines to all the great marts of the world. If we begin now, and, instead of
removing, sell, for a time, the superfluous increase of our slaves, the proceeds, added to the floating capital otherwise accumulated, will enable us

to accomplish all these objects in a much shorter period than twenty years, and bring in upon our State a flood-tide of prosperity, that will cover every hill and valley--every bog and barren--with deposits more valuable than those in California.

But if ample capital were supplied, have we in South Carolina sufficient water power, advantageously located, or can we, on reasonable terms, generate steam power to manufacture our whole crop? The immense pine forests which line our railroads and navigable streams, will, if judiciously managed, furnish fuel for all the factories we shall want, at $1 25 a cord, for generations yet to come.

At this rate, fuel can be supplied as cheaply as the best Cumberland coal at $3 a ton, or 12 cents a bushel, which is cheaper than the same quality of coal is furnished to the English factories. The cost of steam engines, enhanced now only by the charges of transportation, will be proportionably reduced as the mechanic arts advance, under the fostering spirit of manufactures and commerce. . . . As to water power, without looking further, the sand hill streams, which course through the pine barrens of our middle country--the healthiest region, take the year round, on the surface of the globe--are, it is well ascertained, capable of putting in motion millions of spindles and their complimental machinery--spindles enough to consume several times the amount of our crop. . . .

With capital, motive-powers, cheap provisions, and convenient transportation at our command, it would only remain to obtain operatives, on fair terms, to render our capacity to manufacture our cotton crop, complete. For this purpose, about thirty-five thousand, of all ages, would be requisite. There is no question but that our slaves might, under competent overseers, become efficient and profitable operatives in our factories. It may be of much consequence to us, that this fact has been fully fested, and is well known and acknowledged, as it would give us, under all circumstances, a reliable source. But to take, as we should have to do, even three-fourths of the required number from our cotton fields, would reduce our crop at least one-third--a reduction that would seriously affect the great results we have in view. It would also enhance the prices of labor and provisions; not so much by the legitimate and profitable process of increasing the demand, as by diminishing the supply; and it would curtail the relative power of the agricultural class. If purchased by the factories--the only feasible plan of using them--their cost would add fifty per cent. to the capital required for manufacturing. While, in their appropriate sphere, the cultivation of our great staples, under a hot sun and arid miasma, that prostrates the white man, our negro slaves admit of no substitute; and may defy all competition, it is seriously doubted, whether their extensive and permanent employment in manufactures and mechanic arts, is consistent with safe and sound policy. Whenever a slave is made a mechanic, he is more than half freed, and soon becomes, as we too well know, and all history attests, with rare exceptions, the most corrupt and turbulent of his class. Wherever slavery has decayed, the first step in the progress of emancipation, has been the elevation of the slaves to the rank of artisans and soldiers. This is the process through which slavery has receded; as the mechanic arts have advanced; and we have no reason to doubt, that the same causes will produce the same effects here. We have, however, abundant labor of another kind, which, unable at low prices of agricultural produce to compete with slave labor, in that line, languishes for employment; and, as a necessary consequence, is working evil to both our social and political systems. This labor, if not quite so cheap directly, will be found, in the long-run, much the cheapest; since those who are capable of it, will, whether idle or employed, inevitably, in one way or another, draw their support from the community. According to the best calculation, which, in the absence of statistic facts, can be made, it is believed, that of the three hundred thousand white inhabitants of South Carolina, there are not less than fifty thousand, whose industry; such as it is, and compensated as it is, is not, in the present condition of things, and does not promise to be hereafter, adequate to procure them, honestly, such a support as every white person in this country is, and feels himself entitled to. And this, next to emigration, is, perhaps, the heaviest of the weights that press upon the springs of our prosperity. Most of these now follow agricultural pursuits, in feeble, yet injurious competition with slave labor. Some, perhaps,

not more from inclination, than from the want of due encouragement, can
scarcely be said to work at all. They obtain a precarious subsistence, by
occasional jobs, by hunting, by fishing, sometimes by plundering fields or
folds, and too often by what is, in its effects, far worse--trading with
slaves, and seducing them to plunder for their benefit. If the ancient philosopher had the slightest grounds for saying that it would require the
plains of Babylon to support, in idleness, five thousand soldiers and their
families, we may infer how enormous a tax it is on our resources, to maintain to the extent we do now, and are likely to have to do, directly and indirectly, our unemployed, or insufficiently employed poor.

From this class of our citizens, thirty-five thousand factory operatives
may certainly be drawn, as rapidly as they may be called for, since boys and
girls are required, in large porportion, for this business. Nor will there
be any difficulty in obtaining them. Experience has shown that, contrary to
general expectation, there exists no serious prejudice against such labor
among our native citizens, and that they have been prompt to avail themselves, at moderate wages, of the opportunity it affords of making an honest
and comfortable support, and decent provision for the future. The example
thus set of continuous and systematic industry, among those to whom it has
heretofore been unknown, cannot fail to produce the most beneficial effects,
not only on their own class, but upon all the working classes of the State.
And, putting aside the immense contribution of manufactures to the general
prosperity, it would be one of the greatest benefits that could possibly be
conferred on the agriculture of South Carolina, to convert thirty-five thousand of her unemployed or insufficiently compensated population into active
and intelligent workmen, buying and paying for the products of her soil,
which their families consume.

But it has been suggested, that white factory operatives in the South
would constitute a body hostile to our domestic institutions. If any such
sentiments could take root among the poorer classes of our native citizens,
more danger may be apprehended from them, in the present state of things,
with the facilities they now possess and the difficulties they have now to
encounter, than if they were brought together in factories, with constant
employment and adequate remuneration. It is well known, that the abolitionists of America and Europe are now making the most strenuous efforts to
enlist them in their crusade, by encouraging the exclusive use of what is
called "free labor cotton," and by inflammatory appeals to their pride and
their supposed interests. But all apprehensions from this source are entirely imaginary. The poorest and humblest freeman of the South feels as
sensibly, perhaps more sensibly than the wealthiest planter, the barrier
which nature, as well as law, has erected between the white and black races,
and would scorn as much to submit to the universal degradation which must
follow, whenever it is broken down. Besides this, the factory operative
could not fail to see here, what one would suppose he must see, however distant from us, that the whole fabric of his own fortunes was based on our
slave system, since it is only by slave labor that cotton ever has been, or
ever can be cheaply or extensively produced. Thus, not only from natural
sentiment and training, but from convictions of self-interest, greatly
strengthened by their new occupation, this class of our citizens might be relied on to sustain, as firmly and faithfully as any other, the social institutions of the South. The fact cannot be denied, that property is more secure in our slave States than it is, at present, in any other part of the
world; and the constant and profitable employment of all classes among us
will increase, rather than diminish that security. . . .

*James Hammond, "Progress of Southern Industry," Gov. Hammond's Address Be-
fore the South Carolina Institute, 1850, reprinted in DeBow's Review, 8
(June 1850), 513-22 are reproduced here.*

4. A PRO-INDUSTRIAL SLAVERY OPINION

Charleston April 28, 1849

My Dear Sir
        I understand that you are preparing a review of Elwood Fisher's pam-
phlet, a work which I am very glad you have undertaken. As it is a subject
in which we all feel a deep and common interest, I will venture to suggest
one or two considerations to you, even at the hasard of suggesting what may
have passed through your own mind.
        Mr. Fisher has not noticed an important element which makes in favor of
the Slave interest. The products of slave labor are such as can never be
the subjects of competition with white labor. Cotton and Rice are the products of Districts of Country where the white man cannot labor on account of
malaria. They with Tobacco require cultivation during the whole summer with
exposure to a summer's sun. The two chief of them are confined within geographical limits. The other products of agriculture upon which whites are
employed are grains which are planted either in the fall or spring and require but little cultivation. There seems a necessity therefore, if the
world must have Cotton, and if the Rice District is to be cultivated at all,
that slave labor must be resorted to, and the whites can only be furnished
with Cotton Fabrics at the cheap rates which now prevail, by the use of slave
labor. Nay it is questionable, if slavery were abolished, whether the Cotton
Crops would be worth noticing. For without the organized labor of the South,
it could not be produced at all--and it is certain that the negroes themselves would never volunteer to raise it. No free negro now ever attempts
such a thing. They generally go into other pursuits.
        This leads me to another consideration, which is very important to us in
this State and City. I find an opinion gaining ground that slaves ought to
be excluded from mechanical pursuits, and everything but agriculture, so as
to have their places filled with whites; and ere long we will have a formidable party on this subject. The planters generally do not perceive how it
affects their interest, and very frequently chime in with this cry. I think
our friend Gregg of Graniteville, with those who are agog about manufactures,
without knowing it, are lending aid to this party, which is in truth, the
only party from which danger to our Institutions is to be apprehended among
us. Drive out negro mechanics and all sorts of operatives from our Cities,
and who must take their place. The same men who make the cry in the Northern Cities against the tyranny of Capital--and there as here would drive all
before them all who interfere with them--and would soon raise hue and cry
against the Negro, and be hot Abolitionists--and every one of those men would
have a vote. In our Cities, we see the operation of these elements--and if
the eyes of the planting community are opened, the danger may be averted.
Fill Barnwell District with some hundred Lowellers, and how do you think they
will vote at elections. The scheme by which "Brutus" has expected to foment
division among us is based on this element of Discord. For you Know that
even in our lower Country, there are many that could be Marshalled against
the Planter, upon the idea that they were fighting against the aristocracy.
These things I have no doubt you will Keep in view. But I think you would do
much good by giving a timely warning to our agricultural community--as every
body will read your review.

                                        Yours with much esteem

                                        C. G. MEMMINGER [18]

*Christopher G. Memminger to James H. Hammond, reprinted in Thomas P. Martin
(ed.), "The Advent of William Gregg and the Graniteville Company," The Journal of Southern History, 11 (August 1945), 413-14.*

5.   LETTER FROM WILLIAM P. POWELL

Liverpool, March 23d, 1851

. . . it is not necessary for me to visit "the cotton factories of Manchester and Salford, the nail factories of Preston, and, above all, the coal
pits in the north of England, etc. etc." in order to make a just comparison
between the two systems of free and slave labor, for they are, in effect, as
far apart as the Poles. The operatives of those factories and mines are protected in their property and their persons by law; and the scale of prices
for labor performed, especially for the younger branches, and the number of
hours to be employed, are regulated by Parliamentary enactments; and they
realize from THREE shillings sterling to TWO pounds per week for their labor;
and, what is more, they are not chattels personal, subject to corporeal punishment, whips and chains, and separated, parents from their children, and
husbands from their wives. But not so "with the sleek, oily appearances of
the comfortably clothed, well fed, fat and saucy southern slaves." Are there
any laws regulating the price of slave labor, forbidding corporeal punishment for non-performance of task? Are there laws punishing with death the
master, overseer, or driver, for *murder, rape* or *violence* committed daily upon the defenceless slaves? And yet the American negro slaves are better off
than the operatives in the cotton factories and coal mines in England?

William P. Powell. [19]

National Anti-Slavery Standard, May 8, 1851.

PETITIONS AND PROTESTS OF WHITE MECHANICS
AGAINST BLACK MECHANICS

6.   PETITION OF CHARLESTON CITIZENS TO THE STATE LEGISLATURE, 1822

. . . your Memorialists are decidedly of opinion, that the number of negroes to be hired out, should be limited by law, and that no negro should be
allowed to work as a mechanic unless under the immediate control and inspection of his master. By far the greater portion of negroes who work out, are
released in a considerable degree from the controul of their masters--labor-
ing or forbearing to labour, as their interest or inclination prompts, rendering unto their owners, only a monthly account; and provided they but settle the wages with punctuality are permitted to regulate their own conduct;
the consequence is, they assemble together whenever they wish, and having
their time at their own disposal, can be convened at any given and fixed period, and having regular and stated meetings, can originate, prepare and mature their own plans for insurrection. Whereas, the slaves who are kept in
the yards of their masters, are immediately under their eyes, and cannot fix
a period for assembling--they know not at what hour they may be called for
by their owners, or for how long a period they may obtain leave of absence--
they cannot, therefore, act in concert and "concert is the very life of a
conspiracy."
But there is another consideration. The facility of obtaining work is
not always the same. At one period the demand for labor is considerable; at
another the demand is comparatively small; the consequence is, the labor of
the slaves hired out is very irregular, and a quantity of time is consumed
in idleness. Irregularity of habits is thus acquired; this irregularity produces restlessness of disposition, which delights in mischief and detests

quiet. The same remarks will apply to the negro mechanics, who having a
stated portion of labor to perform, are masters of the remainder of the day,
when the work is ended. The time in the evenings, and on the Sabbath is so
entirely at their disposal, that the most ample opportunity is afforded of
forming combinations and devising schemes. Should a law be passed limiting
the number of slaves to be hired out and confining the exercise of the mechanical arts to white persons (except in the cases above specified,) the result will be that a large portion of the black population now in the city,
will be removed into the country, and their places be supplied by white laborers from Europe and the Northern States. In this manner we will exchange
a dangerous portion of our population for a sound and healthy class of persons "whose feelings will be our feelings, and whose interests our interests."

The late intended Insurrection forcibly proves the truth of the above
remarks; for with a very few exceptions, the negroes engaged in that conspiracy were mechanics or persons working out. Great inconvenience, perhaps even
considerable misery, may be experienced by many worthy citizens, who at present are maintained by the hire of their slaves. But to obtain important objects by effecting considerable change or reform, great sacrifices must be
made, and great difficulties encountered. This is an affair in which tempo-
rizing expedients will avail nothing. We must meet the difficulties with
resolution, and overcome them by the most vigorous and determined course of
action. They are difficulties which, if eluded now, will meet us again in
their progress, multiply and crowd upon us until we are involved in confusion
and disorder.[20]

*"Memorial of the Citizens of Charleston to the Senate and House of Represen-
tatives of the State of South Carolina (Charleston, 1822)," as reproduced in
U. B. Phillips (ed.), Documents of American Industrial Society, Vol. II
(Cleveland, 1909), pp. 103-16.*

7. WHITE ARTISANS CLAIM UNFAIR COMPETITION FROM FREE BLACKS

Petition of William J. Grayson, James R. Verdier, and 62 other citizens of
St. Helena Parish as the Senate of South Carolina.

To the Honorbl the President and other members of the Senate, The undersigned
inhabitances of St. Hellena Parish convinced of the perniceous consequences
resulting to the State of So Car from the number of free persons of colour
within her limits beg leave respectfully to bring the subject before you.
The State not only derives no strength from the class of wich we complain,
but is essentially injured, the example of indolence and vice exhibited by
the coloured free persons is perpetually before the Slaves. They encourage
insubordination by precept as well as example. They are rapidly drawing from
the country the valuable class of industrious mechanics, on whose intelegence
and hardihood the safety of So Car must mainly depend. What will be the condition of the State when your carpenters and painters and Blacksmiths, and
the occupants of all the departments of mechanical industry are free men of
colour. Yet such must be the consequences of the competition which the white
mechanic encounters from the coloured labourer, the latter is able to work at
a less price from obvious causes. He has very often no family to support,
his wife and children are Slaves. He lives on the premises of their owner.
He has no house rent to pay no clothing or food but his own to purchase. His
expences are almost nothing, and he can therefore labour for almost nothing.
Your petitioners cannot believe that you will permit a class so useless, perniceous, and degrading, to the character of the State, to Supplant the intel-
legent industrious and vigorous freemen, who in the various mechanical departments would so essentially increase her physical and moral strength. Your
petitioners therefore pray that you will take the whole subject into

consideration, and make such provisions for the removal of the free coloured persons as to your wisdom may seem meet--and as in duty bound they will ever pray.--

[*Post-Revolutionary File, ca. 1831*] *South Carolina Department of Archives and History, Columbia, S.C., as reproduced in Willie Lee Rose (ed.), A Documentary History of Slavery in North America (New York, 1976), p. 95-96.*

8.   NEGRO MECHANICS

A meeting of the Journeymen Mechanics of the town of Petersburg, Va., was held on the 20th ult., the object of which was to oppose the competition brought about by the employment of Negro Mechanics. We copy from the Republican, the following Preamble and Resolutions which were adopted at the meeting and ordered to be published--

While we regard the right of property, and the privilege of the owner to employ his slave in honest labor, our sense of self-respect demands that we put, place, esteem and maintain ourselves a distinct society, and not associates of the Negro. Therefore, be it Resolved,

1st. That we regard the teaching of any Negro any branch of the mechanic arts as prejudicial to the interests, and injurious to the morals of the laboring White man.

2d. That we, whose names are hereunto annexed, will not work for any employer who shall take a Negro in his employ, for the purpose of teaching said Negro any branch of the mechanic arts.

3d. That each member is at liberty to engage with any employer using his own slave at the business, provided they be not published or provided in any way subsequent to this time.

4th. That we form ourselves in a society for our rights, as stated in the preamble.--Signed by the Committee.

The North Star, November 2, 1849.

9.   GEORGIA MECHANICS' CONVENTION

Agreeably to previous notice, between four and five hundred of the Mechanics of Georgia met in council at Atlanta, on the 4th of July, and organised, temporarily, by calling Wm. H. Pritchard, of Richmond county, to the Chair.

The President having taken his position, in a neat address explained the object of the Convention to be the advancement of the Mechanic Arts and the elevation of the Mechanics of Georgia--and returned his thanks for the honour conferred upon him, expressing his earnest wish that the motto of the great seal of the Commonwealth--"Wisdom, Justice and Moderation"--would govern the meeting in its deliberations, and invoking a spirit of concord among the members thereof. . . .

The Committee appointed to prepare and report matter for the consideration of the Convention, reported the following Preamble and Resolutions, which, on motions, were received:

Preamble:

Whereas, the development of the Mechanic Arts in Georgia, and the advancement of the Mechanical and Manufacturing pursuits of the Commonwealth, are no longer matters of questionable importance, as elements of permanent State prosperity, but an admitted necessity; and whereas, it is due to our fellow-citizens that the reasons for the meeting of this Convention, and for its action, should be unreservedly laid before the public, the following considerations are submitted, as embodying the views of its members generally, on the several subjects of interest embraced in this Preamble:

Negro Mechanics.

The policy of Instructing Negroes in Mechanic pursuits is of a very questionable nature. The history of the past proves that nearly all the escapes of slaves from Georgia and several other Southern States, to Free Soil territory, are traceable to the pernicious influence exercised by these persons. It is our firm conviction, that a few Negro Mechanics in towns and cities have done and can do more practical injury to the institution of Slavery and its permanent security than all the ultra abolitionists of the country. Mechanical pursuits elevate the negro's mind and quicken his intellect, leading to a desire to read and write, the gratification of which is often obtained in a clandestine manner, by which he is furnished with facilities for making money, and led into depravity and dissipation, thereby making him restless and unhappy, and an unsafe associate for the dutiful and contented negroes of the State, of a lower grade of condition. Is it not then the dictate of wisdom and prudence, looking merely to the *security* of our institutions, to take such steps as will guard and protect us from such influences, for all time to come?

Mechanical pursuits, moreover, to be fully worthy of Georgia's sons, and rendered capable of competition with other sections, must be honourably associated. Educated young men of the South can seldom be found who will engage in pursuits which lead them into professional competition with persons of inferior morals and minds.

As Mechanics and Southern men, by birth or by adoption, and as slaveholders, we appeal to every class of our fellow-citizens for a just appreciation of our motives, and for encouragement in the work we design to accomplish. That design is to raise and exalt our position as men and as citizens, morally, socially and intellectually. Let that be achieved, and a desire will, it is believed, soon be evinced by our youth to enter at once the workshops of the State, and thus contribute to make it great and independent. We ask only for such encouragement as will raise our calling in the scale of respectability and usefulness, as well as secure, on a permanent basis, the peculiar institution of the South, and promote the general welfare of the people. . . .

Resolved, 6. That in the opinion of this body the instruction of negroes in the Mechanic Arts is a source of great dissatisfaction to the mechanical interest, prejudicial to Southern youths engaging in industrial pursuits, and is believed to be inexpedient, unwise, and injurious to all classes of the community.

The report and resolutions were then taken up separately, and on motion to adopt the preamble as read, W. U. Anderson, of Cowets, moved to strike out all that portion which referred to the subject of Negro Mechanics, which after full discussion was rejected by an overwhelming vote. The preamble was then adopted as it stands.

1st, 2d, 3d, 4th and 5th were then severally read and adopted unanimously.

On a call of the 6th resolution, W. U. Anderson, of Cowets, moved, that it be laid on the table, which after discussion was lost. The 6th resolution was then put and carried.

Resolved, That this Convention individually and collectively do hereby express their firm and abiding devotion to the peculiar institution of the South *as it is,* and their utter and unqualified detestation of those Northern Abolitionists and Fanatics, who are constantly interfering with our interests and property. Carried unanimously and with great enthusiasm. . . .

                                        Georgia Citizen.

National Anti-Slavery Standard, July 31, 1851.

10. NEGRO MECHANICS

There is much that is worthy of consideration in the following remarks
of the Centreville *Enquirer*, which first met our eye in the Pennsylvania *Observer*:--

'We believe the Legislatures of all slaveholding States should pass an
act prohibiting the owners of slaves from making mechanics of them. The
rice, corn and cotton field is the proper place for the negro--and not the
workshop. That should be kept for the white man exclusively. There are
thousands of industrious, enterprising young men, who are driven from the
mechanical trades, rather than work all day side by side with the negro.
Their pride revolts at it, and we think very properly; all cannot be professional men, their inclinations do not lead in that way, but necessity drives
them to business of some kind, and they rush into the learned professions
without one single qualification. And why do they do this? Because they do
not like to be thrown into daily intercourse with the negro mechanics. See
how many young lawyers and physicians are starving, because the country is
overrun with them, and their pride forbids them from following trades. But
exclude the negro race from the mechanical arts, and you at once ennoble the
business. Men who are now ashamed to acknowledge themselves mechanics,
would take pride in it, and there would be but few drones in society. All
parents are not able to give their children education sufficient to be a
professional character, and how far superior is the respectable artisan to
the quack doctor or the jack-leg lawyer, the one scarcely able to distinguish
chill from fever, and the other incompetent to make a speech in a magistrate's court. We hope the Legislatures of the different States will take
this matter into consideration. We are aware that men will say we have the
right to do as we please with our negroes, and convert them to any use we
think proper; but it is not so. The rich have no right to build up fortunes
at the expense of the poor, and this is done whenever you degrade the mechanic to the level of the slave. The only trade entirely excluded from the negro is the printer--he may defy them, for the States have wisely prohibited
them from education.'

No one will pretend that a master who owns a skilful mechanic ought to
be or can be deprived of half of his value by a law forbidding such mechanic
from working at a trade which he has been taught at much expense and loss of
time. The master, beyond dispute, has a vested right in the enhanced productiveness of the mechanic slave's labor at a trade wherein skill, training and
intelligence are as important elements as physical strength.

Nor is it certain that a law, which should permit negroes who have already acquired mechanic arts to work at them, but which should prohibit any
others from being taught and employed at such trades, would be quite equitable and just to the owners of intelligent negroes, whose services would be
doubled in value by being so instructed and employed.

If the proposal to exclude negroes from the mechanic arts were merely a
question of competition between white mechanics and the few owners of negro
mechanics, a satisfactory solution of it might be reached by legislation.
But laws, if just, are not made for classes, but for the whole people. We
are to guard with lynx-eyed vigilance against all that can endanger even re-
motely our vital institution. It is much to be feared that any hasty and
unnecessary tampering with the limits wherein slave labor may be employed
may become a precedent for a greater mischief hereafter.

New Orleans Courier reprinted in The Liberator, September 3, 1858.

11. PETITION OF TEXAS MECHANICS

Marshall, Texas, January 17th 1861

To the Honorable's E.A. Blanch, Eli Craig, E.H. Baxter & George W. Whitmore

Gents

We the undersigned petitioners respectfully wish and request you to endeaver to get a bill passed by the Legislature of Texas to prevent the competition and encouragement of Negro Meachanick as we think that it is not just or right to give Slaves the advantages or liberties that they are now endevering to take or get to put down White whose daily living is made by the sweat of their brow in their industrious pursuits, and men too, who have been reared upon Southern Soil and who have always been with the South and all her institutions.

But we do most solemnly object to being put in competition with Negro Mechanicks who are to rival us in the obtaining of contracts for the construction of Houses Churches and other Buildings--or any other of the Mechanical Branches that are taking by contract

We would therefore appeal to you as your fellow Citizens and constituents to remedy this one feature that is now if let a lone to be greatly to the disadvantage and draw back of our Bright Lone Star State--

We say Negroes forever but Negroes in their places (viz: in Corn & Cotton Fields) and if there are those who have Negro Mechanicks to do their own work let them; have them; but we do not want to be equalized with them by allowing them to go at large contracting for jobs of work up on their own account or on account of those who pretend to be their agents, or to be made the compeditors of Negros in this a true Southern State--

We think that a law might be passed to confine them to the hire of some workman or undertaker whose duty it will be to keep them in their places and under proper control without the owner or Master being at all injured.

W.T. Smith	Phil /Brown
C. W. Slater	J H Van Hook
L. A Henderson	W Miller Johnson
L M Stevens	G W Martin
J C Curtis	G. W. Slants
W A Salmon	etc.
Hames K Fzfee	
R. E. Ramsay	
Henny Jenks	

Ms., File Box No. 42, Library and Historical Commission, State Library, Austin, Texas.

FREE BLACK WORKERS AND THE LAW

12. A SUPPLEMENT TO THE MARYLAND ACT OF 1831
RELATING TO FREE BLACKS AND SLAVES

Sect. 3. And be it enacted, That the Justices of any Magistrate's Court in the several counties of this State, or of any Orphan's Court in the said Counties, in which there is no such Magistrate's Court, upon information given to them that any free negro or negroes, mulatto or mulattoes, male or female, are residing within the jurisdiction, or County in which

said Magistrate's Court or Orphan's Court is situated, without visible means
of support, shall have power to direct the Sheriff, or any Constable of said
County, to bring before the said Magistrate's Court or Orphan's Court, as
the case may be, such free negro or negroes, mulatto or mulattoes, and sum-
mon all necessary witnesses to inquire into the condition or habits of such
negro or negroes, mulatto or mulattoes; and if, upon examination, the Justices of the said Magistrate's Court, or Orphan's Court, as the case may be,
shall be of the opinion, that the said free negro or negroes, mulatto or mulattoes, have not the necessary means of support, and are not of good and
industrious habits, then they shall issue an order in writing, directed to
the Sheriff or Constable to proceed forthwith *to sell the said negro or negroes, mulatto or mulattoes, at public sale, the highest bidder,* to serve in
the capacity of A SLAVE for any [ ] during the year in which said sale
shall be made, first giving ten days public notice of such sale; provided,
that nothing in this section contained shall go into effect until the first
day of January next; and provided, also, that every purchase of any free negro or negroes, mulatto or mulattoes, by virtue of this act, shall, in addition to the prize paid by him for such free negro or negroes, mulatto or mulattoes, find him, her or them during the term for which the said purchaser
shall purchase him, her or them, with good and sufficient food, lodging and
clothing.

     Sect. 4. And be it enacted, That if within ten days from the end of
the term for which any such negro or negroes, mulatto or mulattoes, shall
have been sold by virtue of the third section of this act, he or she shall
not leave the State, or sell him or herself to some respectable white person, to serve as A SLAVE for the following year, then he or she shall be
again sold or disposed of, as required and directed by the said third section, and in like manner in each successive year thereafter.

     Sect. 5. And be it enacted, That the purchaser of any free negro or
mulatto, by virtue of the provisions of the third or fourth sec. of this
act, shall pay to the said negro or mulatto, at the end of the term for
which he or she shall be sold, the amount of money bid for said negro or mulatto at the sale thereof, deducting the necessary costs and charges, the
sum of ten per centum, as commissions to the officer--the sum of 5 dollars
to the informer, if there shall be one, and the sum of one dollar to each of
the justices, as a fee for their services. Provided that the purchase money
aforesaid, after deducting the costs, charges and allowances as aforesaid,
which shall be paid in cash at the time of sale, shall be secured by bond
with security to the Sheriff for the use of said negro, or mulatto at the
end of the term aforesaid, which bond shall be then assigned to said negro
or mulatto, and may be recovered, as small debts now are recovered by law.

     Sect. 6. And be it enacted, That if any free negro or negroes, mulatto
or mulattoes, sold by virtue of the provisions of the third and fourth sections of this act, shall be the father or mother of any child or children,
below the age of 21 years, if male, or 18 years, if female, then the Justices of the said Magistrate's Court, or Orphan's Court, as the case may be,
shall have the infant child or children brought before them, and bound out
to serve as apprentices to good masters, to serve until the age of 21 years,
if male, and until the age of 18, if female, in like manner as orphan children are now bound out; and all indentures made by the Justices of the Magistrate's Court shall be by them returned to the Orphan's court of the County,
in which said Magistrate's Court is situated, and shall be subject to all
the provisions of law, regulating indentures of apprentices in this State.
Provided, that the interest in said apprentices shall be considered personal
property, and shall be liable to be transferred to any person within this
State, but said apprentices shall in no case be removed out of the State.

     Sect. 7. And be it enacted, Provided this act shall not be constructed
to interfere with the provisions of the several acts of Assembly in favor of
free people of color visiting Liberia, Trinidad, British Guiana, or other
Colonies.

     Sect. 8. And be it enacted, That all acts, or parts of acts, inconsis-
tent with this act, are hereby repealed.

     By the Senate, March 21, 1840.

        By the House of Delegates, March 21, 1840.

The Colored American, May 30, 1840.

13. INCENDIARY PUBLICATIONS IN BALTIMORE

John C. Pulley, a free coloured man, has been arrested, says the Baltimore Patriot of the 5th instant, "on the charge of receiving abolition papers, knowing them to be such, in violation of section 1st of the act of
1841, which provides that any free negro or mulatto who shall knowingly call
for, receive, or demand from any Post Office in this State, or have in his
possession, any abolition handbill, pamphlet, newspaper, or pictorial representation of an inflammatory character, having a tendency to create discontent among or stir up to insurrection the people of this State, shall be
deemed guilty of felony and when conviciton thereof, shall be sentenced to
undergo a confinement in the Penitentiary of this State for a period of not
less than ten nor more than twenty years."
        The specific charge in this case was the receiving through the Post
Office the Ram's Horn. The accused was held to bail in the sum of $500 for
his appearance at the next term of the Baltimore City Court. He can scarcely read, it is said, and the paper was sent him by a friend in this city. [21]

National Anti-Slavery Standard, August 20, 1841.

14. OUT OF JAIL

The Black Man Who Was Imprisoned For Reading Uncle Tom's Cabin. [22]

        I am asked to make an appeal for a poor man--a criminal, just out of
jail. He was convicted for three offences:--first, because a black skin
covered his face; second, because the English alphabet came and sat upon his
tongue; and third, because he had read the story of "Uncle Tom's Cabin."
        For these crimes he was tried and convicted by a Maryland Court in 1857,
and sentenced to the Baltimore Penitentiary for ten years. After wearing out
five years of this long penalty, the gate of his cell was opened a few weeks
ago by the new Governor of Maryland, who told him that he might quit the
jail, if he would quit also the United States. He immediately promised to
go to Canada, and is now in New York on his way thither.
        The culprit's name is Samuel Green. He is 62 years of age, though, ex-
cept for his gray hair, he seems younger; good-looking, intelligent, and
amiable; showing in his face God's plain handwriting of a good character; a
man whom a stranger would trust at first sight.
        He was born a slave in Maryland, and wore the chain for 30 years, until
his master died, bequeathing him freedom at the end of five years. The
slave, kindled with this hope of becoming a man, worked extra hours, and
earned in one year enough money to buy his service for the remaining four.
While a slave, he had married a slave-woman, the property of a kind master,
who, after her husband had so handsomely worked out his freedom, sold him
his wife for 25 cents! Mr. Green says, "My wife was worth more, but I was
willing to take her for that!"
        They had two children--son and daughter--both slaves of one master.
Eight or nine years ago, the son, after praying long for freedom, got it at
last, after the manner of Frederick Douglass, who "prayed with his legs."
The boy Green started on a moonlight night, and ran away to Canada. His

master, fearing the sister would follow, sold her straightway to Missouri;
breaking her heart by separating her from her husband and two little children.

About this time, when almost everybody was laughing and crying over the
pages of Uncle Tom, one morning while Samuel Green was going to the mill, a
blacksmith came out of his shop at the roadside--himself a black man, and
since a Methodist clergyman--exclaiming:--

"Sam Green, would you like to see Uncle Tom's Cabin?"

"What is it?" asked Sam, who thought it was some new shanty put up in
the neighborhood.

"It's a book," replied the blacksmith; "it's the story of a slave, and
it goes for Abolition."

"Yes, I'd like to read it," said Sam; and he took home the story, in
two volumes, and began to read. But before he finished, he received a letter from his boy in Canada, saying, "Come and bring mother, and let us all
live together here." It was a good idea, but the old man, before venturing
to take all his little property to a foreign country, made a hurried trip to
Canada, to see what was the prospect of earning a livelihood in the high
latitudes. Meanwhile, the story of his absence made noise enough to reach
the attentive ears of the civil officers. On his return, a constable knocked at his door, and said, "You are suspected of holding correspondence with
the North, and I shall search your house."

"Come in, sir," said Mr. Green; "it is a small cottage; you can soon
search it through; but you will find nothing, for there is nothing to find."

But Samuel Green--unsuspecting man!--found to his cost that he was a
great rogue, and that the proof of it was in his own house. The constable
found three guilty things: first, Uncle Tom's Cabin; second, a map of Canada; third, a picture of a hotel at Niagara Falls. These were all, but were
they not enough? What constable in Maryland would have asked for more?
What Court in the State would have given less than ten years in the State-
prison after such proofs? Besides, even out of Maryland, does not Gov.
Stanly, and the editor of the *Herald,* and other good men, call it a crime
for a black man to know how to read?

But without palliating Samuel Green's crime, if any kind-hearted person
can be persuaded to show kindness to the criminal, by giving a little money
to help the old man off to the penal colony of Canada, it will reach him if
sent to

THEODORE TILTON [23]

The Liberator, July 4, 1862.

15.   FREE COLORED POPULATION OF MARYLAND

We have heretofore called attention to the movement in the Maryland
Legislature for the passage of stringent laws against the free people of col-
or. This effort to expel or enslave that unfortunate class of population
has been agitated for a year or two past, but it received a severe check
last summer from the report and resolutions adopted by the Slaveholders'
Convention at Baltimore, in which good sense and humanity prevailed over the
brutal sentiment which prevails in the lower counties. The agitators, however, have availed themselves of the excitement growing out of the Harper's
Ferry affair and the Helper pamphlet, to renew their efforts, and they now
have high hopes of enacting their diabolical hatred of the poor free colored
people into a law. We are glad to find that there is still spirit enough
among the more enlightened and humane portion of the people to resist this
wicked scheme, as will be seen by the following memorial, which we find inserted as an advertisement in the Baltimore *Sun.*[24]

The following memorial will be immediately presented to the public for
their signatures:

To the Hon. General Assembly of Maryland:

The undersigned, citizens of Maryland, respectfully represent that they have observed with great surprise and sorrow the introduction into the Legislature of various bills which, if enacted into laws, will bear with great severity on the free colored population of the State, and they most earnestly and respectfully ask that neither these, nor any similar measures, may receive the sanction of your honorable body.

The bills have not yet been published for the information of the people, but sufficient has been made known to indicate their general character.

All future manumissions are prohibited, and all those who have been set free since 1832 are to be banished from the State or reduced to slavery.

The noble support which, during the period of her greatest financial embarrassment, the State continued to grant to the scheme of African colonization, is to be withdrawn.

Free negroes are to be prohibited from acquiring real estate, and such as they already possess is to be sold.

Their churches in the counties are to be sold, and everywhere new barriers are to be opposed to their obtaining the rudiments of knowledge, and even the instructions and consolations of religion.

Any free negro convicted of a peniteniary offence, and every free negro now in the penitentiary, is to be sold as a slave for life.

No negro shall preach or conduct any assembly for religious purposes.

Negroes between twelve and fifty-five years of age are to be from time to time hired out for a period of ten years--and those under twelve to be bound out until they are thirty-five.

A new and very large police force is to be established in the counties, for the purpose of carrying out and enforcing these laws, and the regular police of the city of Baltimore is to be charged with the execution of them in the city.

Provision is made for renunciation of freedom and voluntary return to slavery by those who are free.

This is the substance of the bills reported by the committee on the colored population.

The committee of the slaveholders recommend different but very harsh legislation, and, in conformity with their recommendation, bills containing the following provisions have been introduced into the Legislature.

No slave hereafter is to be manumitted, and the fact of a negro going at large, and acting as free, is no longer to be considered as evidence of his freedom. This would deprive many colored people of all testimony of their freedom.

Free negroes are prohibited from acquiring real estate, and, on their death, such as is now held by them is to be sold.

Provision is made for the voluntary return to slavery of all free negroes; and if a mother shall thus return to slavery, all her children under five years of age shall become slaves for life.

Stringent provisions are made against receiving through the post office or otherwise, by any person, white or black, any published matter of an inflammatory character, having a tendency to create discontent among the negroes; and these regulations are so framed as to render innocent white people, as well as black, liable to severe punishment.

Police commissioners are to be appointed throughout the counties and the city of Baltimore to enforce these laws.

They are to have a registry made of all free negroes, and are to cause to be sold until the first day of the ensuing January all such negroes as are not of good and industrious habits, and have not the necessary means of support.

These commissioners are also to bind out all free negro children.

Other harsh laws have been proposed by other persons, one of which prohibits the pursuit of mechanical employment by negroes, and another the granting of them to licenses to trade.

All such legislation, and any legislation which would make the condition of the colored people in any respect less happy and comfortable than it is at present, would be, in the opinion of your memorialists, unjust, oppressive, and uncalled for; not only wrong in itself, but inevitably calculated to inflict deep and lasting injury on the prosperity of Maryland, and to leave an indelible stain on her character.

There are about 90,000 free negroes in the State, many of them respectable, industrious, and religious, constituting a most important part of our
laboring population, and the chief portion of our domestic servants.

The tendency of the proposed measures is to banish them from the State;
and if this should be the result, their places could not for many years be
supplied, and, if supplied at all, would be by a population which would
greatly imperil the security of slave property.

They are helpless before the law, and, by every consideration of humanity and manliness, are entitled to protection.

This is not the time for the agitation of this question. Maryland, as
becomes her character and position, has always been conservative and moderate, although firm and decided, on the subject of slavery, while at the North
and further South bitter controversies have arisen, which, at this moment,
endanger. the stability of the Union itself.

The enactment of laws such as are now proposed would infallibly lead to
an agitation which could do no possible good to any interest or portion of
the State. Already a wide-spread alarm has been excited in the minds not
only of the colored people, but of a large portion of the white population.

Your memorialists pray that such action may be taken by your honorable
body, that all such apprehensions may speedily and forever be put to rest. .
. .

New National Era, February 23, 1860.

16.   NOTE FROM THE DIARY OF A FREE BLACK

the 5 day June 1833 on Wensday my Wife and children philis Shiner wher
sold to couple of gentelman Mr. Franklin and mr John Aremfield and wher
caried down to alexandria on the six day of june 1833 on thrusday the 7 of
June 1833 on friday i went to alexandria 3 times in one day over the long
Bridge and i wher in great distress But never the less with the assistance
of god i got My wife and children clear

i am under ten thousand oBlagation to the Hon Magor general adam lin for
his kindness to me and my wife and children on the 7 day of June 1833 on friday the general laid a Detachment on my Wife and 3 children at Mr. Aremfield
jail and taken them and put them in the county: jail of alexandria to await
action of the court and my Wife and children Remained in the county jail in
alexandria from the 7 of June 1833 on tusday and the same day Mr. levy hump-
rhey executed papers and Manumeited them free the papers wher executed at
the city Hall in Washington She came up from alexandria the 12 day of June
1833 on wensday and i am allso under obligations to Mr Steil and Mrs Steil
for ther kindness to My Wife and children while they wher in the Jail and
may the Allmighty Bless them they gave me such a Race at that time that all
the people that wher acquainted with the affair in alexandria wher sorry for
me and appeared to Be weiling to Believe me of my disstress

i am also under great OBlagation to Comodore isaac Hall for the time my
Wife wher Sold to George he had command of the Washington navy yard fore his
kindness to me and allso to Captain John H Aulie for his kindness to when my
Wife wher sold to George and allso to Captain Joseph Hall for his kindness
to me at that time at that he wher furst lieuntenant of Washington navy yard
and allso under the same OBlagation to Major Cary Selon who wher naval store-
keepper and allso to Mr. John Itheride which at that time he the Commodres
Clerk and also to Mr David eateon Boatswain all those ABoved name gentilmen
all of them wher wiling to help me out of my my distresses in a honest up
right way when my Wif andd Childdren wher snacht away from me and sold on the
5 day of june 1833 on Wensday from near whil alley the Between 7 and eight st
last and May the lord Bless them all i shal never forget them

Michael Shiner Diary, pp. 52-54, Manuscripts Division, Library of Congress.

17. FREE BLACKS IN VIRGINIA

A bill has been introduced into the Legislature of Virginia, proposing a plan for the forcible expulsion of all the free colored people from the State--men, women and children--in all, amounting to about sixty thousand persons, as shown by the returns of the last census. The design is to free the State from this class of its inhabitants, whose presence is, by the projectors and advocates of the measure, deemed to be unsafe for the institution of slavery. The bill has not been passed by the Legislature, and we can hardly think that it will be; yet the proposition to do such a deed of darkness is an outrage, almost without a parallel, upon every rule of justice. The thing seems to us so perfectly barbarous, so flagrantly at war with the civilization of the age, that we cannot believe that the good people of Virginia will tolerate the measure.

Where, let us ask, have these colored people a right to live, to breathe and to die, if not on the spot that gave them birth? Virginia, to most of them, is their *native* land, as much so as it is to the white population; and if they have a right to be *any where* on the face of the earth, then this right applies to the place of their nativity. Surely, there is no sin in being a freeman, even with a black skin: it ought not to be made a crime, and punished as a trespass upon civil society. If, as individuals, they violate the laws, then let them, as such, be punished according to law: but to expel them as a whole class, on the simple charge of freedom and color, would be a most outrageous infraction of justice. We should like to know, also, whither these persons are to be driven, what is to become of them, and where they are to find a home, if forcibly exiled from the one given them by nature? If they have no right to remain in Virginia, where have they a right to stay? Is it in the other slave States? Is it in the free States? Clearly, their claim of residence is not as good upon either of the latter, as it is upon the former: and thence the consequence of the doctrine would be, that free colored people have no right to be *any where;* that is to say, God has made some men, and sent them into this world, that he ought not to have made, since there is no place for them. If Virginia may expel them, without crime, on the mere charge of freedom and color, then other civil communities may refuse to receive them for the same reason. If they have no right to stay where they were born, then obviously they have no better right to go where they were not born.

The Liberator, March 8, 1853.

18. STATE OF DELAWARE VS MOSES MCCOLLY, NEGRO

Indictment no. 10 to April Term 1841

And now to wit, this sixth of April A.D. 1841 it satisfactorily appearing to the Court that the defendent is not able to pay the fine and cost which he has adjudged to pay--It is therefore ordered by the Court that the said defendent be disposed of as a servant to any person or persons residing in this State, for the highest sum that can be obtained for such term as shall be necessary in order to raise sufficient money to satisfy such fine and cost, or any balance remaining after such payment as can be obtained from the said defendent provided such term shall not exceed seven years

Atest

G.M. Manlow C.P.

Ind for cuting sapling
convicted & fined $5.00

Bill of fees

William L. Junit suit   5.19
Zachariah Allen   5.19
Charles Davis   1.79
Atty Genl   2.0
Clerk   3.48
Sheff   5.02   5.55
on costs   53
City   33
fine   5.00
Prison charges 21 days Brd 5.67

34.60

Delaware Archives, Division of Historical and Cultural Affairs, Hall of Records, Dover, Delaware.

19.   PERSECUTION IN DELAWARE

Wilmington (Delaware), March 1, 1850

Our laws are much more severe on the colored than on white persons for the same offence. I have known a colored person charged with stealing a ham that could not pay two-fold its value, and cost of prosecution, sold as a servant for seven years; and in some instances it has been done to a father or mother of a family that have had several children. Many of our petty officers have no principle, and take up our colored people under false pretences, without their having offended in any way just for the sake of the paltry fees allowed in such cases.

Thos. Garret

The Anti-Slavery Bugle (Salem, Ohio), March 23, 1850.

20.   1845 ACT OF GEORGIA LEGISLATURE DIRECTED AGAINST BLACK MECHANICS

An act to prohibit colored mechanics and masons, being slaves or free persons of color, being mechanics or masons, from making contracts for the erection of buildings, or for the repair of buildings, and declaring the white person or persons directly or indirectly contracting with or employing them, as well as the master, employer, manager, or agent for said slave, or guardian for said free person of color, authorizing or permitting the same, guilty of a misdemeanor.

Section 1. Be it enacted by the Senate and House of Representatives of the state of Georgia in General Assembly met, and it is hereby enacted by the authority of the same, That from and after the first day of February next, each and every white person who shall hereafter contract or bargain with any slave mechanic, or mason, or free person of color, being a mechanic or mason, shall be liable to be indicted for a misdemeanor; and on conviction, to be fined, at the discretion of the court, not exceeding two hundred dollars.

W. E. B. Du Bois and Augustus Granville Dill, "The Negro American Artisan," Atlanta University Publications, No. 17 (Atlanta, 1912), pp. 32-33.

21. THE CONDITION OF THE FREE NEGRO IN LOUISIANA

Mr. EDITOR: The legal condition of the free negro in Louisiana, contrasted with his legal condition in the Northern States, is largely in his favor. The free negro in Louisiana is governed by the same laws which govern the free blanc, or white man; and, what is more, they are administered with exact justice to both classes of men. There is no foolish prejudice in that State against the color of the free man, when the law sits upon him. The only question is, is he free? If he is, he enjoys all the immunities of the white man, so far as laws grant them to him. Even socially, the free black has privileges which he does not enjoy in the North. His presence is tolerated where it is not allowed in Northern States. He is suffered to mingle with merchants on 'Change. He is not expelled from traveling vehicles, as Dr. Delany, of Pittsburg, was recently driven out of a coach near Buffalo. He is found in the courts of justice as plaintiff and defendant, and mingles with the whites on perfect equality. This brings me to the point to which I wish to call your attention, and that of your Northern and Western readers. [25]

In the *St. Martin's Creole* of a late date, I find the following advertisement in French, which I translate. It is evidence from the record how impartially the law is administered in Louisiana, whether the parties be white or black.

DISTRICT COURT, PARISH OF ST. MARTIN. NO. 3961. *Ls. Decuir, free man of color, against Rosina Ronchon, free woman of color.*--In this case, according to law and the evidence, which is in favor of the plaintiff, it is ordered, adjudged, and decreed, that he shall be forever divorced from the defendant, and that the parties be restored to that position which they occupied previous to marriage; and by consent of parties, it is agreed that the defendant, Rosina Ronchon, shall keep, at her expense, the child born of the marriage until it is ten years old; and that she shall recover the personal and the real property which she brought in marriage. It is further ordered, &c., that the defendant shall pay the expenses that shall be taxed in this case.

Done and signed in open court, this 23d day of October, 1847.

C. VOORHIES,
Judge of the 14th District.

New National Era, June 29, 1848.

22.   EXODUS OF FREE NEGROES FROM SOUTH CAROLINA

A considerable number have arrived in Philadelphia; but by far the largest portion have been forced into slavery. The process by which they are
made slaves is as follows:--Up to 1822, emancipations were frequent in the
State, but in that year a law was passed forbidding manumission. By that
law, slave owners, upon resigning their ownership in negroes, were to place
them in the hands of trustees, who were to be vouchers for the negroes, pay
their taxes, and a tax, except in the negro's possession, was evidence that
he had been made free.
The law lately passed makes one man their guardian. They are to be entered on the tax list as slaves, and must always wear a badge of servitude,
made of copper, with their number upon it. If found without a trustee, they
are to be sold at the block; if failing to have a badge, they are to be fined
$20, or imprisoned. Under such stringency there was but little hope for
them. They might be robbed of their badges by designing men, then imprisoned, and then sold unconditionally into slavery. To escape such a fate, thousands of the negroes have fled from the State. The Philadelphia *Press* has an
account of the condition of those which have arrived in that city, which we
copy in part. Up to November 1, more than seven hundred and ninety persons
departed from the port of Charleston, about one hundred and fifty of whom
have arrived at Philadelphia.
The facts given by the *Press* are from a personal visit by the editor to
a large number of families. The editor says:

Of the one hundred and fifty mentioned, two-thirds are trades-people.
The men are carpenters, tailors, shoemakers, and masons; the females, mantua-
makers, milliners, laundresses, and nurses. We read a long list of certificates from white ladies of Charleston, stating that one of these was an 'excellent and faithful nurse.' One testimonial was addressed 'to the ladies of
the North,' and certified that the bearer had attended her through a 'long
and dangerous sickness'--a fact which does not go far to show the gratitude
of the recent Palmetto legislation.
Another party bore a certificate of his proficiency in plastering, from
a master-mason of Charleston.

The Liberator, November 23, 1860.

23.   ARRIVAL OF FREE COLORED PEOPLE FROM SOUTH CAROLINA

Since the 1st inst., quite a large number of the intelligent portion of
of the free colored people of Charleston have arrived in this city, among
whom were many first-class mechanics. A part of these, we are pleased to
learn, will find employment here, and the balance will go to Hayti. Among
those who left Charleston on the 13th in the steamer Marion were Mr. H. T.
Graddick, his wife, and mother-in-law. Owing to rough weather, the vessel
was obliged to lay to until the 15th, and during her detention officers came
on board and seized Mr. G., on the authority of the Governor, carried him
back to Charleston, and there detained him until the sailing of the next
steamer. Their excuse was that he, being an old harbor pilot, they suspected that he was leaving for the purpose of bringing Northern vessels into
Charleston harbor. We had the pleasure of an interview with Mr. Graddick,
and learned from him that he and others had to make great sacrifices of property in order to get away--as, for instance, a house and lot valued at $1500
before the excitement, was sold by Mr. G. for $600. It is supposed that the
stampede of this class of persons during this month and next will be very
great, as they do not relish the idea of having their property confiscated
and themselves reduced to bondate, to enable the fire-eaters to raise the

"sinews of war." We copy the following in relation to these people from the
"Tribune:"

A great portion of the Charleston free colored people, they say, read
and write, and become well posted in legislation directly concerning themselves, through the medium of the daily papers. Among the bills suggested
in the South Carolina Legislature relating to the free negroes, they told
our reporter there were no less than six in number, none of which has yet
been adopted. The leading one was that introduced by Mr. Aldridge of the
Barnwell District, about the first of January, which provides that all of
them shall leave the State or be sold, and their property, no matter how
large, be confiscated. Mr. Easton of Charleston proposed that they should
be allowed to remain, but he prevented from carrying on any business; not to
allow even their guardian or agent to hire them, but leaving that alone to
bosses, who were to have the right to hire them by the day. Mr. Lessene had
presented a petition against this which had received about 600 signers in
Charleston. Another amendment was next offered by Mr. Reade, giving the
slaves who, by neglecting to depart, lost their freedom, the privilege of
choosing their own masters, who were each to donate the magnificent sum of
$5 to those coming into their post session by this statute. To this it was
objected because it would be giving them too much privilege.

These and different propositions, they tell us, have been made in the
councils of the Secessionists, and the free colored people have learned
enough about it to become fearful that their liberty may be taken away at
any moment; so that all of them who have the money at hand are leaving.
Among other oppressive features of the day, they inform our reporter, is that
about six months ago the Government stopped their children from going to
school, and about the same time a law was enacted declaring that all who had
purchased their freedom prior to 1822 were yet to be considered as slaves,
on the ground of some point of illegality. This drove about 700 of them
away from Charleston alone. The Mayor's officers had called upon them and
informed them that they were not free, though they had paid the money. They
believed that all this was done because the public treasury was in need of
funds. The authorities also made them pay $20 for not taking out a "badge,"
for which they had to pay $5 more, and mechanics $7. They say that each free
negro has to pay $13.75 annually as "head-tax;" that the amount this year
will probably not be less than $40. Those who own property are, besides,
taxed like other people. They are not allowed to meet in any sort of meeting, social or public, and cannot have a dance or anything of that sort among
themselves, without permission from the Mayor; and if they attempt to disregard this regulation, the police come up and take them to the guard-house.
Even in the streets it is not allowed, they say, that more than two should
engage in conversation together, and this law was strictly enforced. There
was a law now pending which forbids colored people from riding in a carriage.
They are not allowed to buy any sort of liquor, even from a druggist. In the
country, they tell us, the free colored people are considered to be a "thiev-
ing set." At Columbia the head tax was $26 last year. . . .

New York Anglo-African, January 26, 1861.

LABOR VIOLENCE IN BLACK AND WHITE

24. A COAL MINE--NEGRO AND ENGLISH MINERS

Yesterday I visited a coal-pit: the majority of the mining laborers are
slaves, and uncommonly athletic and fine-looking negroes; but a considerable

number of white hands are also employed, and they occupy all the responsible posts. The slaves are, some of them, owned by the Mining Company; but the most are hired of their owners, at from $120 to $200 a year, the company boarding and clothing them. (I have the impression that I heard it was customary to give them a certain allowance of money and let them find their own board).

The white hands are mostly English or Welchmen. One of them, with whom I conversed, told me that he had been here several years; he had previously lived some years at the North. He got better wages here than he had earned at the North, but he was not contented, and did not intend to remain. On pressing him for the reason of his discontent, he said, after some hesitation, that he had rather live where he could be more free; a man had to be too *"discreet"* here: if one happened to say anything that gave offense, they thought no more of drawing a pistol or knife upon him, than they would of kicking a dog that was in their way. Not long since, a young English fellow came to the pit, and was put to work along with a gang of negroes. One morning, about a week afterwards, twenty or thirty men called on him, and told him that they would allow him fifteen minutes to get out of sight, and if they ever saw him in those parts again, they would "give him hell." They were all armed, and there was nothing for the young fellow to do but to move "right off."

"What reason did they give him for it?"

"They did not give him any reason."

"But what had he done?"

"Why I believe they thought he had been too free with the niggers; he wasn't used to them, you see, sir, and he talked to 'em free like, and they thought he'd make 'em think too much of themselves."

He said the slaves were very well fed, and well treated--not worked over hard. They were employed night and day, in relays.

The coal from these beds is of special value for gas manufacture, and is shipped, for that purpose, to all the large towns on the Atlantic sea-board, even to beyond Boston. It is delivered to shipping at Richmond, at fifteen cents a bushel: about thirty bushels go to a ton.

Frederick Law Olmsted, A Journey in the Seaboard Slave States, with Remarks on Their Economy (New York, 1859), pp. 47-48.

25. TROUBLE AMONG THE BRICKMAKERS

The spirit of lawlessness, and interferences with the rights of others, which has exhibited itself in several sections of the city recently, broke out again yesterday among several brick-yards located upon the Ferry road, Federal Hill. During one early part of the day a band of some twenty-five or thirty men, organized for the object visited the brick-yard of Henry Thomas, Esq., for the purpose of driving off the colored employees, and supplanting them in their places. The workmen were attacked by the mob and compelled to run for their lives--pistols, and several instances guns being fired upon them. The colored employees in the yard of the Messrs. Donnelly, adjoining, were also assailed and driven from their work by menace and pistol shots. It was rumored that one colored man was badly shot. Serious difficulty being apprehended, about two o'clock Mr. Thomas was induced to apply to the southern district police station for a force to suppress the riotous proceedings. Capt. Woods at once dispatched to the scene Lieut. Davis, with Sergeants Crouch, Roxenberry, Chambers, Somberton, and a posse of about eighteen officers. This determined movement had the effect to disperse the rioters, and upon the arrival of the police they had disappeared. The aggression, however, caused a perfect *stampede* among the colored workmen, . . .

Baltimore Sun, May 18, 1858.

could be collected again. A number of police remained upon the ground during the day for the protection of the yards. To-day the authorities will
exercise surveillance over the yards to prevent further interference.

Baltimore Sun, May 18, 1858.

26. WHITE WORKERS ATTACK FREDERICK DOUGLASS

     Until a very little while before I went there, white and black ship car-
penters worked side by side, in the ship yards of Mr. Gardiner, Mr. Duncan,
Mr. Walter Price, and Mr. Robb. Nobody seemed to see any impropriety with
it. To outward seeming, all hands were well satisfied. Some of the blacks
were first rate workmen, and were given jobs requiring the highest skill.
All at once, however, the white carpenters knocked off, and swore that they
would no longer work on the same stage with free negroes. Taking advantage
of the heavy contract resting upon Mr. Gardiner, to have the war vessels for
Mexico ready to launch in July, and of the difficulty of getting other hands
at that season of the year, they swore they would not strike another blow for
him, unless he would discharge his free colored workmen.
     Now, although this movement did not extend to me, *in form*, it did reach
me, *in fact*. The spirit which it awakened was one of malice and bitterness,
toward colored people *generally*, and I suffered with the rest, and suffered
severely. My fellow apprentices very soon began to feel it to be degrading
to work with me. They began to put on high looks, and to talk contemptuously and maliciously of *"the niggers;"* saying, that "they would take the country," that "they ought to be killed." Encouraged by the cowardly workmen,
who, knowing me to be a slave, made no issue with Mr. Gardiner about my being there, these young men did their utmost to make it impossible for me to
stay. They seldom called me to do anything, without coupling the call with
a curse, and, Edward North, the biggest in every thing, rascality included,
ventured to strike me, whereupon I picked him up, and threw him into the
dock. Whenever any of them struck me, I struck back again, regardless of
consequences. I could manage any of them *singly;* and, while I could keep
them from combining, I succeeded very well. In the conflict which ended my
stay at Mr. Gardiner's, I was beset by four of them at once--Ned North, Ned
Hays, Bill Stewart, and Tom Humphreys. Two of them were as large as myself,
and they came near killing me, in broad day light. The attack was made suddenly, and simultaneously. One came in front, armed with a brick; there was
one at each side, and one behind, and they closed up around me. I was
struck on all sides; and, while I was attending to those in front, I received a blow on my head, from behind, dealt with a heavy hand-spike. I was completely stunned by the blow, and fell, heavily, on the ground, among the timbers. Taking advantage of my fall, they rushed upon me, and began to pound
me with their fists. I let them lay on, for a while, after I came to myself,
with a view of gaining strength. They did me little damage, so far; but,
finally, getting tired of that sport, I gave a sudden surge, and, despite
their weight, I rose to my hands and knees. Just as I did this, one of their
number (I know not which) planted a blow with his boot in my left eye, which,
for a time, seemed to have burst my eyeball. When they saw my eye completely
closed, my face covered with blood, and I staggering under the stunning blows
they had given me, they left me. As soon as I gathered sufficient strength,
I picked up the hand-spike, and, madly enough, attempted to pursue them; but
here the carpenters interfered, and compelled me to give up my frenzied pursuit. It was impossible to stand against so many.
     Dear reader, you can hardly believe the statement, but it is true, and,
therefore, I write it down: not fewer than fifty white men stood by, and
saw this brutal and shameless outrage committed, and not a man of them all
interposed a single word of mercy. There were four against one, and that

one's face was beaten and battered most horribly, and no one said, "that is enough;" but some cried out, "kill him--kill him--kill the d--d nigger! knock his brains out--he struck a white person." I mention this inhuman outcry, to show the character of the men, and the spirit of the times, at Gardiner's ship yard, and, indeed, in Baltimore generally, in 1836. As I look back to this period, I am almost amazed that I was not murdered outright, in that ship yard, so murderous was the spirit which prevailed there. On two occasions, while there, I came near losing my life. I was driving bolts in the hold, through the keelson, with Hays. In its course, the bolt bent. Hays cursed me, and said it was my blow which bent the bolt. I denied this, and charged it upon him. In a fit of rage he seized an adze, and darted toward me. I met him with a maul, and parried his blow, or I should have then lost my life. A son of old Tom Lanman, (the latter's double murder I have elsewhere charged upon him,) in the spirit of his miserable father, made an assault upon me, but the blow with his maul missed me. After the united assault of North, Stewart, Hays and Humphreys, finding that the carpenters were as bitter toward me as the apprentices, and that the latter were probably set on by the former, I found my only chance for life was in flight. I succeeded in getting away, without an additional blow. To strike a white man, was death, by Lynch law, in Gardiner's ship yard; nor was there much of any other law toward colored people, at that time, in any other part of Maryland. The whole sentiment of Baltimore was murderous.

After making my escape from the ship yard, I went straight home, and related the story of the outrage to [my] Master Hugh Auld. . . .

. . . His indignation was really strong and healthy; but, unfortunately, it resulted from the thought that his rights of property, in my person, had not been respected, more than from any sense of the outrage committed on me as a man. . . . He related the outrage to the magistrate [Mr. Watson] . . . and seemed to expect that a warrant would, at once, be issued for the arrest of the lawless ruffians. . . .

"Mr. Auld, who saw this assault of which you speak?"

"It was done, sir, in the presence of a ship yard full of hands."

"Sir," said Watson, "I am sorry, but I cannot move in this matter except upon the oath of white witnesses."

"But here's the bou; look at his head and face . . . they show what has been done."

But Watson insisted that he was not authorized to do anything, unless white witnesses . . . would come forward, and testify to what had taken place. He could issue no warrant on my word, against white persons; and, if I had been killed in the presence of a thousand blacks, their testimony, combined, would have been insufficient to arrest a single murderer.

Of course, it was impossible to get any white man to testify against my assailants. The carpenters saw what was done; but the actors were but the agents of their malice, and did only what the carpenters sanctioned. They had cried, with one accord, "kill the nigger! kill the nigger!" Even those who may have pitied me, if any such were among them, lacked the moral courage to come and volunteer their evidence. The slightest manifestation of sympathy or justice toward a person of color, was denounced as abolitionism; and the name of abolitionist, subjected its bearer to frightful liabilities. "D---n abolitionists," and "Kill the niggers," were the watch-words of the foul-mouthed ruffians of those days. Nothing was done, and probably there would not have been any thing done, had I been killed in the affray. The laws and the morals of the christian city of Baltimore, afforded no protection to the sable denizens of that city.

Frederick Douglass, My Bondage and My Freedom (New York, 1855), pp. 308-18.

26. A FIENDISH OUTRAGE

A paragraph has recently been published, derived from South Carolina papers, stating that a workman engaged on the State House, in Columbia, S. C., was recently seized by a mob, on account, as was alleged, of holding anti-slavery opinions, and that he received thirty-nine lashes, and was tarred and feathered, and then conveyed to Charleston. The following detailed narrative of the injuries inflicted upon the man, is published in the New York *Independent*. A more inhuman deed is seldom perpetrated. The *Independent* says:

We have seen this unfortunate man, and heard his story, and looked at his wounds. His name is James Power. He is an intelligent young man, about twenty-three years of age, a native of Wexford, Ireland, and a stone-cutter by trade. He went from Philadelphia to the South, and obtained employment in Columbia, where he had worked for nine months.

The only opinion he ever expressed against slavery was that it caused a white laborer in the South to be looked upon as an inferior and degraded man. But this was enough. The remark was reported to the Vigilance Committee, (composed of twelve members,) who immediately ordered the police to arrest him. He was seized two miles away from town, in attempting to escape. He was brought back and put in a cell, where he remained for three days, during which time he was denied the use of pen and ink, and all communication with his friends outside.

At length he was taken before the Mayor. Four persons appeared, and bore testimony to the remark which he had made. The evidence was conclusive. He was returned to prison, and kept locked up for six days. During this time he was allowed only two scanty meals a day, and the food was carried to him by a negro. He was then taken out of jail in the custody of two marshals, who said to him:

'You are so fond of niggers, that we are going to give you a nigger escort.'

He was led through the main street amid a great crowd, hooting and yelling, the marshals compelling two negroes to drag him through the puddles and muddy places of the street, and of the State House yard! As he was taken past the State House, three members of the Legislature, including the Speaker, stood looking on and laughing! The crowd gradually increased until it numbered several thousand persons, headed by a troop of horse.

Douglass' Monthly, July 1859.

OBSERVATIONS ON RACE RELATIONS

27. SOUTHERN WHITES AND BLACKS COULD WORK TOGETHER

. . . He has now there ten or fifteen white men, mechanics, and some twenty or more negroes, working well. As a proof, on Saturday they launched a fine boat built for this river, capable to carry two tow-boats. The scene to us was novel and sublime.

He has another Steam-Boat framed and preparing to receive the plank, and to all appearance, timber sufficient to build three or four tow-boats. This has all been done since the first of January under the immediate direction of Captain Fish, who seems to conduct the business as becomes a master-workman. Besides, this, they have built a small town, as cabbins to live in, shops, etc., and small craft, such as flats to convey timber up and down the river.

Exerpt from a letter to the editor of the Federal Union (Georgia), March 18, 1836.

28. TO THE CONTRACTORS FOR MASON'S AND CARPENTER'S WORK

Gentlemen: I desire your candid consideration of the views I shall here express. I ask no reply to them except at your own volition. I am aware that most of you have too strong antipathy to encourage the masonry and carpentry trades of your poor white brothers, that your predilections for giving employment in your line of business to ebony workers have either so cheapened the white man's labor, or expatriated hence with but a few solitary exceptions, all the white masons and carpenters of this town.

The white man is the only real, legal, moral and civil proprietor of this country and state. The right of his proprietorship reaches from the date of the studies of those white men, Copernicus and Gallileo, who indicated from the seclusion of their closets the sphericity of the earth: which sphericity hinted to another white man, Columbus, the possibility by a westerly course of sailing, of finding land. Hence by white man alone was this continent discovered; by the prowess of white men alone (though not always properly or humanely exercised), were the fierce and active Indians driven occidentally: and if swarms and hordes of infuriated red men pour down now from the Northwest, like the wintry blast thereof, the white men alone, aye, those to whom you decline to give money for bread and clothes, for their famishing families, in the logic matter of withholding work from them, or employing negroes, in the sequel, to cheapen their wages to a rate that amounts to a moral and physical impossibility for them either to live here and support their families--would bare their breasts to the keen and whizzing shafts of the savage crusaders--defending negroes too in the bargain, for if left to themselves without our aid, the Indians would or can sweep the negroes hence, "as dew drops are shaken from the lion's mane."

The right, then, gentlemen, you will no doubt candidly admit, of the white man to employment in preference to negroes, who *must* defer to us since they live well enough on plantations, cannot be considered impeachable by contractors. It is a right more virtual and indisputable than that of agrarianism. As masters of the polls in a majority, carrying all before them, I am surprised the poor do not elect faithful members to the Legislature, who will make it penal to prefer negro mechanic labor to white men's. But of the premises as I have now laid them down, you will candidly judge for yourselves, and draw a conclusion with me, that white bricklayers and house joiners must henceforward have ample work and remuneration; and yourselves and other contractors will set the example, and pursue it for the future without deviation. Yours respectfully

J. J. FLOURNOY.

An open letter from a local citizen published in the Southern Banner (Athens, Ga.), January 13, 1838.

29. A VISITOR COMMENTS ON RACE RELATIONS IN
VIRGINIA COAL MINES

The laborers have each their proper duty to perform--some are employed to dig coal--some to blast rock, and others to attend upon the shafts,
fill and manage the cars, &c. There are about two hundred in all--made up
of Americans, English, Scotch, free blacks and slaves. . . . Though politically and naturally there is a difference in these operatives, yet every
tub here stands on its own bottom--but when they get out of the Pits they
assume to each other their proper attitude. The free blacks in these pits
are very respectable, and make money for themselves and children. It is a
pity that a great number of the free blacks in the State will not or cannot
be made to follow suit, instead of being paupers to the counties. One of
these free hands tried the North, but found that he could do better at home,
and after wasting $150 as an experiment, begged to come back, which he fi-
nally did at the expense of the President of the Company. Many of the
slaves lay up $50 per annum for work done out of the regular hours. This
should teach some of those abolition blatherskites at the North that many of
their stories are too big for this region altogether. They won't go down
any way. The worst slaves in the South are the men who own them.
    "The President of the Company, Maj. Wooldridge, is not annoyed and ha-
rassed for a 'respectable minister' to preach the Gospel to his people, as
District Attorney B. F. Butler was at Sandy Hill--for he has three or four
of them. The colored operatives have a meeting house and a Church organized
here. On Sabbath last three professed to have 'new hearts and new hopes,'
and are soon to be 'buried in baptism.' The place is in a high degree moral
and orderly and affords conclusive evidence that all we need to change the
whose aspect of affairs in this State and to better our condition, is the
WILL to change our WAYS.

*John Smith (of Richmond, Va.) in the Richmond Whig and Public Advertiser,
June 26, 1846.*

30. FREE AND SLAVE LABOR IN VIRGINIA

The white workmen on the Tredegar and Armory Iron Works at Richmond,
Va., have made a strike in consequence of the employment of slaves on a portion of the works. As an indication of the progress of the age, this movement is important, striking as it does, the very root of slave labor. It
sets up a distinction in the slave States themselves between the servile labor of the degraded beings who are held in bondage, and the voluntary labor
of the skilful mechanics who have gone there from the North--a distinction
which the South have not been accustomed to behold, and one they would fain
hope never to see exist. When the principle that "all labor is degrading"
is overthrown, and the mechanic whose capital is his ingenuity and his sinews, begins to be regarded as what he really is by the cotton lords and tobacco growers of the South, they will not, like the Richmond workmen be
thrown upon their dignity as citizens, and their manhood as freemen, to save
themselves from being classed and associated with slaves, and to be treated
in almost every sense like them. The progress of the age is onward, and
light is breaking slowly, though surely on one of the most productive though
badly managed sections of the republic.

                                                Barre Patriot.

Voice of Industry, June 11, 1847.

31.   SLAVE-LABOUR VS. FREE-LABOUR

Our readers will remember the difficulty which occurred recently at the Tredegar Iron Works, in Virginia. The white operatives refused to work because slaves were employed, not, we presume, from any objection to labour with them, but because there could be no fair competition between themselves and the owners of slaves. A slave-owner, who gives to his slaves barely the simplest necessaries of life, and none of the comforts and luxuries, but who gains for himself from the product of their united labours, a large return on the capital invested in their bodies, can afford to let them out at a price which is a miserable remuneration to the free labourer, who has the fruits of his own labour only to support himself and his family. Here is the cause of the wretched condition of the "poor white folks" of all slave-countries, and, to a certain degree, the still more miserable and abject condition of the free coloured people, who are pointed at as evidence of the inherent imbecility of negroes, and of their inability to take care of themselves. [26]

In this proposition, too, is involved the general want of enterprise and prosperity in slave States. Those who constitute the chief portion of the labouring population, do only so much as they are compelled to do, for they are not stimulated by the fear of want, or the hope of gain; they are sure enough to support life, and are certain of receiving nothing more. The remaining portion of the labouring class have little other stimulant than the fear of want, because their labour does not receive an adequate reward,--because their labour is servile and therefore disgraceful,--and because, from both these causes, it cannot be the avenue to wealth and respectability. The remainder of the people are the slave-owners, who are to be sure, a small minority, but who live upon the unrequited toil of their slaves, and through their power over the slave-labour hold all other in check.

The attempts now making at the South to introduce manufactures, must prove abortive for these reasons.--The poor whites cannot, will not work, in competition with the invested labour-capital of the slave-owners; and if the slaves could be made to work enough to render manufactories profitable, they would become too intelligent to labour for nothing but a peck of corn per week, and two suits of clothes per year, and would soon become united enough in large bodies of manufacturing people, either to compel their emancipation, or render it necessary to break up all such establishments. It is impossible, then, that there can be in a slave-country any other prosperity than that which belongs to a rude system of agriculture; for there can be no other than ill-directed, and cramped, and unwilling industry.

All this, perhaps, and much more to the same purpose, the white operatives at the Tredegar Iron Works would have said, in extenuation of their contumacy, to the slave-holders, had they been permitted. But they were not allowed to say anything. Mr. Anderson, the proprietor, published a list of the rates of wages paid at his works, and declared them to be higher than the rates paid at similar establishments at the North. All this might be true, for the simple reason that the demand for the sort of labour he wanted was greater than the supply, inasmuch as the slaves were not yet *educated* up to that point when their labour could come readily into competition with that of white workmen. This, these workmen seemed to understand, declared that they did not demand higher wages, but refused to work till the slaves were discharged. Thereupon they were denounced as conspirators against the peace and prosperity of the "Peculiar Institution," and treated accordingly. It was a struggle between Slave-Labour, and Free-Labour--between the slaveholder, who lives upon the toil of others, and the labouring man, who only asks for a fair field and no favour; and the latter, of course, went to the wall.

Precisely what measures were resorted to the quell these rebellious spirits who thus asserted the dignity of labour, and the right of every man "to eat his own bread in the sweat of his face," we have not learned.--We only know that the strong arm of the law was resorted to, and the operatives were brought to disclaim any purpose of uniting in any unlawful combination, or of violating the laws in any respect. And Mr. Anderson maintains his determination of employing such labour as he sees fit, which of course will be

cheap slave-labor, when slaves enough of sufficient intelligence can be had
to answer his purpose.

National Anti-Slavery Standard, July 1, 1847.

32. RESPONSE TO THE STRIKE OF WHITE WORKERS TO ELIMINATE BLACK COMPETITION AT TREDEGAR IRON WORKS, 1847

The principle is advocated for the first time, we believe, in a slaveholding State, that the employer may be prevented from making use of slave
labor. This principle strikes at the root of all the rights and privileges
of the master and, if acknowledged, or permitted to gain a foothold, will
soon wholly destroy the value of slave property.

Richmond (Virginia) Times and Compiler, May 28, 1847.

33. A FOREIGN TRAVELLER'S OBSERVATIONS ON INDUSTRIAL RACE RELATIONS IN THE SOUTH

. . . It had previously been imagined that an impassable gulf separated
the two races; but now it is proved that more than half that space can, in a
few generations, be successfully passed over, and the humble negro of the
coast of Guinea has shown himself to be one of the most imitative and improv-
able of human beings. Yet the experiment may still be defeated, not so much
by the fanaticism of abolitionists, or the prejudices of those slave-owners
who are called perpetualists, who maintain that slavery should be permanent,
and that it is a blessing in itself to the negro, but by the jealousy of an
unscrupulous democracy invested with political power. Of the imminent nature of this peril, I was never fully aware, until I was startled by the publication of an act passed by the Legislature of Georgia during my visit to
that State, December 27, 1845. The following is the preamble and one of the
clauses:--
    "An Act to prohibit coloured mechanics and masons, being slaves, or free
persons of colour, being mechanics or masons, from making contracts for the
erection of buildings, or for the repair of buildings, and declaring the
white person or persons directly or indirectly contracting with or employing
them, as well as the master, employer, manager, or agent for said slave, or
said free person of colour, authorising or permitting the same, guilty of a
misdemeanor," and prescribing punishment for the violation of this act.
    "Section 1.--Be it enacted by the Senate and House of Representatives of
the State of Georgia in General Assembly met, and it is hereby enacted by the
authority of the same, That from and after the 1st day of February next, each
and every white person who shall hereafter contract or bargain with any
slave, mechanic, or mason, or free person of colour, being a mechanic or mason, shall be liable to be indicted for a misdemeanor; and, on conviction, to
be fined, at the discretion of the Court, not exceeding two hundred dollars."
    Then follows another clause imposing the like penalties on the owners of
slaves, or guardians of *free persons of color,* who authorise the contracts
prohibited by this statute.
    I may first observe, in regard to this disgraceful law, which was only
carried by a small majority in the Georgian Legislature, that it proves that
not a few of the negro race have got on so well in the world in reputation

and fortune, and in skill in certain arts, that it was worth while to legislate against them in order to keep them down, and prevent them from entering
into successful rivalry with the whites. It confirms, therefore, most fully
the impression which all I saw in Georgia had left on my mind, that the
blacks are steadily rising in social importance in spite of slavery; or, to
speak more correctly, by aid of that institution, assuming, as it does, in
proportion as the whites became civilised, a more and more mitigated form.
In the next place I shall endeavour to explain to the English reader the
real meaning of so extraordinary a decree. Mr. R. H. Wilde, formerly senator for Georgia, told me that he once knew a coloured freeman who had been
brought up as a saddler, and was a good workman. To his surprise he found
him one day at Saratoga, in the State of New York, acting as servant at an
hotel. "Could you not get higher wages," he inquired, "as a saddler?"
"Yes," answered he; "but no sooner was I engaged by a 'boss,' than all the
other workmen quitted." They did so, not because he was a slave, for he had
long been emancipated, but because he was a negro. It is evident, therefore,
that it requires in Georgia the force of a positive statute to deprive the
negro, whether he be a freeman or slave, of those advantages from which, in
a free State like New York, he is excluded, without any legislative interference.

I have heard apologists in the North endeavouring to account for the degraded position which the negroes hold, socially and politically, in the
Free States, by saying they belong to a race which is kept in a state of
slavery in the South. But, if they really desired to accelerate emancipation, they would begin by setting an example to the Southern States, and
treating the black race with more respect and more on a footing of equality.
I once heard some Irish workmen complain in New York, "that the niggers shut
them out from all the easiest ways of getting a livelihood;" and many white
mechanics, who had emigrated from the North to the Slave States, declared to
me that every opening in their trades were closed to them, because black
artisans were employed by their owners in preference. Hence, they are now
using in Georgia the power given to them by an exclusive franchise, to pass
disabling statutes against the blacks, to prevent them from engaging in certain kinds of work. In several States, Virginia among others, I heard of
strikes, where the white workmen bound themselves not to return to their employment until the master had discharged all his coloured people. Such combinations will, no doubt, forward the substitution of white for negro labour,
and may hasten the era of general emancipation. But if this measure be prematurely adopted, the negroes are a doomed race, and already their situation
is most critical. I found a deep conviction prevailing in the minds of experienced slave-owners, of the injury which threatened them; and more than
once, in Kentucky and elsewhere, in answer to my suggestions, that the time
for introducing free labour had come, they said, "I think so; we must *get
rid* of the negroes." "Do you not think," said I, "if you could send them
all away, that some parts of the country would be depopulated, seeing how
unhealthy the low grounds are for the whites?" "Perhaps so," replied one
planter,""but other regions would become more productive by way of compensation; the insalubrity of the Pontine marshes would be no excuse for negro
slavery in Italy. All might end well," he added, "were it not that so many
anti-slavery men in the North are as precipitate and impatient as if they believed, like the Millerites, that the world was coming to an end." 27

One of the most reasonable advocates of immediate emancipation whom I
met with in the North, said to me, "You are like many of our politicians,
who can look on one side only of a great question. Grant the possibility of
these three millions of coloured people or even twelve millions of them fifty years hence, being capable of amalgamating with the whites, such a result
might be to you perhaps, as a philanthropist or physiologist, a very interesting experiment; but would not the progress of the whites be retarded, and
our race deteriorated, nearly in the same proportion as the negroes would
gain? Why not consider the interests of the white race by hastening the abolition of slavery. The whites constitute nearly six-sevenths of our whole
population. As a philanthropist, you are bound to look to the greatest good
of the two races collectively, or the advantage of the whole population of
the Union."

Sir Charles Lyell, Second Visit to the United States of North America, Vol.
II (New York, 1855), pp. 97-101.

34. TWO BLACK FOUNDRYMEN PROSPER

'In the foundry of Gaty, M'Cune & Co., in this city, among its two hundred and seventy operatives are two negroes, who began life at the establishment, in 1849, as slaves. By dint of unlagging industry, in due course
of time one of them bought himself, wife and five children, paying for himself $1400, and on an average for his wife and children $800 each. This
negro is now supposed to be worth, in his own right, more than $5000 in real
estate in that city. Another negro entered the factory about the same time,
amassed sufficient money by his attention to duty to purchase himself at the
price of $1500, his wife at $500, and four children at $400, and is now
worth $6000 in real estate. These negroes were bought from their masters by
Mr. Gray, with the understanding that they should work themselves free, and
out of his own pocket he gave two per cent. interest on the deferred payments.'

The Liberator, October 26, 1860.

35. CONSTITUTION OF THE BALTIMORE SOCIETY FOR THE PROTECTION
OF FREE PEOPLE OF COLOUR, 1827

"The Baltimore Society for the protection of free people of colour,"
having been instituted for the purpose of aiding those who are in fact or
prospectively entitled to their freedom, in maintaining their rights against
violation, have deemed it expedient to prefix to their constitution, a short
exposition of the motives which have induced them to associate, and of the
objects they have in view. The members are aware that institutions of this
character are received with jealousy by many intelligent and well disposed
persons, from an apprehension that they are inimical to the rights of slaveholders; they therefore feel it incumbent upon them to declare most explic-
itly, that, whatever may be their individual sentiments in relation to the
policy or justice of slavery, it is *not* among the objects contemplated by
this organization, to promote the abolition of legal slavery or to interfere
with the legal rights which are exercised over slaves. But it is a matter
of public notoriety, that a shameful traffic is carried on, in the persons
of many of these unhappy people; who, possessing a right to freedom and the
precious enjoyment of liberty, are deprived of these inestimable privileges
and entrapped into a state of slavery by theft, fraudulent purchase, and variety of other treacherous artifices, which neither the laws of our country,
& principles of christianity, nor the obligations of moral rectitude, can
for a moment tolerate or sanction. To wrest these unhappy victims from the
fangs of avarice and cruelty, to rescue them from the kidnapper and the un-
principled, and to contribute our efforts in subjecting to the penalties of
the law, the mercenary agents in this infamous traffic, are the purposes and

the designs of this Society; and we believe, that every considerate and
virtuous citizen will admit, that it is not less the interest than the duty
of all classes of the community to lend their aide in suppressing a practice, which is disgraceful to the character of our country, destructive of
the happiness of many of our fellow-creatures, and which requires such a
total destitution of principle in its agents, that they become fitted for
the perpetration of any other act of atrocity affording equal inducements
to their avarice. It is therefore for the interest of owners of slaves, because it is hostile to those who only want an opportunity of totally destroying their legal rights; for it cannot be supposed, that an entrapping
a free person into slavery, they would be scrupulous of robbing a master of
his slave, if they would do it with equal impunity. Instances can be cited
of their having really done so. It is however probable that cases may happen in which, people of colour are illegally detained by persons of very
different character, who would not be guilty of such flagrant outrages as
have been mentioned, and who may be ignorantly infringing upon the liberties of others; but it is unquestionably the duty of every man to become acquainted with the nature and legality of any claims which he may have to a
right of property in persons of colour; and as negligence and innocent intentions ought not to secure him from the operations of justice and law, so
neither ought they prevent the interference of the society in the cases supposed: But it has been said that the law prescribes a mode by which the injured party may obtain redress; and that any man possessed of the common
feelings of humanity would not hesitate to aid in obtaining it for him, that
therefore no necessity exists for such an association. It is admitted that
the law does provide a mode by which those who are illegally detained in
slavery may prefer their claims to the judicial authority and command a
hearing. But the situation in which these poor and friendless creatures are
generally placed, preclude the possibility of their being benefitted by the
benevolent intentions of the law, for, though the law will respect proof
when brought to its view, yet it will not go in quest of it for them, nor
furnish the means by which they may receive it. The proof rests with the
sufferers, and they are subjected to the necessity of proving a negative, of
showing with legal formality and precision that they are not slaves, whilst
they are debarred from all intercourse with those who could furnish it: deprived of the means by which it could be obtained, remote perhaps from the
district of country in which evidence could be procured, ignorant of the
proper mode of proceeding, and destitute of funds to defray the consequent
expenses, they wage an unequal contest with men well versed in legal proceedings, and commanding the immense influence which money can call into exercise in thwarting the intentions of justice. How few men are there among
those who possess the feeling of humanity, even in an eminent degree, that
would be willing to encounter the trouble and expense of affording them such
entire assistance, as only could avail them, and of maintaining vigilant en-
deavours to become acquainted with the numerous cases in which such care is
wanted. To relieve individual exertion and liberality of so unequal a tax
is sufficient to establish the propriety of this institution, which designs
to extend to them this assistance, by furnishing a medium through which they
may carry their complaints to the constituted authorities of our country,
and be enabled to collect the requisite testimony, that when they appeal to
the tribunals of justice a reasonable expectation may be indulged that the
appeals will not be made in vain. In short we only propose to aid them in
maintaining their rights to which they are entitled by law, and in the prosecution of this object we shall pursue the path which the law itself prescribes, and for this purpose we have agreed to the following rules for our
government.

Article 1st

This association shall be called The Baltimore Society for the protection of free people of colour, the stated meetings thereof shall be held
yearly and quarter-yearly. The annual meeting on the first Monday of January and the quarterly meeting on the first Mondays in March, June, September and December.

But the President or any two of the managers may call special meetings
at any time they may deem it necessary.

Article 2nd

Candidates for membership shall be proposed at a meeting of the society and may be balloted in by the votes of two thirds of the members present and when elected shall be notified thereof by the Secretary. Every member upon his admission and signing this constitution shall pay into the Treasury of the society one dollar, and an additional sum of fifty cents at every stated meeting.

Article 3rd

The society may provide for the admission and privileges of honorary members and also for the expulsion of members by a special by-law, which By Law shall not be passed until the next meeting of the society after that in which it has been proposed and read.

Article 4th

Any member who shall absent himself from the meetings of the society for twelve months unless absent from the city, and refuse to pay the dues and fines he may have incurred shall cease to be a member.

Article 5th

There shall be chosen by ballot at the annual meeting from among the members, a President, Vice President, Secretary, Treasurer and eight managers, by a majority of votes of those present. The President, Vice President, Secretary and Treasurer being ex-officio members of the board of managers.

Article 6th

It shall be the duty of the President, to preside in the meetings of the society, to attest when necessary its official acts, to give a casting vote when the meeting is equally divided, and generally to see that all the resolutions and proceedings thereof are duly executed.

Article 7th

The Vice President in the absence of the President shall perform all the duties of the President and when both are absent the meeting shall appoint a President pro-tempore.

Article 8th

The Secretary shall keep fair records of all proceedings of the society and cause a notice of every meeting thereof to be left at the store or dwelling of each member before the hour of meeting.

Article 9th

The Treasurer shall keep all the funds of the society, and where there is any money in the treasury shall pay all orders which the managers may direct, which orders shall be sufficient vouchers for this expenditures. He shall report a statement of his account to every stated meeting.

Article 10th

The board of managers are hereby authorized to appoint such counsellors as they may think necessary and to call to their aid such members as they may deem proper to attend to such cases as require immediate care.

Article 11th

For non-attendance of the meetings of the society and non-payment of the dues at each meeting every member shall be fined twenty five cents for every omission unless a reasonable excuse is offered and accepted by the meeting.

Article 12th

Application for aid in behalf of any person of colour shall be made to the Board of managers who shall cause enquiry to be made into every case for which application is made, and if good reason be afforded for believing it proper to extend aid, they shall render such assistance and protection as they may consider advisable, not exceeding the pecuniary means of the society, and they may adopt at their discretion any proper measures for promoting the execution of the laws against those who may be engaged in violating the rights and liberties of free people of colour.

Article 13th

A history of every case in which the aid of the society shall have been afforded, shall be noted by the managers and recorded by the Secretary who shall report the same at the annual meeting in every year.

Article 14th

The society may pass any By Laws for effecting the object of the association which may be found necessary and not contrary to this constitution, but no By Law shall be passed or repealed but by a vote of three fourths of the members present at a stated or special meeting and no alteration shall take place in this constitution unless it be proposed at one meeting and acted on at the next when if two thirds present agree to the proposed alteration, it shall be considered as forming a part of this constitution.

Thomas Matthews

Joseph Davenport

Wm. E. Bartlett

William Dallam

Aquila Jones

George Appal

Benjamin P. Moore

Jno Q. Hewlett

Jefferson Hough

Gardner Betterton

John Williamson

Wm. Gruyere Jones

John B. Thomsen

George Gillingham

John Needles

Samuel Wilson

At a meeting of a number of citizens of Baltimore held according to previous notice on Monday evening the 9th of July 1827. Thomas Matthews was called to the chair and Wm. Gruyere Jones appointed Secretary.

The object of the meeting was then stated to be divise some method of preventing the numerous instances of kidnapping of free blacks which are constantly occurring in the vicinity of this city and other parts of the country. Several communications were laid before the meeting shewing the necessity of the friends of humanity exerting themselves to prevent such depredations and for the prompt assistance of these oppressed people, when it was unanimously concluded that it is expedient that an association be formed under such regulations as may hereafter be adopted for that purpose, the following gentlemen being present viz,

Thomas Matthews
Joseph Davenport

> Samuel Wilson
> Robert Armstrong
> Stephen Swain
> Joshua Matthews
> Benjamin Lundy
> William Dallam
> Jefferson Hough
> Daniel Pope
> Ephraim Gardiner
> George Gillingham
> Wm. E. Bartlett
> Aquila Jones &
> Wm. Gruyere Jones.

Resolved that Samuel Wilson, John Needles, Wm. Gruyere Jones, George Gillingham, Joseph Davenport & Joshua Matthews be a committee to prepare rules and regulations for the government of the proposed association, and that they report to an adjourned meeting.

When the meeting adjourned to Friday evening next July 15th at 8 o'clock.

Friday evening July 13th 1827.

The company met according to their adjournment Thomas Matthews chairman and Wm. Gruyere Jones Secretary.

Present the same members as at the preceding meeting with the addition of

> Robert Holloway
> William R. Jones
> Garden Betterton &
> George Apple

The committee appointed at the former meeting to prepare rules and regulations for the government of the proposed association, produced a report accompanied by a draft of a constitution. The report of the committee was accepted and the constitution was read, amended an unanimously adopted.

Resolved, that the committee appointed to prepare a constitution be continued to provide a suitable room for the next meeting of the society and notify the members thereof.

When the meeting adjourned to Monday evening the 23rd inst at 8 o'clock.

At a meeting of the Baltimore Society for the protection of free people of colour held on Monday evening July 23, 1827, Samuel Nelson was appointed chairman and Wm. Gruyere Jones secretary.

Ms. Constitution and Minutes of the Baltimore Society for the protection of free People of Colour, Quaker Collection, Swarthmore College Library.

PART III

FREE BLACK LABOR IN THE NORTH

Part III

FREE BLACK LABOR IN THE NORTH

*About five per cent of the total black population lived in the North dur-
the Ante-Bellum Era. Although free Negroes in the northern states enjoyed more personal freedom than their brothers and sisters in the South, this often
meant the freedom to starve. Certainly life was not easy, and northern blacks
encountered gross discrimination, sometimes of the most vicious variety. This
was particularly true during economic depressions when white workers were desperate for employment. Under normal conditions, however, a sort of peaceful
coexistence prevailed, maintained by traditional occupational patterns for the
two races, in which blacks were confined to menial labor and to the service
industries. Only a small percentage of blacks were mechanics, artisans, or
shopkeepers. This pattern is clearly presented for Philadelphia (Doc. 1, 3-4),
New York (Doc. 6-11, 14-15), and Boston (Doc. 16-17, 19-22).*

*Consequently, black workers were concentrated in the lowest paid and most
precarious of jobs. Therefore, they suffered more from economic deprivation,
poor education, housing, and nutritional maladies than whites. This precarious social, economic, and political position meant that Negroes came into
competition with newly-arrived immigrants, such as the Irish, who learned
very quickly that blacks were a ready scapegoat. With the white populace and
their officials disposed against them, black workers all too frequently found
the best of their jobs threatened by the dregs of white society. The result-
ant poverty and injustice is easily demonstrated for Philadelphia (Doc. 2, 5),
New York (Doc. 12-13, 24), and Boston (Doc. 18).*

*One of the most famous cases exemplifying the discrimination against black
artisans in the North is that of Frederick Douglass (Doc. 25). A skilled ship-
caulker, Douglass fled from Baltimore to New Bedford, Massachusetts, a relatively liberal state on racial issues. Once there, however, Douglass was forced to work as an unskilled day-laborer because no one would employ him at
his trade even though New Bedford was a prosperous ship-building community.
The example of Henry Graves, a poor and obscure black handcart peddler in New
York who had his license revoked, is another excellent case in point (Doc. 26-
29).*

NORTHERN FREE BLACK OCCUPATIONS

1. REGISTER OF TRADES OF COLORED PEOPLE IN THE CITY
OF PHILADELPHIA AND DISTRICTS, 1838

Bakers 9	Hatters 4
Basket-Makers 3	Iron-Forgers 1
Blacksmiths 23	Masons 2
Black and White Smiths 5	Millers 3
Bleeders 9	Milliners and Dress-Makers 25
Bleeders and Hair Dressers 5	Nail-Makers 2
Boot and Shoemakers 91	Painters 6
Brass-Founders 2	Painters and Glaziers 11
Brewers 1	Paper-Makers 1
Bricklayers 6	Plasterers 1
Bricklayers and Plasterers 5	Plumbers 3
Brush-Makers 3	Potters 1
Cabinet-Makers 15	Printers 3
Cabinet-Makers and Carpenters 5	Rope-Makers 3
Carpenters 40	Sail-Makers 19
Caulkers 2	(including James Forten,
Chair-Bottomers 2	James Forten, Jr., and Robert
Confectioners 5	B. Forten)
Coopers 5	Scythe and Sickle Makers 1
Curiers 2	Ship Carpenters 4
Dentists 1	Stone Cutter 1
Dress-Makers 74 (women)	Sugar Refiners 3
Dress-Makers and Tailoresses 14	Tailoresses 17 (women)
Dyers and Scourers 4	Tanners 31
Fullers 4	Tanners and Curriers 6
Glass-Paker Makers 2	Tin-Plate Workers 1
Hair-Dressers 95	Tobacconists 2
Hair-Dressers and Hair-Workers 10	Turners 5
	Weavers 5
	Wheelwrights 6

Register of Trades of Colored People in the City of Philadelphia and Districts (Philadelphia, 1838), copy at the Library Company of Philadelphia.

2. COLORED INHABITANTS OF PHILADELPHIA

We have been favored with a copy of an interesting pamphlet, just published, entitled, "A Statistical Inquiry into the Condition of the People of Color of the City and Districts of Philadelphia." "The census (says the preface) which forms the basis of the calculations and statements which follow, was taken near the close of the year 1847, at the suggestion and under the direction of some members of the Society of Friends. It is submitted to the public in the conviction that it presents, so far as it goes, a faithful picture of the condition of our people of color--a picture which should inspire them with hope and confidence in the future, and encourage their friends to persevere in their efforts."

The first table shows the total number of colored residents in Philadelphia to be 20,240, though this is believed to be rather less than the actual number. The increase during the twenty years from 1820 to 1840, is shown to be 14 per cent per annum.

It appears from another table, that 42.7 per cent. of the colored population of Philadelphia have been born out of the State; and it is further
supposed that two-thirds of these immigrants are from the slave States. The
total number of those born slaves is stated as 1,077; manumitted, 767; bought
their freedom, 275; the amount paid for their freedom, $63,043.

It has been attempted by the compilers of this pamphlet, to form an estimate of the real and personal estate held by the people of color; but it is
justly observed, that "no returns of this nature can be more than an approxi-
mation to the actual value," on account of the difficulty of obtaining correct returns from the individuals. The total value of real estate, carefully
computed from the information obtained is $531,809. None of the public prop-
erty, such as meeting-houses, school-houses, &c., is included in this estimate. The increase in the value of the real estate between the years 1837
and 1847, is rated at 50 per cent. This real estate is held by 315 freeholders, who are likewise the owners of personal property to the amount of $194,
318; of these freeholders there are two who own from $5,000 to $10,000, and
two who own from $10,000 to $20,000.

The total amount of rental in 1847; was $199,665.46--paid by 4,019 fam-
ilies--being an average of $49,68 per family. The taxes were in the same
year $6,308.38; the water rents $1,032.

The trades and occupations of 3,358 men, and 4,249 women, forming about
four-fifths of the entire able-bodied population above 21, has been ascertained. Of these, 268 are mechanics; 166 shop-keepers and traders; the rest
are laborers, waiters, hair-dressers, &c. Of the women, 216 are dress-makers; 231 seamstresses; 23 keepers of boarding-houses; 13 school-mistresses.

Under the heading of "Education and Employment of Children," it is
stated that the numbers between the ages of 5 and 20 are computed to be about
4,500. Of this number, 1940, or upwards of 64 per cent of these go to
school; and there are returns of the manner in which 1,340 of those who do
not go to school are disposed of; leaving about 1,200 between 5 and 20 who
are not reported.

The statistics of the Eastern Penitentiary furnish some interesting information. The fact that although the population of the State has been increasing at the rate of 3 per cent., the number of committals for crime has
been steadily decreasing, is peculiarly gratifying--showing as it does, that
the colored population of Pennsylvania are gradually advancing in intelligence and morality.

There are 16 colored churches in Philadelphia. From 12 of these returns
have been received, which state the number usually attending at 6,100. These
twelve congregations all have Sunday schools, employing 107 teachers, and
attended by upwards of 1,000 scholars. The cost of eleven out of the twelve
meeting-houses is given at nearly $67,000.

There are a number of literary associations (says the writer) established among the people of color, several of which appear to be supported with
zeal and ability, and which, no doubt, have an important influence upon those
who are within the sphere of their operations.

There is a marked difference in the condition of the various districts.
As may of course be expected, the immigrant population are chiefly found in
those crowded streets and alleys where destitution and wretchedness most prevail: though some of that class are among the most industrious and thriving
of the people of color. In respect to this state of things, the pamphlet
well remarks

"We may fairly trace these extremes in the condition
of the colored immigrants to the evil influences of slavery. Upon a feeble and common mind it operates like a
blight, withering the active principles of our nature,
and inducing a listlessness and indifference to the future,
which, even should the slave become a freeman, leave all
the vicious habits of slavery worked into the very grain
of his character. To those, on the other hand, who have
resisted these withering influences and bought their freedom with the hard-earned fruits of their own industry,
the love of liberty often imparts a desire for improvement
and a consciousness of their own worth as men, that

invigorate all their powers and give energy and dignity
to their character as freemen."

Here is a statement, written December 18th, 1848, by N. B. Leidy, the
late Coroner, which gives a lamentable illustration of the effects of prejudice and injustice. Let Christian Republican (!) Americans who do not
cease to boast of the freedom and equality of this land, hang their heads for
shame as they read it.--"All men are by nature free and equal!"--Horrible
mockery! "How long, Lord, how long" shall the pale-faced tyrant be permitted
to keep his iron heel upon the necks of the oppressed! Away with Constitutions! away with Republicans! away with governments! if this is the best they
can do for the human family!

> "Many were found dead in cold and exposed rooms and
> garrets, board shanties five and six feet high, and as
> many feet square, erected and rented for lodging purposes,
> mostly without any comforts, save the bare floor, with the
> cold penetrating between the boards and through the holes
> and crevices on all sides; some in cold, wet and damp cel-
> lars, with naked walls and in many instances without floors;
> and others found dead, lying in back yards, in alleys, and
> other exposed situations."

The result of this inquiry is considered by those who instituted it, to
be in a high degree interesting and satisfactory. Say they--

> "Of a large portion of this class of our fellow-citi-
> zens, it may be truly said, that they are steadily advanc-
> ing in all that constitutes a respectable and intelligent
> community. They have numerous skilful and industrious ar-
> tisans and tradesmen--the desire for information and the
> feeling of self-respect are increasing among them; and it
> is upon the influence of the Christian example and the
> steady conduct, both as regards industry and morals of
> those who have thus raised themselves, and upon their be-
> nevolent exertions, that the future welfare and respect-
> ability of the people of color in this city, must, as a
> class in the community, mainly depend.
> "The distinction of color, and the prejudices which
> have grown out of the condition of slavery, are no doubt
> felt by the man of color to be the principal barriers
> against his obtaining that social position to which, by
> his good conduct, intelligence and wealth, he is fairly
> entitled. There are few things in the world more unrea-
> sonable and unreasoning than these prejudices of caste
> and color."

The writer has large hope that these prejudices will speedily die away.

> "Our more intimate connection with the people inhab-
> iting the tropics, where men of color form a large propor-
> tion of the people, and exercise the highest offices of
> state, must, of itself, in the end, obliterate the odi-
> ousness of the distinction here. Let the man of color
> cultivate the spirit of self-respect and independence,
> and without allowing his mind to be disturbed by preju-
> dices which cannot be at once removed, pursue that course
> of quiet industry and unpretending virtue which will make
> him happy and respectable as an individual, and will con-
> tribute more than anything else to elevate the condition
> of his people.
> "This proper feeling of self-respect would tend to
> check the disposition so prevalent among many of the peo-
> ple of color, to indulge in love of show and extravagance,
> in anniversary processions and entertainments, which add

nothing to their respectability in the eyes of their fellow-citizens, and foster tastes and habits most unfriendly
to the real improvement of the people of color.

"There is no way in which the patriotic man of color
can so promote the well-being of his people, as in kindling
and keeping alive the desire for instruction. A good school
is not merely a place for training in knowledge, but in
virtue and morals."

This pamphlet is highly interesting and instructive. Our limits will
not admit of more copious extracts. It should be carefully read and pondered by colored men who are endeavoring to achieve their own elevation; and by
the friends of colored men who are desirous to learn in what way efforts on
their behalf may be rendered most effective.

The North Star, February 2, 1849.

3. TRADES AND OCCUPATIONS IN PHILADELPHIA, 1849

The returns enable us to state the occupations of 3358 men and 4249 wom-
en, who form, it is probable, about four-fifths of the able bodied population, above 21 years of age. These occupations may be thus classified.

Occupations of the Men.

Mechanics	286
Labourers	1581
Seafaring men	240
Coachmen, carters, &c.	276
Shop keepers and traders	166
Waiters, cooks, &c.	557
Hairdressers	156
Various	96
	3358

The principal occupations are as follows: boot and shoe makers 113, bakers 7, carpenters 33, cabinet makers 17, blacksmiths and workers in metal 9,
tailors 18, sailmakers 10, tanners 14, bricklayers 5, plasterers 10, painters
and glaziers 10, basket and mat makers 9, dyers and hatters 7, engineers 5,
second-hand clothes dealers 52, furniture dealers 22, confectioners and cake
sellers 34, hominy dealers 15, hucksters 11, cooks, tavern, oyster and eating
house keepers 77, waiters 453, musicians 32, preachers 22, school-masters 11,
bleeders, dentists, physicians and herb doctors 19, coachmen 111, carters and
draymen 157, labourers and jobbers 603, porters 444, hod carriers 102, work
in brick yards 70, wood sawyers 76, stevadores 57, white washers 40, raggers
and boners 51.

In 1838 a pamphlet was published containing a directory of coloured mechanics and tradesmen, which furnishes us with a point of comparison. It
contained the names of 506 mechanics and tradesmen, of whom 207 were master
workmen, and 299 journeymen. In a note appended to the Register it is
stated, that one half of the latter work as journeymen, and the rest from
choice or necessity follow other occupations. The number working at their
trades in 1838, may therefore be stated at 357; according to the recent enumeration the corresponding number is 481, being an increase of 35 per cent.
Many of these mechanics and tradesmen are excellent and industrious workmen;
75 of them own altogether real estate valued at $230,000, and personal estate
valued at $96,000.

Occupations of the Women.

Washerwomen	1970
Needle-women	486
Cooks	173
Occupied at home	290
Do. day's work	786
Living in families	156
Various	72
Trades	213
Raggers and boners	103
	4249

Among the occupations are 216 dress makers, 231 seamstresses, 19 tailor-esses, 19 milliners, 33 keepers of boarding, eating and oyster houses, 13 school mistresses, 10 cake bakers, 60 white washers, 24 hucksters, 12 con-fectioners, 9 mat makers, 33 sewers of carpet rags, 35 shopkeepers, &c. The aggregate numbers of the occupations thus reported, of the children at school, and at service, and of the children under five years fall about 2500 short of the whole enumeration of those above five years old. Nearly one half of this number, it will be seen, is under 21; and the deficiency is readily explained by the fact, that the occupations of the heads of families only are in many instances reported. . . .

It is greatly to be desired, that there should be more mechanics among the people of colour, and that more of their children should learn mechanical trades. A good master workman, who by steady perseverance and integrity has acquired a reputation of skill and industry, and who trains up his appren-tices in the same knowledge and habits, is a valuable and useful citizen; and instances could be pointed out in which one such man has raised up a succes-sion of skilful and successful workmen in the business he has pursued,--who have received their full share of public patronage.

Statistical Inquiry into the Condition of the People of Colour, of the City and Districts of Philadelphia (Philadelphia, 1849), pp. 17-18, 44.

4. OCCUPATIONS OF BLACKS IN PHILADELPHIA, 1849

I. MECHANICAL TRADES

Bakers	4	Brush Maker	1
Baker and Brewer	1	Cabinetmakers	20
Barbers	248	Cabinet-and Chair-Maker, House	
Barber and Bootmaker	1	Painter and Glazier	1
Barbers and Musicians	6	Cake Bakers	5
Basketmakers	2	Carpenters	49
Blacksmiths	22	Carver	1
Blacksmith and Calico Stamper	1	Carver and Guilder	1
Blacksmith and Shoemaker	1	Carver and Turner	1
Bonnet Presser	1	Caulkers and Gravers	3
Bookbinder and Basket Maker	1	Chair-Maker	1
Boot- and Shoemakers	66	Coach Painter	1
Boot- and Shoemakers and Musi-		Confectioners and Pastry Cooks	7
cians	2	Coopers	9
Boot- and Shoemaker, Musician		Cracker Bakers	3
and Music Teacher	1	Cupper and Leecher and Dress-	
Bootmaker, Barber and Tailor	1	maker	1
Brass Founder	1	Currier	1

Bricklayers	9	Dentists	5
Bricklayers and Plasterers	4	Distillers	2
Brick Makers (Moulders, Setters and Burners)	53	Draughtsman, Sign and Ornamental Painter	1
Brick Maker and Musician	1	Dressmakers	566
Dress- and Shirt Makers and Milliners	2	Printers' Ink Maker	1
Dress- and Shirt Maker and Pastry Cook	1	Rectifier	1
Dyers	9	Rigger	1
Embroiderers	9	Rope Maker	1
Embroiderers and Dressmakers	3	Rope and Brick Maker	1
Embroiderer and Milliner	1	Rope and Brick Maker and Blacksmith	1
Embroiderers and Shirt Makers	2	Saddle- and Harness Maker	1
Embroiderers and Tailoresses	2	Sailmakers	12
Embroiderers and Dress- and Shirt Makers	4	Sandpaper Maker	1
Forgemen	6	Sheet Iron Workers	4
Gardeners	2	Ship Carpenters	5
Garment Cutters	2	Shirt and Dressmakers	70
Glove Maker	1	Shoemakers	46
Gold and Silver Pencil Finisher	1	Shoemaker and Musician	1
Hair Workers	5	Shoemaker and Carpenter	1
Hair Worker and Dressmaker	1	Sign and Ornamental Painter	1
Hatters	4	Silversmith	1
House and Ship Carpenter	1	Spectacle Maker	1
House Painters and Glaziers	7	Stationary Engineer	1
House and Sign Painters and Glaziers	3	Stereotype Moulder and Caster	1
Ink and Blacking Maker	1	Stove Finisher	1
Iron Moulder	1	Stove Maker	1
Ladies' Shoemakers	4	Sugar Refiner	1
Lampblack Maker	1	Tailors	20
Machinist	1	Tailoresses	29
Manufacturing Chemists	2	Tailoresses and Dressmakers	23
Map Mounters	2	Tailoresses, Shirt and Dressmakers and Embroiders	2
Mason and Bricklayer	1	Tallow Chandler	1
Mason and Plasterer	1	Tanners	24
Masonic and Odd Fellow Regalia Makers	2	Tanners and Curriers	6
Millers	4	Tanner and Morocco Dresser	1
Milliners and Dressmakers	45	Tanner and Musician	1
Millwright	1	Tanners and Stationary Engineers	2
Mineral Water Maker	1	Tanner and Type Caster	1
Paper Box Makers	3	Tinsmiths	3
Paperhangers	2	Turners	3
Paper Maker	1	Umbrella Makers	2
Pastry Cooks	10	Upholsterers	2
Plasterers	14	Upholsteresses	2
Plumbers	2	Varnish Manufacturer	1
Portrait, Sign and Ornamental Painter, Teacher of Phonography, the Guitar, Singing, and Daguerreotypist	1	Vest Makers	2
		Weavers	16
Potters	2	Weaver and Blacksmith	1
Pressman	1	Weavers and Dressmakers	2
Printer	1	Wharf Builder	1
		Wheelwright	1
		Wire Workers	2
		Wrought Nail Maker	1

Total.................1,637

(An error occurs in this total which is not accounted for in the original pamphlet.)

II.   OTHER OCCUPATIONS

Artists	5	Midwife	1

Assistant in Pencil Factory....	1	Musicians.................	6
Captains of Coasting Vessels...	2	Music Teachers............	5
Clerks........................	5	Musicians and Music Teach-	
Hat Store.....................	1	ers.....................	4
Indian Doctor.................	1	Physicians................	6
Livery Stablekeepers..........	2	School Teachers...........	16
Lumber Merchants and Proprietors		Trimming Store............	1
of Transportation Lines.......	3		—
		Total.................	59

*Benjamin C. Bacon, Statistics of the Colored People of Philadelphia (Phila-
delphia, 1856), pp. 13-14.*

5. THE COLORED PEOPLE OF PHILADELPHIA, 1860

By some statistics which were published a few years since, there were
4,019 families of colored people, of whom 241 were living in their own
houses. Of these, there were about 5,000 able-bodied men over 21--of whom
1,581 were laborers, 256 mechanics, 240 mariners, 166 shopkeepers, 275 coachmen and carters, 557 waiters, 156 hair-dressers.

The present colored population of the city is from twenty thousand to
twenty-five thousand. They own property to the amount of nearly three millions of dollars, and have churches and schools valued at from four hundred
thousand to five hundred thousand dollars.

The great majority of negroes are poor. They seldom inherit money; many
of them come to the city direct from slavery, destitute of capital wherewith
to make business beginnings, and without education.

It cannot be expected that men of this race--who are said, by certain
statesmen, to be, in their best estate, mere animals--should struggle suddenly on to fortune. That many of them have made money, and advanced themselves
socially, is miraculous; for, be it said to the shame of our people, a free
colored man has more powerful disadvantages with which to contend in the free
States than in the slave. . . .

The prejudice against blacks extends to every class, and may be remarked
in pleasure and in business. At theatres, and concerts, lectures and
churches, the negro is restricted to a remote gallery. In mechanical pursuits, if a colored apprentice or journeyman be employed, there is an immediate rebellion upon the part of the white laborers. It has been to us a
matter of wonder how the black man masters any trade, studies for any profession, or learns anything of the arts. In only the dull, manual labors,
has he a show of equitable competition. He is a hotel-waiter, a vendor of
peanuts and cakes, or a mere beast of burden.

The Colored Man's Avocations in Philadelphia.

Those negroes of this city who pursue what may be called the higher mechanical branches, acquire their knowledge chiefly in the North and East.
The principal of the colored academy of this city is from New Haven; most of
the colored teachers are from Boston, and Providence, and New York. There
are several bona-fide negro physicians in Southern Philadelphia. Some of
these, we are told, managed to acquire odds and ends of medical science in
our own medical colleges, but they perfect themselves in the East. Their
clergymen are as a class, conversant with theological differences, and some
of them acute reasoners. There is not a colored lawyer in this city, that we
have heard of. There are two large African literary societies, one of them
named after Benjamin Banneker, and more than twenty beneficial organizations.
They have fine Masonic, Odd Fellow, and Temperance Halls, lodges of every
kind, several excellent private schools, and some half dozen public libraries. [28]

As caterers, the colored men are remarkably successful. We know of several who keep central saloons, fitted up in gorgeous style. One individual has a fine hotel at Florence Heights, and fine dining-rooms in this city. A number are the owners of carriages and a span of blooded horses. The females are milliners, dress-makers, &c. They frequently exhibit great tact in their respective trades.

Those who look lightly upon the negro as of no practical value to Philadelphia society are unwise, for he fulfills functions distasteful to most whites, and, in certain departments, labors with an aptness which whites could not supply.

Philadelphia Press, September 12, 1860.

6. ADVANTAGEOUS NOTICE

The Subscriber will undertake to furnish colored apprentices, gratis, to the different Mechanical business. *Philanthropists,* on application to him, at his dwelling, in the evening, at No. 272 Spring Street, up stairs, or through the day at No. 118 Anthony, near Elm St., will be attended to.

Colored parents and guardians of our youths, are respectfully requested to give in the names, residence, and age of their boys, in season, so as to secure a place, that will be to their future advantage.

The Colored American (New York), April 15, 1837.

7. BOOT AND SHOE MAKERS

SWAMP Leather and Finding Store, 64 Frankfort-Street, New York. W. P. Johnson thanks the public for patronage already received, and solicits a continuation of the same. Stock, consisting of an assortment of Sole Leather, Calf Skins, Linings, Findings &c. Johnson being a Boot and Shoemaker flatters himself that he can accommodate his Customers a little better than many in his line. N.B. He always trusts after he gets the cash.

The Colored American, June 10, 1837.

William J. Wilson, Boot Maker, has removed to 15 Ann-Street (corner of Theater Alley), basement story, where he continues to manufacture Boots and Shoes in the best manner, and on reasonable terms, for *Cash.*

The Colored American, December 2, 1837.

8. AN ARTIST

PATRICK H. REASON, Historical, Portrait and Landscape Engraver,
Draughtsman and Lithographer, No. 148 Church-Street, New York. Address, visiting and Business Cards, Certificates, Jewelry, &c, neatly engraved.

The Colored American, June 2, 1838.

9. OCCUPATIONS OF FREE NEGROES OVER FIFTEEN YEARS
OF AGE IN NEW YORK CITY, 1850

Occupations	Blacks	Mulattoes
Apprentices...........................	2	...
Architects............................	...	...
Bakers................................	3	1
Barkeepers............................	2	1
Barbers...............................	80	42
Blacksmiths...........................	...	1
Boardinghouse Keepers.................	15	6
Boatmen...............................	25	3
Bookbinders...........................	...	...
Brick-Makers..........................	...	...
Brokers...............................	...	...
Butchers..............................	30	3
Cabinetmakers.........................	...	...
Capitalists...........................	...	...
Carmen................................	28	11
Carpenters............................	10	2
Cigarmakers...........................	6	2
Clerks................................	3	4
Collectors............................	...	...
Coachmen..............................	96	11
Confectioners.........................	2	...
Cooks.................................	78	17
Coopers...............................	7	...
Doctors...............................	7	2
Druggists.............................	1	2
Engineers.............................	...	...
Farmers...............................	12	12
Gardeners.............................	5	2
Gunsmiths.............................	1	...
Hatters...............................	2	...
Hostlers..............................	10	1
Hunters...............................	...	...
Ink Makers............................	5	...
Jewelers..............................	2	1
Laborers..............................	957	187
Lawyers...............................	4	...
Lithographers.........................	...	...
Mariners..............................	316	118
Marketmen.............................	13	2
Masons................................	...	...
Mechanics (general)...................	1	1
Merchants.............................	2	1
Ministers.............................	12	9
Musicians.............................	17	7
Music Teachers........................	...	...

Overseers...........................	...	...
Painters...........................	3	1
Pedlers............................	...	...
Pilots.............................	...	...
Planters...........................	....	...
Printers...........................	2	2
Sailmakers.........................	...	...
Servants...........................	612	196
Sextons............................	9	3
Ship Carpenters....................	...	...
Shoemakers.........................	18	5
Stevedores.........................	...	...
Stewards...........................	34	10
Students...........................	1	...
Tailors............................	18	5
Teachers...........................	6	2
Upholsterers.......................	...	...
Other Occupations..................	160	47
Total........................	2,617	720

Statistical View, Compendium of the Census of 1850, pp. 80-81.

10. TO COLORED MEN OF BUSINESS.

A RARE chance for a partner with a cash capital from three to six hundred dollars to engage in the wholesale and retail new and second-hand clothing trade. To a man of energy this is an inducement rarely offered.

A business of years standing--a large and rapidly increasing run of good
cash customers--a fine store on as good a business street as any city can afford, and a good credit with some of the most respectable firms in the city
of New York.

The partner solicited may employ in the business his time and means, or
the latter only; for which the most undoubted securities will be given. To
a man wishing to engage into a sure and respectable business without hazard,
would do well to communicate immediately to the undersigned when the particulars will be given.

J. N. STILL & CO,
56 Atlantic St., Brooklyn, L. I.

267

Frederick Douglass' Paper, September 5, 1854.

11. A WATCHMAKER AND JEWELLER

EDWARD V. CLARK,

W A T C H M A K E R   A N D   J E W E L L E R ,

891 Canal Street,
NEW YORK,

KEEPS constantly on hand a large assortment Gold and Silver Lever
Watches, Gold guards and Vest chains, Finger rings, Brooches, Gold and Silver Pencil cases, Gold pens, &c. Silver and Plated Ware, Chronometers,

Duplex, Lever, Horizontal and Vertical Watches, Musical boxes, and Foreign clocks carefully reparied.

LIST OF PRICES

Ladies' fine gold watches, as low as	$25
A fine gold lever, full jeweled, at	25
English gold patent levers at 40, 45, &	55
Eng. hunting patent levers, gold faces, at	15
Silver levers, full jeweled, at	10
Cylinder Watches at	1

Each Watch warranted one year

Frederick Douglass' Paper, September 5, 1854.

12. EMPLOYMENT OF COLORED LABORERS IN NEW YORK

It is said to be an ill wind that blows no one any good. The floods of emigration that have flowed in upon us for the last ten or fifteen years—in fact, directly on the heels of the emancipation acts, by the different northern States, were evidently opened with the view of supplying the places of the colored people, and have ever since tended greatly to that end. This, however, was not all. They did not only arrest colored men from the domestic drudgeries and the mechanical pursuits, but they arrested native born white Americans, not only from these, but from the more lucrative ones—from offices of every kind in the gift of the government. This has brought white Americans to a more natural sense of feeling. We are certainly quite glad of it. Colored laborer have now become quite as acceptable as stevedores, porters, &c, &c, as white ones, and a little more so. We are informed that the demand for colored laborers has not been so great in this city for a number of years—while hundreds and even thousands of white foreigners are seeking to vain for employment, colored ones are in constant demand. We really hope that colored men will make well of the present state of favorable feeling in their behalf. Strange as it may appear, yet it is true, that while thousands of whites are begging for labor to enable them to get bread colored laborers who choose to work are in constant demand at a living price.

Frederick Douglass' Paper, February 2, 1855.

13. THE PROBLEMS CONFRONTING BLACK WORKERS IN NEW YORK, 1852

Within ten miles of where I now write there are at least thirty thousand colored people. Out of that number, there are not perhaps over two hundred traders, producers, and manufacturers, conducting business on their own account, to an extent to afford employment for more than one person. The rest are engaged in those occupations generally allowed to the colored man by our enemies, . . . Of course, then, if there are not more than that many fathers, the masters of trades, and conducting business on their own account, there are not, at most, more than that number of boys growing up so engaged. Under existing circumstances, this follows, as neither colored men nor boys can secure situations in white establishments, of a respectable character. Prejudice, aided by the press, is always at work to prevent our reception in

any lucrative pursuit. The poorer classes conceive they will be benefitted
by this, not only by securing that employment themselves, but we shall thereby be kept poor and dependent on them for our means of consumption. They
will allow us to do the drudgery. We may black the boots of the merchant,
whitewash his dwellings, drive his madam and misses; but attempt, even, to
cart the bales of cotton, or boxes of sugar, which he exports or imports--
the very goods which we are to consume, and the white laborer objects; a pretext is made, and the press, the free American, press is called in to villi-
fy, denounce, and abuse us; we must not even sweep in the street the dirt
that falls from their carts, that being more profitable and independent that
those employments assigned to us. We are not only deprived of profitable
labor, but are thereby unable to accumulate and engage in trade.--The consequence is, our want of information, as to cost and price of articles of consumption, allows the same unscrupulous traders to again over tax us in selling to us. We desire but little or no advantage from the poor whites. But
what immense profits are derived from us by the small dealers and domestic
traders; in fact, every branch of trade and manufacturing interest. What are
the profits on the amount required to manufacture, produce, &c, &c, for a
city of thirty thousand? Those who are thus benefitted, think they can well
afford to employ the regard him as having committed the highest outrage
against suffering humanity.

I have delayed this to await the publication of the testimony which you
will find in the *Columbia Spy,* which I will send tomorrow. I felt anxious
to give a true representation and I find that I have nothing to alter, or
take back.

WILLIAM WHIPPER [29]
Columbia, May 3, 1852

Frederick Douglass' Paper, May 13, 1852.

14. BLACK WORKERS IN NEW YORK, 1859

A correspondent of the *Christian Register* thus gives him impressions of
the colored inhabitants of New York city:

Within a few weeks past I have recreated myself by a trip to Africa,
and though I cannot felicitate myself upon any new discoveries, possible the
result of my explorations may fill, not uninterestingly, my weekly column in
the *Register.*

The colored population of this city it is difficult to state with exactness.
The number of names of colored persons in the directory of 1849, out of a
total of 139,801. The latter number represents a population of at least
750,000; this would give a colored population of ten thousand, assuming the
proportion to hold good. This result is probably considerably within bounds.
Of this 1849 adults, 144 are porters, 201 waiters, 150 whitewashers, 80
coachmen and hostlers, 64 cooks, 48 barbers, 182 laborers, 124 seamen, 183
washers, 214 are marked as widows, and no occupation appended. Not more than
40 are in trade, and not above twice that number following regular mechanical
trades, other than those enumerated; 2 are farmers, 1 broker, 3 printers, 6
physicians, 7 teachers, 18 reverend clergy, and 1 ventriloquist.

Douglass' Monthly, March, 1859.

15. HELP! HELP WANTED

Now is the time, at Tilmon's agency for employment, 70 East 13th street, one door east of 4th avenue. Fall is here, and now is the time for all first class help who want to secure good situations for the winter. Families are coming in town and engaging their help for the season, and never was there a greater demand for colored help--cooks, chambermaids, laundresses, waiters, house-workers, seamstresses, coachmen, men and boys to drive and take care of horses, &c.

N.B.--All good colored help coming to this city in search of employment would do well to call. Every attention paid to strangers.

New York Anglo-African, November 24, 1860.

16. DAVID WALKER'S "GROG SHOP" [30]

CLOTHING kept constantly on hand for sale by David Walker, No. 42 Brattle Street, Boston. A great variety of New and Second-hand clothing. He also cleans all kinds of woolen clothing in the neatest manner and on the most reasonable terms.

Freedom's Journal, October 30, 1828.

17. BLACK WORKERS IN BOSTON, 1831

. . . in Boston, where there are near two thousand people of color, it does not appear that there is among them, one merchant, broker, physician, lawyer, blacksmith, shipwright, tinman, caulker and graver, rigger, sailmaker, coppersmith, silversmith, brass-founder, mason, cooper, painter, glazier, printer, bookbinder, cabinet-maker, truckman, baker, or stone-cutter, or any trader in any article except clothes. The Directory for 1830 gives the names of 175 persons of color, with the employment of most of them. The list contains the names of 34 hair-dressers and barbers, 30 mariners, 17 clothes dealers, 15 waiters, 10 laundresses, 9 boot blacks, 9 keepers of boarding houses, 6 laborers, 3 clergymen, 3 cooks, 3 window-cleaners, 3 tailors, 2 sawyers, 1 cordwainer, 1 keeper of a bar-room, 1 servant, 1 clothes cleaner, 1 housewright, 1 handcartman, 1 stevedore, 1 grain measurer, 1 dealer in junk, 1 soap maker, 1 renovator of human hair, 1 confectioner, and 1 blacking maker.

The Liberator, January 22, 1831.

18. COLORED PEOPLE OF BOSTON

We have received from a valued correspondent the following communication respecting the people of color in this city. His statements we are confident are entitled to credit. We are fully persuaded that he has made great
efforts to ascertain the condition of this part of our population, especially
of the poor and destitute. Poor and destitute a great portion of them may
well be, from the disadvantages under which they are placed;--and vicious also may we expect that many of them will be--many more than in the proportion
of their numbers to the whites--since their children are, (we do not say from
what cause) excluded from trades, and in no small degree, by circumstances
beyond their control, from the benefits of the most common education.

MR. EDITOR,--I wish to call attention to the wants of the people of col-
or in this city. They are many and great. For the last nine months I have
taken special pains to inform myself of their wants, and to the utmost of my
ability I have done all I could to assist them--and the more I see of them,
the better I think of them, and feel an increasing interest in their temporal
as well as spiritual affairs. As they are in a deplorable condition, I do
think their case ought to be made public, because I am convinced the people
in this city do not know how much these poor, oppressed and neglected people
suffer for the want of employment and the necessary comforts of life.
In the American Almanac, the population of the colored people of this
county, is set down as 1883. Now how do this great multitude manage to live?
Listen, and I will inform you. It is not by mechanical business; for this
great city has only two colored mechanics--one a blacksmith in Cambridge
street, and another a shoemaker in Brattle street. Of the females, not one
obtains a livelihood as a milliner, mantuamaker, or tailoress. Neither is
there one girl of color in Boston now learning any of these useful trades!
And the boys are equally as bad off. Not one is now learning a mechanical
trade, if printing is excepted, in which there may be two or three. Here
then are near two thousand persons, in Boston, who are obliged to get their
living by the poor means of becoming barbers, clothes cleaners, window washers, servants, domestics, day laborers, &c. Can we wonder at the vanity,
ignorance, idleness or vice of such a people under such circumstances? The
great astonishment is, that they are able to live, and behave as well--and
maintain so much moral courage, virtue and piety, as may be found among them.
Some of these people are now old, some are sick, some without employment,
having families dependent on them; some are in want of every comfort--wood,
clothes and food. I therefore respectfully request my white friends, male
and female, to remember the poor colored people of Boston. Let us feel that
they are men and women, and have wants like ourselves, and have as much
claim on our sympathies as those in Georgia or South Carolina. Let us act on
the principle that 'charity begins at home,' in this case.

A POOR LAYMAN.

We pretend to no wisdom in these matters; but we have no doubt that the
class of people in which our correspondent takes so sincere an interest, have
claims upon the charitable beyond what are community believed. With respect
to their immediate wants, and relief from suffering, we are ready to point
out to any whose charity may flow in that direction, a faithful almoner of
their bounty, as we believe. In a prospective view, it is very possible that
means may be devised without any loss to individuals or to the community, by
which a reasonable number of colored youth may be trained to useful trades,
and thus we may spread among them habits of greater industry and self-respect,
make them more useful, and save many of them from the House of Correction or
of Alms.

The Liberator, November 22, 1834.

19. OCCUPATIONS OF NEGROES IN BOSTON, 1837

Among other inquries, I have ascertained the occupations of every man reported. . . . That you may have every important item of intelligence respecting them before you, to aid you in preparing your report, I present the following table:

Mariners, ...	171	Carpenter, ...	1
Laborers, ...	112	Whitewasher, ...	1
Barbers, (exclusive of apprentices,)	32	Whitesmith, ...	1
		Shoemaker, ...	1
Keepers of clothing shops, &c	23	Blacking Maker, ...	1
Waiters or tenders, . . .	25	Painter, ...	1
Cartmen, ...	8	Paper hanger, ...	1
Tailors, ...	6	Soap Boiler, ...	1
Keepers of Boarding houses, .	5	Measurer, ...	1
Boot Polishers, ...	4	Cobler, ...	1
Blacksmiths, ...	3	Chimney sweep, ...	1
Ordained preachers, . . .	2	Servants not at service, . .	7
Stevedores, ...	2		
Victuallers, ...	2		

The above are as reported to me, and I presume they are nearly, if not perfectly correct.

"Report of Reverend Spaulding to the Boston Auxiliary of the American Union for the Relief and Improvement of the Colored Class," African Repository 13 (March, 1837):89-90.

20. OCCUPATIONS OF NEGROES IN BOSTON, 1850

Occupations		Occupations	
Artists......................	1	Mattress Makers...............	0
Apothecaries..................	1	Mantua Makers.................	0
Barbers......................	26	Mechanics (General)...........	0
Basketmakers..................	0	Merchants....................	1
Blacksmiths..................	7	Millwrights..................	0
Boardinghouse Keepers..........	6	Ministers....................	4
Boatmen......................	0	Millers......................	0
Bootmakers...................	0	Musicians....................	1
Brickmakers..................	1	Machinists...................	1
Bricklayers..................	1	Masons.......................	1
Butchers.....................	0	Painters.....................	4
Bookbinders..................	2	Pasteboard Makers.............	0
Bakers.......................	15	Planters.....................	0
Bootblacks...................	2	Porters......................	4
Cabinetmakers.................	0	Pump Makers..................	0
Capstone Workers..............	1	Printers.....................	1
Carters......................	0	Paperhangers.................	0
Carpenters...................	10	Pavers.......................	1
Cigarmakers..................	4	Riggers......................	1
Clerks.......................	3	Saddlers.....................	1
Clothiers....................	14	Seamstresses.................	0
Coachmen.....................	0	Servants.....................	0
Confectioners................	0	Sextons......................	1
Coopers......................	1	Shopkeepers..................	0
Chimney-Sweeps...............	1	Shoemakers...................	7

Coopersmiths	1	Stewards	0
Cotton-gin Makers	0	Seamen	136
Cooks	9	Saloon-Keepers	1
Daguerreotypers	1	Silversmiths	1
Doctors	1	Ship Carpenters	1
Draymen	0	Stevedores	2
Domestics	15	Tailors	13
Drummers	0	Tinners	0
Engineers	0	Tenders	39
Fruiterers	0	Truckmen	2
Farmers	0	Traders	21
Fishermen	0	Traders	0
Gardeners	0	Traders	0
Gymnasts	2	Tobacconists	2
Glaziers	0	Tavern-Keepers	0
Hairdressers	20	Trimmers	0
Hostlers	3	Upholsterers	0
Laundresses	0	Wheelwrights	0
Jewelers	1	Waiters	26
Job Workers	2	Woodfactors	0
Laborers	135	Whitewashers	0
Locksmiths	0	Curriers	1
Lawyers	1	Teachers	1
Mariners	17	Restorators	1
Marketmen	1	Restaurateurs	2
			0

Total occupations known................ 582

Charles G. Wesley, *Negro Labor in the United States* (New York, 1927), pp.
43-44.

21. COLORED ARTISANS

Boston, hitherto rather tardy in due appreciation of her colored mechanics, business men, &c., is hopefully waking up to encourage those who, thus
stimulated, will prove worthy recipients of her favor.

NELSON L. PERKINS having, for the past few years, filled several stations in an extensive lamp and gas apparatus establishment on Washington
street, has, by dint of close observation and experiment, become very successful in the department of fitting and putting up the various patterns and
fixtures in the drawing-rooms and public houses in Boston and vicinity,--
giving perfect satisfaction to his employers and their patrons.

JOHN T. MATTHEWS has just located himself at No. 17 Howard street, where
he cleans and repairs all kinds of silver and plated ware, jewelry, &c. Appended to his card is the following recommendation, and a better one is not
needed:--

'Boston, April 10th, 1856.
'John T. Matthews has been in our employment nine years, and we commend
him to all as a worthy young man, and deserving of a liberal share of public
patronage.   PALMER & BATCHELDER.'

JONATHAN C. HOGAN, also, at 106 Court street, solicits orders in electro
gilding, fine gilding, silver plating, and working in jewelry.

To all having need of such services, we say, give these young men a
call, and test the American question, whether color of the skin incapaci-
tates a man from the development of mechanical or artistic skill.

Boston, April, 1856.   W. C. N.

The Liberator, April 25, 1856.

22. NEGRO OCCUPATIONS IN MASSACHUSETTS IN 1860

Agents	1	Machinists	3
Apprentices	12	Mariners	279
Artists	2	Marketmen	1
Bakers	1	Masons	6
Barbers	269	Mat Makers	1
Bartenders	4	Merchants and Traders	37
Basketmakers	8	Messengers	2
Beer Makers	2	Millers	1
Billiard and Saloon-Keeper	1	Morocco Dressers	1
Blacking Makers	1	Mill Operatives	3
Blacksmiths	19	Painters	6
Boarding-House Keepers	4	Paperhangers	5
Bookbinders	1	Paper Makers	1
Bootblacks	1	Peddlers	1
Brakemen	1	Photographers	1
Butchers	6	Physicians	14
Cabinetmakers	1	Piano Makers	1
Candle Makers	1	Plasterers	1
Carpenters	20	Porters	42
Carpet Cleaners	2	Printers	5
Caterers	1	Quarrymen	1
Caulkers	7	Riggers	2
Chairmakers	2	Rope Makers	1
Chimney-Sweepers	1	Sailmakers	3
Cigarmakers	1	Saloon and Restaurant Keepers	10
Clergymen	21	Servants	119
Clerks	11	Sextons	1
Clothes Cleaners	3	Shipkeepers	2
Coachmen	2	Shipwrights	4
Cooks	23	Shoemakers	73
Curriers	4	Slaters and Roofers	1
Daguerreotypers		Soap Makers	1
Dentists	1	Sporting-men	1
Draughtsmen	1	Stevedores	5
Drivers	1	Stewards	8
Engineers	2	Stone Cutters	6
Engravers	1	Students	2
Farmers	62	Tailors	112
Farm Laborers	216	Tanners	1
Gardeners	4	Teachers	1
Gentlemen	1	Teachers of Boxing	1
Guilders	2	Teamsters	34
Gymnasts	1	Upholsterers	9
Horse Trainers	1	U. S. Army	1
Hostlers	19	Waiters	62
Inspectors (Flour)	1	Watchmen	2
Jewelers	2	Wheelwrights	6
Jobmen	52	Whip Makers	3
Keepers	1	Whitesmiths	1
Laborers	585	Whitewashers	17
Lamp Lighters	2	Wood Sawyers	1
Lawyers	4	Yoke Makers	1
Lecturers	1		

Total....................2,296

*Abstract of the Census of Massachusetts, 1860, pp. 356-58, as reproduced in
Charles G. Wesley, Negro Labor in the United States (New York, 1927), p. 48.*

23. THE COLORED PEOPLE OF RHODE ISLAND

In Rhode Island, the colored people seem to be doing as much, if not
more, for their own elevation, than is being done in any other State in the
Union. This is doubtless owing to the fact, that in that State there are a
greater number of mechanics among them, according to the number of inhabitants, than is to be found elsewhere. Carpenters, joiners, cabinet-makers,
blacksmiths, printers, and men of various other trades, as well as a large
number of farmers, are among the comparatively small population. The most
finished designer and pattern-maker in the State is Mr. John Mason, of Providence, a man who enjoys the respect and confidence of the entire white population, as well as those of his own color. As a matter of course, these
trades instil into their minds energy and a taste for intellectual pursuits.
'The Rachel Club,' a literary association of Providence, holds its weekly
meetings, at which choice selections from approved authors are read or recited by both male and female members.

We had the good fortune, last week, of attending a dramatic exhibition
of the above Society, and must confess that we were agreeably disappointed.
The characters were well sustained throughout, and some of the acting would
have done credit to professional artists. As self-elevation is, after all,
the great means by which the mass of mankind is to arrive to a high state of
cultivation, we hope the noble example set by the Rhode Islanders will be
followed by the colored population of the other States.

The Liberator, March 28, 1856.

DISCRIMINATION AGAINST FREE BLACK
WORKERS IN THE NORTH

24. EXCERPT FROM REPORT OF PITTY HAWKES ON NEW YORK-AFRICAN [31]
FREE SCHOOL, OCTOBER 13, 1829

. . . after a boy has spent five or six years in the school, and is de-
servedly encouraged by the teacher and the trustees, and (as in many instances is the case) is spoken of in terms of high approbation by respectable
visitors, for his manifest talent and superior intellect, he leaves school,
with every avenue closed against him, which is open to the white boy, for
honorable and respectable rank in society, doomed to encounter as much prejudice and contempt, as if he were not only destitute of that education which
distinguishes the civilized from the savage, but as if he were *incapable* of
receiving it.

All this must be endured, with the additional sensibility which it is
the very nature of education, in some sense, to impart. A case in point is
now before us. A young man, 17 years of age, who about two and a half years
ago, left this school with a respectable education, and an irreproachable
character, which he still retains, was taken as an apprentice to the Black
Smith business, in this City, and served about two years with satisfaction to

his master. Depression of business rendered little or no opportunity of his
obtaining a thorough knowledge of the trade, his father made arrangements
with his master to release him, with a view of the lad's serving his time
out else where: every place that appeared suitable to his object, was closed
against him, *because he was black!* A friend in Philadelphia, agreed to take
him; but when this friend came to make it known in his Factory, he found "an
insurmountable difficulty" in his way; viz. The unwillingness of the workmen to pursue their business in company with poor Isaac, because he was darker than they.

When the lad was informed of this, so far from uttering a word of angry
disappointment, he resolved to leave the country and go to the Colony of Liberia.

Isaac will not only leave in the school the remembrance of a good character, but also several highly creditable specimens of his abilities as a
scholar.

*Charles G. Andrews, The History of the New-York African-Free Schools (New
York, 1830), pp. 117-19.*

25. EX-SLAVE FREDERICK DOUGLASS BECOMES
A FREE BLACK WORKER

Mr. Ruggles was the first officer on the "Underground Railroad" whom I
met after coming North, and was, indeed, the only one with whom I had anything to do till I became such an officer myself. Learning that my trade was
that of a calker, he promptly decided that the best place for me was in New
Bedford, Mass. He told me that many ships for whaling voyages were fitted
out there, and that I might there find work at my trade and make a good
living. . . . Thus, in a fortnight after my flight from Maryland, I was safe
in New Bedford, a citizen of the grand old commonwealth of Massachusetts.

Once initiated into my new life of freedom and assured by Mr. Johnson
that I need not fear recapture in that city, a comparatively unimportant
question arose as to the name by which I should be known thereafter in my new
relation as a free man. The name given me by my dear mother was no less pre-
tentious and long than Frederick Augustus Washington Bailey. I had, however,
while living in Maryland, dispensed with the Augustus Washington, and retained only Frederick Bailey. Between Baltimore and New Bedford, the better to
conceal myself from the slave-hunters, I had parted with Bailey and called
myself Johnson; but in New Bedford I found that the Johnson family was already so numerous as to cause some confusion in distinguishing them, hence a
change in this name seemed desirable. Nathan Johnson, mine host, placed
great emphasis upon this necessity, and wished me to allow him to select a
name for me. I consented, and he called me by my present name--the one by
which I have been known for three and forty years--Frederick Douglass. Mr.
Johnson had just been reading the "Lady of the Lake," and so pleased was he
with its great character that he wished me to bear his name. Since reading
that charming poem myself, I have often thought that, considering the noble
hospitality and manly character of Nathan Johnson--black man though he was--
he, far more than I, illustrated the virtues of the Douglas of Scotland.
Sure am I that, if any slave-catcher had entered his domicile with a view to
my recapture, Johnson would have shown himself like him of the "stalwart
hand."

The reader may be surprised at the impressions I had in some way conceived of the social and material condition of the people at the North. I
had no proper idea of the wealth, refinement, enterprise, and high civilization of this section of the country. My "Columbian Orator," almost my only
book, had done nothing to enlighten me concerning Northern society. I had
been taught that slavery was the bottom fact of all wealth. With this foundation idea, I came naturally to the conclusion that poverty must be the

general condition of the people of the free States. In the country from
which I came, a white man holding no slaves was usually an ignorant and pov-
erty-stricken man, and men of this class were contemptuously called "poor
white trash." Hence I supposed that, since the non-slave-holders at the
South were ignorant, poor, and degraded as a class, the non-slave-holders at
the North must be in a similar condition. I could have landed in no part of
the United States where I should have found a more striking and gratifying
contrast, not only to life generally in the South, but in the condition of
the colored people there, than in New Bedford. I was amazed when Mr. Johnson told me that there was nothing in the laws or constitution of Massachusetts that would prevent a colored man from being governor of the State, if
the people should see fit to elect him. There, too, the black man's children
attended the public schools with the white man's children, and apparently
without objection from any quarter. To impress me with my security from recapture and return to slavery, Mr. Johnson assured me that no slave-holder
could take a slave out of New Bedford; that there were men there who would
lay down their lives to save me from such a fate.

The fifth day after my arrival, I put on the clothes of a common laborer, and went upon the wharves in search of work. On my way down Union street
I saw a large pile of coal in front of the house of Rev. Ephraim Peabody, the
Unitarian minister. I went to the kitchen door and asked the privilege of
bringing in and putting away this coal. "What will you charge? said the lady.
"I will leave that to you, madam." "You may put it away," she said. I was
not long in accomplishing the job, when the dear lady put into my hand *two
silver half-dollars.* To understand the emotion which swelled my heart as I
clasped this money, realizing that I had no master who could take it from me,
--*that it was mine--that my hands were my own,* and could earn more of the
precious coin,--one must have been in some sense himself a slave. My next
job was stowing a sloop at Uncle Gid. Howland's wharf with a cargo of oil for
New York. I was not only a freeman, but a free working-man, and no "master"
stood ready at the end of the week to seize my hard earnings.

The season was growing late and work was plenty. Ships were being fitted out for whaling, and much wood was used in storing them. The sawing this
wood was considered a good job. With the help of old Friend Johnson (blessings on his memory) I got a saw and "buck," and went at it. When I went into a store to buy a cord with which to brace up my saw in the frame, I asked
for a "fip's" worth of cord. The man behind the counter looked rather sharply at me, and said with equal sharpness, "You don't belong about here." I
was alarmed and thought I had betrayed myself. A fip in Maryland was six and
a quarter cents, called fourpence in Massachusetts. But no harm came from
the "fi'penny-bit" blunder, and I confidently and cheerfully went to work
with my saw and buck. It was new business to me, but I never did better work,
or more of it, in the same space of time on the plantation for Covey, the negro breaker, than I did for myself in these earliest years of my freedom.

Notwithstanding the just and humane sentiment of New Bedford three and
forty years ago, the place was not entirely free from race and color prejudice. The good influence of the Roaches, Rodmans, Arnolds, Grinnells, and
Robesons did not pervade all classes of its people. The test of the real
civilization of the community came when I applied for work at my trade, and
then my repulse was emphatic and decisive. It so happened that Mr. Rodney
French, a wealthy and enterprising citizen, distinguished as an anti-slavery
man, was fitting out a vessel for a whaling voyage, upon which there was a
heavy job of calking and coppering to be done. I had some skill in both
branches, and applied to Mr. French for work. He, generous man that he was,
told me he would employ me, and I might go at once to the vessel. I obeyed
him, but upon reaching the float-stage, where others calkers were at work, I
was told that every white man would leave the ship, in her unfinished condition, if I struck a blow at my trade upon her. This uncivil, unhuman, and
selfish treatment was not so shocking and scandalous in my eyes at the time as
it now appears to me. Slavery had inured me to hardships that made ordinary
trouble sit lightly upon me. Could I have worked at my trade I could have
earned two dollars a day, but as a common laborer I received but one dollar.
The difference was of great importance to me, but if I could not get two dollars, I was glad to get one; and so I went to work for Mr. French as a common
laborer. The consciousness that I was free--no longer a slave--kept me

cheerful under this, and many similar proscriptions, which I was destined to
meet in New Bedford and elsewhere on the free soil of Massachusetts. For instance, though colored children attended the schools, and were treated kindly
by their teachers, the New Bedford Lyceum refused, till several years after
my residence in that city, to allow any colored person to attend the lectures
delivered in its hall. Not until such men as Charles Sumner, Theodore Parker, Ralph Waldo Emerson, and Horace Mann refused to lecture in their course
while there was such a restriction, was it abandoned.

Becoming satisfied that I could not rely on my trade in New Bedford to
give me a living, I prepared myself to do any kind of work that came to hand.
I sawed wood, shoveled coal, dug cellars, moved rubbish from back yards,
worked on the wharves, loaded and unloaded vessels, and scoured their cabins.

I afterward got steady work at the brass-foundry owned by Mr. Richmond.
My duty here was to blow the bellows, swing the crane, and empty the flasks
in which castings were made; and at times this was hot and heavy work. The
articles produced here were mostly for ship work, and in the busy season the
foundry was in operation night and day. I have often worked two nights and
every working day of the week. My foreman, Mr. Cobb, was a good man, and
more than once protected me from abuse that one or more of the hands was disposed to throw upon me. While in this situation I had little time for mental
improvement. Hard work, night and day, over a furnace hot enough to keep the
metal running like water, was more favorable to action than thought; yet here
I often nailed a newspaper to the post near my bellows, and read while I was
performing the up and down motion of the heavy beam by which the bellows was
inflated and discharged. It was the pursuit of knowledge under difficulties,
and I look back to it now, after so many years, with some complacency and a
little wonder that I could have been so earnest and persevering in any pursuit other than for my daily bread. I certainly saw nothing in the conduct
of those around to inspire me with such interest: they were all devoted exclusively to what their hands found to do. I am glad to be able to say that,
during my engagement in this foundry, no complaint was ever made against me
that I did not do my work, and do it well. The bellows which I worked my
main strength was, after I left, moved by a steam-engine.

*Frederick Douglass, "My Escape to Freedom," Century Magazine 23 (November,
1881):125-31.*

26. BLACK CARMEN OF NEW YORK

. . . Is it not an OUTRAGE upon revelation and reason, and even a violation of the laws of instinct, by which birds and beast are governed? We have
seen some species of the animal creation, who would wait until the weaker
caught their prey, and then seize upon and take it from them: but it was
left for the Municipality of a christian city, to prevent the hungry poor
from pursuing an honest calling, by which they might get bread for themselves
and their children.

It may be said on the part of those in authority that they have made no
enactments, especially prohibiting colored men from driving carts or rolling
wheelbarrows. This is true: but they have made incorporate laws prohibiting
all men from pursuing these occupations without *special license,* and they
withhold these licenses from colored men, while they give them freely to
white men, without respect to name or nation, and too frequently without respect to character.

It is further pleaded on the part of the authorities, that it is IN
MERCY to the colored man, that they deny him license. Were they, it is said,
to license colored carmen and porters, it would bring them into collusion
with white men of the same calling, and they would get their horses and carts
"dumped" into the dock, and themselves abused and beaten. We confess this is
mercy on the part of our authorities, with A VENGEANCE TO IT!! And it is a

compliment indeed to our worthy carmen and porters.

Who are the carmen of New York, and who are the porters? Are they *illiterate, savage barbarians?* NO, READER--many of them are among our very best citizens, men who for moral worth and industrious enterprise, are the pride of our city, and whose names will ever be united with all that is glorious in our nation. They are, some of them, leaders in the HOLY CAUSE of equal rights, and are laboring to do away, FOREVER, those monopolies and distinctions which are the curse of the nation.

We do not believe, should the authorities license colored men as carmen and porters, there would be any serious difficulties whatever. But were the case otherwise, are not the authorites bound to see every citizen protected in his rights, and sustained in his honest efforts to get bread?--Surely they are. Any colored citizen, who with a respectful petition and recommendation in his hand, applies for license as a carman or porter, is entitled to them: and the authority which withholds them, alike violates the laws of the land, of humanity, and of God.

This illegal proscription of colored men is not practiced in the dark. It is an open violation of law and of conscience. We know an instance in which a worthy citizen, fully convinced of the injustice and cruelty of withholding from colored men THEIR LEGAL RIGHTS, and prohibiting them from pursuing lawful callings, got up and *signed himself,* a petition to the Mayor in behalf of an industrious, worthy man. This same gentleman afterwards *himself* became Mayor of the city, and actually denied the same man a license as a porter?

The spirit of injustice and slavery apparent in this inhuman measure of taking from the colored man the means of getting his bread, is disgraceful to indulge in such feelings of slavery, and resort to, as an apology, the fear of public sentiment. THE CARMEN WILL NOT SUBMIT TO IT!!! . . .

The Colored American (New York), September 16, 1837.

27. HENRY GRAVES AND HIS HANDCART

Here was a worthy gray-headed man arraigned and fined, not for driving a horse with a cart, but for being his own horse, and drawing his own cart, for the accommodation of his friends and neighbors, and as a means to furnish himself and family with bread--fined because he had no license to do so when the City would not grant him a license. One reason urged is, the other cartmen, if they should license a colored man, would push horse, cart, and driver all into the dock. Such an outbreak on the part of the cartmen would be a violation of all law. Does the Mayor presume to suppose that the cartmen are lost to all respect for law?

The Colored American, May 30, 1840.

28. NEW YORK CITY CORPORATION, vs. MR. HENRY GRAVES AND HIS HANDCART

Mr. Editor,--On Monday the 27th ult., Mr. Henry Graves, in obedience to a notice and command of the Corporation, appeared and paid a fine for using his handcart without license. Mr. Graves was not aware that he was violating any law, but as the Corporation made him wise touching that point, he was determined that he would not again violate the law. So, on Tuesday, the 28th inst., Mr. Graves went to the Mayor's office, accompanied by Dr. Sherman and myself, having with him the necessary testimonials of character, and the following petition, in order to get his license:

P E T I T I O N

To the Hon. Isaac L. Varian, Mayor of the city of New York.

The undersigned would recommend to your Honor, Henry Graves, as worthy of a license for a handcart.--We have known him for several years, and always as a sober, honest and industrious man.

A. Sherman,	Charles M. Ray,
J. Stillwell,	George Gurmby,
Amos Upham,	R. McDonald,
Charles S. Benson,	John Parr,
Lawrence Van Wort,	Peter Herbert Hall,
Washington Gordon,	Wm. Redfield,
Gilbert Weeks,	John M. Shepperd,
Lawrence M. Van Wort,	Horace Dresser,

A. M. G. Depew.

New York, April 27, 1840.

By this time, Mr. Editor, I presume you think Mr. Graves has got his license; but not so. The Mayor was absent, and those that were in attendance would not so much as look at the papers, but told us, that it was against the law; but I told the gentleman that there was no law to the contrary. He then said that he had received express orders not to give any license to *colored* people. I told him that there were several colored men who had spring carts, and that I thought they had license, but he said they had no license, and furthermore, they were already fined. Now, Mr. Editor, such insults are too much to bear. It is more than enough to excite the holy indignation, not only of every colored man in these United States, but every man that has one drop of philanthropic blood in his veins. What--chain a man down, so that he cannot get up to go to work, and then lacerate his body because he does not do it! O, sir, the justice of heaven will not much longer sleep o over such consummate wickednesses.

Mr. Graves resides in the 15th Ward, and also the gentlemen who petition for him; some of them are merchants, some carmen, some doctors, and some lawyers, and all of whom are men of education and respectability; and there can be but little doubt, that some of these worthy men aided in placing this functionary into the sacred office that he is thus prostituting; and now hear the excuse: they told us if the Mayor should grant license to colored men to be carmen and porters, white men following the same business would mob the colored ones, shove them off the docks, &c. That is all a sham, Mr. Editor; it is false, because it has been tried both in theory and practice. When C. W. Lawrence filled that important office, I circulated a petition principally among carmen, for a colored man to get license, and they signed it cheerfully, not a few, and it was signed, too, by David Bryson, Charles Collins, Israel Corse and many other leather merchants in the city; and if my memory serves me right, Charles Collins, accompanied by Israel Corse, presented it to his Honor, C. W. Lawrence, and he refused to grant the license for similar reasons that are now made. It will be recollected that Anthony Provost drove his own cart for some time, and was kindly received 'hail fellow well met,' and was treated with as much familiarity and respect as the colored hackmen are treated by the white ones, and the first intimation that Mr. Provost received of a mob, or being shoved in the dock, was by the Corporation, which was bound both by law and justice to protect him. The Corporation lynched him, and exacted a fine from his pocket, which in justice belonged to his wife and children; and then the respectable carmen are insulted by being told that if the Mayor should give a colored man his inalienable right, that they would mob him and shove him in the dock, rights and all.

Now, Mr. Editor, I do not say that we can remedy this evil, that unrighteous distinction of demarkation is daily inflicting upon us, but I do say, that we should immediately arise simultaneously, in the majesty of our nature, and lay hold of the best means to attain that end, and when we shall have done that, then, sir, whether we will have gained our object or not, we

shall not lose our reward, but will be sure to get an equivalent in something, for which I am willing to trust God. The question now arises, what
is the best means? I answer negatively, it cannot be respectability, morality, nor religion, for we have all that, neither can it be the want of education, for we have as much at least as many have, who do not suffer from
the evil. Therefore I am compelled to believe, that it is for the want of
the right of suffrage, and a due appreciation of its value.--Now, sir, I am
sure that if his Honor the Mayor was aware that it was in our power to resent
the wrongs that he is inflicting upon us, at the ballot box, so as to give
him a private instead of a public chair, he would be sure to feel differently, and of course act differently, because a man's feelings are very apt to
be developed in his character; and I am not certain but what we have that
power, if it were only called forth. For instance, I think that there are
enough in several Wards in our city, who have $250 worth of intelligence,
(or real estate) to turn the election either way; and we must take measures
to bring that power into action. I believe, sir, that I am entitled to vote,
and I wish you, as the guardian of my brethren, to examine my claims' and respond to my appeal. I claim the right from the fact that I belong to a
church that owns the ground as well as the walls that are built upon it, and
I am sure that my share is worth more than $250; and, sir, if that principle
be a legitimate one, then all the rest of the members are entitled to vote,
as well as the members of Old Zion, St. Philip's, Bethel, and the Union
church in the village. I hope, Mr. Editor, that you will give us a faithful
and certain sound, touching this important consideration, because if it be
true that we have that much political strength, let us have a knowledge of
it, so that we can immediately begin to tear down the strong holds of the
devil.

I am well aware, Mr. Editor, that I have made this article too long, but
I have ended as soon as I could.--I hope that Mr. Graves will not cease until
he gets his license, for I believe that nineteen-twentieths of the citizens
of New York will endorse his prayer.

W. P. J.

We have some remarks to make upon certain points in the above letter,
which will appear in our next.--ED.

The Colored American, May 9, 1840.

29. HENRY GRAVES AND HIS HANDCART

Our readers will perhaps recollect, that number 150 of this paper contained a communication under the title "New York Corporation, vs. Mr. Henry
Graves and his hand cart," signed W. P. J. We promised to make some comments
upon certain points and inquiries contained therein--but in consequences of a
pressure of matters, have not had time until now.

By referring to the article, our readers will perceive what kind of men
and measures the *inoffensive, innocent* colored people of this city have to
contend with. Here was a worthy, grey-headed man arraigned before a corporate
body, and fined, not for driving a horse with a cart, but for being his own
horse, and drawing his own cart, for the accommodation of his friends and
neighbors, and as a means to furnish himself and family with bread--fined because he had no license to do so, when the Corporation refused, and would not
grant him a license, and his color is the only ground attempted to be urged
for such a refusal. Now it appears to us that in strict justice, the Corporation had as good a right to fine father Graves for sawing wood, or being a
prevate porter, or coachman, as for drawing his own cart, for if in the latter a corporation ordinance was violated, it was not his fault, but theirs,
in refusing to let him comply with the ordinance. This is meeting out justice
with a vengeance.--But *one* reason urged is, it is against the law to license

colored men to drive or draw a cart. Not so fast, Mr. *Substitute for Mayor*--
there is no law about it, and if colored men should all of them draw or drive
carts, they would be good loyal citizens still. It appears to us that the
Mayor in his absence would do well to provide a substitute who understood a
little the duties of the office, at least the laws in the case, and not have
to be instructed as to what was law and what was not, by one of our brethren,
as in this case. Another reason urged is, the other cartmen, if they should
license a colored man, would push horse, cart, and driver all into the dock.
A greater libel upon the civil and honest cartmen of our city, than whom none
of any other city, or any other country are more pure minded and worthy.
Here is also a wonderful regard manifested in one form, for the lives and
property of our people, while the same seeming regard manifests an entire
want of care in life and property in another form. This disposition, cares
not whether our people starve to death for the want of means honorably to
live, or whether for the same reasons they remain poor as the poorest, for if
both should depend upon drawing or driving a cart, such only must be the result, as to all the Mayor or Corporation might care. The Mayor, Corporation,
and no one else, need have any fear as to such a result--they would do much
better to do right, than to fear any such occurrences from their doing justly.
Our honest cartmen, if we know them at all, have too much respect for their
own rights, to interfere with our brethren in the free exercise of theirs.
Besides, such an outbreak on the part of the cartmen would be a violation of
all law, and would render themselves criminals in view of it, and does the
Mayor presume to suppose that the cartmen are lost to all respect for law?

The last reason referred to above for refusing to license colored men as
cartmen, seems to be an old, stereotyped reason, for it has been used successively by every Mayor in almost the identical form. We hope our next will
show that he has more originality, by bringing forward some other reason.

In regard to the inquiry of W. P. J., as to his right to vote upon property he holds in trust with others, we think he can have no right upon property held in trust, as is church property, when held by trustees, and individuals, on whose behalf such property is held in trust, also, we think can have
no right to vote.

The Colored American, May 30, 1840.

PART IV

LIVING CONDITIONS AND RACE RELATIONS IN THE NORTH

LIVING CONDITIONS AND RACE RELATIONS IN THE NORTH

Since most of the crafts and professions were barred to blacks in the North, poverty went hand in glove with African ancestry. Negroes complained bitterly about these barriers but to no avail. The extent and reasons behind this literally pathological poverty are illustrated in Documents 1-5. Even though black people paid taxes, they received few public services without discrimination, and in times of trouble, they were forced to rely on the meager resources which could be supplied by their own institutions, such as the churches and benevolent societies (Doc. 3). The results sometimes meant death from malnutrition or exposure, both of which occurred frequently enough in Philadelphia during the 1840s to prompt the intervention of the city board of health (Doc. 4).

Racial prejudice, which contemporary opponents called "colorphobia," was of course, at the root of the problem. Discriminatory laws existed throughout the northern states. A clear example were the Black Laws of Ohio (Doc. 6), which, among other stipulations, required blacks to exhibit a certificate of freedom in order to settle in the state, to register with the local clerk, and to post a $500 bond for good behavior. Moreover, without a certificate of freedom, it was illegal for an employer to hire a black person. While these codes were not always vigorously enforced, they were not to be taken lightly. Thus, in Cincinnati, authorities in 1829 looked the other way as a white mob rampaged through the city looking for Negroes without certificates. The result was a migration of about 2,000 Negroes to Canada where they could live in peace (Doc. 7). Blacks also encountered mob action in other northern cities, such as Philadelphia (Doc. 9).

Most union leaders were racists also. For example, John Campbell, a Chartist in England who emigrated to the United States and became the leader of the Typographical Union in Philadelphia, published a book at his own expense on the topic of race which portrayed blacks as inherently inferior to whites (Doc. 10). With respect to employment or patronage of black businesses, Afro-Americans could not generally expect much better treatment from the more liberal abolitionists (Doc. 11-16). In 1845, for example, the Pennsylvania Freeman urged its subscribers not to continue in their neglect of black mechanics and artisans who were in desperate financial need (Doc. 12-13). Nor were abolitionists innocent of job discrimination. Martin R. Delany, the noted Afro-American surgeon, complained in 1852 that white anti-slavery men did not practice what they preached, and pointed to the fact that even the abolitionist presses employed black workers only in menial positions (Doc. 15). Even well-educated Negroes found few occupations commensurate with their abilities (Doc. 16).

When blacks could find employment, they frequently encountered white mobs who drove them off the job (Doc. 17-26). The 1834 riot in Philadelphia, for example, was precipitated by the conviction among white workingmen that, because employers preferred black workers, whites were unable to find work (Doc. 20).

The most dramatic evidence of powerlessness among northern blacks, however, was their exposure to kidnapping by unscrupulous whites who, sometimes in collusion with local officials, whisked them off to the South to be sold into slavery. Also, fugitive slaves were sometimes captured by professional slave-catchers and returned South where the catchers received a bounty. Black northerners were particularly outraged by these legal but nefarious captures (Doc. 27-36). Frequently they banded together to rescue captured fugitives, such as in 1845 when Boston Negroes formed an association to assist fugitives in making their escape from authorities (Doc. 35).

PAUPERISM

1. ON PAUPERISM

In approaching this part of our subject, we are well aware of the difficulties we have to encounter in obtaining a just estimate of the value of the
colored people, as a component part of the community, when the census of the
alms-house is made the criterion by which they are to be judged. But when we
consider that, owing to the feelings and prejudices of the community, the
colored people are almost altogether deprived of the opportunity of bringing
up their children to mechanical employments, to commercial business, or other
more lucrative occupations, whereby so many of our white laborers are enabled
to rise above the drudgery in which they commence their career in life, and
in turn, to become the patrons of their younger or less fortunate fellow citizens; it is not matter of surprise that a considerable number of them should
be dependant on public support.
Under these circumstances it certainly cannot be considered unreasonable
that in a gross population of 1,673 individuals in our alms-house, (on the
30th of Twelfth month, 1837,) there should be found 235 people of color, being about one-seventh part of the whole.

*The Present State and Condition of the Free People of Color, of the City of
Philadelphia and Adjoining Districts, as Exhibited by the Report of a Commit-
tee of the Pennsylvania Society for Promoting the Abolition of Slavery, &c.
(Philadelphia, 1838).*

2. IMPEDIMENTS TO HONEST INDUSTRY

In this country ignorance and poverty are almost inseparable companions;
and it is surely not strange that those should be poor whom we compel to be
ignorant. The liberal professions are virtually sealed against the blacks,
if we except the church, and even in that admission is rendered difficult by
the obstacles placed in their way in acquiring the requisite literary qualifications; and when once admitted, their administrations are confined to their
own color. Many of our most wealthy and influential citizens have commenced
life as ignorant and as pennyless as any negro who loiters in our streets.
Had their complexion been dark, notwithstanding their talents, industry, en-
terprize and probity, they would have continued ignorant and pennyless, because the paths to learning and to wealth, would then have been closed against
them. There is a conspiracy, embracing all the departments of society, to
keep the black man ignorant and poor. As a general rule, admitting few if
any exceptions, the schools of literature and of science reject him--the
counting house refuses to receive him as a bookkeeper, much more as a partner
--no store admits him as a clerk--no shop as an apprentice. Here and there a
black man may be found keeping a few trifles on a shelf for sale; and a few
acquire, as if by stealth, the knowledge of some handicraft; but almost universally these people, both in town and country, are prevented by the customs
of society from maintaining themselves and their families by any other than
menial occupations. . . .
In 1836, a black man of irreproachable character, and who by his industry and frugality had accumulated several thousand dollars, made application
in the City of New York for a carman's license, and was refused solely and
avowedly on account of his complexion! We have already seen the effort of
the Ohio legislature, to consign the negroes to starvation, by deterring
others from employing them. Ignorance, idleness, and vice, are at once the

punishments we inflict upon these unfortunate people for their complexion;
and the crimes with which we are constantly reproaching them. [32]

*"On the Condition of the Free People of Color of the United States," The
Anti-Slavery Examiner 13 (New York, 1839):17-18.*

3. CONDITION OF THE FREE PEOPLE OF COLOR IN PHILADELPHIA

The following facts in relation to the free people of color in this
city, are taken from a small paper published here in 1837. We have reason to
believe that their condition has been much improved since then; but as the
statistical information in relation to it is not at present within our reach,
we prefer to give the former statistics, and allow each to make such altera-
tions as truth will warrant.

That there is much vice and misery to be found among these people, we
may not deny--less than this cannot be said of the whites; but it is susceptible of proof, that much of their degradation and suffering is to be attributed to the unholy prejudice that exists against them, and the cruel persecutions that follow them to their very hearth-stone.

They who wish to make themselves acquainted with their *real* condition,
must do more than view them in the lowest grog-shops, whose *white* owners
filch from the poor colored men their little all; they must do more than visit the haunts where congregate the most degraded of them. If they wish to
ascertain their true condition, let them also visit their churches, their
literary institutions, their benevolent associations--let them, in short, be
as anxious to look upon the bright, as on the dark side of the picture, and
they will find abundant cause to admire the perseverance and the moral power
that has enabled them, in spite of the crushing influence of public opinion,
to attain their present elevation.

A FACT.

From a statement published by order of the guardians of the poor in
1830, it appears that out of 549 *out-door* poor relieved during the year, *only*
22 were persons of color, being about four per cent of the whole number,
while their ratio of the population of the city and suburbs, exceeds 8¼ per
cent. By a note appended to the printed report of the guardians of the poor,
above referred to, it appears that the colored paupers *admitted* into the
almshouse for the same period, did not exceed four per cent of the whole
number.

FACT, NO. 2.

The amount of taxes paid annually by the colored people of Philadelphia,
is about 2500 dollars; while the sums expended for the relief of their poor,
out of the public funds, has rarely, if ever, exceeded 2000 dollars a year.
The colored people, then, not only entirely support their own poor, but also
pay 500 dollars a year for the support of *poor whites!!*

FACT, NO. 3.

The colored people in Philadelphia have fifty-five Beneficial Societies,
some of which are incorporated; they expend annually 10,000 dollars, out of
funds raised among themselves, for mutual aid in time of sickness and distress, and for burying the dead, &c. Not a colored person, of any respectability, however poor, is buried at the expense of the poor funds. 'The members of these Societies are bound by rules and regulations which tend to promote industry and morality among them. For any disregard or violation of
these rules,--for intemperance or immorality of any kind,--the members are
liable to be suspended, or expelled. In 1832, it was ascertained that not
one of the members of either of these Societies had ever been convicted in

any of our courts. One instance only had occurred of a member being brought
up and accused before a court--but this individual was acquitted.' We believe no instance has since occurred.

FACT, NO. 4.

The colored people in Philadelphia have fifteen churches belonging to
them, a number of them brick buildings, which, together with their halls,
are worth $172,000. They have thirty-four ministers; seventeen Sunday
schools; a public library, consisting of about 500 volumes, besides 8333 volumes in private libraries; three Debating Societies; three Female Literary
Societies; two Tract Societies; two Bible Societies; and two Temperance Societies.

FACT, NO. 5.

The colored people of Philadelphia pay annually for house rent, 108,121
dollars; for ground rent, 2777 dollars; for water rent, 260 dollars; and for
newspapers, 1578 dollars. A committee recently appointed to investigate how
much property the colored people possess, had not time to ascertain the
amount of more than about two-thirds of the whole population, before they
were required to report. It appeared, however, that these two-thirds possessed, in real estate, 500,000 dollars, and personal property 226,306. Is
it for our *interest* to drive away such a people?

FACT, NO. 6.

'Notwithstanding the difficulty of getting places for them as apprentices, to learn mechanical trades, owing to the prejudice which exist,' in
1832 there were between four and five hundred people of color in the city
and suburbs, who followed mechanical employments. We presume that by this
time the number has considerably increased.

FACT, NO. 7.

'Besides thankfully embracing the opportunities for schooling their
children, which have been opened for them by public munificence and private
benevolence,' the colored people also support several pay schools, and the
pupils in these schools will not suffer by an examination with those of any
other school in the city.

FACT, NO. 8.

Of those colored people who have emigrated from other States to this
State, many are the children of wealthy white planters at the South, by their
slaves. Feeling affection for their own children, they have sent them to a
free State, and settled handsome fortunes upon them. The name of one colored family might be mentioned, which has thus brought 100,000 dollars into the
State; that of another, which has brought from 50,000 to 75,000 dollars, and
the names of a number, all of whom are known to the writer of this, who have
brought from 5000 to 50,000. Now, granting, if you please, that evils do result from having the colored people among us; are not these evils more than
outweighed by the gold and silver which they bring into the State?
Query: Do any of the emigrants from foreign countries bring with them
such sums of money to enrich the State of their adoption? We again ask, is
it for our *interest* to prevent the colored people from emigrating here, or to
drive away those already settled amongst us?

The Liberator, May 14, 1843.

4. POVERTY AMONG BLACKS IN PHILADELPHIA

Philadelphia, Dec'r 18th, 1848

During the fall and winter of 1845 and 1846, I observed much misery and distress among a portion of the coloured population of the city and suburbs, which was much increased in the fall and winter of 1846 and 1847. During the period before named, from September 1837, to April 1848, it increased to such extent as made it necessary to ask the intervention of the Board of Health and Guardians of the Poor. In that time, there came under my notice 76 cases, coloured, male and female (mostly within six blocks or squares, in the district of Moyamensing.) whose deaths after a full and thorough investigation of each case, were attributable to intemperance, exposure, want of nourishment, &c. Of this number eighteen were from 18 to 30 years of age; forty-six, from 30 to 50 years, and twelve from 50 to 90 years, besides some children who also died from exposure and want of proper nourishment and care.

Many were found dead in cold and exposed rooms and garrets, board shanties five and six feet high, and as many feet square, erected and rented for lodging purposes, mostly without any comforts, save the bare floor, with the cold penetrating between the boards, and through the holes and crevices on all sides; some in cold, wet and damp cellars, with naked walls, and in many instances without floors; and others found dead lying in back yards, in alleys, and others exposed situations.

These cases were principally confined to the lowest and most degraded of the coloured population, whose occupations were ragging, boning and prizing. Hundreds were engaged in those occupations and living as others have, that have died; many of whom, unless provided for, must become victims of death through their habits and exposure, should the coming winter be at all severe. Most of them have no home, depending chiefly upon the success of their pursuits through the day, either in earning or begging, (and I may add stealing,) sufficient to pay their grog and lodging. For food, they depend mostly upon begging, or gathering from the street what is thrown from the houses or kitchens of others.

Lodgings are obtained from a penny to six-pence a night according to the extent of the accommodations, with or without an old stove, generally without pipe, a furnace or fireplace, so that a fire may be had if they have means to pay for a few sticks of wood, or some coal; and were it not for the crevices and openings admiting fresh air, many would be suffocated (a few have been) by smoke and coal gas. It is no uncommon circumstance to find several setting around on the floor, with an open furnace in their midst, burning coal. Those places are mostly back from the street, not observable in passing, reached through narrow alleys, or by a back entrance if it be a house fronting the main street, wherein each story is subdivided into numerous small rooms, ofttimes made to accommodate as many as can be stowed into them, without regard to colour or sex. Such articles as an old bed, a carpet, or even straw upon the floor, are not often seen.

Notwithstanding their degrading occupation, yet it is possible for them to earn from ten to fifteen cents per day. There are numerous places for the disposal of their rags, bones, &c., but there are far more numerous places (and constantly increasing) for the disposal of their hard earned (or ill gotten) pennies; namely, at small shops, stocked with a few stale loaves of bread, a few potatoes, a small quantity of split wood, some candles, a few dried and stale herring, &c., exposed to view, serving too often as a cloak; whilst behind and under the counter, concealed from the eye, are kegs, jugs, bottles and measures, containing the poison, some at 4 and 5 cents a pint, and which is the great leading cause of the misery, degradation and death of so many.

Though I have observed much misery and distress both among blacks and whites, in different section of the city and suburbs, yet in no portion to that extent as was found in a small portion of Moyamensing among the blacks, principally in the smaller streets, courts and alleys between Fifth and Eighth and South and Fitzwater streets.

Respectfully your friend,
N. B. Leidy.

A visit to the scene of this distress, made in the latter part of the Ninth month, 1847, is thus described.

"The vicinity of the place we sought, was pointed out by a large number of coloured people congregated on the neighbouring pavements. We first inspected the rooms, yards and cellars of the four or five houses next above Baker Street on Seventh. The cellars were wretchedly dark, damp, and dirty, and were generally rented for 12½ cents per night. These were occupied by one or more families at the present time; but in the winter season, when the frost drives those who in summer sleep abroad in fields, in board yards, in sheds, to seek more effectual shelter, they often contain from twelve to twenty lodgers per night. Commencing at the back of each house are small wooden buildings roughly put together, about six feet square, without windows or fire places, a hole about a foot square being left in the front along side of the door, to let in fresh air and light, and to let out foul air and smoke. These desolate pens, the roofs of which are generally leaky, and their floors so low, that more or less water comes in on them from the yard in rainy weather, would not give comfortable winter accommodation to a cow. Although as dismal as dirt, damp, and insufficient ventilation can make them, they are nearly all inhabited. In one of the first we entered, we found the dead body of a large negro man, who had died suddenly there. This pen was about eight feet deep by six wide. There was no bedding in it; but a box or two around the sides furnished places where two coloured persons, one said to be the wife of the deceased, were lying, either drunk or fast asleep. The body of the dead man was on the wet floor, beneath an old torn coverlet. The death had taken place some hours before; the coroner had been sent for, but had not yet arrived. A few feet south, in one of the pens attached to the adjoining house, two days before, a coloured female had been found dead. The hole from which she was taken, appeared smaller than its neighbours generally, and had not as yet obtained another tenant.

"'Let me introduce you to our Astor House,' said our guide, turning into an alley between two of the buildings on Baker street. We followed through a dirty passage, so narrow, a stout man would have found it tight work to have threaded it. Looking before us, the yard seemed unusually dark. This we found was occasioned by a long range of two story pens, with a projecting boarded walk above the lower tier, for the second story to get to the doors of their apartments. This covered nearly all the narrow yard, and served to exclude light from the dwellings below. We looked in every one of these dismal abodes of human wretchedness. Here were dark, damp holes, six feet square, without a bed in any of them, and generally without furniture, occupied by one or two families: apartments where privacy of any kind was unknown—where comfort never appeared. We endeavoured with the aid of as much light as at mid-day could find access through the open door, to see into the dark corners of these contracted abodes; and as we became impressed with their utter desolateness, the absence of bedding, and of ought to rest on but a bit of old matting on a wet floor, we felt sick and oppressed. Disagreeable odours of many kinds were ever arising; and with no ventilation but the open door, and the foot square hole in the front of the pen, we could scarcely think it possible that life could be supported, when winter compelled them to have fire in charcoal furnaces. With sad feelings we went from door to door, speaking to all, inquiring the number of their inmates, the rent they paid, and generally the business they followed to obtain a living. To this last question the usual answer was, 'ragging and boning.' Some of these six by six holes, had six, and even eight persons in them, but more generally two to four. In one or two instances a single man rented one for himself. The last of the lower story of the 'Astor' was occupied by a blackman, his black wife, and an Irish woman. The white woman was half standing, half leaning against some sort of a box, the blacks were reclining upon the piece of old matting, perhaps four feet wide, which by night furnished the only bed of the three. Passing to the end of the row, we ventured up steps much broken, and very unsafe, to the second story platform, and visited each apartment there. It is not in the power of language to convey an adequate impression of the scene of this property. The filth, the odours, the bodily discomfort, the moral degradation everywhere apparent. Descending with difficulty, we proceeded to examine the cellars and rooms in the building still further back, having the same owner. The same want of accommodations was

observed, few, if any there having a trace of bedding. For the place a few
cents a night were paid generally, 8 cents for the rest. The miserable
apartments in the houses brought about the same prices. Some places, however, rented as high as one dollar per week. . . .

Now for the statistics of this "Astor House," and its appurtenances.
The double row of pens cost perhaps $100 to erect; and if they contain twenty
apartments renting for 8 and 10 cents per night, they produce an income of
$600 per year. When the owner of this property was asked a few years back
to sell it, that a House of Industry might be erected there, he declined;
but in conversation with the individual who asked to purchase it, he stated
that it had cost him $1300. A physician who is frequently called to attend
patients in the place; being curious to know what yearly rent the owner was
receiving, undertook with another white man to visit the apartments, and inquire the amount paid by the dwellers in each. The aggregate amounted to
$1600.

We inquired the daily earnings of those we visited, and the amount they
had to pay for a glass of whiskey. Some earned 50, some 75 cents per day;
but we have reason to believe that many do not realize on an average more
than a few cents over the daily rent. Whiskey, apple or rye, as best suits
the taste of the drinker, is furnished at one cent per glass.

*Statistical Inquiry into the Condition of the People of Colour, of the City
and Districts of Philadelphia (Philadelphia, 1849), pp. 35-39.*

5. EDUCATION AND EMPLOYMENT OF CHILDREN

In my last essay, the pamphlet entitled, "A Statistical Enquiry into the
condition of the People of Color," was examined; the estimate of their numbers, and the value of their real and personal estate noticed, also the increased amount of house rents and taxes paid, and some notice of their trades
and employments by which they earn their subsistence. The subject indicated
by the heading of this essay, forms the next topic of enquiry, and upon which
we are presented with a very interesting chapter. It is there stated that
"the period between 5 and 15 may be regarded as comprising the children sent
to school; while that between 10 and 20 comprise those whose services are
made available to their parents. The number of colored children between
those ages, that is, between 5 and 20, are computed to be about 4500. Of
this number, 1940, or agreeably to a recent correction in the return of the
Abolition Society's school of 100 additional scholars, which gives us 2040
of those between 5 and 15 that go to school." Besides which, "we have returns of the manner in which 1340 of those who do not go to school, are disposed of, leaving about 1100 minors between 5 and 20, who are not reported."

The returns upon the subject of schools are admitted "to be imperfect,
which is much to be regretted, as any comparison between the state of the
colored schools within the last period of ten years, must consequently be
very incomplete. According to the Society's report, published in 1839, there
were 25 schools, public and private, having 1732 scholars on the rolls. By
the late report, there were in 1847, 12 free and 20 pay schools, in which it
is stated there are 1940 scholars on the lists, or as corrected above 2040,
showing an increase within the last ten years, of only about 300 colored children, who are in the way of attending school. In the concluding paragraph of
this interesting chapter they say, "When we call to mind that there are 1100
children between the ages of 5 and 20, of whom no account is received, the
greater part of who are probably growing up in idle and vicious habits; it is
clear that this is one of the most painful facts brought to light by this enquiry, and one which should promptly and earnestly engage the attention of
the friends of the people of colour." That a large number of colored children are suffered to grow up, without partaking the benefits of school education, is a fact which cannot be doubted. But the discrepancy between the

reports for 1837 and 1847 is so striking, as to encourage a hope that the number of 11 or 1200 delinquents from the privilege, or rather the duty of attending school, may also be proportionately over-rated. Taking the lowest estimate of the colored population for 1837, compared with the number for the late report for 1847, the difference is upwards of 3000, of which number one-fifth, equal to 600, may reasonably be set down as the increase of scholars within the last ten years.

"The Beneficial Societies" form the next subject treated of in the pamphlet under consideration. The funds of these associations, arising from contributions of the members varying from 25 to 37½ cents per month, are appropriated to the support of the members in time of sickness, and to bury the dead. The writers of the pamphlet say: "On comparing the list (prepared from the report of their agents) with that published by the Abolition Society in 1837, we find the number of Societies increased from 80 to 106. That more than one-half of those then reported, have disappeared, or have assumed new names." "The permanent funds of 76 of these Societies, (details of which have been furnished,) exceed those reported in 1837 by upwards of $7,000. Six hundred and eighty-one families have been assisted by them in 1847, and the sums furnished to 517 of those families, are slated at $7,189." "It is clear that these charitable funds must very considerably relieve the distress attendant on the sickness of the heads of families, and maintain a large portion of the people of color under privations, and in circumstances, which would otherwise throw them upon the public for relief." This is evident from the returns from the almshouse for 1847. By reference to the Society's report for 1837, and comparing it with "the Statistical Inquiry" for 1847, it will appear that the number of colored paupers admitted into the house has declined very considerably. Agreeably to the former account, out of 1673 individuals in the almshouse in the 12th mo., 1837, there were 235 people of color equal to about one-seventh of the whole; the recent investigation shows that of an average almshouse population of 1704 persons in 1847, only 196 or 11.5 per cent were colored people. The total number admitted in the year was 4,403, of whom 522 or 12.15 per cent. were colored. When we advert to the character of the pauperism of the people of color during that year (1847,) the number of ordinary patients admitted is a matter of surprise. Of the 523 as above (including 23 born in the house) 117 were from the city proper, 21 from Southwark, 16 from the Districts north of Vine Street, and 10 from the Prisons and Hospital. From Moyamensing, which has not quite one-fifth of the colored population, there was 334, equal to one-third of the whole. "Of the white residents of the almshouse, 14.3 per cent. died, of the colored inmates 44.6 per cent died. Of the number of 523, 277, or more than one half, were cases of fever; seven out of every nine were from Moyamensing, and most of these were cases of low typhus fever from the neighborhood of Baker, Bedford and Small streets." These facts afford strong proof of the evil effects of the people of color crowding together in narrow and confined streets, courts and alleys.

"The amount of out door relief furnished to the people of colour, is likewise quite small," being, as stated in the returns received, only 442.

On page 24 of "the Statistical Inquiry," we are presented with a table exhibiting the manner in which the 4262 families of the colored population are distributed in the city and districts, and the proportions receiving public assistance. The amount claimed from the public funds by the people of color, is found to be small, thus the relief bestowed upon the 250 families residing in the city, consists in the greater number of cases of donations of wood, or from a quarter to half a ton of coal, some receive a small supply of groceries in addition, and a few fifty cents per week during sickness.

The following sketch exhibits the main features of the table alluded to, to wit:

		Families.		Assisted.
City,		2562		320
S. Garden,	202		3	
N. Liberties,	272		6	
Southwark,	287		7	
W. Philada.,	73	834	2	18

Moyamensing,	866	104
	4262	442

By which it will appear that only about one-tenth of the whole number of families receive a small pittance of public out-door relief. Another circumstance developed by this tabular statement, is the superior advantage of a sparse, over that of a dense population of our colored people, as will be seen above. In Spring Garden, Northern Liberties, Southwark and West Philadelphia, comprising an aggregate of 834 families, only 18 received support as out-door paupers, which is only one in 46--while in the single district of Moyamensing, with a population very little larger, the number requiring assistance is 104--equal to 1 in 8.32.

There are other subjects of considerable importance contained in the pamphlet, which would perhaps be interesting to examine, beside the valuable remarks upon the general aspect of the concern, which the authors had been investigating, are well worthy of further notice. This review, however, has already occupied so much space, that the expediency of pursuing the subject further, becomes a question yet to be determined. Should it be deemed proper, I may, in a subsequent number present such observations as the subjects yet to be treated of may suggest.

E. N.

Pennsylvania Freeman, February 25, 1849.

COLORPHOBIA

6.   THE BLACK LAWS OF OHIO

Below will be found all the enactments that we are aware of in the Statutes of Ohio, imposing disabilities on the Coloured portion of our citizens, now in force. They are mostly inoperative, on account of their unreasonable requirements; but sometimes, in cases of great excitement among the people, they have been productive of mischief.

An Act to Regulate Black and Mulatto persons.
Passed and took effect, January 5, 1804, 29 v. Stat.
439

1. SECT.I. Be it enacted by the General Assembly of the State of Ohio, That from and after the first day of June next, no black or mulatto person shall be permitted to settle or reside in this state, unless he or she shall first produce a fair certificate from some court within the United States, of his or her actual freedom; which certificate shall be attested by the clerk of said court, and the seal thereof annexed thereto by the said clerk.

2. SECT. II. That every black or mulatto person residing within this state, on or before the first day of June, one thousand eight hundred and four, shall enter his or her name, together with the name or names of his or her children, in the clerk's office, in the county in which he, she or they reside, which shall be entered on record by said clerk; and thereafter the clerk's certificate of such record shall be sufficient evidence of his, her or their freedom; and for every entry and certificate, the person obtaining the same shall pay to the clerk twelve and a half cents: provided, nevertheless, that nothing in this act contained, shall bar the lawful claim to any black or mulatto person.

3. SECT. III. That no person or persons, residents of this state, shall be permitted to hire, or in any way employ, any black or mulatto

person, unless such black or mulatto person shall have one of the certificates as aforesaid, under pain of forfeiting and paying any sum not less
than ten, nor more than fifty dollars, at the discretion of the court, for
every such offence; and one-half thereof for the use of the informer, and
the other half for the use of the state; and shall moreover pay to the owner,
if any there be, of such black or mulatto person, the sum of fifty cents for
every day he, she or they shall in any wise employ, harbor or secrete such
black or mulatto person; which sum or sums shall be recoverable before any
court having cognizance thereof.

4.   SECT. V.   That every black or mulatto person who shall come to reside in this state with such certificate as is required in the first section
of this act, shall, within two years, have the same recorded in the clerk's
office, in the county in which he or she means to reside, for which he or
she pay to the clerk twelve and a half cents; and the clerk shall give him or
her a certificate of such record.

5.   SECT. VI.   That any person or persons who shall attempt to remove,
or shall remove from this state, or who shall aid and assist in removing,
contrary to the provisions of this act, any black or mulatto person, without
first proving, as hereinbefore directed, that he, she or they is, or are legally entitled so to do, shall, on conviction thereof, before any court having cognizance of the same, forfeit and pay the sum of one thousand dollars;
one-half to the use of the informer, and the other half to the use of the
state; to be recovered by action of debt, quitam, or indictment; and shall
moreover be liable to the action of the party injured.

An act to amend the last named act.

Passed January 25, 1807.   Took effect April 1, 1807.
29 v. Stat., 440.

6.   SECT. I.   Be it enacted by the General Assembly of the State of
Ohio, That no negro or mulatto person shall be permitted to enter into, and
settle within this state, unless such negro or mulatto person shall, within
twenty days thereafter, enter into bond with two or more freehold sureties,
in the penal sum of five hundred dollars, before the clerk of the court of
common pleas of the county in which such negro or mulatto may wish to reside,
(to be approved by the clerk,) conditioned for the good behaviour of such negro or mulatto, and moreover to pay for the support of such person, in case
he, she or they should thereafter be found within any township in this state,
unable to support themselves.   And if any negro or mulatto person shall mi-
grate into this state, and not comply with the provisions of this act, it
shall be the duty of the overseers of the poor of the township where such negro or mulatto person may be found, to remove immediately such black or mulatto person, in the same manner as is required in the case of paupers.

7.   SECT. II.   That is shall be the duty of the clerk, before whom such
bond may be given as aforesaid, to file the same in his office, and give a
certificate thereof to such negro or mulatto person; and the said clerk shall
be entitled to receive the sum of one dollar for the bond and the certificate aforesaid, on the delivery of the certificate.

8.   SECT. III.   That if any person being a resident of this state, shall
employ, harbor or conceal any such negro or mulatto person aforesaid, contrary to the provisions of the first section of this act, any person so offending shall forfeit and pay for every such offence, any sum not exceeding one
hundred dollars, the one-half to the informer, and the other half for the use
of the poor of the township in which such person may reside; to be recovered
by action of debt, before any court having competent jurisdiction; and moreover be liable for the maintenance and support of such negro or mulatto, provided he, she or they shall become unable to support themselves.

9.   SECT. IV.   That no black or mulatto person or persons shall hereafter be permitted to be sworn or give evidence in any court of record, or
elsewhere, in this state, in any cause depending, or matter of controversy,
where either party to the same is a white person; or in any prosecution which
shall be instituted in behalf of this state against any white person.

10. SECT. V. That so much of the act entitled "an act to regulate
black and mulatto persons," as is contrary to this act, together with the
sixth section thereof, be and the same is hereby repealed.

This act shall take effect and be in force from and after the first day
of April next.

An act to amend the act entitled "an act to regulate
black and mulatto persons," passed Jan. 5, 1804.

Passed and took effect, Feb. 27, 1834. 32 v. Stat., 29.

11. SECT. I. Be it enacted by the General Assembly of the State of
Ohio, That in all cases wherein a certificate is granted to any black or mulatto person, resident within this state, agreeably to the second section of
the act to which this is an amendment, the clerk of the court issuing the
same shall make or cause to be made, a record of the same, in a book provided for that purpose, and carefully preserved in said office; and on such
record of the same being made, the said clerk shall endorse thereon the number of the same, the book in which, and the page or pages where such record
is made; and shall forthwith, if required, deliver over the same to the individual for whose benefit it was intended. And it shall furthermore be the
duty of the presiding judge of such circuit in which said certificate may be
issued, on application being made to him by the holder of the same, to endorse thereon his certificate of the genuineness of the same: provided, that
nothing in this act contained shall be so construed, as to bar the lawful
claim to any black or mulatto person thus obtaining a certificate within
this state.

BLACK LAWS IN OHIO

The Legislature of Ohio has refused to annul or amend her black laws.
Not one of the members of that body would hesitate about denouncing
Slavery generally.--Very few of them who do not condemn the South for holding on to the institution. Yet they deny justice to the negro, and refuse
to take his testimony in any of their courts.
There are hundreds of planters in this State who refuse to emancipate
their slaves--and who oppose emancipation because of free State legislation
of this character. They ask--"What can the slave do if he be set free?
Where can he go?" And fearing that he may be worse off, they conclude to do
the best they can with him, and for him!
Most of the free States deal shamefully in this matter. The majority
of the Ohio Legislature, certainly, merit a rebuke for their inhumanity in
sustaining laws which a Kentucky Statesman calls "atrocious," and most men
admit to be disgraceful.--*Louisville Examiner*.

The Non-Slaveholder 3 (1848):117-19.

7. INQUIRY INTO THE CONDITION OF BLACKS
IN CINCINNATI, 1829

The Anti-Slavery Society, late of Lane Seminary, appointed a Committee
in March last, to inquire into the condition of the Colored People of Cincinnati. For the following statement, exhibiting the result of their investigation, we are indebted to them. Mr. Wattles, whose personal examination secured the facts here stated, is the superintendent of the colored
schools in that city. [33]

Statement in regard to Cincinnati.

In the spring of 1829, an effort was made to enlist the citizens of Cincinnati in the plan of removing the free people of color from the United
States. This effort was vigorous and protracted. Whatever were the *motives*
which prompted the effort its particular *effect* was to excite the powerful
against the weak, to countenance the lowest class of the whites in persecut-
ing the victims of public scorn and contempt.

The township trustees issued a *proclamation* that every colored man who
did not fulfil the requirements of the law in thirty days should leave the
city. The law here referred to had lain a dead letter since it passed the
Ohio Legislature, in 1807. It provided, that every negro or mulatto person
should enter into bonds with two or more freehold sureties, in the penal sum
of $500, conditioned for the good behavior and support of such negro or mu-
latto person, if they should be found in the state, unable to support themselves. It also made it the duty of the overseers of the poor, to remove all
such persons as did not comply with the above laws, in the same manner as is
required in the case of paupers.

Another section of the same law provided that any person who should employ, harbor, or conceal any such negro or mulatto person, should, for every
such offence, forfeit and pay any sum not exceeding one hundred dollars and
be liable for their maintenance and support, should they ever be unable to
support themselves. This proclamation was fully sustained and urged into execution by the public sentiment of the city. The colored people immediately
held a meeting to consider what should be done. They petitioned the city
authorities for permission to remain thirty days longer, and forthwith sent
a committee to Canada to see what provisions could be made for them there.
The sixty days expired before their return.

The populace finding that few, if any, gave security, and seeing no
movement made, became exasperated, and determined to expel them by force.
For three nights the fury of the mob was let loose upon them. They applied
in vain to the city authorities for protection. Despairing of succor from
the whites they barricaded their houses and defended themselves. Some of
their assailants were killed and the mob at last retired.

The deputation to Canada returned with a favorable answer. The reply of
Sir James Colebrook, Governor of Upper Canada, is characteristic of a noble
minded man. "Tell the Republicans" said he, "on your side of the line, that
we royalists do not know *men* by their colour. Should you come to us, you
will be entitled to all the privileges of the rest of his Majesties subjects."

On the receipt of this grateful intelligence a large number removed to
Canada, and formed what is called the Wilberforce Settlement. It cannot be
ascertained, definitely, how many went to Canada. But, one of the two men,
who took the census a short time previous to the excitement, states, that
the colored people numbered 2200. About three years after, the same gentleman assisting in taking the census again, when they numbered only 1100.
"This" he added "is not guesswork, but matter of fact."

The wrongs suffered by those who remained behind, either from inability
to remove, or other causes, cannot well be imagined. The mechanical associations combined against them. Public schools were closed by law, and prejudice excluded them entirely from such as were selected. A general desire
among the white population that they should remove to Liberia, or elsewhere,
rendered the operation of these laws too effective. They were by no means a
dead letter. One or two facts will be sufficient.

A respectable master mechanic stated to us, a few days since, that in
1830 the President of the Mechanical Association, was publicly tried by the
Society, for the crime of assisting a colored young man to learn a trade.
Such was the feeling among the mechanics, that no colored boy could learn a
trade or colored journeymen find employment. A young man of our acquaintance,
of unexceptionable character and an excellent workman, purchased his freedom
and learned the cabinet making business in Kentucky. On coming to this city
he was refused work by every man to whom he applied. At last he found a
shop, carried on by an Englishman, who agreed to employ him--but on entering
the shop, the workmen threw down their tools, and declared that he should
leave or they would. *"They would never work with a nigger."* The unfortunate
youth was accordingly dismissed.

In this extremity, having spent his last cent, he found a slave holder who gave him employment in an iron store as a common laborer. Here he remained two years, when the gentleman finding he was a mechanic, exerted his influence and procured work for him as a rough carpenter. This man by dint of perseverence and industry has now become a master workman, employing at times, six or eight journeymen. But he tells us he has not yet received a single job of work from a native born citizen of a free state. This oppression of the mechanics still continues. One of the boys of our school last summer, sought in vain for a place in this city to learn a trade. In hopes of better success his brother went with him to New Orleans when he readily found a situation. Multitudes of common laborers at the time alluded to above, were immediately turned out of employment, and many have told us that they were compelled to resort to dishonorable occupations or starve. One fact--a clergyman told one of his laborers who was also a member of his church, that he could employ him no longer for the laws forbade it. The poor man went out and sought employment elsewhere to keep his family from starving, but he sought in vain, and returned in despair to the minister to ask his advice. The only reply he received was "I cannot help you, you must go to Liberia."

This combined oppression of public sentiment and law reduced the colored people to extreme misery. No colored man could be a drayman or porter without subjecting his employer to a heavy penalty, and few employers had the courage or disposition to risk its infliction. Many families, as we *know,* have for years been supported by the mothers or female part of the family. This they have done by going out at washing, or performing other drudgery which no one else could be procured to do.

The schools, both common and select, remain shut against them to the present day although they have always paid their full proportion of taxes for all public objects. A short time since, it was discovered by a master of the common school, a presbyterian elder, that three or four children who attended had a colored woman for a mother. Although the complexion of these children is such that no one could distinguish them amongst a company of whites, they were told they could not stay in school, and were sent home to their parents.

The law not only placed the colored population in a situation where they must remain in ignorance and deprived them of the means of procuring a honest living, but it went still further and took from them their oath in courts of justice in any case where a white person was one of the parties. Thus they were placed by law at the mercy of their cruel persecutors. A few cases have accidentally fallen under our own observation. Last spring a colored man had his house broken into and property to a considerable amount stolen. The evidence was entirely conclusive as one of the thieves turned State's evidence and confessed the whole. At the court, one of the pleas put in by the counsel was that neither the oath of the man nor that of his family could be taken to prove the property to be his. The jury returned a verdict of *not guilty* and the robbers were cleared.

At the same court a white man was arraigned for murdering a colored man. The case was a plain one,--eight or ten men who were standing near, saw the murder. Only two of them, however, were white. On the day of trial one of the white men could not be found. The testimony of the other was received, while that of the colored men, though equally respectable, was refused. As it was a capital crime, where two witnesses were necessary, the murderer escaped unpunished. Subject to such disabilities is it strange that this population should be ignorant and degraded? Especially when we remember that nearly one half of them were formerly in bondage. They have grown up under its blighting influences. The charge is *true, they are a degraded people.* But this charge, true as it is, should not make them objects of contempt. It is the proof that they have *minds* and are susceptible of moral influence. We wonder as we sometimes sit and listen to their tale of sufferings and of woe, that black despair has not entirely palsied every energy. To those acquainted with the system of slavery, it is known that not only law but even brute force is frequently exerted to prevent the dawn of intellect. Said a colored woman to us the other day, "When I was little, I used to long to read. After prayers, master would often leave the bible and hymn book on the stand, and I would sometimes open them to see if the letters would not tell me something.

When he came in and catched me looking in them he would always strike me and
sometimes knock me down. . . ."

*Proceedings of the Ohio Anti-Slavery Convention (Cincinnati, 1830), pp. 19-
21.*

8. THE DIFFERENCE BETWEEN THE NORTH AND THE SOUTH

In most of the States in which slavery is tolerated, the laws in relation to free colored persons are severe in the extreme. Though their freedom
is recognized, yet they have not the rights of other freemen. . . .
Few whites will eat with blacks. Even where blacks and whites are domestics in the same kitchen, the blacks, as I have been told, are often compelled to eat at a separate table. So it is said that white journeymen and
apprentices of mechanics often refuse to work with blacks. The prejudice
has taken two different forms in the different parts of our country. At the
North, few blacks are mechanics, because the whites will not allow them to
work with them. At the South, on the contrary, few of the mechanics are
whites, because they will not do the same sort of work as blacks. . . .

The Liberator, January 22, 1831.

9. COLORPHOBIA IN PHILADELPHIA

The Commissioners of the pious and orderly District of Moyamensing, the
hotbed of Sunday riots, the place where no decent person, can walk after
nightfall, without being robbed or insulted, have recently had their sense of
propriety outraged, and their tender hearts lacerated by a most iniquitous
proposal to erect a House of Industry for colored persons in that District.
In consideration of this fearful atrocity, these Commissioners met on the
evening of Monday, Oct. 2d, (a day forever hereafter to be held sacred in the
annals of Hunkerism,) and passed the following preamble and resolutions:[34]

Whereas, a petition has been presented to this Board, which sets forth
that a building is about to be erected on Catharine, near Seventh street,
within this District, which is to be occupied as a *House of Industry* for poor
and degraded negroes;
And, whereas, it is represented by the petitioners that the erection of
a building to be occupied for such a purpose, in a thrifty and improving
neighborhood, which is densely settled by white people, will create a disturbance or will drive away the white population, and thereby depreciate the
value of property; therefore,
Resolved, That in the opinion of this Board the black population of our
city and county is already sufficiently cared for, and the charities that now
exist are ample to supply the wants of all of them that are worthy and deserving.
Resolved, That the erection of a building for such a purpose, in such a
neighborhood as that within which it is intended that this shall be erected,
manifests a wanton and reckless disregard of public sentiment, and contempt
for the feelings of the neighboring inhabitants.
Resolved, That if those who have contributed to the fund for the erection
of this building, are determined to waste their means in visionary schemes of
philanthropy, justice dictates that they should concentrate the objects of

their charity in their own neighborhood--near their own doors, where, if they
create a nuisance, they may suffer the consequences of it, or if it is a public benefit, they may be eye-witnesses of its great advantages.

Resolved, That all buildings to be used for purposes to which public
sentiment is opposed and which are thereby likely to create a disturbance or
commotion, should be erected within the limits of the City of Philadelphia,
whose great resources enable it to keep a powerful police, and thereby extend at all times ample protection to both persons and property.

Oh, the hardness of heart that can be guilty of the wickedness of driving away the respectable and liberal-minded "white population" of that District! None but a Nero or a Caligula could be guilty of such an atrocious
wickedness. Besides, "the black population of our city and county (and they
might have added, "of our country") is already sufficiently cared for." The
chivalry of the Old Dominion, act towards them the part of fathers--they
feed them, lodge them, clothe them, and chastise them, and lest they should
get intelligent and discontented, keep them in ignorance! One of the candidates for the Presidency has 280 of the "colored population" living on his
farm in Louisiana, whom he purchased with the express intention of "caring
for them." Another of the candidates says he will veto the Wilmot Proviso,
or any other proposed act of legislation which would so grossly violate all
the claims of justice as to exclude the "colored population. . . ."

And in Pennsylvania, and other Northern States, the colored people are
prevented, as far as possible, no doubt as an act of charity towards them,
from engaging in any but the most menial and dependent employments; and in
Philadelphia, the city of brotherly love and benevolence, which it is proposed to erect a House of Industry for the colored inhabitants, the District
Commissioners meet and vote that it is a nuisance, and that such a manifestation of partiality is likely to create a disturbance among the white people.
Verily, the colored people are "cared for"--as the wolf cares for the lamb!

Shade of William Penn! Is not Philadelphia a glorious city--a Christian
city--a liberal-minded city--a city of philanthropists! A lack a day!

The North Star, October 13, 1848.

10. THE RACIAL ATTITUDES OF A LEADING WHITE LABOR SPOKESMAN

A couple of years ago men were afraid in Philadelphia to speak out their
opinions of the Negro; that day is past--his equality and humanity can be
talked of now in any and every company. Were one to have said that no amount
of education, or circumstances, or food, or climate, or all united, could
ever make aught of a negro than a negro, there were not wanting a certain
number of sham humanitarians, fierce as wolves, ready to pounce upon the unfortunate utterer of the truth, and willing to hunt him to the death. This
evil had to be arrested--public opinion had to be changed--and the only way
to accomplish this was by open and free discussion. I dared the abolitionists to the contest; nearly every speaker was upon their side at the commencement, but one after another changed their opinions, the nature of the
evidence, and the character of the authority I cited were so irresistible
that the *honest and disinterested, having no selfish motives to blind their
eyes to the evidence adduced,* readily adopted the ideas of the great names
who had made the science of man and the history of races their especial study.

Open, full, and free discussion will settle this question. In every contest of this kind the Negroites have been ignominiously driven from their
strongholds. This must ever be the case where truth and falsehood come in
contact. The truth must and shall prevail; and I am of opinion that a new
turn will be given to public opinion in the free States, and the fact be believed, that whenever the white man and the Negro inhabit a warm climate together, there is no other state of society than mastery for the white and

slavery for the black race; but this has been so clearly demonstrated by
Hammond, Blackwood, and others, that I need not do more than allude to it.

In this place it may not be inappropriate to say something about the
free colored people. I speak now of Pennsylvania. Here we have a negroid
population numbering over fifty-three thousand. I hold that he would be a
pure patriot, and a philanthropist, in every sense of the term, who could
rid us of this intolerable curse; who could point out a plan by which this
vicious, idle, lazy, mongrel race would be safely deposited in Liberia.

The Shams denounce any attempt at colonization as cruel and tyrannical,
thereby displaying their usual ignorance of negro nature. They claim for
this species of man the same rights the whites possess; whereas, if they understood the matter, they would know that Negro nature is not Celtic or Saxon nature; they would know that the destiny, constitution, intellect, civilization, and even diseases of the negro are all essentially different from
the white. These things the abolitionists know, or ought to know. The
plain fact of the matter is, that we must take efficient steps ere long to
get rid of our negroes, either by *colonization or otherwise;* but get rid of
them we must, and must is the word. We must appropriate a certain sum annually, to enable those who are willing to emigrate so to do. We must prohibit the introduction of free negroes into out State. We must alter our State
constitution for the purpose of enabling us to get rid of this population.
And after we have made ample provision to send them in comfort to Africa,
should there be any left who would prefer being slaves to the whites instead
of free blacks in Liberia, they should have the power to choose, but they
must either go there as free, or remain here as slaves. Aside of us they
cannot be on terms of equality.

Will the white race ever agree that blacks shall stand beside us on
election day, upon the rostrum, in the ranks of the army, in our places of
amusement, in places of public worship, ride in the same coaches, railway
cars, or steamships? Never! never! nor is it natural or just that this kind
of equality should exist. God never intended it; had he so willed it, he
would have made all one color. We see clearly that God himself has made the
distinction--has made him inferior to the white. Could any body or tribe of
negroes maintain the warlike attitude which the Circasian, a typical stock
of the Caucasian race do against the armed forces of the Russian Bear.
This, I presume, none will attempt to answer in the affirmative. Why, then,
all this rant about negro equality, seeing that neither nature or nature's
God ever established any such equality. . . .

John Campbell, Negro-Mania: Being An Examination of the Falsely Assumed
Equality of the Various Races of Men (Philadelphia, 1851), pp. 543-45.

WHITE ABOLITIONISTS AND JOBS FOR FREE BLACKS

11. ABOLITIONISTS! DO GIVE A HELPING HAND!

A correspondent in Philadelphia informs us that a number of colored people have abjured intemperance and other kindred vices, under the influence
of the "Society for the Mental and Moral Improvement of the Colored Population." They have kept their pledges faithfully, but they are surrounded by
fiery temptations, and *they cannot get employment.* Most earnestly do they
beg to be set to work, and be removed from evil influences. Farmers and
mechanics, all over the country, in the name of humanity we beseech you not
to turn a deaf ear to their appeal! *Do* employ these brethren, and help them
to return to their Father's House.

National Anti-Slavery Standard, June 30, 1842.

12. WHITE ABOLITIONISTS AND COLORED MECHANICS
IN PHILADELPHIA, I

Some of our abolitionists seem not to know that there is any such thing in Philadelphia. Bootblacks and barbers are known to abound and are pretty well patronised, but as for artizans in any other line, they are either supposed to have no existence, or are most culpably neglected. Such at least is the testimony of respectable colored workmen with whom we have lately conversed, and who (we must confess) have made us feel not a little ashamed of the remissness of abolitionists, (including ourselves) in this particular. Colored mechanics, notwithstanding some of them are thoroughly proficient in their business, receive but very little encouragement or patronage from abolitionists. Their main support is derived from persons either hostile or indifferent to the anti-slavery cause. This ought not so to be, and must not so continue. We must be true to our professions, and extend a helping hand to our brethren who are struggling, against an iniquitous prejudice, to introduce among themselves those useful arts of which their oppressors have hitherto had almost an entire monopoly. There are *some* skilful workmen among them as we can testify--slight as has been our experience --and all that is wanted, greatly to increase their number, is the encouragement which they have a fair right to expect from their professed friends.
Taylors and shoemakers are the classes of mechanics who are in most requisition, and if abolitionists, when they have occasion for the services of workmen in either of these branches, would employ colored persons, many a respectable, and struggling family would be made comfortable and much good would be done every way for the whole colored population.

Pennsylvania Freeman, September 25, 1845.

13. WHITE ABOLITIONISTS AND COLORED MECHANICS
IN PHILADELPHIA, II

Since writing the article under this heading in our last number we have been making some further inquiries, and find all we there said in regard to the claims of our colored tradesmen to the support of white abolitionists, and the remissness of abolitionists in meeting these claims, fully sustained by the facts in the case. The facilities for getting work done by respectable and competent colored mechanics, particularly in regard to the articles of boots, shoes and clothing, which are in most frequent requisition, are greater than we had supposed, while the patronage extended to them by abolitionists is less than any one would imagine. A colored tailor informs us that while the principal part of the work which he does is for white persons, and while his main customer is one of the most distinguished lawyers at the bar of this city, he has never been called upon to make but a single suit of clothes for an abolitionist. This he feels to be bad treatment on the part of those who profess to be his friends.
We happen to know the abolitionist here alluded to: he has since removed from the city, but we remember to have heard him say before he left, alluding to this circumstance, that for neatness of fit and cheapness of price he could not have been better accommodated by any white tailor in the

city; and the handsome black suit which he was wearing at the time bore
testimony in part of the truth of his statement.

Now our colored friends should not have such grounds for complaint;
they should not be made to feel that they are badly treated by those who
profess to be their best friends. They have a right to a fair share of the
custom which abolitionists have to give and we hope for their sakes and for
the sake of the cause that they will hereafter receive at least a larger
portion of what is their due.

Supposing that some of our friends may be inclined to profit by these
remarks and to look out for a colored tailor the next time they have any
clothes to make we would recommend them either to N. W. Depee, 334, South
st., or Francis Moore, 150 Locust st., or Jno. Gilberry, 147 Locust st., or
Wm. Tollson 200 N. 8th. st. And we would add that by giving one or other of
these men their patronage, they will not only be consulting duty but economy.
Colored tradesmen from the necessity of their circumstances, are compelled
to work cheaper than the whites, in order to get what little custom falls to
their lot. This is perhaps a low motive to urge for the performance of a
duty, but it is one, the force of which we all feel more or less.

Pennsylvania Freeman, October 9, 1845.

14.   COLORED MECHANICS--FREE LABOR BOOTS AND SHOES

It is well known that colored persons have to encounter great difficulties in attempting to learn any mechanical business; and it too frequently
happens, when individuals of this class have, through perseverance, become
qualified to engage in such business for themselves, that they are deprived
of a proper share of public patronage by the general but cruel prejudice
against color.

These facts suggest to the true friends of the colored man, the propriety and, we may perhaps say, the duty of giving special encouragement in
such cases; and we have great satisfaction in recommending our friend Peter
Lester, boot and shoe maker, No. 76 north 7th street, Philadelphia, to the
patronage of our readers. He recently commenced the manufacture of Boy's
shoes in addition to his former business of making men's boots and shoes;
and we are particularly gratified in being able to state that he not only
uses leather of the best quality, but so far as muslin is used in his work,
it is exclusively made of FREE cotton.

The Non-Slaveholder 4 (1849):226.

15.   MARTIN R. DELANY PROTESTS JOB DISCRIMINATION
AMONG WHITE ABOLITIONISTS

The cause of dissatisfaction with our former condition, was, that we
were proscribed, debarred, and shut out from every respectable position, occupying the places of inferiors and menials.

It was expected that Anti-Slavery, according to its professions, would
extend to colored persons, as far as in the power of its adherents, those
advantages nowhere else to be obtained among white men. That colored boys
would get situations in their shops and stores, and every other advantage
tending to elevate them as far as possible, would be extended to them. At
least, it was expected, that in Anti-Slavery establishments, colored men

would have the preference. Because, there was no other ostensible object in view, in the commencement of the Anti-Slavery enterprise, than the *elevation* of the *colored man,* by facilitating his efforts in attaining to equality with the white man. It was urged, and it was true, that the colored people were susceptible of all that the whites were, and all that was required was to give them a fair opportunity, and they would prove their capacity. That it was unjust, wicked, and cruel, the result of an unnatural prejudice, that debarred them from places of respectability, and that public opinion could and should be corrected upon this subject. That it was only necessary to make a sacrifice of feeling, and an innovation on the customs of society, to establish a different order of things,--that as Anti-Slavery men, they were willing to make these sacrifices, and determined to take the colored man by the hand, making common cause with him in affliction, and bear a part of the odium heaped upon him. That his cause was the cause of God--that "In as much as ye did it not unto the least of these my little ones, ye did it not unto me," and that as Anti-Slavery men, they would "do right if the heavens fell." Thus, was the cause espoused, and thus did we expect much. But in all this, we were doomed to disappointment, sad, sad disappointment. Instead of realising what we had hoped for, we find ourselves occupying the very same position in relation to our Anti-Slavery friends, as we do in relation to the pro-slavery part of the community--a mere secondary, underling position, in all our relations to them, and any thing more than this, is not a matter of course affair--it comes not by established anti-slavery custom or right, but like that which emanates from the proslavery portion of the community, by mere sufferance.

It is true, that the "Liberator" office, in Boston, has got Elijah Smith, a colored youth, at the cases--the "Standard," in New York, a young colored man, and the "Freeman," in Philadelphia, William Still, another, in the publication office, as "packing clerk;" yet these are but three out of the hosts that fill these offices in their various departments, all occupying places that could have been, and as we thought, would have been, easily enough, occupied by colored men. Indeed, we can have no other idea about anti-slavery in this country, than that the legitimate persons to fill any and every position about an anti-slavery establishment are colored persons. Nor will it do to argue in extenuation, that white men are as justly entitled to them as colored men; because white men do not from *necessity* become anti-slavery men in order to get situations; they being white men, may occupy any position they are capable of filling--in a word, their chances are endless, every avenue in the country being opened to them. They do not therefore become abolitionists, for the sake of employment--at least, it is not the song that anti-slavery sung, in the first love of the new faith, proclaimed by its disciples.

And if it be urged that colored men are incapable as yet to fill these positions, all that we have to say is, that the cause has fallen far short; almost equivalent to a failure, of a tithe, of what is promised to do in half the period of its existence, to this time, if it have not as yet, now a period of twenty years, raised up colored men enough, to fill the offices within its patronage. We think it is not unkind to say, if it had been half as faithful to itself, as it should have been--its professed principles we mean; it could have reared and tutored from childhood, colored men enough by this time, for its own especial purpose. These we know could have been easily obtained, because colored people in general, are favorable to the anti-slavery cause, and wherever there is an adverse manifestation, it arises from sheer ignorance; and we have now but comparatively few such among us. There is one thing certain, that no colored person, except such as would reject education altogether, would be adverse to putting their child with an anti-slavery person, for educational advantages. This then, could have been done. But it has not been done, and let the cause of it be whatever it may, and let whoever may be to blame, we are willing to let all pass, and extend to our anti-slavery brethren the right-hand of fellowship, bidding them God-speed in the propagation of good and wholesome sentiments --for whether they are practically carried out or not, the professions are in themselves all right and good. Like Christianity, the principles are holy and of divine origin. And we believe, if ever a man started right, with pure and holy motives, Mr. Garrison did; and that, had he the power of making the

cause what it should be, it would all be right, and there never would have
been any cause for the remarks we have made, though in kindness, and with
the purest of motives. We are nevertheless, still occupying a miserable position in the community, wherever we live; and what we most desire is, to
draw the attention of our people to this fact, and point out what, in our
opinion, we conceive to be a proper remedy. [35]

*Martin Robison Delany, The Condition, Elevation, Emigration, and Destiny of
the Colored People of the United States (Philadelphia, 1852), pp. 26-30.*

16. "IS THERE ANYTHING HIGHER OPEN TO US?"

The position of the colored man to-day, is a trying one; trying, because the whole country has entered into a conspiracy to crush him; and it
is against this mighty power that he is forced to contend. Some persons
think we are oppressed only in the South: this is a mistake. We are oppressed everywhere on this slavery-cursed land. To be sure, we are seldom
insulted here by the vulgar passers by. We have the right of suffrage. The
free schools are open to our children, and from them have come forth young
men who have finished their studies elsewhere, who speak two or three lan-
guages, and are capable of filling any post of profit and honor. But there
is no field for these men. Their education only makes them suffer the more
keenly. The educated colored man meets, on the one hand, the embittered
prejudices of the whites, and on the other the jealousies of his own race.
Perhaps you may think that there are exceptions. This is true; but there
are not enough of them in the whole United States to sustain, properly, a
half dozen educated colored men. The colored man who educates his son, educates him to suffer. When La Martine said to an Armenian chief at Damascus,
'You should send your son to Europe, and give him that education you regret
the want of yourself,' the Armenian answered, 'Alas! what service should I
render to my son, if I were to raise him above the age and the country in
which he is destined to live? What would he do at Damascus, on returning
thither with the information, the manners, and the taste for liberty he has
acquired in Europe? If one must be a slave, it is better never to have
known anything but slavery. Woe to the men who precede their times: their
times crush them.' And woe to the black man who is educated: there is no
field for him.
The other day, when a man who makes loud anti-slavery pretensions, and
who has the reputation of being the friend of the blacks, had it in his power to advance the interests of a colored man, and was asked to do so, he
said, 'Colored men have no business to aspire--the time has not come'! This
gentleman no doubt regrets that he did not originate the ideas that 'black
men have no rights that white men are bound to respect,' and that 'a white
skin is the only legitimate object of ambition.' He has now only to sigh
for 'a plantation well stocked with healthy negroes,' and his cup of pleasure
will be full. Some men are ruined by success. I remember very well that
about five years ago, he was an active laborer with us, and I am certain he
did not say, 'the time has not come,' when he asked us to elect him to the
Legislature. (Applause.)
No where in the United States is the colored man of talent appreciated.
Even here in Boston, which has a great reputation for being anti-slavery, he
is by no means treated like other talented men. Some persons think that because we have the right to vote, and enjoy the privilege of being squeezed
up in an omnibus, and stared out of a seat in a horse-car, that there is
less prejudice here than there is farther South. In some respects this is
true, and in others it is not true. For instance, it is five times as hard
to get a house in a good location in Boston as it is in Philadelphia, and
it is ten times as difficult for a colored mechanic to get work here as it
is in Charleston, where the prejudice is supposed to be very bitter against

the free colored man. Colored men in business here receive more respect and less patronage than in any other place that I know of. In this city, we are proscribed in some of the eating houses, many of the hotels, and all the theatres but one. Boston, though anti-slavery and progressive, supports, in addition to these places, two places of amusement, the sole object of which is to caricature us, and to perpetuate the existing prejudices against us! I now ask you, is Boston anti-slavery? Are not the very places that pro-scribe us sustained by anti-slavery patronage? Do not our liberal anti-slavery politicians dine at the Revere House, sup at the Parker House, and take their creams and jellies at Copeland's? We have several friends, (whose tested anti-slavery is like gold tried in the fire, which comes out purer every time it is tried,) who speak occasionally upon platforms that are claimed to be anti-slavery, and which are dependent upon their eloquence for support, which have, up to this time, refused to give any colored man a hearing. The Boston Theatre, an institution which has been fighting death ever since it came into existence, could not survive a single year without anti-slavery patronage!

The friends of slavery are everywhere withdrawing their patronage from us, and trying to starve us out by refusing us employment even as menials. Fifteen or twenty years ago, colored men had more than an even chance in me-nial employments; to-day, we are crowded out of almost everything, and we do not even get the patronage of our professed friends. The colored stevedores who could once be found all along the wharves of Boston, may now be found only about Central wharf, where they meet with just encouragement enough to keep soul and body together. Such is the progress of the public sentiment and of humanity in Boston!

Last summer, a colored servant who was stopping at the Revere House with a gentleman from New York, was maltreated by the Irish servants. He told his employer, who made complaint to Mr. Stevens. Mr. Stevens replied, that he would not interfere in anything that his servants should do to any colored man--that if gentlemen travel with colored servants, they must ex-pect to be insulted, and he would rather that such gentlemen would stop some where else. That is the idea--colored men have no right to earn an honest living--they must be starved out.

Fifteen or twenty years ago, a Catholic priest in Philadelphia said to the Irish people in that city, 'You are all poor, and chiefly laborers; the blacks are poor laborers, many of the native whites are laborers; now, if you wish to succeed, you must do everything that they do, no matter how de-grading, and do it for less than they can afford to do it for.' The Irish adopted this plan; they lived on less than the Americans could live upon, and worked for less, and the result is, that nearly all the menial employ-ments are monopolized by the Irish, who now get as good prices as anybody. There were other avenues open to American white men, and though they have suffered much, the chief support of the Irish has come from the places from which we have been crowded.

Now, while we are denied the humblest positions, is there anything high-er opened to us? Who is taking our boys into their stores at a low salary, and giving them a chance to rise? Who is admitting them into their workshops or their counting-rooms? Who is encouraging those who have trades? With the exception of a handful of abolitionists and a few black Republicans, there are none. If a few more of those who claim to be our friends would patron-ize us when they can, and in this manner stimulate us to be industrious, they would render us infinitely more service than all of their 'bunkum' speeches.

You can have but a faint idea of the charm their friendship would carry with it, if they would spend a dollar or two with us occasionally. It will not do to judge men by what they say. Many speak kindly of us when their hearts are far from us. Or, as Shakespeare has it,

> 'Words are easy like the wind,
> Faithful friends are hard to find.

This is our experience, and we have learned to appreciate the Spanish proverb, 'He is my friend who grinds at my mill.' In New England, we have many mechanics, who get very little patronage. Indeed, a trade appears to be of but little service to any of us unless we can, like the tailor of Campillo, afford to work for nothing, and find thread.

John S. Rock at Crispus Attucks Meeting in Boston, The Liberator, March 16,
1860.

ANTI-BLACK LABOR RIOTS

17. THE LATE RIOTS IN PROVIDENCE

   The committee of citizens appointed at the town meeting in Providence
on the 25th ult. to investigate and make a statement of facts, have made a
report. It is stated that for several years there has been in Olney's lane
and in that part of Providence called 'Snow Town,' a number of houses inhabited chiefly by idle blacks, others by whites, and others by a mixture; constituting a continual nuisance, from their riots and affrays; that the town
authorities had been remiss in not correcting the nuisance, as so hateful
was it to those who lived within its sphere, that they made no efforts to
discountenance the mob, whose proceedings on the night of the 22d inst. were
scarcely interrupted in the presence of nearly 100 satisfied and passive
spectators. Yet those who thus countenanced the mob, are now convinced that
of all the evils that can be inflicted upon civil society, that of a lawless
and ferocious mob is the most capricious in its objects, the most savage in
its means, and the most extensive in its consequences.
   The first of the recent riots took place on Wednesday evening, Sept. 21.
Five sailors, after supper, started from their boarding houses in the south-
erly part of the town to go 'on a cruise.' They arrived at the foot of Olney's lane about eight o'clock, where they met six or seven men, of one of
the steam boats, with sticks or clubs in their hands, and without hats or
jackets. They stated that they had been up and had a row with the 'darkies,'
and asked the five sailors to go up and aid them. About a hundred persons
were assembled, all of whom appeared ready for an affray. The five sailors
admit that they proceeded up the lane with the multitude. A great noise was
made, the crowd singing and shouting until they came near the elm tree, when
a gun was discharged and stones thrown from the vicinity of the houses occupied by the blacks. Stones were also thrown by the crowd against the houses.
The committee have received no satisfactory evidence whether the discharge
of the gun and stones by the blacks preceded or succeeded the stones thrown
by the crowd, or whether they were simultaneous. It is pretty certain that
upon the firing of the gun, the main body of the crowd retreated to the foot
of the lane. The five sailors, however, continued up the lane, and when
nearly opposite the blacksmith's shop, another gun was discharged. Wm. Henry, one of the five sailors, put his hand to his face and said he was shot.
George Erickson and Wm. Hull proceeded to the house the farthese east but
one, on the south side of Olney's lane, occupied by blacks. A black man
standing on the steps presented a gun, and told them to keep their distance
at their peril. Hull proposed taking the gun from him, but Erickson thought
it best to leave him. They accordingly joined their three comrades, and proceeded up the lane about 100 feet to a passage leading from the south side
of the lane to a lot in the rear. They saw three or four men, one of whom
Hull knew. The black whom they had seen on the steps with a gun, perceiving
that they had stopped, ordered them again 'to clear out,' or he would fire
upon them. He said, 'Is this the way the blacks are to live, to be obliged
to defend themselves from stones?' The sailors refused to go any farther.
One of them, Hull thinks it was George, told the black to 'fire and be damned.' Two attempts to fire were made, a flash and a snap; upon the third, the
gun went off.
   George fell, mortally wounded, with a large shop in the breast. William
Hull and John Phillips were wounded, but not dangerously. George died in

about half an hour, during which time Hull states that he could obtain no
assistance from the crowd below. Before he was removed, and within half an
hour after his death, as Hull states, the crowd had increased to a large mob,
and they proceeded up the lane, and demolished two of the houses occupied by
blacks, and broke the windows and some of the furniture of others.

On the 22d, the knowledge that a white man had been shot by the blacks,
made a great excitement, and the mob assembled at 7 o'clock, and the sheriff
arrested seven and committed them to jail, but in three or four other instances, the mob made a rescue. Twenty-five soldiers of Capt Shaw's company
being ordered out, they were pelted by the mob with some injury, and it being
perceived that nothing short of firing would have any other effect than to
exasperate the mob, they were marched off, and no further attempt made that
night to quell the mob. On Friday morning, it was generally reported that an
attempt would be made to break into the jail and rescue the prisoners. A
meeting of the State Council was had, three infantry, one cavalry, and one
artillery company ordered to be under arms. Four of the rioters were liberated for want of evidence, and three bound over for trial, that the mob might
have no pretense to attack the jail. In the afternoon, the following placard
was posted.

NOTICE.

'All persons who are in favor of Liberating those Men who are confined
within the walls of the Providence Jail are requested to make due preparation,
and govern themselves accordingly'

'N B--No quarters Shone'

Most of the evening from 30 to 50 collected in front of the jail, many
threats were uttered, and it was with difficulty that the mob could be made
to believe that all the prisoners had been discharged. Soon after, a man
who had an instrument under his arm, apparently a sword, appeared and ordered
the mob to Snow Town, whither they went, but did but little damage.

On Saturday evening, 6 o'clock, the same companies mustered about 130
men at their armories, and the Sheriff repaired to Snow Town at 8½. There
was a great crowd, and stones were thrown at the houses; he waited on the
Governor, who at his request ordered out the troops, who on their way to
their post on the hill west of the buildings the mob were destroying, were
sorely pelted, and in clearing the hill, one of the mob seized an Infantry
soldier's musket, and pulled him down the bank 20 feet. A skirmish ensued
between two or three soldiers and some of the mob, in which an artillerist
gave the man who had seized the soldier, a sabre cut. After the military had
taken their position, the riot act was read, audibly by W. S. Patten, Esq. a
Justice of the Peace, the mob listening in silence, after which all persons
were repeatedly warned to disperse peaceably, and told that all who remained
would be considered rioters. The night was still, and the proclamation and
statements were plainly heard at a great distance; but the multitude answered
by huzzas, shouts and threats. The Sheriff then gained attention, and stated
that all must disperse, or in 5 minutes they would be fired upon. The shouts
and stones were redoubled, and exclamations of 'fire and be damned' were
heard from all quarters. The civil officers were constantly employed in trying to induce the mob to depart. Soldiers being injured from an opposite
hill, the Sheriff directed the crowd to retire from that, or he would have to
fire upon them; one party moved off towards Mr. Newell's residence, and another portion towards the houses near the bridge.

The mob then again attacked one of these houses, throwing stones and demolishing the windows. The Sheriff, in a very loud voice, commanded them to
desist, but no attention was paid to him. The violence of the attack increased, so that it was supposed they had begun to tear the building down.
At this time, the Sheriff requested the Governor to detach a portion of the
force to suppress the riot. The Light Dragoons and the first Light Infantry
were accordingly ordered to march under the Sheriff's directions. The Governor advised the Sheriff not to fire unless in self defense.--As these two
Companies approached Mr. Newel's in order to gain the road, they found a portion of the tumultuous crowd still posted in that quarter, who threw stones
upon them. The soldiers halted, and musketry was discharged into the air,
with a view to intimidate the rioters, and thus cause them to disperse without injury, but this firing produced no other effect than a shower of

missiles, accompanied with hootings and imprecations. The Sheriff left this detachment, returned to the Governor, and said he did not deem it prudent to move down the hill, leaving this large body of the mob in the rear. The Governor then directed the Company of Cadets to occupy a position to protect their rear, which they did accordingly. The Sheriff with the two companies first detached, then marched down, the infantry in front, he constantly directing all persons to retire, and moving sufficiently slow to give them an opportunity to do so. As he approached the house, the mob desisted from their work.

During this march, the stones were continually heard rattling against the muskets, and fall thick among the soldiers. As the troops approached the bridge, part of the mob retired before them, some occupied the ground upon each flank, and the sides of the bridge were filled. They slowly crossed the bridge, the Sheriff continually and earnestly repeating his request for the rioters to disperse, warning them of their danger. The crowd immediately closed in upon their rear with great clamor, throwing stones without cessation. After the detachment had gained the street east of the bridge, the assaults upon them increased to so great a degree of violence, that the Cavalry were forced against the Infantry, and the rear platoon of Infantry nearly upon the front. The Dragoons called out to the Infantry that they could not withstand the incessant shower of missiles, and unless the Infantry fired upon the rioters, it was impossible that they could remain. The Cavalry were without ammunition. The Infantry also exclaimed that they could no longer sustain these dangerous vollies of stones, and if they were not permitted to defend themselves, they felt they were sacrificed. The detachment halted in Smith-street near its junction with North Main-street, at a distance of about forty rods from the residue of the military on the hill. The Infantry faced about to present a front to the assailants, and the Light Dragoons who had been compelled to advance partly along their flanks, filed past them, and formed upon the left.

After they halted, the stones were still hurled unremittingly. Many of the soldiers were seriously injured. The stocks of several of the muskets were split by the missiles. The air was filled with them. The Sheriff, who was by the side of the Captain of the Infantry during the whole march, repeatedly commanded the mob to desist, but those orders were wholly unavailing. It having now become manifest that no other means existed by which the riot could be suppressed, or the lives of the men preserved, the Sheriff directed the Captain to fire.--The Captain then gave the word, 'ready.' Here a momentary pause took place. The stones were still thrown with the greatest violence, and exclamations were vociferated 'Fire and be damned.' The Captain turned to the Sheriff and asked, 'Shall I fire?' Perceiving that the crisis had at length arrived, and that the danger was imminent, he replied, 'Yes, you must fire.' The further orders were then given, 'Aim--Fire.' A discharge followed in a somewhat scattering manner. After the order was thus executed, a second was immediately given to cease firing. The most perfect silence ensured, not a sound was heard, and all violence instantly ceased. In about five minutes, it being evident that the mob was now quelled, the Infantry assumed a new position in line on the east side of Main street, facing westwardly with the cavalry on their left.

At the moment these two companies passed the bridge on their march eastward, the shouts were so violent, and the attacks upon them appeared so alarming, that the Governor, apprehensive for their safety, ordered the Company of Cadets to march in double quick time to their support. The firing of the Infantry was heard immediately after. The Cadets were then moving down, but had not passed below the point where the Governor with the artillery and volunteer companies remained. They however continued their march, crossed the bridge, and proceeded down Canal street to Weybourne bridge, dispersing the mob before them. After the firing ceased, information was brought to the Governor, that the multitude was separating. Before leaving the hill, the Governor requested Dr. Panter, who was with him to attend upon the wounded, and render them every possible assistance.

Throughout this investigation, the committee have not been able to conceal from their view the disastrous consequence of a predominance of the mob over the Infantry, on the night of the 24th. The Dragoons had been driven upon the Infantry, and forced partly around their flank; the men could stand

the pelting no longer. Surrounded as they were, no effectual use could be
made of the bayonet. They were obliged to fire, or suffer their ranks to be
broken. Had their ranks been broken, the lives of many if not all of the
soldiers would have been sacrificed, and their arms fallen into the possession of the mob.

The Committee therefore are of unanimous opinion, that the necessity of
a discharge by the Infantry was forced upon them by the mob, and that it was
strictly in defence of their lives.

The Liberator, October 1, 1831.

18. LETTER FROM AN OBSERVER OF THE PROVIDENCE RIOT, 1831

Father--

. . . Last Wednesday night, some disturbance taking place in Olney's
Lane, a sailor, a young and promising fellow, 2d mate of the Anna H. Hope,
who was in search of the cook of the ship with two or three others, was shot
dead from a house occupied by negroes, and the rest wounded. The alarm
spread rapidly, and a large company assembled, and tore down the house and
one or two other small ones, occupied by negroes. The next night, the moon
shining bright, an immense multitude gathered in the Lane, and began to show
signs of tearing down more houses. The Governor, Sheriff and all the watchmen were on the spot ready to prevent it, if they could. The first who commenced, were immediately seized by the Sheriff and watchmen, who succeeded in
holding only two of them, after hard fighting; the mob then burst forward,
and drove all the watchmen off, and commenced pulling down all the bad houses
in the Lane. They stationed sentinels, and went to work as busy as bees,
first pulling down the chimneys and then with a firehook and plenty of axes
and iron bars tearing down the buildings and rolling them into the street.
The air was so still, and the weather so pleasant that Elish tells me he
could hear them talk when he was at the mill.

The whole street was full of spectators, a great many of whom were
cheering the mob every time a house fell. About 11 o'clock the Governor ordered out the 1st Infantry, and they marched up the lane, but the mob stopped
work and surrounded them, throwing stones at them, hissing and hooting, etc.
Several of them were badly wounded by the stones, and they had to retreat.
As soon as they were gone, they began work again, and levelled 8 or 9 buildings with the ground. They then marched over to Snowtown, and tore down two
or three houses there, breaking windows in others, &c. It was then near 4 in
the morning, and they dispersed. The next day the whole of the military companies were warned to meet at 6 oclock and wait further orders, but it rained
very hard, and but few of the mob assembled, they having threatened to tear
down the hall, to liberate some of their companions. This was Friday night;
but the worst was yet to come.

Yesterday, Saturday, the companies were again ordered to meet at sunset,
at their alarm posts, and wait further orders, the ringing of the Court House
but being the signal for them to march. As soon as it began to grow dark,
the streets were thronged with persons moving up towards Snowtown that being
the place it was expected they would meet. The whole of Canal street, from
the basin up to Shingle Bridge was filled with spectators, and about 9 o'
clock, the stones began to rattle against the negro houses, and the axes to
fly. The Court House bell then rang, and the whole town was alarmed. Four
companies with the Governor and Sheriff then marched up to Main st. and over
Shingle Bridge, and up on to the hill, where the rioters then principally
were. By this time, the whole street was full (over the Bridge) of citizens.
The Sheriff then read the riot act, amid a shower of hisses and stones, which
severely wounded some of the troops. Before the act was read, they drove the
mob off the side of the hill, and among them was Daniel Branch, the carpenter, who had his face badly cut by a sword, so that they had to carry him

home. He wounded some of the troops badly after he was struck. The riot
act allowed them one hour to disperse, but they continued to pour stones into the corner house, owned by Mrs. Granger, breaking all the windows. The
military then fired across the street, into the side hill, towards Fletchers,
some of the balls hitting his shop, but the mob only renewed their attacks.
As soon as the hour was out, they marched down the street, towards the bridge
driving the crowd before them. The Sheriff kept telling them to disperse,
but was only answered by showers of stones. He then ordered the companies up
the street by Janny's, in front of Metcalf's shop, wheeled round, gave orders
to fire down the street on to the bridge, and *killed* two men, and badly
wounded several others. I, with hundreds of others stood at the time, at the
corner shop, just round the corner, and the men dropped in the dirt right before us. No one had any idea of their firing, and the street was full.
Wethermore, a bookbinder, a young man, and Walter Lawrence were killed. The
town was in the utmost a larm all night, and to-day a town-meeting was called
to raise patrols for to-night, in addition to the military. I never knew
such an excitement before, Many blame the Governor and Sheriff, and threaten
hard, so that we look for something perhaps worse.

*J. A. Randall to Mowry Randall, September 25, 1831, Ms., Brown University Li-
brary.*

19. BLACK WORKERS ASSAILED IN PHILADELPHIA

Though gatherings of large numbers of people at Philadelphia to commit
acts of violence, had ceased after the third night--many excesses subsequently took place, and colored persons, when engaged in their usual vocations,
were repeatedly assailed and maltreated, especially on the Schuylkill front
of the city. Parties of white men have *insisted* that no blacks shall be employed in certain departments of labor. This is going a "considerable
length."

Niles' Weekly Register, August 30, 1834, p. 441.

20. COMMITTEE REPORT ON THE CAUSES OF THE
PHILADELPHIA RACE RIOTS, 1834

At an *adjourned* meeting of the citizens of the City of Philadelphia and
the adjoining districts, held at the District Court Room, September 15, 1834.
JOSEPH R. INGERSOLL, Esq. the Chairman, being absent, John Goodman, Esq. of
the Northern Liberties, was called to the Chair. The minutes of the first
meeting having been read, John Binns, Esq. from the Committee appointed to
make inquiries as to the origin, character and extent of the riots in the
month of August, made the following

REPORT.

The Committee appointed at a Town Meeting of the Citizens of the City
and County of Philadelphia, held in the District Court Room, September, 3,
1834, "to inquire into the origin and progress of the late riots in Philadelphia, and the means taken to suppress them; and to ascertain the extent of
personal injury inflicted, and the damage done to property, real and personal;" with instructions, to make report to an adjourned meeting of the Citizens of the City and County of Philadelphia, to be held at this place, this
evening--respectfully Report:--

. . . It is notorious--indeed, a fact not to be concealed or disputed, that the "object of the most active among the rioters, was a destruction of the property, and injury to the persons, of the colored people, with intent, as it would seem, to induce, or compel them to remove from this district. A similar feeling and intent, had previously manifested itself in the city of New York, and has subsequently been in active operation in the interior of this state, as well as in the state of New York. These events are called to mind, for the purpose of remarking, that general principles and convictions, rather than local feelings or interests, must have been in operation thus extensively to influence public opinion, and disturb the peace of so many districts in our heretofore tranquil country. Whatever those principles and convictions may have been, their consequences are deeply deplored, and by this community, sincerely regretted. . . .

Among the causes which originated the late riots, are two, which have had such extensive influence, that the committee feel they would be subject to censure, if they did not notice them. An opinion prevails, especially a-mong white laborers, that certain portions of our community, prefer to em-ploy colored people, whenever they can be had, to the employing of white peo-ple; and that, in consequence of this preference, many whites, who are able and willing to work, are left without employment, while colored people are provided with work, and enabled comfortably to maintain their families; and thus many white laborers, anxious for employment, are kept idle and indigent. Whoever mixed in the crowds and groups, at the late riots, must so often have heard those complaints, as to convince them, that the feelings from which they sprung, stimulated many of the most active among the rioters. It is neither the duty, or the intention of this committee, to lay down rules for the public, or the government of individuals, but they deem it within the obligations imposed upon them, to make the statements they have made, and to leave the matter for correction, to the consideration and action of individ-uals.

The other cause, to which the committee would refer, is the conduct of certain portions of the colored people, when any of their members are arrest-ed as fugitives from justice. It has too often happened, that when such cases have been under the consideration of the judicial authorities of the country, the colored people have not relied on the wisdom and justice of the judiciary; on the exercise of the best talents at the Bar, or on the active and untiring exertions of benevolent citizens, who promptly interest them-selves in their behalf; but they have crowded the Court Houses, and the ave-nues to them, to the exclusion of almost all other persons; they have forci-bly attempted the rescue of prisoners, and compelled the officers of justice to lodge them for safety, in other prisons, than those to which they had been judicially committed. Scenes like these, have given birth to unfriendly feelings, for those who have thus openly assailed the officers of justice. The committee hope and expect, that such disgraceful scenes will not, again, be exhibited in our city, causing disrespect for the laws; instilling a spir-it of subordination; familiarizing the public to breaches of the peace; and a resistance to the judicial authority, and stimulating the violent and the turbulent, to make war upon the officers of the Courts, and exhibit, in our most public places, an armed and a riotous people.

These, and other causes, have long operated in the minds, and occupied the thoughts of no inconsiderable portion of our fellow citizens. Nearly twenty years ago, there was, in this district, an out-breaking of popular discontent, which issued in the destruction of a place of worship, of the colored people, in the Northern Liberties. As a small frame building, used by the same description of people, as a meeting house, was torn down, and the windows of another broken, during the late riots in the Southern Liberties, the Committee deem it proper to remark, that the directions thus taken by the rioters, was, in no instance, given by any prejudice against any religious sect, or from any indisposition to seeing the people of color assemble to-gether, for the purpose of public worship. It is believed to have been caused by the disorderly and noisy manner in which some of the colored con-gregations indulge, to the annoyance and disturbance of the neighborhood, in which such meeting houses are located.

The earliest facts immediately connected with the origin of the late riots, of which the committee have been able to obtain authentic information,

are the occurrences on the evening of Tuesday, the 12th of August. On a lot
in the rear of South street, and above Seventh, there had been for some time
before, an exhibition of what were called, Flying Horses. On these horses,
a limited number of persons, for a certain sum of money, were allowed to
ride a limited time. On these horses, the whites and the blacks rode indiscriminately, and seats were eagerly sought after, angry words and quarrels
would arise, as to the rights of preference to a seat. On the night stated
there was an unusual crowd of young men, and it was at the time remarked,
that they were principally strangers, persons not residing in the vicinity.
What was the immediate cause of the riot, or whether, as is, by many believed, it had been preconcerted, the committee have been unable, with certainty,
to ascertain; but a disturbance arose in a very short space of time, the
whole of the Flying Horses, were torn to pieces. The magistrates and peace
officers of that vicinity, did their duty courageously, and except the damage
done on the premises, where the riot commenced, and where some wounds were
inflicted, the public peace was not again disturbed that night.

The next evening, the 13th of August, a considerable mob unexpectedly
presented itself in the vicinity of the premises, which had been destroyed
the night before. There having been no expectation of such a visit, no preparation had been made, and the resistance to the mob, on that evening, was
principally by the local authorities and inhabitants, until, at a late hour,
and after much mischief had been done, they were reinforced by the Constables, Watchmen, and Police from the City. In Seventh, Shippen, Bedford, and
Small streets, and in the Lanes in that neighborhood, the mob did much injury
to property, breaking into houses, destroying the furniture, and greatly
abusing and beating the inmates, all colored people, many of whom, after having labored hard through the day, had retired to rest, without a thought
that their dwellings would be invaded, and their lives endangered by the inhumanity of persons to whom they were strangers. We record such facts with
deep regret, but trust that their record will act as a warning, and deter
other persons from being seduced into a participation in such an outrage.

On Thursday, the 14th of August, the President Judge of the Court of
Common Pleas, and the Attorney General wrote to the Sheriff, and, on their
representations, he promptly took the necessary steps to preserve the public
peace. As the execution of Murray had been fixed for the next day, the 15th,
and no reprieve had then arrived, the time and attention of the Sheriff, was
so much occupied in making arrangements for that melancholy event, that he
entrusted to his Counsel, P. A. Browne, Esq., the calling out of a sufficient
force to ensure the public peace. In a communication from this gentleman to
the committee, he expresses an entire conviction, that the civil authority,
is, in this district, without the aid of any of our Volunteer Corps--which,
however, was promptly tendered--abundantly sufficient to quell any riot,
which unfortunately may take place. The attendance of nearly every individual summoned on the Posse Commitatus, and the facility with which, by volunteers, the places of the few who were absent, were supplied, affords gratifying evidence of the general determination of our citizens, that the laws
should be respected, and the public peace preserved. If any additional evidence was required, it is to be found in the obedience, discipline, and good
order, which was, at all times observed, whenever the citizens were called
out, wherever they were directed to go and whatever they were ordered to do,
by those under whom they were organized. It is due to these citizens, and to
the volunteers, horse and foot, who were out during the riots, to remark,
that, nowithstanding their determination at all times, to do their duty,
they were in no instance, guilty of a wanton exercise of power, but, were as
forbearing, as they were resolute. This evening, (Thursday,) although the
number of the people assembled, was greater than before, in the neighborhood,
where persons and property had been assailed, yet was there little, or no,
mischief done, so well had the constituted authorities made their arrangements, and so overwhelming was the force they had called out.

This night, however, was marked by the complete destruction of a small
frame building, used as a place of worship by the colored people, near Whar-
ton Market, a distance of a mile and a half from where the riot had commenced. This was an event so unexpected, that conjecture was busy to account
for it. The committee have ascertained the cause why this building, thus
situated, and thus used, was prostrated.--The evening before Wednesday, there

had been some excitement in that vicinity, but of no great extent, and without any marked character or object. Between 9 and 10 o'clock, of Wednesday night, as three lads, strangers to each other, were passing the south end of this frame meeting, they were fired upon from a house, and the general belief was that it was an officer of the meeting, a colored man, who fired. The young man, about 17 years of age, most injured, the committee have examined. He was shot in the hand and in the leg. It was this unprovoked firing, and the general belief, that it was done by an officer of the meeting, which excited popular indignation, and directed it against the frame building.

On the night of Friday the 15th, serious and not unfounded apprehensions were entertained that blood would be shed. In Seventh street, below Lombard, some colored men had taken possession of a house called Benezet Hall, into which, it was said, they had conveyed arms and ammunition. The crowd in front of the Hall was great, and made violent threats. The Mayor of the city, with an effective force of constables and watchmen, came on the ground. The windows of the hall and the doors were fastened on the inside, the tumult without increased every every hour, and some stones were thrown at the hall. The Mayor, justly apprehensive of the consequences, and feeling the deep responsibility resting on him, addressed with energy and effect, those who were in the hall, as well as those around him. Soon after the effect produced by this address, High Constable Garrigues stationed four watchmen in front of the hall, and then went round, and made his way in, at the back of the building.--He made known who he was: some of the colored men were turbulent and disposed to resist, but the mass of them, (there were about 60,) were willing to submit, and were only anxious for their safety. He took them all quietly out the back way, announced to the crowd that the hall was cleared, and quiet was restored. The weapons found in the hall were swords, sword canes and clubs--there were no fire-arms.

This evening, Friday, in consequence of many assemblages of young men, and some threats thrown out against the colored people in the Northern Liberties, strong apprehensions of a riot were entertained in that district. The Sheriff organized the citizens--the Police Magistrate, and the other local authorities were on the alert; a few individuals were arrested, and happily the peace was preserved. An occurrence which took place on Saturday night, and which was wonderfully distorted and magnified, again endangered the peace of this district. Two black men were fighting in their own yard; a watchman interfered to keep the peace, and was, by one of the black men, cut with a scythe on the head, arm, and shoulders, in a very dangerous manner. A correct account of this affair was industriously and actively circulated, the public mind was informed and tranquilized, and peace preserved.

In the district of Spring Garden, an apprehension at one time prevailed, that an attack was contemplated on Type alley, inhabited principally by coloured people. Dispositions were made by the Police Magistrate of that district to avert the threatened calamity, but happily the peace of that neighborhood remained unbroken.--Since the night of the 15th, no attempt has been made to disturb the tranquility of any part of Philadelphia.

The committee have taken pains to ascertain the damage done, and the personal injuries inflicted. All the houses injured were occupied by colored people.--The houses in the same neighborhood, inhabited by white people, were preserved from injury by the white inhabitants showing themselves, with lights, at the doors and windows. More than thirty houses were, more or less, injured--a frame meeting house torn down, and the windows and sashes of another meeting house much broken. As the rioters broke into the houses, their inhabitants fled, many of them nearly naked, to save their lives. The furniture of the houses was utterly destroyed. The whole amount of damages is probably less than $4000. The damage sustained does not average to the sufferers a hundred dollars; but small as is that sum, it had been hardly earned, and it would require much time and labor to replace the things which were destroyed. They were the little all, of those to whom they belonged, and as the cold weather approaches, they will more and more feel the want of their stoves and their beds, and other necessities.--Many of these people were forced from their abodes, and for days were afraid to return; others were beaten severely, and one, we regret to say, died of his wounds. . . .

The case of Stephen James is entitled to some consideration. He was an honest, industrious colored man; a kind husband and a good father. He had retired to rest on the night of the 14th of August, but was aroused by the clamor of the mob. The cries which met his ears soon informed him that he was in danger, and he fled for safety; he was however overtaken, and wounded in many places, even unto death. He never spoke after he was found wounded, in the yard. The Committee do not believe that among all the persons, who made up the mob assembled on this occasion, there was one wicked enough to contemplate taking the life of an inoffensive and unoffending aged man--yet, in truth, they did this accursed thing. These facts are stated, to induce men to reflect upon the desperate deeds, which mobs, without desperate intentions, may commit. It may be proper here to state, that more than one of the peace officers were so seriously wounded that their lives were despaired of.

Some of the coloured population are yet under apprehensions, that, at no distant day, another attack will be made on their persons and property. The committee have diligently sought to acquire information as to the ground on which these apprehensions rest, and they have been unable to ascertain any facts which authorize them. As, however, the peace of every community, however large and peaceably disposed, may be endangered and broken, by the machinations of a few designing or turbulent persons, it is deemed a portion of the duty of this committee, to make such suggestions, as, in their opinions may tend to avert so dreaded an event, as an irruption upon the quiet of any portion of our population. Nothing will tend to win the good opinion, and secure the good offices of the community, more than a respectful and orderly deportment. It would do much good if those of the coloured population, whose age and character entitle them to have influence, would take the trouble to exercise it, and impress upon their younger brethren, the necessity as well as the propriety, of behaving themselves inoffensively, and with civility at all times, and upon all occasions; taking care, even as they pass along the streets, or assemble together, not to be obtrusive, thus giving birth to angry feelings, and fostering prejudices and evil dispositions. . . .

Resolved, That it is due to justice and to the character of this community, that the losses sustained by the unhappy sufferers, among whom are included those who were wounded in defence of the public peace, should be compensated.

Resolved, That a committee of fifteen be appointed to investigate the claims of the sufferers, to collect subscriptions from our fellow citizens, and distribute them in the most speedy and equitable manner, among those who have suffered, in proportion to their losses.

> JOHN BINNS,
> J. GOODMAN,
> PETER HAY,
> JAMES MOTT,
> A. HOOTEN,
> MORTON M'MICHAEL,
>   Committee. . . . .

Hazard's Register 14 (September 27, 1834):200-04.

21. ROBERT PURVIS' REACTION TO THE PHILADELPHIA RIOT [36]

Philadelphia, August 22, 1842

My dear friend Wright:

I have been absent from the city all of the past week. This I offer in excuse for not acknowledging your letter before this.

I am even now, in every way, disqualified from making proper answers to your [questions] in reference to one of the most ferocious and bloody-spirited mobs that ever cursed a Christian (?) community. I know not where I should begin, nor how or when to end in a detail of the wantoness, brutality and murderous spirit of the actors in the late riots, nor of the apathy and *inhumanity* of the *whole* community in regard to the matter. Press, Church, Magistrates, Clergymen and Devils are against us. The measure of our sufferings is full.

From the most painful investigation in the feelings and acts of this community in regard to us, I am convinced of our utter and complete nothingness in public estimation. I feel that my life would find no change in death, but a glorious riddance of a life weighed down and cursed by a despotism whose sway makes Hell of earth--we the *tormented,* our persecutors the *tormentors.*

But I must stop. I am sick--miserably sick. Everything around me is as dark as the grave. Here and there the bright countenance of a true friend is to be seen. Save that--nothing redeeming, nothing hopeful. Despair black as the face of death hangs over us--and the bloody *will* of the community [is] to destroy us.

In a few days perhaps I will write you again. To attempt a reply to your letter now is impossible.

Your brother,
Robert Purvis

Antislavery Collection, Boston Public Library.

22. PECUNIARY COST OF THE PHILADELPHIA RIOTS OF 1838

It is well known that the Anti Abolition mob of '38 was, to a great extent, a mercantile speculation--a bid for Southern trade, and that Pennsylvania Hall was a burnt-offering to both Mammon and Slavery. Whether our Esaus who bartered away order, peace and liberty have ever received their pottage in pay is doubtful. The table below which gives merely the *pecuniary* losses from the riots, bred by that great courage, does not tell much for the shrewdness of these speculators in honor and justice.

The *Philadelphia Inquirer* says: From the official sources, we learn that the following sums have been paid by the County of Philadelphia for riots, pay of military and civil posse, since the year 1842 up to 1849, inclusive:

1842	Lombard and St. Mary st. riots,	$6,363 50
1843	Kensington, pay of military, &c.	790 70
1843	Harper's brick yard,	22 50
1845	Damages from riots, pay of military, &c.	35,301 23
1846	Riot in Southwark, 1844	7,647 91
1846	Riot in Kensington, 1844	23,421 66
1847	Claims of troops,	8,000 69
1848	Judgment for damages in late riots,	53,498 69
1849	do. do. do.	34,815 59
	Total.	$172,866 84

Could we have added to these statistics the losses of life, of moral principle, and social restraints, of security at home, and reputation abroad, which are the most alarming expenses of those mobs, it would make a fearful balance against this city. But the end is not yet, nor know we when it will be. We have but just begun to reap the bitter harvest of our sowing. The future we hardly dare to explore in thought. Still the past may do one service to ourselves and the world, if we will heed its warning against the first step of wrong or violence.--

The Non-Slaveholder 5 (1850):167.

23. THE COLUMBIA (PA.) RACE RIOTS, 1834

Excitement ran high everywhere. Some idea of the state of affairs in Columbia at this time may be had when we read the following, which the chief burgess of the borough caused to be issued two days after the town meeting:

"Proclamation.

"Whereas there is at present an undue excitement in this town, and whereas there have been unlawful assemblages doing much damage and destroying the peace of the borough, and whereas numerous assemblages of people of color are particularly to be avoided, I do hereby command and enjoin it upon all colored persons from and after the issuing of this Proclamation and until publicity revoked, to cease from the holding of all public religious meeting whatsoever, of any kind, after the hour of 8 o'clock in the evening, within the borough limits. And I do further request of and enjoin it upon all good citizens to aid in the suppression of all disturbances whatsoever, and particularly to aid in the execution of this Proclamation and in all proper ways to prevent the good order of the town from being destroyed, the laws broken and the lives and property of the citizens endangered, so that all persons concerned, or aiding or abetting in such disturbances may be arrested and dealt with according to the utmost extent of the law.

"Given under my hand and seal of office as Chief Burgess of the Borough of Columbia, August 22, 1834.

"Robert Spear."

On Saturday evening, August 23, 1834, the day following the issuance of the Chief Burgess' proclamation, a meeting of the working men, and others favorable to their cause in the borough, was held in the town hall. Dr. Thomas L. Smith was appointed chairman and Joseph M. Watts, secretary. The following preamble and resolutions were passed at this meeting, without a dissenting voice:

"When a body of citizens assemble to concert measure for the protection of those inestimable rights secured to them by the constitution, they owe to the public a distinct statement of the grievances they meet to redress, so that disinterested and patriotic persons may not labor under any mistake or imbibe prejudices against them. We therefore, willingly detail to the people the causes that urged us to meet this evening, confident that the intelligent will approve and coincide with us in support of our measures. We cannot view the conduct of certain individuals in this borough, who by instilling pernicious ideas into the heads of the blacks, encourage and excite them to pursue a course of conduct that has caused and will continue to cause great disturbance and breaches of the peace, and which we are fearful if not checked will ultimately lead to bloodshed, without feeling abhorrence, disgust and indignation. The practice of others in employing Negroes to do that labor which was formerly done entirely by whites, we consider deserving our severest animadversions; and when it is represented to them that the whites are suffering by this conduct, the answer is, 'The world is wide, let them go elsewhere.' And is it come to this? Must the poor honest citizens that so long have maintained their families by their labor, fly from their native place that a band of disorderly Negroes may revel with the money that ought to support the white man and his family, commit the most lascivious and degrading actions with impunity, and wanton in riot and debauchery. Who in this town does not know in what manner many Negroes spend their leisure hours; and who, but one that has lost all sense of right and justice, would encourage and protect them? As the negroes now pursue occupations once the sole province of the whites, may we not in course of time expect to see them engaged in every branch of mechanical business, and their known disposition to work for almost any price may well excite our fears, that mechanics at no distant period will scarcely be able to procure a mere subsistence. The cause of the late disgraceful riots throughout every part of the country may be traced to the efforts of those who would wish the poor whites to amalgamate with the blacks, for in all their efforts to accomplish this diabolical design, we see no intention in them to marry their own daughters to the blacks, it is therefore intended to break down the distinctive barrier between the colors that the poor whites may gradually sink into the degraded condition of the Negroes--that, like them, they may be slaves and tools, and that the blacks are to witness their disgusting servility to their employers and their unbearable insolence to the working class. Feeling that this state of things must have a brief existence if we wish to preserve our liberties, therefore be it

"Resolved, That we will not purchase any article (that can be procured elsewhere) or give our vote for any office whatever, to any one who employs Negroes to do that species of labor white men have been accustomed to perform.

"Resolved, That we deeply deplore the late riots and will as peaceable men assist to protect the persons and property of the citizens in case of disturbance.

"Resolved, That the Colonization Society ought to be supported by all the citizens favorable to the removal of the blacks from the country.

"Resolved, That the preachers of immediate abolition and amalgamation ought to be considered as political incendiaries, and regarded with indignation and abhorrence.

"Resolved, That the editor of the Spy be requested to publish the proceedings of this meeting."

Another meeting of the citizens of the borough of Columbia assembled at the town hall on Tuesday evening, August 26, 1834, in pursuance of a printed call "to take into consideration the situation of the colored population, and to devise some means to prevent the further influx of colored persons to this place." James Given, Esq., was called to the chair, and Thomas E. Cochran appointed secretary.

The following resolutions were offered by Chief Burgess Robert Spear and adopted at the meeting:

"Resolved, That a committee be appointed whose duty it shall be to ascertain the colored population of this borough, the occupation and employment of the adult males among them, and their visible means of subsistence.

"Resolved, That a committee be appointed whose duty it shall be to communicate with that portion of those colored persons who hold property in this borough and ascertain, if possible, if they would be willing to dispose of the same at a fair valuation; and it shall be the duty of the said committee to advise the colored persons in said borough to refuse receiving any colored persons from other places as residents among them; and the said committee shall report their proceedings to the chairman and secretary of this meeting, who are hereby empowered and requested to call another meeting at an early period and lay before said meeting the reports of said committees that such order may be taken thereon as may be most advisable.

"Resolved, That the citizens of this borough be requested, in case of the discovery of any fugitive slaves within our bounds, to cooperate and assist in returning them to their lawful owners."

The last resolution was offered by Henry Brimmer.

The following committees were then appointed by the meeting:

On the first resolution, Messrs. James Collins, Peter Haldeman, Jacob F. Markley, John McMullen and William Atkins. On the second resolution, Robert Spear, Esq., Messrs. Henry Brimmer and James H. Mifflin.

At the adjourned meeting of the citizens convened at the town hall on Monday evening, September 1, 1834, to receive the reports of the committees appointed to inquire into the state of the colored population and to negotiate with them on the subject of a sale of their property, the officers of the former meeting resumed their seats.

The committees having made their reports, it was on motion

"Resolved, That these reports be remanded to the committees who offered them for the purpose of having resolutions attached to them, and that this meeting do adjourn until Wednesday evening next."

The meeting convened pursuant to adjournment on Wednesday evening, September 3, 1834. The committee appointed to inquire into the state of the colored population of the borough presented the following report and recommendation, which were adopted:

"Number of black population found in Columbia, Penna., on August 28, 1834; --214 men, 171 women, 264 children-- total 649.

"It is supposed that a good number have left the place within a few days, and that a number were scattered through the town that were not seen by the committee. Among the above men, the committee consider the following named persons as vagrants: William Rockaway, Henry Holland, Wash Butler, Charles Butler, Jacob Coursey, Joe Dellam, James Larret, Joseph Hughes, Abraham Waters, William Malston, Jr., and Lloyd Murray.

"A house occupied by John Scott and William Stockes, is considered by the committee as a house of ill fame; it is rented by Joshua P. B. Eddy to them.

> "James Collins
> "William Atkins
> "John McMullen
> "J. F. Markley
> "Peter Haldeman."

The committee also recommended the attention of the proper authorities as early as practicable to the above named vagrants and nuisances.

The committee appointed to negotiate with the blacks on the sale of their property, reported as follows:

"That they have endeavored to give that attention to the subject which its importance justly demands.

"They have, in the first place, ascertained as nearly as possible the names and number of colored freeholders in this borough, which according to the best information they could obtain they lay before you as follows, viz: Henry Barney, William Brown, Aaron Brown, James Burrell, Michael Dellam, Charles Dellam, Joshua Eddy, Walter Green, John Green, George Hayden, Widow Hayden, James Hollinsworth,--Henderson, Glascow Mature, Edward Miller, William Pearl, Nicholas Pleasants, Philip Pleasants, Jacob Dickinson, John Johnson, Ephraim Malson, Sawney Alexander, Robert Patterson, Stephen Smith, Peter Swails, John Thomas, James Richards, Betsey Dean (formerly Roatch), George Taylor, George Young, Stephen Wilts, Eliza Park, Thomas Waters, Samuel Wilson, Patrick Vincent, John Vincent and Washington Vincent--making all thirty-seven.

"They have called on most of them in person and think the disposition manifested by most of them decidedly favorable to the object of the committee. Some of them are anxious, many willing, to sell at once provided a reasonable price were offered--others would dispose of their property as soon as they could find any other eligible situation.

"All to whom your committee spoke on the subject of harboring strange persons among them, seemed disposed to give the proper attention to the subject. Your committee deem the result of their observation decidedly satisfactory.

"In presenting this report your committee would respectfully call your attention to the impropriety of further urging the colored freeholders to sell until some provisions are made to buy such as may be offered, lest they should be led to consider it all the work of a few excited individuals, and not the deliberate decision of peaceful citizens. They therefore recommend the subject of the attention of capitalists; having no doubt that, independent of every other consideration, the lots in question would be a very profitable investment of their funds, and that if a commencement were once made nearly all of the colored freeholders of the borough would sell as fast as funds could be raised to meet the purchasers. Your committee would further remark if everything was in readiness, considerable time would be required to effect the object; they would therefore recommend caution and deliberation in everything in relation to this important object.

"In conclusion your committee offer the following resolution:

"Resolved, That an association be formed for the purpose of raising funds for the purchase of the property of the blacks in this borough.

> "Robert Spear
> "H. Brimmer

"Jas. H. Mifflin."
The report and resolution were adopted, and the following committee of
five was appointed to form an association for the purpose of purchasing the
property of the blacks in the borough: Joseph Cottrell, Dominick Eagle,
John Cooper, Robert Spear and Jacob F. Markley. . . .

*William Frederick Warner, "The Columbia Race Riots," 26 (October, 1922):178-
82.*

24. ABOLITION RIOTS IN NEW YORK

Since the evening of the 9th instant, there have been nightly riots and
mobs in the city of New-York, *caused by the mad conduct of a class of visionary and fanatical zealots* in that city, who have taken the lead in the
wild scheme of *immediate* and unqualified emancipation of the blacks, and by
openly advocating the amalgamation of the blacks with the whites. Degraded
as are the instigators of these riots, the *cause* is still more disgraceful
and degrading to the character of an enlightened community. We had occasion
to allude to this subject nearer home some months since, and to express our
opinion of the impropriety and bad effects produced in community by the discussion of a question in itself so exciting, and so entirely out of the power of the people of this State to afford any salutary remedy. We regret to
learn that the subject has again been publicly broached in this city, and
that there is a *certain religious class among us* desirous of agitating the
subject at this time. *The example of New-York should deter them from so doing*. We have no desire to see the disgraceful scenes of that city re-enacted here; but if the matter should be carried to the same lengths in Utica,
may we not fear the same consequences to result from it? We trust the good
sense of our citizens will be directed against any public discussion of this
nature.--*Utica Observer*.

The Liberator, August 21, 1834.

25. ALLEGED RIOTING OF THE STEVEDORES

The Evening Post, last evening, contained the following statement relative to the longshoreman:
"*Riot of the Stevedores--The Strike for Higher Wages--Compelling Men
to Leave their Work--The Police called Out*.--A most high-handled measure is
now pursued by the stevedores on a strike for higher wages. Because merchants refuse to pay more than one dollar and a half per day these men are
determined that no work shall be done. Hundreds of poor men are desirous of
labor at the present price. No sooner, however, do they begin to work, than
they are pounced upon by these disturbers of the public peace.
"This morning, between 9 and 10 o'clock, about two hundred of the dis-
contended stevedores went to the packet-ship Lease Allerton, at Pier No. 50
East River. A large number of men were discharging the vessel under the orders of Wm. Nelson & Son, shipping merchants, in South, st. The rioters did
not go on board the ship, but demanded that the men should cease work.
Afraid of their lives, they complied with the request of the mob, and come
ashore.
"The rioters then fell upon the men and beat them severely. Mr. Nelson
sent for the Seventh Ward Police, who soon arrived and dispersed the rascals.

The men again resumed work on the ship, and the stevedores scattered. The
owners of Holmes's line of New Orleans packets have been paying one dollar
and fifty cents a day to the longshoremen for the past four weeks. They
load their vessels at the foot of Pine st., and have had occasions frequently to call upon the Police to protect their men.

"Negroes have been employed in the vessels of Morgan's London Line. At
dusk, last evening, while one of the colored men was going home from the
Margaret Evans, at Pier No. 48 East River, he was attacked by an Irishman,
who struck him on the head. The colored man was armed, drew a pistol upon
his assailent, and fired. The Irishman took to his heels, and it is not
known whether he was shot. At the time of the attack, only the two men were
present but in a few moments afterward, as if by magic, several hundred
longshoremen were gathered upon the wharf. The negro escaped from the crowd.

"The Police are stationed along the wharves of the North and East Rivers to day, to maintain order and to guard men at work in loading and discharging vessels. No disturbances have taken place on the North River side.
We observed squads of policemen at the wharves of the Charleston and Savannah streamers. . . .

New York Tribune, January 18, 1855.

26. ANOTHER MOB IN CINCINNATI

Sometime since a dispute arose between a negro fireman on a steamboat
and one of the white hands, which occasioned an altercation at St. Louis.
Last week, the negro arrived in our city, and met his antagoist on the landing, who was armed with a dray pin. Blows were exchanged, the negro snap-
ping a pistol, and it failing fire, threw it at his adversary and struck
him on the head. He was arrested and brought before the Mayor and held to
bail for farther examination on Monday, yesterday. It was rumoured that the
security intended to pay the amount and let the negro escape. This drew a
crowd around the house of the bail on Saturday, which was dispersed after
some threats had been made. The negro was brought before the Mayor yesterday morning for farther examination.--The Mayor ordered him to be committed.
A crowd having gathered in the street in front of the Mayor's office when
the marshal and his assistants brought out the prisoner on the way to the
jail, they were surrounded by the crowd--stones and other missiles were
hurled at them. The mob seized the negro, rescued him from the officers,
carried him to the river, and across into Covington, Ky. followed by the
officers and a great crowd of persons. The negro man was taken to a point
in Covington, where was a scaffold erected and ropes provided, and other
preparations made for hanging him without law or trial. They placed the
rope round his neck, and were deliberately proceeding to execute their purpose, when the Mayor of Covington with a police posse appeared on the ground,
cut the ropes and commanded the crowd to disperse, assuring them that if
they would proceed in their work of violence, they must go back to Cincinnati for that purpose. The resolute and honorable course of the Mayor of
Covington was successful in preventing a farther violence there. The mob
then took the negro man down the river and landed him in the lower part of
Cincinnati, when he was recaptured by our city police, and taken to prison.
They were pursued on their way by the excited and noisy crowd, hurling
stones at the officers. The police maintained their ground and committed
the negro man to jail. The last we heard of them they were in pursuit of
the rioters.

Cincinnati Gazette, September 14, 1847.

NORTHERN FREE BLACKS KIDNAPPED AND SOLD INTO SLAVERY

27.   BOSTON BLACKS PETITION THE GENERAL COURT ON
BEHALF OF THREE VICTIMS

To the Honorable the Senit and House of Riprisentetives of the common Welth
of Massachsetts bay in general court assembled February 27 17C3:
    The Petition of greet Number of Blacks freemen of this common welth
Humbly sheweth that your Petetioners are justly Allarmed at the enhuman and
cruel Treetment that Three of our Brethren free citizens of the Town of Boston lately Receved; The captain under a pertence that his vessel was in des-
tres on a Island below in this Hearber haven got them on bord put them in
irons and carred them of, from their Wives & children to be sold for slaves;
This being the unhappy state of these poor men What can your Petetioners expect but to be treeted in the same manner by the same sort of men; What then
are our lives and Lebeties worth if they may be taken away in shuch a cruel
& unjust manner as these; May it pleas your Honnors, we are not uncensebel
that the good Laws of this State forbedes all such base axones: Notwithstanding we can aseuer your Honners that maney of our free blacks that have
Entred on bord of vessels as seamen and have been sold for Slaves & sum of
them we have heard from but no not who carred them away; Hence is it that
maney of us who are good seamen are oblidge to stay at home thru fear and
the one help of our time lorter about the streets for want of employ; were-
as if they were protected in that lawfull calling thay might a hanceum
livehud for themselves and theres: which in the setturation they are now in
thay cannot. One thing more we would bege leve to Hint, that is that your
Petetioners have for sumtime past Beheald whith greef ships cleared out from
this Herber for Africa and there they either steal or case others to steal
our Brothers & sisters fill there ships holes full of unhappy men & women
crouded together, then set out to find the Best markets seal them there like
sheep for the slarter and then Returne near like Honest men; after haven
sported with the Lives and Leberties fello men and at the same time call
themselves Christions: Blush o Hevens at this.
    These our Wattey greevences we cherfully submeet to your Honores With-
out Decttateing in the lest knowing by Experence that your Honers have and
we Trust ever will in your Wisdom do us that Justes that our Present con-
dechon Requires as God and the good Laws of this commonwelth shall [one word
illegible--ed.] you—as in Deutey Bound your Petetioners shall ever pray.

*Herbert Aptheker (ed.), A Documentary History of the Negro People in the
United States (New York, 1950), pp. 20-21.*

28.   CAUTION! TO THE COLORED PEOPLE

    Beware of kidnappers! Two villains from Boston visited Salem a few
days since, and introduced themselves to some of the colored people there,
as particular friends of Garrison & Knapp, and as being there at their request; and also desiring to see a certain person supposed to be a runaway
slave.
    We all understand that a certain Constable in this city, is very active
in entering the dwellings of colored people, pretending to have search warrants, and ransacking their houses from cellar to garret, in search of fugitives from slavery. *Constables have no right to enter a house, without a
special Warrant for that purpose from some Judge, granted for a special
case.* Colored People, beware! put confidence only in such persons as you

know to be your friends.

The Liberator, August 3, 1836.

29. KIDNAPPING IN THE CITY OF NEW YORK

It is too bad to be told, much less to be endured!--On Saturday, 23d instant, about 12 o'clock, Mr. George Jones, a respectable free colored man, was arrested at 21 Broadway, by certain police officers, upon the pretext of his having 'committed assault and battery.' Mr. Jones, being conscious that no such charge could be sustained against him, refused to go with the officers. His employers, placing high confidence in his integrity, advised him to go and answer to the charge, promising that any assistance should be afforded to satisfy the end of justice. He proceeded with the officers, accompanied with a gentleman who would have stood his bail--he was locked up in Bridewell--his friend was told that 'when he was wanted he could be sent for.' Between the hours of 1 and 2 o'clock, Mr. Jones was carried before the Hon. Richard Riker, Recorder of the city of New York. In the absence of his friends, and in the presence of several notorious kidnappers, who preferred and by oath sustained that he was a runaway slave, poor Jones, (having no one to utter a word in his behalf, but a boy, in the absence of numerous friends who could have born testimony to his freedom,) was by the Recorder pronounced to be a SLAVE!

In less than three hours after his arrest, he was bound in chains, dragged through the streets, like a beast to the shambles! My depressed countrymen, we are all liable; your wives and children are at the mercy of merciless kidnappers. We have no protection in law, because the legislators withhold justice. We must no longer depend on the interposition of Manumission or Anti-Slavery Societies, in the hope of peaceable and just protection; where such outrages are committed, peace and justice cannot dwell. While we are subject to be thus inhumanly practised upon, no man is safe; we must look to our own safety and protection from kidnappers; remembering that 'self-defence is the first law of nature.'

Let a meeting be called--let every man who has sympathy in his heart to feel when bleeding humanity is thus stabbed afresh, attend the meeting; let a remedy be prescribed to protect us from slavery. Whenever necessity requires, let that remedy be applied. Come what will, any thing is better than slavery.

Yours, &c.   DAVID RUGGLES.

The Liberator, August 6, 1836.

30. THE CALL AT LYNN

Important Meeting!

The citizens of Lynn and vicinity are requested to meet at Lyceum Hall, on Friday evening, at 7 o'clock, to adopt some effectual measures to prevent kidnappers from stealing, and carrying off to the South, the peacable inhabitants of this Commonwealth. The case of George Latimer, who, a few days since, was kidnapped in the city of Boston, and manacled in the very halls of justice, and in presence, and under the direction of the sworn protectors of our liberty, and who is now lying in Leverett street jail, waiting the order of the Court to consign him to interminable slavery, ought to

arouse every working man in the country to a sense of his own personal insecurity.

Already the clank of chains is heard in our streets! The kidnapper is
allowed to go abroad, in open day-light, unharmed, while spotless innocence
is consigned to the felon's cell.

Husbands and Fathers! one and all, turn out! Let the New Cradle of
Liberty rock on Friday evening, as the Old one did, in the days of Hancock
and Adams.

If our present Government fails to protect us from the blood-hounds of
the South, it is high time to fall back upon our reserved rights!--LIBERTY
BEFORE CONSTITUTIONS!! The times demand a second rovolution!!!

The People's Advocate (Concord, New Hampshire), November 18, 1842.

31. LIABILITY TO BE SEIZED AND TREATED AS SLAVES

An able-bodied colored man sells in the southern market for from eight
hundred to a thousand dollars; of course he is worth stealing. Coloniza-
tionists and slaveholders, and many northern divines, solemnly affirm, that
the situation of a slave is far preferable to that of a free negro;--hence
it would seem an act of humanity to convert the latter into the former. Kidnapping being both a lucrative and a benevolent business, it is not strange
it should be extensively practised. In many of the States this business is
regulated by law, and there are various ways in which the transmutation is
legally effected. Thus, in South Carolina, if a free negro "entertains" a
runaway slave, it may be his own wife and child, he himself is turned into a
slave. In 1827, *a free woman and her three children* underwent this benevolent process, for *entertaining* two fugitive children of six and nine years
old. In Virginia all emancipated slaves remaining twelve months in the
State, are kindly restored to their former condition. In Maryland a free negro who marries a white woman, thereby acquires all the privileges of a
slave; and generally, throughout the slave region, including the District of
Columbia, every negro not known to be free, is mercifully considered as a
slave, and if his master cannot be ascertained, he is thrown into a dungeon,
and there kept, till by a public sale a master can be provided for him.--
But often the law grants to colored men, *known to be free,* all the advantages
of slavery. Thus, in Georgia, every *free* colored man coming into the State,
and unable to pay a fine of one hundred dollars, becomes a slave for life; in
Florida, insolvent debtors, *if black,* are SOLD for the benefit of their cred-
itors: and in the District of Columbia, a free colored man, thrown into jail
on suspicion of being a slave, and proving his freedom, is required by law to
be sold as a slave, if too poor to pay his jail fees. Let it not be supposed
that these laws are all obsolete and inoperative. They catch many a northern
negro, who, in pursuit of his own business, or on being decoyed by others,
ventures to enter the slave region; and who, of course, helps to augment the
wealth of our southern brethren. On the 6th of March, 1839, a report by a
Committee was made to the House of Representatives of the Massachusetts Legislature, in which are given the *names* of seventeen free colored men who had
been enslaves at the South. It also states an instance in which twenty-five
colored citizens, belonging to Massachusetts, were confined at one time in a
southern jail, and another instance in which 75 free colored persons from
different free States were confined, all preparatory to their sale as slaves
according to law.

But it is not at the South alone that freemen may be converted into
slaves "according to law." The Act of Congress respecting the recovery of
fugitive slaves, affords most extraordinary facilities for this process,
through official corruption and individual perjury. By this Act, the claimant is permitted to *select* a justice of the peace, before whom he may bring
or send his alleged slave, and even to prove his property by *affidavit.* Indeed, in almost every State in the Union, a slaveholder may recover at law a

human being as his beast of burden, with far less ceremony than he could
his pig from the possession of his neighbor. In only three States is a man,
claimed as a slave, entitled to a trial by jury. At the last session of the
New York Legislature a bill allowing a jury trial in such cases was passed
by the lower House, but rejected by a *democratic* vote in the Senate, democracy in that State being avowedly only *skin* deep, all its principles of liberty, equality and human rights depending on complexion.

Considering the wonderful ease and expedition with which fugitives may
be recovered by law, it would be very strange if mistakes did not sometimes
occur. *How* often they occur cannot, of course, be known, and it is only
when a claim is *defeated,* that we are made sensible of the exceedingly precarious tenure by which a poor friendless negro at the north holds his personal liberty. A few years since, a girl of the name of Mary Gilmore was
arrested in Philadelphia, as a fugitive slave from Maryland. Testimony was
not wanting in support of the claim; yet it was most conclusively proved
that she was the daughter of poor *Irish* parents, having not a drop of negro
blood in her veins; that the father had absconded, and that the mother had
died a drunkard in the Philadelphia hospital, and that the infant had been
kindly received and *brought up in a colored family.* Hence the attempt to
make a slave of her.--In the spring of 1839, a colored man was arrested in
Philadelphia, on a charge of having absconded from his owner *twenty-three*
years before. This man had a wife and family depending upon him, and a
home where he enjoyed their society; and yet, unless he could find witnesses
who could prove his freedom for more than this number of years, he was to be
torn from his wife, his children, his home, and doomed for the remainder of
his days to toil under the lash. *Four* witnesses for the claimant swore to
his identity, although they had not seen him before twenty-three years! By
a most extraordinary coincidence, a New England Captain, with whom this negro had sailed *twenty-nine* years before, in a sloop from Nantucket, happened at this very time to be confined for debt in the same prison with the
alleged slave, and the Captain's testimony, together with that of some other
witnesses, who had known the man previous to his pretended elopement, so
fully established his freedom, that the Court discharged him.

Another mode of legal kidnapping still remains to be described. By the
Federal Constitution, fugitives from *justice* are to be delivered up, and under this constitutional provision, a free negro may be converted into a
slave without troubling even a Justice of the Peace to hear the evidence of
the captor's claim. A fugitive slave is, of course, a felon--he not only
steals himself, but also the rags on his back which belong to his master.
It is understood he has taken refuge in New York, and his master naturally
wishes to recover him with as little noise, trouble, and delay as possible.
The way is simple and easy. Let the Grand Jury indict A. B. for stealing
wearing apparel, and let the indictment, with an affidavit of the criminal's
flight, be forwarded by the Governor of the State, to his Excellency of New
York, with a requisition for the delivery of A. B. to the agent appointed to
receive him. A warrant is, of course, issued to "any Constable of the State
of New York," to arrest A. B. For what purpose?--to bring him before a magistrate where his identity may be established?--no, but to deliver him up to
the foreign agent. Hence, the Constable may pick up the first likely negro
he finds in the street, and ship him to the South; and should it be found,
on his arrival on the plantation, that the wrong man has come, it will also
probably be found that the mistake is of no consequence to the planter. A
few years since, the Governor of New York signed a warrant for the apprehension of 17 Virginia negroes, as fugitives from justice. Under this warrant, a man who had lived in the neighborhood for three years, and had a
wife and children, and who claimed to be free, was seized, on a Sunday evening, in the public highway, in West Chester County, New York, and without
being permitted to take leave of his family, was instantly hand-cuffed,
thrown into a carriage, and hurried to New York, and the next morning was on
his voyage to Virginia.

Free colored men are converted into slaves not only by law, but also
contrary to law. It is, of course, difficult to estimate the extent to
which illegal kidnapping is carried, since a large number of cases must escape detection. In a work published by Judge Stroud, of Philadelphia, in

1827, he states, that it has been *ascertained* that more than *thirty* free colored persons, mostly children, have been kidnapped in that city within the last two years.

The Colored American, March 21, 1840.

32. INFORMATION WANTED

A colored man named Horace Hitchcock, is now confined in New Orleans Jail, on charge of being a slave. He affirms he is a free man—says he was born in New Lebanon, N. Y., in the year 1805; is known to Messrs. Brown & Morris, Hardware Merchants, J. Wilson, Dry Good Merchant, and Mr. Woodruff, Public Notary. Any information respecting this man, tending to establish his claim to freedom, will be thankfully received. Ministers of colored churches will serve the cause of humanity by reading this notice in their congregations.

Any communications may be directed to the office of the Colored American, post paid, or to 198 Hudson street, New York city.

Editors friendly to the cause of liberty, will please to insert this notice.   J. JOHNSTON.

The Colored American, June 6, 1840.

33. RALLY IN BOSTON

. . . Then rally, ONE AND ALL, to the meeting on Sunday evening, and let the OLD CRADLE OF LIBERTY rock as it did in "the times that tried men's souls," and let the majestic voice of a FREE PEOPLE be heard, "like the voice of many waters," in favor of IMPARTIAL LIBERTY and UNIVERSAL EMANCIPA-TION! Even now, kidnappers infest our community! Even now, one made in the Divine image—created free by the power and grace of God—a MAN, a BROTHER, lies incarcerated in Leverett street jail, charged with no crime, guiltless of all wrong-doing against society, *without even the forms of law, or any legal authority whatever,* at the bidding solely of the kidnapper—claimed as a SLAVE—a THING—and in a few days to be hurried to the South, to be cut to pieces by the infernal lash of the slave driver—unless he be rescued by THE STRONG ARM OF LIBERTY! No citizen is safe! The color of the skin has ceased to protect any of us from the doom of slavery! Are we not able to protect ourselves! SHALL WE NOT DO IT! Or shall we basely consent to give up our rights to any ruffians who may choose to take them from us? Let FANEUIL HALL answer! [37]

The meeting will be addressed by several distinguished advocates of equal rights and impartial liberty.

Boston, October 29th, 1842.

The People's Advocate (Concord, New Hampshire), November 18, 1842.

34. THE CHIVALROUS JAMES B. GRAY

MR. EDITOR:--I happened to be present last evening at a conference of
citizens at the house of S. Hill, of South Boston, and had an opportunity of
seeing the man at whose *dictum* Boston jail is converted into a yard, and a
Boston jailor into a paid herdsman for one of his human cattle; and as it may
be interesting as well as *important* to some to know how a soul-hunter looks,
I will just say, that he is about five feet nine inches high, dark complexion. Whoever looks in his face will perceive at once a want of one of the
most important properties of a man, viz, a soul; which, however, is supplied
by a sort of hyena energy. His object obviously was to take vengeance upon
the sympathizing benevolence of the citizens towards his victim, George Latimer, for the trouble and expense which he had been at in the pursuit of his
victim, which in his estimation was considerable, as he said he had put $200
in the hands of his lawyer, &c. &c.--not forgetting his heardsman.

It was truly painful, in listening to his talk about the *nigger,* to see
how slavery can eat out all that is lovely in human nature. The following,
as near as can be recollected, was the conversation which passed between him
and those present.

Citizen--Have you a wife and children, sir?
Answer--Yes.
Citizen--Then you know the feelings of a father and husband?
Ans.--I didn't come here to talk about that.
Another citizen--How much are you willing to sell Latimer for?
Gray--Put yourself in my situation and what would you do?
Cit.--Adopting your sentiments, and putting myself in your situation, I
should expect he would run away again if he could, and to save myself, if I
got him back to Norfolk, I should sell him to the highest bidder, to go far-
ther South.
Gray--If I get him back, *he'll not run away again.*
Another cit.--You will be under the necessity of using great severity
to prevent him from attempting it.
Gray, with a slaveholder's look--*I know how to keep him.*
Cit.--How much are you willing to take for him?
One of his Guardians--[He had two men with him, who seemed to exercise
a watchful supervision over him]--You have left it with your attorney, have
you not?
Gray--Yes, I have left the figures with him; he will tell you.
Cit.--What was the character of Latimer before he left you? was he
honest?
Gray--I shouldn't think he was honest, to treat me so; this is the sec-
ond time he has run away from me, and the second time he has stolen from me.
Cit.--Well, as to his running away, that was quite natural. Would not
you run away if any one should attempt to hold you as a slave?
Gray--Me! I hope you don't think I'm a *nigger!*
Cit.--But as to the money, don't you think he had earned it?
Gray--Earned it! when?
Cit.--When in your service.
Gray--He was my slave.
Cit.--That may be; but that does not alter the justice of the case.
Gray--Justice! Don't you think that slavery has existed from the begin-
ning?
Cit.--There has been a devil from the beginning; but that makes neither
slavery nor him any better.
Gray--I didn't come here to talk about that.
Cit.--How could Latimer get at your money to steal it?
Gray--He was my salesman; I trusted him with the store; he could get as
much as he wanted.
Cit.--Is it not singular, Mr. Gray, if, as you say, Latimer was dishon-
est and had stolen from you before, that you should trust him in that manner
again?
Gray--Ahem, ahem--I forgave him that time.
Cit.--Has Latimer a wife?

Gray--A woman he lived with.
Cit.--How long had he lived with her?
Gray--About ten months.
Cit.--Don't you think Latimer has the feelings of a man?
Gray--I shouldn't think he had, or he wouldn't have given me all this trouble.
Cit.--Don't you think he loves his wife?
Gray--He love his wife? Niggers!--I didn't come here to talk about that.
Cit.--Latimer is part white, is he not?
Gray--He's touched with white; he's *merlatter*.
Cit.--They are apt to get "touched" in that way at the South, are they not?
Gray--They mix 'em here at the North; I see black and white walking together since I been here.
Cit--Yes; but at the South you seem to have the faculty of mixing black and white in one person.
Gray--Well, I didn't come here to talk about that.
Cit.--Does his wife belong to you?
Gray--She didn't; but she does now.
Cit.--Did you buy her since she ran away?
Gray--I have a power of attorney, and shall take her back.
[Mark that, colored men! and keep your eye out for Judases.]
Cit.--Has she any children?
Gray--She's had one since she came here.
Cit.--Well now, Mr. Gray, as Latimer loves his wife and child, and wants freedom, would you not find pleasure in making some sacrifice yourself and allow us to pay the rest, and let him have his freedom?
Gray--I didn't come here to talk about that. I've told you what I'd take for him, and I wont take a cent less. [Rising up to go.]
Cit.--You mean you have left the figures with your attorney. But, Sir, instead of carrying back your man or the money for him, you may carry back the frowns of God for your heartless cruelty. Good night.

Really, Mr. Editor, while listening to this rare specimen of Southern humanity, this soulless thing, which by the partiality of Southern law, is "second among sentient things," I could but think, were the slaves half as soulless, it were less crime to reckon them among "things," "chattels." He is just one of those petty tyrants, subjection to whose caprice is worse than death. Poor Latimer! Poor Latimer!!
A SPECTATOR.

The People's Advocate (Concord, New Hampshire), November 18, 1842.

35. ASSOCIATION OF FREE BLACKS TO AID FUGITIVE SLAVES [38]
FREEDOM ASSOCIATION, BOSTON, 1845

The object of our Association is to extend a helping hand to all who may bid adieu to whips and chains, and by the welcome light of the North Star, reach a haven where they can be protected from the grasp of the manstealer. An article of the constitution enjoins upon us not to pay one farthing to any slaveholder for the property they may claim in a human being. We believe that to be the appropriate work of those at the North, who contend that the emancipation of the slaves should be preceded by the compensation of the masters. Our mission is to succor those who claim property in themselves, and thereby acknowledge an independence of slavery.
Fugitives are constantly presenting themselves for assistance which we are at times unable to afford, in consequence of the lack of means. Donations of money or clothing, information of places where they may remain for a temporary or permanent season as the case may demand, are the

instrumentalities by which we aim to effect our object. We feel it to be a
legitimate branch of anti-slavery duty, and solicit, therefore, in the name
of the panting fugitive, the countenance and support of all who "remember
those in bonds as bound with them." . . . Donations are punctually acknowledged in some of the anti-slavery papers.

The Liberator, December 12, 1845.

36. KIDNAPPING IN HARRISBURG

Harrisburg, Sept. 30, 1849.

FRIEND DOUGLASS.--During the past week a family of five or six persons
arrived in this place, from the peculiar, contented, happy, religious, pious
and Christian Institution of the South, and feeling themselves secure from
the grasp of bloodhounds of the south and north, who are ever ready to scent
the track of the flying bondman.

They dismantled themselves of those habiliments by which a fugitive from
the peculiar institution may be known, and set themselves now to rest. They,
however, were not permitted to rest in peace.

On Saturday the 29th inst., as one of their number was passing along
Front street on the river bank, he was pursued by two men, and after a considerable chase they overtook him, and endeavored to get him to the bridge.
Fortunately, two colored men observing the chase, joined the parties, and effected the release of the fugitive, his pursuers making good their escape
across the river.

The seizure of a man in open day in one of the most public thoroughfares
of the Capital, for the purpose of reducing him to bondage, did, as might be
expected, create a considerable excitement among the citizens. [39]

The North Star, October 12, 1849.

PART V

BLACK WORKERS IN SPECIFIC TRADES

BLACK WORKERS IN SPECIFIC TRADES

Even though black workers were barred from many occupations by racial discrimination, and sometimes by mob violence, there were certain occupations where large numbers of blacks labored. Waiting on tables in northern hotels, restaurants, and saloons represented one of those occupations employing conspicuously large numbers of blacks. Wages and conditions were generally poor enough among waiters that they occasionally formed unions to improve their lot. One such organization, the Waiters Protective Association, after winning concessions from the employers, received an invitation to attend a meeting of white waiters and advise them how they might do the same (Doc. 1). This is the only known example before the Civil War of a white union requesting a black union to participate in a joint meeting. The Negroes were not invited to join, only to participate. A rival black waiters' union had been formed about the same time, and it pledged to work even if the white union did strike for higher wages (Doc. 3). The Waiters Protective Association denounced these black brothers as traitors, charging that they were in collusion with the employers (Doc. 4-5).

One of the most glaring deficiencies in Afro-American historiography is the almost total lack of interest in black seamen. Although they have been ignored for the most part, blacks represented a very important percentage of the workers in that dangerous, exploited, and underpaid occupation. One of the earliest studies of black seamen was published in a series of articles printed in the National Anti-Slavery Standard n 1846. The articles reveal the atrocious conditions of life for black sailors, such as excessively hard work, brutal officers, excessive fees for food and lodging while ashore, and countless other harassments. All too often these problems were compounded by too much alcohol and too little education (Doc. 6-10). The black sailor faced his gravest danger, and degradation, if his ship anchored in a southern port. Beginning in the 1830s, southern port towns from Charleston to New Orleans imprisoned free black seamen at their own expense until the ship took sail. Every southern coastal state passed these legal restrictions as security precautions against the possible importation of seditious ideas about slavery, the proliferation of which they associated with free Negroes (Doc. 16-32). This constituted a serious breach of federal law in the case of black citizens from the North and produced a storm of controversy until the Civil War. On several occasions black subjects of Great Britain were detained, producing scandalous international incidents with potentially serious repercussions (Doc. 25-29).

Black ship caulkers, who practiced the skilled craft of sealing the seams of newly-built wooden ships with hot tar to waterproof them, also encountered serious racial handicaps as they pursued their labor. The Baltimore shipyards, which employed large numbers of Negroes, both slave and free, was the scene of innumerable acts of violence perpetrated by white caulkers attempting to drive off black competitors (Doc. 33-39). Violence was a fact of life at the yards, and ranged from individual fisticuffs to mob murder, and illustrates the depth of animosity produced by economic competition exacerbated by racism.

FREE BLACK WAITERS

1. MEETING OF THE HOTEL AND SALOON WAITERS --
FORMATION OF A PROTECTIVE UNION

One of the most numerously attended, harmonious and efficient meetings
which has been convened since the commencement of the general movement for
an increase of remuneration among the working class, we held last evening at
the Grand Street Hall, near Broadway, in this city. It was composed of the
waiters employed in the various hotels, saloons and restaurants, as well as
ballmen and waiters in private families. At half-past 8 o'clock, the room
was crowded to suffocation, there being nearly five hundred men present,
among whom the colored population of the profession was very well represented.

The meeting was called to order by Mr. William Hamilton, of the Union
Place Hotel. Mr. H. said: Gentlemen, we have assembled here for the purpose of forming, in this city, a Waiters' Protective Union Society. It is
well known to you that such associations exist in almost all other large
cities. Heretofore, it has been the idea among waiters that they were altogether depending for employment and support upon the landlords. This is a
mistake, for it is the landlords who are depending upon us. But, however
widely this may be known, even then the landlords will scarcely acknowledge
it, and will not give us more wages than they can help. The aspect of the
times demands that you should receive more for your services than twelve
dollars a month. With the present high rents and rates of provisions, your
families are brought to the verge of starvation. The same causes -- rents
and rate of market -- have caused the landlords to raise the price of board
and hotel charges; and, if they press so heavily on them, how must they be
felt by the poor waiter, who has his wife and family still, but only has his
twelve dollars? Rents have rendered it impossible that we can be generous to
the landlords. The colored waiters are before us in this respect -- they
won't work for less than sixteen dollars a month; and in the Metropolitan
Irving House, and another house downtown, where they are employed, they get
the sixteen dollars. The main reason why white men work for ten, twelve and
fourteen dollars a month, is that they are generally driven, by a combination
of unfortunate circumstances, to become waiters, and are, in a manner,
ashamed of being so, and are consequently indifferent. Another reason is
that the white men put too much confidence in the head waiters, who, most
generally, have laid down a fixed standard which the under men shall work
for, and thus, while they themselves are receiving from thirty to fifty dollars a month, and do not find the pressure at all, the real working man is
not paid for his labor as he ought to be. There is no disgrace, gentlemen,
attached to the profession of a waiter, for it requires an active, intelligent man, of good moral character and honesty, to be cone, and if you now be
true to yourselves, you will dignify your calling and character.

Mr. HAMILTON read the preamble, constitution, and by-laws of the Waiters' Protective Society.

The preamble recited the necessity of an organization. The rules were
proposed to be twenty in number, and make provision for the formation of the
society, admission of members, duties of officers, and initiation fees. It
is proposed that all honest, sober waiters join the Union; that members
shall not work with expelled members or others who have not joined; that the
standard rate of wages shall be $18 a month; and that an office be hired for
the transaction of business, where regular members can obtain situations,
and employers form all parts of the States help of the waiter class.

The reading of the paper was received with loud and repeated cheers.

Mr. ADOLPHUS SWIN was appointed President pro tem, and made a very forcible speech upon putting the question of the adoption of the rules.

Mr. S. then pointed out the general rise in the price of board in Boston and New York. It was caused by high rents; but the poor waiter had to
pay rent also, and his means were not increased. Many amongst you are

prevented from marrying, and thus adopting a barrier against vice and dissipation, owing to the impossibility of sustaining a family upon twelve dollars
a month. Your Sundays and your week days are all alike. If you ask the religious hotel keeper, who heaps in his twenty or sixty thousand dollars a
year, "if you can go to church or to mass," what does he reply? Just this,
"I do not employ you to go to church; I pay you to work." And yet perhaps
this hotelkeeper is a member of a Bible Society, or subscribes to send missionaries out to the countries of the far Pacific, or the desert of Sahara,
at the moment he refuses you a just remuneration for your time, and thus
contributes to your moral and social degradation.

Mr. FLORNEY of the Mercantile, made a very eloquent speech in favor of
the formation of the union.

Mr. HICKMAN (colored), of College place, said the colored men are the
pioneers of the movement, and would not work for less than eighteen dollars
a month, only they dreaded that the numerous body of white man would have
taken less if they left. Gentlemen, I advise you to strike upon the 15th of
April for $18 a month, and if the landlords do not give it, that you turn
out, and be assured that we will never turn in in your places at less.
(Cheers.)

Mr. Swin, Mr. Hamilton, and Mr. Florney, were appointed a committee to
revise the by-laws, which are to be submitted for final adoption, at a mass
meeting to be held upon the 15th of April. The contribution of members was
fixed at 12-1/2 cents per month.

The great unanimity and good humor prevailed, and the meeting was excel-
lently managed. The objects will be more completely developed upon the 15th
of April.

New York Herald, March 31, 1853.

2. ADVERTISEMENTS OF THE WAITERS UNION

WAITERS -- WE HAVE RAISED THE STANDARD. Let us defend it. We, the
waiters of the New York Hotel, return our sincere thanks to Messrs. Coleman
& Stetson, the worthy and generous proprietors of the Astor House, for their
speedy compliance with the demands of our Union, and to the waiters of that
establishment for their firmness in demanding their rights.

WE, THE WAITERS OF THE NATIONAL HOTEL, Cortlandt street, take this
method of expressing our sincere and hearty thanks to Mr. George W. Seely,
the worthy proprietor of the National Hotel, for the very gentlemanly and
satisfactory manner in which he not only expressed his willingness, but also
delcared his intention, to increase our wages from its present standard to
that of $18 per month, to take effect on the first proximo.

WE, THE WAITERS OF THE ASTOR PLACE HOTEL, return our sincere thanks to
Messrs. Coleman and Stetson, for being the first in giving the wages demanded at our first union protective meeting; may you long enjoy the good name
you have so justly earned, by your boarders and helps, for being the first
in everything that's good. May those who first get up our Protective Union
long live to see it go on prosperously and may their names be as dear to the
waiters of this country as Washington's is to the people of the United States.
The poor African that's stole from his native land, sold a slave, he buys his
freedom, has got more than we white men, and sons of freemen; we have demanded eighteen dollars, so come on, come all, get your shoulder to the wheel;
the colored men are at your back, and never stop till you roll eighteen

dollars to the top. There are one or two houses to come forward yet. The
Union must and shall be protected.

New York Herald, April 5, 1853.

3. FIRST UNITED ASSOCIATION OF COLORED WAITERS

At a meeting of the First United Association of the colored waiters of
New York, held on the 11th day of April, at 156 Church street, it was unanimously
     Resolved, That a committee of three be appointed to prepare and publish
an exposition of the general objects of this Association.
     On a motion being made, the following persons were appointed to carry
out the object of the resolution:--T. G. Campbell, Jeremiah Dickerson and
Ezekiel Buston.
     The general objects and intentions of the First United Association of
the Colored Waiters of the city of New York are these:--
     1. Seeing the generally degraded position that waiters, as a class,
hold in the scale of society, and knowing that moral and intellectual improvement is the only sure method by which any class can be elevated, we have
therefore resolved to improve our minds, and by precept and example try to
reform all with whom we may hereafter become associated, and endeavor to make
gentlemanly deportment with a practical knowledge of the professional indispensable requirements to membership and advancement in the Association.
     2. In view of the encouragement given to us by the keepers of the ho-
tels, saloons, and boarding houses in this city, we feel that in gratitude it
becomes our duty to remain in the city, and not go to the Springs and water-
ing places, as we have heretofore done, (unless such prices as will renumer-
ate us, and being poor, we owe it as a duty to our families and to ourselves
to seek employment where it is most to our advantage,) knowing that permanent
employment is the only sure way of producing identity of interest between the
employer and the employed. We, as a society, recommend all our members to
remain in the city, and by so doing, show their interest in the business in
which they are engaged; and we trust, by this means, to establish a mutual
feeling of confidence and good will between the employer and the employed,
and that each will feel that the interest of either is the interest of both.
     3. Therefore, the resolutions which we have published contemplates the
raising the wages in the country, because, in the city the wages have always
been regulated by the demand for all classes of help, and hence we are willing to trust to the proprietors themselves, from the encouragement already
given, to arrange such a scale of prices as will be satisfactory to us -- the
colored waiters of the city of New York.
     And we, the members of the First United Association of the Colored Wait-
ers of the city of New York, take this method of expressing our sincere and
hearty thanks to Mr. George W. Seely, the worthy proprietor of the National
Hotel, for the very gentlemanly and satisfactory manner in which he not only
expressed his willingness, but also declared his intention, to increase our
wages from its present standard to that of $18 per month, to take effect on
the first proximo.
     We, also, hereby deny any connection with the contemplated strike of the
waiters on the 15th inst., as that idea never was countenanced by this Association. We, therefore, hope that all will definitely understand that we
have nothing to do with the contemplated strike, either directly or indirectly.
                              T. G. CAMPBELL   )
                              JEREMIAH DERICKSON) Committee
                              EZEKIEL BUSTON   )

The following are the resolutions of the First United Association of the Colored Waiters of the city of New York, adopted at a meeting held on the 9th day of March last, at No. 18 Thomas street.--

Resolved, In review of the encouragement given by the proprietors of the hotels of the city of New York, that we, the waiters of New York, will not leave the city, as heretofore, unless such prices are paid as will justify poor men in making such change.

Resolved, That we will discharge our duties faithfully, as waiters, or in any occupation we may be engaged to fill.

Resolved, That in no instance will we leave the city of New York for the purpose of acting as waiter, or other calling, for a sum less than $16 per month, with passage, &c., paid.

Resolved, That it shall be the duty of every head waiter, when taking charge of a house out of the city, to secure for all men under him $16 per month, and any person having such charge, and refusing to make said demand, shall be considered incapable of filling the place to which he aspires, and all shall be at liberty to leave him.

Resolved, That, in our opinion, it is better to remain in the city, and work for the current prices than to leave, even in case the same prices and our passage, &c., are paid.

Resolved, That no second waiter shall go out of the city for a sum less than $20 per month, and passage, &c., paid.

JOHN CAMPBELL, JR.)
TUNES G. CAMPBELL) Committee
PETER J. HICKMAN)

NOTICE.-- A public meeting of this Association will be held at the El Dorado Hotel, Church street, on Friday evening next, April 15.

New York Herald, April 13, 1853.

4. AROUSE WAITERS

TRAITORS IN THE CAMP

To the white waiters of New York City--

We the colored waiters of New York city, hereby declare that we have no communion with the meeting of April 11 (as may be supposed,) or with T. G. Campbell, J. Derickson, and E. Buston, or with the meeting assembled there on that night.

And we hereby declare our intention of intending the meeting of the 15th inst., at Grand Street Hall, and so abide by the decision of that meeting. We are sorry to see the name of any man in connection with the abovementioned individual, for they are traitors to the Union.

New York Herald, April 14, 1853.

5. MEETING OF THE WAITERS' PROTECTIVE UNION

Between seven and eight hundred waiters assembled in Grand Street Hall last evening, to adopt measures to secure an advance of wages from twelve and fourteen dollars a month to eighteen. The first meeting was held about two weeks ago, since which time the proprietors of several eating houses, saloons, hotels, &c., have granted the increase demanded. Those who have not, it is expected, will not hold out much longer; but should they still persist in refusing, it is the intention of the waiters to strike. A society of colored waiters has also been formed, and they are prepared to co-operate with the white waiters in any movement of the kind that may take place. To prevent inconvenience to their employers by such action, should they desire to reengage their own men on a strike, a general place of meeting will be designated at which both employers and employed can assemble and reconcile their differences.

The meeting was called to order at eight o'clock by the President, Adolphus Schwind. The minutes were read by the Secretary, W. F. Hamilton, and received with repeated cheering and a unanimous approval. The Secretary stated that the committee had engaged an office at 483 Broadway for the agency of the society. He then read the constitution and by-laws which were adopted at the last meeting. A list of such waiters as desired to join the society was handed in from the different hotels, eating houses, &c., with their initiation fees, which amounted in the aggregate to about four hundred dollars.

The President made an appropriate address, when the preliminary business was transacted. He recommended union among the waiters as the only means by which they could secure their demands. Several hotel keepers had granted the advance, while others offered to do so, but only on condition that they should not join the society. This, said Mr. S., they refused to do. (Applause.) He spoke also of an editorial article in yesterday's HERALD, as a proof that the press of the city supported the movement of the industrial classes for increased wages. This allusion was received with three cheers for the HERALD.

Mr. Florey next addressed the meeting. He disavowed on behalf of the waiters any intention to indulge in riotous proceedings, or to interfere with the peace of society. They were determined, nevertheless, to have their rights, and for this purpose they had formed a society, which would procure from them a fair remuneration for their labor. He mentioned several proprietors of hotels who had acceded to the demands of the waiters; among them were Messrs. Coleman & Stetson, Mr. Judson, and Mr. Ford. He also read a long list of head waiters who had joined the society, and expressed the opinion that there would be no occasion for a strike, as all their employers would grant the advance which had been asked. The society of waiters, he said, was calculated not only to benefit them materially, but to give them a more respectable position in society and in public opinion, than they had hitherto occupied. Mr. F. concluded by calling for three cheers for the HERALD for the manner in which it had supported the just demands of the waiters. The cheers were given and repeated.

Mr. JOHN THOMAS (colored) of the Irving House, made a few remarks in relation to an advertisement published in the HERALD a few days ago, by some society of colored waiters, which he said was calculated to injure all who had joined in the present movement, both colored and white. That society, he desired it to be understood, did not represent the majority of the colored waiters of the city, and what they had done should not therefore be regarded as the action of that majority. He concluded by promising, on behalf of the colored waiters, a hearty co-operation with the whites.

Addresses were also made by Mr. J. REID and Mr. HAMILTON, after which the following song was sung by Mr. W. E. Topley, the audience joining in the chorus:--

> Waiters, all, throughout the nation,
>   Why will you every be
> Overburdened by oppression --
>   Overawed by tyranny?
>
> Wait for the good time coming no longer;
>   Claim at once what is your due;
> Toil no more like slaves, and hunger,
>   To support an idle few.
>
>   CHORUS:

Be of good cheer, and do not fret.
A golden age is coming yet.

See your wives and children tender
   Badly clothed and pine for bread,
While your bosses live in splendor,
   And off dainty dishes fed.

If, united, you are the stronger,
   Why not to yourselves prove true?
Toil no more like slaves, and hunger,
   To support an idle few.

Be of good cheer, &c.

At the conclusion of this song, the meeting adjourned.

New York Herald, April 16, 1853.

BLACK SEAMEN

6.   COLOURED SEAMEN--THEIR CHARACTER AND CONDITION.

NO. I

   1st. *Statistics of coloured Seamen in the United States.*
--It has always been to me a matter of surprise why measures have not been
taken long to ascertain, if possible, the number of coloured seamen in the
United States. Thousands of our people have lived and died in the naval service; and many of our fathers, brothers, and friends, yet live to tell the
tales of their perilous adventures. As I have said, very little, if anything, is recorded in history as to the active part our people took in the
great struggle for national rights. So that so far as my knowledge extends,
I am only enabled to present such facts as will confirm whatever may appear
to some minds to be doubtful.
   In the debates of the New-York Convention, for amending the Constitution
of the State, in 1821, Dr. Clarke, the delegate from Delaware county, speaking of the coloured inhabitants, said: "In the war of the Revolution these
men helped to fight your battles by land and sea. In the late war they contributed largely towards some of your most splendid victories. On Lakes Erie
and Champlain, our fleets were manned in a large proportion with coloured
men."
   Governor Morrill, of New Hampshire, in a speech in Congress, in 1820,
said: "Your soldiers of colour have fought your battles. They have defeated
your country, they have preserved your privileges, but they have lost their
own."
   By an estimate recently made, England, the greatest commercial country
in the world, only exceeds this country in tonnage of ships a few thousand
tons. Now, add to this fact the gigantic strides of this infant Republic in
agriculture, which has brought the mother-country to our doors begging for
bread, the increase of her commerce, and, as we shall hereafter show, that
the increase of coloured seamen most assuredly keeps pace with the prosperity
of the country, the unconstitutional Southern laws to the contrary, notwithstanding; because, whilst they do prohibit coloured seamen coming into their
ports sailing from Northern ports, they *do not* prohibit and imprison coloured
seamen when sailing from one Southern port to another, so that whilst the

Charleston, Mobile, and New-Orleans ports are closed against us, it opens a
market and gives employment to Southern coloured seamen. It does not reduce
the number of coloured seamen, whilst it may throw them out of employment in
the Southern trade. Will the North see to it, how this invidious distinction
is made between her commercial interests and that of the South?

By a careful estimate I have prepared a table of the number of coloured
seamen sailing from the principal and minor ports in the United States, viz:

Coloured Seamen sailing from port of	New-York,	2200
" " " " "	Boston,	1000
" " " " "	Baltimore,	600
" " " " "	Philadelphia,	500
	all other ports,	1700
	Total,	6000

There are eighty vessels of war in the United States Navy, including
ships of the line, first and second class frigates, sloops, brigs, schooners,
steamers, and storeships. Of thus number we must also include vessels in the
Revenue service, (say about twenty,) making one hundred vessels of all
classes. The highest number of coloured men on board the Pennsylvania at one
time was eighty, and on board the North Carolina, fifty. The number of coloured men on board the other vessels varies according to the number of guns
they carry. But it is not a regulated rule in the service to apportion coloured men according to the rate of the vessel. Though a successful motion
was made and passed in Congress in 1843, to exclude coloured seamen from the
naval service, *waiters* and *musicians* excepted, yet, to my certain knowledge,
no regard is paid to this law. Subsequent to the passage of this law, in
fitting ships for the African station, the Secretary of the Navy issued a
special order to ship a larger proportion of coloured men than usual. Then
again, another rule is to ship one coloured to every twenty white seamen; but
in either case it is at the discretion of the Secretary of the Navy.

Of the one hundred vessels of war, there are eighty-five in actual service, in commission, or as receiving ships, and including those in the revenue service. The number of coloured seamen in the naval service, as near as
can be ascertained, (the largest vessels having eighty, and the smallest
five, would give us an average of eighteen, or an aggregate of fourteen hundred and thirty, deducting the fractions,) in round numbers, is *fourteen
hundred*.

In the absence of official documentary evidence, I venture to offer so
much to this table as being correct. But in order to satisfy the most scrupulous, I will endeavour to remove any objections upon which they may hang a
doubt. I have laboured seven years in this city in behalf of coloured seamen, during which time I have closely investigated every fact in connection
with this interesting subject, and whenever a vessel of war arrived in this
or other ports, more especially those within my personal knowledge, I have
endeavoured to ascertain the number of coloured seamen on board each vessel.
In doing this, I have generally selected the most intelligent of the crew,
either white or coloured men, of undoubted veracity, who have kindly furnished me with all the necessary information.

In the summer of 1839, when the North Carolina arrived from her last
cruise, her complement of men being eight hundred, there were fifty coloured
men. So with regard to the Independence, in 1840, the Ohio, Delaware, Columbus, and the Pennsylvania, (the latter having eighty coloured men.) All of
these were ships of the line. Then there also arrived at this port several
frigates, sloops-of-war, brigs, and schooners, having on board from forty,
thirty, twenty-five, eighteen, down to five coloured men in each of the several classed vessels. Of this number discharged from the navy, one-third,
and in some cases one-half have boarded at the Coloured Sailors' Home. I
think I am safe in my estimated table; if not, the errour can only be detected at *head quarters*. Will the Secretary of the Navy correct the table
if wrong?

Statistics of coloured men sailing from the different whaling ports in
the United States, with a table of the number of ships sailing from each
port, viz:

TABLE.

Ports.	Ships, Brigs, and Schrs.	Coloured Men.
New Bedford,	252	1,008
Dartmouth,	2	8
Falmouth,	4	16
Fairhaven,	49	196
Mattapoisett,	11	44
Sippican,	5	20
Wareham,	5	20
Westport,	11	44
Nantucket,	73	292
Edgertown	10	40
Holmes' Hole,	4	16
Provincetown,	23	92
Plymouth,	5	20
Boston,	2	8
Fall River,	7	28
Freetown,	2	8
Portsmouth,	1	4
Providence,	9	36
Bristol	6	24
Newport,	12	48
Warren,	24	96
Lynn,	3	12
Salem,	2	8
Somerset,	1	4
Mystic,	17	68
New London,	77	308
Stonington,	27	108
Sag Harbour,	63	252
Greenport,	11	44
New Suffolk,	2	8
New-York,	1	4
Cold Spring,	8	32
Bridgeport,	3	12

Total number of ships	732	Total number of coloured men, 2930

In the table for coloured seamen engaged in the whaling service, I have
given the average number to each vessel. Some ships manning five boats, very
often have from ten to twelve coloured men, second and third mates, three
boat-steerers, five foremast hands, and cook, and steward. There is not that
nice distinction made in the whaling as there is in the naval and merchant
services; a coloured man is only known and looked upon as a MAN, and is promoted in rank according to his ability and skill to perform the same duties
as the white man; his opportunities for accumulating pecuniary means--invest-
ing his earnings in whaling capital, is equally the same. Hence the necessity, and in fact it is to the INTEREST of the whaling merchants, to keep
constantly in their employ a large proportion of coloured men. Very few
ships carry less than six coloured men, while many have more. In fact, there
can be no doubt about the actual number of coloured men engaged in the whaling service; the table may vary, but in my opinion, not enough to effect it
materially. The number of ships are correct, and from my knowledge of whaling, having performed one voyage myself, and resided eleven years in New Bedford, one of the largest whaling ports in the Union, I think I am nearly correct. If in errour even in this, I stand corrected.

The number of coloured men engaged in the international navigation cannot be less than three thousand six hundred. For instance, there are four
thousand canal boats on the inland transportation in different sections of
the Union: add to this the number of steamboats on the Lakes, the Mississippi, and other rivers of the Southwestern States; say one thousand--allow the
number of coloured men to the one thousand steamers to be fourteen hundred,
and this would give us five thousand coloured men engaged in the internal

canal and steam navigation, or an average of one to each vessel.

RECAPITULATION.

Coloured men in the merchant service,				6,000
"	"	naval	"	1,400
"	"	whaling	"	2,900
"	"	internal navigation,		5,000
	Total,			15,300

The estimated marine of the United States according to Capt. Thomas B. Sullivan, (exclusive of the internal navigation) is 150,000, including the naval and merchant service, the whale, cod, and mackerel fisheries. Of this number, 25,000, or 16 2/3 per cent are Americans, the remainder being foreigners representing every tribe under heaven. Allowing the ratio of coloured seamen to be 1-15 of the estimated marine, (and this, I am informed on good authority, is the common ratio in this case,) it would give us ten thousand now in service, excluding those engaged in internal navigation. There is, however, one important fact which I wish to notice; of the one hundred and fifty thousand seamen in the United States, only twenty-five thousand are Americans. We claim one-half of the American seamen in the merchant and naval service, &c. &c. to be coloured men.

National Anti-Slavery Standard, September 14, 1846.

7.   COLOURED SEAMEN--THEIR CHARACTER AND CONDITION.

NO. II

Statistics of coloured seamen imprisoned in Southern and foreign ports.

In order to get at the truth, in regard to the number of coloured seamen imprisoned in Southern and foreign ports, I shall be under the necessity of making further extracts from the laws of the State of Louisiana, enacted in the spring of 1842, which makes the person liable to be punished by imprisonment FIVE YEARS--and if found in the State thirty days after, shall be indicted therefor, and on conviction, shall be punished by *imprisonment at hard labor for life.*

SECTION 1. Be it enacted by the Senate and House of Representatives of the State of Louisiana, in General Assembly convened, that from and after the time specified in this act, no free negro, mulatto, or person of colour, shall come into this State, on board of any vessel or steamboat, as a cook, steward, mariner, or in any employment on board said vessel or steamboat, or as a passenger; and in case any vessel or steamboat shall arrive in any port, or harbour, or landing, on any river of this State, from any other State or foreign port, having on board any such free negro, mulatto, or person of colour, the harbour master, or other officer having charge of such port, or any person or persons residing at or near said landing, shall forthwith notify the nearest Judge or Justice of the Peace, in the parish in which said port or harbour or landing is situated, of the arrival of said vessel, or steamboat, whereupon the said Judge or Justice of the Peace shall immediately issue a warrant to apprehend and bring every such free negro, mulatto, or person of colour, before him; and on the execution of said warrant, by bringing before him such free negro, mulatto or person of colour, he shall forthwith commit him or her to the parish jail, there to be confined until said vessel or steamboat shall be ready to proceed to sea, or to her place of destination, when the master or commander of such vessel or steamboat, shall, by the written permit or order of the said Judge or Justice of the Peace, take and carry away out of this State, every such free negro, mulatto, or person of colour, and pay the expenses of his or her apprehension and detention.

SEC. 3. Be it further enacted, etc.--That if the master or commander of any vessel or steamboat, on board of which any free negro, mulatto, or person of colour, shall have been brought into this State, shall refuse or neglect to transport and carry out of this State, such free negro, mulatto, or person of colour, then the said Judge or Justice of the Peace shall order the same to be done by the Sheriff of the parish, and in the parish of New Orleans by either of the sheriffs or marshal of New Orleans, who shall thereupon be bound to transport or send out of the State, such free negro, mulatto, or person of colour, at the proper cost and charge of such free negro, mulatto, or person of colour, if he or she have the means to pay the same, and if not, at the expense of the State, to be paid out of the penalty recovered under this act or otherwise, on the warrant of the said Judge or the Justice of the Peace.

SEC. 4. Be it further enacted, etc.--That every free negro, mulatto, or person of colour, who, after having been transported or sent out of this State, in pursuance of this act, shall return into it, shall on conviction thereof, before a court of competent jurisdiction, be punished by imprisonment at hard labor for five years; and if such free negro, mulatto, or person of colour, shall be found in this State, thirty days after the expiration of said imprisonment, he shall be indicted therefor, and on conviction, shall be punished by imprisonment at hard labor for life.

SEC. 6. Be it further enacted, etc.--That any person who shall introduce or bring into this State any free person of colour, in violation of this act, shall be punished on conviction thereof, by fine, not exceeding two hundred dollars for the first offence, and for the second, by imprisonment not exceeding six months, and by a fine not exceeding one thousand dollars.

SEC. 7. Be it further enacted, etc.--That any person who shall employ, or harbor, or entertain as a boarder, or lodger, any person of colour, residing in this State contrary to law, shall, on conviction thereof, be punished by a fine not exceeding two hundred dollars for each offence.

The reader will please notice that in the laws of Louisiana, no provision is made, (as is the case with South Carolina,) that these acts shall not extend, or that coloured seamen shall be exempted from imprisonment who have arrived in the State by SHIPWRECK, or STRESS of WEATHER, or UNAVOIDABLE accident, or who shall arrive in the State, in any port or harbour, employed as mariners, cooks, or stewards, in any vessel of WAR of the United States, or on board any national vessel of the navies of any European or other powers in amity with the United States; but all are liable to be seized upon and thrust into prison on account of their colour. A case in point. Here is a letter addressed to me three years ago, by a Robert Anderson. It will speak for itself:

NEW-YORK, March 7th, 1843.

Mr. William P. Powell--Dear Sir:--I have been in New Orleans six months, in the United States schooner Essex, Captain Charles Wolf. I sailed from New Orleans to Florida, and then back to New Orleans; on our arrival, two officers came on board the schooner and wished to know my name. I told them Robert Anderson, and they asked the steward his name, and he told them John Burton. They took us both out of the vessel, and put us in prison, and kept us there TWENTY-ONE days. We had to pay fifty cents a day for board. They gave us ONE loaf of bread, which costs THREE cents, and ONE half pound of beef and pork, and TWO potatoes, which is to last TWENTY-FOUR hours. No tea or coffee unless we put our hands in our pockets and buy it. If we want any hot water to shave or to use we must pay extra. They don't give us any bed to lay on, unless we get bed and bedding from our ship. We had to pay our jail fees, the Recorder's and officers' bills. They do treat coloured seamen very bad. Indeed, they refused to take the Captain as bail for us.

ROBERT ANDERSON.

As I depend mainly upon facts, in order to make my case good, I will give a few of the many brutal outrages committed upon the liberties of the poor defenceless coloured sailor, in his own country, and in the same State

where, thirty-two years ago, coloured men POURED out their life's blood, to
defend their wives, their children, and their homes, from British bayonets,
rapine and murder!

JOHN H. SLATE, a native of Connecticut, shipped as steward of the bark
Gulnare, and sailed from the port of Boston to New Orleans--was taken from
on board his vessel at New Orleans, and imprisoned for want of evidence to
prove his freedom, was compelled to work in the chain-gang FOUR YEARS and
SIX MONTHS, employed ditching in the winter, and digging graves for the public cemetery. If sick, charged ONE dollar per day, to increase the jail
fees--was allowed only TWENTY-FIVE cents per day for labour, food, stinking
meat and corn. Slept on the naked plank floor; he was finally released
through the interference of lawyer Randolph, who was paid for his services
out of the balance of the money due him from the State. This poor fellow arrived in this city destitute and crippled, the iron shackle which he wore on
his ancle for four years and six months, having chafed the FLESH off to the
BONE. Oh! I shall never forget the shadow of that poor boy, as he crossed
the threshold of the coloured Sailors' Home, and asked for charity--his emaciated form reduced to a mere skeleton. To look at his ancle made my heart
sick. "Shall I not visit for these things," saith the Lord, "shall not my
soul be avenged on such a nation as this."

In the year 1840, CHARLES BECKET, an inmate of the Sailors' Home, shipped as cook on board ship Chester, of this port, and sailed for New Orleans.
Was discharged there, sick--took a boarding-house, and had not been long
there when, he was taken from his place of abode, late in the evening, and
taken before the Recorder and imprisoned. Not having any free papers, he
was sentenced to work in the chain-gang till he could prove his freedom. He
was three years in the chain-gang. Lawyer Randolph secured his liberty.
Charles Becket also returned to this city, and boarded at the Sailors' Home.
He was a native of the State of Delaware.

WILLIAM THOMPSON, a native of Pennsylvania, and whose father was ten
years in the United States naval service during the last war, shipped on
board of ship Havre, of Boston, Captain McClown, bound to New Orleans; was
discharged, and joined the ship Mary Elizabeth. Was on board the said ship
three weeks--was discharged from her, and joined another ship for Europe.
Had liberty to go ashore for a few hours. When his liberty had expired, he
returned to his ship. A police officer came on board, and asked him for his
free papers. Not having any, he was taken to prison, and there kept till
tried--was sentenced to work in the chain-gang. Was ONE year and five days
a prisoner. William Thompson says he is well acquainted with John H. Slate
and Charles Becket. Were all prisoners together, and worked in the same
gang. He was also released through the influence of lawyer Randolph.

Another way in which colored seamen lose their liberty in New Orleans,
which I must mention in order to account for a large number who cannot be
found in the parish jail, and whose friends suppose them to be dead.

It is customary in New Orleans for masters of vessels, that is if they
lay two or three months waiting for freight, to discharge the crew; previous
to the law of 1842, a large number of ships carried coloured crews, who were
either discharged, or left the vessel of their own accord, the same also with
white seamen. The wages in New Orleans, generally, is for seamen, cooks, and
stewards, from eighteen, to twenty-five dollars per month, which is a sufficient inducement for seamen to sail out of the port. Large ships generally
lay down to the Balize, several miles below the city, and these finish loading, and when ready the crew are articled, and sent down to the ships in tow-
boats. If seamen are scarce, it is a matter of no consequence whether they
get white or coloured; either are shipped in a great hurry--take the advance
money of twenty-five dollars per month, not knowing what kind of vessel they
are to join. All they know is, that the vessel lays down to the BALIZE, and
they are ready to go on board when called for. Now, very often the coloured
sailors get deceived. Instead of going on board of a ship at the Balize,
they are transferred and distributed among the pilot boats, where they are
compelled to work, sometimes for LIFE, like galley slaves. The pilots will
not pay them one cent of wages, and if they dare to say they are free, they
are whipped and punished with such cruelty, that they are glad to have the
opportunity at any and at all times, to say that they are SLAVES.

I have seen and conversed with eight who have been fortunate in getting
away. Some have been discharged by the pilots, (after having been five
years in Slavery,) and put on board ships outward bound, without a cent of
wages, and glad to get off at that, others are released through the interference of friends, or the civil authorities and thrust into jail, and if
free, they are shipped, and get off that way, others NEVER get their freedom.

On the first of this month a young man called on me for assistance to
enable him to get home to Boston. His name is John H. Roberts, the son of
Deacon Roberts, a worthy coloured man, and I believe a member of "the old
South Church."

The following is the substance of his written statement. I sailed from
Boston, October 26th, 1845, for Rio de Janeiro, in the bark Effort, Capt.
Hussey, was taken sick three weeks on the passage out, and remained so during the voyage--the Captain refused to give me any medicine. He also refused to let me go ashore at "Rio," and go to the hospital, but told me to
go to h--l. He did, however, make the attempt the next day to get me into
the hospital, but the day being a great festival, he was unable to get a
permit, so, without medical aid, I was compelled to remain on board till I
arrived in New Orleans, when I was taken out of the ship, and shut up in
prison; my disease, the dysentery, preying upon my system--obliged to lay on
the naked floor--my food uncooked except the bread. I had about fifty dollars due me from the ship. I wrote a note to the Captain (as also did the
keeper of the prison) to send me some money, but he did not. I was confined
twenty-eight days, when the Captain, finding me unable to join my ship and
go to work, cursed and swore at me, and sailed for Marseilles. I was finally taken out and put on board one of the New-York packets, and arrived at
this port. The Captain made me pay my jail-fees, which was *fifteen* dollars.
In consequence of the neglect and treatment I received at New Orleans, my
health is entirely prostrated.

National Anti-Slavery Standard, October 8, 1846.

8. COLOURED SEAMEN--THEIR CHARACTER AND CONDITION.

NO. III

*Statistics of coloured seamen imprisoned in Southern
and foreign ports.*

JACOB BROWN, a native of Nova Scotia, shipped as cook of the brig Oce-
ana, of Boston, and sailed for New Orleans in January, 1841. The captain
and mate conspired to sell him as a slave in New Orleans. Was compelled to
leave the vessel without his wages. Soon after shipped as cook to join the
ship Lafayette, for Liverpool, laying at Slaughter-House Point--wages twenty-
five dollars per month. Put his clothes on board the tow-boat Tiger, to
join said ship. When near the Point, inquired for the ship, and was told
the ship had gone down further--when upon the second inquiry, was told that
he had shipped to the pilot boats at the Balize. There were eight other
coloured men shipped the same way, and all compelled to work without pay.
There were sixty-eight free coloured men on board the several pilot boats at
the Southwest and Southeast Pass, all made to work as slaves, some employed
as pull-away boys, others repairing sails and rigging. A large number of
these men were finally released by the civil authorities.

In my humble efforts to vindicate the character and condition of coloured seamen, I am aware that in order to bring my country to the bar of
public opinion, and the world, to be adjudged for the outrages and cruelties
inflicted upon the poor defenceless coloured sailor, when in the prosecution
of his lawful business, much depends upon the WEIGHT of evidence, and to use
a legal phrase I must keep a single eye to the LAW and the TESTIMONY.

Doubtless there are many who will not believe all the statements in the last number, as to the treatment the individuals therein named received at New Orleans; then again, there is another class who do not believe that a sailor can *tell* the truth, but sneeringly treat their story as a *forecastle yarn,* to enlist the sympathies of credulous citizens. But the difficulty does not lay here--it is the Southern States and their Northern apologists, who will not believe, and hence the difficulty to get the truth before them, and even if they should believe, you cannot get the newspapers to publish these *wrongs,* even as an item of information. There is, however, some fairness now and then to be found, of which the following extract from the report of the grand jury of the parishes of New Orleans, &c. &c. is a specimen. It is Southern testimony, and corroborates the statements of the principal sufferers.

"In this prison, our attention was attracted to several *negroes,* principally females, *who are detained from inability to prove their freedom, some more, some less, than from one to four years.* They most of them represent themselves to be from other States of the Union; and name persons of respectability therein, who can furnish proof of their being free, could they but find the means of informing each persons of their present situation. It occurred to the members of the jury that it might be an act of charity, on the part of the Mayor, to procure a weekly or other periodical report of such cases, accompanied with a statement from each party so committed, the truth of which he could ascertain by applying to the references given, either by correspondence, or otherwise; then deal with the parties accordingly; for if these people are really free, and only require means to establish their freedom, it would certainly not be a praiseworthy act to detain them incarcerated two years, and then sell them as *slaves,* as the laws provide for; whilst with a little trouble their freedom might be substantiated, and they sent back to the State to which they belong; and on this point, we feel authorized to state that Mr. Planchard, the present keeper, is ready and willing to take any trouble that humanity and justice call for in such cases. . . .

The police prison of the second municipality, cannot be denounced in too strong terms, to the reprobation of the public. The prisoners, principally black, are kept locked up in small rooms . . . without a blanket to lay on; although the keeper admitted that they were supplied to the establishment. The rooms are floored on the ground, six or eight inches below the level of the ground, are filthy, full of vermin, several of them are not closed, having none but iron-railed doors and windows, thereby leaving the inmates exposed to the cold and wet.

"Painful as it may be, it is, nevertheless, our *duty* to present a series of malpractices connected with this prison. *There are men now in it, who have been there for months and years, without having had a hearing before the Recorder.* On our inquiring into the cause of this, the reply of the keeper was, 'I don't know. The Recorder receives regularly every morning a report of the prisoners, and orders before him those he thinks proper.'--Others are detained from inability to prove their alleged freedom, being *foreigners,* and not having the means of producing such proof, they are kept in prison for years, without further notice; to what good purpose, it is difficult to understand.

"That the public may judge by facts, we beg leave to report the following cases, merely remarking that the dates of their respective imprisonments are taken from the books of the prison, corroborating, in most instances, the report of the prisoners, who represent themselves as free persons:

No. 1. *Augustus Smith,* 18th August, 1840. This is a mulatto man, says he is a native of the Spanish Main. Has never been before the Recorder.

No. 2. *John Harvey*--imprisoned 24th April, 1839: a black man. Says his free papers have been taken to the Recorder by Mr. Jacob Barker--but he himself has never been before the Recorder.

No. 3. *Louis Polony,* imprisoned 28th September, 1839: a *Griffe*--says he is a native of Gaudaloupe--came here in the American brig Lucy, from New York; had his certificate of baptism on board, and lost the opportunity of producing it, the vessel having left the port shortly after; was never before the Recorder.

No. 4. *Charles Banks,* a black; imprisoned 18th September, 1843; never before the Recorder.

No. 5. *John Booyes,* called Buckett, --imprisoned 19th September, 1840-- a free black, native of Nassau, New Providence--never taken before the Recorder.

No. 6. *Jeremiah Carroll,* February, 1841--a black man. Says his case was investigated by the Mayor, in whose hands his free papers now are. Was taken up in second Municipality shortly after--never taken before the Recorder.

No. 7. *Solomon Mandlop,* a black, imprisoned above a year; had been taken up in the first Municipality, found here contrary to law, and discharged by the court, and subsequently taken up in the second Municipality; never taken before the Recorder.

No. 8. *William Wallace,* a mulatto, imprisoned 22d January, 1839; never before the Recorder.

No. 9. *Francis Quin,* a black, imprisoned 25th December, 1840; never before the recorder.

No. 10. *Solomon Jones,* an Indian, imprisoned 25th of August, 1849; is a native of Philadelphia, his mother is an Indian; has been once before the Recorder.

"Most of these persons, and many others now confined, came to this port from different ports of the United States, and are all made to work in the chain-gang as *Slaves*.

"All of which is respectfully submited,
                                    "CHARLES J. DARON, Foreman.
"New Orleans, February 4th, 1842."

The States of Virginia, Georgia, and Alabama, like South Carolina and Louisiana, have enacted similar laws imprisoning coloured seamen. At the port of Norfolk, coloured seamen when discharged from the Naval service, are not permitted to leave without first having their discharge signed by the Mayor of the city. He is under police regulations till north of Mason & Dixon's line, and before he leaves Baltimore he must produce personal white evidence to prove his identity as the person holding said certificate of discharge as countersigned by the Mayor of Norfolk. Below is a copy of a discharge from the naval service; the holder being sick and unfit for duty:

No 1346.--This is to certify that *John Blossom,* landsman, being considered as unfit for duty, is, by order of the Hon. Secretary of the Navy, regularly discharged from the United States ship Pennsylvania, and from the sea-service of the United States.
        (Approved.)   JOHN DE BREE, *Purser*
    J. PAUL ZANTZINGER, *Captain.*
    Norfolk, 13th January, 1843.

On the back of this certificate is the following permission from the Mayor:

John Blossom, landsman. Colour, black, Age. 20 years. Height, 5 feet 6 inches. Hair, woolly. Eyes, black. Complexion, negro. Born--New Hampshire.

The bearer, John Blossom, is at liberty to proceed to New-York, in the Virginia packet.

                                          M. KING, Mayor.

No. 186.--This is to certify that Andrew Robinson is regularly discharged from the United States ship Cyane, and from the sea-service of the United States. Norfolk, 10th October, 1844.   JOHN D. GIBSON, *Purser.*
    GEORGE NICHOLAS HOLLINS, *Commander*

Norfolk Borough, to wit:
    I, William D. Delany, a Justice of the Peace of the Commonwealth of Virginia, in and for the said Borough, do hereby certify that John Bedell, master of the schooner, Ann D. now lying in Norfolk, and bound for New-York, has this day produced before me a certain negro man, named ANDREW ROBINSON, who has been regularly discharged from the United States ship Cyane, as proved by the certificate of John D. Gibson, purser, and approved by Captain Hollins, Commander of said ship.

Given under my hand and seal, this 15th day of October, 1844
      [seal.]   WM. D. DELANY, Mayor.

So much for the laws of Virginia, that when a coloured sailor having
served his country from two to four years in the naval service, and honourably discharged from the sea-service by the Hon. Secretary of the Navy, he
is seized upon by the laws of Virginia, and not permitted to leave without
the *consent* of the corporate authorities at an expense of *two* dollars. Will
the Secretary of the Navy please turn his attention to this matter, and extend to coloured seamen at least the protection of the Government whilst
thus employed? Or will he suffer the broad seal of the United States to be
trampled in the dust by the authorities of Norfolk?

The Legislature of Alabama have passed a law to imprison all the coloured seamen that may arrive in the port of Mobile from sea, and to retain them
in prison at the expense of the owners of the vessels to which they may belong, until the vessel is ready for departure.

Some inquiries having been made by the writer of this of an intelligent
ship-master relative to the law, and the presumed reasons for passing it, he
has given us the information, which we herewith communicate to you for publication.

The avowed reasons for passing this law, was the alleged fear, that the
coloured seamen of the North, having experienced the blessings of freedom,
might contaminate their slaves, and thus cause insurrection.

Ships bound to Mobile, anchor off Cedar Point, distant thirty miles from
the city, and in a wide, open roadstead. In almost every case, the boats are
hoisted in, and no communication permitted by the masters with the city, except through passing steamboats, or return lighters. The coloured portion
of the crew, are never permitted to go on shore, and the ship-masters have
informed the authorities, that in case any coloured seamen go on shore, they
would--however illegal to imprison a seaman, charged with no crime except
having a black skin--interpose no objection to his detention. This would
seem to be sufficient to satisfy the people, or rather the mob city of Mobile.

The law further provides, that the Marshal shall receive a fee of *five*
dollars for taking, and *five* dollars for retaining each coloured seamen,
which must be paid by the ship-owners.

The necessity of this law is yet to be explained.

It is the custom in the Bay of Mobile for crews of unemployed vessels to
assist in loading the ships taking cargoes; for this service they receive, or
rather the loading ship is charged, at the rate of two dollars per day, one-
half of which goes to the seamen employed. This is a service they are eager
to perform. The extra pay furnishes them with their small stores. Now the
whole purport of this law is, to break up the loading ships by their crews,
as far as possible, and to give to the slave-owners of Mobile employment for
their slaves, at high prices. The merchants and men of business are opposed
to it, but in vain.

It is seen by all men that this great question must be met by the people of the North; it obtrudes itself everywhere; the spirit of Slavery requires us to violate the trial by jury under penalties known to be unconstitutional Menaces of dissolution of the Union, have been again and again
thrown out; and now the free coloured people of the North are to be kept in
prison, that the slave owners of Alabama may find profitable employment for
their slaves. We shall meet this great question; and if our great statesmen
of the North desert us in the hour of need, other and worthier leaders of the
people will not be wanting; one that at least, though borne down with the
weight of years, will leave a bright example of faithfulness to the cause of
human freedom.

The more I look at this subject, the more I see of Slavery. It is evident the South in this matter (as well as in Church and State) are determined
to reap a rich harvest; there is no satisfying our *Southern masters*.

The people of the North have given them two-thirds of all the offices,
both civil, military, and naval, in the gift of the National Government, in
order to replenish the exhausted pockets of their profligate sons. The *Tar-
iff*, the laws, and indeed everything is made to bend to the wishes of the

South, who live upon the toils of unrequited labour. They prate about *protection* to American industry--protection to slave property. They claim the
right, under the law of 1792, to come into the free States and pounce upon
the coloured man, be he ever so free, and consign him to perpetual slavery.
And now with the same high-handed injustice, enact laws to seize and imprison free coloured men when coming into their ports, as an excuse to prevent
insurrection among their slaves, when the truth is, these laws operate pecu-
niarily to the benefit of slave owners.

The *island of Cuba,* taking advantage of the example of the Southern
States, have also framed laws to imprison coloured seamen, except Indian,
Malays, Lascars, subjects of China, and the South Pacific Ocean. Every negro seized with *woolly* hair, no matter how *white* his complexion may be, is
thrust into prison.

Now as it regards the number of coloured seamen imprisoned in Southern
and foreign ports. I think the foregoing facts are sufficient to deduce the
following table. The reader will bear in mind that there are no slaves condemned to work in the chain-gang at New Orleans. All are free coloured men.
I have been particular to ascertain the number of coloured men imprisoned at
New Orleans, and learn that the average number is not less than *thirty-five*
per month, for twelve months, whilst in some months, the number upon an
average (say six months) is not less than fifty. *Nineteen* coloured men were
taken out of vessels in one day; in fact, according to the statement of men
who have been in prison, and the sworn testimony of not less than one hundred
can be had, if desired, there is not a day passes without prisoners coming in
under this law.

From the same authority I learn that the ports of Charleston, Savannah,
Mobile, and the different ports of CUBA average, for Charleston, *twenty* per
month. Savannah, seventeen; Mobile, seventeen; Cuba, eight. A provision is
made in the laws of Cuba, that captains may give bonds for *one thousand dollars,* and thereby prevent the imprisonment of cooks, stewards, or seamen,
amenable to this law; or else the number of *Cuba* would be much greater. I
have been told by Mr. William H. Davis, who was imprisoned in Charleston
Jail, that there were seventy coloured seamen, belonging to different vessels, in prison at the same time.

I think I am safe, (relying as I do, mainly upon the testimony of men
whose veracity I have good reason to believe,) in my table, viz:

No. of col'd seamen in New Orleans Jail in one year				420
"	"	Charleston	"	240
"	"	Savannah	"	204
"	"	Mobile	"	204
"	Islands of Cuba		"	100
				1168

Eleven hundred and sixty-eight American citizens imprisoned in different
parts of their own and foreign countries, for no other crime than for the
crime of colour! Americans, look at this and blush!!

Before I finished this number, for the benefit of the generous North--
the lavishing non-slaveholding States, to help their *dear* Southern brethren
to defray the expenses of their own State Government, I will now foot the
bill.

The general rule is to charge the vessel fifty cents per day for board
for every coloured prisoner, besides charges for commitment. Then each vessel must employ a cook, at one dollar per day; the cook is generally a female slave, especially in Charleston.

The result will be as follows, viz:

For board and other incidental expenses, the North are
made to pay for imprisoning coloured seamen at New Orleans,
for one year,

"	"	$159,600
"	" Charleston	91,200
"	" Savannah	78,120
"	" Mobile	80,160
"	" Island of Cuba	37,940
		$447,020

Add to this charges for commitment,
        discharges, and jailors' fees   52,980
                                                    ──────────
                                                       $500,000

National Anti-Slavery Standard, October 15, 1846.

        9.   COLOURED SEAMEN--THEIR CHARACTER AND CONDITION.

                            NO. IV

        Statistics of Coloured men -- Captains and Officers of
                Merchant and Whaling Vessels.

        It is difficult, as I before observed, to ascertain the whole truth in
relation to definite numbers which go to make up a fair and correct estimate
of the character and condition of coloured seamen, as it regards the number
of coloured men, captains and officers of whale-ships. As I have said in a
former number, there is not that nice distinction in the whaling as there is
in the merchant and naval services. In the former there is no barrier, no
dividing line, no complexional distinction, to hedge up the cabin gangway or
the quarter-deck, to prevent the intrepid, enterprising, and skillful coloured sailor from filling the same station as the white sailor, but *all* are
alike eligible, and stand upon a common level. There are some redeeming
traits in the characters of the owners and captains of whale-ships which
would be well for the Government of the United States, and the owners of mer-
chant-ships to imitate. On board of whale-ships the crews are generally unlettered men, or rather, a large proportion are ignorant of the rudiments of
a good common school education. No one can imagine, but those who have performed a whaling voyage, the thirst the men have for mental cultivation.
The forecastles are turned into schoolrooms. There you will see the *cook,*
the *steward,* and two or three of the crew, under the tuition of their several
teachers, busily engaged in their primary lessons: and others studying *navigation,* and taking *Lunars,* under the instructions of the captain or mates.
By close application during the voyage, an unlettered man may acquire the
art of reading, writing, and arithmetic. Now this is the case with a large
majority of coloured men in the whaling service, that when having acquired a
thorough knowledge of the art and skill in capturing whales, together with
navigation and seamanship, it qualifies them to fill the offices of boat-
steerers, third, second, and first mates, and sometimes captains of whaling
vessels.
        A fair inference from the above can be drawn to insure a correct esti-
mate. There are more than seven hundred vessels engaged in the whale fish-
ery, each vessel averaging one coloured officer. I have known some ships to
have second mate, and three boat-steerers; others to have chief mate and two
boat-steerers. There are, without exception, any quantity of coloured men
constantly employed as officers out of the different whaling ports--suffi-
cient, in my humble opinion, to warrant the following table:--

No. of captains in the State of Massachusetts,   8
    "   masters' mates   "   "   12
    "   captains in the State of Delaware in the
            merchant service,   3
    "   mates in the State of Delaware in the
            merchant service,   7
    "   captains in the State of Maryland, and
            owner of two vessels,   1
    "   captains in the State of New-York, in
            the merchant service,   4

<table>
<tr><td>"</td><td>mates in the State of New-York in the merchant service,</td><td>4</td></tr>
<tr><td>"</td><td>second and third mates, and boat-steerers in the whaling service,</td><td>700</td></tr>
<tr><td></td><td>Total,</td><td>739</td></tr>
</table>

In 1836, the brig "Rising States," owned, and entirely manned and officered by coloured men, sailed from New Bedford on a whaling voyage, and returned in 1837, partially successful, re-fitted and sailed on the second voyage, which was unfortunately interrupted by the vessel's being unseaworthy. The effort, however, gave satisfactory practical evidence of the coloured man's ability to navigate vessels to any part of the world. It is not necessary for me to refer to this as an evidence what coloured seamen can do. Facts, overwhelming facts, can be given, if required, that for thirty years coloured men more or less have been in command of vessels without any material intermission.

I am confident that sufficient justice has not been awarded to all, for the very reason that I am not in possession of all the facts in relation to this one subject; and if sufficient pains were taken to collect all the facts, what a mass of evidence we could have at hand to refute the *foul* calumnies daily heaped upon us by those whose chief study is to degrade us.

National Anti-Slavery Standard, October 29, 1846.

10.   COLOURED SEAMEN--THEIR CHARACTER AND CONDITION.

NO. V

Their Social, Civil, Moral, and Religious Character.

The time was when no man cared for the temporal and spiritual welfare of the sailor; he was looked upon only as an article of merchandise. Imported and exported from one country to another, and bartered for, sold, transferred from his ship to a rum-selling boardinghouse--to the brothel, and those sinks of pollution, where he is exchanged for what he is worth, until, like a depreciated currency, he is shipped at a discount to some foreign port, and passed off as current coin.

The sailor's occupation necessarily shuts him out of the pale of social, civil, moral, and religious society; he is constantly forming new acquaintances in foreign and distant ports, and associating with a class of men whose habits of life very often (especially foreigners) compel them to seek refuge at sea from the vengeance of the sword of Justice for violating the laws of their country.

To those acquainted with a sea-life, and the vicissitudes and snares which follow in the *wake* of the sailor--his hard usage at sea, wholly at the mercy of tyrant captains and brutal officers, (more especially the coloured sailor,) subject as he is to the unholy prejudice, in consequence of the *usage, customs,* and *laws* of his native country, seized upon when entering a Southern port of discharge, and thrust into prison for no other crime than that of having a coloured skin, where in some cases he is stripped of his hard earnings, and not permitted to depart until he has paid the utmost farthing,--it is not at all surprising that when on shore and unrestrained, he is careless and thoughtless, and gives way to his passions and appetites, and drowns all his troubles in a glass of grog.

Thus we see the mind and physical energies of the generous, free-hearted sailor, steeped in vices of all kinds. His social and civil rights, few--his moral and religious privileges as things that have no existence; his hopes crushed; his manhood reduced to the mere title of a brute, he is easily made the willing dupe of myriads of landsharks, pimps, and false-hearted landlords and base friends--he is stripped of his hard earnings, beaten, and left to wallow in misery and wretchedness. And alas! is there no help for old Ocean's sons? was the cry that greeted the ears of Christian philanthropists, coming from every point of the compass, until it had reached high heaven: and the spirit of God moved upon the waters of the mighty deep and caused the inhabitants thereof to sing a new song of deliverance from the powers of Satan and his kingdom! Now Bethel Churches, Seamen's Friend Societies, and Sailors' Homes, are established: magazines and papers are published advocating his claims, and Christians throughout the world unite in the glad sound, Glory to God in the highest, the *Sailor is free*.

It is not my purpose to disparage, or undervalue the many sterling virtues which, as a general rule, characterize the true-hearted sailor, for I am intimately acquainted with many who are an ornament to society and an honour to their country. Allowance must be made for the many precious gems that glitter amid the ruins of dissipated humanity.

For seventeen years I have been associated with this interesting class of people; five of which were spent at sea, in the capacity of a sailor. I have been twelve years engaged in seamen's affairs, and with this experimental knowledge, I feel safe in saying that there is a decided improvement in the social and civil habits of the coloured sailor.

Again, about one-third of the coloured seamen in the United States were born and reared in the States of Delaware, Maryland, and Virginia; in these States education so far as the coloured man is concerned, is to a great extent prohibited, and many make choice of a sea-life as a means of subsistence. At an early age he is deprived of a good parental education, which is the foundation upon which rests the mighty intellect of man, and of his future hopes for good. His social and civil habits depend mainly upon paternal and maternal cultivation. Blessed is that wandering but reclaimed prodigal sailor who can date his redemption from the fact that he has a praying mother and father, or sister, and friends, at home, supplicating the Throne of Grace in his behalf! Now take into the account all of the disadvantages under which the coloured sailor labours, and it is astonishing that there should be any redeeming trait in their character left.

It has been more than twenty-seven years since the first effort was made in this country to evangelize seamen, during which time thousands and hundreds of thousands of dollars have been expended for the benefit of white seamen, yet not one cent ever benefited the coloured sailor (within my knowledge) till 1839. Well, now what is the difference of character between the two classes, the one having been operated upon twenty-seven years, and the other but seven! You will bear in mind, that the ratio of the native American sailor is only 16 2/3 per cent. of the 150,000 seamen in the United States, all the rest being foreigners. The coloured seamen are eight per cent of the whole. I have proven that the coloured sailor is every way qualified to man and command vessels of any class to any part of the world-- that he has surmounted superhuman difficulties, and placed himself side by side with his white brother sailors, the prejudice against his colour, the usages of society, and the customs of this slaveholding republic, to the contrary notwithstanding.

I do not consider this fact a phenomenon to be gazed upon as one of the seven wonders of the world, but simply as an evidence that his social and civil habits are susceptible of the same improvement as that of the white sailor, provided always that his opportunities are the same.

National Anti-Slavery Standard, November 12, 1846.

11. BOARDING HOUSE FOR SEAMEN

UNDER THE DIRECTION OF THE
AMERICAN SEAMEN'S FRIEND SOCIETY,
C O L O R E D   S E A M E N ' S   H O M E,

KEPT BY

WILLIAM P. POWELL,

No. 70 John, corner of Gold-street, New-York.

Cooks, Stewards, and Seamen, who come to this house will have their
choice of ships, and the highest wages; and if they are not satisfied after
remaining twenty-four hours, no charge will be made.

The Colored American, March 21, 1840.

12. COLOURED SAILORS' HOME

Since the first of May, 1841, the experiment has been tried to sustain
this establishment without the aid of the Society. From that time to the
present there has been received and accommodated two hundred and eighty-three
boarders, at an expense of $970 32; to defray which, the receipts during that
time for board amounted to $804 73--not including the outstanding dues, some
of which may be collected.

Independent of the expenses sustained for the support of the Home, and
other incidental expenses, one of the present proprietors, William P. Powell,
has been to an expense of $262, in lowering and finishing the basement, al-
tering and finishing the attic, &c. The alteration and repairing thus made,
it is believed, were necessary for the comfort and convenience of the inmates.

Of the two hundred and eighty-three boarders who have found a *home* in
this house, many have duly appreciated the advantages of having a strictly
temperance, and otherwise well conducted house, where, after escaping the
dangers incident to the life of a sailor, they can enjoy repose and quiet,
and none to molest nor make them afraid.

The proprietors acknowledge, with gratitude, their many thanks to Messrs.
Goin, Poole & Pentz, shipping agents, for their large and increased patronage
to the "Coloured Sailor's Home," since its establishment up to the present
time.

With many thanks to the Seamen's Friend Society, and to the friends of
seamen, for the praiseworthy stand they have taken in their behalf; we humbly
commend them and the cause to the care of our Heavenly Father: and with renewed zeal begin the new year with brighter prospects.

WILLIAM P. POWELL
NATHANIEL A. BORDEN.

New-York, Jan. 1, 1842.

Sailor's Magazine, February, 1842, p. 197.

13. WILLIAM P. POWELL ON THE COLOURED
SAILOR'S HOME

It is hardly necessary to call the attention of our readers to the following statement which we find in the last number of the *Sailor's Magazine*. Mr. Powell is well known for his devotion to the improvement of that most neglected and abused of all classes, the coloured sailors, who, both from complexion and position, are exposed to a thousand dangers, temptations, and wrongs, which do not fail to the lot of those who are only black, or only sailors. Without having made a single inquiry as to the present exigencies of the "Home," we feel quite confident that nothing but dire necessity would prompt Mr. Powell to make this appeal, for we know that the enterprise has for years past been a perpetual struggle, and that in a pecuniary point of view it has been to him a source of considerable loss. And this result is owing not to any want of good management on his part, but simply to the intrinsic difficulties with which he has had to contend--the unfortunate relations of coloured sailors, and the prejudices which pursue them no less than others of their race in other positions. The appeal we hope may find a fitting response on the part of those who are able of their abundance to aid a good purpose and an excellent man:

COLOURED SAILOR's HOME, NEW YORK.--The undersigned, keeper of the Coloured Sailor's Home in the city of New York, begs leave to submit to the Christian community the following statement:
In 1839, nearly ten years ago, the condition of the 2000 coloured seamen sailing out of this port was urged upon his attention. He found them subject to all the vices common among seamen, with very little motive for self-respect, and less encouragement of gaining the respect of others. *Can they be elevated and saved?* was a question most seriously pondered.
Two years before the American Seamen's Friend Society had made a successful movement in the establishment of a Home for other sailors; and the same friends asked 'why not also have a home for the coloured? At their instance and advice, accompanied by some pecuniary aid, the Coloured Sailor's Home was opened. Notwithstanding the narrowness of its accommodations, and much pecuniary embarrassment, it has continued to be a refuge for the tempted, a protection for the virtuous, and a house of mercy for the wrecked and destitute. The whole number of boarders has been about 4,275, or an annual average of 450. Of the whole number, 560 destitute sailors, true objects of charity, have received relief in board and clothing, or an average of $3 each, amounting to $1,680. In the mean time many have refused admittance for the want of *means* to assist them.
Finding it necessary either to abandon the enterprise of keeping up a Home for coloured seamen, or to have a house commodious and comfortable for such a purpose. The undersigned has hired the three story brick building at 330 Pearl st. On the 1st of May he hopes to open it under auspices of greater good to his coloured brethren of the sea than ever enjoyed by them before. But in order to do it, he is compelled to make his first public appeal to the friends of the cause for aid. To procure beds and bedding and furniture, and to pay his additional rent, will sink the enterprise, unless friends voluntarily come to his relief. And this *relief* he *earnestly* asks; not on his own account, but on account of his *brethren,* who may, through the instrumentality of a well regulated home, be saved from wretchedness here and hereafter. Grateful acknowledgements are due for early and recent aid; and among the recent $20 worth of necessary articles from the Ladies' Bethel Society, Newburyport, Mass. The friends of the cause are respectfully referred to any of the officers of the American Seamen's Friend Society to ascertain the necessities of this case, and whether the much needed aid will be most wisely and usefully expended.

WILLIAM P. POWELL,
Keeper of Coloured Sailor's Home,
330 Pearl street, New York.

April 1, 1849.

National Anti-Slavery Standard, April 5, 1849.

14. A SENSIBLE PETITION

MR. WM. P. POWELL of this city, who, although of an unconstitutional and sinful color, is well known as a man of cultivated mind and great respectability, is about to leave this country with his family for England. In that kingdom he is sure that his children are not shut out by the laws of the country and the customs of society from such share of knowledge and such opportunity of obtaining and maintaining a respectable position among their fellow-men as law and custom offer to them. Though happily successful in life, this success has been in spite of the obstacles which every day of his life have been thrown in his way because of his complexion. He does not know that his children may be blessed with equally good luck, or that energy and enterprise, should they possess an unusual share of these qualities, will, under no circumstances command with them, the success which they have in his own case. Having the means of removing to another country where they will not, because of their color alone, be compelled to fight the battle of life at a disadvantage, which he, too well, knows how to appreciate, he does not feel that he would be discharging a parental duty by retaining them in a land which though theirs by birth, makes them alien to the protection of its laws and the benefits of its social relations.

Before leaving, however, Mr. Powell chose to present to the Legislature of his native State those claims upon her which from his birth to the present moment have been denied him by society. He asks her aid to assist him in the removal of his family to a new home. The petition, though its very presentation would be a cutting sarcasm, is a very proper one, and would have come with peculiar appropriateness before the assembled wisdom of the State, at a moment when its wise and Christian legislators were discussing the propriety of refusing its aid to a seminary of learning, because that Institution would not refuse to colored youth the advantages which it gives to others. Had Mr. Powell asked permission to sell his children at auction to the highest bidder, or have asked assistance to emigrate to Liberia, we have no doubt he would have gained a hearing, but a petition for aid to remove them where the buying and selling of their brethren would not consign them to contempt and degradation, it was not deemed proper by his representative even to present to the Legislature, and doubtless this gentleman estimated truly the character of the body of which he is a member. They might not, perhaps, hesitate to do an act not too palpably outrageous to degrade a colored man, but it was useless to ask them to aid in bettering the position of a whole family.

Mr. Powell sent his Memorial to the representative of his ward with the following letter:

TO HON. H. G. ALLEN.

Dear Sir:--Please present this petition and advocate its reception, and oblige your constituent, and twelve years a resident of the 4th Ward.
New York, July 7, 1851.

M E M O R I A L.

To the Honorable the Senate and House of Assembly of the State of New York Convened:
Your memorialist an inhabitant of the city and county of New York, and citizen of the State aforesaid represents,
That he is the Grandson of ELIZABETH BARJONA, one of the many Heroines

who, during the Revolutionary war with Great Britain, rendered *aid* and *comfort* to the rebels of the first Continental Congress, that when these patriots were driven from one State to another, and when large rewards were offered for their persons dead or alive, and when it was declared a penal offence, punishable with death, for any person to *aid,* assist or even to give them a morsel of bread or a drink of water, struggling as they were for national Independence from British rule, your petitioner's Grandmother, the said Elizabeth Barjona did in the capacity of Cook to the said Congress, carefully and regularly supply to the members thereof, every possible luxury which in those days of darkness and despair could be procured; and your memorialist feels therefore that his venerable relative though an humble was an important instrument in the deliberations of that body. It is not for your memorialist to remind your honorable body of how much the mind depends upon the wholesome, vigorous condition of its dwelling-place, nor to point out to you the disastrous consequences which might have ensued had not they eaten and drunken and been daily filled with the good things of this life, whereby the strength was given them to conceive, sign and proclaim to the world the great and noble truths of the American Declaration of Independence, "that all men are created free and equal and are entitled to life, liberty, and the pursuit of happiness," and your petitioner further sheweth that notwithstanding his grandmother did directly and indirectly contribute all her youthful energies to cement the "Union of the States," yet the "States of the Union" have violated the contract, securing LIFE, LIBERTY, and the PURSUIT OF HAPPINESS to all persons without regard to the color of their skin. And your petitioner further sheweth that, his father EDWARD POWELL was held a *slave* for life by the laws of New York, whereby your petitioner was deprived of a HOME and of a *father's* protection; and your petitioner further showeth that, owing to the prejudices, customs, and usages of the people of this State and of the Union that, it is impossible for him though freed from the disabilities which weighed upon his father, to give his own children, of whom he has a large family, that education and to secure to them those opportunities for a livelihood and a respectable position in society, to which, as human beings, and as American Citizens they are entitled.

Now in view of all these facts above stated, and in view of the fact that, one branch of the Legislature did enact a bill this session appropriating monies from the State Treasury to aid colored persons emigrating from this country; which bill was lost in the Senate, your petitioner respectfully asks your honorable body to appropriate by special act----Dollars which will enable him to emigrate with his family from this country, which denies to him and them the rights guarrantied by the Declaration of Independence, in which he has as above shown so great an hereditary interest, to the Kingdom of Great Britain, where character and not color--capacity and not complexion, are the tests of merit; and your petitioner will ever pay &c.

New York July 7th 1851

WILLIAM P. POWELL

National Anti-Slavery Standard, July 17, 1851.

15. EXTRACT FROM A LETTER OF WM. P. POWELL, DATED
ON BOARD PACKET SHIP DE WITT CLINTON

MY DEAR FRIEND GAY: In a few hours, with a strong breeze from "old blow hard," and a few rolls of ocean's billows between you and myself, I shall be beyond the reach of American Institutions; Institutions without a parallel in the civilized world. To enumerate their peculiarities would be a waste of labour and time. Much has been said in praise of them; the Pulpit--the Press --the State and National forums have groaned under the weight of religious and civil declamation in admiration of the wisdom of the Temple whose foundation and chief corner stone is Slavery. How long, oh! how long shall men,

women, and children, be sacrificed on the altar of this god of oppression?
how long shall humanity's voice be stifled by the din and clamour of his wor-
shippers? It is the voice of a god they exclaim, and *you* who oppose must
obey it. Great God, shall it be so! Shall this wicked nation trample the
poor black man in the dust any longer? Oh! for another miracle, another manifestation of they displeasure, such as befel Herod, the persecutor of *thy
people,* in the days of the Apostles!

Sorry I am to leave you, but the way of duty is the way of safety. I
have *tried* to do my duty to my *brother* man, whilst with you, and I mean to be
found trying, not forgetting my family, wherever it may please God to cast my
lot.

The success of my undertaking I leave in the hands of God; in Him do I
put my trust; may I never be confounded.

Farewell, my friend; be true to principle; be true to the slave, and
comfort my afflicted nominally free coloured countrymen, and the blessings
of them that are about to perish, and the approbation of "Our Father, who
art in heaven" "well done good and faithful servant," &c., shall be your reward.

Mrs. Mercy A. Powell, Wm. P. Powell, Edward B. Powell, Sylvester H.
Powell, Mary O. Powell, Isaiah A. Powell, Sarah A. Powell, and Samuel Powell,
wife and seven children, accompany me in my journey to England. You will
confer a favour by publishing the names, for the information of my relatives
and friends.

Truly and faithfully yours, in the bonds of American Slavery,
                                                WILLIAM P. POWELL.

Monday, Nov. 17, 1851.

National Anti-Slavery Standard, November 27, 1851.

16. BLACK SEAMEN AND ALABAMA LAW

MR. EDITOR--It of course is well known to you that the legislature of
Alabama have passed a law, to imprison all the colored seamen, that may arrive in the port of Mobile from sea, and to retain them, at the expense of
the owners of the vessels to which they may belong, in prison, until the vessel is ready for departure.

Some inquiries having been made, by the writer of this, from an intelligent shipmaster, relative to the law, and the presumed reasons for passing
it, he has given us the information, which we herewith communicate to you for
publication.

The avowed reason for passing this law, was the alledged fear, that the
colored seamen of the North, having experienced the blessings of freedom,
might contaminate their slaves, and thus cause insurrections.

Ships bound to Mobile anchor off Cedar Point, distant 30 miles from the
city, and in a wide, open roadstead. In almost every case, the boats are
hoisted in, and no communication permitted by the masters with the city, except through passing steamboats, or return lighters. The colored portion of
the crew are never permitted to go on shore, and the shipmasters have informed the authorities, that in case any colored seamen be found on shore,
they would--however illegal to imprison a seaman, charged with no crime, except having a black skin--interpose no objections to his detention. This
would seem to be sufficient to satisfy the people, or rather the mob of the
city of Mobile.

The law further provides, that the marshal shall receive a fee of five
dollars for taking, and five for retaining each colored seaman, which must
be paid by the ship owner.

The present mayor of Mobile has hitherto refused attempting the execution of this law; and application having, it is stated, been made to the
captain of one of our revenue cutters for assistance, be, *of course,* refused;

consequently, no attempt has as yet been made to enforce this horribly unjust law; but the same interest from the city of Mobile, which was powerful enough to cause the passage of this law, will probably elect their own Mayor, and thus a collision will yet take place. Whether the British government will permit *their* free colored seamen to be forcibly taken from their ships, is yet to be seen; meanwhile the present Secretary of State for the United States, will have time to prepare an elaborate opinion, justifying the law in anticipation. After his published letter in the Creole case, he may as well be considered as the exponent of any ultra southern claim; the "necessity of the case," &c., may furnish him with arguments.

The "necessity" of this law is yet to be explained. It is the custom, in the bay of Mobile, for the crews of unemployed vessels to assist in loading the ships taking in cargoes; for this service they receive, or rather the loading ship is charged, at the rate of two dollars per day, one-half of which goes to the seamen employed; this is a service they are eager to perform--the extra pay furnishes them with their small stores. Now the whole purport of this law, is to break up the loading of ships by their crews, as far as possible, and to give to the slave owners of Mobile employment for their slaves, at high prices. The merchants and men of business, and the present city authorities, were opposed to it, but in vain.

It is seen by all men, that this great question of slavery must be met by the people of the North; it obtrudes itself every where; the spirit of slavery requires us to violate the trial by jury; under penalties known to be unconstitutional, menaces of dissolution of the Union have been again and again thrown out; and now the free colored citizens of the North are to be kept in prison, that the slave owners of Alabama may find profitable employment for their slaves. We shall yet meet this great question; and if our great statesmen of the North desert us in the hour of need, other and worthier leaders of the PEOPLE will not be wanting--one at least, though borne down with the weight of years, will leave a bright example of faithfulness to the cause of human freedom.   B. J.

National Anti-Slavery Standard, March 17, 1842.

17. FREE NEGROES IN LOUISIANA

An act has just been passed by the general assembly of Louisiana, to oblige every master of a vessel arriving at any of the ports of that State, and having blacks on board, to give notice of the fact to a judge or justice of the peace, and cause them to be confined in the jail during his stay there; the vessel being liable for all charges. Also, that he shall give his bond for five hundred dollars to pay said charges. If he fails to take said blacks out of the State on his departure, this shall be done at the expense of the State. If the colored person thus removed returns, he is liable to imprisonment for life. This bill does not affect the right of property of a master to a slave, who, contrary to his will, has gone out of the State. Any captain of a foreign vessel is bound to report, on his arrival at New-Orleans, to the mayor or recorder, on oath, the name, &c. of every colored person on board of his vessel, under penalty of $100. A penalty of $200 dollars is laid upon any person harboring a free person of color residing in the State contrary to law. The bill does not refer to free negroes who have resided in the State since 1st of January, 1825.

National Anti-Slavery Standard, June 23, 1842.

18.   COLORED MEN IN LOUISIANA

WARNING TO SHIPOWNERS AND SHIPMASTERS!--We have just seen an act, passed by the authorities of Louisiana the present year, entitled, "An act more
effectually to prevent free persons of color from entering into this State,
and for other purposes." The act is not only arbitrary, but undoubtedly unconstitutional, and is exceedingly onerous and unjust in its operations, with
regard to the free States; and the very essence of tyranny and oppression in
its operation on free colored persons, who are not by the Constitution debarred from the rights and privileges of American citizens. The bill consists of fifteen sections; the first is as follows:

> Sec. 1. Be it enacted by the Senate and House of Representa-
> tives of the State of Louisiana, in general assembly convened, That
> from and after the time specified in this act, no free negro, mulat-
> to, or person of color, shall come into this State, on board of any
> vessel or steamboat, as a cook, steward, mariner, or in any employ-
> ment on board said vessel or steamboat, or as a passenger; and in
> case any vessel or steamboat shall arrive in any port or harbor,
> or landing, on any river of this State, from any other State or
> foreign port, having on board any such free negro, mulatto or per-
> son of color, the harbor master, or other officer having charge
> of such port, or any person or persons residing at or near said
> landing, shayl forthwith notify the nearest judge or justice of
> the peace in the parish in which said port, or harbor, or landing
> is situated, of the arrival of said vessel or steamboat; where-
> upon the said judge or justice of the peace shall immediately
> issue a warrant to apprehend and bring every such free negro,
> mulatto, or person of color before him; and on the execution of
> said warrant, by bringing before him such free negro, mulatto,
> or person of color, he shall forthwith commit him or her to the
> parish jail, there to be confined until said vessel or steamboat
> shall be ready to proceed to sea or to her place of destination,
> when the master or commander of such vessel or steamboat shall,
> by the written permit or order of the said judge or justice of
> the peace, take and carry away out of this State every such free
> negro, mulatto, or person of color, and pay the expenses of his
> or her apprehension and detention.

In the other sections, various penalties are prescribed to aid in carrying out the principles of this act. Every master of a vessel, on board which
a free black or mulatto may have been brought into Louisiana, must give a
bond, with securities to an amount not exceeding five hundred dollars, that
he will pay all expenses of arrest and detention, and carry the proscribed
individual out of the State. The penalty for refusing to give such security,
is one thousand dollars. Every free black or mulatto person, who may return
after having been sent out of the State, shall be liable to imprisonment at
hard labor, for five years; and if he shall be found in the State, thirty
days after such imprisonment, he shall be liable to imprisonment at hard labor for life.

It is further enacted, that any person who brings into the State any
free person of color, in violation of this act, shall be punished, on conviction, by a fine not exceeding two hundred dollars, for the first offense; and
for the second, by imprisonment not exceeding six months, and by a fine not
exceeding one thousand dollars. Also, that any person who shall employ or
harbor, or entertain as a boarder or lodger, any free person of color, residing in the State contrary to law, shall, on conviction thereof, be punished
by a fine not exceeding two hundred dollars, for each offense.

It behooves our merchants and shipmasters to examine the provisions in
the above unjust law, before they leave a northern port on a voyage to New
Orleans.

National Anti-Slavery Standard, October 6, 1842.

19.   RESOLUTIONS ADOPTED AT A MEETING OF BOSTON
NEGROES, OCTOBER 27, 1842

Resolved, That the legislative enactments of South Carolina, Georgia, Alabama, Mississippi and Louisiana, prohibiting all free colored citizens of the United States entering those several States under penalty of imprisonment, are manifestly unconstitutional; insomuch as the Constitution declares that the citizens of each State shall be entitled to all the rights and immunities of citizens of the several States.

Resolved, That Congress possesses the power to invalidate any State Legislative enactment which tends to restrain the liberties of any portion of the citizens of the United States.

Resolved, That the voice of the Massachusetts Legislative should be heard in the Congress of our nation, remonstrating against the unjust and unconstitutional deprivation of the liberties of her citizens. . . .

Resolved, Therefore, That we, the colored citizens of Boston, memorialize Congress, and our Legislature, at their next sessions, for their action in this case; especially that on some fitting occasion the point may be carried by this State before the Supreme Court of the United States, in order that such laws may be pronounced unconstitutional by that tribunal.

A committee was appointed to prepare and circulate petitions, and also to correspond with our friends in the several States, to awaken an interest in behalf of their own seamen. Committee as follows, viz: William C. Nell, Victor W. Barker, Robert Wood, Benjamin Weeden, John Thompson, Charles A. Battiste, Eli Cesar.

The Liberator, November 4, 1842.

20.   FREE BLACK SEAMEN OF BOSTON PETITION
CONGRESS FOR RELIEF, 1843

To the honorable the Senate and House of Representatives of the United States in Congress assembled:

Your petitioners, citizens of the United States, and some of them owners and masters of vessels,

Respectfully Represent:

That on board of that large number of vessels accustomed to touch at the ports of Charleston, Savannah, Mobile, and New Orleans, it is frequently necessary to employ free persons of color:

And whereas it frequently happens that such crews are taken from the vessels, thrown into prison, and there detained at their own expense, greatly to the prejudice and determinent of their interest, and of the commerce of these States:

They pray your honorable body to grant them relief, and render effectual in their behalf the privileges of citizenship secured by the Constitution of the United States. . . .

Majority Report (Committee of Commerce) on Memorial of one hundred and fifty Citizens of Boston

. . .The committee are aware that the laws in question have sometimes been vindicated upon considerations of domestic police; and they have no disposition to deny, that the general police power belonging to the States, by virtue of their general sovereignty, may justify them in making police regulations even in relation to matters over which an exclusive control is constitutionally vested in the National Government.

But the committee utterly deny that provisions like these can be brought within the legitimate purview of the police power. That American or foreign

seamen, charged with no crime, and infected with no contagion, should be
searched for on board the vessels to which they belong; should be seized
while in the discharge of their duties, or it may be, while asleep in their
berths; should be dragged on shore and incarcerated, without any examination
other than an examination of their skins; and should be rendered liable, in
certain contingencies over which they may have no possible control, to be
subjected to the ignominy and agony of the lash, and even to the infinitely
more ignominious and agonizing fate of being sold into slavery for life, and
all for purposes of *police;*--is an idea too monstrous to be entertained for
a moment. It would seem almost a mockery to allude to the subject of police
regulations in connection with such acts of violence. . . .

   Report of the Minority of the Committee

   . . .the undersigned need hardly state, what is notoriously a part of
the social and political history of the times, that these State regulations
have grown out of incendiary efforts to light up a servile war in the South.
Not only do the non-slaveholding States tolerate, within their limits, these
affiliated societies, whose professed object is to destroy the institutions
of the South, no matter by what means; whose daily efforts are directed not
only to the protection of runaway slaves, but to the instigation of insurrection and servile war; but these leagued bands of incendiaries send their
emissaries to the South, to operate in secret, regardless of all the social
obligations and fraternal feelings which should bind the various sections of
the Union together. The opportunities offered, by the means and through the
agencies of free negro sailors, of disseminating their mischievous purposes,
have not been lost sight of by the abolitionists of the North. The ports of
the Southern States have of late years frequently been agitated with rumors
of intended insurrections; and, as the undersigned is informed, these disturbances have mostly had their origin in the agency of colored seamen in
Northern vessels, who annoy the slaves with a glowing description of the efforts which their white brethren of the North are making in their readiness
to co-operate with them in their struggles for freedom. The undersigned does
not allude to these things with any wish to aggravate the difficulties already existing, or to exasperate the feelings, already too highly excited, of
the respective sections of the country; but simply for the purpose of showing, that these police regulations of the Southern States, complained of, are
not the result of unfriendly feelings toward the North, but of stern necessity; that they have been adopted as a means of self preservation, of preserving order and domestic tranquility, and of preventing commotion, violence,
and bloodshed. . . .

*"Free Colored Seamen--Majority and Minority Reports, January 20, 1843," Re-
port No. 80, House of Representatives, 27th Cong., 3d Sess., pp. 3, 7, 38.*

21. "AN ACT FOR THE BETTER REGULATION AND GOVERNMENT OF
     FREE NEGROES AND PERSONS OF COLOR, AND FOR
     OTHER PURPOSES," SOUTH CAROLINA, 1822

   Section 1. *Be it enacted by the honorable the Senate and House of Representatives now met and sitting in General Assembly, and by the authority of
the same,* That, from and after the passing of this act, no free negro or person of color, who shall leave this State, shall be suffered to return; and
every person who shall offend herein shall be liable to the penalties of the
act passed on the twentieth day of December, in the year one thousand eight
hundred and twenty, entitled "An act to restrain the emancipation of slaves,
and to prevent free persons of color from entering the State, and for other
purposes."
   Sec. 2. *And be it further enacted,* That every free male negro or person
of color, between the ages of fifteen and fifty years, within this State, who

may not be a native of said State, or shall not have resided therein five
years next preceding the passing of this act, shall pay a tax of fifty dollars per annum; and in case said tax shall not be paid, the said free male
person of color shall be subject to the penalties of the act against free
persons of color coming into this State, passed on the twentieth day of December, one thousand eight hundred and twenty.

Sec. 3. *And be it further enacted by the authority aforesaid,* That if
any vessel shall come into any port or harbor of this State, from any other
State or foreign port, having on board any free negroes or persons of color,
as cooks, stewards, mariners, or in any other employment on board of said
vessel, such free negroes or persons of color shall be liable to be seized
and confined in jail, until said vessel shall clear out and depart from this
State; and that, when said vessel is ready to sail, the captain of said vessel shall be bound to carry away the said free negro or free person of color,
and to pay the expenses of his detention; and, in case of his neglect or refusal so to do, he shall be liable to be indicted, and, on conviction thereof, shall be fined in a sum not less than one thousand dollars, and imprisoned not less than two months; and such free negroes or persons of color shall
be deemed and taken as absolute slaves, and sold in conformity to the provisions of the act passed on the twentieth day of December, one thousand eight
hundred and twenty, aforesaid.

Sec. 4. *And be it further enacted by the authority aforesaid,* That the
sheriff of Charleston district, and each and every other sheriff of this
State, shall be empowered and specially enjoined to carry the provisions of
this act into effect, each of whom shall be entitled to one moiety of the
proceeds of the sale of all free negroes and free persons of color that may
happen to be sold under the provisions of the foregoing clause: *Provided* the
prosecution be had at his information.

Sec. 5. *And be it further enacted,* That it shall be the duty of the
harbor master of the port of Charleston to report to the sheriff of Charleston district the arrival of all free negroes or free persons of color who
may arrive on board any vessel coming into the harbor of Charleston from any
other State or foreign port.

Sec. 6. *And be it further enacted,* That, from and after the passing of
this act, it shall be altogether unlawful for any person or persons to hire
to any male slave or slaves his or their time; and in case any male slave or
slaves be so permitted by their owner or owners to hire out their own time,
labor, or service, the said slave or slaves shall be liable to seizure and
forfeiture, in the same manner as has been heretofore enacted in the act in
the case of slaves coming into this State contrary to the provisions of the
same.

Sec. 7. *And be it further enacted,* That, from and after the first day
of June next, every free male negro, mulatto, or mestizo, in this State,
above the age of fifteen years, shall be compelled to have a guardian, who
shall be a respectable freeholder of the district in which said free negro,
mulatto, or mestizo, shall reside; and it shall be the duty of the said
guardian to go before the clerk of the court of the said district, and before
him signify his acceptance of the trust, in writing; and at the same time he
shall give to the clerk aforesaid his certificate, that the said negro, mulatto, or mestizo, for whom he is guardian, is of good character and correct
habits; which acceptance and certificate shall be recorded in said office by
the clerk, who shall receive for the same fifty cents; and if any free male
negro, mulatto, or mestizo, shall be unable to conform to the requisitions of
this act, then and in that case such person or persons shall be dealt with as
this act directs for persons of color coming into this State contrary to law;
and the amount of sales shall be divided, one-half to the informer, and the
other half for the use of the State.

Sec. 8. *And be it further enacted by the authority aforesaid,* That if
any person or persons shall counsel, aid, or hire, any slave or slaves, free
negroes, or persons of color, to raise a rebellion or insurrection within
this State, whether any rebellion or insurrection do actually take place or
not, every such person or persons, on conviction thereof, shall be adjudged
felons, and suffer death without benefit of clergy.

Sec. 9. *And be it further enacted by the authority aforesaid,* That the
commissioners of the cross roads for Charleston neck be, and they are hereby

declared to be, justices of the peace, ex-officio, in that part of the parish of St. Philip's without the corporate limits of Charleston, for all purposes except for the trial of causes small and mean.

In the Senate house, the first day of December, in the year of our Lord one thousand eight hundred and twenty-two, and in the forty-seventh year of the independence of the United States of America.

JACOB BONDTON,
President of the Senate.
PATRICK NOBLE,
Speaker of the House of Representatives.

22. LAWS OF SOUTH CAROLINA RESPECTING COLORED
SEAMEN

Our readers may remember that last year a commissioner was appointed by the Executive of this Commonwealth to attend to the interests of the State with regard to colored seamen in the port of Charleston, S. C. The same gentleman who was named for this duty has since been the chairman of a Committee of the South Carolina Legislature to investigate the existing laws on the subject, and to report on a bill which had been brought in to modify those laws. The report of this Committee is now before us, and we proceed carefully to give its purport for the information of our readers, interested on either side of the question.

The report acknowledges that 'the practical enforcement of the existing laws tends to abuses, which may compromise the State, both with the other States of the confederacy, and with foreign friendly powers,' and proceeds to recommend the passage of the proposed bill, as agreeable to the *meaning* of the Constitution of the United States, and the inalienable rights of an independent sovereignty. This 'bill requires all colored seamen, while within the territorial limits of the States to remain on board their vessels, or within such limits as the municipal authority of the port shall prescribe; and a violation of this law incurs a penalty or fine, with security that the offender shall be detained on board his vessel, and depart with it. No expense is incurred by those who do not violate the law. But, to secure its enforcement, the captain or agent of the vessel, within three days after his arrival, is required to deposit in the sheriff's office a list and description of all colored seamen brought in. The omission involves a penalty of fine for each day until the law is complied with. So that colored seamen are required to remain on board their vessels, and depart with them, under the penalty prescribed.'

We now proceed to the arguments in favor of the bill, as we find them in the report. It has been said that any law restraining, because of color, the free ingress, stay, and departure, of the subjects of foreign States, or of those who are citizens of other States of the Union, is a violation of the courtesy due to friendly powers, to the treaty stipulations of the general government, and to the Constitution of the United States, which provides that 'the citizens of each State shall be entitled to all privileges and immunities of citizens in the several States.' To prove the falsity of these notions, it is necessary to establish two positions. First, that a State, every way distinct and sovereign, may enact such laws without violating the law of nations; and secondly, that South Carolina has not given up such right by joining the confederacy of the United States. As to the first position, we think it cannot be doubted by any reasonable person that such a right exists, or, at any rate, is the common usage among civilized nations. The police and quarantine regulations of Europe, at the present time, are as

annoying to strangers as they are (oftentimes) needless; but they are acquiesced in without demur. Vattel, in several places, is very explicit on the
right of a sovereign power to admit what aliens he pleases within his dominion, and under what restrictions. We shall not, therefore, quote arguments
on what seems to us to be indisputable. But, with regard to the present
matter, the report adds-- [40]

> 'This liberty to adapt its laws to its own circumstances
> is indispensable to self-preservation. Such regulations depend
> on this right, and it is quite immaterial whether the disease
> is a physical or moral one; whether destruction is threatened
> from pestilence, or domestic insubordination, the right is the
> same. If South Carolina apprehends the baleful effects which
> a free intercourse with foreign negroes will produce, she has,
> by the primary law of nature, a right within her own limits to
> interdict it. She is not bound to wait until her citizens are
> involved in the conflagrations and murders of a servile out-
> break. Humanity, as well as a proper caution, warn us not to
> suffer our slaves to be drawn into schemes which must end in
> their own punishment or destruction; while those who have se-
> duced them from their fidelity are safe beyond the dangers
> and inflictions which must ever attend such attempts.

As to whether or not South Carolina has yielded any of her natural
rights in joining the confederacy, the report answers in the negative, by declaring, first, because the right of self-preservation is *inalienable,* and
self-preservation signifies the maintenance of the *body politic* as it was at
the formation of the Union. At that time, the body politic of South Carolina
consisted of 'white citizens'--the negroes constituted no part of it, but
were held, by her fundamental laws, to be 'absolute slaves,' *personal property* of their owners, and this relation cannot be changed without the destruction of the body politic, according to well established principles.

'The preservation of a nation consists in the duration of the *political
association* of which it is formed. If a period is put to this association,
the nation or State no longer exists, though the individuals who composed it
still exist.' Any alteration in the relation of master and slave, and introduction of equal political power on the part of our colored population,
would so entirely change the body politic as to render it a different State
for all political purposes. Her very representation in Congress would be
affected. Nay, the attempt to confer on negroes the right of citizenship is
a clear violation of the principles of the federal Union. Negroes were no
parties to the Constitution of the United States, and although the States
may, in regard to their civil rights, introduce them into the class of white
men--negroes are a race originally introduced by the English settlers as
slaves; and although many of them have been released from servitude, they
have not been, and public feeling and the natural antipathy to association
has kept them, like the gypsies of England, an anomalous population, protected it is true by the humanity of the laws, but separated in habits, associations, and duties. They constitute no part of the militia, who are composed
only of 'free *white* men;' as servants and laborers they may be used, but the
flag of the Union is under the protection of 'free white men.' Even fanaticism itself has not yet polluted the ranks of the militia or the jury box
with the associations of negroes.
But whatever folly and fatuity may bring about elsewhere, South Carolina
entered the Union a slaveholding State, and as such she will continue unaf-
fected by the terms of the Union. She declines to defend her position, because she admits no authority to question it. She is as absolutely beyond
inquiry as Russia in relation to her boors, or subjugated Poland, or England,
in relation to her Irish population, her starving operatives, or her millions
of enslaved and conquered natives of India, held in cruel bondage, not by the
rod of a driver, but the bayonets and cannon of her mercenaries. On these
matters each State is responsible only to heaven, by the laws of nature and
of nations.'

This ground is supported by strong quotations from Vattel.

The Committee again alludes to the quarantine laws, but with regard to them as enacted by different States of the Union. The report continues--

'South Carolina never intended to yield her *absolute right* to secure the subordination of her slave population. It is a vital interest, as much so as that of New-York to establish health laws to prevent the importation of disease, or that of Massachusetts to prevent the importation into her State, of the paupers and felons of Europe.'

Again it is said, that South Carolina has no right to pass laws respecting citizens of other States, because she has given up to Congress the power to *'regulate commerce.'* The report remarks--

'If Congress alone can pass laws regulating those concerned in commerce, then the quarantine laws are unconstitutional. If not, then our laws also are no violation of that instrument. It is felony to quit the quarantine ground against the law, because the people of New-York believe that the presence of citizens of this State, leaving home in particular seasons, is dangerous to the bodily health of their fellow-citizens of that region, and the punishment is absolute slavery for a long term in their State's prison--where hard labor, coarse diet, and the most cruel and bloody bodily punishment are indicted by keepers, who are the arbitrary judges and merciless executioners of their helpless victims. In South Carolina, we think the presence of a free negro, fresh from the lectures of an abolition society, much more infectious, and we confine him to the vessel, or prescribed limits. Each State acts for itself, upon a matter believed to be vitally important. It is proper to show that in this matter our State acts in good faith, and on sound principles. In the first place, it is a subject on which our people are peculiarly sensitive. It is connected with no immediate and pressing apprehensions, but interest and humanity unite in moving us to obviate the necessity for severity, which is alike painful to our feelings, and injurious to our interests.'

On another ground, also, the right of South Carolina to enact the laws under notice, is denied.

'The first article of the second section of the Constitution of the United States provides that 'the citizens of each State shall be entitled to all privileges and immunities of citizens in the several States;' and under this clause, it is supposed, that if a negro is a citizen of Maine, he may come to South Carolina and claim here the rights and immunities of a white man. White or black, if a citizen of Maine, we must treat him as a citizen. The folly of such a claim is only equalled by the recklessness with which the pretension is urged. If true, this State would rather yield her place in the Union than submit to it. But it has no foundation in the Constitution. All that instrument means is this: Citizens of each State shall be entitled to the same rights in the other States as if they had been born there. A white man born in Maine, and removing to South Carolina, is on an equal footing with a white citizen; and so, a negro, born in Maine, is no better than one born here, and if he comes here, he must abide by our negro laws. Were not this so, this State might be infested with runaway negroes, who, having acquired the rights of citizens in Maine, would return to beard their masters and claim the protection of the federal Constitution. This may be illustrated by other cases. In some States, a service in the militia for a number of years, exempts one from ordinary duty, but he cannot carry that privilege out of the State, and insist upon it elsewhere. He must abide the laws of the State where he is. So, if by the laws of Maine every citizen can vote for President, a citizen of Maine living in Virginia must abide her laws, and unless he has a freehold he cannot vote, for her own native citizens are subject to that law. All then that the Constitution means is, that, white or black, the inhabitants of any State will stand in every other as her own citizens, white or black; not that if Maine chooses to permit her negroes to vote, or marry white persons, they can do so in other States where the same thing is forbidden to her own negroes. Massachusetts for years prohibited the marriage of blacks with whites; establishing a precedent that a State may make a color a distinction, as well as any other peculiarity. One State may prohibit the marriage of minors; if so, all minors within her limits must

obey the law. So all negroes within our limits must abide our laws as to
that population.'

The remainder of the paper is devoted to a consideration of the extent
of the treaty-making power of our general government, and to answering those
who affirm that the laws respecting negro seamen, &c., when affecting English
subjects, are contrary to the Convention of 1818, with Great Britain. The
ground taken on the latter topic is, that 'all treaties, and the Convention
in particular, are subject to the internal laws of the respective countries.'
This stipulation was absolutely made, and though, if the proviso were not
literally written in the treaty, the construction would be the same, yet as
it was made, the matter is settled beyond question.

'The laws of a nation are not to be repealed by the construction of
treaties; the parties to which would, if they intended to do so, expressly
stipulate upon the point. And it is equally true, that not only existing
laws, but such internal laws as the necessities of each may require, may be
enacted; provided they do not directly impair the obligations of the contract. It would be no violation of our Convention if Great Britain should
make any regulations as to shipping generally, which affected the mode of
carrying on the trade guarantied by the Convention; she might exclude our
ships from specified parts of the river, or compel them to load their cargoes in specified docks. This would be but a mode of carrying on commerce;
and if she may designate where our ships shall lie, why may we not prescribe
limits to her black seamen? If the necessities of one of the contracting
parties existing at the time or supervening afterwards, require regulations
to be adopted to preserve the health, the morals, or the political safety of
such party, they are by the just application of what is termed the 'restrictive interpretation,' exceptions to the general terms of the contract.'

We conclude with the remarks of the treaty-making power of the central
government--

'The Constitution vests in the President the 'power to make treaties,'
by and with the advice of the Senate, &c. I hold that this power, however
general in its terms, is limited by the other provisions of the Constitution.
The treaty-making power cannot extend to impair those rights which the States
have not delegated. It would otherwise be the most sweeping and dangerous
power vested in the federal government, and being exercised in conjunction
with the Senate only, where the smallest States are represented equally with
the largest, might be exercised in a way to destroy the most cherished rights
of the States. If the federal government could do by *treaty* what Congress
could not by law, then have the large States yielded to a Convention of
States what they have denied to a Congress, in which the preponderance of
their population is justly felt. I then hold it as a fundamental maxim, in
relation to the treaty-making power, that it is but a mode of exercising
those powers which are expressly delegated by the States, or which are necessary to the perfect exercise of those powers; but does not authorize the
President and Senate to invade those rights reserved to the States respectively, or to the people. That it is not an unlimited grant, but is restrained
and modified by the nature of the federal compact, and the express powers
therein delegated. Each State has an undoubted right to lay taxes upon all
who reside within its limits, and the United States could not, by treaty,
stipulate that the subjects of any foreign State should be exempt. If so,
they might as well stipulate that they should be liable to trial only in the
courts of the United States, and not subject to the criminal process of the
States. It might be advantageous to surrender some town or post to a foreign
government, with the privilege of exercising martial law, yet no treaty could
invade the domain of a State in these particulars. In short, the States retain their domestic legislatures and natural powers, and all the acts of the
general government must leave the exercise of them, as far as necessary for
their preservation and protection, unimpaired. It will never be admitted as
a sound interpretation of the Constitution, that the President and Senate
possess powers controlling the States, which were purposely withheld from
Congress; but the extent of the authority of the treaty-making power must be
limited to the delegation of powers by the States. Construction has already
gone far to swallow up the state sovereignties, and it will be fearful if the

treaty-making power is to be the bottomless gulph into which they are eventually to sink.

I thus have attempted to maintain that South Carolina, as a sovereign
State, does possess the power to pass the law. That is a power upon the
exercise of which her dearest and most vital interests depend. That such a
power is the rightful and inalienable attribute of a sovereign State--that
its exercise must depend upon the views of policy, and upon the individual
discretion of the State, which can alone safely decide in matters involving
self-preservation--that it was not either expressly or by implication ever
surrendered, and from its nature could not be--that the treaty-making power
does not extend so far as to authorize stipulations destructive of this
power--that is but a police regulation, and not inconsistent with any commercial convention.

It was due to our sister States, and to those foreign powers with whom
we trade, to thus demonstrate our respect to national law, and our regard to
treaties entered into with friendly States. The objections against the act
of 1835, we have endeavored to remove, as far as they were well-founded--and,
at the same time, to preserve the just rights of the State to secure her domestic tranquility.'

The Liberator, January 12, 1844.

23.   COLOURED SEAMEN IN SOUTHERN PORTS

As in many other cases, the information which Anti-Slavery lecturers and
Anti-Slavery papers have, from time to time, for years past, brought to public notice of the cruel injustice and unconstitutional character of Southern
laws in regard to Northern coloured seamen, is beginning to have due effect.
The principle of *quid pro quo* is one to which politicians are very sensible,
and several of our contemporaries of the political press have lately had the
boldness to question whether, inasmuch as anybody may be made a slave of, at
the North, to oblige the South, it is asking too much that free Northerners
who go South shall be permitted to remain so. Considering that that never
has been the case, and that the only religion now thought worth having is,
that we should believe the Constitution as the only revealed law of God, and
that we should love the slaveholders better than ourselves, the only wonder
is that somebody, beside the Abolitionists, has not before discovered that to
imprison Northern seamen in Southern ports if they are not of the pale tint,
and sell them for slaves, if they are not themselves able to pay the expense,
of their imprisonment, is not in accordance with all the articles of the popular "higher law." However, we must be thankful for things as they come,
hoping to live long enough to look at the Declaration of Independence and the
Constitution without laughing.

It must be confessed, however, that the late discovery of this unconstitutional conduct of the Southern brethren had been brought about by the aid
of "Foreign Interference." The British Consul at Charleston, Mr. Matthews,
has done much to assist the Northern sight, in the salve he has been using
for Southern blindness. Great Britain seems quite determined to make it a
recognized and fixed fact, that a British subject is a man, and can, by no
possibility, be permitted to be made a slave of. The correspondence of Consul Mathew with the Governor of South Carolina was, as far forth, more than
mere diplomatic correspondence, that it meant something. It is now to be
followed up by something more. We quote a paragraph current in the papers of
the week:

IMPRISONMENT OF COLOURED SEAMEN IN SOUTH CAROLINA--MR. CONSUL MATHEW
AGAIN.--The validity of the law of South Carolina, requiring the imprisonment of coloured seamen, who may arrive in the ports of that State, has at
length been controverted in a form which will put it to the test before the
judicial tribunals of the country. Manuel Pereira, a coloured Portuguese

sailor, articled to service on an English brig which was recently driven in-
to Charleston by stress of weather, having been arrested and committed to
jail, Mr. Mathew, the British Consul at that port, has applied to Judge
Withers, through his counsel, Mr. Pettigru, for a writ of *habeas corpus*. The
Judge has refused to grant the writ, and notice of appeal has been given.
The issue, therefore, has been legally raised, and there is every probability
that it will ultimately be carried up to the Supreme Court of the United
States for final adjudication.

If the British Government shall not be more successful in this attempt
to get a decision of the Supreme Court on this question than Massachusetts
was when she tried to do the same thing, the Minister for Foreign Affairs
will probably have a question to put to some body at Washington. *Hinc illa
lachryma* perhaps, of our contemporaries.

A paragraph in the Charleston (S. C.) *Mercury,* of the 27th ult., though
it does not promise that that State will open any way out of this embarrassment, shows that one other Southern State at least prefers to be discreet
rather than valorous:

THE LAW REGARDING COLOURED SEAMEN.--The Legislature of Louisiana, after
full consideration of the representations that have been addressed to them,
have repealed those provisions of their law which provided for the imprisonment of coloured seamen from abroad, and have substituted for this a provision allowing such seamen to land for their necessary duties with passports
from the Mayor. We have not yet seen the statute, and cannot say whether it
applies to coloured seamen from the North as well as from foreign countries.
In regard to the former, we should be decidedly opposed to placing them on
the same footing as the latter, except where they are driven into our ports
by stress of weather. But even in regard to them it seems to us that our
law ought to be changed on the principle of the Indiana and Illinois constitutions. Let coloured seamen from the North be forbidden to enter our ports,
and let their introduction subject the vessel to a fine of a thousand dollars
for every one, and we venture to say we should be more troubled with the
visits of those precious "citizens of Massachusetts." We shall publish the
Louisiana statute as soon as we can get a copy.

National Anti-Slavery Standard, May 6, 1852.

24. THE LAW REGARDING COLORED SEAMEN

The Legislature of Louisiana, after full consideration of the representations that have been addressed to them, have repealed those provisions of
their law which provided for the imprisonment of colored seamen from abroad,
and have substituted for this a provision allowing such seamen to land for
their necessary duties with a passport from the Mayor. We have not yet seen
the statute, and cannot say whether it applies to colored seamen from the
North as from foreign countries. In regard to the former, we should be decidedly opposed to placing them on the same footing as the latter, except
where they are driven into ports by stress of weather. But even in regard
to them, it seems to us that our law ought to be changed on the principle of
the Illinois and Indiana constitutions. Let colored seamen from the North
be *forbidden* to enter our ports, and let their introduction subject the vessel to a fine of a thousand dollars for every one, and we venture to say we
should be no more troubled with the visits of those precious "citizens of
Massachusetts." We shall publish the Louisiana statute as soon as we can
get a copy.--*Charleston Mercury.*

Frederick Douglass' Paper, June 17, 1852.

25.   IMPRISONMENT OF BRITISH SEAMEN

Shortly after President Taylor's cabinet was formed, the attention of
his Secretary of State was invited to the systematic violations of our treaty
stipulations, by South Carolina, under a law authorizing the arrest, imprisonment and conditional enslavement of free colored people. Mr. Clayton regretted that South Carolina was so naughty, but he said he could not help it;
this confederacy was a collection of independent sovereignties, and the general government had no power to compel a refractory State to respect treaties, or the Constitution, or anything else. This was duly communicated by
the British Minister to Lord Palmerston, and by him, with well-affected grav-
ity, communicated to Parliament. [41]

The Premier's statement created some amusement in political circles in
England, and a great deal of mortification in the United States, but it was
accompanied by none of the threats or denunciation which we had a right to
have anticipated from the English government. Mr. Clayton thought it was
very kind of the Queen to take the matter so quietly, and congratulated himself that he had extricated himself and his party, as he imagined, from a
vexatious dilemma, with no greater loss than his own self-respect.

He supposed that the matter was here to end, and that England, appreciating the defects of our Constitution, and the lamentable weakness of our
government, and the general imperfections of our political institutions,
would forbear to insist upon her rights, and would be grateful for the obser-
vance of such portions of the treaties existing between her government and
ours, as could be enforced without distracting the Whig party or unsettling
the government.

But such is not England's usual way of doing things. Lord Palmerston
very naturally thought that if South Carolina was independent of the federal
authority in questions of this nature, hers was the government for England to
treat with, and the next thing we hear is the arrival at Charleston of Mr.
George Mathew, commissioned as Consul-General for the Carolinas, and specially charged to present the wrongs sustained by free colored British seamen in
the ports of those States, to the consideration of their respective governments, for redress.

Mr. Mathew did as he was bid; he addressed the Executive at length upon
the subject, and made out a very strong case--a *casus belli* for a quarrelsome
nation--unless the amplest reparation was promptly offered. This letter appeared in our columns last winter. Governor Means immediately communicated
it to the Legislature, who adjourned, however, without acting upon it.

At the last season of the Legislature, which commenced, we believe, in
November, Gov. Means, at the request of Mr. Mathew, brought the subject again
to the attention of that body, expressing himself, however, averse to any
modification of the law in question. The substance of his doctrine upon this
point appeared in the *Evening Post* immediately after the Message was delivered. A Committee was appointed, in each branch of the Legislature, to consider the subject, and both reported in conformity with the sentiments of the
Governor.

This conclusion, at war with the treaties and with the Constitution of
the United States, with the Constitution of the State of South Carolina, with
the decisions of her tribunals, and with the written and printed opinions of
some of her most eminent lawyers, evidently took Mr. Mathew by surprise, and
he has taken occasion to address Governor Means once more upon the subject.
His letter will be found in another column of this sheet.

He wishes it to be understood that his government has not modified or
abated a particle of their claim, but are desirous of maintaining a good temper on both sides, if possible, and of getting the redress, which they are
determined to have, in the way it will be most agreeable to the Carolinians
to grant it.

We understand that the aid of the Courts will now be invoked, and the
question whether the Supreme Court of South Carolina will adhere to its former decision against the constitutionality of the imprisonment laws, and, if
so, whether its decrees will be enforced by the executive authorities, will
be tested.

The Liberator, February 13, 1852.

26. THE BRITISH SEAMEN AT CHARLESTON

A case of hardship occurred some months ago, which can hardly be forgotten; and which, if forgotten, ought to be brought into remembrance. On the 22d of last June, Mr. Milnes inquired of Lord Stanley, in the House, what had been, or would be, done in aid of Manuel Pereira, a British subject, who had been imprisoned in Charleston on account of the colour of his skin, being charged with no other offence, and being, moreover, a reluctant intruder in that port, into which he was drifted for refuge in a sinking ship. Lord Stanley gave hopes that the poor man would be watched over by our Consul at Charleston, and intimated that the case was one of "peculiar delicacy," from the intricacy of the relations between the Federal and "Provincial" governments. The error of calling the State Governments *provincial* was pointed out at the time by several authorities. It is a mistake of serious consequence to ourselves to think of the American States--which are all sovereign--as provinces. The safety of our seamen, and other fellow-subjects, is deeply concerned in that difference, as may be seen in a moment. If any seaman is put in jail, in any provincial port of a friendly foreign power, we have simply to demand his release, and are sure to obtain it, with due apology for the improper conduct of local authorities. But the case is very different when we have to do with a Federal Government, whose function of managing the foreign relations of the whole nation is invaded by the legislation of any particular State. This was so clearly seen and admitted six months ago, that there was a kind of promise all round that the case of Manuel Pereira should not be lost sight of, and that its treatment by the two American Governments --the General Government and that of South Carolina--should be regarded as an indication of what we may have to do, in regard to the safety of British subjects who may enter the port of Charleston. The Governor of South Carolina, in a recent message to the Legislature, gives a report of the matter, and his view of it.

It appears that just two years ago, our Consul at Charleston addressed a communication to the Legislature on the subject of a modification of the law by which "the Sheriff of Charleston is required to seize and imprison coloured seamen who are brought to that port." Committees of the two Houses were appointed to consider the suggestion; and they reported against any modification of the law. Last March, the ship in which Pereira served was driven into the port in distress, and the Sheriff put the poor fellow in jail. The British Consul applied to Judge Withers for a writ of *habeas corpus;* and Judge Withers refused it. The Governor laid his commands on the Sheriff not to release the prisoner, even if the writ were granted. Anxious to get rid of the prisoner, the Sheriff procured a passage for him in a ship to Liverpool; an act which the Governor lauds as one of great kindness, adding that Pereira was at liberty to take a passage anywhere beyond the limits of the State--as if a man in prison, whose ship had gone to pieces, had any means of letting his services as a free and innocent man should always be able to do! To get free, Pereira signed the articles offered to him in the prison, and was on his way to the ship when our Consul interfered, and prevented his departure. A few days after, the Consul paid his passage to New York, and saw him off--having, no doubt, by that time, assurance that the Federal Government meant to move in the case. On the 19th of May another coloured seamen, named Reuben Roberts, also a British subject, was seized on the arrival of his ship, the *Clyde,* and imprisoned till her departure on the 26th. And now comes the interesting sequel to the story. "On the 9th of June, a writ in trespass, for assault and false imprisonment, from the Federal Court, was served upon Sheriff Yates, laying the damages at four thousand dollars." Such is the Governor's news; but he does not tell us which case the writ relates to. No matter! The Federal Government has taken up the case against South Carolina, and our dispute is with the little State, and not with our ally at Washington. The Governor recommends the Legislature whom he addresses to add to the law in question some means of protection to the sheriff, whom it compels to occupy the position of Sheriff Yates.

Governor Means is like Southern politicians in general in his faculty of wonder. He is amazed that anybody should have dared to annoy a Sheriff of Charleston by calling him to account. He is amazed that any one dares to complain of any law that South Carolina thinks proper to make. He is amazed that any one ventures to interfere with the operation of State laws. Will he be amazed when the day comes for merchants--American and foreign--to sail past the port of Charleston, and seek one where innocent men are not marched to jail in sight of a whole city? Louisiana has provided by law for the liberty and safety of coloured seamen in her ports. And Louisiana is wise; for there are two constitutional provisions which it might be dangerous for any State to infringe. By the one, every free citizen has a right to the same liberty in every part of the country that he has in his own State; and by the other, the management of foreign relations is vested in the central Government. South Carolina has infringed the latter, and threatens to violate the former, by forbidding the entrance of free coloured men from Massachusetts and other Northern States into her port. The Supreme Court will see to the matter; and it will be very interesting to witness the result of the controversy. There is probably no one outside the boundaries of the blustering little State who has any doubt of what the verdict will be in the first place. The Supreme Court is not likely to rule that any State of the Union can, under pretence of police necessity, give cause of war to any foreign power or sister State. If the verdict is against Sheriff Yates, what next? The men of his State boast that they never yield. Well--it is not now our affair. The two Governments must settle the matter; we, meantime, keeping a careful watch over the safety of our seamen who may go to Charleston, whether in the regular course of trade, or as Pereira did, as the only alternative from going to the bottom. There are two or three points, however, worthy of notice in the Governor's statement and pleading. He expressly, without the slightest disguise, avows that the obnoxious law was made in self-defence against a grave danger, and will be maintained on that ground. When strangers let fall a remark on that same danger, in which the citizens of Charleston are living, the fact is denied, and allusion to it is resented. Yet Governor Means calls this law "a police regulation which is so essential to the peace and safety of our community. In fact," he proceeds, "it is neither more nor less than the right of self-preservation, a right which is above all constitutions, and above all laws, and one which never was, and never will be, abandoned by a people who are worthy to be free. It is right which," he is pleased to say, "has never yet been attempted to be denied to any people except to us." Without going into any historical review which may affect this last statement, we may indulge, in our turn, in a little wonder that this ruler does not see that every Pereira and Roberts, and other Britons, and every Boston and New York seaman, has a similar right; and that if the self-preservation of South Carolina is incompatible with that of the whole world besides, South Carolina must succumb. That is a fact clear to the meanest capacity. She may be comforted, however. It is not the destruction of South Carolina that will be found necessary, but only of that peculiarity in her which places her at war with the rest of mankind, including her own federal head. That she should choose to live in bondage to such a fear as her ruler confesses, is strange to those who live in a State of freedom. That these recent transactions may teach her a better wisdom, and suggest to her the means of emancipating herself from a life of conflict, isolation, and terror, is the best thing that her friends could desire.

The Governor declares that, if the Supreme Court had not taken up the question, piquing the pride of the State, he should have advised some modification of the law, to the extent of sparing coloured seamen the penalties of imprisonment, if their captains were prohibited to allow them to land. They might be imprisoned, he thinks, on board their ships instead of in the jail. No doubt it would be convenient to the Charleston people to be spared the dangerous spectacle of a black man being marched to prison because he is free. It would be convenient that their slaves should know nothing about such a fearful anomaly as a free mulatto. But it is not at all convenient to Britons, or to Salem or Boston merchants, to turn their ships into jails to please the men of Charleston. It is not convenient to them to make such distinctions of complexion. It is not convenient to the world to relinquish constitutional rights, or rights under treaty, to spare the alarms of the men of Charleston. The Governor speaks of this proposal of his as a concession of the spirit of the age. If the age had not got on further than that, we would just as soon have lived in any other. One word more. Whatever South Carolina may think, there is a world outside her borders, which will serve the world's turn well enough for traffic and other intercourse. There are ports in other States where cotton may be got without seeing our seamen carried to jail. We expect relief from the General Government, but, if South Carolina chooses to fight it out with the General Government, we need not wait. Cotton can be bought at other ports.--*London News.*

National Anti-Slavery Standard, January 20, 1853.

27. THE CASE OF MANUEL PEREIRA

In the present state of public feeling with respect to American Slavery, it is probable that some sensation was created by an official argument upon the subject which we published. . . . It will, perhaps, be recollected that attention was called some two years ago to the State Laws of South Carolina, as exemplified on the person of Isaac Bowers, a British seaman of colour, who, on no charge excepting the tint of his skin, was forcibly taken from the vessel and lodged in Charleston jail. It proved that this proceeding was in strict conformity to the laws of the State, which, in order to prevent any possible contagion of negro liberty, enacted that any free black coming even upon the waters of South Carolina should be arrested and locked up forthwith till the ship's departure. On this law, thus exemplified, the Governor of South Carolina, in his recent message to the Legislature of the State has offered some remarks of considerable decision and importance. It appears that the ordinance in question has, since the case of Bowers, been again put in force, and, on one occasion especially, under circumstances of peculiar notability. On the 24th March in the present year, a vessel was driven into the port of Charleston *in distress.* On board the unfortunate ship was a coloured seaman named Manuel Pereira, who, notwithstanding the involuntary character of his visit to the shores of South Carolina, was immediately seized and thrust into prison. This proceeding, as well as another of a similar kind in the May succeeding, provoked certain legal measures on the part of the British Consul, and it is on a general review of these transactions that Gov. Means founds the official remarks to which we allude. In this communication the Governor observes that when, upon the case of Isaac Bowers, the British Consul had applied for some modification of the law, committees of the State Legislature were appointed to consider the subject, and that these committees "reported adverse to any modification." The Governor himself, as appears from his own acknowledgement, was "anxious that the modification should be made," and he would even have recommended such a measure in his first message, had not the subject been already taken into consideration. Now, however, he avows such unbrage at the legal proceedings referred to, that he positively refuses to "abate one jot or tittle of the law."

We should be extremely sorry to import into this question any assumption injurious to either the rights or feelings of an independent people. We may even venture to grant the premises from which Governor Means proceeds. There is no doubt that the laws of South Carolina do plainly provide for the capture and incarceration of unoffending mariners being of negro blood. It is equally certain, we may presume, that the skins of Manuel Pereira and Reuben Roberts brought them under the penalties of the statute; nor are we entitled to argue that this provision was made without visible warrant. Very possibly

the question may, to use the Governor's own expression, be one of "self-preservation," and we certainly cannot interfere in the regulation of State
rights and federal duties under the Act of Union. But the unsoundness of
the argument--for unsound it assuredly is--lies somewhat deeper. It lies in
the character of Slavery itself--in the utterly indefensible nature of those
institutions which this particular law was directed to maintain. It is absolutely true--and we do not gainsay the fact--that a large portion of the
population of South Carolina is kept in such a condition as to render the
very sight or company of a free negro dangerous--that is the strongest possible evidence against the institutions themselves. The rights of "self-
preservation," spoken of by the Governor, are not unconditional. A slaver
or a pirate might resist an American sloop-of-war in direct "self-defence,"
but any homicide committed in this proceeding would be treated as murder.
True it is, undoubtedly, that every State has "a right to make police regulations of its own," but is it not also true that this right is also qualified by the forbiddance to inflict injury upon others? We are now addressing
Americans themselves--men of our own blood and lineage--and not Free Soilers
or Abolitionists merely, but all the right-thinking people of the Union.
They have lately dispatched an armed expedition to Japan, and one of the
soundest justifications of this menacing embassy is based upon the inhospi-
table treatment experienced by foreign seamen at the hands of the Japanese.
Now, in what does this treatment differ from that inflicted upon similar
visiters in an American port, and justified by an American Governor? The
Japanese look upon a stranger as dangerous to their institutions, and they
frame their own police regulations accordingly, in virtue of which a shipwrecked mariner is consigned to severe custody. The Americans of South Carolina profess the same views, and adopt the same precautions. They make no
exception or allowance for the perils of the deep; and, if a vessel from the
Republic of Liberia were driven upon Charleston strand, every passenger who
escaped the fury of the waves would be instantly incarcerated in Charleston
jail. Excepting the probable difference between Oriental and Christian prisons, there is literally no distinction between these two cases, and we request Americans to consider what answer they could return if an African State
powerful enough to fit out a 300-gun squadron should send to Carolina exactly
such a message as they are sending to Japan. [42]
     Much has been recently said and written about the proprieties or advan-
tages of external interference in a case like this, and the example of Governor Means himself, whose assent was converted into opposition by provocation from without, is an opportune verification of the arguments employed by
"A States'-Man" in our paper of Thursday. On these arguments, however, we
cannot avoid remarking that they would tell with greater force against pressure from without, if more movement be observed within. If those Southern
proprietors, who, as "A States'-Man" informs us, are "anxious to surrender
their slaves without a penny in exchange," would but give some sign of their
resolutions, or lay some visible foundation for negro emancipation at any
day, however distant, it would be a cogent fact against that unreasoning and
irresponsible agitation, which, we freely acknowledge, is fraught with incalculable peril to blacks and whites alike. Institutions which have taken
root and ramification like those of domestic Slavery in the Southern States
cannot be violently destroyed without extreme danger to the whole community,
and the magnitude of the hazard is enormously increased when the scene of experiment, instead of being laid, like our own, in a distant colony, is among
the very homes and dwellings of the people concerned. But, if there is to
be no external interference, and nothing is done in the State itself, what is
to be the end of institutions which the universal voice of mankind has condemned?
     Much, again, has been said of British "complicity"--of the responsibil-
ity which rests upon ourselves as originators of the evil, and of the immunities which the Americans thus derive. But is the argument really either
sound or becoming? Doubtless the New England colonists carried with them
many old English principles, and among them not the least settled was that of
treating witchcraft by combustion. Would this be thought a justification for
burning old women in New York at the present day? Do the free and enlightened people of America really hold that they are bound to model their own practices in the 19th century on those of English in the 17th? Do they hang for

shoplifting? do they press men to death for refusing to plead? or do they
maintain any other civil disabilities, except those created by the colour of
the skin? And what was thought of the force of this whole argument on tra-
dition on another occasion? There was an institution in America more ancient and more universal than that of Slavery; more intimately connected
with the daily business of the population, and more inextricably linked with
the thoughts and principles of society. This was allegiance to Great Britain. Less than ninety years ago--within the recollection, indeed, of men
not long dead--this institution was not only in existence, but influencing
and governing all the proceedings of the States. In pursuance, as they
stated in their Declaration of Independence, of the right to "assume the
station to which the laws of Nature and of Nature's God entitled them," the
Americans destroyed this institution utterly, and succeeded, through all the
vicissitudes of a dangerous struggle, in superseding it by others. Is the
case of the slave, according to these same "laws of Nature and of Nature's
God," less plain or less urgent than that of the colonists? or is the "institution" in the former instance less amenable to change than in the latter? We do not think "A States'-Man," or any of his countrymen, will venture on an affirmative reply.--*London Times*.

National Anti-Slavery Standard, April 21, 1853.

28. COLOURED SEAMEN

We would not mind having a dark complexion if we were sure of never going to the Southern States of America. In that country, a tinge of brown on
a man's cheek renders him more or less an object of suspicion, and we strongly advise all brunettes who may contemplate a trip to the Southern States,
to provide themselves before leaving their country, with credentials establishing the fact of their Caucasian origin. In all seriousness we are not
certain that such a precaution is unnecessary. If brown-complexioned men
may be legally seized by the American authorities of the South, conveyed to
jail, scourged, and finally sold into Slavery, we know of nothing to prevent
them from laying violent hands on women, whose olive complexion may excite
doubt as to their descent. The ready and the legal excuse would be, that all
coloured persons entering the States of North and South Carolina, may be law-
fully incarcerated. Women are not exempted from the operation of this law.
It is, then, clearly resolved into a question of shade. Now some of the enslaved population of America are even fairer than the Spaniards or the English, and are in no wise distinguishable from them. The same may be truth-
fully asserted of a large proportion of the free population of the North, of
African descent. The Southern legislatures have not left in doubt what fate
awaits these persons, should they trespass upon the territories which the
slaveholders have taken under their especial patronage. The laws of North
and South Carolina, in providing "that no persons shall enter these who are
labouring under any contagious or infectious diseases; who are foreign paupers; or convicts; or persons of vicious character" (and we do not quarrel
with them for attempting in such manner to preserve their health and their
virtue): comprise in this not by any means distinguished category, "free
persons of colour," because they are "a dangerous class of persons." We are
informed that the law which prohibits them from entering into these States,
was introduced by the local legislature about thirty years ago, subsequent to
the detection and suppression of an insurrectionary movement, devised and set
on foot by a free negro who had been for some time in the habit of going and
coming at his pleasure, and whose frequent excursions were proved to have
been connected with this attempt at revolt. "Therefore," says the authority
from whom we quote, "it is certainly very far from being unreasonable or
surprising that free persons of colour, coming from abroad into North and
South Carolina, should be deemed a dangerous class of persons, and dealt with

accordingly." This is slaveholders' logic, which carried out in its integrity would prove that one swallow *does* certainly make a summer. If it could be shown that at any time an Englishman had rendered himself obnoxious to the charge of infringing the laws of these States, the Legislature might, by a parity of reason, urge this circumstance as a reasonable pretext for passing a law prohibiting all Englishmen from entering the country, on "pain of being incarcerated for the first offence; whipped for the second; and sold at auction as slaves for the third." And this, in point of fact, is the law of North and South Carolina as it stands at present; and under it, British subjects, men and women may be imprisoned, whipped and sold, if they be so unfortunate as to possess a complexion of African hue. The thing has actually been done.

Sometime in March, 1852 (we believe it was on [illegible]). . . Jamaica, was driven into the port of Charleston by stress of weather. The captain and the crew had scarcely landed, before she went to the bottom. One of the crew, Manuel Pereira by name, was immediately seized and conveyed to jail. He was of African descent, and therefore belonged to a "dangerous class." He was guilty of no greater offence than that of being a man of colour, and even the misfortune of shipwreck did not save him from the black law of the States. According to it, he would have had to remain in prison until the vessel that brought him should sail again, when the captain would have to pay the cost of the poor fellow's keep, the jail-fees, and two dollars as a fee to the justice of the peace for entering Pereira's name in a book, with a specification of his age, occupation, height, and distinguishing marks. In case of a refusal on the part of the captain, Pereira might have been sold to pay these fees: sold into Slavery. In the present instance, the vessel had sunk, and the captain and the crew procured a passage in another vessel. Pereira therefore remained in jail; although Governor Means asserts, in his late message, that "the man was at perfect liberty to depart at any moment he could get a vessel to transport him beyond the limits of the State." How the unfortunate prisoner was to "get a vessel," under these circumstances, Governor Means does not inform the public. The British Consul, George Mathew, Esq., thought this a favourable opportunity for trying the question how far the forcible detention of a British subject is in accordance with the treaties existing between the Federal Government and that of Her Britannic Majesty. He had sometime before mooted the same subject, and suggested a modification of the existing laws, to the extent of simply restricting coloured persons to their vessels (except when engaged in loading or unloading on the wharfs), under a police passport or ticket. Governor Means says that this suggestion was under consideration when Mr. Consul Mathew, on behalf of Pereira, sued for a *Habeas Corpus* in the Courts of the State, but his application was rejected. He then appealed to the higher Court, pending which the authorities, getting somewhat alarmed, made an attempt to ship Pereira off, with the obvious intention of thus preventing any further legal steps being taken. But Mr. Consul Mathew, finding that his great object would thus be defeated, intercepted the sheriff, on his way to the vessel, with Pereira still in custody, and had the latter reconveyed to prison, until, having completed the requisite arrangements for carrying on the suit in appeal, and given due notice thereof to the Sheriff, he paid Pereira's passage to New York, and he recovered his liberty.

Here is another case. On the 19th of May, the steamer Clyde arrived at Charleston, from the Bahamas. On board of her was a coloured seaman named Reuben Roberts, who was, in like manner, forthwith seized by the Sheriff and conveyed to jail, where he remained until the 26th, when the Clyde being ready to sail, Roberts was once more put on board, and departed the same day.

If Pereira or Roberts return, they will not only be imprisoned, but flogged: should they return a second time, they may be sold, for the law says, speaking of such persons thus offending a third time, "he or *she* shall be sold at public sale as a slave, and the proceeds of such sale shall be appropriated and applied, one half thereof to the use of the State, and the other half to the use of the informer."

We are informed, upon the very best authority, that in 1851, thirty-seven British subjects were seized and incarcerated and forty-two in the course of last year; and that there is no doubt of many free coloured British subjects having been sold into Slavery under the operation of this law, all

traces of whom have been lost. The cases of Pereira and Roberts are, however, now being prosecuted, with a view of bringing the subject before the
Supreme Court of the United States. The Legislature of South Carolina asserts its intention of resisting to the last any attempt to abate one jot or
tittle of the law, alleging as its reason for making so resolute a stand,
that an attempt has been made to defy the law, and bring the States of North
and South Carolina into conflict with the Federal Government. On the other
hand her Majesty's Government will allow the case to go on until the decision of the Supreme Court is known, when it will no doubt, in the advent of
an adverse verdict, take that course which is at once consistent with what
is due to its own dignity, to the spirit of our treaties, and to the freedom
of British subjects.

We may mention that besides the barbarous penalties which an infraction
of the above-mentioned law involves, it operates most injuriously in other
respects. The commerce of the West Indies with the Southern ports of the
United States is (in winter especially), of great importance to those islands, where the state of the population and the nature of the climate pre-
cludes the employment of any considerable number of white seamen. The vessels are chiefly of small tonnage, and suited only for coast-wise navigation.
They are mainly sailed on what is called the share-system: that is, the captain and the crew agree to receive remuneration according to a certain scale
determined upon amongst themselves, the superior officers of course receiving more or less according to their rank, and the total amount to be divided, pro rata, depending upon the proceeds of the voyage. It is obvious that
the operation of the law under review must prove detrimental to the commercial success of these coasting enterprises. In the first place it takes
from the master of the vessel a portion of his paid and articled labourers,
and forces him to employ slave-labour, to load and unload his cargo, at the
rate of a dollar per man per day, whilst he has to maintain his own hands in
jail, at considerable cost, and pay the registration fees besides. In the
next place it always causes a longer detention of his vessel in port, so
that he frequently finds himself fore-stalled in the market, and compelled
to dispose of his cargo at a disadvantage. In the third place it checks the
enterprise of the free-coloured seamen, who are naturally deterred from entering upon a vocation which to pursue with profit, they should be able to
pursue constantly, but in attempting to do which they must risk their liberty, since they may be sold as slaves for paying a third visit to the same
port or State, though they be engaged in a perfectly legitimate calling.
These arbitrary laws are in reality intended as a precaution to prevent the
free-coloured seamen from having access to the slaves. This is openly avowed, for the authorities are quite aware that with a population of nearly
9,000,000 free persons of colour, and with the constant transit of travel-
lers from other States and countries, it is next to impossible to prevent
the slaves of North and South Carolina from acquiring the knowledge of the
existence of negro freedom, or of the geographical limits of Slavery. It is,
therefore, they think, to their interest to perpetuate ignorance, by shut-
ting up the coloured men who come in from foreign parts, and who, from their
being generally intelligent, enterprising, and above all, free, might engen-
der a contagion for liberty amongst their enslaved brethren. Such is the
nature of this abominable system: it is actually afraid of its own victims.

We conclude this notice with a statement which will be found in Mr. Consul Mathew's letter to Governor Means, under date of the 5th January, 1852.
He says:

"On Saturday, and again on this very day, the spectacle has been exhibited in the streets of Charleston, of unoffending British seamen taken forcibly from the protection of the flag of their country, and marched along to
a jail."--(London) Anti-Slavery Reporter.

National Anti-Slavery Standard, April 21, 1853.

29.   THE COLORED SEAMEN QUESTION IN
THE HOUSE OF COMMONS

On the 20th, in the Commons, Mr. Kinnaird put the following question:
"In what state the correspondence between the British and United States
Governments, with reference to colored seamen, being British subjects, on
the vessels to which they belong arriving at a port in any of the Southern
States being imprisoned on account of their color, now is; and whether there
would be any objection to lay the correspondence on the table of the House?"
    Lord John Russel, in reply, stated that there had been a great deal of
correspondence, and beneficial changes had been proposed in Georgia and Carolina, which would soon be carried into effect. He thought it was better
not to produce the correspondence as hopes were entertained that there would
be great improvement in the legislation of the States he had mentioned.

Frederick Douglass' Papers, May 15, 1854.

30.   COLORED SEAMEN IN SOUTH CAROLINA

In regard to the imprisonment of colored seamen visiting ports in South
Carolina, which has long been a subject of complaint and remonstrance on the
part of foreign nations, Governor Adams makes some important suggestions.
He says:
    "I recommend that the law be so modified as to permit colored seamen,
the subjects of *foreign nations,* to remain on board their vessels, to be allowed to land whenever the duties of the vessel may require it, upon their
receiving a written permit to that effect from the Mayor of the port; and
that while on land they be subjected to the ordinary restrictions applied to
the native colored population. Such a modification would relieve the law of
all its harshness, without compromising our right or endangering our domestic quiet."

New National Era, December 13, 1855.

31.   PERSONAL ACCOUNT OF A BLACK SEAMAN IN THE
PORT OF CHARLESTON

U.S. Steamer *Walker,* Pensacola, Florida
January 8, 1858

Dear Sir:
    I must first tell you of my adventures in Charleston. My duty on
board this ship required that I should go on shore. The laws of South Carolina forbade my doing so. The day after I arrived I was ordered ashore and
obeyed. When I was walking up King Street I was seized and arraigned before
the mayor. Fortunately for me, a young gentleman, an acquaintance of Captain Huger (the Capt. of the *Walker)* saw the arrest and informed him immediately. The Captain rendered securities and I was released.
    You, sir, have not perhaps been south of Mason and Dixon line, and
judge slavery therefore by the testimony you receive. You must witness it
in all its loathsomeness. On the 5th of December I was seated in the stern
sheets of one of our boats going on shore. As I neared the wharf I saw a
crowd of half-clad, filthy looking men, women and children go on board the

Savannah steamer. Poor wretches. In all that vast number, 2 or 300, I did
not notice one smile. All were moody, silent, sorrowful. I see in this
gang both sexes and all ages from the suckling babe to the decrepit old, all
bartered and sold to the rice swamp.

I walked up a large thoroughfare. The first thing that attracted my
[attention] was a sign: "Negroes and Land for sale." I passed on a little
farther and I see a large open room, over the door "Brokers' office." This
means, a Negro Seller. Two or 3 half starved looking wretches were seated
around. The very Earth seemed to tremble for the guilt of the oppressor.

A few days after my perambulation about the streets of Charleston I met
a young man with whom I had become acquainted in Philadelphia. I invited
him to take a cigar with me. He informed me that it was against the law for
a colored man to smoke a cigar or walk with a cane in the streets of Charleston. And if the streets (sidewalk) are crowded the Negro must take the middle of the street. I met several white women. They did not move an inch--
so I had always to give way to them. If I had run against one of them, they
would have had me flogged.

One can witness here what education can effect. The blacks here invariably believe that white men are superior not merely mentally but physical-
ly. I had occasion to have some clothes washed and called on an old [slave]
woman for that purpose. Several little white children were running about
the house, and she called them "Master" and "Mistress." I could not stand
this and reprimanded her. She was perfectly astonished, commenced an argument with me to prove that those children were entitled to this distinction.
She told me I must not talk this way--some of the people might overhear me
and tell master.

G. E. Stevens

*Jacob C. White Collection, Moorland-Spingarn Collection, Howard University
Library.*

32. APPEAL TO THE PUBLIC

We trust that the following appeal to the Northern public by four colored seamen, now in prison in Wilmington, North Carolina, will meet with a
cordial response. This case is one of peculiar hardship. The poor fellows
are far from home, without friends, without money to employ counsel; popular feeling is against them, and however meager the evidence, they are likely, unless help come speedily, to be convicted of a crime of which the penalty is death. Were it the worst of crimes, they would be entitled to counsel and to an impartial trial. The charge is, that they have 'abducted' a
piece of property, which was and is a part of the real and personal estate of
a clergyman--the Rev. Michael Robbins. The culprits shipped in Boston last
month. Shall they be hung because the servant of a minister of the Gospel
chose to take passage northward on board of their schooner?--Tribune.

WILMINGTON, N. C., Aug. 31, 1859.

We are here in jail on the charge of abducting a slave, the property of
the Rev. Michael Robbins, who was found secreted on board the schooner
George Harriss, while on a passage to your city from this port, which caused
us to be brought back, when an investigation was had, and we were committed
to jail, and are to be tried for our lives in October. The penalty for same,
by the laws of this State, is 'DEATH.'

The vessel is owned here, and the loss to her owners being great, we
cannot expect help, or even sympathy from them--nor can we obtain a lawyer
without means, and can only appeal to Northern friends for help in this our
'time of need.' Public sentiment is against us. We are all colored men.
The excitement is great, and if funds can be raised to employ a lawyer, and
we succeed in having our trial removed to an adjoining county, with the

meager testimony bearing on the case, we will be acquitted. If without
counsel, and our case is tried here, with popular feeling against us, we
fear the result. The only witness is the slave himself, whose evidence is
admissible against his own color, but not against a white. The other witnesses are gentlemen who found the slave on board, but are not aware how he
came there.

    We shipped on board the schooner George Harriss, in Boston, as seamen,
early in this month. We have written our friends for help and appeal to you
for assistance, and all who feel for suffering humanity, for aid.

    Please publish this, if practicable, and get all papers friendly to us
to copy. Your servants,

    William Tubbs, Taunton, Mass., born in Elizabeth City, N. C. William
Weaver, Boston, Mass, born in Sierra Leone. John Williams, Boston, Mass,
born in Sandwich Islands. Tom Winisfield, New York, born in the Island St.
Kitis; well known in St. Thomas as an English subject.

Douglass' Monthly, October, 1859.

BLACK CAULKERS

33. STRIKE ON THE FRIGATE COLUMBIA

    . . . they wher Rebuilding of the Columbia frigate and Commodore Hull
issued a order that no Mechanics or laborer should eat ther Dinners in rooms
of those shops in Dinner hour and at that time they wher Shop Carpenters her
from difrent parts of the cuntery at work on the Columbia frigate and they
got unsulted at the order that Commodore Hull isshued and every one of them
struck and said they wouldent work anny moore and at the same time they wher
a collered man from Baltimore By the name of Isral Jones a Caulker By trade
he was the forman Caulker of those collered Caulkers and they wher fifteen
or twenty of them here at that time Caulkin on the Columbia and the Carpenters made all of them knoc off too.

*Micheal Shiner Diary, July 28, 1835, Manuscript Division, Library of Con-
gress.*

34. BLACK CAULKERS DESERT BALTIMORE

    So great is the fear excited in the minds of the colored caulkers by the
frequent attacks made upon them that a number have deserted the city and
sought labor in other seaboard cities.

Baltimore Sun, July 5, 1858.

35. THE TROUBLE AMONG THE WHITE AND BLACK CAULKERS

The difficulty between the white caulkers and the colored caulkers
still exists, we learn, to such an extent that Messrs. William Skinner &
Sons have ceased operations at their ship yeard, and are about to commence
to suit against the city for damages growing out of the interruption of their
business, on the alleged ground of the failure of the authorities to afford
them adequate protection. Messrs. Skinner in a card, state that the police
having refused to accompany the colored caulkers from the yard, Mr. Jeremiah
P. Skinner proceeded with them in a boat, and was intercepted by a number of
armed men who had taken possession of the schooner Cambria in the river, and
pointed their weapons at them and threatened to fire, and it was only by Mr.
Skinner presenting his own weapon and calling out to some of the parties by
name that the lives of the negroes were prevented from being sacrificed.
The posse of police who were sent over to prevent any infraction of the peace
at the yard of Messrs. Skinner were we learned instructed to remain on duty
there until 6 o'clock in the evening, and another force started about five
o'clock under the charge of Marshal Herring, to escort the colored caulkers
from the yard, and protect them on their way to their homes, but on arriving
found that they had stopped work a half hour previous, and that their services were then not wanting. Had they remained until the usual hour of
stopping work adequate protection would doubtless have been afforded them.
It is a difficult matter to obtain all the facts with regard to outbreaks of this description, and still more difficult to give satisfaction to
all parties concerned. As to the origin of this outbreak both parties defend themselves and give their own version of the matter. The white caulkers complain that a most stringent combination and association exists among
the black caulkers, who, from their superior numbers, have not only oppressed the whites, but have obtained control of most of the yards. A case is
cited of a party of black caulkers having been induced, after considerable
persuasion, to caulk a schooner ready for launching in a ship yard in which
the proprietors had refused to acknowledge the sway of their society. When
the work was done they received their pay, and the schooner was no sooner
launched than she filled with water, the caulking having been done so bad in-
tentionally that the vessel had to be hauled up and recaulked. Another case
is mentioned of a white foreman in a yard that acknowledged the society's
regulations having done a day's work in another yard that resisted its authority, and his employers were compelled to discharge him forthwith, the
black caulkers refusing any longer to work under him. It is also asserted
that a party of black caulkers having found a white man at work on a vessel
on which they were engaged threw down their tools and refused to work until
he was discharged from the vessel. These charges, if true, were certainly
provocative of resistance, but do not justify any violence or infraction of
the rights and interference with the business of employers. The black caulkers on the other hand allege that there not, or was not until very recently,
any white caulkers in the city, that the business has always been in their
own hands, and that the regulations of their society were exclusively applicable to their own members--They also say that those men who are interfering
with them are not caulkers, or such bad workmen that they are unwilling to
work with them, and share in the blame that would fall on all if the work
should prove defective. It is an undoubted fact that for many years past all
of the caulking done in the city has been performed by blacks, and it was not
until this outbreak occurred, that we were aware that there were any white
men who claimed a knowledge of the business.
The parties who committed the acts of violence at the yard of Messrs.
Skinner are known to these gentlemen, and should be at once arrested and prosecuted to the full extent of the law. Every employer should be allowed,
without let or hindrance, to employ black or white men, as he may think proper, and if the white caulkers have, as has been alleged, resolved, that no
black caulkers should work on the south side of the basin, so long as the
work is not more than sufficient for their employment, they should be taught
that such resolve cannot be carried into execution.
We visited the yards on the south side of the basin yesterday afternoon,
and found black caulkers at work in some of the yards, and white caulkers in

others, and great activity visible everywhere. Perfect calm prevailed, and
some to whom we spoke on the subject remarked that they had witnesses or
heard of little of the outrages that they had read in some of the papers.
Those employers who refuse to employ black caulkers, allege many grievances
that they have suffered at their hands, besides being compelled to pay them
$1.75, being fifty cents more per day than they could get the work done by
white men, whilst each journeyman caulker has two or three apprentices for
whom they are compelled to pay $1.50 per day. Other employers, however, al-
lege that they are perfectly satisfied with the blacks, that they are good
workmen and are in such numbers that the work can be done much more rapidly
than by white men, who do not number at present more than thirty, whilst a
hundred or more are sometimes required in that locality. They also allege
that the white men are, generally speaking, not as good workmen as the
blacks, whilst others assert that the whites do better work than the blacks.
It appears that there is also a Ship Masters' Society, the operations of
which, are alleged to be connected with the difficulty, and that the black
caulkers have been used to bring refractory members to terms.

The appearance of white caulkers in the city, who are now here in considerable numbers, we learn has been occasioned by the oppressive action of
the blacks, who formerly monopolized the business and effectually excluded
the whites from participation from them.--We were yesterday informed by one
of our most extensive firms that they were compelled to advertise for them
on account of the refusal of the blacks to work in their yards, leaving them
at a time when they were crowded with business, and willing, as they always
had been, to pay them the wages they demanded. The following substance of
an affidavit yesterday voluntarily made to Mayor Swann by Captain Adams
Gray, formerly engaged in ship building, will probably throw some light on
the subject:

"In 1850 Captain Adams Gray rented on Fardy's ship yard. He followed
the business of building and repairing ships for four years. There was then
an association of black caulkers, whose President was Mr. Flannigan. It is
the same association that exists now, but they have another President. Captain Gray was not a regular ship builder, and gave dissatisfaction on this
account. The colored caulkers were ordered to leave working for Captain
Gray, and he was left without hands in his yard. He had had not difficulty
with the colored men and had always given the highest wages. Captain Gray
determined not to be made the victim of what he supposed to be a combination,
and Mr. Cully, who was then in his employ, was instructed to go to Wilmington
and procure *white* caulkers. He also threatened the foreman of the black
caulkers, who had contracted to do the work, that he would sue him for damages for suffering himself to be controlled by the association. The Captain
considered himself entirely at the mercy of the colored association. The
black caulkers, finding Captain Gray determined and resolute, afterwards returned to their work."

Baltimore American and Commercial Advertiser, July 8, 1858.

36. THE CAULKERS' DIFFICULTY

We learn that the ship-yard of Messrs. Skinner & Sands, Federal Hill,
which had been closed since Saturday in consequence of the difficulty between
the white and colored caulkers was reopened yesterday morning, and a number
of the white class were set to work on the vessels in the yard.

Baltimore Sun, July 9, 1858.

37. THE DIFFICULTY AMONG THE CAULKERS

We received yesterday various statements with regard to the hostility
assumed by the white caulkers on the south side of the basin against the
black caulkers, none of which, however, conflict in the least with the review of the difficulty contained in yesterday's American.--There have been
faults on both sides, and causes for provocation and resentment, and the exercise of arbitrary power by both when circumstances gave them the strength
to resist and oppress each other. Heretofore the association of blacks,
when the pursuit was altogether in their own hands, by combination, sought
and did maintain an exclusive monopoly of the business, and effectually
excluded white men from this field of employment. In this course they were
sustained, and acted, we believe, under the direction and advisement of the
association of employers. Indeed it has been no fault of the blacks that
this difficulty has been brought upon them, but rather in being required to
submit to the dictation of their employers, in withdrawing from the employment of refractory members as a means of forcing them into an obedience to
the rules and regulations of the association of employers. The blacks may
perhaps have been the willing instruments in this species of oppression, but
it was a regulation originally adopted by the consent of all the shipwrights
of the city, with one or two exceptions, and consequently beyond their
powers of resistance, had they so desired. The rule was that in case of any
members of the Association of Employees disregarding the rules of the Association, he should be fined $50 and the caulkers withdrawn from his service
until the fine was paid. It was the enforcement of this rule on Messrs,
Fardy & Brothers that brought the white caulkers to the city, and was the
incipient step to the present difficulty.

However, both the society of employing shipwrights and the association
of black caulkers have now been dissolved, and all rules and regulations,
whether oppressive or otherwise, have been abandoned. The employers at
Fell's Point all desire to continue the employment of their old hands, most
of whom have been brought up in their yards, and some have been in their
employment for ten or fifteen years, and for whom they have a sincere regard.
All they ask and demand is, that they shall be protected in their inalienable
right to give employment to whoever they choose, whether white or black,
without let or hindrance, and in this they should be protected and doubtless
will be protected by the city authorities. The violence that has been exercised by the white caulkers on the south side of the basin should be at once
checked and the perpetrators punished.--They have committed high-handed outrages, and have established a tyranny that must become still more oppressive
if continued to be countenanced by any portion of the employers. They should
at once, and before it is too late, deny the right of this white association
to assume the power to say who they shall or shall not employ, or it may
still further extend its powers by limiting a day's work to six hours, or demand a per centage on the profits of employers. Above all, the poor negro
should be protected, and not be beaten and intimidated from seeking employment in the business to which he has been reared. If employers prefer the
black caulkers, they should be protected in their preference, their interest
to use their influence to maintain the rights of all in this respect. There
is abundance of work for all the real caulkers in the city, both black and
white, at the present time, and if the effort to force on employers inex-
perienced and incompetent white men is countenanced, it will lead to greater
troubles than any that have yet been encountered.

We learn that the Messrs. Skinner yesterday resumed business at their
yard on the south side of the basin, taking into their employment twelve
white caulkers, having been compelled to yield to their demands. The colored caulkers at work on the south side of the basin we learn were allowed to
work by permit from the President of the white caulkers' association, which
certainly exhibits a sad state of affairs.

We are requested by Captain Adam Gray to state that he was summoned to
testify before the Mayor, and did not appear voluntarily to give his testimony as published in the American yesterday. Mr. Fianigin also requests us
to say that Captain Adams is mistaken in his supposition that he was

President of the Caulkers' Association at the time of the difficulty in his shipyard, and neither is he President at the present time.

Baltimore American and Commercial Advertiser, July 9, 1858.

38. MORE VIOLENCE IN THE BALTIMORE SHIP YARDS

Highhanded Proceeding.--Yesterday afternoon an outrageous proceeding was enacted at the screw deck, Fell's Point, in which Mr. Hugh O. Cooper was knocked down and several colored caulkers were severely beat. As far as the facts could be ascertained, it appeared that a brig was placed on the screw-dock for the purpose of being coppered, which had been caulked by white caulkers, and the party employed to put the copper on engaged the colored caulkers, who do all their work in that line. Shortly after one o'clock a party of three or four white men went to the dock and threatened the colored men with summary vengeance if they did not desist from the work, and after knocking down three or four them left.--Some two hours later a larger force of white men appeared, headed by Joseph Edwards, and again ordered the colored men to cease work. They exhibited some hesitation about complying with the order, when the white men fell upon them and beat several severely, and finally drove them from the work. Hugh A. Cooper was standing on Thames street, when Edwards followed one of the colored men, and Mr. Cooper called to him, saying that if he committed any breach of the peace he would lay it before the grand jury. Edwards ceased his pursuit of the colored man and turning on Mr. Cooper, dealt him a blow which felled him to the ground, and then kicked him severely in the abdomen.

By this time information had been sent to the middle district police station, and Capt. Lynch, with a posse of officers, proceeded to the scene of riot--The assailants, however, had been busily at work, and had inflicted severe wounds on several of the colored men. An apprentice boy on the rail of the vessel was struck with a club and knocked to the deck. One of the colored men, named Anthony Miller, living in Happy alley, had his right cheek cut open, severing the facial artery, which bled profusely. Dr. Monkur took up the artery and dressed the wound. Another named Wm. Hudlow was struck over the left eye with a club, inflicting a severe wound. Several others were beat, and nearly the whole of them driven from work. As soon as the police approached the assailants fled to their boat, in which they crossed the harbor, and tried to make the south shore of the harbor, but Captain Lynch at once procured a steam-tug, gave chase and soon overhauled them. Joseph Edwards, George Gardner, James Carr and Wm. Kirwan, all the parties in that boat, were arrested and conducted to the office of Justice Griffin.--There were no white witnesses to appear against Gardner, Carr and Kirwan, and they were dismissed from custody. Edwards was held to bail in the sum of $300 for the assault on Mr. Cooper, George Gardner becoming his security. The whole thing was said to have been entirely unprovoked, but anticipated, from previous threats which had been made.

Baltimore Sun, June 28, 1859.

39. THE FELL'S POINT OUTRAGE

The outrage at Fell's Point on Wednesday afternoon, it appears was not confined to the attack on the colored men in coppering the barque Virginia. After Edwards and his associates had been arrested and released, George Gardner, the party who entered bail for Edwards, took the command and went to the ship David Stewart, when they made an attack on a man named Hammond, employed on that vessel.--When the attack was first made, H. endeavored to defend himself with a barrel stave and struck Gardner one blow; the others then rushed upon him, beating him over the head and in the face, until he sought refuge in the hold of the ship.--They followed him to the hatchway, and fired pistols into the hold. After his assailants left, Hammond procured a carriage and went to the office of Dr. Monkur, where his injuries were dressed and then went to his home. The assailants then left that part of the city. Yesterday morning the grand jury found a true bill against Joseph Edwards for the assault on Hugh A. Cooper, one of their number, and a bench warrant was ordered for his arrest.

Baltimore Sun, June 29, 1859.

PART VI

THE FREE BLACK WORKERS' RESPONSE TO OPPRESSION

THE FREE BLACK WORKERS' RESPONSE TO OPPRESSION

The relatively small number of northern blacks in the crafts and mechanical pursuits, compared with menial labor and the service industries (as waiters, porters, barbers, and the like), caused difficulties beyond simple poverty; over time this came to mean that whites expected blacks to work only in those occupations, which created an oversupply of labor in those areas which were open to black workers.

To counter this pattern of employment, blacks fashioned several institutional responses. The American League of Colored Laborers was organized in New York City in July 1850 with Frederick Douglass as vice president. Its main objectives were to promote unity among mechanics, foster training in agriculture, industrial arts, and commerce, and assist members in establishing business for themselves. Clearly, the League was interested in industrial education rather than trade union activity, and was oriented toward the self-employed artisan (Doc. 1).

The Negro Convention Movement was another institutional response to the problems of restricted labor mobility. During the Ante-Bellum Era, black leaders gathered in conventions, both on the local and national level, to discuss issues of mutual concern, and to reach some agreement as to the appropriate group response. Many of the documents in Part VI refer to the proceedings of these conventions (Doc. 2-17). One of the most interesting corrective proposals called for the construction of an "industrial college" for black youths (Doc. 15-17). This idea gained currency at several conventions during the 1840s and 1850s, and won support from the most prominent black leaders, including Alexander Crummell and James McCune Smith (Doc. 8), and Frederick Douglass (Doc. 15). Several eminent white abolitionists also favored the concept, among them William Lloyd Garrison (Doc. 5), and Harriet Beecher Stowe (Doc. 12). No one phrased the alternatives more starkly than Douglass, who suggested that blacks must "Learn Trades or Starve" (Doc. 11).

The gradual expulsion of blacks by immigrants from traditional jobs, as waiters and porters for example, further necessitated this reassessment regarding the long-range strategy for black workers. The question broke over the age-old dilemma of whether blacks should integrate into or separate from American society (Doc. 18-20). Some, such as Martin R. Delany, saw no end to the oppression and therefore advocated emigration (Doc. 19), while others, such as Frederick Douglass, were determined to fight against discrimination and for integration (Doc. 20).

FREE BLACK UPLIFT: UNIONS, COOPERATIVES,
CONVENTIONS, SCHOOLS

1. AMERICAN LEAGUE OF COLORED LABORERS

An Association under this name was formed in New-York during the anni-
versary week, the object of which is to promote union and concert among the
people of color in means for their own improvement; especially in their social and physical condition.

They recommend as general and thorough an education of their youth in
agriculture, the mechanic arts, and commerce as in science; that every colored mechanic should, if able, carry on business for himself, and for such
as have not the means, that

"A fund should be established in every community, for the purpose of
loaning sums of money to colored men of integrity to assist them to go into
business on their own account, or in such way as they may find most convenient and profitable.

They "recommend skillful, honorable, profitable labor to the free colored men of the United States, not merely because it is productive of wealth,
and all its accompanying advantages; but because it is indispensable to that
development and perfection, both of body and mind, which we so much need, and
which many of us so much desire."

The following plan of organization and list of officers, were adopted:

1. That the editors present, and all friendly, be requested to publish,
repeatedly, the propositions adopted by this meeting.

2. That there be an Executive Committee whose office shall be in the
City of New-York, the members of which, residing in said City, shall be a
quorum for the transaction of business for the Association generally, and
said City in particular; all other Committees or Associations, for the same
object, shall correspond with said Executive Committee at least once a month;
and said Committee shall consist of 23 members.

3. That the details of carrying out the work be left to the colored
communities in the various parts of the country, who are hereby respectfully
recommended to form Associations in co-operation with the Executive Committee.

4. Every Association or Committee, when formed, shall publish its proceedings in our papers, (and pay for the same,) and also in one local paper.

5. That an Industrial Fair shall be held in New-York City in the second week in May, 1852; of the proceeds of which 70 per cent shall be given
to the producers, and 30 per cent. shall be devoted to carrying out the
views of this organization; and that colored mechanics, artisans and agricul-
turists, be earnestly requested to exhibit at the several national Fairs,
specimens of their skill and industry.

6. That an Agent shall be employed by the Executive Committee to lay
these views before the Colored People of the United States.

S. R. WARD, President.

L. Woodson,)
) Vice Presidents.
F. Douglass,)

New York Tribune, July 3, 1850.

2. CONVENTIONS OF COLORED PEOPLE

There is now in session in this City a Convention composed entirely of colored citizens. The object of the Convention is to consider the present condition of the Negro race, and to devise means for its improvement. On Tuesday evening, Dr. J. McCune Smith read a report from the Committee on the Social Condition of the Colored Race. It was an elaborate document, containing a great many curious facts. The first question discussed was, whether the colored people should endeavor to organize themselves in the City, or devise a plan of settling in the country. The report made, considers the subject: [43]

The advantages about city life with us are, that a larger number of us can be within short distances of each other, and thereby may easily organize without such disadvantage as would grow from the same number being banded in a single country.

We get a large amount of friction without being so condensed as to be reached by a law for removing us from any rural locality--such laws as expatriated Indians and Mormons. We can be, if we will, much better provided for in the matter of education in the city than we could in the country. We can, if we shoose, throw vastly more trade of our own and of other people, in the way of each other in the city, than we could in the country.

The disadvantages of our City life--I mean those peculiar to us, for all city life is, after all, a kind of hot-house forcing of human beings--are the following:

1st. Our lives are much shortened. Look at the preponderance of widows and children among us. They so far exceed the calamities of mere sickness, that our benevolent societies have been obliged to cut off the widows and orphans, in order to help the sick.

2nd. Next, the seductions of the City--policy gambling, porter houses, with their billiards and cards, create a gang of lazaroni of both sexes, women hastening through the streets, with their bonnets untied; men, shirtless and shoeless, hanging round the corners, or standing, walking, gutter-tumbling--signs which our foes call the type of our condition.

3d. City life shuts us from general mechanical employment; while journeymen in the cities refuse to work with us, and colored bosses have either too little capital, or too little enterprise, to bring up and employ apprentices and journeymen.

4th. From the necessity of seeking employment in the city, as servants, porters, &c., our manhood is, in a measure, demeaned, lowered, kept down; and I doubt much whether manhood flourishes very much among citizens of any class.

5th. The enormous combination of capital, which is slowly invading every calling in the city, from washing and ironing to palace steamers, must tend more and more to grind the face of the poor in the cities, and render them more and more the slaves of lower wages and higher rents.

No sane man can doubt, from this or any comparison of the kind, that country life is the better choice of our people; not consolidated, isolated country life, but a well mixed country and village life. The matter of education, the great disadvantage of country life, might be remedied by concert of action.

As to the practicability of removing to the country, it was argued, that savings might be effected by the two thousand colored families in the city, in a rigid economy of house-rent and fuel, enough to establish a bank, which would soon colonize the entire class. The topic was first illustrated in the matter of house-rent thus:

In the rear of No. 17 Laurens-street, is a back lot which cost $2,500; on it are erected two buildings, which cost $6,000, Total, $8,500. Interest on which, at 7 per cent, is $595; and add for taxes, insurance and wear $100, making full cost $695 per year. These two buildings are occupied by twenty colored families, who pay an average of $7 each per month; that is $1,680 per year. Here is a clear profit to the landlord of $985 per year, above interest and expense.

Here then, in the single item of rent, twenty families are paying enough to fit out two families a year most amply and abundantly for the country.

Again: If those buildings were owned by a colored Savings Institution, whose surplus funds should be devoted to setting up colored young men on farms, such institution, after paying depositors six per cent would have a splendid surplus for starting farmers or men in others business. If we take a larger view of this matter of house rent, the results are amazing. According to the above estimate, each one of the twenty families in the rear of 17 Laurens-st. are paying $37 per year too much for house rent.

There are some 2,500 colored families in New York and its vicinity; say that each family pays only $10 a year too much for house rent, and that these families could, by organization, retrench and accumulate that sum per year, and we would save, in this one item, $25,000 per year!

In respect to the use of fuel, it was also shown, that it is next in importance. Our 2,000 families consume at least two and a half tons coal each year per year, making 4,500 tons. At least two-thirds of these 2,000 families buy their coal by the bushel or peck, thereby paying $2 per ton more than the market price, which is a sacrifice of $6,000 per year. Then, if these 2,000 families combined to buy their own coal at the wharf, they could save, by purchasing cargoes, $1 on each ton, at least, which is $10,500. Allowing the hire of a coal yard at $800 per year, and the pay of two good clerks at $800 each, there would be clear gain of $8,100 in the single matter of coal, if we would thoroughly organize the matter.

By similar calculations, it can be shown that we could easily save $20,000 on groceries and food, and $10,000 on wearing apparel; beside setting up in successful and commanding business such men as are capable, intelligent and trustworthy.

In order to accomplish these, the report proposed the establishment of a mutual bank, in which all the depositors should be at the same time stockholders, and which should have power to buy and sell real estate, to discount paper, to lend money on bond and mortgage, and to deal in merchandise. The Doctor, after concluding the reading of the report, said that there were $40,000 or $50,000 belonging to colored people invested in savings banks in Wall-st., and he then presented the following resolution:

Resolved, that a Committee of three be appointed, with power to present the form of a Mutual Savings Institution, embracing the matters of house rent, fuel and other domestic wants, and that one of the conditions of membership of said institution shall be a pledge to abstain from policy-gambling.

A discussion of the subject at great length took place, in the course of which fearful revelations were made of the extent of policy gambling among the blacks, and the resolution adopted.

New York Daily Tribune, March 20, 1851.

3. THE QUEST FOR EQUALITY

White Fellow Citizens:

The great truth of moral and political science, upon which we rely and which we press upon your consideration, have been evolved and enunciated by you. We point to your principles, your wisdom, and to your great example for the full justification of our cause this day. That "ALL MEN ARE CREATED EQUAL," that "LIFE, LIBERTY AND THE PURSUIT OF HAPPINESS" are the right of all; that "THE CONSTITUTION OF THE UNITED STATES WAS FORMED TO ESTABLISH JUSTICE, PROMOTE THE GENERAL WELFARE AND TO SECURE THE BLESSING OF LIBERTY TO ALL THE PEOPLE OF THIS COUNTRY."

We address you as American citizens asserting their rights on their own native land.

WE ASK to be disencumbered of the load of popular reproach heaped upon us -- for no better cause than that we wear the complexion given us by our God and Creator.

WE ASK that in our native land, we shall not be treated as strangers.

WE ASK that, speaking the same language, and being of the same religion, worshipping the same God, owing our redemption to the same Savior, and learning our duties from the same Bible, we shall not be treated as barbarians.

WE ASK that, having the same physical, moral, mental, and spiritual wants, common to other members of the human family, we shall also have the same means which are granted and secured to others to supply those wants.

WE ASK that the doors of the schoolhouses, the work-shop, the church, the college, shall be thrown open as freely to our children as to the children of other members of the community.

WE ASK that as justice knows no rich, no poor, no black, no white, but, like the government of God, renders alike to every man reward or punishment according as his works shall be -- the black and white may stand upon an equal footing before the laws of the land.

WE ASK that the complete and unrestricted right of suffrage, which is essential to the dignity even of the white man, be extended to the colored man also.

We shall invite the cooperation of good men in this country and throughout the world -- and above all, we shall look to God, the Father and Creator of all men, for wisdom to direct us and strength to support us in the holy cause to which we solemnly pledge ourselves.

In numbers we are few and feeble; but in goodness of our cause, in the rectitude of our motives, and in the abundance of argument on our side, we are many and strong. The number in our land who already recognize the justice of our cause, and are laboring to promote it, is great and increasing.

As a people, we feel ourselves to be not only deeply injured, but grossly misunderstood. Our white fellow-countrymen do not know us. They are strangers to our character, ignorant of our capacities, oblivious of our history and progress. It is believed that no other nation on the globe could have made more progress in the midst of such universal and stringent disparagement. In view of our circumstances, we can, without boasting, thank God, and take courage, having placed ourselves where we may fairly challenge comparison with more highly favored men.

Among the colored people we can point with pride and hope, to men of education and refinement, who have become such, despite of the most unfavorable influences.

While conscious of the immense disadvantages which beset our pathway, we are encouraged to persevere in efforts adapted to our improvement, by a firm reliance upon God, and a settled conviction, as immovable as the everlasting hills, that all the truths in the whole universe of God are allied to our cause.

"Address of the Colored National Convention to the People of the United States," held at Rochester, N.Y., on July 6-8, 1853.

4. INTRODUCTORY ADDRESS,

Spoken by a pupil at a public examination 1819, embracing also his Valedictory on that occasion.

RESPECTED PATRONS AND FRIENDS,

To me is allotted the honor of inviting the attention of this philanthropic assembly to the various specimens of improvement, which the constant efforts of the Trustees and Teachers of this school, have caused us to make, since the last public examination, and I am happy in having been one of the favored number who have enjoyed the blessed advantages of this Institution. We have been the objects of your care, and I still earnestly solicit your sympathy. Had I the mind of a Locke, and the eloquence of a Chatham, still, would there not be in the minds of some, an immeasurable distance that would divide me from one of a white skin? What signifies it! Why should I strive hard, and acquire all the constituents of a man, if the prevailing genius of the land admit me not as such, or but in an inferior degree! Pardon me if I feel insignificant and weak. Pardon me if I feel discouragement to oppress me to the very earth. Am I arrived at the end of my education, just on the eve of setting out into the world, of commencing some honest pursuit, by which to earn a comfortable subsistence? What are my prospects? To what shall I turn my hand? Shall I be a mechanic? No one will employ me; white boys won't work with me. Shall I be a merchant? No one will have me in his office; white clerks won't associate with me. Drudgery and servitude, then, are my prospective portion. Can you be surprised at my discouragement? Child as I am, of the same Almighty Being, and equally accountable both here and hereafter, as much so as any of the great human family!

You will not have an opportunity of seeing that many of us have acquired a commendable knowledge of the various branches taught in this School. This, the exercises now to be introduced, will, I hope, more fully demonstrate.

Charles G. Andrews, The History of the New-York African-Free Schools (New York, 1830), p. 132.

5. SCHOOL FOR COLORED YOUTH

At the meeting of the Anti-Slavery Society at Franklin Hall on Monday evening last, the following resolution was passed.

Whereas, Education must be regarded as the first and principal means of improving the moral condition and character of the Free People of Color in this country; and whereas those people do not at present enjoy the privilege of obtaining an education on terms of equality with others, such as is necessary to qualify them to become highly useful as teachers:

Therefore, Resolved, That this Society will immediately take measures to raise, by voluntary contributions, subscriptions and donations, the sum of Fifty Thousand Dollars, for the purpose of establishing a school on the manual labor system, for the education of Colored Youth; and that a committee now be appointed to have the special Charge of this subject, and to promote its accomplishment by all reasonable ways and means, as to them shall seem right and proper.

The Committee chosen were, the Rev. Moses Thacher, Samuel E. Sewall, Esq., Mr. Arnold Buffum, Mr. James G. Barbadous, and Mr. John T. Hilton.

Proposals for establishing a School on the Manual Labor System, for the Education of Colored Youth.

It appears by the official census of 1830, that there were then in the United States of America 600,000 free people of color, and 2,000,000 slaves. This great multitude, constituting one fifth part of our whole population are by the influence of an unholy prejudice virtually excluded from our seminaries of learning, and but very few of them are able to obtain an education to qualify themselves for usefulness as teachers of persons of their own color. We know not that there is in the whole country a single institution above that of a common grammar day school, established for their benefit.

We regard them as a deeply injured and suffering people, having claims upon us which are as imperative and obligatory as the positive injunctions

of the gospel can make them, to do for the promotion of their welfare, all
that Christianity requires at the hand of man for his brothers and we believe that nothing short of an improved system of education, the benefits
whereof may be diffused through the entire community, can ever place them in
that rank of society to which they are justly entitled, as a portion of the
American family, and which will prove an legislatible argument against the
[illegible] objections to the safety and propriety of gaining the blessing of
universal freedom to their brethren who are now in bondage. We are assured
that there are numbers of unfortunate individuals who are the offspring of
white fathers and that are now held in bondage by their near relatives, who
would gladly embrace the opportunity to free them, and place them in an institution where they might receive a liberal as well as a moral and virtuous
education to fit them for usefulness and respectability. Deeply impressed
with the importance of speedily entering upon the discharge of the duties
which we owe to the people of color among us, and not doubting the liberal
patronage and support of the stewards of the bounties of indulgent heaven,
we have resolved to make an appeal, not to the avarice of the sordid miser,
but to the spirit of benevolence, the swift winged messenger of love from on
high, for the pecuniary means necessary for establishing a seminary on the
manual labor system for the education of colored youth of both sexes, where
at the same time that the males are instructed in such useful employments in
agriculture and the mechanic arts, and the females in such domestic concerns,
as will qualify them for extensively promoting the improvement of the condition of the people of color in our country, they will also be educated in
useful literature and science, and where the most careful and persevering
guardianship will be exercised over their habits and morals, and all those
virtues which adorn life and render it a blessing, may be cultivated.

It is therefore proposed to raise by voluntary donations and subscriptions the sum of *fifty thousand dollars* to be applied, under the direction of
a board of trustees, to be chosen at a general meeting of those who have contributed to the amount of $10 and upwards for the establishment and support
of such an institution, under an act of incorporation to be obtained from
the legislature of the State in which it may be situated.

Considering that the degradation and sufferings of the unfortunate people in whose behalf we now present ourselves before a liberal and enlightened generation, have been entailed upon them through the mistaken policy of
the government under which our fathers lived, at a time when they constituted
a dependent portion of the British Empire, and knowing that distinguished
philanthropists of that empire at the present day, with their abundant means,
posses abundant feelings of sympathy and benevolence toward those people,--
we regard this as one of those very peculiar cases in which it is not only
our right, but our duty, to invite them to participate with us in the prosecution of our plan for conferring upon the unfortunate children of sorrow
and oppression in our land, those inestimable benefits which arise from cul-
tivating and enlightening their intellectual and moral powers. We therefore
propose simultaneously to solicit, both in England and America, precuniary
contributions from the friends of virtue, justice, humanity and religion, for
the promotion of this interesting object.

Relying upon the benign influence of the spirit of the gospel, to in-
cline those who are blessed with means, to contribute liberally and freely,
and more especially to qualify for their high duties those on whom the government of the institution may devolve, we reverent commend our cause to
whom we are bound by the highest obligation, to devote all that we have, and
all that we are.

In behalf of the New England Anti-Slavery Society.
ARNOLD BUFFUM, President.
Wm. Lloyd Garrison, Corresponding Sec.
Joshuan Coffin, Recording Sec'y.
Boston, Sept. 26, 1832.

The Liberator, September 29, 1832.

6. PROGRAM OF THE PHOENIX LITERARY SOCIETY,
NEW YORK CITY, 1833

This Society will aim to accomplish the following objects: To visit
every family in the ward, and make a register of every colored person in it
--their name, sex, age, occupation, if they read, write, and cipher--to invite them, old and young, and of both sexes, to become members of this society, and to make quarterly payments according to their ability--to get the
children out to infant, Sabbath, and week schools, and induce the adults also to attend school and church on the Sabbath--to encourage the women to
form Dorcas societies to help clothe poor children of color if they will attend school, the clothes to be loaned, and to be taken away from them if
they neglect their schools; and impress on their parents the importance of
having the children punctual and regular in their attendance at school--to
establish mental feasts, and also lyceums for speaking and for lectures on
the sciences, and to form moral societies--to seek out young men of talent,
and good moral character, that they may be assisted to obtain a liberal edu-
cation--to report to the board all mechanics who are skillful and capable of
conducting their trades and with respectable farmers for lads of good moral
character--giving a preference to those who have learned to read, write and
cipher--and in every way to endeavor to promote the happiness of the people
of color, by encouraging them to improve their minds, and to abstain from
every vicious and demoralizing practice.

The Liberator, June 29, 1833.

7. MANUAL LABOR SCHOOL FOR COLORED YOUTH

To promote the virtuous and guarded education of the free Colored Youth
in the United States; to form in them habits of industry, economy, and morality, as well as to extend to them the benefits of literature and science:
--we, the subscribers, agree to pay to the Trustees, to be chosen as hereinafter expressed, the sums affixed to our respective names, for the purpose
of establishing a School in some part of New-England, for the education of
colored youth on the Manual Labor System, on the following terms:

ARTICLE I. Such part of the sums subscribed, as may be necessary, shall
be invested in lands, buildings, and farming and mechanical stock and apparatus, and other things requisite for the establishment and support of the
proposed institution, and shall remain forever a fund for the support of an
institution for promoting an economical and judicious system of education for
young persons of African descent, having especial reference to their qualifications to become extensively useful as teachers and examples and benefactors to their brethren.

ART. II. The Trustees may invest such part of the funds as to them
shall seem advisable in permanent stocks, the income to be appropriated to
defray the expense of educating such pupils as may be otherwise unable to
enjoy the benefits of the institution.

ART. III. While virtue and piety are to be regarded as essential parts
of the education to be given in the proposed institution, and while Christianity will form the basis of the system, young persons of all sects and
denominations shall be equally admitted to the school, and shall enjoy equal
rights and privileges therein; there shall be no infringement of the liberty
of conscience in any manner whatever; and no measures shall ever be adopted
tending to give any denomination the ascendancy in the government of the
proposed seminary. In order to preserve these fundamental principles from

violation, a majority of the Trustees shall never consist of persons of the same denomination of Christians. This article is to be unalterable.

ART. IV. As soon as it shall be ascertained that ten thousand dollars or upwards have been subscribed, the President of the New-England Anti-Slavery Society shall call a meeting of the contributors, by giving notice in at least three newspapers published in Boston, and one or more in Providence, New-Haven, New-York, Philadelphia, and Washington, and by giving notice by mail to every person who may have subscribed to the amount of one hundred dollars or upwards, to assemble in Boston at such time and place as he may designate, then and there, in conjunction with the Board of Managers of the New-England Anti-Slavery Society, to elect twenty Trustees, who, with their successors, shall have the perpetual government of the institution and management of its funds. If practicable, the Trustees thus chosen shall obtain an act of incorporation from the Legislature of the State in which the seminary may be situated, for the better security of the funds and interests of the institution, and embracing the principles of these articles as far as possible.

ART. V. After the first election, the Trustees shall be chosen annually, by a joint ballot of the existing Trustees and the Board of Managers of the New-England Anti-Slavery Society.

ART. VI. No subscription shall be called for until the amount of *Ten Thousand Dollars* has been subscribed, while such sums as may have been paid will be invested in stocks by the Treasurer of the New-England Anti-Slavery Society, to remain until Trustees are chosen, when it shall be paid to them.

Boston, January 28, 1833.

The Liberator, February 16, 1833.

8. COMMITTEE ON EDUCATION REPORT, 1848 NATIONAL COLORED CONVENTION, CLEVELAND, OHIO

Resolved, That the founding of a collegiate institution, on the manual labor plan, well endowed, placed in some central position, is calculated to lessen the restraint and timidity, which must long exist, from the existence of caste in social and consequently college life; to call forth larger numbers in the pathway of learning, and to rouse a new spirit and temper among our people, wholly favorable to learning and intellectual advancement.

Therefore, Resolved, That this Convention places before the colored people of the United States, the founding of a college, as its leading and most prominent object.

Resolved, That a committee of twenty-five be appointed, with full powers to devise a plan, and, if possible, to commence obtaining subscriptions and funds, to designate proper and capable persons to conduct such an institution, to fix upon a site, and to make such other arrangements as may seem to them fit and proper, for the founding of a collegiate institution, where the facilities of education of colored youth may be abundantly increased, but which shall not be exclusive; and this committee report to this convention at its next annual session.

ALEX. CRUMMELL,[44]
JAS. M'CUNE SMITH.
P. G. SMITH.

The North Star, January 21, 1848.

9. TO PARENTS, GUARDIANS AND MECHANICS

A corporation, having in charge a fund to be applied to the instruction of coloured boys in trades, literature and agriculture, having requested that a committee of coloured persons should be appointed to assist them in carrying out this important object, the following named persons have been appointed for this purpose.

Rev. William Douglass, Rev. S. H. Gloucester, Peter Lester, Nathaniel W. Dupee, Morris Brown, Jr., Samuel Nichols, John P. Burr, James M. Bustill, Nicholas G. Bolivar, J. J. G. Bias, Chas. Simpson, Morris Hall, Clayton Miller.

The name of this organized body will be, The Board of Education, auxiliary to the guardianship of the estate of the late Richard Humphreys bequeathing a legacy for the instruction of coloured boys in trades, literature and agriculture.

Officers.--President, Rev. William Douglass; Vice President, John P. Burr; Rec. Sec., James M. Bustill; Cor. Sec., Nicholas G. Bolivar.

Examining Committee.--J. J. G. Bias, Morris Hall, Samuel Nichols.

Committee for securing places for Boys.--Rev. Stephen H. Gloucester, Clayton Miller, Morris Brown, Jr.

Committee on Guardianship.--Peter Lester, Nathaniel W. Dupee, Charles Simpson.

The applicants for the benefit of the fund must be intelligent, of good moral character, and instructed in the elementary branches, such as reading, writing and arithmetic, when the selections are made. A reasonable compensation will be paid to respectable mechanics, white or coloured, who will take the boys on condition that they shall be well instructed in their several trades. An evening school will also be opened for their instruction in the higher branches of education.

Mechanics who wish apprentices will apply to G. W. Taylor, N. W. corner of 5th and Cherry streets, Rev. S. H. Gloucester, Lombard street above 5th, Morris Brown, Jr., South street above 9th, or Clayton Miller, No. 13 Currant Alley. Persons who wish *places* for boys will apply to J. J. G. Bias, 6th street below Pine, Morris Hall, Cherry street above 7th, Samuel Nichols, Shippen street near 9th, John P. Burr, and N. W. Dupee, South street below 8th, N. G. Bolivar, office of the Lebanon Cemetery, or to any other member of the Board.   N. G. BOLIVAR, Cor. Sec.

The Non-Slaveholder, 4 (1849):141.

10. "MAKE YOUR SONS MECHANICS AND FARMERS, NOT WAITERS, PORTERS, AND BARBERS "

TO COLORED MEN:--Such is the caption of an article of advice to black men, in *Douglass Paper* of 18th inst. It is the key note for the redemption of your race--strike it often. Apprentice your children to useful and honorable employments. Waiting upon those who should wait upon themselves, shaving those who should perform such service themselves, or go unshaven, if as honorable, is not as useful employment as building houses, or ships, or engines, or cars; make your son's mechanics, therefore, not waiter, and let the latter position be occupied by those who can afford to bear the estimation society has for those thus employed.

The black man cannot afford longer to occupy such position; he has difficulties to overcome, lost ground to gain, an elevation of character and social standing to acquire. He must make himself useful, and his usefulness will be acknowledged. In proportion to his usefulness as a part of the great industrial force of the country, will be the necessity of his remaining with us, and being of us. Up, then, and make yourselves men, useful men,

necessary men. Let the anvil ring back the echo of your determination to
work out your own redemption. Let you saw, your hammer, and trowell ring
around the rising cottage and the proud dome. "Put money in your purse."
Yes, put money in your purse; take to yourselves land, enough of it for a
home; or, at least enough to entitle you to suffrage. You have seen with
how much more respect a $250 man is treated, than one who has no land. With
your work get money--with your money get land--with your land get respect
that you can never obtain for your mere manhood.

The Jews, in most Christian countries have been under as severe disabilities as the free blacks in this. Even employments were denied them,
that are open to black men here. These very disabilities were incentives to
exertion and economy. Thrift and wealth were the consequences, until the
Jew monarchs of Europe dictate peace, war, policy, to the moneyless kings
and emperors of the continent. I would not make you Jews; but I would have
you remember that what you regard as obstacles in your path may be the necessary stimulants to arouse your energies to the employment of the means not
only to remove them, but to give you a preeminence. The demand for builders
and artizans is rapidly increasing in this country, while a foolish pride or
ambition is deminishing the supply and overcrowding the professions of the
merchandizing, pedling and half idle classes. If the present generation
must live on in the habit that have become too strong to be broken, (and to
a great extent it must be so,) let the young men devote themselves to useful
mechanical employments and we shall soon cease to hear of colonization
schemes or such statutes as disgrace Illinois. Let the black man get land
and exercise their right of suffrage, and they will command a respect (however mean the feelings that prompt it) that will be important and useful to
them.

The white natives of this country are becoming rapidly enervated by idleness and easy life; and this will continue while foreigners and the blacks
are willing to do the drudgery and menial services. Acquaint yourselves
with the pursuits most indispensible and necessary--have a proper self-respect without that foolish vanity, ruinous to the black as well as the white
man--and then shall a good time come even for the black man. In slavery,
black men become superior mechanics--prove that by freedom they do not love
this capacity.

(We thank our friend "B," not only for his valuable words on this subject, but for the "material aid" which accompanied them. We hope to hear
from him often--a hope which we are sure our readers will participate, especially if his future contributions shall be marked with the same wisdom as
the present.)--Ed.

Frederick Douglass' Paper, April 8, 1853.

11.   LEARN TRADES OR STARVE!

By Frederick Douglass

These are the obvious alternatives sternly presented to the free colored
people of the United States. It is idle, yea even ruinous, to disguise the
matter for a single hour longer; every day begins and ends with the impres-
sive less that free negroes must learn trades, or die.

The old avocations, by which colored men obtained a livelihood, are
rapidly, unceasingly and inevitably passing into other hands; every hour sees
the black man elbowed out of employment by some newly arrived emigrant, whose
hunger and whose color are thought to give him a better title to the place;
and so we believe it will continue to be until the last prop is levelled beneath us.

As a black man, we say if we cannot stand up, let us fall down. We desire to be a man among men while we do live; and when we cannot, we wish to

die. It is evident, painfully evident to every reflecting mind, that the
means of living, for colored men, are becoming more and more precarious and
limited. Employments and callings, formerly monopolized by us, are so no
longer.

   White men are becoming house-servants, cooks and stewards on vessels--
at hotels.--They are becoming porters, stevedores, wood-sawyers, hod-carriers, brick-makers, white-washers and barbers, so that the blacks can scarcely find the means of subsistence--a few years ago, and a *white* barber would
have been a curiosity--now their poles stand on every street. Formerly
blacks were almost the exclusive coachmen in wealthy families: this is so
no longer; white men are now employed, and for aught we see, they fill their
servile station with an obsequiousness as profound as that of the blacks.
The readiness and ease with which they adapt themselves to these conditions
ought not to be lost sight of by the colored people. The meaning is very
important, and we should learn it. We are taught our insecurity by it.
Without the means of living, life is a curse, and leaves us at the mercy of
the oppressor to become his debased slaves. Now, colored men, what do you
mean to do, for you must do something?   The American Colonization Society
tells you to go to Liberia. Mr. Bibbs tells you to go to Canada. Others
tell you to go to school. We tell you to go to work; and to work you must
go or die. Men are not valued in this country, or in any country, for what
they *are;* they are valued for what they can *do*. It is in vain that we talk
about being men, if we do not the work of men. We must become valuable to
society in other departments of industry than those servile ones from which
we are rapdily being excluded. We must show that we can *do* as well as *be;*
to this end we must learn trades. When we can build as well as live in
houses; when we can *make* as well as *wear* shoes; when we can produce as well
as consume wheat, corn and rye--then we shall become valuable to society.
Society is a hard-hearted affair.--With it the helpless may expect no higher
dignity than that of paupers. The individual must keep society under obligation to him, or society will honor him only as a stranger and sojourner.
How shall this be done? In this manner: use every means, strain every nerve
to master some important mechanical art. At present, the facilities for doing this are few--institutions of learning are more readily opened to you
than the work-shop; but the Lord helps them who will help themselves, and we
have no doubt that new facilities will be presented as we press forward. [45]

   If the alternative were presented to us of learning a trade or of getting an education, we would learn the trade, for the reason, that with the
trade we could get the education, while with the education we could not get
the trade. What we, as a people, need most, is the means for our own elevation.--An educated colored man, in the United States, unless he has within
him the heart of a hero, and is willing to engage in a lifelong battle for
his rights, as a man, finds few inducements to remain in this country. He is
isolated in the land of his birth—debarred by his color from congenial association with whites; he is equally cast out by the ignorance of the *blacks*.
The remedy for this must comprehend the elevation of the masses; and this
can only be done by putting the mechanic arts within the reach of colored
men.

   We have now stated pretty strongly the case of our colored countrymen;
perhaps some will say, *too* strongly; but we know whereof we affirm.

   In view of this state of things, we appeal to the abolitionists, What
boss anti-slavery mechanic will take a black boy into his wheelwright's shop,
his blacksmith's shop, his joiner's shop, his cabinet shop? Here is something *practical;* where are the whites and where are the blacks that will respond to it? Where are the anti-slavery milliners and seamstresses that will
take colored girls and teach them trades, by which they can obtain an honorable living? The fact that we have made good cooks, good waiters, good barbers, and white-washers, induces the belief that we may excel in higher
branches of industry. *One thing is certain: we must find new methods of obtaining a livelihood, for the old ones are failing us very fast*.

   We, therefore, call upon the intelligent and thinking ones amongst us,
to urge upon the colored people within their reach, in all seriousness, the
duty and the necessity of giving their children useful and lucrative trades,
by which they may commence the battle of life with weapons commensurate with
the exigencies of the conflict.

Frederick Douglass' Paper, March 4, 1853.

12. A PLAN FOR AN INDUSTRIAL COLLEGE PRESENTED BY FREDERICK
DOUGLASS TO HARRIET BEECHER STOWE, MARCH 8, 1853

You kindly informed me, when at your home, a fortnight ago, that you
designed to do something which should permanently contribute to the improvement and elevation of the free colored people in the United States. You especially expressed an interest in such of this class as had become free by
their own exertions, and desired most of all to be of service to them. In
what manner, and by what means, you can assist this class most successfully,
is the subject upon which you have done me the honor to ask my opinion.
Begging you to excuse the unavoidable delay, I will now most gladly
comply with your request. . . . What can be done to improve the condition of
the free people of color in the United States? The plan which I humbly submit in answer to this inquiry--and in the hope that it may find favor with
you, and with many friends of humanity who honor, love and co-operate with
you--is the establishment in Rochester, N. Y., or in some other part of the
United States equally favorable to such an enterprise, of an Industrial College in which shall be taught several important branches of the mechanical
arts. This college is to be opened to colored youth. I will pass over, for
the present, the details of such an institution as I propose. It is not
worth while that I should dwell upon these at all. Once convinced that something of the sort is needed, and the organizing power will be forthcoming.
It is the peculiarity of your favored race that they can always do what they
think necessary to be done. I can safely trust all details to yourself, and
the wise and good people whom you represent in the interest you take in my
oppressed fellow-countrymen.
Never having had a day's schooling in all my life I may not be expected
to map out the details of a plan so comprehensive as that involved in the
idea of a college. I repeat, then, I leave the organization and administration to the superior wisdom of yourself and the friends who second your noble efforts. The argument in favor of an Industrial College--a college to
be conducted by the best men--and the best workmen which the mechanical arts
can afford; a college where colored youth can be instructed to use their
hands, as well as their heads; where they can be put into possession of the
means of getting a living whether their lot in after life may be cast among
civilized or uncivilized men; whether they choose to stay here, or prefer to
return to the land of their fathers--is briefly this: prejudice against the
free colored people in the United States has shown itself nowhere so invin-
cible as among mechanics. The farmer and the professional man cherish no
feeling so bitter as that cherished by these. The latter would starve us out
of the country entirely. At this moment I can more easily get my son into a
lawyer's office to learn law than I can into a blacksmith's shop to blow the
bellows and to wield the sledge-hammer. Denied the means of learning useful
trades we are pressed into the narrowest limits to obtain a livelihood. In
times past we have been the hewers of wood and the drawers of water for American society, and we once enjoyed a monopoly in the menial employments, but
this is so no longer. Even these enjoyments are rapidly passing away out of
our hands. The fact is--every day begins with the lesson, and ends with the
lesson--the colored men must learn trades; and must find new employment; new
modes of usefulness to society, or that they must decay under the pressing
wants to which their condition is rapidly bringing them.
We must become mechanics; we must build as well as live in houses; we
must make as well as use furniture; we must construct bridges as well as pass
over them, before we can properly live or be respected by our fellow men. We
need mechanics as well as ministers. We need workers in iron, clay, and
leather. We have orators, authors, and other professional men, but these
reach only a certain class, and get respect for our race in certain select

circles. To live here as we ought we must fasten ourselves to our countrymen through their every day cardinal wants. We must not only be able to
black boots, but to *make* them. At present we are unknown in the Northern
States as mechanics. We give no proof of genius or skill at the county,
State, or national fairs. We are unknown at any of the great exhibitions of
the industry of our fellow-citizens, and being unknown we are unconsidered.

The fact that we make no show of our ability is held conclusive of our
inability to make any, hence all the indifference and contempt with which
incapacity is regarded, fall upon us, and that too, when we have had no means
of disproving the infamous opinion of our natural inferiority. I have during the last dozen years denied before the Americans that we are an inferior
race; but this has been done by arguments based upon admitted principles
rather than by the presentation of facts. Now, firmly believing, as I do,
that there are skill, invention, power, industry, and real mechanical genius,
among the colored people, which will bear favorable testimony for them, and
which only need the means to develop them, I am decidedly in favor of the
establishment of such a college as I have mentioned. The benefits of such
an institution would not be confined to the Northern States, nor to the free
colored people. They would extend over the whole Union. The slave not less
than the freeman would be benefited by such an institution. It must be confessed that the most powerful argument now used by the Southern slaveholder,
and the one most soothing to his conscience, is that derived from the low
condition of the free colored people of the North. I have long felt that
too little attention has been given by our truest friends in this country to
removing this stumbling block out of the way of the slave's liberation.

The most telling, the most killing refutation of slavery, is the presentation of an industrious, enterprising, thrifty, and intelligent free
black population. Such a population I believe would rise in the Northern
States under the fostering care of such a college as that supposed.

To show that we are capable of becoming mechanics I might adduce any
amount of testimony; dear madam, I need not ring the charges on such a proposition. There is no question in the mind of any unprejudiced person that
the Negro is capable of making a good mechanic. Indeed, even those who
cherish the bitterest feelings towards us have admitted that the apprehension
that Negroes might be employed in their stead, dictated the policy of excluding them from trades altogether. But I will not dwell upon this point as I
fear I have already trespassed too long upon your precious time, and written
more than I ought to expect you to read. Allow me to say in conclusion, that
I believe every intelligent colored man in America will approve and rejoice
at the establishment of some such institution as that now suggested. There
are many respectable colored men, fathers of large families, having boys
nearly grown up, whose minds are tossed by day and by night with the anxious
enquiry, "what shall I do with my boys?" Such an institution would meet the
wants of such persons. Then, too, the establishment of such an institution
would be in character with the eminently practical philanthropy of your
trans-Atlantic friends. America could scarce object to it as an attempt to
agitate the public mind on the subject of slavery, or to *dissolve the Union*.
It could not be tortured into a cause for hard words by the American people,
but the noble and good of all classes, would see in the effort an excellent
motive, a benevolent object, temperately, wisely, and practically manifested.

Frederick Douglass' Paper, December 2, 1853.

13. RESOLUTIONS ADOPTED BY THE NEGRO NATIONAL CONVENTION,
ROCHESTER, 1853

WHEREAS. The social condition of the colored inhabitants of this country, in its developments shows, beyond a question, the necessity of social
reform, and a better regulation of our domestic habits; therefore,

Resolved. That this Convention urge upon the clergy, who are not only
our spiritual, but our social and moral instructions to begin the reform, by
urging upon the people who attend their preaching the necessity of a social
reform; to use more untiring exertion than heretofore; to induce parents to
pay more attention to the domestic education of their children; to prepare
them for a better condition in society; to instill in them a desire for their
elevation in society; to instill in them a desire for better occupations than
the mass are brought up to; to give them higher notions of what the genius
and spirit of the country requires of us, than they now have; to teach them
more regular habits; and this Convention would urge upon parents the fact,
that while the mass of the people are generally employed in menial service,
from necessity, while this may not, of itself, bring reproach upon a people,
yet it must be admitted that, should we bring up our children to the same
employment, it will of necessity, engraft upon them unstable habits--a disregard for the mechanical branches, as well as unfit them for regular employments; and instead of elevating their character for the future, we shall
place them beneath our own position and give them rather the downward, than
the upward tendency.

Resolved. That to secure a more permanent attention to business habits
than heretofore, and the acquisition of mechanical branches, it is necessary
that some decisive measure be taken to open and secure the avenues of mechanical trades to our youth; and that, as a primary measure, it is necessary
that it be known to parents and youth who are willing to take colored apprentices in their workshops; and further, that it is now expedient that intelligence offices be established, which shall register the names and places of
business of such mechanics as are willing to employ colored youth; and also
the names, age, [illegible] youth as are desirous of learning trades.

Resolved. That it is the duty of colored men, in any way connected with
mechanical or business houses, enjoying the confidence of their employers, to
use all fair and honorable means to secure for themselves business advantages, and especially, to secure the admission of their children, or the
children of others into mechanical establishments; and in every way practicable to use their influence to secure and extend business advantages and
business connection to those now excluded from it.

Frederick Douglass' Paper, July 22, 1853.

14.   REPORT, COMMITTEE ON MANUAL LABOR, NATIONAL NEGRO
CONVENTION, ROCHESTER, NEW YORK, 1853

Our earnest youth have gone asking to be cared for by the workshops of
the country, but no acknowledgement has been made of their human relationship; their mental and bodily fitness, have had the same contumely heaped
upon them, as is received by those unfortunate beings who in social life
bear upon their persons the brand of illegitimacy. As a consequence, we have
grown up to too large an extent--mere scholars on one side and muscular gi-
ants on the other. We could now equalize these discrepancies--We would produce a harmonious development of character. In the sweat of their brows, we
would have our scholars grow powerful, and their sympathies run our for humanity everywhere. On the altar of labor, to whom have every mother dedi-
cate her child to the cause of freedom; and then, in the breeze wafted over
the newly plowed field, there will come encouragement and hope; and the ringing brows of the anvil and the axe, and the keen cutting edge of the chisel
and the plane will symbolize how on one hand human excellence is rough, by
self-exertion, and on the other fashioned into models of beauty by reflection
and discipline.

Let us educate our youth in such wise as shall give them means of success, adapted to their struggling condition, and are long following the enterprise of the age, we may hope to see them filling everywhere positions of

responsibility and trust, and gliding on the triple tide of wealth, intelligence and virtue, reach eventually, . . . distinction and happiness.

Respectfully submitted.

Chas. L. Reason
Geo. B. Vashon
Chas. H. Langston [46]

Frederick Douglass' Paper, August 5, 1853.

15. PLAN OF THE AMERICAN INDUSTRIAL SCHOOL

The undersigned, the Committee on Manual Labor School, appointed by the
National Council of the colored people, in offering a plan for the organization of the school, beg leave respectfully to state,

1st. That the *location* of the school, which is to be within one hundred
miles of the town of Erie, Pennsylvania, will be selected as soon as three
thousand dollars are paid in; the school building and work-shop will be commenced as soon as fifteen thousand dollars are paid in; and that in no case
will a contract be made beyond the sum of money actually paid in. The site
of the school will be at least two hundred acres of land, one hundred and
fifty of which shall forever be used as a farm or agricultural instruction.

2d. In accordance with a vote of the Rochester Convention, the teachers are to be selected for, and pupils admitted into, the school without reference to sex or complexion.

3d. Special provision will be made to make this, from the beginning,
an industrial school for females as well as males; a prominent principle of
conduct will be to aid in providing for the female sex, methods and means of
enjoying an independent and honorable livelihood.

> Frederick Douglass,
> John D. Peck,   Committee
> Amos G. Beman,   on Manual Labor
> J. D. Bonner,   School.
> J. McCune Smith,

1. The title shall be "THE AMERICAN INDUSTRIAL SCHOOL."
2. The foundation fund shall be thirty thousand dollars.
3. Twenty thousand dollars shall be in stock of 2000 shares, at ten
dollars per share.
4. Ten thousand dollars shall be in donations to be solicited from the
friends of the cause.
5. The shares shall be payable, *ten* percent, at the time of subscrib-
ing, and *ten* percent, every first day of July, October, January and April
thereafter, until the whole is paid in.
6. The School shall be organized and conducted entirely by a board of
fifteen trustees.
7. Six of these trustees shall be the Committee on Manual Labor School,
appointed by the National Council of the People of Color; and nine of the
trustees shall be elected by the stockholders when three thousand dollars
shall have been paid in by them, (the Stockholders) and annually thereafter.
Each share of stock shall count as one vote at all such elections. And
stockholders may vote by proxy, on affidavit made and acknowledged before a
Commissioner of Deeds.
8. In organizing the School, the following regulations shall be strictly enforced:
a. For every branch of Literature taught, there shall be one branch of
handicraft also taught in the School.
b. Each pupil shall occupy one half his time when at School, in work at
some handicraft, or on the farm.

c. The handicrafts shall be such that their products will be articles
saleable for cash, or money's worth, at a market within easy access from the
School.

The agent appointed by the Committee, Frederick Douglass, Esq., shall
be empowered to receive donations and take subscriptions for stock, giving a
receipt for the latter, signed by himself and Rev. Amos G. Beman, the Secretary of the Committee. As soon as, and as often as the Agent aforesaid shall
receive two hundred and fifty dollars, either in subscriptions or donations,
he shall pay the same over to the Treasurer, John Jones, Esq., of Chicago,
who shall deposit the same forthwith in the Bank of America, Chicago, Ill.:
the Treasurer aforesaid, as soon as he shall receive one thousand dollars,
and for every thousand dollars hereafter, shall give bonds with two sureties
to the President and Secretary of the National Council of the Colored People,
for double the amounts aforesaid. For his services, the Agent shall receive
five per cent on all stock instalments paid in by him, and ten per cent on
all donations above two hundred dollars paid in by or through him.

10. The members of the Committee on Manual Labor School shall also be
empowered to receive donations for the same; and they shall transmit all
said donations to the Treasurer, by draft, within ten days after receiving
the same. They shall also be entitled to five per cent on all such donations
paid in *by* him.

11. The Treasurer shall publish at least once a fortnight a list of all
the donations and subscriptions of stock received by him; and shall transmit
to each donor or stockholder, a copy of the paper, (*Frederick Douglass' Paper*, or *Aliened American*,) which shall contain the acknowledgement of their
gift or subscription.

Frederick Douglass' Paper, March 24, 1854.

16. THE COLORED PEOPLE'S "INDUSTRIAL COLLEGE"

What Some of the Builders Have Thought

A word oft-times is expressive of an entire policy. Such is the term
Abolition. Though formerly used as a synonym of *Anti-Slavery,* people now
clearly understand that the designs of those who have ranged themselves under
the first of these systems of reform are of deeper significance and wider
scope than are the objects contemplated by the latter, and concern themselves
not only with the great primary question of bodily freedom, but take in also
the collateral issues connected with human enfranchisement, independent of
race, complexion, or sex.

The Abolitionist of to-day is the Iconoclast of the age, and his mission
is to break the idolatrous images set up by a hypocritical Church, a Sham
Democracy, or a corrupt public sentiment, and to substitute in their stead
the simple and beautiful doctrine of a common brotherhood. He would elevate
every creature by abolishing the hinderances and checks imposed upon him,
whether these be legal or social--and in proportion as such grievances are
invidious and severe, in such measure does he place himself in the front rank
of the battle, to wage his emancipating war.

Therefore it is that the Abolitionist has come to be considered the especial friend of the negro, since *he,* of all others, has been made to drink
deep from the cup of oppression.

The free-colored man at the north, for his bond-brother as for himself,
has trusted hopefully in the increasing public sentiment, which, in the mul-
tiplication of these friends, has made his future prospects brighter. And,
to-day, while he is making a noble struggle to vindicate the claims of his
entire class, depending mainly for the accomplishment of that end on his own
exertions, he passes in review the devotion and sacrifices made in his behalf: gratitude is in his heart, and thanks fall from his lips. But, in one

department of reformatory exertion he feels that he has been neglected. He
has seen his pledged allies throw themselves into the hottest of the battle,
to fight for the Abolition of Capital Punishment--for the Prohibition of the
Liquor Traffic--for the Rights of Women, and similar reforms,--but he has
failed to see a corresponding earnestness, according to the influence of Abolitionists in the business world, in opening the avenues of industrial labor to the proscribed youth of the land. This work, therefore, is evidently
left for himself to do. And he has laid his powers to the task. The record
of his conclusions was given at Rochester, in July, and has become already a
part of history.

Though shut out from the workshops of the country, he is determined to
make self-provision, so as to triumph over the spirit of caste that would
keep him degraded. The utility of the Industrial Institution he would erect,
must, he believes, commend itself to Abolitionists. But not only to them.
The verdict of less liberal minds has been given already in its favor. The
usefulness, the self-respect and self-dependence,--the combination of intelligence and handicraft,--the accumulation of the materials of wealth, all
referable to such an Institution, present fair claims to the assistance of
the entire American people.

Whenever emancipation shall take place, immediate though it be, the
subjects of it, like many who now make up the so-called free population, will
be in what Geologists call, the "Transition State." The prejudice now felt
against them for bearing on their persons the brand of slaves, cannot die out
immediately. Severe trials will still be their portion--the curse of a
"taunted race" must be expiated by almost miraculous proofs of advancement;
and some of these miracles must be antecedent to the great day of Jubilee.
To fight the battle on the bare ground of abstract principles, will fail to
give us complete victory. The subterfuges of pro-slavery selfishness must
now be dragged to light, and the last weak argument,--that the negro can never contribute anything to advance the national character, "nailed to the
counter as base coin." To the conquering of the difficulties heaped up in
the path of his industry, the free-colored man of the North has pledged himself. Already he sees, springing into growth, from out his foster *work-
school,* intelligent young laborers, competent to enrich the world with necessary products--industrious citizens, contributing their proportion to aid on
the advancing civilization of the country;--self-providing artizans vindicat-
ing their people from the never-ceasing charge of a fitness for servile positions.

Abolitionists ought to consider it a legitimate part of their great
work, to aid in such an enterprise--to abolish not only chattel servitude,
but that other kind of slavery, which, for generation after generation, dooms
an oppressed people to a condition of dependence and pauperism. Such an Institution would be a shining mark, in even this enlightened age; and every
man and woman, equipped by its discipline to do good battle in the arena of
active life, would be, next to the emancipated bondman, the most desirable
"Autograph for Freedom."

Chas. L. Reason

Julia Griffiths (ed.), Autographs For Freedom (New York, 1854), pp. 12-15.

17. COLORED NATIONAL COUNCIL

At the Conference referred to, only the States of New York, Pennsylvania,
Rhode Island, Connecticut and Illinois were represented.

WM. C. NELL, an original member from Massachusetts, although happening
to be present, was predisposed against any participation, because of valid
objections, constitutional and otherwise. As, however, the Council insisted
upon his voting, he negatived all the questions submitted during his stay.

REV. AMOS G. BEMAN, also an original member from Connecticut, refused to vote, for reasons satisfactory to himself.

The principal topic discussed was the Industrial College, on which ability and earnestness were exhibited on both sides.

Mr. BONNES, of Illinois, thought the colored people had too long been dependent upon what might be done for them by the whites. It was time that they did something for themselves. He hoped this report would be adopted, for he did not believe that the colored youth could otherwise find channels through which to elevate themselves to a position of independence and respectability.

Mr. DOUGLASS fully concurred with the last speaker in the propriety of adopting the report; but he deemed the Industrial College of so much moment, that he hoped it would be more fully discussed. He believed that if an agent had been appointed at the time the plan was first proposed, it would now be placed in a position of success beyond all doubt. This scheme had been pronounced, by the first periodical in the world, to be the greatest and most comprehensive for elevating the colored race in this country yet proposed. That is the opinion of the New York *Tribune*. He was aware that some of the abolition papers had opposed the plan, but if the colored people would ever arrive at a respectable place in society, *they must do their own thinking*. The colored people are now the sick man of America; those who pretend to be their friends measure their place and guage their ideas and pat them on the back, but if they step beyond that narrow place, those friends become villifiers and enemies. He wanted the colored men to feel that they possessed the power to overcome the prejudice against their color. He did not see why colored men's enterprises should be stigmatized by their color. When white men start a school for their children, no one stigmatizes it as proscriptive; why, then, do they charge the colored man with proscriptiveness when he seeks to overcome the disabilities attendant upon his position? The proscription is theirs, not his.

Mr. D. said he hoped that if they voted down this proposition, the Council would remember that they decided that it was proscriptive for the colored people to make an effort to elevate themselves; that they were incompetent to do any thing to help themselves. The fiat had gone forth from the central organ at Boston, that all efforts to elevate the free colored people, while slavery existed in America, are useless. He expected to see the school voted down, and should say no more.

Mr. STEPHEN SMITH, of Philadelphia, said that most of the colored mechanics in Philadelphia had received their education in the South, and he knew that the colored people of the city of Philadelphia could not obtain opportunity to learn mechanical trades. But wherever a colored man understood a trade he was sustained in Philadelphia.

Dr. PENNINGTON thought that the colored people ought to do their part in educating men with the whites. The white people established schools for black and whites; why should not the colored people start schools and workshops for white and black? [47]

Dr. J. McCUNE SMITH, in a speech answering objections, asked--Is not this school practicable? Gentlemen, we have to do impracticable things. We must sing, as sings the Black Swan,--we must write, as writes Dumas,--speak, as Douglass speaks,--before we are acknowledged. We have to struggle harder to be on the level of society than those already there. The impracticability of this measure is one of its choice features, in my mind: but I think it to be practicable; for, make it a fact before the free colored people, and you will find that you will gather up the mass of public sympathy, which now can find no real vent, for our benefit.

[The query here arises--Did Dumas learn rhetoric or Frederick Douglass oratory in a colored college?]

Mr. EDWARD V. CLARK, of New York, differed from Mr. Douglass in regard to the cause of the opposition manifested by the colored people to the proposed school. The Manual Labor School never could develop any degree of perfection in mechanical or agricultural education among its pupils. At Oberlin, Oneida, and elsewhere, this fact had long since become apparent. And if they established it, what white man would teach colored children a trade? How could such an institution be self-sustaining? What would the $30,000-- not the first cent of which had been collected--amount to? He would suggest that social communities of colored people be established, so that the mechanic arts could be nurtured within their limits.

Mr. GEORGE T. DOWNING, of Rhode Island, was not able to see clearly the practicability of this plan. There is, and the truth must be spoken, too much apathy on our part. We might, if we pleased, find plenty of opportunities of learning trades and working at them afterward. He enumerated many instances in proof of his position. The only argument that could be advanced in favor of this school was that it might tend to induce colored people to feel the necessity of educating their children to trades. The natural tendency of proscriptive measures is depressive. An instance of this kind is shown by the schools of Worcester, where, at the wish of the colored citizens, a separate school was started, and failed. Such, he thought, would be the fate of the Manual Labor School. [48]

Mr. Douglass had stated that the will is all that is wanted--there is the rub! There is actually not interest enough in the matter to carry it into effect. He believed there was no necessity for it, and that conviction had been strengthened by the remarks of to-day.

Mr. J. E. BROWN, of Elmira, New York, instanced several colored workshops and workmen in Elmira, where white and colored are employed. He believed that colored mechanics could always find employment.

Mr. PHILIP A. BELL, of New York, opposed the establishment of the Manual Labor College, contending that the whole plan was impracticable, and had been proved to be so at Oberlin, Oneida, Central College, and every where else. Even in Prussia, where Labor Colleges are largely endowed by the government, they have not been self-supporting. The colored people had frequently made efforts to establish educational institutions, and always failed, and they would not succeed in this.

The members of State Councils present being invited to an expression of opinion, J. W. DUFFIN, of Geneva, N. Y., hoped that the report would not be adopted. I feel, said he, that we are not yet prepared for its passage. I have been convinced of this by the speeches this afternoon. I live in the pro-slavery county of New York. The Abolitionists have abandoned our ground to the heathen, and there, out of three hundred colored people, I can get any number of colored youth, from one to twenty, into any educational institution, from the blacksmith shop to an entrance into the free college.

I do not go to abolitionists--I do not believe they are more ready to do us good than others. Where is the necessity for establishing such an institution as is proposed, when we feel assured it will fail for want of patronage?

CHARLES LENOX REMOND, of Massachusetts, held that what the colored race most wanted in this country was equal rights in the community--a fair field and no favor. This he believed the Anti-Slavery party would afford him. And with such a field, he did not need any such school as the one proposed. The great want was a public sentiment recognizing the colored man as an American citizen. Whatever position the colored race had attained to in this country, was due to the efforts of the abolitionists, and whatever they had to hope for would be through their assistance, and he was not prepared to turn his back upon them. [49]

Of the thirteen present, seven voted in the affirmative, and the Chairman decided the report adopted.

It is an undeniable fact, that the colored people of the several States are not in harmony with the National Council and its proceedings. At a meeting of colored citizens, recently held in New York, in Rev. Mr. Hodges' church, the following resolutions were adopted, which we copy from the Salem (Ohio) *Bugle:*--

Resolved, That we do not acquiesce with the National Council of Colored People in the establishment of proscriptive institutions, or in other measures set forth by that body.

Resolved, That we protest against any attempt, by any body of men, of any color, to strengthen that which is dying out of itself.

Resolved, That it is unwise and impolitic, at this time, to establish an Industrial School, or erect a building for free colored youth. If free, let them have the freedom of schools in free States.

Resolved, That we hail with pleasure the example of the Star in the East, (Massachusetts,) which shines brighter than ever. She has opened the doors of her schools to youth, irrespective of complexion, and we look forward to the day when the State of New York will follow her example.

A Committee of the Council have issued a call for a National Convention in Philadelphia next October, to which delegates are to be chosen in September. Should they conclude to make it an Anti-Slavery Convention, and invite those friendly, irrespective of complexion, some good might be anticipated. Otherwise, in the present advanced state of public sentiment, it looks like taking steps backward.
Boston, July, 1855.   W. C. N.[50]

The Liberator, July 27, 1855.

INTEGRATE OR SEPARATE?

18. EDITORIAL: THE AFRICAN RACE IN NEW YORK

All persons having a shade of philanthropy in their composition, must have that feeling excited by witnessing the poverty and degradation in which the African race exist in this city. Systematically shut out from all mechanical pursuits, and expelled from almost all the inferior positions they were once allowed to hold here, they have seen their places filled by Germans and Irish; and now there are not more than half a dozen occupations in which they can engage. Even as waiters in our hotels—one of the last and best strongholds left them—they find that they are constantly losing ground by the abler competition of immigrants from Europe. The expulsion of the negroes from almost every branch of industry has had its natural effect in thinning their numbers. And while during the last ten years they have increased in the Southern States at the ratio of thirty per cent, the negro population of this State has fallen from fifty to forty-seven thousand.
Under such circumstances, would not the wisest and most philanthropic measure be, to promote, by all possible means, the emigration of the colored people of this State to the republic of Liberia? and would it not be prudent and politic in our government to appropriate a certain annual sum for this purpose? The States of New Jersey, Pennsylvania, Maryland, Virginia, and Indiana, have, from time to time, made considerable appropriations in favor of the scheme of colonization, which has been found to work admirably. The State of New York should not remain passive to the wretched condition of so many of her colored citizens, but do what humanity and sound policy alike suggest—make such an appropriation as would enable all negroes wishing to emigrate to Liberia to do so free of expense. We trust that the Legislature, at its next session, will not be unmindful of the claims of the poor African, condemned to a life of abject penury and estitution in this State, and longing for means to enable him to become a good citizen of the modern black republic. Let him have them.

New York Herald, April 12, 1853.

19. MARTIN R. DELANY, "WHY WE MUST EMIGRATE"

To the colored inhabitants of the United States

   Fellow-Countrymen! The duty assigned us is an important one, compre-
hending all that pertains to our destiny and that of our posterity--present
and prospectively. And while it must be admitted, that the subject is one
of the greatest magnitude, requiring all that talents, prudence and wisdom
might adduce, and while it would be folly to pretend to give you the combined result of these three agencies, we shall satisfy ourselves with doing
our duty to the best of our ability, and that in the plainest, most simple
and comprehensive manner.
   Our object, then, shall be to place before you our true position in
this country--the United States--the improbability of realizing our desires,
and the sure, practicable and infallible remedy for the evils we now endure.
   We have not addressed you as *citizens*--a term desired and ever cherished by us--because such you have never been. We have not addressed you as
freemen--because such privileges have never been enjoyed by any colored man
in the United States. Why then should we flatter your credulity, by inducing you to believe that which neither has now, nor never before had an existence. Our oppressors are ever gratified at our manifest satisfaction, especially when that satisfaction is founded upon false premises; an assumption on our part, of the enjoyment of rights and privileges which never have
been conceded, and which, according to the present system of the United
States policy, we never can enjoy. . . . Were we content to remain as we
are, sparsely interspersed among our white fellow-countrymen, we never might
be expected to equal them in any honorable or respectable competition for a
livelihood. For the reason that, according to the customs and policy of the
country, we for ages would be kept in a secondary position, every situation
of respectability, honor, profit or trust, either as mechanics, clerks,
teachers, jurors, councilmen, or legislators, being filled by white men,
consequently, our energies must become paralysed or enervated for the want
of proper encouragement.
   This example upon our children, and the colored people generally, is
pernicious and degrading in the extreme. And how could it otherwise be,
when they see every place of respectability filled and occupied by the
whites, they pandering to their vanity, and existing among them merely as a
thing of conveniency. . . .
   Where, then, is our hope of success in this country? Upon what is it
based? Upon what principle of political policy and sagacious discernment,
do our political leaders and acknowledged great men--colored men we mean--
justify themselves by telling us, and insisting that we shall believe them,
and submit to what they say--to be patient, remain where we are; that there
is a "bright prospect and glorious future" before us in this country! May
Heaven open our eyes from their Bartemian obscurity. . . .

*"Political Destiny of the Colored Race, on the American Continent," Proceed-
ings of the National Emigration Convention of Colored People. . . . 1854
(Pittsburgh, 1854), pp. 33-43.*

20. FREDERICK DOUGLASS, "WHY WE SHOULD NOT EMIGRATE"

   Sir, I am not for going anywhere. I am staying precisely where I am in
the land of my birth. Here I can hope to be of most service to the colored
people of the United States. . . . Our minds are made up to live here if we
can, or die here if we must; so every attempt to remove us, will be, as it
ought to be, labor lost. Here we are, and here we shall remain. While our
brethren are in bondage on these shores; it is idle to think of inducing any

considerable number of free colored people to quit this for a foreign land.

For two hundred and twenty-eight years has the colored man toiled over the soil of America, under a burning sun and a driver's lash---plowing, planting, reaping, that white men might roll in ease, their hands unhardened by labor, and their brows unmoistened by the waters of genial toil; and now that the moral sense of mankind is beginning to revolt at this system of treachery and cruel wrong, and is demanding its overthrow, the mean and cowardly oppressor is meditating plans to expel the colored man entirely from the country. Shame upon the guilty wretches that dare propose, and all that countenance such a proposition. We live here---have lived here---have a right to live here, and mean to live here.

The North Star, January 26, 1849.

PART VII

THE NORTHERN BLACK WORKER DURING THE CIVIL WAR

THE NORTHERN BLACK WORKER DURING THE CIVIL WAR

The hostilities which had been brewing between blacks and the Irish immigrants, who competed for America's menial jobs, came to a head during the Civil War as physical violence erupted between the two struggling groups. The flames of hatred were often fanned by irresponsible newspapers which openly taunted one group or the other. The Irish Catholic Boston Pilot, for example, spewed forth its racist venom against blacks, while the Liberator sympathized with Afro-Americans and denounced the Irish as hoodlums (Doc. 2-3).

In 1862 blood was shed along the levee in Cincinnati when Irish stevedores and draymen attempted to drive the black workers off the job (Doc. 5-10). Similarly, Brooklyn witnessed an assault by white workers upon defenseless Negro men, women, and children (Doc. 11-13). The following year, in 1863, numerous race riots erupted, one of the worst in Detroit where the military was called in to stop the bloodshed and destruction of property (Doc. 14-16).

The New York Draft Riots represented the worst of these anti-Negro outbursts. On July 11, 1863, the Provost Marshal's office opened for conscription in New York City. That same day wild mobs began to riot, and for five infamous days they stormed through the streets of New York City, unleashing their hatred against the National Conscription Act and committing unspeakable atrocities against the black community, murdering or maiming any Negro whom they came upon. The riots went unchecked until eleven Union regiments were released by the Secretary of War to quell the rioters. The Draft Riots resulted from a combination of factors. The city's poorer classes, sympathetic to the Democratic party, were not, in the main, sympathetic to the war's purposes and feared the emancipation of the slaves would be followed by an influx of black workers who would compete for their jobs. There was a huge criminal class in the city, and the riots gave an opportunity for looting. The Conscription Act passed by the government aroused indignation because it allowed richer members of the community to buy their way out of the draft. More than 400 blacks were either killed or wounded and an estimated five million in property damage was sustained. Everywhere black workers were driven from their jobs. Documents 21-29 illustrate the breadth of the tragedy.

The federal government steadfastly refused to accept black recruits into the Union army, telling many applicants that this was a "white man's war." After considerable pressure by black leaders, however, coupled with growing manpower needs, Negro men were put into uniform. Afro-Americans experienced fewer obstacles enlisting in the navy where they had always constituted a large percentage of the personnel, about one-half in 1850. Documents 38-44 reveal the occupations of Negro enlistees and the degradation heaped upon blacks even as they wore the Union uniform.

When the war ended in 1865, the future still appeared bleak for Negroes. Whites feared that the ex-slaves would inundate the northern job market, rendering inevitable a new round of racial conflict among the working classes. Many responsible whites, therefore, concluded that the freedmen must be forced to remain upon the soil in the South, or be exported to colonies outside the United States (Doc. 45-48).

THE WORSENING STATUS OF FREE BLACK WORKERS IN THE NORTH

1. JOHN S. ROCK AT THE FIRST OF AUGUST CELEBRATION, [51]
LEXINGTON, MASSACHUSETTS

The present condition of the colored man is a trying one; trying because
the whole nation seems to have entered into a conspiracy to crush him. But
few seem to comprehend our position in the free States. The masses seem to
think that we are oppressed only in the South. This is a mistake; we are
oppressed everywhere in this slavery-cursed land. Massachusetts has a great
name, and deserves much credit for what she has done, but the position of
the colored people in Massachusetts is far from being an enviable one. While
colored men have many rights, they have but few privileges here. To be sure,
we are seldom insulted by the vulgar passers by, we have the right of suffrage, the free schools and colleges are opened to our children, and from
them have come forth young men capable of filling any post of profit or hon-
or. But there is no field for these young men. Their education aggravates
their suffering. The more highly educated the colored man is, the more
keenly he suffers. The educated colored man meets, on the one hand, the embittered prejudices of the whites, and on the other the jealousies of his
own race. The colored man who educates his son, educates him to suffer. The
more ignorant the colored man, the more happy he must be. If we are never to
derive the benefits of an education, it would be a misfortune for us to see
inside of a school-house. You can hardly imagine the humiliation and contempt a colored lad must feel in graduating the first in his class, and then
being rejected everywhere else because of his color. To the credit of the
nineteenth century, be it said, the United States is the only civilized
country mean enough to make this invidious distinction. No where in the
United States is the colored man of talent appreciated. Even in Boston,
which has a great reputation for being anti-slavery, he has no field for his
talent. Some persons think that, because we have the right of suffrage, and
enjoy the privilege of riding in the cars, there is less prejudice here than
there is farther South. In some respects this is true, and in others it is
not true. We are colonized in Boston. It is five times as difficult to get
a house in a good location in Boston as it is in Philadelphia, and it is ten
times more difficult for a colored mechanic to get employment than in
Charleston. Colored men in business in Massachusetts receive more respect,
and less patronage, than in any place that I know of. In Boston we are proscribed in some of the eating-houses, many of the hotels, and all the theatres but one. Boston, though anti-slavery and progressive, supports, in
addition to these places, two places of amusement, the sole efforts of which
is to caricature us, and to perpetuate the existing prejudices against us.
I now ask you, is Boston anti-slavery? Are not the very places that pro-
scribe us sustained by anti-slavery patronage? Do not our liberal anti-slavery politicians dine at the Revere House, sup at the Parker House, and take
their cream and jellies at Copeland's?
The friends of slavery are everywhere withdrawing their patronage from
us, and trying to starve us out by refusing to employ us even as menials.
When our laboring men go to them for work, as heretofore, they reply, "Go to
the Abolitionists and Republicans, who have turned the country upside down"!
The laboring men who could once be found all along the wharves of Boston,
can now be found only about Central wharf, with scarcely encouragement enough
to keep soul and body together. You know that the colored man is proscribed
in some of the churches, and that this proscription is carried even to the
grave-yards. This is Boston--by far the best, or at least the most liberal
large city in the United States.
Now, while our enemies are endeavoring to crush us, and are closing the
avenues from which we have wrung out our humble subsistence, is there anything higher opened to us? Who is taking our boys into their stores at a
low salary, and giving them a chance to rise? Who is admitting them into
their work-shops, or into their counting-room? Or who is encouraging those

who are engaged in trade or business? With the exception of a handful of
Abolitionists and Republicans, there are none. This is the kind of friendship that we need. . . .

The Liberator, August 15, 1862.

2. RIGHTS OF WHITE LABOR OVER BLACK

        The historic misfortunes of America commenced *when Abolitionism broke
the shell;* they will not have disappeared until the blind virtue itself, its
champions and its objects, *be driven from the soil.* Our country is now on
the verge of lasting ruin, *chiefly from mad philanthropy for the African.*
The greater part in the cause of the accursed rebellion of the South issued
directly from it; and when the rebellion is trampled to death in mud and
mire, the integrity of the republic will be yet in jeopardy, *unless Abolitionism be made to feel its military weight,* and unless the black be taken
off to the climate intended for him by nature. *To expel the negro,* and to
shut down the race of fanatic men whom he has bewitched, are indispensable
remedies for a permanent restoration of the Union. *While they are in the
land, we shall have tumult and sedition.*
        After the war—*which is the first consequence of Abolitionism*—we have
already upon us bloody contention between white and black labor—the second
issue of that *insanity.* The North is becoming black with refugee negroes
from the South. These *wretches* crowd our cities, and by overstocking the
market of labor do incalculable injury to white hands. In Cincinnati, employers along the wharves have taken the negro by the arm, and given him the
place of the white man. The result has been a terrible riot. The evil is
increasing. Philadelphia, New York, and Boston may soon follow the example
of the Western metropolis. In fact, it is a certainty that the exodus of
plantation blacks now going on will lead to the most unfortunate excesses in
the Northern cities.
        What is to be done? That which the State of Illinois has very saga-
ciously done, namely, *made a stringent law forbidding blacks to cross its
boundaries. This is pre-eminently just.* The negro indeed is unfortunate,
and *the creature* has the common rights of humanity living in his breast; *but,*
in the country of the whites where the labor of the whites has done everything, but his labor nothing, and where the whites find it difficult to earn
a subsistence, what right has the negro either to preference, or to equality,
or to admission? When rights collide, it is the stronger that should prevail: for it has the more reason—without which there can be no right—to
support it. What has the African done for America? What great or even decent work has his head conceived, or his hands executed? We pity his condition: *but* it is unjust to put him in the balance with the white laborer.
To white toil this nation owes everything; but *to black, nothing.* Furthermore, there is decided unnaturalness in preferring the negro to the white;
therefore has Illinois done a just and prudent piece of legislation. It has
saved itself from much tumult, and has done common justice to its own members.
        If the other States of the North be true to themselves and just to their
inhabitants, *they will imitate Illinois.* It is the whites that made and are
to perpetuate this nation. The perpetuity of it may be measured by the circumstances of its chief props—its laborers in brain and hand. The condition
of the negro—whether he be in dependence or misery—can have no effect whatever on the continuance of the Republic; neither himself nor his children can
ever constitute a true part of the State. But such is not the case with the
white laborer. He is a citizen, and his descendants have the rights of the
Presidency before them with as much certainty and with greater probability
than the descendants of the rich. It is they, more than the offspring of
more fortunate parents, that will increase the population and constitute the

soldiers and magistrates of America. Now the national value of those de-
scendents greatly depends on the condition of the parent. The better paid
he is for his toil, the better the culture he gives his offspring. And the
better they are cultured, the better for the future of America. This is incontestible. No one calls it into doubt. So that improving the condition
of the white laborer, no matter what the means may be, cannot have bad consequences on the future greatness of the empire.

Will our Northern Legislatures act with just and patriotic wisdom? But
we prefer appealing to *all* the white operatives--the people--the bone and
sinew of the nation. This country is theirs exclusively. It will belong
exclusively to the generations that succeed them. As they are now, so will
those generations be--so will their grand country be in the future. Therefore, by justice, and by patriotism, they have the right and duty to resist
this black current that is invading them, for it will injure their condition.
So, without violence, down with Abolitionism, and away, from the certainty
of injuring the white laborer, with the African!

We counsel no tumult. The black is loaded with misery. *But* the author
of the greatness of the country, he who owns the country, and who perpetuates
it best with members, and with brain and muscle, must be preferred to him.
As he is treated, so will the country be. *Let no man employ a black while
he can get a white laborer.* He who prefers the black to the white may yet
find his own injured by the choice.--*Boston (Catholic Irish) Pilot.*

The Liberator, August 22, 1862.

3.   RIGHTS OF WHITE LABOR OVER BLACK   (REBUTTAL)

To the Editor of the Liberator:

SIR--The article under this caption, copied into your paper of the 22d,
from the Boston Irish *Pilot*, is of a piece with the infuriate and blind prejudice entertained by the Irish and their descendants in America towards the
African race; and it is the effects of such counsels as this we see cropping
out in the riots at Brooklyn, Cincinnati and elsewhere, between the Irish
and black. It is this narrow-sighted and unphilanthropical advice to Irishmen, by those who set themselves up as their leaders, that serves to
strengthen the Slave Power of Rebeldom, by maintaining an element in our
midst of disloyalty to humanity, to true liberty, and the common rights of
man.

This blind leader of the blind, who *will* not see the hand of God in the
present fearful reformation; who will not see that this glorious and extensive country if man were free everywhere in it, would be large enough for
all; who will not wait until society, within the bounds of our common territory, rights and settles into its natural position, after this state of con-
vulsion and unrest it is now in be past; who can see no destiny for the black
man, no place for the sole of his foot, but the cities and towns of the
Northern States, should be, in the Providence of God, become free,--sets himself up as the counsellor of the people, and stimulates this condition of un-
quiet by stirring up hatred for those who have as good a right in this land
as himself. He does not stop to take a broad or rational view of the question, "What will become of the black man?" such a view as we would expect
taken by an educated man; but, with nineteen out of twenty of the lowest intellectually and most ignorant Irishmen you could meet in the neighborhood
of Fort Hill to-day, he falls into their groove of thought, and says--"Liberate the slaves throughout the land, and they will overrun the North, looking for work, and the white man will be destroyed by their attempt to find
it."

A few years ago, no voice than that of this *Pilot* was more loud in its
denunciation of the cry of "America for Americans." Now none is more furious

in its own cry of America for the white man. By white man he means, of
course, Irishman, as no other white man in the length and breadth of the
land is the least afflicted at the prospect of general emancipation of the
slaves, unless it be slaveholders and their political sympathizers. [52]

A philosopher, such as, I have no doubt, the writer of that article
would delight to have himself considered, would take a philosophical view of
this question, and argue, *a priori*, that, wherever they are free to do so,
like seeks like and run together, as do drops of water or grains of sand;
that were the black man no longer restrained by the bond of slavery in this
nation, he would prefer to dwell where he was born; and he who had wandered
from there would seek happiness in that climate most favorable to his growth,
which his very nature covets, and which he left to gratify but one object,
the instinct of freedom implanted by nature in the heart of every man who is
born upon the earth. From a high stand-point, and uncontaminated by the influences of his locality, in which is generated the belief that there is but
one god--the institution of slavery--of which the faubourg of Franklin and
Milk streets enjoy and were built up by the profit,--he would see some ten
thousand of the black race in Massachusetts, some driven here by the instinc-
tive desire for freedom, others born here, all Americans by birth and such
education as they possess; all entitled, therefore, to the rights which the
political privileges of this free land confer upon its inhabitants; and all
fully as intelligent, as a class, as the same number and intellectual grade
of Irishmen. That in the object for which those not born here came hither,
both classes present an exact analogy--both came here seeking freedom, and
to better their natural and political condition beyond what it was where
they were born; and that were the reasons for that condition not being as
good in the land of their birth as it is here, *to be removed,* thousands of
them would instinctively desire to go back; for each love the land of their
birth, and in that love exhibit the oneness of their humanity.

But neighbor *Pilot* (oh, what a misnomer! Heaven preserve us from such a
pilot for our ship of State as he would make!) can see nothing but an exodus
of black men setting towards the North Star, should the Abolitionists obtain
the object for which they have striven alone, and been persecuted for thirty
years; and that they are going on, in the course of the next twelve months,
he is too sharp a Pilot not to see. Hence his uproarious cry of Down with
the black man! enslave him! kill him! do any thing with him! but if you will
make him free, drive him instantly out of the country, which is only large
enough for the white man, and particularly for white Irishmen, this *Pilot's*
flock!

"To white toil," says this *Pilot,* "the nation owes everything--to black,
nothing." Well, if that is not the height of audacious and cold-blooded lying, the height has never been reached! The four million slaves, not to
speak of the one million free blacks and colored, have done nothing for this
country! Why! before an Irish laborer had a foothold on this soil, the
blacks were the only laborers the South had for fifty years. Does the *Pilot*
know this? or is he so grossly ignorant of the chart of the country that has
received him, and thousands like him, not for the benefit they would be to
the country as a first cause, but to relieve them from that oppression which,
if Irishmen are to be believed, (and I believe them,) they have groaned under
for ten generations? So atrociously profligate an untruth as this is without
a parallel. The blacks, the bone and sinew of some thirteen States, the
toiling millions who, for a hundred years, have known nothing but labor, who
are crucified by work, and die daily to supply the wants and luxuries of
their owners and taskmasters, have done nothing for this country! while the
few hundred thousand Irishmen and their descendants in that time have done
all! Preposterous and unjust decision!

As mere laborers, hewers of wood and drawers of water, as the mass of
the Irish emigrants to our Free States are, I deny them no jot nor tittle of
all they deserve. They have hedged and ditched and borne burdens, built the
earthwork of railroads, and dug out canals; they have extended a ready hand
for labor wherever they have found it to do. As a class, they are industrious and willing to work; but in that particular, they are not superior, by
one jot or tittle, to the black man in a state of freedom; and, as a class,
it is well known that, for all the purposes of intelligent citizenship, free
black men are more tractable and thoughtful, less inclined to fight among

themselves or with others, to brawl, to quarrel about trifles, to drink whiskey and get themselves into the hands of the police authorities, than free Irishmen. Yes, I say boldly, and call for proof to the contrary, that in peace or in war, free black men--who have been long enough free to know the value and privileges of freedom--are as serviceable to the country as a like number of Irishmen, or any other nationality of their degree of intelligence. I would not take one grain of credit from the thousands of Irishmen who have gone forward to fight for the republic. They have done nobly. But I say, let the free black men of America have a chance, and they will do as well. History, wherever it has a chance, will support me in this assertion. And it is this fact that the *Pilot* fears. Of all things, he dreads that the opportunity should be given the black man to distinguish himself as a soldier of the republic upon the battle-field. That is a privilege not for the black man to enjoy, lest he should prove, by the most irresistible evidence, that he is in this particular, as in everything else, the equal of the Irishman of equal attainments and education. But even in the face of such proof, the *Pilot* would be found cursing him, and desirous to expel him from the land; and, basing its reasons upon the few isolated facts recorded within the past month, and which such incendiary publications have been the generating cause of riot between blacks and Irish, it would again hurl forth its manifesto that, "While they are in the land, we shall have tumult and sedition."

This blind leader proposes no means of diverting the fertilizing stream of black emigration he so much dreads, but at once to open a way for it into the sea. Instead of going to the source of the stream, and there providing means for it to go gladly on its way into a thousand fields of usefulness and freedom on its own soil, and, by embankments properly constructed, keeping it within its natural bounds, he calls his laborers around him to dig deep and wide a single channel, through which it may rush out of the country, and thus deprive the country of the benefit of its teeming strength, its thousands of toiling hands, which know no direction but to work in the soil-- know no art nor handicraft, but possess the main strength, the bone and muscle to till the soil, to grasp the plow and hoe, which provide bread for a nation of freemen. And what substitute does he provide? Nothing, unless it be a sparse future emigration of Irish laborers--an emigration that cannot, in the very nature of cause and effect, be but slender for years.

O, thou blind leader of the blind, who can see the mote in thy brother's eye, but not the beam in thine own, didst thou suppose that any but thy slavish, ignorant followers would believe thy doctrines, thy incorrect statements, thy gross untruths? No, thou couldst not do so. Written and printed only for them, thou believedst they would help to leaven that spirit of riot natural to them, and which Jeff. Davis, whom thou indirectly servest, doth glory and rejoice to see, as it is as good for his cause as 20,000 men. [53]

Boston, August 23, 1862.   JUSTICE.

The Liberator, September 5, 1862.

4. BUTTS AND PORK-PACKERS AND NEGROES

The human form is often called divine and many other agreeable names, but after all it only affords presumptive evidence of manhood. Man is worked upon by what he works on. He gets something of all he touches. Vile and loathsome beasts do often get themselves better expressed in the human form than in the forms appropriated to them by nature. The Scribes and Pharisees were called wolves and vipers by Him who knew what was in man. The characterization was just they were men to the eye, but wolves and snakes to the touch--sleek and beautiful without, but full of hate and poison within. . . This train of thought was suggested by reading the following preamble and resolution, copied into the Rochester Union of yesterday, and by that every respectable journal evidently approved. Here they are:

Whereas, It has come to the knowledge of this meeting that it is the intention of one or more of the leading packers of this town to bring negro labor into competition with that of the white man, for the purpose of reducing the wages of the latter to the lowest possible standard.

Resolved, That we, the packing-house men of the town of South Chicago, pledge ourselves not to work for any packer, under any consideration, who will, in any manner, bring Negro labor in competition with our labor.

In all this may be seen the veritable swine. This preamble and resolution might have emanated from a body of "porkers," rather than of pork-packers, had the former the gift of speech. A slight change in the wording would bring out the genuine animal:

"Whereas, It has come to the knowledge of the big pigs of this meeting, that it is the intention of one or more of the pig-owners of this town to bring little pigs into competition with big pigs, for the purpose of reducing the amount of swill to the lowest possible standard, therefore,

Resolved, That we, the big pigs of the town of South Chicago, will do our utmost to drive the little pigs away from the trough, and have all the swill ourselves."

The Rochester Union is not surprised at the proceedings of the Pork-packers of South Chicago. No piggish development of Selfishness could possibly surprise that journal. It will one day be ashamed of the disgusting meanness of daily fanning the flame of prejudice and persecution against the humblest and least protected class of the community.

Douglass' Monthly, November, 1862.

5. RIOT ON THE CINCINNATI LEVY

The levee was the scene of a disgraceful riot yesterday morning. It appears that the India laborers or deck hands, deeming $25 to $30 per month--the customary wages on black boats since the outbreak of the rebellion--too low, have seen fit to demand $40 per month. In the first place German laborers were abundent at $30 per month, but the Irish laborers, through threats and intimidations, finally succeeded in driving the Germans from the levee, a week or two since. Since then, the negro laborers have been a source of annoyance to the Irish. During the present week there have been several disgraceful assults on the negroes, while they were passing from the boat's on which they were engaged to their homes up town. In no instances, however, have the police seen fit to interfere and simply discharge their sworn duty by keeping the peace.

As before stated, yesterday morning, a gang or mob of Irish attacked the negro laborers employed in loading the steamer Aurora, above the foot of Sycamore. The negroes were stoned and pursued on board of the Aurora, notwithstanding the timely remonstrance of the officers of the boat. Several of the negroes, after being chased on board, turned and "pitched" into their pursuers,--the result being several Irishmen pretty well whaled. On went the mob from boat to boat, in pursuit of every negro they could find. One poor "contraband," who was in no way implicated in the melon was finally over taken and pelted with boulders. His teeth were knocked out, or down his throat, while his jaw bone was fractured, eight or ten of the rowdies having pounced on him at once. Several of the negroes were pursued up town through the principle streets up into Second Street, where they sought refuge in a tenement occupied exclusively by their race. There being no police about, as is usual in such cases, Capt. Lightner of the Aurora, called on Mayor Hatch and stated the case, when his Honor promised to send down a posse of police, and see that the officers of the boat were protected in the pursuit of their business. During the afternoon, gangs of Irish were standing about

the levee, and at the gangway of the boat, out no violent demonstration was
made, except the frequent exclamation that "no d--d niggers should work on
the levee." The police and protection guaranteed by the Mayor, did not arrive however. The levee police is inefficient, or at least, if we have a
police force detailed in that quarter, they always manage to make themselves
scarce when their services are needed. If Mayor Hatch, and his very efficient police force cannot find time to preserve order, and see that boatmen
are protected in the pursuit of their business, it behooves the latter to at
least make the usual preparations to protect their own lives and property.
Our steamboat men are heavily taxed in wharfage fees, &c., and it is a hard
case if our vigilent police can't preserve order along that importance
thoroughfare--the levee.

Cincinnati Commercial, July 11, 1862.

6. FURTHER RIOTING

There was a shameful and most deplorable riot in the Thirteenth Ward
last night. The houses of negroes were stoned, a number of windows being
broken and doors battered.--The negro church on Sixth street was stoned, and
several shops were fired. We did not hear that any persons were seriously
hurt, but the wonder is they were not. The city is indebted to the forbearance of the unoffending negroes, whose houses were assulted, for the
fact that the riot was not made a bloody one. It is imperatively necessary
that this rioting should be stopped. If it continues any longer there is no
telling how far it may go. The negroes are the victims thus far, but if the
mob spirit is permitted to gather force, it will soon proceed to assualt
and destroy irrespective of color or condition. The rioters at our wharf,
who have been permitted to have their own way for several days, have not
only driven off the negro, but the German laborers. This is exactly the
way it goes.

Cincinnati Commercial, July 14, 1862.

7. WHITE FEAR OF EMANCIPATION

How do our white laborers relish the prospect that the emancipation of
the blacks spreads before them? What do they think of the inundation of two
or three hundred thousand free into Ohio, which inundation will come, if we
carry out the emancipation policy of President Lincoln. How many whites will
be thrown out of employment. How much will it reduce the price of labor?

Cincinnati Enquirer, July 15, 1862.

8. BLACK AND IMMIGRANT COMPETITION FOR JOBS

The Irish, who along with the German, may be regarded almost as the sole representative of white labor in the United States, regards with the bitterest feeling of hate and dislike, the race who now begin to share with him the source of subsistence which he has always hitherto monopolized, and which habit has taught him to regard as peculiarly belonging to him.

Cincinnati Gazette, July 16, 1862.

9. "MORE RIOTOUS AND DISGRACEFUL CONDUCT"

There was more riotous and disgraceful conduct on the levee yesterday. About noon, several Irish draymen indulged in a free fight near the intersection of Water and Main. About the same time a gang of Irish stevedores, spying a solitary negro crossing the grade, pursued and peppered him with boulders chasing him on board of the steamer Golden Era. They only offense on the part of the negro, it appeared, was his color and the fact that he was engaged on a boat in the capacity of fireman or deckhand. The stones flew thick and fast, several boatmen and passengers on the Cricket and Golden Era barely escaping being struck. During the afternoon, the same party of rioters ran another negro across the levee, and finding that he was hemmed in by the Irish at or near the foot of Sycamore, he pulled trigger on his assailants, who escaped injury, however. Still later, the same offenders chased another disconsolate negro. In this case, however, several respectable and responsible citizens having urged on a policeman the importance of arresting the ringleader, the aforesaid officer very graciously acceded to the request. He perhaps led the chap up street a square or two, when he was doubtless released. Our boatmen having called upon the authorities for protection against mobs of this character, and the desired relief being promised but not executed, the fraternity, for their better protection are now discussing the propriety, as a matter of self defense, of taking the law in their own hands. It behooves the police authorities to give a little more of the valuable times and attention to these rioters.

Cincinnati Commercial, July 17, 1862.

10. THE MOB

It has been justly said that a man who abuses a dumb brute is a coward. The common instincts of men acknowledge the principle, and civilized communities punish the offence by the infliction of severe penalties. But how much more cowardly are they who want only insult and maltreat defenceless men, women, and children. We are ashamed to confess that there are gangs of miscreants in this city who thus degrade the name of men, and disgrace the community, but it is still more humilitating to know that the people of Cincinnati tamely submit to gross outrages upon both the property and persons of a humble class of persons whom they are bound by every principle of justice, humanity, and decency, to protect.

In view of a current riotous spirit, however, the question begins to come home to us sternly; shall we put down the germ of rebellion against the peace and order of society, or shall we wait until it expands into strength

that will tax our whole municipal power to suppress? The trouble which now
ripples the surface of society may seem trifling, but it is obvious that it
has been long gathering head, and that it daily increases in strength. Not
many days hence, unless it is crushed, it may become dangerous both to the
property and persons of a very different class of people from those who are
now stiffled.

Yesterday afternoon quite a large number of respectable citizens held a
meeting to consider the condition of the city. Their resolutions were very
well, but some of the speeches were unfortunate in being open to injurious
misinterpretation. No question of riches or poverty is involved. The mob
is nothing more or less than the effect of the influence of cunning and designing knaves and covert traitors, who are working upon classes who have
not been accustomed to think upon any subject disconnected with their necessities, and who are too ready to atribute poverty and distress to any but the
real cause. Besides, the shrewd rascals who take advantage of the ignorant
and unthinking, adroitly seize upon the instrument that best serves their
evil purposes, and that instrument is the unfortunate negro. The poor
wretches who have been maltreating the helpers colored people of the city,
are not morally responsible for the crimes they have committed, but the
guilty are they who designedly encouraged them to disturb the peace and good
order of the community to promote their own infamous projects.

The riots begun among the Irish stevedores on the public landing. They
were instigated by the political clamor against negroes. They were wickedly
deceived into belief that an alleged competition of negro with white labor
would injuriously affect their interests, and they proposed to abate the supposed evil by violence. The feeling was contagious, and it extended to the
most populous negro quarters of the city, designated in local slang as "Buck-
town," where there are also many poor Irish people. The antipathy of the
latter towards the former was possibly, aggravated by the misconduct of some
very disreputable negroes who live in that district. But the riot once begun, the rioters, did not discriminate, and some very worthy colored people
were grossly insulted and abused, and the property of both white and black
persons was injured or destroyed. As usual, the only person seriously injured was an innocent spectator--one WM. Burke, a young Irishman, whose father is a grocer on the corner of Sixth and Culvert streets, near the scene
of the disturbances. Young BURKE was shot in the side, but it has not been
ascertained by whom the shot was fired. The assailants and assailed are mutual accusers. It is just to say, however, that the negroes, were assulted
and altogether they displayed extraordinary forbearance. The Irish people
who sympathise with the rioters try to justify their conduct on two allega-
tions--firstly, on the ground that the colored residents of that neighborhood
are not virtuous, and secondly, that the negroes are the cause of war, want
low wages and heavy taxes.

Cincinnati Commercial, July 17, 1862.

11. THE DISGRACEFUL RIOT IN BROOKLYN

Brooklyn, the city of churches and noble charities, is usually so well
behaved, we could scarcely credit the report that a riot had actually taken
place there; but a careful and impartial investigation of facts show that the
fair fame of our sister city has been sullied by a riotous mob of half-drunk-
en and ignorant white men and women, whose jealously of the blacks was kindled by a fight, on Saturday afternoon, between a negro and a white man in
front of grog-shop. The negro had taken a bill to the liquor-shop to get it
exchanged for postage stamps or small coin, and was standing on the threshold, when a white man of the name of Spaulding pushed him aside. The indig-
nity was resented by hard words, which soon ripened into hard blows, and the
negro had the best of the fight, when Policeman Oats interfered and seperated

the belligerents. The idea of a white man being whipped by a black man was
a source of humiliation too grievous to be endured. Sunday being a day of
leisure, grog-shop and street-corner committees had the subject of retalia-
tion under discussion and finally determined to mob the black women and
children on Monday, while the majority of the men were absent at a public
demonstration at Myrtle-avenue Park, in another part of the city.

On Monday forenoon three or four scouts, wishing to ascertain the
strength of the 'enemy,' called at Mr. Lorillard's tobacco factory, and were
denied admittance. The foreman, anticipating trouble, sent all the colored
parents in his employment at their homes, and closed the front doors and
windows of the establishment. Soon a committee of eight Irishmen effected
an entrance, and searched the premises for 'nagers;' but finding none, they
retired for reenforcements, which were easily obtained. They soon returned
with thirty or forty other rioters, and forthwith commenced hurling bricks
and paving-stones at the doors of windows of Mr. Watson's shop, in which two-
sets of hands are employed--a set of white hands under a white foreman, and
a set of black hands under a black foreman. These parties work side by side
without quarreling or jealousy.

In this factory where the fire originated seventy-five persons are employed, of whom fifty are colored and twenty-five white. The establishment
was started eight years ago, and some of the negroes employed there at the
time of the row have been faithful workers from the commencement of the concern.--Negroes have always been employed in Mr. Lorillard's establishment,
which is next door but one to Mr. Watson's; but there have been no sign of
disturbance there before, although it has been no sign of disturbance there
before, although it has been in operation eight or nine years.

At the time of the commencement of this riot, which was 12 o'clock at
noon on Monday, the white employees of the establishment had gone to their
dinners--and there were only twenty colored persons within the walls of the
building, five of whom were men, and the remainder women and children. These
colored employees not having homes in the neighborhood, had brought their
dinners with them, and were quietly eating at the time of assault.

Scarcely had the first missile been hurled by the leaders of the gang,
when four or five hundred men and boys, some of them intoxicated, came rushing with shouts and yells toward the factory, from the vicinity of Columbia
and Harrison streets, and at once surrounded the building, crying out, 'Down
with the nagers,' 'Turn out the nagers,' some of them entering the lower
story to look for the objects of their hatred. The mob continued to increase
until it numbered thousands. Although it was well known for hours before
this time that a riot was contemplated, no additional police force was sent
to the neighborhood. The two officers, Oats and Burns, who belong to that
beat, were on hand, but they could not control a drunken and infuriated mob.
The negroes, who were on the upper floor, barricaded the stairway in the best
manner they could, and then threw at their assailants, when they attempted
to approach them, whatever they could find at hand. In this way these five
men and fifteen women kept the mob at bay for two hours until Inspector Folk,
with a strong detachment of policemen, made his appearance.

Just before the arrival of the police force the rioters finding it impossible to get at the negroes, at the suggestion of a grogseller near by,
determined to set fire to the building and roast the niggers alive. A pot of
licorice and whisky, which was mistaken for tar, was emptied, and an attempt
was made to set it on fire, but the flame was put out by the police.

While Officer Donnelly was standing at the foot of the stairs keeping
the rioters away, he received a wound on the head from a box thrown by a colored man named Baker, at the rioters. The police finally drove away the rioters, and arrested Patrick Canna, the grogseller, who is charged with arson
and riot; Michael Maher, Wm. Morris, John Long, Charles Baker (colored),
Charles Baylis, Thomas Clark, Jos. Flood, Patrick Day, and Elias P. Riddle.

The rumor that fifty negroes had armed themselves with pistols purchased
at a gun shop on Court street on Tuesday morning is untrue. It is not true
that the negroes insulted white women in the neighborhood or the factory, as
reported by *The Hearald*.--That report was circulated on Sunday by a number
of evil-disposed fellows, who lounged about the liquor shops in that vicinity
for the purpose of creating the riot that followed.--It is not true that the
Irish assaulted the negroes because they had taken up their residence in that

neighborhood, for the negroes live in New York and on the outskirts of
Brooklyn. It is not true that they are a poor shiftless set, unable to take
care of themselves or that they caused this disgraceful riot.

The riot raged from 12 o'clock until about half-past 2, when it was
quelled by the police. Why did not the police officers in charge of that
district, knowing as they must have known that a row was anticipated, send
force there to protect the lives and property of peaceable citizens?

After the riot commenced, why were the police authorities so slow to
move? It is not more than twenty minutes' walk from the City Hall in Brooklyn to the tobacco manufactories, near the corner of Columbia and Sedgwick
streets, where the riot occurred.--When this force arrived, why did it behave so strangely as to merit the following rebuke from *The Brooklyn Eagle?*

"It is stated that the officers who were first at the scene of the riot
allowed their feelings against the negroes to interfere with their duties,
and that instead of attacking the white rioters they struck at the negros
with their clubs."

Mr. Watson's establishment, with its broken doors and windows, is
closed and unoccupied, and the hands, white as well as black, are for no
fault of theirs thrown out of employment. The colored people dare not return to Mr. Lorrillard's factory even. Threats of future demolition and assault are made, and yet we found only five policemen there yesterday to defend the just rights of the people.

Douglass' Monthly, September, 1862.

12. PERSECUTION OF NEGROES

Months ago, when the Rebel cause seemed at its last gasp, its partisans
in the loyal States were secretly impelled to get up a diversion in its favor by instigating riotous assaults on the unarmed and comparatively defenseless Blacks of our Northern cities. In furtherance of this plot, stories
were started that thousands of negroes at Washington, Fortress Monroe, and
elsewhere, were being subsisted in idleness at the public cost; next, that
fugitive slaves were so abundant in Chester County, Pa. and its vicinity,
that they were taking the bread out of the mouths of white laborers by working for ten cents per day! This was of course a falsehood, as the absence
of laboring men in the army has produced a scarcity of laborers in Chester
County, as almost everywhere else; no tolerably efficient white laborer having failed of finding constant employment there at $1 to $1½ per day. We
published repeated and explicit contradictions of the lie, but to no pur-
pose--could be impelled to assault and despoil the poor fugitives, taking
good care never to look into The Tribune.

Attacks on the negro population were commenced weeks ago at Cincinnati,
and have since tried at Evansville, Ind., and Toledo, Ohio. In the latter
place, they have been traced directly to the instigation of emissaries from
this City. Probably no one has given them a whisper of encouragement who
would not split his throat in cheering   Jeff Davis if that potentate should
ride by him in triumph.

The recent attack on the negro women and children employed in a tobacco
manufactory at Brooklyn is most disgraceful to our sister city, and--if it
be true that they were fore warned of it--to our Metropolitan Police, or at
least to the Brooklyn branch of it. That a ruffian mob should be enabled to
hold women and children in mortal terror for hours, gratifying meantime their
groundless malice by earnest and all but successful attempts to roast them
alive in their workshop, is a stain which Brooklyn will not soon efface.

Douglass' Monthly, September 1862.

13. BRUTAL AND UNPROVOKED ASSAULTS UPON COLORED PEOPLE

A species of violence and persecution towards colored people has been revived in Northern towns and cities during the present and past month, which can only be accounted for by the presence of some deadly inciting cause. Assulting individual negroes in the streets, and bodies of negroes at their work was years ago, of frequent occurrence even in the best of our Northern towns and cities.--But of late, this savage practice had well nigh ceased--and colored men were nearly as little liable to personal assault as other people. The case is now changed for the worse, and the unarmed black man, on the streets, at his work, and in his house, is constantly marked out for violence and persecution such as would disgrace a community of savages.

Cincinnati and Brooklyn have of late had their mobs of this character, and the colored people of those cities have suffered much in person and property from them, while scarcely a day passes when we do not hear of some individual assaults without any visible cause. The writer of these lines was standing in the Rail Road Station at Springfield Massachusetts, awaiting the departure of a train to Albany, perfectly silent and engrossed with his own thoughts, when he was confronted by a stalwart Irishman, who demanded two cents for an old and worthless postage stamp, and on being refused, poured out upon him a loud stream of vile abuse attempting meanwhile to clutch the writer by the throat. He laid the ruffian on the ground and mounted the cars and was off with the train, before he could rally to a second assault-- though not without leaving the sleeve of a tolerably good coat behind him.

On reaching home we heard of similar outrages in Rochester, and in other parts of the country. The number, character, and simultaineous occurrences of such assaults all over the Northern States, render them highly significant, and suggests the idea that the poor miserable human brutes who openly perpetrate them are really the least guilty parties. The pretense that colored men are elbowing white men out of employment cannot be alleged as explanation. Work for all classes is abundant, and there are few of the whites who wish to compete with the negro in those few departments of labor which are still open to him. Nor is mere wantonness an explanation. There never was a time when this vice was more visibly checked in this country. Our young, daring, dashing young white men have gone to the war from all our towns and cities, and the wanton gaiety which sometimes leads to a brush at street corners, has been sobered down, and has in some instances wholly disappeared. If the base and brutal assaults made upon the colored people arose from wantonness, there would be less cause of concern. They would soon die out. But, if as some think, there is a secret slaveholding organization all over the free States, in secret sympathy with the rebels, and full of hatred to the negro, and who thinks the ends of the rebels can be better served by stirring up hate and wrath against our long abused and unprotected people, these assaults become just cause of alarm and searching enquiry.

It is remarkable that these demonstrations of hostility came along about the same time when it became probable that the necessities of the Government would lead to arming the negroes in common with others to fight the battles of the Republic. We can conceive of any number of base motives for opposing such arming, and for endeavoring to defeat it by all means. We take the following timely remarks on the subject from the New York Tribune!

Yesterday afternoon a colored man, was quietly walking along Furman street, in Brooklyn. Some white men hooted at him, or made offensive remarks. He had the audacity to answer. The whites set about the pleasing pastime of beating him. He defended himself as best he could--kept off five or six--when five or six more mixed to whip the negro because he was black. He picked up a stone, and knocked a man named Lyno on the head. Then a crowd collected and about a hundred brave, chivalrous white men undertook to kill the negro not only because he was black, but because he would not stand quietly at ease and be murdered for the sport of the Knickerbocker Ice men. The black man escaped from the infuriated crowd by being arrested and taken to the Station-House. There being no charge against him, he was set at large. It does not appear that any of the sportive crowd who hunted the negro down were arrested. We understand that many less prominent events of the

kind have recently occurred in Brooklyn. Will not all good citizens unite
in stopping this wicked business? If suffered to go on, their may be a
fearful reckoning ere long. The men who instigate as well as those who make
these outbreaks against a handful of helpless creatures are, playing with
burning torches in a powder-house. If men are to be killed like dogs because they are black, the same spirit will kill them because they are anything else that an unreasonable mob may not like.-'They that sow the wind
will reap the whirl wind.'

Douglass' Monthly, September, 1862.

14. BLOODY RIOT IN DETROIT

A despatch from Detroit, dated Friday, 6th, says--"A negro, who had committed an outrage upon a young white girl, was being taken from the court-
room to the jail, under escort of the military, this afternoon, when an attempt to take the negro from the hands of the officers was made by a gang of
rowdies. The crowd was fired upon, and one man killed and several wounded.
Being foiled in their attempt to get possession of the negro, the mob perpetrated the most horrible outrages upon the colored people residing in the
vicinity of the jail."

The Liberator, March 13, 1863.

15. ANTI-BLACK MOB IN DETROIT

*Assault upon a Negro Hovel, and Murder of the Inmates--A Blood-thirsty and
    Unmanageble Mob--The City Fired in Twenty Places--The Military Called
    Out to Suppress the Riot.*

Yesterday was the bloodiest day that ever dawned upon Detroit. Up to
twelve o'clock, no disturbance of a serious nature had occurred. At about
half past twelve, after the adjournment of the court, the clouds which por-
tended the coming storm began to gather. The mob first inaugurated the day
by petty persecutions of any negroes who chanced to come in the vicinity of
the City Hall. Any of that unfortunate race who happened along were subjected to kicks, cuffs and blows, and were liable to be butchered upon the
streets. Even women and children were not exempt, several of them being
abused in a most shameful and outrageous manner.
    In order to quell the disturbance, and to deliver the prisoner safe to
the jailer, the Detroit Provost Guard had been ordered to escort him to the
jail. Their arrival in front of the City Hall was greeted by threats of defiance from the crowd, who became more excited as the prospect of gratifying
their blood-thirsty vengeance upon the negro became less favorable. The
Guard formed in line upon Monroe Avenue, and everything being prepared for a
vigorous defence, Faulkner was led down by the officers into the street. As
the mob got sight of their intended victim, the yells, groans and hisses were
almost deafening, and nothing but the fixed bayonets of the soldiers could
have prevented them from rushing upon and tearing him in pieces. And it was
with great difficulty they could be kept back. The throng of people which
followed the prisoner to the jail was immense, and could only be estimated
by thousands.

It was not until they had neared the jail that the riot commenced in earnest. Notwithstanding the array of flashing bayonets, and the danger of being shot down in the attempt, a large number of rioters simultaneously rushed for the prisoner, and came very near rescuing him. But he was got into the prison inclosure unharmed, without a single sacrifice. All would have been well, and the mob would have soon dispersed, had it not been for a wanton and malicious act of certain members of the provost guard toward the exasperated citizens. Without orders from any reliable authority, a number of random shots were fired promiscuously into the crowd, several of them taking effect, and one man, Chas. Langer, being instantly killed, shot through the heart. The Provost Guard, after this display, then hurried back to the barracks, leaving the crowd to disperse at their leisure. The cry of death and vengeance ran through the crowd like an electric shock. The sight of the bleeding corpse of the dead man, and the groans of a half dozen who were wounded, kindled anew the flames of insubordination and frenzy. The germans, especially, were maddened beyond description, because their countryman had been sacrificed, as they thought and expressed it, to protect a negro who was deserving of torture and death. The excitement among all classes, however, was intense. Being baffled in their attempt to rescue the criminal, they sought other channels to give vent to their malice.

The first house where a negro family resided, one end of which was used as a cooper shop, situated on Beaublen street, was assaulted with bricks, paving stones and clubs. About a dozen negroes were at work in the shop or stopping in the house at the time. The most of them were armed, and fired several shots into the crowd from the windows, taking effect in several instances, but not fatally injuring any one, as far as could be ascertained.

As each shot from the negro hovel reverberated through the vicinity, the fiendishness of the mob became more manifest, and their desperation more dreadful. The firearms in possession of the negroes deterred them from entering, for it would have been almost certain death for any man to attempt it. Any missile that could be obtained was hurled at the rendezvous of the negroes, the windows and doors burst open, and everything destroyed which could be seen by those outside. Finally, finding that they could not be forced out of their hiding place in any other manner, the match of the incendiary was placed at one end of the building, and in a very short time the flames spread so as to envelop almost the entire building.

The scene at this time was one that utterly baffles description. With the building a perfect sheet of livid flame, and outside a crowd of bloodthirsty rioters, some of whom were standing at the doors with revolvers in their hands, waiting for their victims to appear, it was a truly pitiable and sickening sight. The poor wretches inside were almost frantic with fright, undecided whether to remain and die by means of the devouring element, or suffer the almost certain terrible fate which awaited them at the hands of the merciless crowd. There was no more mercy extended to the suffering creatures than would have been shown to a rattlesnake. No tears could move, no supplications assuage the awful frenzy and demoniacal spirit of revenge which had taken possession of that mass of people.

One colored woman made her appearance at the door with a little child in her arms, and appealed to the mob for mercy. The monstrous fact must be told, her tearful appeals were met with a shower of bricks, stones and clubs, driving herself and the babe in her arms back into the burning building. At this juncture one man, moved to mercy at this cowardly and inhuman act, rushed to her assistance, bravely and nobly protecting her person from the violence which threatened her. But the negroes found no such protection. They were driven gradually to the windows and doors, where they were murderously assailed with every species of weapons, including axes, spades and clubs, and everything which could be used as a means of attack. The frightened creatures were almost as insane with fright as their persecutors were with madness. As they came out, they were beaten and bruised in a terrible manner, their shrieks and groans only exciting the mob to further exertions in their brutal work. Several of them were knocked down with axes and left for dead, but who afterwards recovered only to be again set upon and cruelly beaten to insensibility.

The scenes which followed were of a similar nature. Old men, eighty years of age, were not in the least respected, but knocked down with the

same fiendish vindictiveness which characterized all the other proceedings
of the day. After the first building had been reduced to ashes, the appe-
tite for arson had only been whetted, and not at all appeased. As night approached, they grew bolder, and did not scruple to commit the worst crimes
upon the calendar with perfect impunity. The houses on Lafayette st., between Beaublen and St. Antoine, were literally sacked of their contents, and
the furniture piled in the middle of the street and burned.

Among the articles constituting the bonfires, a large number of musical
instruments could be discovered--bass viols, violins, banjos, guitars, ac-
cordeons, and almost every musical instrument in existence. Feather beds
were ripped open, and their contents scattered over the streets, and everything valuable totally destroyed. Then, no satisfied with having destroyed
every vestige of furniture, the torch was applied to the buildings, and
nearly the whole of the entire blocks, on both sides of the street, were
soon levelled to the ground. The steamers were on the spot promptly, but
would only be permitted to throw water on the houses of white men, to prevent the conflagration from becoming general. The mob threatened that the
engines would be torn to pieces if they attempted to play upon any other
buildings than those designated.

As there was no room for doubt that these threats would be summarily
executed, if necessity compelled that course, it was deemed proper to cater
to the wishes of the mob in that respect.

The work of destruction then progressed with fearful rapidity. No sooner was one building burned than another was set on fire, some of them being
several blocks apart.

The notorious Paton Alley was totally destroyed, as were also several
buildings in that vicinity.

It was impossible last night to ascertain the number of buildings destroyed, but it is safe to say that they will aggregate not less than forty
or fifty.

An hour or two previous to this, the authorities, becoming alarmed, and
being satisfied that no force that could be mustered in Detroit would be
sufficiently powerful to quell the riot, or stop the outrages of the rioters,
telegraphed to the commander of the Twenty-seventh Infantry, in camp at
Ypsilanti, requesting him to forward a battalion of his men, by special
train, to assist in dispersing the mob. About this time, a despatch was received, stating that the request of the city officials had been complied
with, and that five companies were on the way. This news, together with the
appearance of several squads of armed men in various parts of the city, had
no influence in overawing the crowd, but rather tended to increase their rage
and activity.

Great alarm and distress prevailed everywhere, as these fires successively burst forth, and in some localities the citizens armed themselves, and
turned out to protest their families and property.

After the last fire had been extinguished, the rioters suddenly dispersed, completely worn out and dispirited by their labors.

It is impossible to give the names of all the persons injured.

Perhaps a dozen or more were struck, and more or less injured, by the
bullets and shot fired by the soldiers and negroes. At one volley from the
negro house on Beaublen street, several people were struck, including a boy
ten or twelve years old, and a girl a little older.

Of the negroes there are all sorts of rumors. It is believed that several were killed, but as far as known, nothing is positive concerning the
matter. Our reporter saw a large number in an insensible condition in the
gutters and alleys, but none entirely dead. A large number, however, were
very seriously injured, and it is probable that many of them will never recover.

The colored population of the city, frightened and distracted, hurried
from the mob, scattering in every direction, a large number going over the
river to Canada, while many actually fled to the woods, with their wives and
little ones. They were perfectly panic-stricken, and run hither and thither
with a recklessness which rendered them totally unfit to take proper care of
themselves. Those who did not leave the city huddled themselves together in
the kitchens and out-houses of the buildings adjoining the places where the
riotous proceedings were had.

Detroit Free Press, March 7, 1863.

16.   EYEWITNESS TO THE DETROIT RIOT

LOUIS HOUSTON AND SOLOMON HOUSTON--We were working in Mr. Reynold's cooper shop, between Fort and Lafayette streets. An immense crowd came to the shop, and the first thing we knew they smashed in the front window and door, and said: "Come out ye sons of b---h." They came around in the alley and smashed in the back windows. We did not go out, but they seemed too cowardly to come in, and they continued to smash and break up Mr. R's house. Finding the mob directing their fury on the dwelling house where there was none but the wife of Mr. Reynolds, Mrs. Bonn and child, and Mrs. Dale and four children, all exposed to all kinds of missiles that could be thrown through the doors and windows, we all went to the house to try to defend the women. Then the mob set the shop on fire. During our stay in the shop, none of them dared to come in; but after we left it they then put the torch to it, and soon it was in flames! The mob then surrounded the house in every direction, as if determined to burn up the property and all the men, women and children that were therein; during which time they were throwing brickbats and missiles from every direction. I came to the front door of the house, and it was then partly consumed. A gentleman that I knew called me to come to him, and I made my way to him, and he forbade the mob interfering with me. He knew me well, and I was a peaceable man. Several laid hold of me and said they were intent on taking my life; that they saw me shoot. A German man rushed on me with a spade, and struck me with it over the head, inflicting a severe wound at each blow. A person who stood by him, as he raised the spade the third time, asked him what he intended to do? Said he, "I intend to kill him!"

The man said to him: "You ought to be ashamed to strike a man with such a weapon, whom you have never seen, nor has done you any harm!" At this, the assassin threw the spade down.

A gentleman, who I did not know at that time, being much excited, but I very well knew him afterwards, came to me and took me down Lafayette street to Mr. Thairs', and the mob surrounded me again, and prevented the friend from taking me on. Here they knocked me down again. Mr. T. then came out and bade them not to interfere with me any more, and came and took me in. He sent for a doctor to examine my wounds, and washed me and took care of me kindly, till the next day.

I suffered for a couple of weeks severely; but, thank the Lord, I am now recovering, but have not been able to do a stroke of work since the 6th of March, five weeks, with a helpless family depending on me for protection!
. . .

JOSEPH BOYD, a young man, and an excellent mechanic, was knocked in the head with an axe. After this he was unconscious, and was dragged out of the way of being destroyed by the flames. Officer Sullivan, who appeared the only authorized officer of peace that discharged his duty in the face of the mob, as was known as such. He gave poor Boyd some aid, and after having him taken to a saloon, the mob found out that the innocent victim was there, and they made a rush and dragged him out, though he was unconscious! His head gaping wide from the wounds by the axe, which were sufficient to kill him; and enough was the affliction inflicted upon him to have satisfied the most savage of a heathen tribe, even had he been guilty of some crime! But astonishing to tell, Dutch and Irish fell on him with hellish fury, and with all kinds of missiles; they beat and dragged him back as if determined to end his suffering in the flames, but came to a halt, as if their rage was abated, when they saw no stroke moved him. They considered him dead.

Detroit Free Press, March 7, 1863.

17. STRIKE AMONG THE NEGROPHOBISTS AT THE NAVY YARD. BOSTON

The Navy Yard is a great institution for strikes among the workmen, and
if they don't have something for excitement at least once a month, it is set
down as a remarkable event. A very respectable colored man from Baltimore,
a day or two since, applied for a situation as a caulker and graver, being
recommended by parties who knew him as a good workman. He was hired, and
went to work. There are about two hundred and fifty men in the caulker's
department, and yesterday, without taking any preliminary steps in the matter, such as a meeting or a consultation among the members of the whole
gang, about one hundred and sixty of the workmen came to a conclusion that
they would not work if the colored man was allowed to remain in the yard,
and refused to answer to their names at the roll call. The Captain of the
Yard, Mr. Taylor, who is acting Commodore, in consequence of the death of
Commodore Montgomery's daughter, upon learning the facts of the case, ordered the discharge of these men who refused to answer to the call.

There are now about one hundred caulkers left, and most of these did
not know the intentions of their brother workmen until they learned of the
discharges. A few strong-minded ones led on the rest and the result was,
instead of compelling Uncle Sam to accede to their demand, they all lost
good situations.

Douglass' Monthly, June, 1863.

18. THE COLORED SAILOR'S HOME IN NEW YORK

COLORED SAILOR'S HOME--WM. P. POWELL, *Superintendent.*

On Mr. Powell's return from England, whither he had been for the education of his children, because the foolish and wicked prejudices of Americans
would not permit them to enter our institutions, he has again opened a Sail-
or's Home for the seamen of his race. The Society became responsible for
furnishing the house, and aided at the outset in the payment of rent.
Though a few boarders had been received previously, the Home was hardly in
operation till the first of August. The whole number of boarders received
during the nine months is 270. Of this number 61 were shipwrecked and des-
titute--several of them captures of the pirate Alabama--and relieved at the
expense of the Society. For a time this new and worthy enterprise for the
benefit of colored seamen was bitterly opposed by a combination of colored
sailor landlords preventing the shipping of seamen from Mr. Powell's house.
Through the persuasive influence of the Home Committee, however, that has
happily ceased, and the New Colored Sailor's Home is prosperous.

A Beneficial self-protective Society for colored seamen has been organized among themselves which promises good to that class and to the interest
of commerce, so far as affected by the improvement of our colored seamen.

Sailor's Magazine (June, 1863):312.

19.   REPORT OF THE COLORED SAILORS' HOME

WM. P. POWELL, *No. 2 Dover Street, near Franklin Square.*

Gentlemen:--With the close of the year 1864 ends the *second* year of the operations of the Colored Sailors' Home. The difficulties, hopes and fears of its success from its opening up to the present, and the opposition with which it had to contend, to say nothing of the terrible riot of July, 1863, have all passed into the history of the AMERICAN SEAMAN'S FRIEND SOCIETY, in its Christian efforts to promote the moral and religious elevation of the colored sons of the ocean. Although the Home has not been patronized, so as to make it self-supporting, as well as we could wish, yet the problem, to make the *sailor* a better *man,* and the *man* a better *sailor,* in so far as our humble labors are concerned, in providing him with all the comforts of a well-regulated home, with all its moral and religious surroundings, is being daily worked out. For example, the *vital* statistics and the *mode* of life of colored seamen boarding at the Home, show only *one* having died in the hospital in *two* years, and he from old age, and not from dissipation; and only *six* have been sent to the hospital sick out of *all* the boarders since opening; and, also, *not one* imprisonment for *mutiny* or bad conduct. This is all owing to the sanitary regulations, and a due regard to the *moral* health of the boarders. In our visits to the various hospitals, we often find as many as *five* colored seamen from *one* boarding house. Then, again, with few exceptions, the boarders provide themselves with plenty of clothing, and save their money, sending their parents and families, through our agency, more than half of their earnings.

Since our last Report in September, *one hundred* stewards, cooks and seamen have boarded at the Home. Total number since the July riots *four hundred and ninety-eight.* Total amount received for board since September, 1863, $1,727 00. Total amount due from destitute shipwrecked seamen and delinquent boarders, $551 52. Total amount of expenses, *current,* since September, 1863, $2,693 01.

To sum up, taking into consideration all the contingencies incidental to every well-directed effort for good, we have every encouragement.

New York, Dec. 27, 1864.

Sailor's Magazine (February, 1865):169-70.

ANTI-NEGRO RIOTS IN NEW YORK CITY

20.   TROUBLE AMONG THE LONGSHOREMEN.

A disturbance occurred, to-day, among the longshoremen, on the line of the East River, above the battery. The cause of the difficulty was the fact that negroes were employed on the docks, and white laborers, who were principally Irishmen, objected. To-day they undertook to beat the negroes.

The plan was arranged in an underground bar-room in South street, and simultaneously this forenoon the Irishmen, among whom the mode of operations appeared to have been previously agreed on, set out upon a negro hunt. The largest proportion of the Irishmen proceeded to the docks, where about two hundred of the negroes were employed, and they pommelled them without mercy. The negroes defended themselves as well as they could, and one of their number presented a pistol at the rioters, which he fired three or four times, but it does not appear that any shots took effect. The police interfered and drove off the assailants, arresting the negro who fired the pistol, and one of the rioters. The others fled.

Meanwhile, the Irishmen who had gone into the ward attacked all the negro porters, cartmen and laborers whom they could find, and subsequently the
police went after the rioters, who were routed without a conflict. They
were desirous of assaulting negroes, but declined to face the policemen, on
sight of whom they made their escape.

The negroes are all at work. They are represented by the police as sober, peaceable men, industrious, but declining to work for less than usual
rates, and as being of a better class relatively than their persecutors.

New York Evening Post, March 13, 1863.

21. THE RIGHT TO WORK

If longshoremen or any other class of laborers do not choose to work
with negroes they need not. But no law compels them. But the negro, as well
as the white man, has a right to work for whoever will employ and pay him,
and the law, and courts, and police, and public opinion ought to protect him
in that right, and will.

New York Tribune, April 14, 1863.

22. DISGRACEFUL PROCEEDING - COLORED LABORERS,
ASSAILED BY IRISHMEN

A disgraceful riot occurred among the longshoremen at pier No. 9, New
York, on Monday, May 29. A number of unoffending negroes were brutally assailed, while quietly pursuing their labors, by a body of Irishmen who had
struck, for higher wages. Most of the Negroes took refuge in flight, but
not until many of them had become severely wounded with the stones and clubs
employed by their assailants. One of them in self-defence, drew a revolver,
which he fired several times, and succeeded in wounding one of the rioters.
The arrival of the police checked any further hostilities. Two of the rioters and the negro who discharged the revolver were arrested. The latter
was afterwards discharged, as he had acted only in self-defence. The two
Irishmen were committed for trial.

Douglass' Monthly, June, 1863.

23. REIGN OF TERROR

A perfect reign of terror exists in the quarters of this helpless people, and if the troubles which now agitate our city, continue during the
week it is believed that not a single negro will remain within the metropolitan limits.

New York Herald, July 15, 1863.

24.   "REPORT OF THE COMMITTEE OF MERCHANTS FOR THE RELIEF OF
COLORED PEOPLE, SUFFERING FROM THE LATE RIOTS IN THE CITY
OF NEW YORK"

Report of the Secretary

Driven by the fear of death at the hands of the mob, who the week previous had, as you remember, brutally murdered, by hanging on trees and lamp
posts several of their number, and cruelly beaten and robbed many others,
burning and sacking their houses and driving nearly all from the streets,
alleys and docks upon which they had previously obtained an honest though
humble living--these people had been forced to take refuge on Blackwell's
Island, at Police Stations, on the outskirts of the city, in the swamps and
woods back of Bergen, New Jersey, at Weeksville and in the barns and out-
houses of the farmers of Long Island and Morrissania. At these places were
scattered some 5,000 homeless and helpless men, women, and children.

The first great point to be gained was the restoring of the confidence
of the colored people in the community, from which they had been driven. To
do this a central depot was to be established to which they should be invited
to come and receive aid with the fullest assurance that they should be protected.

Temporary aid might be sent them to their residences, as was done
through the hand of Rev. Mr. Dennison, and through the Society for improving
the condition of the poor.

This plan met your approval, and that evening, Tuesday, July 21st, I
was instructed to look up an office and announce in the morning papers the
contemplated purpose, and I did so.

On Wednesday, the present office, No. 350 Fourth Street, was secured,
vacated by its former occupants, cleansed and opened for business the following day, Thursday, July 23d, when 38 applicants received aid. On Friday,
July 24th, the wants of 318 were attended to, and on Saturday, July 25th,
the streets in the neighborhood were literally filled with applicants. The
N. Y. Express thus describes the scene:--

At ten o'clock, Fourth street, near Broadway, was filled with colored
people of both sexes, and all ages. They presented an aspect of abject poverty; and many of them bore evidence of the assaults made on them during the
riots.

The building where relief was given to the applicants at No. 350 Fourth
street, was soon surrounded by nearly three thousand negroes. Some of them
had come into the city from woods and fields in different parts of the
State, where they took refuge. They appeared to be no strangers to hunger;
for when the good soldiers of the Twelfth Regiment, who are quartered up
stairs in the building, "brushed" out their rations to the throng, there was
a pitiable scramble to obtain them, and the lucky blacks retired to eat them.

The method of conducting business is thus described in the *N. Y. Times:*

The above institution, located at No. 350 Fourth street, is doing an
immense amount of good in relieving the immediate wants of the colored people
who suffered during the late riots. Yesterday the building was thronged with
applicants, all of whom were provided for to some extent. The amount of
money already collected for this fund amounts to over $28,000, of which some
$7,000 has thus far been distributed.

Yesterday, males only were admitted to the apartments. Last Saturday
was devoted exclusively to females. That order will be observed in future--
the males having the privilege of the institution every other day, commencing
from yesterday, and the females the alternate days. The hours of business
are from 9 A.M. to 4 P.M. From 8 to 9 A.M. and from 4 to 5 P.M. the use of
the room is extended to the legal profession, members of which assemble to
give their services gratuitously to such of the colored sufferers as may desire to avail themselves of their valuable assistance. Yesterday over $2,500
was distributed to 900 men. A considerable amount of clothing has been received by the Committee, but as yet none of it has been given out, the great
want of the applicants being, at present, money. In the basement of the

building a receptacle for clothing is being fitted up, so that, when the proper time arrives, it will be systematically and judiciously distributed.

It is well worth the attention of any one who takes an interest in the objects of the institution, to witness with what regularity and quietness business is conducted. The applicants enter the building by the basement, arranged with railings, so that, although full, only a single line can be formed, and in the order in which they enter. On the floor above are the officers and clerks seated at desks inclosed with railing, and as applicants enter the room they are taken by policemen in attendance to them. By this means confusion is avoided, and each clerk has no more at one time than he can promptly give relief to. Policemen are on duty in and about the establishment, and they perform their duties well and kindly. Each clerk notes in a book the name of the applicant, his occupation and residence, the amount of loss sustained, and other particulars bearing upon his means and condition. If the person proves himself to be a worthy object of charity, he is furnished with a ticket which entitles him, on presenting the same to the Cashier, to receive a certain amount of money specified thereon. In no instance does the amount exceed $5, unless the Committee are satisfied upon evidence adduced, that the party is actually in need of more. It is the intention of the Committee to send out missionaries next week for the express purpose of looking up special cases of destitution. Rev. H. GARNETT (colored) is at present engaged at the institution in investigating the special cases which offer themselves there, as his extensive acquaintance among the colored people enables him to decide upon the veracity of the statements made by many of them.

The first object of the Committee is to relieve the immediate wants of the colored people who have suffered by the riots. When that has been accomplished measures will be taken to increase the sphere of their usefulness.

The New York daily *Tribune* speaks as follows:

The rooms devoted to this charitable enterprise are easy of access, and centrally located on a quiet street not far from Police Headquarters, where protection can soon reach the sufferers in the event of a disturbance. These rooms have been temporarily fitted up with benches and tables for the accommodation of those who apply for assistance.

The distribution of funds has been reduced to such a perfect system, that in a few hours a dozen men can record the names, give out the tickets and disburse the money appropriated for that purpose, to three thousand persons. A set of books containing the name, occupation, residence, and necessities of each applicant is kept in the same exact and nice manner that a merchant or a banker would keep his accounts. The funds are not filtered through many hands. The sufferer has not to wait until patience ceases to be a virtue before his case is considered. There are no harsh or unkind words uttered by the clerks--no impertinent quizzing in regard to irrelevant matters--no partizan or sectarian view, advanced. The business is transacted in a straightforward, practical manner, without chilling the charity into an offense by creating the impression that the recipient is humiliated by accepting the gift. To the credit of the colored sufferers they gratefully receive the small sums given to them without criticism or jealousy, knowing that they can call again in the hour of need without being "bluffed" away with an unpleasant reminder that they had been assisted before. Those who are prudent and honest need not be afraid to repeat their requests in the time of necessity. The object of the fund is to help the sufferers along over the slough during this low tide in their affairs, and as fast as they can take care of themselves, they are expected to cease their applications for help from the committee. Among the volunteers who have put their shoulders to the wheel in this work, are the Rev. S. H. Tyng. Jr., Rev. H. B. Barton and George Hancock, Esq., the Rev. H. H. Garnett, the Rev. Mr. Ray, and others. [54]

During the month cirling August 21st there have been 3,942 women, and 2,450 men, making a total of 6,392 persons of mature age, relieved; full one-third being heads of families, whose children were included in the relief afforded by your committee, making a total of 12,782 persons relieved.

From these persons 8,121 visits were received and aid was given; to which add 4,000 applicants whose calls were not responded to, as they had previously been aided sufficiently, and you have 12, 121 applicants whose cases were considered and acted upon at the office during the month. Add to this the work of the members of the legal profession, Messrs. JAS. S. STEARNS and CEPHAS BRAINERD, who have been indefatigable in their labors, assisted by several other gentlemen, by whom 1,000 notices of claims for damages against the city, have been made out, copied and duly presented to the Comptroller, while our clerks have recorded on the books over 2,000 claimants for a sum of over $145,000, together with a considerable distribution of clothing by two colored clerks, and a fair idea of the work done in this office, during the month may be obtained and a reason for what might otherwise appear a large amount of expenditure.

Of the 2,450 men relieved, their occupations were as follows:

1,267 Laborers and Longshoremen,	4 Tailors.
177 Whitewashers	3 Artists.
176 Drivers for Cartmen,	3 Music Teachers.
250 Waiters,	3 Coopers.
124 Porters,	2 Engravers.
97 Sailors and Boatmen,	2 Janitors.
72 Coachmen,	2 Measurers.
45 Cooks,	2 Oystermen.
37 Barbers,	2 Undertakers.
34 Chimney Sweepers,	1 Landlord
25 Tradesmen,	1 Flour Inspector.
20 Butchers,	1 Teacher.
15 Bootblacks,	1 Copyist.
11 Ministers or Preachers,	1 Farmer.
11 Shoemakers,	1 Botanist.
11 Tobacconists,	1 Physician.
11 Wood sawyers,	1 Book-binder.
8 Carpenters,	1 Tin Smith.
7 Basket-makers,	1 Upholsterer.
6 Scavengers	1 Black Smith.
5 Carpet shakers,	

Of the 3,942 women, were

2,924 Day's work women,	13 Hucksters.
664 Servants hired by month,	4 Teachers.
163 Seamstresses,	1 Artist.
106 Cooks,	1 Boardinghouse keeper.
19 Worked in Tobacco factory,	1 Basket-maker.
13 Nurses,	32 Infirm.

In the height of the crowd of applications it was found necessary to employ as many as ten clerks, and several special policemen. These last, together with one regular patrolman who is still with us, preserved excellent order and were kindly furnished by Mr. Acton, of the Metropolitan Police, free of charge.

As soon as the most pressing necessities of the sufferers were relieved through the office, colored clergymen were employed by your direction as missionaries to visit the applicants for relief at their residences, four of the clerks were discharged and four clergymen employed in their places--The Rev. Mr. Ray, Rev. Mr. Leonard, Rev. Mr. Carey and John Peterson in addition to the Rev. H. H. Garnett, who was with us, and whose services have been invaluable from the first. These missionaries made 3,000 visits, relieving the wants of 1,000, and examining the cases of 3,000 persons, and nearly all the payments of the last week were made upon their representation.

I refer with pleasure to the valuable aid rendered the Committee by the City Tract Missionaries as Secretaries of the Association for improving the condition of the poor, not only in promptly supplying on our behalf, the pressing wants of the colored people in the different wards, but in giving such reports of applicants as facilitated our work at the office.

A good many applications for servants have been made, and as it seemed desirable that places should be provided for many of the sufferers as soon as possible, a book was kept open for employers needing servants and servants needing employment to register their names. Constant pressure of business, however, and the demand for servants in most cases far exceeding the supply, left this branch of useful mission work quite incomplete.

A large number of workmen having been discharged by their employers, who were in fear of damage to their property by the mob, the following appeal from the Executive Committee was printed and sent on 31st July to merchants and corporations employing colored laborers.

TO THE MERCHANTS AND OTHER EMPLOYERS OF LABORERS IN NEW YORK:

The undersigned, an Executive Committee appointed at a large and influential meeting of the Merchants of New York, to dispense the funds contributed by them in aid of the colored sufferers by the late riot, have been instructed by the General Committee to address their fellow-citizens in relation to the objects of their care. The Committee have learned, with deep regret, that in various ways obstacles have been thrown in the way of the attempt of colored laborers to resume their wanted occupation, cases having occurred where men, who had labored faithfully for years in a situation have been refused a restoration to their old places. Street railroads, by which many had been accustomed to pass from their distant homes to their usual places of business, have refused them permission to ride, and have thus deprived them of the ability to perform their customary duties and earn their needful pay. The undersigned, in behalf of the Merchants of this great Metropolis, respectfully but urgently call upon their fellow-citizens to unite in protecting the injured and persecuted class, whose cause the Committee advocate. The full and equal right of the colored man to work for whoever chooses to employ him, and the full and equal right of any citizen to employ whoever he will, is too manifest to need proof. Competition is indispensable to the successful management of commercial business; surely the energetic, enterprising merchants of this city will not allow any interference with their rights. On the other hand, if the colored population, from a want of firmness on the part of the whites, be deprived of their just rights to earn an honest living, they will become a dependent, pauper race. The Committee, therefore, earnestly appeal to the good feelings, to the sense of justice, to the manliness of every employer of whatever class, to restore the colored laborers to his customary place, and to sustain him in it. They appeal to the Board of Directors of our Street Railroads to give them all the immunities they ever enjoyed; and to the managers of all associations and corporations requiring many operatives, to restore the old order of things. While they enjoin upon merchants and others to maintain their right to employ whoever they please, it is no part of their purpose to recommend the discharge of one class and the substitution of another. What they do ask is that where colored laborers have been employed, they should not be discharged in this emergency; and the Committee would appeal to those laboring men who would drive colored men from the city, to consider the principle they would thus establish, and see how it may react upon themselves. Should they succeed in this attempt they would compel many white laborers now in the country to seek employment in the city, and before they were aware of it a new class of laborers would be brought into the city, and the wages of labor would be reduced. The laws of the demand and supply of labor cannot be permanently changed by combinations or persecutions.

The merchants of New York, the main supporters of every enterprise undertaken in our city, ask that this appeal may have the favorable consideration and support of every citizen.

In conclusion the Committee are fully authorized to state that the Police of our city who behaved so nobly during the recent troubles will render any aid which may possibly be needed, but the want of which is not anticipated.

J. D. McKENZIE, Chairman.

The work before us, is now, chiefly to take care of the claims against the city of those who have lost property by the riots. In the pressure with

which sufferers applied for relief, it was not possible to do more than
take a general estimate of their losses. These have now been revised and a
more particular statement of items obtained. Others have been sought out at
their residences, and notified to come and have their claims made out, and
it will be our duty to see that they are properly presented to the Comptroller and prosecuted against the city, within the time prescribed by the law.
. . .

Incidents of the Riot.

ABRAHAM FRANKLIN.

This young man who was murdered by the mob on the corner of Twenty-seventh St., and Seventh avenue, was a quiet, inoffensive man, 23 years of age,
of unexceptionable character, and a member of Zion African Church in this
city. Although a cripple, he earned a living for himself and his mother by
serving a gentleman in the capacity of coachman. A short time previous to
the assault upon his person, he called upon his mother to see if anything
could be done by him for her safety. The old lady, who is noted for her piety and her Christian deportment, said she considered herself perfectly safe;
but if her time to die had come, she was ready to die. Her son then knelt
down by her side, and implored the protection of Heaven in behalf of his
mother. The old lady was affected to tears, and said to our informant that
it seemed to her that good angels were present in the room. Scarcely had
the supplicant risen from his knees, when the mob broke down the door,
seized him, beat him over the head and face with fists and clubs, and then
hanged him in the presence of his mother.
While they were thus engaged, the military came and drove them away,
cutting down the body of Franklin, who raised his arm once slightly and gave
a few signs of life.
The military then moved on to quell other riots, when the mob returned
and again suspended the now probably lifeless body of Franklin, cutting out
pieces of flesh and otherwise mutilating it.

PETER HEUSTON.

Peter Heuston, sixty-three years of age, a Mohawk Indian, with dark
complexion and straight black hair, who has for several years been a resident of this city, at the corner of Rosevelt and Oak streets, and who has
obtained a livelihood as a laborer, proved a victim to the late riots.
His wife died about three weeks before the riots, leaving with her husband an only child, a little girl named Lavinia, aged eight years, whom the
Merchants' Committee have undertaken to adopt with a view of affording her a
guardianship and an education. Hueston served with the New York Volunteers
in the Mexican War, and has always been loyal to our government. He was
brutally attacked on the 13th of July by a gang of ruffians who evidently
thought him to be of the African race because of his dark complexion. He
died four days at Bellevue Hospital from his injuries.
At the end of the Mexican War Heuston received a land warrant from the
government, which enabled him to settle on a tract of land at the West, where
he lived but a short time previous to his coming to this city.

WILLIAM JONES.

A crowd of rioters in pursuit of a negro, who in self defence had fired
on some rowdies who had attacked him, met an innocent colored man returning
from a bakery with a loaf of bread under his arm. They instantly set upon
and beat him and after nearly killing him, hanged him to a lamp-post. His
body was left suspended for several hours and was much mutilated.
A sad illustration of the painful uncertainty which hung over the minds
of the wives and children of the colored men was found in the fact that two
wives and their families, were both mourning the loss of their husbands in
the case of this man, for upwards of two weeks after its occurrence. And so
great was the fear inspired by the mob that no white person had dared to
manifest sufficient interest in the mutilated body of the murdered man while

it remained in the neighborhood to be able to testify as to who it was. At the end of two weeks the husband of one of the mourners to her great joy returned, like one recovered from the grave.

The principal evidence which the widow, Mary Jones, has to identify the murdered man as her husband is the fact of his having a loaf of bread under his arm. He having left the house to get a loaf of bread a few minutes before the attack.

One of our colored missionaries is still investigating the case.

From an old man in Sullivan street, a very patriarch in years and progeny, we gathered the following

INTERESTING STATEMENT.

I am a whitewasher by trade, and have worked, boy and man, in this city for sixty-three years. On Tuesday afternoon I was standing on the corner of Thirtieth street and Second avenue, when a crowd of young men came running along shouting "Here's a nigger, here's a nigger." Almost before I knew of their intention, I was knocked down, kicked here and there, badgored and battered without mercy, until a cry of "the Peelers are coming" was raised; and I was left almost senseless, with a broken arm and a face covered with blood, on the railroad track. I was helped home on a cart by the officers, who were very kind to me, and gave me some brandy before I got home. *I entertain no malice and have no desire for revenge* against these people. Why should they hurt me or my colored brethren? We are poor men like them; we work hard and get but little for it. I was born in this State and have lived here all my life, and it seems hard, very hard, that we should be knocked down and kept out of work just to oblige folks who won't work themselves and don't want others to work.

We asked him if it was true that the negroes had formed any organization for self-defence, as was rumored. He said no; that, so far as he knew, "they all desire to keep out of the way, to be quiet, and do their best toward allaying the excitement in the City."

The room in which the old man was lying was small, but it was the kitchen, sitting-room, bedroom and garret of four grown persons and five children.

Instances of this kind might be multiplied by the dozen, gathered from the lips of suffering men, who, though wounded and maimed by ruffians and rioters, are content to be left alone, and wish for no revenge.

The following

CASE OF BRUTALITY

is one of the worst, so far as beating is concerned, which, has come under our observation: At a late hour on Wednesday night, a colored man, named Charles Jackson, was passing along West street, in the neighborhood of Pier No. 5, North river. He was a laboring man, and was dressed in a tarpaulin, a blue shirt, and heavy duck trousers. As he was passing a groggery in that vicinity, he was observed by a body of dock men, who instantly set after him. He ran with all the swiftness his fears could excite, but was overtaken before he had gone a block. His persecutors did not know him nor did they entertain any spite against him beyond the fact that he was a black man and a laborer about the docks, which they consider their own peculiar field of labor. Nevertheless they knocked him down, kicked him in the face and ribs, and finally by the hands of their leader, deliberately attempted to *cut his throat*. The body, dead they supposed it, was then thrown into the water and left to sink. Fortunately life was not extinct and the sudden plunge brought the poor fellow to his senses, and being a good swimmer he was enabled instinctively to seek for the net work of the dock. This he soon found, but was so weak from the loss of blood and so faint with pain that he could do no more than hold on and wait for day. The day after, Messrs. Kelly and Curtis, of Whitehall, discovered him lying half dead in the water. They at once attended to his wants, gave him in charge of the Police-boat and had him sent to the hospital. The escape of the man from death by the successive abuses of beating, knifing, and drowning, is most wonderful. So determined and bitter is the feeling of the longshoremen against negroes that not one of the latter dared show themselves upon the docks or piers, even when a regular employee of the place.

Report of the Committee of Merchants for the Relief of Colored People, Suffering From the Late Riots of the City of New York (New York, 1863).

25. PERSONAL RECOLLECTIONS OF THE DRAFT RIOTS

All this time the fighting was going on in every direction while the fire-bells continually ringing, increased the terror, which was, every hour becoming widespread.

Especially true was this of the negro population. From the first day they had been made to feel that they were to be the objects of mob violence, and those who could fled into the country.

They crowded the ferry-boats and trains, fleeing for their lives in all directions.

But many, old men and women, were compelled to remain and meet the fury of the mob which made a regular hunt for them.

Deeds were done, and scenes occurred that one would not believe could have occurred in a civilized community.

C. L. Chapin, "Personal Recollections of the Draft Riots, New York City, 1863," Ms., New York Historical Society.

26. A PERSONAL EXPERIENCE

On the afternoon of July [13th], a rabble attacked our house, breaking windowpanes, smashing shutters and partially demolishing the front door. Before dusk arrangements had been effected to secure the safety of our children. As the evening drew on, a resolute man and a courageous woman quietly seated themselves in the hall, determined to sell their lives as dearly as may be. Lights having been extinguished, a lonely vigil passed in mingled indignation, uncertainty and dread. Just after midnight a yell announced that a second mob was gathering. As one of the rioters attempted to ascend the front steps, father advanced into the doorway and fired point blank into the crowd. The mob retreated hastily and no further demonstration was made that night. The next day a third and successful attempt at entrance was effected. This sent father over the back fence while mother took refuge on the premises of a neighbor.

In one short hour, the police cleared the premises. What a home! Its interior was dismantled, furniture was missing or broken. From basement to attic evidences of vandalism prevailed. A fire, kindled in one of the upper rooms, was discovered in time to prevent a conflagration.

Under cover of darkness the police conveyed our parents to the Williamsburg ferry. There steamboats were kept in readiness to transport fugitives or to outwit rioters by pulling out into midstream. Mother with her children undertook the hazardous journey of getting to New England. After a brief rest in New London, we reached Salem tired, travel-stained, with only the garments we had on.

Lyons-Williamson Papers, Schomburg Collection.

27. THE LONGSHOREMEN'S ATTITUDE TOWARD BLACKS

So determined and bitter is the feeling of the 'longshoremen against
negroes that not one of the latter dares show himself upon the docks or
piers even when a regular employee of the place. The white workmen have resolved, by concerted action, to keep colored men from this branch of labor,
and have evinced, by their conduct toward their former comrades in work, a
spirit as murderous and brutal as it is illiberal and selfish. It is a
prevalent rumor, to which the authorities give full credence, and which the
'longshoremen seem proud of, that scores of these unfortunates have been
thrown into the river and drowned, for no other reason than that they were
abnoxious to the sensitive-minded individuals of a lighter color.

New York Times, July 17, 1863.

Longshoremen made no attempt to conceal their determination to keep negroes . . . from that sort of labor. They insist upon it that the colored
people must and shall be driven to other departments of industry, and that
the work upon the docks, the stevedoring, and the various job-work therewith
connected, shall be attended to solely and absolutely by members of the
'Longshoremen's Association, and such white laborers as they see fit to permit upon the premises.

New York Daily Times, July 17, 1863.

28. THE COLORED REFUGEES AT POLICE HEADQUARTERS

Upward of two hundred colored persons have found shelter from the fury
of the mob at Police Headquarters. They are of both sexes and all ages, from
the infant at the breast to the white-haired grandfather. Notwithstanding
their misfortunes and losses they are calm and cheerful. They are not unconscious of the dangers from which they have escaped, nor of the difficulties which surround them, but they have a strong faith in the power and justice of God. While they express the deepest gratitude to their benefactors,
they show no spirit of vindictiveness toward the rioters, who with torches,
halters, and firearms drove them from their homes.

They are furnished with rooms in the upper story of the Station-House.
Trunks and boxes are used for seats and their beds are on the floor. They
are abundantly supplied with good substantial rations, such as the officers
and other persons connected with the Station have. Many of them make themselves useful by scrubbing and sweeping the rooms, waiting upon those who
used their help and doing with the utmost cheerfulness any task assigned to
them.

The following facts related in the language of the sufferers will give
the reader an idea of the trials to which these poor unoffending negroes
have been exposed. We omit their names and places of residences at their
own request. Mrs. S—a very intelligent woman, the mother of three children—the eldest, a daughter, married, said:

"One of the rioters came into my house suddenly on Wednesday, and asked
me for my man, I told him he had gone to sea. The rioter then said, I will
give you just ten minutes to clear out, and then I will tear down your house
and burn it. Just then another rioter spoke a word in my behalf, when the
tall, savage looking man drew his revolver and hit my little boy over the
head, and threatened to shoot the man who manifested sympathy for me. I
then picked up my babe and sought shelter in a house on Lexington avenue.
The next day I went to Police Headquarters, and soon after my arrival, some

fireman of No. 39 Co. found my little boy hid in a box. I lost him in my
haste from the rioters, and was almost crazy until they brought him here.
The child still suffers in consequence of the blow he received at the hands
of the rioter. Her oldest daughter had previously gone to headquarters for
protection."

    William -- makes the following statement of the manner in which he and
two other men escaped, leaving the women and children in the house, knowing
they had a better chance to get away from the rioters:

"On Wednesday evening a tall man with red whiskers and moustache, came
to my house; with him were two boys with ropes in their hands, and a crowd
followed crying, 'Hang the niggers.' We then made our escape from the
third story window by means of a rope, and hid away in the furnace in the
cellar. The women and children (ten in number), then fled into the street
and sought refuge at Jefferson Market Precinct. After remaining in our hiding place until 2 o'clock in the morning we made our escape, and we all met
at Police Headquarters on Saturday. There were white families in the same
house, consequently it was not burned, but everything was stolen from it."

    G -- is blind and lame. Here is in brief the plain account of his es-
cape:

"A mob burst my door open on Wednesday afternoon. I had an aunt there,
an old woman of sixty. I was hid in the wood-house. The mob said to the old
lady that if she would give me up they would not harm her. She said I was
lame and blind, and had to go on crutches, and was afraid of them. They
found me, however, and carried me into the house, and gave me an hour in
which to make my escape. I went to the Station House in the Eighteenth Ward,
guided by my aunt, and there some kind friend--I wish I knew his name--put
me into a carriage and conveyed me to this place."

    A mother with her two children, one of them very ill, said:

"Last Wednesday I went to the Station-House on Twenty ninth street, and
the officer in charge told me to return to my house. He said no person
would injure me. I went home with my two children, and as soon as I entered
the house a mob kicked the door open; he was followed by a crowd of men and
boys who drove me away. One of my children was very sick at the time."

    Mrs. D., a very nice looking woman, gives the following statement:

"I was driven from my own home on Tuesday, and from the house where I
sought refuge on Wednesday. I and my three children finally reached the Police Headquarters. I supposed that my husband had been killed--his death
having been announced in the newspapers, but he made his escape by hiding
away in outhouses, and moving from place to place under the cover of darkness, and is here with me."

New York Tribune, July 21, 1863.

29. THE COLORED SUFFERERS BY THE RECENT RIOTS--
MEETING OF MERCHANTS

    In accordance with a call issued at a meeting of merchants held on Sat-
urday last, a second meeting convened at 2 o'clock yesterday afternoon, at
McCallough's salesrooms, corner of Front street and Maiden lane, for the
purpose of taking into consideration means to be adopted to aid colored men
and their families whose homes and property have been destroyed during the
pendency of the recent riots. The meeting was well attended, there being between 100 and 200 merchants present.

    JONATHAN STURGIS occupied the chair, and on calling the meeting to order
he said:

For the information of those who were not present at the meeting held
here on Saturday, it is proper that I should state its origin and object.
The meeting was called on the suggestion of several gentlemen in Front
street, at a very short notice, to consider the destitute condition of the

colored people of this city, who have been deprived of their homes, and
their little property, by a mob during the past week, to devise means to relieve their immediate wants and to secure them in their peaceable and honest
labor hereafter. I have been 41 years a merchant in my present location.
During this period I have seen a noble race of merchants pass away. I cannot help calling to mind the many acts of charity which they performed during their lives. I hardly need to name them; you all know them. You all
know how they sent relief to Southern cities when they were desolated by
fire or pestilence; how they sent shiploads of food to the starving people of
Ireland; this last act of brotherly love we have had the privilege of imitating during the past Winter--and as often as occasion requires, I trust we
shall be quick to continue these acts of humanity--thus showing that the race
of New-York merchants is not deteriorating. We are now called upon to sympathize with a different class of our fellow men. Those who know our colored people of this city, can testify to their being peaceable, industrious
people, having their own churches, Sunday-schools, and charitable societies
and that as a class they seldom depend upon charity; they not only labor to
support themselves, but to aid those who need aid. This is their general
character, and it is our duty to see that they are protected in their lawful
labors, to save themselves from becoming dependent on the charity of the
city. We have not come together to devise means for their relief because
they are colored people, but because they are, as a class, persecuted and in
distress at the present moment. It is not necessary for our present purposes
to inquire who the men are who have persecuted, robbed, and murdered them.
We know they are bad men, who have not done as they would be done by. Let
us not follow their example; let us be quick to relieve those who are now in
trouble, and should we ever find those who have persecuted the negroes in
like trouble, let us be quick to relieve them also, and thus obey the injunc-
tion of our Divine Master, "Bless those who persecute you."

On motion, the President, Mr. Sturgis, was made the treasurer of the
fund to be raised in accordance with the objects of the meeting.

Mr. MACKENZIE, Chairman of the Committee appointed at the previous meeting, submitted the following resolutions:

The condition of the colored people of this city, who have recently
been deprived of their kindred by murderers of their homes by fire, and of
their accustomed means of support, having been forcibly driven therefrom by
an infuriated mob without cause or provocation, is such as not out to excite
the sympathy of every good member of the community of all parties and all
creeds, but also demands and should receive prompt pecuniary assistance and
aid.

That this may be effectually accomplished, we do hereby

Resolved, That a Committee of five merchants be appointed by the Chairman of this meeting, who, with the Treasurer of the fund to be collected as
a member of same, shall have full power to receive, collect and distribute
funds in the purchase of necessary food and clothing and in relieving the
wants of the suffering colored population.

Resolved, That to said Committee are hereby granted full powers to assist all colored people whose property has been destroyed by the mob, in making the needful proof of the facts to obtain redress from the county, under
the staute laws of the State of New York, and that they have authority to
collect funds and employ counsel for that purpose.

Resolved, That we will exert all the influence we possess to protect the
colored people of this city in their rights to pursue unmolested their lawful
occupations, and we do hereby call upon the proper authorities to take immediate steps to afford them such protection.

Resolved, That we will not recognize or sanction any distinction of persons of whatever   nation, religion or color, for their natural rights to labor peaceably in their vocation for the support of themselves and those dependent upon them, and that so far as we are able to contribute to the wants
and necessities of our fellow men it shall be done without reference to their
distinctions. And further that what we now propose doing for the colored
man, we shall ever be ready to do for any of our fellow men under like circumstances.

New York Tribune, July 21, 1863.

30. "THE MOB EXULTS"

The mob exults in the belief that, if it failed in its other objects,
it has at least secured possession of the labor of the city, and has driven
the blacks to seek work elsewhere. . . . It is the duty of merchants and
other employers to take pains to recall their workmen immediately, and as-
sure them of permanent protection.

New York Tribune, July 21, 1863.

31. THE COLORED SAILORS' HOME,

OR GLOBE HOTEL, NO. 2 DOVER-STREET
NEW YORK

This Institution, which owes its existence and former prosperity and
usefulness to the energy and perseverance of its proprietor, Mr. Wm. P.
Powell, under the patronage and aid of the American Seamen's Friend Society,
was completely rifled of all its furniture, books and clothing, by the mob
of July 13th, the building greatly damaged--Mr. Powell, his family and
boarders compelled to escape over the roof for their lives. After a consequent suspension of nearly three months, the building has been thoroughly repaired, newly painted, and re-furnished with new furniture, beds and bedding,
is heated throughout with hot air, abundantly supplied with hot and cold water baths for the use of the boarders; is kept neat; airy, and well arranged
for the promotion of health, and is designed to be a *Home,* with its religious, moral and social influences for our colored seamen. During the
eleven months previous to the riot, 450 seamen had been inmates of this Home.
    Mr. Powell is well known in the business community, as an enterprising,
intelligent, and worthy citizen, though of dark complexion, as his ancestors,
on one side, came from Africa. He is entitled to great credit for his persistent efforts in behalf of our colored seamen, and to the protection of the
Law, and the patronage of the friends of humanity.
    We confidently commend him, and his Home to the patronage of seamen and
their friends.

Sailor's Magazine (November, 1863):83.

32. ATTEMPT TO DROWN A NEGRO

Joseph Marshall, a boatman, was arrested yesterday by Officer Cornell
of the Harbor Police, charged with a felonious assault and battery on Joseph
Jackson, a colored man, residing on the corner of Broadway and Houston
street. On the 15th inst. Jackson was attacked by a gang of rioters, and to
escape them ran down to Pier No. 4, North River, where he had some business.
The mob pursued him, crying "Here's a d--d nigger," and the prisoner, as is
alleged, made a rush for him, and, seizing the frightened negro, beat him in
the most terrible manner about the head and body with a large stone. Jackson
was then thrown into the river for dead, but the plunge in the water revived
him so that he was enabled to crawl under the pier, where he remained for
nearly twenty-four hours before daring the venture from his hiding-place.
The rioters robbed their victim of his watch and chain and $36 in money. The

prisoner, who is reported to be a newly-imported rowdy from New-Orleans, was taken before Justice Quackenbush and locked up. He was positively identified by Jackson as one of the men who beat him.

New York Tribune, July 25, 1863.

33. FEARFUL OF BEING KNOWN

For the last few days General Superintendent Kennedy and Inspector Carpenter, have received numerous anonymous communications, to the effect that the writers know who had mobbed and hung negroes, and committed other acts of violence against both persons and property, but they feared violence at the hands of the rioters should they betray them. Any person possessing such information, by making the necessary affidavits before Inspector Carpenter, will be protected from harm, and assurances given that their names will not be divulged, except by their consent.

New York Tribune, July 25, 1863.

34. THE MERCHANTS RELIEF COMMITTEE

The following notice was issued yesterday afternoon:

MERCHANTS' RELIEF COMMITTEE FOR SUFFERING
COLORED PEOPLE, DEPOT, NO. 350 FOURTH STREET,
NEW YORK, July 21, 1863.

At a meeting of the Committee of the Merchants, for the relief of suffering colored people, held this morning, the following resolutions were unanimously adopted:

Whereas, It has come to our knowledge that many parties heretofore employing colored men and women are now declining their further employment, from fear of molestation by the mob, therefore,

Resolved, That merchants, warehousemen, transport companies, and others are respectfully urged to employ colored men as heretofore, and are requested to rely upon the public authorities for protection.

Resolved, further, That all such cases be reported to the Board.

Resolved, That responsible persons residing out of town, knowing of colored refugees from the city in their neighborhood, be requested to report them to the Committee at their rooms, No. 850 Fourth street, and aid the Committee in returning such refugees to their accustomed labor as soon as possible.

JONATHAN STURGIS,	GEO. C. COLLINS,
A. R. WETMORE,	J. D. McKENZIE,
J. S. SHULTZ,	JOS. B. COLLINS,
	Executive Committee.

New York Tribune, July 25, 1863.

35. EMPLOYERS TURN TO NEGROES RATHER THAN IRISHMEN
BECAUSE OF THE RIOTS

Quite a number of large corporations and mercantile firms are determined
--not from any idle notions of venegeance, but on sound business considera-
tions--to secure hereafter labor which shall not be liable to interruption
from Irish prejudices. The longshore business is going to pass into the
hands of negroes. Foundries and factories, whose business was interrupted by
the striking of workmen who turned rioters, are going to gradually make such
changes as will effectively preclude accidents hereafter. Employers who
heretofore have preferred Irishmen to negroes are now going to take into consideration the riotous propensities of the former, and for the sake of their
business--to which interruption is loss and possible ruin--at all events to
dilute their operative force with enough colored men to secure themselves
against the chance of another Irish riot. Individuals who never dreamed of
employing negroes are being led by consideration of humanity and manhood to
extend a helping hand to the oppressed race.

Harper's Weekly, August 18, 1863.

36. HOW BLACKS SHOULD MEET THE RIOTERS
BY J. W. C. PENNINGTON

Let us look at the labor question a little more closely, and see what
must be the greed of those who would have us believe that there is not room
and labor enough in this country for the citizens of foreign birth and the
colored people of native growth. The legitimate territory of these United
States, is about 3,306,863 acres. That is ten times larger than Great Britain and France together; three times larger than Britain, France, Austria,
Prussia, Spain, Portugal and Denmark; and only one sixth less, in extent,
than the fifty-nine or sixty republics and empires of Europe put together.
And yet there are those who would teach the British and other foreigners the
selfish and greedy idea that there is not room enough in this country for
them and the colored man. Such a notion is ridiculous.
The foregoing state of fact suggests some lessons of duty.
First, we must study the use of arms, for *self-defense*. There is no
principle of civil or religious obligation that requires us to live on in
hazard and leave our persons, property and our wives and children at the mercy of barbarians. Self-defense is the first law of nature.
Second, we must enter into a solemn free colored *Protestant industrial
or labor league.*
Let the greedy foreigner know that a part of this country *belongs to us,*
and that we assert the right to live and labor here, that in New York and
other cities we claim the right to buy, hire, occupy and use houses and tene-
ments, for legal considerations, to pass and repass on the streets, lanes,
avenues and all public ways. Our fathers have fought for this country and
helped to free it from the British yoke. We are now fighting to help to free
it from the combined conspiracy of Jeff Davis and Company; we are doing so
with the distinct understanding, that *we are to have all our rights as men
and as citizens,* and that there are to be no side issues, no reservations,
either political, civil or religious. In this struggle we know nothing but
God, manhood and American nationality, full and unimpaired.
The right to labor, earn wages and dispose of our earnings for the support of our families, the education of our children and to support religious
institutions of our free choice is inherent. No party or power in politics
or religion can alienate this right.
No part of our influence has been used to prevent foreigners from coming
to this country and enjoying its benefits. We have done them no wrong. What

we ask in return is nonintervention. *Let us alone.*

Third, let us place our daughters and younger sons in industrial positions, however humble, and secure openings where they may be usefully employed. Every father and every mother may be of service, not only to their own children, but also to those of others. You will have many applications for "colored help." Be useful to applicants. Prepare your sons and daughters for usefulness in all the branches of domestic labor and service.

From address, "The Position and Duties of the Colored People," August 24, 1863, Philip S. Foner (ed.), The Voice of Black America: Major Speeches by Negroes in the United States, 1797-1971 (New York, 1972), pp. 271-80.

37. COLORED ORPHAN ASYLUM

On the same day that Irish Catholics destroyed the institution for colored orphans, they received a check of $50,000 from the city, for the establishment of a Roman Catholic Orphan Asylum!

It has been erroneously stated in all the city papers that warning was given at the Asylum for Colored Orphans of the intention of the mob, in order that the inmates might be removed. This, says a correspondent of the *Independent,* is a very grave mistake. No notice whatever was given, and nothing saved the children from the flames and from the fury of these demons, except the fidelity and coolness of the Superintendent, and the protecting hand of God. The children did not leave the building until the wretches were thundering at the front door. A fireman who saved a sick child from being burned, was twice knocked down, and another, in endeavoring to direct the fugitives to a place of safety, was pulled away and had his clothes torn from his back for attempting to assist the "damned nagers."

The Liberator, August 21, 1863.

BLACKS IN THE UNION ARMY AND NAVY

38. STATISTICS OF ENLISTED MEN

Number who had been slaves. 247
" pure blacks. 550
" mixed blood. 430
" who could read 477
" who could read and write 319
" church-members 52
" married. 219
Average age . . . . 23½ years.
" height. . . . . 5 7/12 feet.

BIRTHPLACE.

Maine	1	North Carolina	30	Kentucky	68
Vermont	1	South Carolina	6	Tennessee	24
Massachusetts	22	Georgia	6	Michigan	8
Rhode Island	3	Alabama	5	Wisconsin	7

Connecticut. . . 4
New York . . . 23
New Jersey . . . 8
Pennsylvania . 139
Delaware . . . 13
Maryland . . . 19
Virginia . . . 106

Mississippi. . . . 9
Louisiana. 1
Arkansas 1
Missouri 66
Ohio 222
Indiana. 97
Illinois 56

Iowa 9
District of
   Columbia. . . 10
Nova Scotia. . 1
Canada 3
Africa 1
Unknown. . . . 11

TRADES AND OCCUPATIONS.

Farmers. . . . 596
Laborers . . . 76
Barbers. . . . 34
Waiters. . . . 50
Cooks. 27
Blacksmiths. . 21
Painters . . . 7
Teamsters. . . 27
Grooms 7
Hostlers . . . 9
Coachmen . . . 3
Coopers. . . . 5
Sailors. . . . 20
Butchers . . . 8
Iron-workers . 2
Shoemakers . . 9

Masons and Plas-
   terers. 16
Brickmakers. . . . 3
Whitewashers . . . 2
Stonecutters . . . 2
Printers 3
Boatmen. 6
Teachers 6
Clerks.. 5
Porters. 5
Carpenters 6
Wagon-makers . . . 2
Millers. 2
Engineers. 3
Firemen. 2
Coppersmith. . . . 1

Machinist. . . 1
Rope-maker . . 1
Fisherman. . . 1
Tinker 1
Harness-maker. 1
Caulker. . . . 1
Glass-grinder. 1
Musician . . . 1
Moulder. . . . 1
Confectioner . 1
Tobacco-
   worker. . . . 1
Clergyman. . . 1
Broom-maker. . 1
Baker. 1
Student. . . . 1

Record of the Service of the Fifty-Fifth Regiment of Massachusetts Volunteer Infantry (Cambridge, Mass., 1868), pp. 110-12.

39.   OCCUPATIONS FOR BLACK ENLISTEES

	1861	1862	1863	1864	1865	Total
Artist			1			1
Baker	3	5	4	9		21
Barber	69	70	75	114	15	343
Bartender		1	1			2
Basketmaker	1			1		2
Blacksmith	7	15	17	20	2	61
Boatman		4	34	19	9	66
Bookbinder		1				1
Brakeman				1		1
Bricklayer	4		6	22		32
Brickmaker	3	3	13	20		39
Burnisher			1			1
Butcher	1	3	10	15	2	31
Cabinetmaker			3			3
Carder					1	1
Carman				1		1
Carpenter	16	13	20	36	3	88
Caulker	3	3	6	24	1	37
Chairmaker		3	3		1	7
Cigarmaker		6	2	2		10
Clerk		1				1
Coachmaker			1		1	2
Confectioner	3		3	4		10
Contraband	21	46	383	44	4	498
Cook	95	144	336	460	89	1124

	1861	1862	1863	1864	1865	Total
Cooper	3	3	2	4	1	13
Coopersmith				1		1
Dentist		1				1
Druggist		1				1
Drummer		1				1
Dyer			1			1
Electrician				1		1
Engineer			3	3		6
Farmer	5	18	55	159	13	250
Fireman			49	79	26	154
Florist					1	1
Gardener		1	3			4
Grocer			2			2
Groom	1			2		3
Harnessmaker		1				1
Hatter	2				1	3
Hostler		2	5		1	8
Huckster				1		1
Jeweler	1					1
Jockey			1			1
Laborer	3	2	301	526	23	855
Machinist	1	3		2		6
Mason		4	2	2		8
Miller				4		4
Mill-wright			2			2
Moulder		1	1			2
Musician				3		3
Oysterman			4	6		10
Painter	10	7	4	7	1	29
Photographer		1	1			2
Pilot			3			3
Plasterer		2		2		4
Porter	1		7	12		20
Potter			1			1
Printer		1	2		1	4
Ropemaker			3	1		4
Sailmaker		2	2			4
Sashmaker			1			1
Seaman	18	31	135	389	51	624
Servant	1	6	18	27	2	54
Shoemaker	13	14	26	15	3	71
Silvermaker			1			1
Silverplater	3					3
Soapmaker				1		1
Soldier				3		3
Stevedore	1	2	2			5
Steward		47	39	7	12	105
Stonecutter	1					1
Stovemaker			1			1
Stove mounter				1		1
Tailor	4	3	5	6	1	19
Tanner	2	4		2		8
Teacher		1	1	1		3
Teamster	1	1	25	53	1	81
Tilemaker				1		1
Tinman		1				1
Tinsmith	3					3
Tobacconist		1	3	11	1	16
Upholsterer	1					1
Waiter	88	140	403	595	53	1279
Waterman	1			4		5
Weaver	1		2	1		4
Wheelwright			2	4		6

	1861	1862	1863	1864	1865	Total
Whitewasher			2			2
Woodcutter	1					1
Occupation unlisted	559	535	708	1659	50	3511
Total	951	1154	2748	4387	370	9710

BLACK-WHITE
OCCUPATIONAL COMPARISON
1861 - 1865

Percentage

	Black	White
Professional	.0012	.0089
Proprietors Managers	.0003	.0032
Skilled	.0500	.3000
Semi-skilled	.4000	.3400
Unskilled	.1800	.1200
Student	.0000	.0075
Occupation Unlisted	.3600	.2000
n =	(9610)	(9778)

Rendezvous Reports for 1861-1865, RG 24, National Archives.

40.   GIVE US EQUAL PAY AND WE WILL GO TO WAR

By Rev. J. P. Campbell [55]

. . . If we are asked the question why it is that black men have not more readily enlisted in the volunteer service of the United States government since the door has been opened to them, we answer, the door has not been fairly and sufficiently widely opened. It has been opened only in part, not the whole of the way. That it is not sufficiently and fairly opened will appear from the action of the present Congress upon the subject of the pay of colored soldiers. It shows a strong disposition not to equalize the pay of soldiers without distinction on account of color.

When the news of the first gun fired upon the flag of the Union at old Sumner reached the North, the friends of the Union were called upon to defend that flag. The heart of the black man at that hour responded to the call. He came forward at once and offered his services to the government, and failed to act immediately, because he was denied the opportunity of so doing. He was met with the cold, stern and chilling rebuke, that this was

not the Negro's war, not a war upon slavery, and that in it the services of
the Negro were not wanted; that slavery had nothing to do with the war, or
the war with slavery; that it was purely a war for the safety of the Union
and its preservation, without reference to the slavery question.

But the time came when it was thought that under very great restrictions, as by giving him unequal pay and restraining him from being an officer
in the Army, the Negro might be allowed to bear arms. Afterward, the black
man, saying nothing about officeholding for the time being, asked the government to acknowledge the justice of his claim to equal pay with the white soldier and to recommend the same to the then ensuing Congress, to be made law.
The government pledged itself to this recommendation, and many colored men
enlisted upon the faith which they had in the government and the future good
legislation of Congress upon the subject of giving to black soldiers equal
pay and equal bounties with white soldiers, and that all other necessary and
needed provisions would be to both the same. Congress met, and the good
President Lincoln, with the excellent Secretary of War, Mr. Stanton, proved
faithful to their promise. They laid the matter before Congress in their
Annual Message and Report. But, alas, that honorable body hesitates to act,
and that, too, while the country and its liberties are in danger and calamity
by armed rebellion against the government.

Now, we say to our honorable Senators and Representatives in Congress,
gentlemen, don't be afraid to do the black man justice. He will not abuse
your confidence in his fidelity to the Constitution and the Union. He will
never prove himself a traitor by his acts. He will never prove himself to be
unworthy of receiving at your hands the rights and privileges which justice
and equity demand.

Give to the black man those simple demands set forth in this bill of
particulars, and he will rush to the defense of his country by thousands.
His heart within him pants for the opportunity to show himself a man, capable
of discharging all the duties of a common manhood, in whatever sphere that
manhood may be called to act. Here we are, by thousands and ten thousands,
standing ready to move at the nod of your august and mighty fiat. The state
of Maryland wants to fill up her last quota of men demanded by the call of
the President. This, with a little more time allowed, may be done, if she
will do justice to the black citizens of her own soil. They are strong men,
and true to the country which gave them birth. They will be ready, at the
first sound of the bugle, to fill up the balance of Maryland's apportionment.

The law requires that black men shall pay as much commutation money as
white men pay. We ask, then, that the same pay, bounty, pensions, rights and
privileges be given to black men that are given the white men, and they will
go to war, without paying the commutation money.

We want an equal chance to show our equal manhood and love for the Constitution and the Union. Under the above-named circumstances, we are standing ready to respond to the call of the government and go to defend our common country against the encroachments of an armed rebellion.

In conclusion, we ask the question, Will you have us? Will you accept
of us upon equal terms with white men in the service of our country? We
await, with deep solicitude and anxiety, the action of a government and people whom, with all their faults, we love, and whom we are willing to defend
with our lives, liberty and sacred honor in common with white men. Will you
have us so to do? That is the question. We ask for equal pay and bounty,
not because we set a greater value upon money than we do upon human liberty,
compared with which money is mere trash; but we contend for equal pay and
bounty upon the principle that if we receive equal pay and bounty when we go
into the war, we hope to receive equal rights and privileges when we come out
of the war. If we go in equal in pay, we hope to come out equal in enfranchisement.

Is that an unreasonable hope or an unjust claim? It takes as much to
clothe and feed the black man's wife as it does the white man's wife. It
takes as much money to go to market for the black man's little boys and girls
as it does for the white man's little boys and girls. We have yet to learn
why it is that the black soldier should not receive the same compensation for
labor in the service of his country that the white soldier receives. There
is no financial embarrassment, as in the case of Mr. Jefferson Davis's government at Richmond. Our great and good financier, Mr. Salmon P. Chase,

Secretary of the Treasury, has money enough to carry on the war, and some
millions of gold and silver to sell. Give us equal pay, and we will go on to
the war--not pay on mercenary principles, but pay upon the principles of justice and equity.

The Christian Recorder, March 19, 1864.

41. TWENTY PER CENT. OFF THE WAGES OF COLORED WAGONERS

     And now another of those outrages practiced upon colored men during the
war has come to light. It appears, from the correspondence published in
another column, that all the colored men, numbering many thousands, employed
during the war as wagoners, laborers, etc., were actually cheated out of five
dollars of their wages per month under the pretence that the five dollars
thus deducted was to be a contraband fund for the support of the liberated
slaves. It is said the deductions were by the order of Hon. E. M. Stanton,
We hope the statement will prove to be untrue. As it seems incredible that
that gentleman would be guilty of what we conceive to be a crime. We do not
understand that the President of the United States or the Secretary of War
has authority to impose any such tax upon government laborers. It is evident
it was not a legislative enactment else the public would have known all about
it, and if Mr. Stanton issued the order without congressional authority, it
is in our opinion plainly a usurpation and an outrage. Even if it was a congressional enactment it was unjust, for by what mode of reasoning can it be
established that colored wagoners more than any one else, should support the
liberated slaves. These people were properly the wards of the government,
and it should have provided for them better than it ever did. If there was
ever a class of people who deserved the sympathy of and protection by the
American government, it was the people just liberated as a war necessity.
They did not liberate themselves. They were not responsible for being thrown
homeless, friendless and destitute upon the government. Neither were the
slaves or the free colored people of the country responsible for their helpless condition, the white population alone were to blame. But one of the
worst features in this deplorable condition of things is there is much doubt
that not one cent of the money deducted from poor colored wagoners ever went
toward the support of the freedmen. Then in whose pockets did it go?

The Christian Recorder, June 20, 1875.

42. PROSCRIPTION IN PHILADELPHIA

     MR. EDITOR: I wish to jot down a few thoughts if you will be kind
enough to give them a place in your columns, in regard to the intolerable and
incomprehensible prejudice which shows itself toward the colored people of
this city on every possible occasion. The dividing line of light and darkness is not more distinctly drawn than are the lines of caste and prejudice,
drawn between the white and colored people of this city. There is no more
regard shown by the whites for the common and natural rights of the colored
people here, than there is at Richmond; and nothing but an upheaval in this
community, like that at New York, will bring the people to a sense of common
justice. Proscription is written on the door post of every useful institution, from the church down to the lowest hovel kept by some Pat Murphy. If
you go out of the city by railroad you will see posted up in each end of the

cars, a notice like the following: "Colored people must take the back end of the car or ride in the baggage car;" and this is made imperative. It is not enough that you take the first end of the car, if you get in there, but you must go through to the lower end, which means behind all white folks. If you are going to Salem, N.J., or any other like insignificant town, you will meet in your journey around the boat, forward of the wheel, of course, a device like this over some door, "Colored People's Room," and, no mistake about it, you will find them there, as meek and as gentle as we ever saw them in old times on board the steamer Louisiana, plying between Baltimore and Norfolk, and apparently thinking and talking about everything under the sun, but their proscribed condition. In fact I have met a good number of colored people right here in Philadelphia, who are entirely averse to any sort of agitation whatever, whether in regard to their social or political rights; and you ask them the reason, and they will tell you, that it will make the case worse and injure our cause--that the white people will become still more prejudiced against us, and therefore it is best to wait until they shall see fit to treat us better.

Now I look upon this conduct as abominable sycophancy, for there is no colored man who has had his residence in the free States, a single twelve months, but who knows that the colored people as a class, get nothing so to speak, in the way of social and political privileges, only by long, persistent and obstinate agitation, and if the Abolitionists had been governed by such a feeling their time would have been thrown away, for in all the past thirty years of anti-slavery work we have not obtained anything by consent of the Northern people--every reform has been wrung from and comes to us by express statute. We do not melt and fuse into place and position as does the most outlandish foreigner, and the reason is obvious; from the very beginning of Southern slavery, the Northern whites have made color and condition a life-long barrier between them and us, and the legislation of the free States for the last sixty or eighty years, from the date of the Constitution, proves that that barrier has broadened and kept pace with the race, until caste has become an established American Institution, to be got rid of only by the success of the moral and physical forces which are now at work around us. We must open our eyes to this fact; that social and political equality will be harder to win back in Pennsylvania and New Jersey than in the South. Here prejudice to color is the effect of slavery, and the constant observer of a race held in bondage by the whites and at all times liable to be made slaves of by the latter, at any time, when they might desire to practice slave-holding. In the South, slavery actually existed in form without prejudice to the race or its color, save the law of subjugation, and now slavery once effectually abolished there by no matter what method, and all other social difficulties will melt away with the progress of the school.

The former dictators of Southern institutions will be more or less dependent upon the emancipated laborers. Force, no longer available; money worth nothing without labor will bring about instantly at the close of the war a degree of social and political privileges such as we have never enjoyed in the North, and I believe this state of equality will take place sooner at the South than here. What are the facts?

A few days ago the first regiment of colored men raised in Maryland for the war were marched through the streets of Baltimore, the very city which mobbed the Massachusetts 6th Regiment two years ago, and the New York *Herald* has not been refreshed with the news which it would have published with avidity, were they interrupted or had a single insult been offered to them; while on the other hand, the Third Regiment of Colored Pennsylvania Volunteers which left this State two months ago to give their bodies a living sacrifice for the white man's Union and Constitution, could not parade through the streets of Philadelphia, from apprehension, which was not without a good deal of foundation too, that they would be mobbed by the Copperheads, those sickly vermin, which have always insiduously dragged the North along upon their slimy backs and made her kiss the feet of her Southern masters--and for what. Why for the sake of that ill-established trade which never had any real life in it, but whose vitality was just sufficient to enable this very class to float along, the hired and only lovers of Southern brutality and man-stealing, and who would today, to retrieve their lost Southern pottage and political hopes sell out the North and all the little hope left in her for mankind, a

308 THE BLACK WORKER   I

perpetual sacrifice to Jefferson Davis and his confederacy. Not until slaveholding Baltimore had set free Philadelphia an example would the Mayor allow
the 6th Regiment which is to leave in a few days for the South to be paraded
in this city.

From the railroad and steamboat we come to the eating-house. In this
city it is thought impudent for a colored person to go into an eating-house
where white people dine, and ask for a meal, and you are notified of the
fact as soon as you try it. And that your readers may not think what I am
saying over-stated, I will give you my experience: I went into Mr. F. Ford's
eating-house, 804 Market St., a few days ago; it was the only one I saw where
I was then passing. Being quite hungry I took a seat, but had not fairly got
seated before I felt the paw of a lame, swarthy-looking-white man, upon my
shoulder, saying to me: "Out with you! Don't you know better than to come
where white people eat and take a seat, and ask for something to eat? You
are an impudent fellow!" If I had made a mistake could he not treat me civilly? I was a colored man, that was enough, and I ought to know better.
Now, this is Philadelphia, where 25,000 colored people are seen in the
streets every day. And if in the past thirty years of anti-slavery labor
here, the most progressive of us have not yet been able to penetrate the social atmosphere of the white, so as to ride in the same railroad car with
them, or take a hasty meal in business hours in the same public eating saloon, or sit with suavity of mind anywhere in the same church, pray, what
have we to expect from silence? Go from the eating house to the freest and
most liberal church in this city, which is the Rev. Mr. Furness', corner of
10th and Locust Sts., and colorphobia meets you at the door, and points you
to a place in the gallery appropriated especially for the colored people,
where if you go up you will see seated members and heads of a few families
whose well-known business character, money and reputation ought to entitle
them to a seat any where in that church.

But the dividing line is so visible and strongly drawn, that no colored
person thinks of entering the body of that church save to a back seat, where
you are almost hid in the darkness of the gallery. A man of keen sensitive-
ness might have as much religion as St. Paul had, and he could not enjoy it
in a church where he knows he is pointed to the most diminutive corner in it.
And palliate as we may, we cannot get over the fact that while colored people
are so proscribed, they are nothing less than objects of constant remark, and
will continue to be so long as the Negro pew is known to be in existence in a
church where they may congregate, however few.

Mr. Furness is a good man, but he converts but few over to the faith.
He is now approaching that after-life which seeks quest and would turn aside
from the contentions of the hour, and be content to slide along in the
smoother grooves which his labors of a more active date had helped to carve
out.

What we want in this city is not a pulpit, but a platform, which shall
give the scorching light of a Theodore Parker--that will penetrate through
this immoral soil which has been hardened by the tread of a wicked, unrelent-
ing prejudice, and discover to the people the grievous injustice they have so
long practiced upon us. And among the worst prejudice here is that hateful
feeling which excludes the colored people from the city horse cars. However
remote may be their homes from the centre of the city, or whatever may be the
emergency of their case, they cannot use this public conveyance, or if they
do, they are compelled, women and men, to stand upon the front platform, by
the side of the driver, in all weather, and under no circumstances are they
allowed to go inside of the cars. We often see women, with their little
children in their arms, standing upon the front platform of the cars. Yes,
think of it, civilized and Christian white people of Philadelphia: colored
women, unless they are white enough to run the gauntlet, have to stand upon
the front platform of your city horse-cars, surrounded on either side with
the vulgar, and compelled to listen to all the obscenity of the brothel
which is invariably directed towards them! At the same time take a look into the cars through the window as they pass, and you will see dotted all
through it the long white bonnets worn by a class called friends, but no word
of remonstrance do they raise against the inhumanity which they witness every
day practiced upon the colored women of Philadelphia, their own sex.

The altercation between Mr. Thomas Smith, President of the North
American Bank, and a few roughts who wished to have a colored volunteer removed from the horse-cars, and which you have already noticed works no observable change in the public feeling, and this mean prejudice will have its
way until it shall wreak itself out on some noble soul like the above, defending his weaker brother in these simple rights, and then Philadelphia
will begin to remember justice. If communities will not do right, then
God's justice will carve its own way.

The Christian Recorder, October 31, 1863.

43. OUT OF THE FRYING-PAN INTO THE FIRE

The subjoined statement is from the New York correspondent of the Philadelphia *Press,* of Jan. 4. We have heard rumors of similar transactions in
this city; and many assert that agents are employed to visit the border
States for the purpose of kidnapping slaves and emancipated negroes, and for-
warding them to different Northern recruiting stations, where the darkies are
put off with $25 or $50, and the balance of the $300 bounty is pocketed by
these organized thieves. We have always avoided the "nigger question," because we considered the discussion of it, in any shape, as foreign to the interests of this paper; but when it comes to the enactment of such scenes as
those described below, the rascals should have their villainy heralded by
every press in the country. The darkies thus treated, can scarcely feel ju-
bilant over their emancipation from slavery, since they have only "jumped out
of the frying-pan into the fire." The statement is as follows:

The matter of kidnapping of negroes and their compulsory enlistment, is
exciting much comment in the community. As far as is known, the outrages are
committed on behalf of Gen. Spinola's "recruiting" office only. It appears
by statements that some one hundred and forty-eight men have been mustered in
at Spinola's headquarters, who have been partially defrauded out of their
bounties, some receiving only $50 out of the $300 to which they are entitled,
and this in defiance of an order forbidding the mustering of recruits who
have not received the entire sum. The following facts, extracted from an affidavit which has just been given to the public, will convey some idea of the
modus operandi of this abominable system.

The deponent states that while walking in Broadway, near the headquarters of Gen. Spinola, he observed a colored man walking between two men in
uniform, who were talking to him. The negro showed some evidences of fright
in his actions, and the deponent, following them, passed into Lafayette Hall,
where the negro was thrust into "the crib." Deponent, who is himself colored, had some brief altercation with one of the men in uniform, and was ultimately seized by them, with the remark: "You d--d nigger, you've got to
stay here now." At the same time he was told that he must enlist, and the
guard at the door was ordered to run him through with his bayonet should he
attempt to escape. Fortunately, the deponent was already connected with a
colored regiment, and, on representing this fact to the kidnappers, they allowed him his liberty. He states, in his deposition, that he saw five or
six negroes "in the crib or pen," all of whom complained to him that they
had been kidnapped. One had his face swollen from a blow received while resisting his captors. All this occurred at mid day, in a building nearly opposite the Metropolitan Hotel, and in the very central portion of Broadway.
How much better this "crib" is than the slave pens of the South, let thinking
men decide. And if a thrust of the bayonet is better than a blow from the
slave-driver's lash, it is only because it has less of the elements of torture and degradation in its results. Not the slightest doubt of the reality
of the devillish crime can exist, and Heaven only knows how many more of
these slave-pens may exist in other portions of this city, in connection with
the brigade of this same political general. When General Spinola shall march

out his regiment, and claim the enthusiasm and respect of the people as the
reward of his recruiting services, it will be well for the country to ask
how many of the men, in his blue-coated ranks, are the victims of a cruelty
and an abominable traffic, whose details are scarcely less revolving than
those of the genuine slave trade, and how many of them are bullied into a
desperate silence regarding their wrongs, by threats of court-martials, or
the hideous and unnatural punishment of camps. General Spinola will, of
course, disclaim all knowledge of these outrages; but a quibble of the tongue
is no vindication. What the public knows, and has known for weeks, General
Spinola knows; and so long as he retains uniformed men-stealers in his service, so long is he chargeable with their misdeeds.

Fincher's Trades' Review, January 9, 1864.

WHITE NORTHERNERS ANTICIPATE THE ADDITION OF EX-SLAVES TO
THE LABOR FORCE

44. GENERAL JAMES S. WADSWORTH TO HENRY J. RAYMOND,
ACCEPTING THE NEW YORK GUBERNATORIAL NOMINATION OF
THE REPUBLICAN PARTY

I think I cannot be mistaken in assuming that the election will turn
upon the necessity of sustaining our National Government in its effort to
uphold itself, and maintain its territorial integrity, and especially upon
the Proclamation of the President, issued to that end, and referred to the
fourth resolution of the Convention.
I entirely approve of that proclamation, and commend it to the support
of the electors of New-York, for the following reasons:
1. It is an effectual aid to the speedy and complete suppression of
this rebellion.
Six or eight millions of whites, having had time to organize their government, and arm their troops, fed and supported by the labor of four millions of slaves, present the most formidable rebellion recorded in history.
Strike from this rebellion the support which it derives from the unre-
quired toil of these slaves, and its foundation will be undermined.
2. It is the most humane method of putting down the rebellion, the
history of which has clearly proved that the fears of slave insurrections
and massacres are entirely unfounded. While the slaves earnestly desire
freedom, they have shown no disposition to injure their masters. They will
cease to work for them without wages, but they will form, throughout the
Southern States, the most peaceful and docile peasantry on the face of the
earth.
The slave-owners once compelled to labor for their own support, the war
must cease, and its appalling carnage come to an end.
3. The emancipation once effected, the Northern States would be forever
relieved, as it is right that they should be, from the fears of a great influx of African laborers, disturbing the relations of these Northern industrial classes who have so freely given their lives to the support of the
Government.
This done, and the whole African population will drift to the South,
where it will find a congenial climate and vast tracts of land never yet
cultivated.

New York Times, October 6, 1862.

45. GEN. WADSWORTH'S ACCEPTANCE: AN EDITORIAL

Upon one point of considerable importance, Gen. WADSWORTH'S view will
be read with interest. One of the favorite devices of the enemies of the
Government in the North is to endeavor to alarm the laboring population by
the cry that emancipation will fill the Northern States with freed negroes,
and bring them largely and disastrously into competition with Northern labor.
Gen. WADSWORTH meets this very directly. "Emancipation once effected," he
says, "the Northern States *would be forever relieved, as it is right that
they should be, from the fears of a great influx of African laborers,* disturbing the relations of those Northern industrial classes who have so freely
given their lives to the support of the Government. This done, and *the whole
African population will drift to the South,* where it will find a congenial
climate and vast tracts of land never yet cultivated." There can be no reasonable doubt of the substantial soundness of this view of the case. The negro is a creature of local attachments to a far greater degree than the white
race, and nothing will induce him to leave the South; if he can possibly remain there. Emancipation would be much more likely *to draw all the free negroes South,* than to send the slaves North.
      Gen. WADSWORTH thus takes direct issue with Gov. SEYMOUR and the party
which has put him in nomination. The latter opposes the Government--Gen.
WADSWORTH supports it. Gov. SEYMOUR denounces the proclamation--Gen. WADS-
WORTH upholds it. Gov. SEYMOUR is for maintaining and preserving Slavery,--
in face of the fact that it is the main stay and strength of the rebellion,
--Gen. WADSWORTH, on account of that fact, is for destroying and exterminating it. Gov. SEYMOUR bestows all his censure upon our own Government, and
devotes all his effects in weakening and crippling it in its contest with
the rebellion,--Gen. WADSWORTH summons all the enemies and resources of the
State to the support of the Government and the extermination of those who are
in arms for its overthrow.

New York Times, October 6, 1862.

46. NEGRO APPRENTICESHIP

To the Editor of the *New York Times:* colonization in Florida. Waiving
the consideration of all incidental questions, such as the derangement of labor over the whole face of the country, as well as others that would require
to be considered in any thorough examination of this matter, let us suppose
the whole race transferred to the soil of Florida, and to be so distributed
and so circumstanced as to be immediately self-supporting. At the rate of
the natural increase of the race, how long would it be before their numbers
would be so great as that, in sheer self-defence, they would require additional territory for even their bare subsistence. I will not pursue the argument. The measure, if it were even practicable, would be inexpedient, and
the difficulties of our position would be intensified to an utterly unmanage-
able degree.
      The black race must be dealt with substantially upon the soil where they
now are, and public sentiment must be brought to the point of dealing with
them honestly and fairly as men, and for the most part upon the soil where
they now are. Any legislation in regard to them in the future must follow in
the track of Providential laws, or we shall continue to pay the penalty of
transgression. We are now suffering the penalty of a violation of God's laws
in having taken a race of men from its normal position on the surface of the
earth, and transferring it to an abnormal one. The negro race is a tropical
race, and we have undertaken, in violation of natural laws, to adapt it to a
temperate climate, and to subject it to unnatural relations, and we are simply paying the penalty of our transgression. But they are here, and have

become a nation in numbers. They cannot be removed, and we must deal with
them, therefore, not as heretofore, regardless of God's laws, but in harmony
with them--with becoming modesty. I beg leave to say that hereafter any
policy that tends to concentrate the blacks to a point territorially, or as
slaves in few hands, as the present system of Slavery does, will only increase the evils under which we now labor with respect to them. On the
other hand, any policy that tends to scatter them widely among the dominant
race, and to gradually remove all artificial dams across the natural flow of
the race South, will tend to diminish the evils of our situation, and if
this is carried to an extent which the writer believes to be practicable,
the dangers of our situation will, in time, if not very soon, wholly disappear.

Considering the present numbers of the black race now on this Continent,
and considering that for the present, at least, they must for the most part
be subjected in a measure to the control and direction of the white race, it
is submitted that the relations of the two races are continental in their
proportions and significance. Under these circumstances the whole subject of
their general treatment should be remitted at once to the General Government.
State legislation is wholly unequal to the task of duly providing for all
the contingencies involved. We have already painful evidence of this, and
if this method is to continue, the nation has greater sorrows still to endure. Let the President, as Commander-in-Chief, decree the abolition of
Slavery, and let the whole system of legislation in relation to the blacks be
remitted to Congress and this will simplify the problem materially. Then let
a wise and beneficient apprenticeship system be adopted, spplicable to the
whole country; one that shall not only not outrage, but recommend itself to
the commendable philanthropy of the age, and in this way the race will become
widely scattered again, and then they will slowly, but surely, gravitate
South to those regions relatively more congenial to their nature, and where
they may be useful to themselves and us. It is admitted that there are difficulties in the way of executing such a plan as this; but they are far from
insuperable, and are of vastly less magnitude than those we are now suffering. I do not now go into details in regard to such a system, having neither
time nor space to do so. I am confident, however, there is no serious difficulty in the way, and the change, I am fully warranted in saying, will, if
brought about in a proper manner, be hailed by the black race as a breat
boon.

                                                           W. L. B.

New York Times, October 12, 1862.

                        47. THE NEGRO AND FREE LABOR

A somewhat extended acquaintance with the colored population in several
of the seceded States induces me to believe that you will regard the following lines as not altogether inopportune or unimportant. From education, and
still more, from experience, I confess myself thoroughly Anti-Slavery, but I
must admit, at the same time, that I never felt satisfied of the negro's capacity for self-government until convinced of it by several months' residence
in the South. Lest I should be accused of negro-phobia, I will say, in as
few words as possible, that I do not regard this country, or any section of
it, as a suitable home for the colored man, and his speedy removal to other
climes will inure not less to his own advantage than to that of the white
population. Nature placed him originally in the torrid zone, as she placed
us in the temperate, and, if left to his own volition, he will move further
and further South, until a negro or mulatto will be as much a curiosity in
the United States as in Europe. This I believe to be only possible by placing him on a perfect quality with white laborers, and leaving him to himself
as you do them; and, if my conclusions be correct, the institution of

Slavery must perpetuate the existence of the two races side by side, inasmuch as you compel the negroes to remain within your confines. The tendency of all races is to separate themselves into distinct nationalities, and we need go no further than the City of New-York to find that the negro is not an exception to the rule, for he dwells with his own people away from the whites, and many streets are almost wholly given up to him. History proves that where two or more races are thrown together in the same territory, the more numerous or powerful absorbs the other, or the weaker moves off into other regions. The Britons are an example of the latter, and such will assuredly be the case in reference to the colored population of this country, when they are left to battle, unassisted, with the energetic, domineering Saxon.

I shall, of course, be met with the objection that the negro alone can labor in the fields of the South. This defence of Slavery, or, if you will, this assumed necessity of colored labor there, is either based upon ignorance or purposed misstatement. In no portion of this country is the climate too hot for white men to labor at all seasons, and, what is more, the hardest work in the South, such as railroad and other engineering operations, is performed to a great extent by whites, and *imported* whites at that. I have seen Northern troops at Port Royal felling tree after tree with the sun at 95 in the shade, others throwing up earthworks with no lack of energy, blacksmiths and carpenters at their trades, and yet scarcely one of these had ever before been further south than this State of New-York. Furthermore, I have no less authority than the official report of the Seventh Census of the United States for asserting that the ratio of mortality amongst the white population of the South is considerably below that of their fellow citizens in the North, a fact somewhat incompatible with the assumed unhealthiness of the former region.

Wherever I have traveled among the negro population, in South Carolina, Georgia, Virginia or Maryland, I have always found them docile, tractable and unassuming--much more so, I am afraid, than whites would be under similar circumstances. Nor have I ever found amongst them the slightest disposition to quit their plantations, or their runaway owners, when the latter had treated them with humanity and kindness. I have not seen the slightest evidence of any chimerical ideas of prospective freedom, nor the faintest anticipation of political advantage accruing to them from emancipation. If I may be allowed the expression, they all, men and women alike, take a practical, common-sense view of future liberty, regarding it as simply a right to keep what they make by their labor, not by any means as placing them socially or politically on a par with the white man. A conversation I had with a coal-black negro at Port Royal, last December, proved satisfactorily to my mind that he at least was actuated by much the same motives as the pale faces; and although he put the issue more tersely than most of his race are accustomed to do, yet I have invariably found that similar views are held by others in the same position as himself. JIM had formerly belonged to Miss PINCKNEY, but at the period in question he earned his living and wages as cook and servant to the Postmaster of the Expedition, and a better servant no man could possibly desire. I asked him one day, "To whom did you belong, JIM, before the Uankees came here?" and the following conversation ensued: "To Miss PINCKNEY, Sar." "Was she a kind mistress, JIM?" "Oh, very kind, Sar." "Were you a field-hand or house-servant?" "A house-servant, Sar." "And was Miss PINCKNEY kind to the field-hands, too, JIM?" "Oh, yes, Sar. When any ob them war sick she always went to them, and 'tended to them herself." "Well, JIM, if Miss PINCKNEY was so kind as you say, don't you want to return to her?" "Oh, no, Sar." My question, "Why not?" seemed to hurt the poor fellow; but at last he replied, with much discomposure, as though ashamed to acknowledge such a motive, "Why, Sar, all I made before was Miss PINCKNEY'S, but all I make now is my own."

This unsophisticated remark of JIM'S reminded me of a circumstance, which, at this moment, strikes me forcibly. I was dining with a wealthy planter several years ago, and observing the peculiar flavor of the ham that was served at the table. I took the liberty of asking whether it was his own raising or foreign produce. "I am not astonished at your observation," he replied, "because the pork you generally eat has been permitted to run loose and to feed upon any and everything it came across, but I make it a point to buy mine from my own negroes, for you must know that our servants are allowed to raise pork and poultry on their own account, and sell them in the market. *Self-interest,* as you are aware, is a great incentive to exertion, for the negroes are particularly careful in feeding their stock so as to obtain the highest price for their produce. Hence the superiority of this over other hams!"

I might multiply such examples as the above to an indefinite extent, and cite the experience of American naval officers on Southern stations as to the willingness of the colored man to labor for his own interest, even without the supervision of the whites. We need not, however, go outside the City of New-York to prove this position. The colored people here are a very slight burden, if any upon the community. Happening lately to be in the store of a merchant in Front-street, a negro entered the office and solicited charity. The merchant surveying the applicant from head to foot, and, having cross-questioned him, finally took out a five dollar bill and gave it him. Knowing my friend's conscientious scruples against bestowing eleemosynary aid upon beggars, aware also of his strong bias against the negro, this circumstance took me by surprise, and I could not help telling him so. Thereupon he replied, "You may depend upon it that little assistance is well bestowed, for no negro will beg unless he is forced to it by absolute necessity."

The colored people and their children, as a class, are much cleaner and better clothed than other portions of the laboring population. A peregrination through Church, Thompson, Laurens and contiguous steeets--particularly on Sundays--will satisfy any one of the correctness of this statement. Where they get their clothes from has always been a mystery to me. The love of the negro for dress is very much greater than that of any other race, and this fact, which nobody can possibly deny, should be an additional inducement with Northern men to set them free in their labor. Four millions of people offer a magnificent market for manufactures--a market which, for cotton goods, will certainly be greatly more valuable than any other community of equal numbers.

I would repeat in conclusion that all my acquaintance with the negro in this country convinces me that he regards emancipation as naught else than a freeing of his labor and the protection of his right to live and amass property. Emancipate labor and you place him immediately in conflict with the more energetic and shrewd Caucasian, and to save himself from the competition and rivalry in which he is certain to be beaten, he will move gradually away into other regions, and leave this "a white man's country." Continue to recognize Slavery as an institution and you compel him to remain here; but, rely upon it, if he do remain here, designing politicians will soon find means to build up anew that domineering sectionalism which the Northern armies are in a fair way to destroy.

I am, Sir, yours respectfully,
FREDERICK MILNES EDGE.

New York Times, October 13, 1862.

PART VIII

CONDITION OF THE BLACK WORKER DURING EARLY RECONSTRUCTION

CONDITION OF THE BLACK WORKER DURING EARLY RECONSTRUCTION

Even though blacks were overjoyed by the destruction of the institution of slavery, freedom brought unparalleled problems as well. Throughout the South, blacks suffered from inadequate food, housing, and other vital necessities. Since specie was scarce, many employers who remained "unreconstructed" fell back on former methods of coercion, such as the whip, to force the ex-slaves to continue in their previous capacities. Conflict was inevitable where whites demanded that blacks remain subordinate, and Negroes were determined to exercise their hard-won freedom (Doc. 3-5). While illiteracy further hampered blacks, not all Negroes confronted that obstacle. Many items in Part VIII are from the New Orleans Daily Tribune, the first black daily in the South. The Tribune was published in both English and French.

Because the old economic system had collapsed and a new one had yet to emerge, blacks fell back on traditional institutions for relief, such as the church and the numerous benevolent societies which flourished in the black community (Doc. 6). New black organizations appeared almost immediately after the war; however, most of them were founded along occupational lines. The Universal Suffrage Party (Doc. 9), the Freedmen's Aid Association of New Orleans (Doc. 10), and the Commercial Association of Laborers of Louisiana (Doc. 14), are representative examples. Most black people agreed, however, that the only effective solution to the difficulties lay in a division of land ownership among the ex-slaves (Doc. 7).

While some white southerners were not convinced that conversion to a free labor system spelled certain destruction (Doc. 16) most of them envisioned the demise of "civilization" as they knew it (Doc. 19). On the other hand, the newly-founded National Labor Union saw in the new free labor system a fertile field for labor organization (Doc. 21). The growing discontent and militancy among the black and white working classes lent credence to such a view (Doc. 23-50). Undoubtedly, the source of this militancy among Negro workers lay in the passage of the hated "black codes," passed in 1865 and 1866 by the white state legislatures, which attempted to control the mobility of blacks (Doc. 26-27, 37).

In fact, the determination of black workers to exercise their freedom of choice often was the immediate reason for many of the labor disputes. Thus, on one Louisiana plantation in 1865, blacks laid down their tools and refused to work when they suspected their employer of trying to trick them (Doc. 25). Many ex-slaves simply left the plantations behind and moved to the cities where wages were higher (Doc. 31). Once there, labor organization was facilitated, and grievances were often channelled into local strikes, protests for higher pay, or petitions (Doc. 32-34, 39-50).

Economic privation was not confined to southern blacks during the early Reconstruction period. The Civil War failed to alter the prevailing patterns of discrimination which had existed in northern cities, and blacks continued to be concentrated in the menial categories (Doc. 54-55). Nor had the root cause evaporated, as white prejudice against black workers remained as strong as ever (Doc. 53), and social discrimination remained rigid (Doc. 52).

RECONSTRUCTION IN THE SOUTH

1. DIGNITY OF LABOR

One of the most disastrous results in slavery was the contempt for the laborer, and the repulsive disposition shown for labor, by the aristocratic class of planters. Labor is the only true element of prosperity, strength and grandur in modern societies. The prize is no longer won, among nations, by bodily qualities, such as the power of endurance and the athletic forms which gave the Greeks the superiority over their rivals. The future of civilized countries is no longer at stake upon the issue of a "single fight." We, now, use gun-powder and steam-engines. The time when Ajax knocked down the Trojan chief, with a rock that two ordinary men were hardly able to raise from the ground, is past for ever. No other Horatius will, in the nineteenth century, defend a bridge against a whole army, or even a whole regiment. No modern Robert Bruce will crush at one blow the helmet and head of Sir Henry Bohun, in the presence of a large army. No other Lion-Hearted Richard will, in our days, gallop for two hours in front of the enemy's lines, without finding his match and fight to death. The invention of fire-arms has equalized all men; and the bullet from the gun of the meanness and weakest recruit may strike the heart of the highest officer in command of the enemy.

The steam-engine has, in a similar way, equalized the powers of men in master of navigation, traffic, industrial works and commerce. The competition of nations, on the market of the world, is now based upon the extent of their productive means, that is to say upon the quantity of labor. Every man who fairly works—be he an humble field hand on a plantation, or a distinguished engineer at the head of an important workshop—contributes to the power, greatness and renown of his country. National strength and national fame are, in our time, the offsprings of labor.

The contempt for the laborer is therefore, a great injustice, and a capital error. It is unjust, because the labor is the true fountain of life for modern nations. The isolated man, whatsoever be his purity of birth and his individual elegance or courage, or audacity, no longer has a sufficient power by himself. Men become useful by their co-operation in the great work of producing the national riches only. Labor is, therefore, the first requisite of modern societies, and it ought to be regarded in consequence and duly praised and honored.

New Orleans Daily Tribune, November 26, 1865.

2. BIOGRAPHICAL INFORMATION ON BLACK LEADERS IN NEW ORLEANS
DURING RECONSTRUCTION

SOURCES: Manuscript Census Returns, Eighth Census of the United States, 1860, Louisiana, Records of the U.S. Bureau of the Census, Record Group 29; Muster Rolls, Returns, and Regimental Papers, Volunteers. Civil War, U.S. Colored Troops, 73rd, 74th, 75th, 76th, and 77th Regiments, Records of the Adjutant General's Office, Record Group 94; Pensions, Records of the Veterans Administration, Record Group 15; New Orleans, Mayor's Office, Register of Free Colored Persons Entitled to Remain in the State, 1856-1864; New Orleans, Conveyance Office, Record of Conveyance, 1855-1862; New Orleans, Treasurer's Office, Tax Ledger, 1859-1861; New Orleans, Office of Vital Records, Record of Birth, 1819-1857; New Orleans, Office of Vital Records, Record of Death, 1865-1900; St. Louis Cathedral, Baptismal Register of Negroes and Mulattoes, 1831-1840; *New Orleans Directory,* 1855-1862; New Orleans press, especially *L'Union,* 1862-

1864; *Tribune*, 1864-1869; *Black Republican*, 1865; *Republican*, 1867-1876; *Louisiana*, 1870-1880; *Times*, 1873-1880; and various other primary and secondary sources, published and unpublished.

KEY: In the listings below the asterik (*) means that the exact place of residence in New Orleans in 1860-1861 is known for the person concerned; the dagger (+) means that the person was a slaveowner at some time before the Civil War. The abbreviations have the following meanings: F--free; S--slave; M--mulatto; B--black; N.O.--New Orleans; L--literate; I--illiterate.

Name	Ante- bellum Legal Status	Color	1860-1861 Place of Residence	1860-1861 Occupation	Ante- bellum Literacy
Joseph Abelard*	F		N.O.	Carpenter	L
C. J. Adolphe					
Joseph B. Alexis*	F	M	N.O.	Cooper	L
James W. Allen				Minister	
Madison Allen*	F		N.O.	Painter	
Caesar Carpentier Antoine*	F	B	N.O.	Barber	L
Felix C. Antoine	F	M	N.O.	Mechanic	L
Charles Aubert	F		N.O.	Carpenter	
Laurent Auguste*	F	M	N.O.	Cigar store	
Adolphe Augustin	F	M	N.O.	Cigar maker	L
Moses B. Avery	F				L
Noel Jacques Bacchus	F	M	N.O.	Carpenter	L
Lewis Banks+	F	M	N.O.	Minister	
Alexander Eusibius Barber	S	B		Steward	L
William B. Barrett	F	M	N.O.	Barber	L
Richard C. Baylor	S		N.O.	Laborer	L
Armand Belot*	F	M	N.O.	Cigar factory	L
Octave Belot*	F	M	N.O.	Cigar factory	L
E. Arnold Bertonneau*	F	M	N.O.	Wine merchant	
Imanuel B. Bijou	F	B	N.O.	Carpenter	
Thomas Bland*	F		N.O.	Drayman	
Ovide C. Blandin	F				
Ludger B. Boguille*	F	M	N.O.	Teacher	L
Francois Boisdore*	F	M	N.O.	Accountant	L
Henry Bonseigneur*	F		N.O.	Cigar store	
J. B. D. Bonseigneur*+	F	M	N.O.	Grocer	L
Paulin C. Bonseigneur*	F	M	N.O.	Shoe store	L
Anatole Louis Boree*	F	B	N.O.		
Pierre Boyer*	F		N.O.	Tailor	
Numa Brihou	F				
Bazile Brion*	F		N.O.	Shoemaker	
Clement Isaac Camp*	F		N.O.	Mason	L
Edmund Campenel	F	M	N.O.	Turner	L
J. Manuel Camps*+	F		N.O.	Grocer	L
Pierre Canelle*	F	M	N.O.	Cotton weigher	L
Placide Z. Canonge*+	F		N.O.		
Lucien Jean Pierre Capla*	F	M	N.O.	Shoe store	L
Edward Carter					
Jefferson B. Carter				Minister	I
St. Felix Casanave*	F	M	N.O.	Used furniture	L
Jean Pierre Cazelar, Jr.	F	M	N.O.	Planter	L
Eugene Chesse*	F		N.O.		
Charles B. Chevalier*	F	M	N.O.	Carpenter	
Henry Chevarre*	F		N.O.		
Firmin C. Christophe	F		N.O.		
John Racquet Clay*+	F	M	N.O.	Broker	L
David Copeland*	F		N.O.	Baker	

Name				Occupation	
Myrtile Courcelle*[+]	F	M	N.O.	Broker	L
Joseph A. Craig	S			Printer	L
Robert I. Cromwell	F	B	Wisc.	Physician	L
Joseph Curiel*	F	M	N.O.	Grocer	L
Victor Darinsbourg	F	M	N.O.	Carpenter	I
Edgard Charles Davis	F	M	N.O.	Cooper	L
L. Theodule Delassize[+]	F		N.O.	Bldg. materials	
Jules Desalles*	F	M	N.O.	Cigar maker	
Emile Detiege	F	M	N.O.	Mason	L
W. A. Dove				Minister	
Adolphe Duhart	F	M		Teacher	L
Francis Ernest Dumas*[+]	F	M	N.O.	Clothing store	L
Oscar James Dunn	F	M	N.O.	Plasterer	L
Pierre Guillauim Dupin*	F		N.O.	House furnishings	L
Edmond Dupuy[+]	F	M			
Joseph Ebb*	F	M		Warehouseman	
James Edwards*	F		N.O.	Drayman	
Francois Escoffie*	F		N.O.	Teacher	L
J. B. Esnard	F	M	N.O.		
Francois Esteve	F		N.O.	Tailor	L
Louis Ferry*	F		N.O.	Clerk	
Alphonse Fleury, Jr.*	F	M	N.O.	Tailor	L
Florian Fleury	F	M	N.O.	Shoemaker	L
Joseph Follin*	F		N.O.	Carpenter	
William P. Forrest				Minister	
Louis Nelson Fouche*	F	M	N.O.	Mason	L
Henry Francis				Minister	
August Gaspard*	F	M	N.O.	Mason	
Charles W. Gibbons*	F	M	N.O.	Painter	L
Achille Glaudin	F		N.O.	Cigar store	
Clement Glaudin	F		N.O.		
Jean Baptiste Glaudin*[+]	F	M	N.O.	Cigar store	L
Maurice Glaudin	F	M	N.O.	Cigar store	L
Placide Glaudin	F		N.O.	Cigar store	
Joseph C. Graves*	F		N.O.	Carpenter	
J. B. Grounx*	F		N.O.	Carpenter	
James H. Henry					
Joseph W. Howard					
Charles H. Hughes	F		N.O.	Baker	
James H. Ingraham	F				L
Robert Hamlin Isabelle	F	F			
Thomas H. Isabelle	F			Merchant	
William C. Johnson	F	M	N.O.	Mason	
Blanc F. Joubert[+]	F	M	France	Grocer	L
Jean B. Jourdain*	F	M	N.O.	Cigar maker	L
Victor Jourdain*	F	M	N.O.		L
John F. Keating	F	M	N.O.	Mason	
John Keppard				Cafe owner	
Francois Lacroix*[+]	F	M	N.O.	Tailor	L
Thomy Lafon*	F	M	N.O.	Merchant	L
J. Othello Lainez*	F		N.O.	Shoemaker	
Louis Lainez	F				
Joseph Jean Pierre Lanna*	F	M	N.O.	Dry goods	L
Armand Lanusse*	F	M	N.O.	Teacher	L
Louis Duqueminy Larrieu*[+]	F	M	N.O.		L
George W. Levere				Minister	
A. W. Lewis	S	B		Physician	L
James Lewis*	F	M	N.O.	Steward	
Charles E. Logan*	F	M	N.O.	Plasterer	
Ernest Longpre, Jr.					L
Drauzin Barthelemy Macarty*[+]	F	M	N.O.	Broker	L

Name			Location	Occupation	
Victor Eugene Macarty*+	F		N.O.	Musician	
Robert McCary, Jr.				Minister	
Joseph Francis Mansion	F				
Lucien Mansion*	F		N.O.	Cigar factory	L
Theodule A. Martin*	F	M	N.O.	Barber	
Charles Martinez*	F		N.O.	Merchant	L
Alexander Aristide Mary	F	M	N.O.	Real Estate	L
J. A. Massicot			N.O.		L
Eugene G. Meilleur	F	M	N.O.	Carpenter	L
John Willis Menard	F	M	Ohio		L
Thomas A. Miles				Minister	
Louis Monde*	F		N.O.	Mason	
Julien J. Monette	F	M	N.O.	Tailor	
Felix Montegut*	F	M	N.O.	Mason	L
Joseph Leonie Montieu*	F	M	N.O.	Clerk	L
Manuel Moreau*+	F.	M	N.O.		L
Eugene Moret	F	M	N.O.		L
C. Clay Morgan	F			Lawyer	L
Ernest C. Morphy	F		N.O.		
George P. Nelson*	F	B	N.O.	Soda shop	
Jordan B. Noble*	F	M	N.O.		L
Jacob A. Norager	F	M		Cabinetmaker	
John Parsons*	F		N.O.	Barber	
W. H. Pearne				Minister	L
P. B. S. Pinchback	F	M	N.O.	Steward	L
Armand Populus*	F		N.O.	Mason	L
Ulysse Populus*	F	M	N.O.	Barber	L
Francois Poree*	F	M	N.O.	Clerk	L
Paul Poree*	F	M	N.O.	Carpenter	L
Thomas Medard Poree*	F	M	N.O.	Carpenter	
John Pullum, Jr.*	F		N.O.	Barber	
John Pullum, Sr.*	F	M	N.O.	Drayman	
Joanni Questy*	F		N.O.	Teacher	L
James W. Quinn			La.		
P. B. Randolph	F		N.Y.	Reporter	L
Eugene Rapp*	F		N.O.	Tailor	
Robert Ray		M	N.O.	Mason	L
Joseph Auguste Raynal*	F	M	N.O.		L
Eusebe Reggio*+	F		N.O.	Dry goods	L
Anthony Remoir		B	N.O.	Mason	
Joseph Renaud	F	M	N.O.	Cigar maker	
Henry Louis Rey*	F	M	N.O.	Clerk	L
Octave Rey*	F	M	N.O.	Cooper	L
Edmond Rillieux*+	F	M	N.O.	Dry goods	L
Charles W. Ringgold*	F		N.O.	Cigar maker	
Thomas P. Robinson*	F		N.O.		
Lazard A. Rodriguez*	F	M		Shoemaker	
Stephen Walter Rogers*	F	M	N.O.	Minister	L
Anthony Ross				Minister	
Jean Baptiste Roudanez*	F	M	N.O.	Builder	L
Louis Charles Roudanez*	F	M	N.O.	Physician	L
Antoine St. Leger	F	M	N.O.	Jeweler	L
Henry Sanders				Minister	
Charles Satchell				Minister	
Bernard Saulay*	F		N.O.	House furnishings	
Charles S. Sauvinet			N.O.		
A. Lucien Scott					
John Scott*	F		N.O.	Carpenter	
John Sidney			N.O.		
William G. Smoot*+	F		N.O.	Drayman	
Louis A. Snaer	F				
Philomene S. Snaer	F	B	N.O.	Cigar maker	
Joseph Simon Soude	F		N.O.	Carpenter	L
Bernard A. Soulie*+	F	M	N.O.	Comm. merch.	L
Victor Souterre*	F		N.O.	Clerk	L

John F. Spearing[+]	F		N.O.	Sailmaker	
Eugene Staes*	F		N.O.	Clerk	L
George W. Steptoe				Minister	
Robert H. Steptoe[+]	F	M	N.O.	Minister	L
Mitchell M. Sturgess	F	M	N.O.	Minister	L
George B. Taylor*	F		N.O.	Carpenter	
William W. Taylor	F		N.O.	Steward	
Sidney Thezan*	F		N.O.	Tailor	L
Camille Theirry	F	M		Shoemaker	L
Jacob L. Tosspot	F		N.O.	Railroad worker	
Pascal M. Tourne*[+]	F		N.O.		L
Moses Townsend	S				
Paul Trevigne*	F	M	N.O.	Teacher	L
Raymond Trevigne*	F	M	N.O.	Cigar maker	
William Troy	F		Canada	Minister	
Maure Parquitto Valentin*	F	M	N.O.	Shoemaker	L
James Madison Vance	F		N.O.	Minister	L
Eugene Vessier*	F		N.O.		
Charles Joseph Veque*	F		N.O.	Painter	L
William F. Vigers	F		N.O.	Merchant	L
Norbert Villere	F	M	N.O.	Lawyer	L
Henry White*	F	M	N.O.	Drayman	L
Emperor Williams	F	M	N.O.	Minister	
P. M. Williams	F			Teacher	L
David Wilson*	F		N.O.	Barber	
John F. Winston					L
Francis Xavier*	F		N.O.	Carpenter	
Adolphe Zemar	F	M	N.O.		L

David C. Rankin, "The Origins of Black Leadership in New Orleans During Reconstruction," Journal of Southern History, 40 (August, 1974):436-40.

3. GENERAL SCHURZ ON BLACK WORKERS [56]

Bureau of Free Labor

Montgomery, Alabama, Aug. 19th, 1865.

Genl. C. Schurz

I take pleasure in laying before you my replies to the interogations you handed me yesterday.

1st General experience as to the efficiency of the negroes as free laborers.

For nearly two years I have labored exclusively with the colored race. Part of the time as an officer in colored organizations, part of the time with children, as Superintendent of colored schools in the Mississippi Valley, and finally as Superintendent of Freedmen in this city since May last, where I have had better opportunity than ever before of becoming acquainted with the plantation system of labor, its requirements and the negro as a tiller of the soil.

In my varied experiences I have found the race exceedingly patient and generally industrious. If they do not work with such rapidity as white men they do it as willingly and as surely. I have the grestest confidence that the freedmen will become reliable & efficient laborers in every branch of industry. There is among them a vast amount of mechanical skill, which has heretofore rendered many very valuable slaves. Many planters whose plantations I have visited have pointed to one of the negroes and said, "that man built this house he framed it all alone," "that man is my blacksmith, he makes all my ploughs and plantation tools." I find in this way good Shoemakers,

Carpenters, Masons, Blacksmiths, Weavers, Spinners, and Seamstresses, Cooks, &c. as well as negroes familiar with agricultural pursuits, truly & competent foreman, who have had charge of large plantations during the war. As the providence of God led the children of Israel to Egypt to learn the mechanical arts and then go forth from bondage no more as a family but as a nation competent no itself to perpetual national existence, so that same kind Prodience has thought the colored race under similar bondage alike the useful arts, so that in due time, when the privilege is granted to these people of seeking employment like other laborers in any part of the world they are prepared to step in and fill successfully any & every branch of manual labor. Their hands are familiar with the tools of the Artisan. This diversity of talent of is inestiamable value and a great relief in the present emergency. If such men have been efficient under a slave I am confident they will be under a free system. This is the basis of my confidence.

I have observed as a race they love thrift & prosperity--& can endure success far more advantageously than the Irish nation. My residence in this city has forcibly convinced me of this statement. Some of the most prosperous men of this city are negroes. Some at this early day of their freedom, are ready to purchase land & many others are anxious to become owners of real estate. On closer inspection, one can readily detect among some, a foundness for trade, the germ of a commercial spirit, which is rapidly developing. Present to such people accustomed to labor incessant and in part inspired by a newly aquired freedom and stimulated by the love of gain, the proper rewards of industry, and they will, they must become efficient and reliable laborers. The might that slumbers in their sable arms will cause these desolate fields to whiten with returning prosperity. Some I confess are indolent, preferring to live in a dishonest way, rather than toil for an honorable support. But it is not strange if persons who have labored for years with no profit, do not realize at once the advantages of a directed labor, or see that nothing is attained without it.

2nd The second interrogatory, "Do they work well or not & under wath circumstances do they work well, and under wath badly," is answered under the 4th head.

3d. "What are the ideas of the planters as to the efficiency of the free labor system" in this part of the country." Poor enough. Many of the larger slaveholders, who have grown rapidly wealthy by slave labor declare the country ruined *for ever;* that cotton cannot be made by 'free nigghers.' I have heard many say that they never intended to try it again, nor would they have anything to do with the free niggers."

Not a day passes but I am told many times that they *won't work*. If asked who will cultivate fields, I have heard them reply that their plantations should grow up in the weeds before free negroes should attempt their culture. The depression of spirits, this unwarranted despondency, has its natural results in depreciating real estate. Good corn & cotton lands which before the war sold at from $25.00 to $40.00 per acre, and now offered for $10.00 and $15.00 per acre. Whit this wealthy class slavery was every thing when that was taken away it left them helpless. It destroyed all energy and was like the going out of life itself. These are the men who are most anxious to sell & cherish the poorest ideas as to the success of free labor. And what astonishes me most of all, is their despondency increases as they witness the negroes coming into the possession of rights and privileges which alone render them valuable as a free laborer. Happy for the South if some of them would leave the country for ever.

There is a class of small planters who have been accustomed to work themselves, who have always had the supervision of their own plantations and had not committed it to an overseer, who have much more confidence in the efficincy of the free labor. The people of this class have had much less trouble in controlling their hands this year than that of the former.

They are disposed to treat the freedmen more as white laborers are treated. These men, I doubt not, will be in a few years the wealthy men of the South. They are inclined to give better wages to their employees and express a determination to plant as in former years. They yielded more readily to the changing conditions of things & will make good loyal citizens.

4th Are Southern men far better adapted. At present there is no confidence existing between the late masters & slaves in but very few cases is there

any good will existing between them. The planters say, "they won't believe
any thing I tell them," & in most cases I know that this is true & Southern
men realize this fact & are anxious to secure Northern men as partners so
that they may better control their labor for the ensuing year.

5th What is the treatment free negro laborers are generally receiving
from Planters?

Much better than it was months ago.

During June & July there was much suffering in consequence of ill & abusive treatment. But the change for the better of late, has been generally &
rapid. The negro is gaining friends even in his own country. The friends of
justice dare now to make their will heard in his behalf.

For their labor the freedmen generally are receiving nothing more than
a support & their food & clothing is of the coarsest & poorest quality. Many
negroes are working upon food which a white man would not touch. Corn meal &
vegetables are the principal food in many instances. For the fall months the
prospect is still more gloomy so far as compensation for labor is concerned,
it is not worth mentioning. The free men are working simply for a livelihood, & we cannot expect men will work very hard for such meagre support.
When the wages are fair, the money paid monthly, I have never heard a word of
complaint, but on the other hand, I have heard planters say that they never
had men do better. They work badly when the pay is nothing & they have no
hope of bettering their condition.

6th There are many cases of differences arising constantly, some of a
serious nature, between planters and freedmen. The difficulties arise as the
planters alledge, because the negroes are "indolent & insolent." We have
eight men in hospital now under treatment for gun shot wounds inflicted by
white men. In all my experience here I have not seen a white man shot by a
negro. This, at best is severe punishment for such harmless crimes. There
are plantations not far from this city upon which a negro will not work another year, because of the bad treatment this year. The negro is far from receiving that treatment and consideration which is due a free laborer. Our
hope is that the great patience of the race will not wear away till they come
into their rightful position as freemen.

I have the honor to be,
General,

with much regards,
Your ob't serv't

(sig) C. W. Buckley,
Asst Supt. Freedmen

Carl Schurz Papers, Library of Congress.

4. WORK ONLY FOR GOOD EMPLOYERS

The freedmen have, by this time, made a distinction between men, on one
hand, who act fairly with them, who treat them manfully, give them their
rights, and exact from them no more than what is just and fair; and men, on the
other hand, who look upon them as upon an inferior class of beings, who distrust them, treat them harshly, and try every means of cheating their employees. With these last employers, freedmen have to act defensively all the time;
. . . .

When these planters of the old school;--of the whip school--will see that
they cannot obtain laborers, unless by a fair treatment, the system will undergo a sudden and remarkable change on the plantation. It will be done away with
cursing, cheating and robbing; it will be done away with harsh treatment; and a
better condition will then be made to the country laborer.

It is therefore in the power of freedmen to obtain fair dealing. Good
or tolerably good employers are numerous enough; nobody is under the absolute
obligation of contracting with the worse planters. Let these unjust and unnatural men stay alone. Let them cultivate their lands the better they can.
Let them look after white laborers, if they like. They will have to pay them
full prices, and to treat them as men. It will be at all events a lesson for
the unfair employer. The remedy to your wrongs is in your hands. Do not
neglect to apply it to the sore, at the proper time.

New Orleans Daily Picayune, October 13, 1865.

5. WHITELAW REID'S OBSERVATIONS ON NEWLY LIBERATED SLAVES [57]
IN SELMA, ALABAMA

The burnt houses in the business part of the city were being rapidly re-
built. Negro carpenters and masons seemed to have exclusive control of the
work. An old negro, who worked as hod-carrier, explained that he was paid a
dollar a day. "By de time I pays ten dollars a month rent fo' my house, an'
fifteen cents a poun' for beef or fresh po'k, or thirty cents fo' bacon, an'
den buys my clo'es, I does n't hab much leff. I's done tried it, an' I knows
brack man cant stan' dat." He had been "refugeed" from Tuscumbia; now he
could not get back. He had been doing his best to save money enough, (forty
dollars,) but he couldn't seem to get ahead at all with it.
His people were all going to work well, he thought, on cotton plantations
where they were sure of good pay. Of course, they would work better for the
Yankees, 'cause dey freed 'em. There was no talk of insurrection among them
--had never heerd of sich a thing. What should they rise for? There were no
secret societies among them.
On the other hand, the people had many complaints of insubordination, so
great that they were in actual fear for the lives of their families! Some of
the newspapers thought "the scenes of bloodshed and massacre of St. Domingo
would be re-enacted in their midst, before the close of the year." "We speak
advisedly," continued one frightened editor, "we have authentic information
of the speeches and conversation of the blacks, sufficient to convince us of
their purpose. *They make no secret of their movement.* Tell us not that we
are alarmists. After due investigation and reflection upon this matter, we
have determined to talk plainly, without fear or favor, and if our voice of
warning is not heeded, we, at least, will have the consoling reflection that
we have performed our duty."
All this silly talk was, doubtless, utterly without foundation. Negroes
neglected to touch their hats to overseers or former masters whom they dis-
liked; and straightway it was announced that they were growing too saucy for
human endurance. They held meetings and sung songs about their freedom,
whereupon it was conjectured that they were plotting for a rising against the
whites. They refused to be beaten; and, behold, the grossest insubordination
was existing among the negroes*
Near the ruins of the Selma armory was a village of huts, filled with the
lowest order of plantation negroes. One or two were riding about on abandoned
Government horses; more were idly watching them. They were "joying their
freedom." A little round furnace stood some distance from the huts. At its
mouth sat an old negro, far gone with fever and greatly emaciated. His story
was a simple one. He had been sent here, by his master, from Northern Alabama,
to work for the Government. Yankees had come along, and his paper to go home
(his transportation) done wuf nothing no more. He begged a little, picked up
a little, slept in the furnace, and so got along. He might last through the
winter, but it was very doubtful. He was, apparently, sixty or seventy years
old, and there was not a soul, black or white, to care for him.
Most of the negroes congregated here had either been sent to work in the
Rebel shops, or had come since the end of the war to "joy their freedom."

"You were just as free at home as here," I said to one who had patched
up an abandoned tent, under which he lived.

"But I's want to be free man, cum when I please, and nobody say nuffin
to me, nor order me roun'."

"De Lo'd tole we to come heah," another said. "De Lo'd him'll take car'
ob us now."

*Carl Shurz gave an instance in point:

One of our military commanders was recently visited by a doctor living
in one of the south-eastern counties of Georgia. The doctor looked very much
disturbed.

"General," says he, "the negroes in my county are in a terrible state of
insubordination, and we may look for an outbreak every moment. I come to im-
plore your aid."

The General, already accustomed to such alarming reports, takes the matter with great coolness. "Doctor, I have heard of such things before. Is not
your imagination a little excited? What reason should the negroes have to resort to violence?"

"General, you do not appreciate the dangers of the situation we are
placed in. Our lives are not safe. It is impossible to put up with the demonstrations of insubordination on the part of the negroes. If they do not
cease, I shall have to remove my family into the city. If we are not protected, we can not stay in the country. I would rather give up my crop to the negroes than the lives of my wife and children."

"Now, Doctor, please go into particulars, and tell me what has happened."

"Well, General, formerly the slaves were obliged to retire to their cabins before nine o'clock in the evening. After that hour nobody was permitted
outside. Now, when their work is done, they roam about just as they please,
and when I tell them to go to their quarters, they do not mind me. Negroes
from neighboring plantations will sometimes come to visit them, and they have
a sort of meeting, and then they are cutting up sometimes until ten or eleven.
You see, General, this is alarming, and you must acknowledge that we are not
safe."

"Well, Doctor, what are they doing when they have that sort of a meeting?
Tell me all you know."

"Why, General, they are talking together, sometimes in whispers and sometimes loudly. They are having their conspiracies, I suppose. And then they
are going on to sing and dance, and make a noise."

"Ah, now, Doctor," says the imperturable General, "you see this is their
year of jubilee. They must celebrate their freedom in some way. What harm is
there in singing or dancing? Our Northern laborers sing and dance when they
please, and nobody thinks anything of it; we rather enjoy it with them."

"Yes, that is all well enough, General; but these are negroes, who ought
to be subordinate, and when I tell them to go to their quarters, and they do
n't do it, we can't put up with it."

"By the way, Doctor, have you made a contract with the negroes on your
plantation?"

"Yes."

"Do they work well?"

"Pretty well, so far. My crops are in pretty good condition."

"Do they steal much?"

"They steal some, but not very much."

"Well, then, Doctor, what have you to complain about?"

"O, General," says the Doctor, dolefully, "you do not appreciate the dangers of our situation."

"Now, Doctor, to cut the matter short, has a single act of violence been
perpetrated in your neighborhood by a negro against a white man?"

"Yes, sir; and I will tell you of one that has happened right in my family. I have a negro girl, eighteen years old, whom I reaised. For ten years
she has been waiting upon my old mother-in-law, who lives with me. A few days
ago the old lady was dissatisfied about something, and told the girl that she
felt like giving her a whipping? Now, what do you think? the negro girl

actually informed my old mother-in-law that she would not submit to a whipping, but would resist. My old father-in-law then got mad, and threatened
her; and she told him the same thing. Now, this is an intolerable state of
things."

*Whitelaw Reid, After the War: A Tour of the Southern States 1865-1866 (New
York, 1965), pp. 385-89.*

6. TO THE MASS MEETING AT THE SCHOOL OF LIBERTY

New Orleans Sept. 11th 1865

Ladies and gentlemen -- I would respectfully submit to your consideration the following plan to aid, by pecuniary means, the "Central Executive
Committee" of the Friends of Universal Suffrage, which Committee stands in
want of funds to carry out the "good cause."

I will now proceed to demonstrate by facts and figures, the great case
by which a sum of money may be raised, that may materially assist the above
named "Committee" to carry out the great work.

There exist, at this present time, in this city, forty-two organized and
"Benevolent Association," with an average membership of fifty persons to each
association. My proposition is as follows:

First--That each Association or Society contribute from its treasury,
the sum of ten dollars.

Second--That each and every individual member of every Association or
Society aforesaid, pay the sum of twenty-five cents to round a general fund,
this fund amounting to twelve dollars and fifty cents; that is to say fifty
members at twenty-five cents each, $12 50 cents.

This sum, twelve dollars and fifty cents, to be added to the ten dollars
contributed from the treasury, footing up a total of twenty-two dollars and
fifty cents, $22 50 cents.

Now the sum $22 50 cents thus raised by each Association, be enclosed in
an envelop giving on a slip of paper therein enclosed the amount contributed,
and name of the Association or Society contributing it, and forward the same
to the chairman of said Central Executive Committee, taking a proper receipt
therefor.

The facts being given now for the figures:
Forty-two Associations or Societies at $10 each . . . $420 00
Fifty member of any one Association or
      Society paying 25 cents each 12 50
Forty two Associations or Societies paying
      $12 50 each 525 00
Making a grand total as follows: Forty-two
      Associations or Societies each
      contributing $22 50 as before stated $945 00

I would also suggest that the Pastors of each and every colored Congregation, throughout the city, would take immediate steps to take up collec-
tions for this good object and forward the amount thus collected to the
Chairman of the Central Executive Committee of the Friends of Universal Suffrage, giving the names of Congregations contributing and amounts forwarded;
and I truly believe that all concerned will get due credit for what they may
accomplish as herein proposed.

I hope that the facts and figures herein given will go to prove with
what little trouble we may be of real use to our real friends and co-labor
in the cause of "equal human rights."

Very respectfully,
RICHARD C. BAYLOR.

New Orleans Daily Tribune, September 15, 1865.

7. THE LABOR QUESTION

The following letter, addressed by our friend S. Seiler to Major Gen. C. Schurz, will be read with interest. The division of the lands is the only means by which a new, industrious and loyal population may be made to settle in the South. Large estates will always be in the hands of an aristocracy. Small estates are the real element of democracy.

Mr. Seiler considers the question from a twofold stand-point. For us, we will be permitted to let aside, for the present, the question of foreign emigration. We must, first of all, begin our good work at home. There is a large population of freedmen that has to settle on the divided lands. We have also to bring on our field of labor the numerous refugees and soldiers who suffered and fought for the cause of freedom. Those are the men who have the first and unquestionable right to receive a part of the abandoned lands. The future will achieve the work.

We see with satisfaction that Gen Howard's policy is favorable to the division of the lands. It is the first step in a good direction. The high importance of that question gives more than a common interest to M. Seiler's letter.

To C. Schurz, Maj. Gen. U. S. V. Commissioner to the South.

General, different essays published by Louisiana planters during the last two years, but especially an article from the N.Y. copperhead World 'on labor in the restored States,' reproduced by our copperhead organ, the Times, of the 13th inst., pleasantly inviting all planters to form joint stock companies, induce ine to suggest in the Tribune, the features of another plan.

Next to Universal Suffrage, the grand issue in Congress will be the partition of rebel property. Insist, upon dividing, at once, all large real estates, confiscated, abandoned, or still in the hands of traitors, into lots suitable for small families. Provide first for the million freedmen available for agricultural purposes in the fourteen rebel States; then encourage foreign immigration. Establish at Mentz, Hamburg, and London, Central Immigration Bureaus, and declare Charleston and New Orleans, in spite of the jealousy of New York, as two great entrepois for immigrants, by converting the magnificent Judah-Touro-A-yium on the left bank of the Mississippi, at the latter place into a Southern Castle [illegible], where new comers from all nations may find shelter and protection on their arrival.

Thus, you will not only attract loyal labor to the South, but save many lives which are cost by compelling laborers from the old world to reach via New York their friend-along the Ohio, Mississippi, and Missouri.

Respectfully yours,
SEBASTIAN SEILER,
Member C. E. C.

New Orleans, 14th Sept. 1864.

New Orleans Daily Tribune, September 15, 1865.

8. AN APPEAL TO THE COLORED COTTON WEIGHERS, COTTON PRESSMEN, GENERALLY, LEVEE STEVEDORES AND LONGSHOREMEN

Gentlemen and Friends, I beg leave to state to you that I have already made an appeal to the Benevolent Societies, and all Colored Congregations in the city, for the object hereinafter set forth; and now friends, I would respectfully appeal to you all.

I have worked with you on the Levee, in the Cotton Presses, and around the cotton scales; and as a consequence I know well what you all can do, *if you only will.*

Friends, the most of you have voted at the first trial of your ability so to do, now I call upon you to sustain your ballots. Your late vote was cast only for the purpose of choosing delegates to a Convention, which Convention met, chose and nominated a delegate who is to proceed to Washington, to lay before the Government and Congress, your wants and grievances as citizens of the "United States" and this State. This delegate you will again have to vote for (ratifying the action of the Convention) at the next general election in this State, which will be held on Monday 6th of November next. On that day, I hope you all, my friends, will go to the polls and vote like men for the chosen delegate, and after voting, let each man of you go peaceably about his business or to his home. I, for one, if living, intend to vote on that day, and I will do so quietly and coolly, if God will be my helper, which in his own promises I faithfully believe he will. I am in hope, friends, that you will all do the same and please not let the idea of a failure in this respect dwell for a moment on your minds.

Remember the "Republican party" which has been for the last thirty-five years, working in your behalf. See the result of its labors our white friends to lead the cause, for your own sake, for the good of your children, and your generations that are to come after you. I appeal to you to do what you can in raising funds to defray expenses of our delegate. Do not let it be said by those who oppose you so much, that you had the means and did not give them, and were too miserly to contribute for the good of yourselves and children. My fellow laborers, come together like men, and prove to the world that you mean to do good for your country, yourselves and your posterity.

Now, my friends, I would respectfully suggest to you all the adoption of the following plan, whereby you all may contribute the necessary means towards a "General Fund" to defray the expenses of our delegates to Washington, for the purposes herein stated.

First   To you, the levee laborers:--Form yourselves into companies of one hundred men, and choose one from among you to act as captain.

Second. After forming companies as above, let each man arm himself with "one dollar" and then all the companies meet on Claiborne street, on Sunday 29th inst., and proceed in a body to No. 49 Union street, quietly and peaceably, and each man march into the office, and deposit on a table his dollar; after doing which, quietly go to your various homes. The Secretary of the "Executive Committee of the Republican party," and other of your friends, will be there to receive your contributions.

Third. I propose that the same plan be adopted by the "Cotton Press Men," "Cotton Weighers," Stevedores and Longshoremen, on the day and date above specified to-day. Four millions of bond-men enjoying the blessings of liberty. The remainder left for us to accomplish is to prove, and show to the Government that we, as freemen, are worthy of and entitled to all the rights and privileges of men, that is to say, citizenship, in its broadest and fullest sense and meaning. I believe that I can safely say in your behalf, that *you are entitled to all the rights and privileges accorded to other citizens in the country where you are born and where you live; they are not only God given rights that we ask for, but rights that we have earned by long toils and many sufferings*. By our labors when in bondage, we have made the Southern portion of this Republic wealthy, and many of its inhabitants happy.

We have fought in three wars of our country: that of Washington, that of Jackson, and I thank God that I have lived to wear the blue and carry the musket in defense of the honor of my country during the late rebellion, and helped to open the door of Freedom to my fellow-bond-men. In these three wars we have assisted to conquer or subdue the enemies of our country. For the good of your country, you have done thus much, and though your record is honorable in that respect, yet, for yourselves and your children, you are called upon to fight another battle with the pen and the brain. To fight it, you well know that you require means to do it with, as well as in any other warfare. Friends, you have the means, and you know it. I call upon you all to contribute the means to assist and contribute your dollar as above individuals who may feel disposed to contribute more than the amount above specified, of course can do so, as the amount to be contributed by each man, is in nowise limited. Fellow citizens, do this, and God will bless you for your good work.

Friends, I beg of you to loose sight of him who thus appeals to you and your generosity,--for your own and your children's good, and look at the

object for which you contribute, steadfastly in the face, and excuse your
humble servant for annoying you so often with his name. The work in which
you are called upon to assist, is for your own good and benefit.

Respectfully,
RICHARD C. BAYLOR.

New Orleans Daily Tribune, October 22, 1865.

9. APPEAL TO SUPPORT THE UNIVERSAL SUFFRAGE PARTY

We publish on the other page an appeal to the colored working men, more
particularly to the numerous class of cotton weighers, cotton press-men,
Levee stevedores and longshoremen. This call is signed by a citizen well
known to the people for his constant and active devotion to the cause of progress. The name of Richard C. Baylor is synonimous of disinterestedness and
patriotism. The new suggestion of this good citizen is worthy of the approbation of our friends. Mr. Baylor, who has himself, worked on the Levee, and
who knows well his late fellow laborers, advises them to make a common move,
on behalf of the Central Executive Committee.

The Committee needs money to carry out the purposes of its organization;
and Mr. Baylor suggests that every colored workingman in the city should make
a donation of one dollar to the Treasury of the Universal Suffrage Party.
Most of the city laborers can afford to give the sum above mentioned, and
many of them can afford to give even more. The sacrifice will be light for
each man in particular, and the result, however, will be great, on account of
the large number of contributors.

But, although this question of material aid be unquestionably of great
consequence, we deem that the moral effect will be more important still. Mr.
Baylor calls upon the colored laborers to go and bring on their donation on
the same day, at the same time, by forming themselves in a civic procession.
He invites them to meet on Sunday next, the 29th inst., on Claiborne street,
and thence to proceed, in good order--two abreast--to the room of the Central
Executive Committee. In order to give to that mass some organization, he
suggests that companies of one hundred men or thereabout be formed, during
the week, and that these companies should fall in line on Claiborne street,
each man "armed," as Mr. Baylor says, with the "one dollar" he intends to
contribute to the success of our cause.

This would be a two fold display--display of force, and display of patriotism. We have no doubt that the people will readily cooperate in this kind
of celebration. It will be a holiday for the disfranchised. Their sole
presence on Claiborne street will show that they take an interest in their
political future. Not only the laborers will be there, but all the citizens
who actively work for the advancement of the oppressed race.

New Orleans Daily Tribune, October 22, 1865.

10. NOTICE

FREEDMEN'S AID ASSOCIATION OF NEW ORLEANS

[Resolutions passed on Tuesday, 28th inst.]
   Resolved. That it is due to the honor and dignity of the State of Louisiana to encourage, reward and elevate labor, as the only safeguard for the

lives, liberties and happiness of her inhabitants.

Resolved. That in the opinion of this Association labor is or should be free; and that any attempt to control the inhabitants of this State, and particularly the freedmen, by legislation or otherwise, through contracts spre spreading over many months, is deprecated by this Association.

Resolved. That in the opinion of this Association it is wise on the part of the freedmen of this State, at the present time, to make short contracts with their employers and insist upon regular weekly cash payments of their wages.

New Orleans Daily Tribune, December 12, 1865.

11. SHORT CONTRACTS

It is clear, therefore, that the laborer must not alienate his freedom, for any term of months. The only means for him to escape the injustice and exactions of a bad master, is to remain free to leave the plantation and go elsewhere. This is the only way to teach the employers how they have to treat their employees. It is the condition of most of the laborers throughout the civilized world; and this kind of freedom is more essential in a State directly emerging from the de-potism of slavery than it would be anywhere else.

The laborer has nothing to lose by making short contracts or no written contract at all, but working by the week or by the day. On the contrary, by doing so he preserves his freedom. We now assert that the planter will neither be the loser.

It is freely and voluntarily that a free man has to work. Compulsion is nothing short of disguised slavery. And when the planters speak of sheriffs and soldiers to keep their laborers, when they speak of retaining their wages, of pursuing them on the roads, bringing them back in chains, and putting them to work "without compensation," we cannot refrain from telling them that they take the wrong end of the horn.

New Orleans Daily Tribune, December 12, 1865.

12. THE EIGHT HOUR SYSTEM [58]

Our readers are probably aware that a meeting of workingmen was held on Wednesday evening, at the St. Charles Opera House, in regard of the "eight hours system." This great move has been fairly and fully inaugurated throughout the North and the Great West, and ought to find its way into the Southern States. We believe it to be a move in the right direction, as upon the broad platform of Republicanism it is intended to harmonize the two classes of laborers. The white laborer and the black laborer, whose interests are one and the same, will thus be brought together, and the prejudices of caste will eventually die away. The laborer is the bone and sinew of the land, and it is right that he should have time to cultivate his mind and prepare himself for the duties of citizenship.

New Orleans Daily Tribune, December 17, 1865.

13. A TYPICAL LABOR CONTRACT

State of South Carolina
District of Beaufort

Articles of agreement made and entered this twenty Sixth day of March 1866
and between *Wm. Henry Heyward* and the Freedmen and women whose names are
herewith attached.

I. The said Freedmen and Women agree to have their time and labor on the
plantations of the said Wm. Henry Heyward from this date of signing this
agreement to the first day of January 1867. They agree to conduct themselves
honestly and civilly, to perform diligently and faithfully, all such labor on
said plantation as may be connected with and necessary for, the raising, har-
vesting, and protecting of the crop. The said freedmen further agree not to
invite visitors upon the premises, or absent themselves from the same, during
working hours, without the consent of the employer or his agent.
II. The said freedmen agree to perform reasonable daily tasks on said plantation, and in all cases when such tasks cannot be assigned, they agree to
labor diligently, ten hours per day, unless the weather be such as to actually forbid labor, or the employer or his agent excuse them from work. In either case, no deduction for loss of time shall be made.
III. For every days labor lost by absence.
                              (refusal)

The National Archives.

14. CONSTITUTION OF THE COMMERCIAL ASSOCIATION OF THE
LABORERS OF LOUISIANA

SECT. 1. The officers of the Association are: A President, a Vice President, a Treasurer and three Inspectors. These officers will from the Board
of Managers. They will be elected for one year from the 1st of January, 1866,
by a plurality of the members present at the meeting.
SECT. 2. The Board of Managers will make all by-laws and regulations
which will be necessitated in order to secure the success and good administration of the several shops under their care, such by-laws and regulations
to be dictated by a spirit of justice and equity. They shall report, every
quarter, about the situation of the work, from the stand point of the practical operations as well as from that of the social progress. The President,
when prevented from attending to his duties, will cause the Vice-President,
or any other member of the Board, to fill his place.
SECT.3--The Treasurer shall keep the books in a clear and correct manner.
He shall be responsible for all money entrusted to his care and for all mistakes he may make. He will have to give security to an amount double of the
money kept in his hands.
SECT. 4.--All persons, without discrimination of nationality, origin or
color, may become members of the Association, by giving in their adhesion to
the present deed.
SECT. 5.--The Association intends first to organize a Bakery, and then to
extend their operations as fast as the capital will accumulate.
SECT. 6.--The initiation fee will be $5, till the first declaration of
dividend. Afterward such fee will be raised by adding to it twice the amount
of the dividend paid to each member, in accordance with sect. 7. The initiation fee will, in that way, be, at all time, equal to the amount of capital
forming each and every share; and such addition will be made at each time
that a new dividend will be declared. In case that the investments made prior
to the 1st of January 1866 be deemed insufficient, the Board of Managers may
authorize the members present to lend to the Association the amount needed to

immediately organize the first shop, said loan, however, not to exceed the
sum needed to make up a capital of ten thousand dollars, and said loan to be
made voluntarily, and to be reimbursed as fast as new members come in. The
interest on said loan will be the legal interest, and the Association will be
security for it.

SECT. 7.--Every six months one third of the net proceeds of the Bakery
or any other shop is to be divided among the members. The balance, making
two-thirds of said proceeds, will be devoted to the getting up of other workshops or business places, such as groceries, butcher-shops, stores, etc. To
have a right to share in the profits it will be necessary to have been a member of the Association for at least six months.--Full weight and good measure
will in all classes be one of the benefit to derive from our system, and all
products will be of first rate or quality.

SECT. 8.--No limitation is fixed to the existence of the Association.
One third of the members will have power to prevent its dissolution, and will
be sufficient to continue the Association itself.

SECT. 9.--By-laws will be made, according to the operations exigencies.
The Constitution may be amended annually, at the General Meeting which will
be held on the first Sunday in January, provided that the amendments be offered by two-thirds of the members present. Moreover said Constitution will
be posted on in the room of meeting, and printed in the form of hand-ills--at
least one thousand copies.

New Orleans Daily Tribune, December 24, 1865.

15. LABOR NOTES

The Charleston *South Carolinian* chronicles a new phenomenon in that city,
namely, a demand by the blacks for higher wages.

Chicago Workingman's Advocate, April 28, 1866.

16. TO THE EDITOR OF THE WORKINGMAN'S ADVOCATE [59]

As you have frequently notified your readers that you are not responsible for the opinion of your correspondents, I take the liberty of using your
columns (with your permission) to discuss a question of which, in my opinion,
is assuming too much importance. The subject I allude to is
NEGRO LABOR.
In time gone by the subject of negro slavery served to agitate the public mind, and furnished the key to second rate politicians, designing knaves
and ambitious fools, whereby they unlocked the popular heart and elevated
themselves to place and power. The result of their suicidal policy and political machinations was a bloody and fratricidal war, in which over half a
million of the best blood of America was slain or mutilated, and a debt of
$3,000,000,000 entailed upon the American people, for which the LABOR of the
republic is *mortgaged to the bondholders,* and the *interest of which the child
yet unborn, will have to pay without liquidating the smallest particle of the
principal.*
Now that slavery is abolished that fruitful source of agitation has become extinct, and in its place that ghastly shadow of negro labor is looming
up in the distance. To those who are satisfied with a glance at the surface
of things, negro labor may have a terrible significance, and it may scare the

timid into the contemplation of some terrible things against this unfortunate
race. But I cannot see what direful consequences are to result from free negro labor. By emancipation the *relation* only of the slave to the master was
changed and NOT THE NATURE of the negro; the masters of the negro remains the
same whether in the condition of freedom or slavery.

I take it as an incontestible truth that the Caucasian, mentally considered, is the superior race; and, though the negro may be more muscular,
yet the former is capable of the greater endurance, and, therefore, for all
practical purposes--mentally and physically--the superior of the latter. It
is safe then to conclude that in the mechanic or fine arts, there is nothing
to fear from negro labor or competition.

Previous to the consumation of emancipation there was full employment
for this class of labor south, and there can exist no reasonable doubt, in a
rational mind, but that if things were restored to a healthy condition in the
south, this class of labor or so much of it as would be dispensed to labor,
would be fully absorbed, thereby not only diminishing but practically destroying the probability of negro labor competition south of Mason and Dixon's
line.

But by far the most important feature in the consideration of this matter as the probable existence of the negro race on this continent. The negro
is naturally improvident, he is lacking in parental affection and that care
which is a prerequisite to the preservation of a race is not a quality of his
nature; hence, is a condition of freedom, being self dependent, he must doci-
mate. In their condition of slavery there was an interest, and a great interest too, in preserving the race and in bringing it to as high a state of
perfection as was possible, and under such a regime, and the accessions made
to it by the slave trade, the negro population of the south increased, while
that of the north decreased. But now things are changed; the negro is no
longer a slave; the relation between master and slave is destroyed. The incentives to the care and preservation of the race by the Caucasian south no
longer exists; the place of the negro can be supplied by the German and
Irish emigrant, and the necessity for negro labor will with time pass away.
Thus the negro, naturally improvident and indolent, will be reduced to pauperism, and the extinction of the race becomes a question of time and not of
fact.

It is true this will not take place in a day, a month, nor a year; but
every decade of time, as it rolls around, will make it, to those who choose
to observe it, more perceptable, and the unfortunate negro, like the poor
Indian, will have to move out of the path of the over-conquering Caucasian.
Why then should the white man fear his competition? To do so is a weakness
incompatible with his nature. Leave the negro to work out his own salvation,
extending to him all rights and privileges to which his nature, relation, and
condition entitles him. Let us study and understand ourselves, and closely
scrutinize the motives of men, particularly political leaders and demagogues,
and the ghost of negro competition need no longer haunt the mind of the white
workingman.

Veritas, Baltimore

Workingman's Advocate, April 25, 1868.

17. FROM LOUISIANA

The election in the city and state is over, and has proved to be more
favorable to the city than state, and the democrats have elected over two-
thirds of their candidates, viz; eleven representatives, two sheriffs, district attorney, five assessors, five judges (out of six), all the clerks,
three state tax collectors, mayor, comptroller, street commissioner, and over
two-thirds of the city councilmen. A majority of over 500 in the city, were
cast against the (famous) constitution, and we may be sure that at least

one-quarter of the colored population voted against it, although the partial
returns from the interior gives a majority for it of from 10,000 to 12,000,
so that we may look upon that instrument as soon to become the law of the
state.   However, full official returns have not yet been recorded or published, and an order from the commanding general was issued yesterday, ap-
pointing a new committee of tellers in order to count the votes over if needed, or to discover the frauds, if any. Mr. Warmothe (the negro worshipper)
will be our next governor by a majority of 10,000 votes over Mr. Taliferro,
with the whole negro carpet-baggers for state officers. [60]
     By the results of the election, as far as known, New Orleans is to be
found in a rather gloomy mood, and our people look as though they were doomed
to a reign of ruin, many of the negroes are, and will continue, suffering
from its results, and from voting the ticket of Distructiveness, Warmoth &
Co.   They are now being discharged in great multiples by those who have heretofore given them employment, which will cause them to work on the plantations or farms as heretofore, thus opening the way and giving inducements for
white labor.   Negroes who openly declare themselves the enemies of their employers, can expect no favors here in future, and must look to the carpet-
baggers for work and support; and this sentiment pervades the whole city.
They will soon learn who their friends are.
     The order and talk of the day is, at present, the scene of impeachment,
which may result in a war of races, and a war between them would be much
worse than any of the revolutions or insurrections known heretofore.
                                             P. J. K.

Workingman's Advocate, May 9, 1868.

18.   BLACK SHIP-BUILDERS IN NORTH CAROLINA

     The colored mechanics when employed command the usual wages paid, al-
though in the days of slavery no colored man according to the law, could act
as master workman upon a job, but must always be subordinate to the white man;
yet the freed mechanics are now constantly taking work upon their own responsibility and doing it to the satisfaction of their employers.   One of the most
interesting sights which it was my good fortune to witness while in the state
of North Carolina was the building of a steamboat on the Cape Fear River by a
colored ship-builder with his gang of colored workmen. [61]

*John M. Langston, Bureau of Refugees, Freedmen, and Abandoned Land, July,
1868, pp. 108-09.*

19.   A LOUISIANA CORRESPONDENT'S VIEW OF RADICAL RECONSTRUCTION

     Over this land the evils of anarchy have hovered, and never suffered more
than it at present endures under the rule of the carpet-baggers and their new-
made voters, who are worse than a nuisance to all good citizens, even to many
who have hitherto been followers of the Radical party.   It is now apparent to
all that the tribe of carpet-baggers only work for themselves, by stealing,
and that they have robbed the people of this state alone of many millions of
dollars; and that the plundering horde is fastened upon an outraged people, and
maintained by a galling military despotism, unparalleled in the history of
the civilized world.   Hence, it is not wonderful that our oppressed people
should look forward with hope to the election of Seymour and Blair for

deliverance. The demonstration of last Saturday, in which 20,000 voters marched in procession, carrying thousands of torches and calcium lights, amid the blaze of rockets, Roman candles, &c., was a scene to be remembered. [62]

The WORKINGMAN'S ADVOCATE has often written of the corruption of our Congress, but to witness bare-faced corruption and unblushing villainy, you should observe the shameless transactions carried on in our legislative halls.

White and black children shall go to the same school, and if white parents refuse to "mix" their children, school Superintendent Conway will take them from their homes and incarcerate them in a prison, called an asylum to be indoctrinate with Radical doctrines--Radicial "religion." I, for my part, have the happiness to be the father of a family; and feel the degradation inflicted upon us by this horde of adventurers, who, while they do much in the way of bleaching the incoming generation, have no intention of remaining long enough to hear their dusky offsprings call them father.

P. J. K.

The Workingman's Advocate, September 12, 1868.

20. THE NEED FOR A SECOND EMANCIPATION PROCLAMATION

Whatever our opinions may be as to immediate causes of the war, we can all agree that human slavery (property in man) was the first great cause; and from the day that the first gun was fired, it was my earnest hope that the war might not end until slavery ended it. No man in America rejoiced more than I at the downfall of Negro slavery. But when the shackles fell from the limbs of those four millions of blacks, it did not make them *free* men; it simply transferred them from one condition of slavery to another; it placed them upon the platform of the white working men, and made all slaves together. I do not mean that freeing the Negro enslaved the white; I mean that we were slaves before; always have been, and that the abolition of the right of property in man added four millions of black slaves to the white slaves of the country. We are now all one family of slaves together, and the labor reform movement is a second emancipation proclamation. [63]

James C. Sylvis, The Life, Speeches, Labors and Essays of William H. Sylvis (Philadelphia, 1872), p. 82.

21. TWO LETTERS FROM THE SOUTH BY WILLIAM H. SYLVIS

Augusta, Ga., Feb. 19, 1869

We have not said anything yet about the state of the South, socially and politically. We think it best not to until we have gone over the whole South, and from the people get their views, learn their wants, and see Southern life in all its phases. We are keeping our eyes and ears both open, and we are conversing with men in all the walks of life, white and black, and we promise the readers of the *Advocate* that, when we have gone over the country and made a thorough examination of everything, we will give them a *true* account of things here as we see them, and our opinions of the situation. The National Labor Union is but little known in this country, but everybody we come in contact with is delighted with it. Careful management, and a vigorous campaign, will unite the whole laboring population of the South, white and black, upon our platform. The people down here will be a unit on the great money

question, because everybody is poor, and ours is a war of poverty against a
moneyed aristocracy.

Mobil, March 8, 1869

. . . During our stay in Montgomery, friend Casey remained with us, and
took all pains to show us the sights. We visited the court-house, where, for
the first time, we saw a "mixed" jury, nine blacks and three whites; from the
verdict rendered, we concluded it was a "mixed" jury. The case on hand was
that of a villanous-looking loafer, charged with arson. He keeps the lowest
kind of a negro dance-house, where he dispenses bad whiskey and other refreshments. There was no doubt as to his guilt, but he belonged to the right side,
and was acquitted. The judge failed to make the jury comprehend the meaning
of "arson," or of circumstantial evidence. This is the way justice is dispensed in this part of the world. The readers of the *Advocate* have often
heard of what are known in the South as "carpet-baggers." There are many bad
stories told of these men that are not true. Many of them are good men, and
are esteemed and respected by all the people here; but there are many bad
ones. We met two of them in Montgomery; one of them, a fellow by the name of
Barber, from Saratoga, N. Y., is sheriff of Montgomery County. He is a man
without brains, education, or character. He is a common drunkard, and his
looks stamp him as a common blackguard, and excludes him from all respectable
society. The other is John C. Keffer, from Philadelphia, Pa., who is Commissioner of Internal Improvements, a man that could not get a position as engineer of a train of night-cars at home. He came down here a practical adventurer, destitute of brains, honor, or honesty, and by worshipping his
superiors--negroes--he obtained position. He has a family of daughters, who
entertain young negro gentlemen in their parlors. It is just such low scoun-
drels as this Barber and Keffer, that has been the cause of so much bad feeling between the two sections of our common country; and one of the very best
evidences to be found, that there is no such organization as the Ku-Klux
Klan, and that the people are orderly and well disposed, having patience,
charity, and sincerity, desiring peace and harmony, is the fact that such
scamps are permitted to live here unmolested.

*James C. Sylvis, The Life, Speeches and Essays of William H. Sylvis (Philadel-
phia, 1872), pp. 339-40, 345-46.*

22.   COOPERATION AMONG THE FREEDMEN

Cooperative farming in England is no longer an experiment. In various
localities it has been successfully tried, and found to work to the mutual
advantage of all concerned. We printed not long since, as our readers will
remember, some account of two of these English Cooperative farms, from the
London *Social Economist*. We commended the subject to the careful consideration of capitalists here, who are interested in promoting the welfare of the
freed people of the South. The desire of the freedmen for land is equalled
only by their desire for education. They should have been provided with home-
steads from the confiscated estates of the rebels, their former slave-masters.
The day for this, however, Congress has allowed to pass. The next best thing
is undoubtedly cooperation, the union of small sums of money, and of laborers,
for the purchase and cultivation of land.

We are glad to see that so competent and intelligent a man as WILLIAM
CRAFT, whose history is well known to our readers, is already at work to inaugurate a movement for practical cooperative farming among the freed people
of the South. He thoroughly understands the peculiarities and the needs of
the freedmen, and he is familiar, by his long residence in England, with cooperative farming as it exists there. We doubt not that the movement he
seeks to inaugurate in the South will accomplish great good, not only in a

material point of view, but as an educational help, and a corrective of the
lingering evils of slavery. We find the following in the *Manchester* (Eng.)
Examiner of April 22d:

"Mr. William Craft, a negro, is at present in this country, endeavoring
to raise a fund for the purchase and stocking of a cooperative farm in the
United States, with a view to the employment of the freedmen. The *New-castle
Chronicle* says Mr. Craft proposes to raise a capital of 1,500 by subscription, with which he will proceed to one of the Southern States, secure a suitable tract of land, probably on lease, purchase all the necessary implements,
and make advances to the people employed on the estate until they understand
the system. He believes that the undertaking may be made self-supporting in
a year or two. It is not too much to expect that the greater part of the
freedmen who possess a little money will be most anxious to join in the
scheme, and that associated labor on the land, combined with cooperation in
the purchase and distribution of the ordinary necessaries of life, will take
root in the Far West on a most extensive scale. It must be borne in mind
that the cooperative movement is not merely productive of material benefit;
it is also a great educational agency, and, under this aspect, promises to
confer inestimable benefits upon the population on whose behalf Mr. Craft is
exerting himself. No man living, perhaps, is better fitted for the conduct of
this philanthropic enterprise than he who has undertaken it. The past history
of Mr. Craft points him out as the man specially adapted for the successful
execution of the project. Throughout his interesting and romantic career,
from the epoch of his perilous excape from slavery to his daring mission to
the King of Dahomey, he has given the most abundant proofs of ability, energy,
and integrity. To those who are unacquainted with Mr. Craft, and who lack
the materials from which to form a judgment of the merits of his plan, it may
be some assurance to know that amongst its active supporters and promoters
are Mr. W. E. Forster, M. P., Mr. T. Hughes, M. P., and the executive committee of the National Freedmen's Aid Union of Great Britain and Ireland. The
latter body has passed a resolution expressing its warm approval of the design, and its conviction that Mr. Craft is qualified, by his intelligence,
aptitude, and integrity, to prosecute it to a triumphant issue. [64]

National Anti-Slavery Standard, May 15, 1869.

LABOR DISCONTENT IN THE SOUTH

23. REGULATIONS FOR FREEDMEN IN LOUISIANA, 1865

Whereas is was formerly made the duty of the police jury to make suitable
regulations for the police of slaves within the limits of the parish; and
whereas slaves have become emancipated by the action of the ruling powers;
and whereas it is necessary for public order, as well as for the comfort and
correct deportment of said freedmen, that suitable regulations should be established for their government in their changed condition, the following or-
dinances are adopted with the approval of the United States military authorities commanding in said parish, viz:

Sec. 1. *Be it ordained by the police jury of the parish of St. Landry,*
That no negro shall be allowed to pass within the limits of said parish without special permit in writing from his employer. Whoever shall violate this
provision shall pay a fine of two dollars and fifty cents, or in default
thereof shall be forced to work four days on the public road, or suffer corporeal punishment as provided hereinafter.

Sec. 2. . . Every negro who shall be found absent from the residence of
his employer after ten o'clock at night, without a written permit from his

employer, shall pay a fine of five dollars, or in default thereof, shall be compelled to work five days on the public road, or suffer corporel punishment as hereinafter provided.

Sec. 3. . . No negro shall be permitted to rent or keep a house within said parish. Any negro violating this provision shall be immeidately ejected and compelled to find an employer; and any person who shall rent, or give the use of any house to any negro, in violation of this section, shall pay a fine of five dollars for each offence.

Sec. 4. . . Every negro is required to be in the regular service of some white person, or former owner, who shall be held responsible for the conduct of said negro. But said employer or former owner may permit said negro to hire his own time by special permission in writing, which permission shall not extend over seven days at any one time. Any negro violating the provisions of this section shall be fined five dollars for each offence, or in default of the payment thereof shall be forced to work five days on the public road, or suffer corporeal punishment as hereinafter provided.

Sec. 5. . . No public meetings or congregations of negroes shall be allowed within said parish after sunset; but such public meetings and congregations may be held between the hours of sunrise and sunset, by the special permission in writing of the captain of patrol, within whose beat such meetings shall take place. This prohibition, however, is not to prevent negroes from attending the usual church services, conducted by white ministers and priests. Every negro violating the provisions of this section shall pay a fine of five dollars, or in default thereof shall be compelled to work five days on the public road, or suffer corporeal punishment as hereinafter provided.

Sec. 6. . . No negro shall be permitted to preach, exhort, or otherwise declaim to congregations of colored people, without a special permission in writing from the president of the policy jury. Any negro violating the provisions of this section shall pay a fine of ten dollars, or in default shall be forced to work ten days on the public road, or suffer corporeal punishment as hereinafter provided.

Senate Executive Document, no. 2, 39th Cong., 1st sess., p. 93.

24. RESOLUTIONS OF THE FREEDMEN'S AID ASSOCIATION
OF NEW ORLEANS

Our readers will find below the resolutions adopted by the Freedmen's Aid Association, at their last meeting, on Tuesday night. These resolutions bear on the labor question, and express the sense of the Association on that subject. They are worthy of being well considered. We will have to call attention upon that very point at an early day.

FREEDMEN'S AID ASSOCIATION OF NEW ORLEANS.
[Resolutions passed on Tuesday, 28th inst.]

Resolved, That it is due to the honor and dignity of the State of Louisiana to encourage, reward and elevate labor, as the only safeguard for the lives, liberties and happiness of her inhabitants.

Resolved, That in the opinion of this Association labor is or should be free; and that any attempt to control the inhabitants of this State, and particularly the freedmen, by legislation or otherwise, through contracts spreading over many months, is deprecated by this Association.

Resolved, That in the opinion of this Association it is wise on the part of the freedmen of this State, at the present time, to make short contracts with their employers and insist upon regular weekly cash payments of their wages.

New Orleans Daily Tribune, Novenber 30, 1865.

25. WHITELAW REID WITNESSES A PLANTATION "STRIKE"

On one of the "best-stocked" plantations that I visited in Louisiana, I witnessed, in March, a "strike" of the entire force. It was a curious illustration, at once of the suspicions and the docility of the blacks.

The negroes had been hired by a Southern agent, who had formerly acted as factor for the plantation. These gentlemen are never likely to fail in magnifying their offices; and in this particular case it happened that the agent left very distinctly upon the minds of the negroes the impression that he was hiring them on his own account. When, therefore, a month or two later, the proprietor went out and assumed charge, they became suspicious that there was something wrong. If they had hired themselves to the old factor, they didn't see why this new man was ordering them around, unless, indeed, he had bought them of the factor, which looked to them too much like the old order of things. Not one word of this, however, reached the ears of the proprietor. Before him all was respectful obedience and industry.

It happened that some little difficulty occurred in procuring the large amount of fractional currency needed to pay them off, and pay-day came and passed before it was obtained. The negroes had never mentioned payment to the proprietor. He asked the overseer, who replied that probably they would never know it was the beginning of a new month, unless he told them, and that therefore it was best to say nothing about the payment till the money came up from New Orleans.

One afternoon, a day or two later, the proprietor spent in the field with the laborers. Riding up among the plow-gang, he dismounted, talked with the plowmen about the best way of working, took hold of one of the plows himself, and plowed for some little distance. Everybody seemed cheerful. Going over to the trash-gang, he found there the same state of feeling; and after mingling with them till nearly sun-down, he returned to the house without the remotest suspicion of any latent discontent; or, indeed, as he said afterward, without having himself once thought of the deferred payment.

Next morning the overseer came dashing up to the house, before breakfast, with the alarming news that "the hands were on a strike; declared that they didn't hire with the man who was now on the plantation, that he hadn't paid them, and they wouldn't work for him." Not one, he said, would leave the quarters; and they were complaining and plotting among themselves at a great rate. The proprietor took the matter coolly, and acted on a shrewd estimate of human nature. Fortunately for him, the house was, in this case, some distance from the quarters. Directing the overseer to hurry off to the Freedman's Bureau and bring down the agent, he quietly resumed his easy chair and newspaper. The mules had all been taken from the plowmen as soon as they refused to work, and brought up to the house. They could not go to work, therefore, without asking permission.

The negroes expected to see the proprietor down at the quarters the moment he heard of their action. He had peremptorily refused to give them an acre of land apiece, to plant in cotton; and their plan was to refuse now to work till he promised them this land, and satisfied them about the payments. But hour after hour passed, and no proprietor was seen. Growing uneasy, they sent out scouts, who speedily returned with the news that he was reading his paper on the front gallery, just as if nothing had happened. Manifestly, he was not alarmed, which greatly disappointed them; and was waiting for something or somebody, which might be cause of alarm to *them*. In short, instead of being masters of the situation, they were suddenly eager to get out of a scrape, the outlet from which began to look very uncertain. By-and-by, they sent the plow-driver up to the house to ask if they could have the mules again. The proprietor told him "not just at present," and added that after a while he should go down to the quarters. Meantime no person must on any account go to work.

About twelve o'clock the overseer returned with the agent of the Freedman's Bureau, a one-armed soldier from the Army of the Potomac. They rode down to the quarters where the whole force was gathered, uneasily watching for developments. He asked what was the matter.

"We;s not been paid di's monf."

"Did you ask for your pay?"

"N-n-no, sah."

"Did you make any inquiry whatever about it, to find out why you weren't paid?"

"N-n-no, sah."

"Didn't you have plenty of chance to ask? Wasn't Mr.-----out among you all yesterday afternoon? Why didn't you ask him whether it wasn't time for your payment?"

"Well, sah, we dono Missah-----; we hired ou'selves to Missah-----, (naming the New Orleans factor,) and we's afread we git no money. We nebber heern o' dis man."

The agent read over their contract; and explained to them how, being busy, the proprietor had simply sent an agent to attend to the business for him. All professed themselves satisfied at once, save one lank, shriveled, oldish-young fellow, who said, in a very insolent way, that "He'd done been cheated las' yeah, and he wanted his money now, straight down. He was as good as any other man; but tree o' four time now dis yeah new man, wat pretended to be boss had passed him in de fiel' without ever lookin' at him, much less speakin' to him fren'ly-like; and he was'n' agoin' to stand no sich ways." The agent sharply rebuked him for such language; and finally told him that he had already broken his contract, by refusing to work without sufficient cause, and that if he gave a particle more trouble, he would arrest him for breach of contract, and throw him into jail. The rest seemed ashamed of his manner. As it subsequently appeared, he had been the leader in the whole matter. The plowmen had gone to the stable in the morning, as usual, for their mules. This fellow met them there, persuaded them that they were going to be cheated out of their money, and induced them to return to the quarters. Several of them wanted to go to work; and took good care to inform the proprietor that, "Dey didn't want to quit,. . . .

"Y-yas, sah; but may be, if you'd tink 'bout it, it'd be better for us."

"Didn't you say though that you must have an answer right off?"

"Y-yas, but"--

"*Stop!* Didn't you get your answer right off?"

"Yas, but"--

"*Stop!* You got it. Well, I always keep my word. If you had waited, I might have given a different answer; but you wouldn't wait so you got your answer; and it is all the answer your going to get."

Meantime the crowd was chuckling at the discomfiture of Berry. It didn't seem to concern them so much that they were losing their case, as it amused them to see how Berry had entrapped himself. Every time he attempted to renew the discussion, the lessee stopped him with the reminder that he had demanded an answer in Natchez, and had got it; and each time the laughter of the crowd at their own champion grew more uproarious.

Whitelaw Reid, After the War: A Tour of the Southern States 1865-1866 (New York, 1965), pp. 546-50.

26.   CHAIN-GANG FOR "IDLE NEGROES"

The Columbus (Ga.) Sun indulges in the following:

Preparations have now been completed to have a chain-gang of the idle negroes found in Columbus. All colored people, who have no visible means of support, are to have a ball and chain attached to them, and set to work at leveling the fortifications around the city, the city to feed them the while. It is the determination of both the civil and the military authorities that no idlers, who can only exist by pilfering and robbery, will be allowed to remain in the city, unless they can be forced to earn their bread. Some eight are to be put to work this morning.

New Orleans Daily Tribune, November 30, 1865.

27. THE SUBSTITUTE FOR SLAVERY

From the Cincinatti Gazette.

What is included in the Mississippi constitutional amendment that the Legislature shall make laws to guard the freedmen and the State from any evils that may arise from their sudden emancipation, may be seen by an "ordinance relative to the police, of recently emancipated negroes or freedmen within the corporate limits of the town of Opelousas," recently published in the Natchitouches (La.) *Times:*

"By this ordinance no 'negro or freedman' is permitted to visit the town without permission from his employer, under penalty of imprisonment and fine. Any 'negro or freedman' found in the streets at night after 10 o'clock without the written pass from his employer, shall suffer the same penalty. Section 3 of the ordinance enacts that "No negro or freedman shall be permitted to rent or keep a house within the limits of the town, *under any circumstances,* and any one thus offending shall be ejected and compelled to find an employer or leave the town within twenty-four hours.' Even the white lesser in such case is fined. No negro shall reside in the town unless in the regular service of a white person. No public meetings or congregations of negroes shall be held, under any circumstances, or for any purpose, without the permission of the Mayor or President of the Board.' No negro shall preach without the same permission. No freedman shall carry arms without permission. No freedman shall sell, barter or exchange any article of merchandise or traffic, without permission in writing from his employer, or the Mayor, or President of the Police. Penalties in all the foregoing cases are fine or imprisonment, or both."

When we have added to this the combination of the planters to pay no wages to the freedmen, or to pay them such wages as they see fit, and at their convenience, and to report any inhabitant who shall hire a negro without his master's permission, as was resolved upon in Virginia, we shall have slavery re-established, so far as the negro is concerned, without the obligation of support on the part of the master. Do these black regulations indicate a disposition in the late slaveholders to submit to the emancipation of the blacks? Is it strange that the loyal people of the North distrust their good faith when they see such atrocious regulations as these enacted against the only class in the South that has ever earned its subsistence by labor? How long shall common intelligence be insulted by this charge that the negroes will not work in the condition of freedom, made against them by whites who never labored, and whose first principle is to live by the unrequited toil of other men? All that is necessary to restore the labor and production of the South is common honesty on the part of the whites toward the blacks. It is a substitute for honest wages and fair dealing that these black codes are made.

National Anti-Slavery Standard, September 18, 1865.

28. BLACK WAGES

The Richmond *Republic* reports that a meeting of the farmers representing seven counties in Virginia, held to consider the question of the wages of negro labor, after due deliberation, fixed the hire of field hands at five dollars a month, the hand to clothe himself and pay his own doctor's bills; also, the sum of one dollar a day for hands in harvest was fixed upon. The *Republic* supposes this will fix the wages throughout Virginia and the South.

These wages for first class hands, subject to the usual contingencies of sickness and seasons, will prevent the liberty of the blacks from being made dangerous by riches. We suppose that if the blacks of the aforesaid counties should hold a meeting to deliberate on the subject of wages for labor, and should fix the rate without which they would not work, it would be regarded as proof that the negro would not work in a state of freedom, and that slavery was the only condition he is fit for.--*Cin. Gazette*.

National Anti-Slavery Standard, June 24, 1865.

29. NORTHERN LABORERS--ATTENTION!

New York, June 10, 1865.

To the Editor of the Standard.

RESPECTED SIR: In your issue of the 10th inst., you give, from the Richmond *Republic*, under the heading of "How the Freedman Fares," a report of a meeting of the farmers of Virginia, held at Louisa Court House, in which the following rate of prices was ordained as a proper remuneration for their workingmen:

For agricultural laborers $5 per month--the negro finding his clothing and paying his doctor's bills.

In harvest time $1 per day.

The extract closes with the following ominous words: *These prices far exceed those paid for agricultural labor in Europe and should be satisfactory to all parties.*

Thus the minimum price of agricultural labor in the United States is fixed by Virginia employers to suit themselves. Workingmen of the North, now is the time to speak out! It pertains to you to reply to this. Your wages will soon be re-adjusted on the above mentioned basis. If your Christianity permits you to stand by idly, and see your colored brethren oppressed, have a little respect for your own interest. The labor system of the country is one now, and the blow that is aimed at your brother in the South to-day, will strike you full in the breast to-morrow.   JOHN.

National Anti-Slavery Standard, June 24, 1865.

30. LETTER TO A NEW YORK EDITOR FROM A FREEDMAN

Some have withheld just compensation, or such pay as would not support the laborer and his family, while others have driven the hands away without any pay at all, or even a share of the crops they have raised. Women with families of children, whose husbands have been sold, have died, or have wrongfully deserted them, have in some cases been driven away from the homes where, under Slavery, they have spent a lifetime of hard service. Is it just or Christian thus to thrust out upon the cold world helpless families to perish?

These grosser forms of evil, we believe, will correct themselves under wise and humane legislation, but we do most respectfully and earnestly urge that some suitable measures may be adopted to prevent unscrupulous and avaricious masters from the practice of these and other similar acts of injustice and cruelty toward our people.

Our first and engrossing concern in our new relation is how we shall provide shelter and an honorable subsistence for ourselves and families. You will say, "Work." This we are willing and expect to do, but without the aid of just legislation, how shall we secure adequate compensation for our labor? If the kindly relations we so much desire shall prevail, must there not be mutual cooperation? As our longer degradation cannot add to your comfort, make us more obedient as servants, or more useful as citizens, will you not aid us by a wise and just legislation to elevate ourselves? We desire education for our children that they may be more useful in all the relations of life.

We most earnestly desire to have the disabilities under which we have formerly lived removed; to have all the oppressive laws which make unjust discriminations on account of race or color wiped from the statutes of the State. We invoke your protection for the sanctity of our family relations. Is this asking too much?

We most respectfully and urgently pray that some provision may be made for the care of the great number of orphan children, and the helpless and infirm who, by the new order of affairs, will be thrown upon the world without its protection. Also, that you will favor, by some timely and wise measures, the reunion of families which have been long broken up by war, or by the operation of Slavery.

Though associated with many memories of suffering as well as of enjoyment, we have always loved our homes, and dreaded, as the worst of evils, a forcible separation from them. Now that freedom and a new career are before us, we love this land and people more than ever before. Here we have toiled and suffered, our parents, wives and children are buried here, and in this land we will remain, unless forcibly driven away.

Finally, praying for such encouragement to our industry as the proper regulation of the hours of labor, and the providing the means of protection of our property and of our persons against rapacious and cruel employers, and for the collection of just claims, we commit our cause into your hands, invoking Heaven's choicest blessings upon your deliberations and upon the State.

New York Daily Tribune, October 7, 1865.

31. WHY FREEDMEN WON'T WORK

The following extract from the Charleston (S.C.) correspondent of the New York Tribune, who has just returned from an extensive tour through the Southern States, shows the principal reason why "the freedmen will not work." He says the stereotyped expression all through the country, South, is: "Why, yes, the nigger is needed here. We want him to work our farms. There's plenty of work if he'll only do it."

This extract, concerning his experience at Branchville, is, substantially, but a repetition of his experience at the other places where he investigated:

I stopped at Branchville two hours, and there I saw a large company of negroes, numbering probably 200, and forming a most motley, yet, to me, interesting group,—ol men and women,—young men and women, and little children.

I walked up to one whose countenance indicated a good degree of intelligence, and said, "What are all you folks doing here?" He replied, quite guardedly, "Nothing much, just goin' down the road." I said, "I am from the North and have come out to see how you folks are getting along, and what you are going to do." He said, "I reckoned you're from the North. Well, I'm goin' to Charleston to make contract. I kin do better there 'n whar I bin." I said to him, "What makes you come away from work upon an uncertainty? The city is full now of negroes, and some of them must be suffering." He answered me, "Well, I let myself to a man up in Aubeville three months ago for $12 a month. Now you'se know that's mighty little for a man and his wife and two little chil'en what can't walk, an' when I came t' settle up for Christmas he didn't give me but $22 50; said I hadn't earnt it, do' I worked hard all de time, and didn't pay me no attention to his aliens complainin'. Now, I've been called good hand, and no white man wouldn't work for tree times dat."

I thought he knew what he was doing better than I could tell him, and wondered if this story, which is hourly and daily repeated and corroberated from mouths which four trying years have proved to have been truthful, and be a lie! Perhaps the vacant wharf stores of Charleston would never have been occupied by the poor blacks if employer and employee had alike fulfilled the contracts.

344   THE BLACK WORKER I

Boston Daily Evening Voice, January 15, 1866.

32. COMPLAINT OF TOBACCO WORKERS

Dear Sirs We the Tobacco mechanicks of this city and Manchester is worked
to great disadvantages. In 1858 and 1859 our masters hiered us to the Tobacconist at a prices ranging from $150 to 180. The Tobacconist furnished us
lodging food and clothing. They gave us tasks to performe. all we made over
this task they payed us for. We worked faithful and they paid us faithful.
They Then gave us $2 to 2.50 cts, and we made double the amount we now make.
The Tobacconist held a meeting, and resolved not give more than $1.50 cts per
hundred, which is about one days work in a week we may make 600 pounds apece
with a stemer. The weeks work then at $1.50 amounts to $9--the stemers wages
is from $4 to $4.50 cents which leaves from $5 to 4.50 cents per week about
one half what we made when slaves. Now to Rent two small rooms we have to pay
from $18 to 20. We see $4.50 cents or $5 will not more then pay Rent say
nothing about food clothing medicin Doctor Bills. Tax and Co. They say we
will starve through laziness that is not so. But it is true we will starve at
our present wages. They say we will steal we can say for ourselves we had
rather work for our living. give us a chance. We are Compeled to work for
them at low wages and pay high Rents and make $5 per week and sometimes les.
And paying $18 or $20 per month Rent. It is impossible to feed ourselves and
family--starvation is Cirten unles a change is brought about.
    Tobacco Factory Mechanicks of Richmond and Manchester

*J. T. Trowbridge, A Picture of the Desolated States; and the work of restora-
tion, 1865-1868 (Hartford, 1888), pp. 230-31.*

33. THE FREEDMEN - A STRIKE EXPECTED

    We hear that a number of the freedmen at Jackson held a meeting the other
day in the Baptist Church for the purpose of regulating the price of wages,
and, if possible, to get up a strike on the part of those employed for higher
rates. The meeting was presided over by a burly darkey--who is an itinerant
vender of ice cream. A similar movement has been going on by the colored washerwomen and they have presented an address to Mayor Barrows, which we publish
below. Desiring the welfare of the colored people of Jackson, we regard this
agitation so ill-timed, unfortunate and calculated to injure instead of better
their condition. Besides, we believe it originated wi ore or two Northern
adventurers who have come here to fill their pockets a. the pense of the ignorant negro, under the pretense of philanthrophy and benevolence. Whether
one of the aforesaid adventurers presided at the conclave of washerwomen, we
are not advised, but he acted as their amanuensis, as it is said the petition
comes up in his writing. There are now twice as many negroes in Jackson as
have any regular employment. Little business is doing; it is the dull season
of the year; the wages that have been given as a general thing are liberal,
and any demand for higher rates would only end in many of those now employed,
and who have comfortable homes losing their situations. Idleness and a disposition to change from one place to another without sufficient reason, are
injuring the prospects of the freedmen more than low rates of wages, and if
the itinerant vender of ice cream and the Northern Secretary of the washerwomen's convention had liad these facts before their assemblages, they might
have done something to ameliorate the condition of their brethren. As it is,

if the matter is persisted in, some temporary inconvenience may result to the
residents of that city. It has heretofore been difficult to procure reliable
servants, no matter what the price: but in the end, their places will be supplied, and the only result will be that the already large number of black
loafers and vagrants will be increased.

Jackson (Mississippi) Daily Clarion, June 24, 1866.

34. JUNE 18, 1866 FIRST COLLECTIVE ACTION OF BLACK WOMEN WORKERS

"Petition of the Colored Washerwomen."

Jackson, Miss., June 20, 1866.

Mayor Barrows--Dear Sir:--At a meeting of the colored Washerwomen of this
city, on the evening of the 18th of June, the subject of raising the wages was
considered, and owing to many circumstances, the following preamble and resolution were unanimously adopted:
Whereas, under the influence of the present high prices of all the necessaries of life, and the attendant high rates of rent, while our wages remain
very much reduced, we, the washerwomen of the city of Jackson, State of Mississippi, thinking it impossible to live uprightly and honestly in laboring
for the present daily and monthly recompense, and hoping to meet with the support of all good citizens, join in adopting unanimously the following resolution:
Be it resolved by the washerwomen of this city and county, That on and
after the foregoing date, we join in charging a uniform rate for our labor,
that rate being an advance over the original price by the month or day the
statement of said price to be made public by printing the same, and any one belonging to the class of washerwomen, violating this, shall be liable to a fine
regulated by the class.
We do not wish in the least to charge exorbitant prices, but desire to be
able to live comfortably if possible from the fruits of our labor.
We present the matter to your Honor, and hope you will not reject it as
the condition of prices call on us to raise our wages. The prices charged are:
$1.50 per day for washing
$15.00 per month for family washing
$10.00 per month for single individuals
We ask you to consider the matter in our behalf, and should you deem it
just and right, your sanction of the movement will be gratefully received.
Yours, very truly,
THE WASHERWOMEN OF JACKSON.

Jackson (Mississippi) Daily Clarion, June 24, 1866.

35. MEETING OF PLANTERS TO REGULATE THE PRICE OF LABOR

We give below the proceedings of a meeting held by the planters of Cumberland county, Va., for the purpose of regulating the prices of labor among the
freedmen. The mere publication of these proceedings, without a word of comment, would be sufficient for the intelligent reader, and were it not said by
commenting upon them, we can thereby answer some of our contemporaries' outrageous falsehoods respecting colored laborers, we should not bear a single word

346   THE BLACK WORKER   I

to either prefer or append to this most infamous schedule of prices:

HIRING FOR NEXT YEAR.

A meeting of the citizens of Cumberland county, Va., was held at the Court-House, on November 27. The meeting was for the purpose of adopting some regulations between the farmers and the negroes. The meeting adopted resolutions expressing kind feelings toward the negroes, but asserting that up to this time, they had, too generally, been guilty of idleness, insubordination, vagrancy and theft. The following scale of prices for the ensuing year was adopted:

For men, strictly No. 1 in every respect, $6 per month.
For next class, $50 per year.
For ordinary men, $40 per year.
For boys between fifteen and twenty, from $25 to $40 per year.
For strictly No. 1 house women, cooks or washers, $60 per year.
For strictly No. 2 house women, cooks or washers, $40 per year.
For No. 3 house women and field hands, from $20 to $30 per year.
For girls from fifteen to twenty, from $10 to $30 per year.
For boys and girls under fifteen, food.

One-half the annual pay is to be paid in July—the other half in January. The men will not be allowed to converse during working hours; they will not be allowed to raise stock or fowls for their own use; they will be charged with all the property, stock, or fruit on the farm that may be lost or stolen; they will have 30 minutes for breakfast, and 45 minutes for dinner; they will be fined one dollar for each time they are impudent, or are guilty of swearing, quarreling, fighting, or wilful disobedience.

The above may be taken as a fair specimen of the prevailing ideas of justice and fair dealing among many of the planters in different sections of our own and neighboring States. We presume this action of the planters in Cumberland county, to be one link in the solution of the all-absorbing question, "Will the negro work?" Should the freedmen of said county find that, during the months of July and August, they have no clothes to wear, no money to pay doctor's bills, or to meet the thousand other incidental wants of their families, and should, in consequence thereof, express the slightest word of dissatisfaction or discontent, these self-appointed regulators of capital and labor will undoubtedly consider the great problem solved, and will exhibit to the world new and conclusive proof that the "negroes are inclined to idleness, insubordination, vagrancy and theft."

The most infamous portion of the rules laid down for the government of the colored laborers, is that relating to their *personal liberty*. They are not allowed "to converse during working hours." Even the small enjoyment of enlivening the weary hours of toil with "small talk," is denied them, and their mouths are locked in silence. The birds chatter while building their nests; the industrious bee hums while storing his hive, and a republic of busy ants hold converse with each other while laying up their winter food, but a community of human beings, endowed with reason and intellect, must transform themselves into dumb oxen, and work. Again, they will not be allowed "to raise stock or fowls for their own use." Here we have "Shylock" with a vengeance. The planter, in substance, says, "your labor is *mine,* and I will exact all, even to the last quiver of a muscle." Again we see cropping out that same disposition to discourage industry and enterprise among the freedmen. They must do nothing, be nothing, say nothing except what will profit their *masters,* alias employers. They are to be charged with everything "that may be stolen or lost;" they will be "allowed 30 minutes for breakfast and 45 minutes for dinner." "They will be fined one dollar for each time they are impudent." These are the enactments of professedly Christian planters, in a civilized land in the nineteenth century.

National Anti-Slavery Standard, February 10, 1866.

36. FREEDMEN'S BUREAU MEETING IN NORFOLK, VIRGINIA

REPORT OF AN INTERVIEW BETWEEN GENS. STEADMAN AND FULLERTON WITH THE LEADING
COLORED CITIZENS OF NORFOLK, VA., HELD AT THE COURT-ROOM OF THE FREED-
MEN'S BUREAU, CORNER FEN CHURCH AND MARSH STS., NORFOLK, VA., ON SUNDAY
AFTERNOON, APRIL 22, 1866, at 3½ O'CLOCK.

Nearly all the seats being filled and the hour having arrived, the audience was addressed by Capt. A. S. Flagg, in charge of First District R. F.
and A. L. He stated in a brief and eloquent manner the object of the meeting
to be, that Gens. Steadman and Fullerton wish to converse with the colored
freemen and get their ideas concerning the wants and necessities of the people
relative to the Freedmen's Bureau in the South, and also obtain from them
their views as to existing state of affairs here and the best way to adjust
the difficulties between the whites and blacks in the States lately in rebellion. Cap. Flagg referred to the idea entertained by some gentlemen that "the
agents of the Bureau were mere sticks of wood" and incapable of rendering any
assistance to the colored freemen.

At the close of his remarks, he enjoined that the colored people work
quietly, orderly and industriously to bring about the desired results.

Gens. Steadman and Fullerton arrived, accompanied by Gen. O. Brown, Capt.
C. E. Johnson and others, who took seats on the platform.

Cap. Flagg introduced Gens. Steadman and Fullerton. The audience receiving them by rising to their feet.

Gen. Steadman stated that his mission was to converse with them as to the
general state of feeling between the whites and blacks in this community, and
said that he was with them in an official capacity, with Gen. Fullerton as a
Commissioner, sent by President Johnson to inquire into the affairs of the
Freedmen's Bureau in the South, and to obtain information as to the benefit
derived from the Bureau by the people. He said that he could not talk to all
of them, but if they would appoint a delegation, that he would talk with them
in behalf of the people.

Accordingly, the following gentlemen were chosen said delegates, viz.:
Wm. Keiling, J. T. Wilson, J. G. Selden, A. A. Portlock, N. Barbour and James
Bryant.

Mr. Keiling--I hope the Freedmen's Bureau will not be abolished until law
and order is restored here, and to the whole country; were the government to
remove it now, while we are not recognized as men by the whites of the South,
it would be leaving us and the white Union men at the mercy of the ignorant
and still rampant rebels and enemies of the government.

Jos. G. Selden--I am a discharged seaman, and I thank God that I helped
to suppress the rebellion. I know, having been an old resident here, that the
great mass of the whites are against the blacks, and against the United States
government. The colored people are true to the government, are quiet and lawabiding, but there are *many* of them ignorant of the existence of certain laws.
The rebellious spirit is now rife against the blacks; they say that had it
not been for the blacks they would have whipped the Yankees. The rebel sympathizers and the Copperheads are bitter against both the black man and the
Union. The rebels say they hate the negroes because they were once their pro
property. They say that one Southern man is *better* than ten Yankees. One
man (a Mr. Marsden) told me the other day that he was "as good as ten Yankees
at any time." Marsden was in the rebel army during the war.

Mr. Wilson--Can we render the white loyalist any protection in the position that we are in?

Gen. Steadman--In every way, *except* as a witness. A black man cannot
(according to the civil law of Virginia) act as a witness in cases between
white men; but where either party is colored, his evidence will be taken.

Mr. Wilson--Then if we were to see a rebel shoot down a loyalist, we
could not act as a witness in such a case?

Gen. Steadman--No; you could not.

Mr. Wilson--Suppose the combatants were both colored, could a white man
act as a witness?

Gen. Steadmen--Yes, according to Virginia law; you can make the white
man a witness in your case, there is where you have the advantage of a white
man.

A. A. Portlock--I have been in the United States Navy and was honorably discharged after the war; I would like to cite you a case where a rebel is trying to rob my mother-in-law of a piece of property; it is all she owns; the case was brought up before the Virginia Civil Court, Mr. Pepper being counsel; it has been postponed, and I expect the civil authorities are waiting so that the Bureau may be abolished and the military withdrawn, then they will dispossess this poor woman of all she has.

James Nickles (late First Sergeant, Co. I, 1st U. S. C. C.)--We know that we cannot get justice at the State courts; they do not recognize that we have any rights as white men have. We must have a say as to who shall compose the courts, then we can get justice, and not *until* then.

I know that my former master (Geo. Bramble) would shot me down if he could get a chance because I went into the Union army. When I returned from the battle-field I was willing to take his hand, but he scorned me with contempt. At the breaking out of the war, my old master was a cripple; he had his leg broken. I nursed and attended to him faithfully, and I thought he would be glad to see me on my return from the war; so I went to see him, and took hold of his hand and shook it three times, but he failed to return the compliment, so I let him alone ever since. If he needs my assistance at any time, I am ready to do what I can.

Mr. Wilson--Does the government recognize the Virginia courts?

Gen. Steadman--It does. If the action of the State courts is oppressive, application can be made to the United States courts, the same as in cases between white men.

Mr. Wilson--I think if we had the exercise of the right of suffrage, it might *then* be safe to abolish the Bureau, and until we do this, we are unsafe and cannot enjoy our freedom. We are anxious to vote because it is *our right* to do so. Our forefathers exercised this right in the dark days of our country, and why cannot we in this enlightened age? We have polled our vote on the battle-field; why cannot we poll it at the ballot-box? If we are allowed the use of the bullet to *suppress* rebellion, why can we not *as intelligently* use the ballot to *keep down* rebellion?

Educate the people of the South; learn them that we have laws, that we have a country and a government, and that the laws of the government must be enforced; then remove the great barrier, inequality, and put us all on the same footing, and we will then all be respected by the whites of the South and by all men. I hope the Bureau may yet remain until this is done. I hope the military will not be removed until this question is settled.

National Anti-Slavery Standard, May 26, 1866.

37. SOUTHERN CODES FOR FREEDMEN

From a statement of the laws and provisions of the reconstructed States, regarding the freedmen, called for by Congress, April 27, and recently sent to that body, we condense some of the most important facts

THE SOUTH CAROLINA APPRENTICESHIP CODE.

In the negro code of the Palmetto State, while "the statutes and regulations concerning slaves are now inapplicable to persons of color," yet it is thought necessary to declare that such persons are inadmissable to "social or political equality with white persons." They are privileged to make contracts, to sue and be sued, and to be protected under law in person and property. But an act to amend the criminal law, passed and approved December 19, declares in the first section that certain crimes specified shall be declared *felony* (which of late was punishable with death), viz.: for any person to raise an insurrection or rebellion in this State; fpr any person to furnish arms or ammunition to other persons *who are in a state of actual insurrection or rebellion,* or permit them to resort to his house for advancement of their

evil purpose; * * * for any person who had been transported under sentence,
to return to this State within the period of prohibition contained in the
sentence; or for a person to steal a horse or a mule, or cotton packed in a
bale ready for market. Another section forbids farm laborers to sell produce of any kind without written leave from the "master;" and the punishment
is for the buyer, $500 or imprisonment; for the seller, a lighter fine, $5,
or twice the value of the products; "and if that be not *immediately* paid, he
shall suffer corporeal punishment."

The section devoted to corporeal punishment is well furnished to make
flogging the rule and fining the exception. It forbids colored persons, under penalty of fine or flogging, to keep fire-arms or weapons of any kind;
to keep a distillery, or to sell liquor; to come into the State from another
State, unless he gets two freeholders to be his security for good behavior in
a bond of $1,000. Section 30 provides that upon view of a misdemeanor com-
mitted by a person of color, *any person present may arrest the offender* and
take him before a magistrate, to be dealt with as the case may require. In
case of a misdemeanor committed by a white person toward a person of color,
any person may *complain to a magistrate*.

Section 29 of the District Court act provides that indictment against
a white person for the *homicide* of a person of color shall be tried in the
Superior Court of law, and so shall other indictments in which a white person is accused of a capital felony in the same regard. Not so, however,
with "persons of color." The accused, in a colored criminal case, and the
parties in every such civil case, may be witnesses; and so may every other
person who is a competent witnesses, and in every such case, either party
may offer testimony as to his own character, or that of his adversary, or of
the third person mentioned in an indictment;" and Section 35 secures to persons of color the same rights as to whites, in regard to the distribution of
property by will.

The act to regulate the "domestic relations of persons of color" is
worthy of attention. "Colored children between the ages mentioned, who have
neither father nor mother living in the district in which they are found, or
whose parents are paupers, or unable to afford to them maintenance, or *whose
parents are not teaching them habits of industry and honesty,* or are persons
of notoriously bad character, or are vagrants, or have been, either of them,
convicted of an infamous offence, may be bound as apprentices by the district judge, or one of the magistrates, for the aforesaid term." Section 22
of this law provides that the apprentice shall be well treated in certain
useful respects, "and if there be a school within a convenient distance in
which colored children are taught, shall send him to school at least six
weeks in every year of his apprenticeship, after he shall be of the age of
ten years, provided *that the teacher of such school shall have the license of
the district judge to establish the same.*"

Section 29 provides that a mechanic, artisan or shopkeeper, or other per-
person, who is required to have a license, shall not receive any colored apprentice without having first obtained such license.

Section 35 provides that all persons of color who make contracts for
service or labor shall be known as *servants,* and those with whom they contract shall be known as *masters.*

Section 39 provides that a person of color who has no parent living in
the district, and is ten years of age, and is not an apprentice, may make a
valid contract for labor or service for one year or less.

Section 60 provides that upon the conviction of any master of larceny or
felony, the district judge shall have the right, upon the demand of any white
freeholder, to annul the contract between such convict and his colored servants. *If any white freeholder shall complain to the district judge that any
master so manages and controls his colored servants as to make them a nuisance
to the neighborhood, the judge shall order an issue to be made up and tried
before a jury,* and if such issue is found in favor of the complainant, the
district judge shall annul the contract between such master and his colored
servant or servants. It would appear that this act is obliquely directed at
the innovating Yankees.

More wonderfully made is the following section, which prescribes that no
person of color shall pursue or practice the art, trade, or business of an
artisan, mechanic, or shopkeeper, or any other trade, employment, or business

(beside that of husbandry, or that of a servant under a contract for service
or labor), on his own account and for his own benefit, or any partnership
with a white person, or as agent or servant of any person, until he shall
have *obtained a license* thereof from the Judge of the District Court, which
license shall be good for one year only. This license the judge may grant
upon petition of the applicant, and upon being satisfied of his skill and
fitness, and of his good moral character, and upon payment by the applicant
to the Clerk of the District Court of *one hundred dollars, if a shopkeeper
or peddler,* to be paid annually, and $10 if a mechanic, artisan, or to en-
gage in any other trade, also to be paid annually: Provided, however, that
upon complaint being made and proved to the District Judge of an abuse of
such license, he shall revoke the same: And provided, also, That *no person
of color shall practice any mechanical art or trade* unless he shows that he
has served an apprenticeship in such trade or art, or is now practicing such
trade or art.

GEORGIA, ALABAMA AND TEXAS.

The laws of Georgia make the average provisions in vogue as to the
right of freedmen to contract, sue, and be sued; to testify and inherit; purchase, lease, and otherwise dispose of their property, and to have full and
equal benefit of laws accordingly, without being subject to other depriva-
tions or punishments than white persons. These are contained in the Act of
March 17. An Act of Dec. 15 declares free persons of color shall be compe-
tentwitnesses in all the courts of this State, in civil cases, whereto a free
person of color is a party, and in all criminal cases wherein a free person
of color is defendant, or wherein the offence charged is a crime or misdemeanor against the person or property of a free person of color.

The law of Alabama declares that freedmen shall be competent to testify
only in open court, and only in cases in which freedmen, free negroes and
mulattoes are parties, either plaintiff or defendant, and in civil and criminal cases, for injuries in the persons and property of freedmen, free negroes and mulattoes, and in all cases, civil or criminal in which a freedman,
free negro or mulatto is a witness against a white person, or a white person
against a freedman, free negro or mulatto, the parties shall be competent
witnesses, and neither interest in the question or suit, nor marriage, shall
disqualify any witness from testifying in open court.

Section 2 of a law of Texas, passed April 2, states that "Africans and
their descendants shall not be prohibited, on account of their color or race,
from testifying orally, as witnesses in any case, civil or criminal, involving the right of, injury to, crime against, any of them in person or property, under the same rules of evidence that may be applicable to the white
race; the credibility of their testimony to be determined by the court or
jury hearing the same; and the Legislature shall have power to authorize
them to testify as witnesses in all other cases, under such regulations as
may be prescribed as to facts hereafter occurring."

FLORIDA PILLORY LAWS.

The law of Florida affecting negro testimony is much the same as the
foregoing. But an act of the 15th of January provides in the twelfth section
that it shall not be lawful for any negro, mulatto or other person of color
to own, use or keep in his possession or under his control any bowie-knife,
dirk, sword, fire-arms or ammunition of any kind, unless he first obtain a
license to do so from the Judge of Probate of the county in which he may be
a resident for the time being; and the said Judge of Probate is hereby authorized to issue such license upon the recommendation of two respectable
citizens of the county certifying to the peaceful and orderly character of
the applicant; and any negro, mulatto or other person of color so offending
shall be deemed guilty of a misdemeanor, and upon conviction shall forfeit
to the use of the informer all such fire-arms and ammunition, and in addition
thereto shall be sentenced to *stand in the pillory for one hour, or to be
whipped,* not exceeding thirty-nine stripes, or both, at the discretion of the
jury.

Section 14 provides that if any negro, mulatto, or other person of color,
shall intrude himself into any religious or other public assembly of white
persons, or into any railroad or car or other public vehicle set apart for

the exclusive accommodation of white people, he shall be deemed guilty of a misdemeanor, and, upon conviction, shall be sentenced to *stand in the pillory for one hour, or be whipped,* not exceeding thirty-nine stripes, or both, at the discretion of the jury; nor shall it be lawful for any white person to intrude himself into any religious or other public assembly of colored persons or into any railroad car or other public vehicle, set apart for the exclusive accommodation of persons of color, under the same penalties.

Section 4 provides that in addition to cases in which freedmen, free negroes and mulattoes are now, by law, competent witnesses, freedmen, free negroes or mulattoes shall be competent in civil cases, when a party or parties to the suit, either plaintiff or plaintiffs, defendant or defendants; also in cases where freedmen, free negroes and mulattoes are either plaintiff or plaintiffs, defendant or defendants, and a white person or white persons is or are the opposing party or parties, plaintiff or plaintiffs, defendant or defendants. They shall also be competent witnesses in all criminal prosecutions where the crime charged is alleged to have been committed by a white person upon or against the person or property of a freedman, free negro or mulatto; provided, that in all cases said witnesses shall be examined in open court on the stand, except, however, they may be examined before the grand jury, and shall in all cases be subject to the rules and tests of the common law as to competency and credibility.

Section 5 provides that every freedman, free negro and mulatto shall, on the second Monday of January, 1866, and annually thereafter, *have a lawful home or employment, and shall have written evidence thereof, as follows,* to wit: If living in any incorporated city, town or village, a license from the Mayor thereof, and if living outside of any incorporated city, town or village, from the member of the Board of Police of his beat, authorizing him or her to do irregular and job work, or a written contract, as provided in section 6 of this act; which licences may be revoked for cause at any time by the authority granting the same.

Section 7 provides that every civil officer shall and *every person may* arrest and carry back to his or her legal employer any freedman, free negro or mulatto who shall have quit the service of his or her employer before the expiration of his or her term of service without good cause; and said *officer and person shall be entitled to receive for arresting and carrying back every deserting employe aforesaid the sum of five dollars,* and ten cents per mile from the place of arrest to the place of delivery, and the same shall be paid by the employer and held as a set-off for so much against the wages of said deserting employe; provided, that said arrested party, after being so returned, may appeal to a justice of the peace or member of the board of police of the county, who, on notice to the alleged employer, shall try, summarily, whether said appellant is legally employed by the alleged employer, and has good cuase to quit said employer; either party shall have the right of appeal to the county court, *pending which the alleged deserter shall be remanded to the alleged employer,* or otherwise disposed of, as shall be right and just; and the decision of the county court shall be final.

National Anti-Slavery Standard, May 29, 1866.

38. AN APPEAL FOR JUSTICE

Auburn, June 3d/1866

Gen. Pope: [65]

I have to appeal to you or have injustice shown me. I contracted to stay at the Isaid Hills of this place for this year, but after staying there a while found out that I could not do the work—that what had been done by them before & went there, I told them I was disatisfied and wished to leave. They told me I could not do so—If I attempted it they would put me in jail,—

I have no husband--but one man by the name of Manuel Mitchell had been coming to see me for nearly two years. Mr Hill told me if I agreed to stay
with him this year, he would not say anything but stand between me and the
law, after I left them he has prosecuted me for living in adultery although
the man has quit coming to see me. Mr Hall says I will have to either go
to jail, pay, or go back to his house and work it out. The court is in session in oblilitra now and I understand I will have to go this week There is
no justice in it--what can I do--can you not help me..If so I would be ever
lasting grateful

Your obedient servant
Elizabeth Gleenn

*Records of the Assistant Commissioner for the State of Alabama, Bureau of
Refugees, Freedmen, and Abandoned Lands, Letters Received, 1865-1870, National Archives.*

39. WHITE AND BLACK LABOR UNITY IN NEW ORLEANS, 1865

I thought it an indication of progress when the white laborers and Negroes on the levee the other day made a strike for higher wages. They were
receiving $2.50 and $3.00 a day, and they struck for $5.00 and $7.00. They
marched up the levee in a long procession, white and black together.

*J. T. Trowbridge, The South: A Tour of its Battlefields and Ruined Cities,
etc. (Hartford, Conn., 1866), p. 405.*

40. A STRIKE IN SAVANNAH

Some time since the Common Council of Savannah, Ga., adopted a municipal
ordinance imposing a poll tax of $10 each on all stevedores and persons em-
ployed on the wharves. It does not appear that the City Fathers of Savannah
really intended to discriminate against labor. But they were driven to a
corner for money, and adopted means of raising it that were just as distasteful to the merchants and capitalists, as the ten dollar poll tax was to the
stevedores. But the latter, who are chiefly colored men, managed to resist
the impost, and refused to pay the tax. They flatly refused to work on such
terms, and for several days there was great excitement in the city. The work
of loading and unloading the cotton ships and steamers was brought to a
standstill, to the great loss of the whole community. The merchants who
suffered severely from the suspension of work on their vessels, offered to
pay the poll tax for the stevedores. But the latter manfully refused. They
felt that the tax was unjust, and opposed it to the last.
Finally, the force of public opinion being on the side of the stevedores,
the Common Council met and reconsidered and repealed the tax, and the men
promptly resumed work. We cordially congratulate our colored friends in Savannah upon their victory. This is not the first time since their emancipation, that they have resolutely asserted and vindicated their rights. The
fact is that the black man likes to be paid for his work just as well as
white men, and are rapidly learning how to secure their demands.

National Workman (New York), February 9, 1867.

41. DISCONTENT AMONG NEGRO LABORERS

For ten days or two weeks past a growing feeling of dissatisfaction and discontent has been manifested among the entire negro laboring population, including alike those engaged on the levee, those employed in saw-mills, and those who work odd jobs and day's-work generally.--That this is a combined movement is easily discerned by the manner in which the matter has been carried on. And that white men are the instigators of the trouble is equally evident from the same reason. The first public demonstration was made on Saturday, the levee laborers demanding an advance of 25¢ per hour for their services, the strenuous exertions of the police, alone preventing a very serious disturbance of the public peace. Yesterday and last night meetings were held by the leaders among the negroes, and resolutions were adopted by all of them, at the suggestion of the same white men who first incited the trouble, sustaining the strikers of Saturday and pledging themselves to stand by any of those who might become amenable to the law in the carrying out of the proceedings. This morning, Wylle Brown, a mulatto, formerly in the employ of Mr. Jewett, proprietor of a saw-mill in the lower part of the city, went to the lumber yard of Mr. Jewett, and attempted to persuade the negro hands at work there to leave, giving them to understand that nothing more was necessary to insure a large advance in their wages. Mr. Jewett, learning what was going on, went to the yard and ordered Brown from his premises, Brown refused to go, and Mr. J. had him arrested and sent to the station house, charging him with disorderly conduct in interfering with matters which did not concern him. After the news of his arrest became circulated among the other negroes, a large crowd assembled and moved up Royal street towards the city prison, evidently under excitement. The crowd, on reaching the side walk under the verandah of the building situated on the northeast corner of Royal and St. Michael streets, halted, and, after some consultation, gradually dispersed. The case of Brown came before Ald. Overall, acting Mayor, at this morning's session of the Municipal Court, and he was discharged, the officiating justice not deeming the evidence sufficient to sustain the charge made against the prisoner. The crowd, which had dispersed, as above stated, had assembled in front of the City Hotel, opposite the Mayor's Court room, and received the news of Brown's dismissal from custody with cheers and other manifestations of approbation.

We learn that after adjournment of the Court Brown was re-arrested by Officer Shelton, of the day police, but upon what charge we have been unable to ascertain. A small crowd of negroes followed the officer and his prisoner to the station-house, but made no demonstration towards his rescue.

We also learn that the negroes declare that no white men shall be employed in the work of discharging and loading steamboats until the present difficulty is arranged. The steamer Lucretia, from New Orleans, is now at her wharf laden with corn, and if, according to the ring leaders of the disaffected negroes, white men should go to work discharging her, it is feared that there will be serious trouble.

There is a rumor, for the truth of which we cannot vouch, that the Chief of Police dispatched a messenger to the Commandant of the Post requesting him to send a squad of men to the stationhouse to aid in preserving the peace, but we have not learned the result of the message.

LATER.--We are informed that a large crowd of negroes started for Broad street, where the chain-gang is employed, with the avowed intention of releasing the prisoners that were in charge of the officers of the Street Commissioner, but that the advice of the better disposed among the negroes prevailed, and the attempt was abandoned.

It is thought that the trouble is over, and that no serious disturbance will occur.

The Post Commandant has assured the Mayor that in the event of the service of the troops being required they will be promptly ordered out.

Mobile (Alabama) Register and Advertiser, April 2, 1867.

42. "A SINGULAR CASE"

During the excitement on the wharf last Saturday, growing out of the strike of the negro laborers for higher wages, Capt. Charpentier, the Chief of Police, ordered the arrest of James Watson, one of the ringleaders, who was more boisterous and turbulent than the rest. He was taken to the station-house, where he was confined for one hour, when he was released by order of Capt. Charpentier. Whereupon Watson went before a justice of the peace and sued out two warrants against the Chief of Police, one for assault and battery and the other for $1,000 damages for false imprisonment. This morning the case of alleged assault and battery was brought before Justice Mac-Donald. Six white witnesses testified that Capt. Charpentier did not touch the complainant, but stood at least six feet from him when the arrest was ordered. The negro witnesses, however, of whom there were three, testified that Capt. Charpentier put his hand upon Watson and pushed him towards the officer ordered to make the arrest. Complainant's lawyer submitted the case upon the evidence, and it was dismissed.

The case of damages for false imprisonment will come up before the City Court.

We give simply a plain statement of the facts of the remarkable affair, without comment. In fact, comment is unnecessary.

Mobile (Alabama) Register and Advertiser, April 3, 1867.

43. A DIFFICULTY BETWEEN WORKINGMEN AND A CONTRACTOR

Yesterday morning, about half past seven, a crowd of colored stevedores, numbering about five hundred, assembled on the levee to deliberate upon some difficulty which existed between themselves and certain contractors. It appears that for some time the contractors who undertake to load and unload boats have been practising a swindle upon the workmen, and the latter were determined to prevent any further such abuses. The workmen were generally paid only one half of what was justly due them by these contractors.

Under the state of excitement the working men soon seized a contractor named Moses, and attempted to lynch him, but the man was soon rescued by Sergeant Stewart, of the river police, and he was placed in the station-house for safe keeping. Considerable resistance was made and many efforts attempted to rescue him.

The contractor employed in discharging the steamer Irene was also attacked, but the swiftness of his legs put an end to the assault.

Mayor Heath, with the Chief of Police, went to the scene of tumult and made an effort to appease their riotous dispositions by addressing them a few words of advice. But, as the Mayor has lost much of the affection of the colored people, very little attention was paid to his remarks. Mr. Heath then applied to the military authorities to quell the disturbances, and a company of soldiers was soon under arms. Meanwhile the disturbers had proceeded toward Julia street, going to the New Basin for the purpose of catching some other contractor; but passing the headquarters of Gen. Mower, the rioters were advised by Gen. Mower to desist in their conduct, which they did.

After 2 o'clock P. M., peace and quiet were completely established.

New Orleans Tribune, May 18, 1867.

44. "SWEARING" MOWER

Gen. Mower, Assistant Commissioner of the Freedmen's Bureau, has earned the title of "Swearing Mower," as Gen. A. J. Smith earned a similar title during the late war.

Gen. Mower can swear at poor freedmen as readily as he can swear at rebels. "By the eternal God" is a big thing to say. Pious people, as most of the freedmen are, on hearing such language from their assistant commissioner, must have opened their eyes and exclaimed: "What sort of a man is that?" Gen. Jackson, the hero of the Battle of New Orleans, is credited with a similar stretch of speech when he was arraigning South Carolina for her secession proclivities in former days.

If Mower should have uttered this speech when he was upbraiding rebels for the crime of rebellion and treason he might have been justified with the same sort of justification which charitable patriots usually extend to our illustrious ex President.

But to have met a few freedmen who felt indignant because they had worked hard under the burning sun and then been cheated out of their earnings, and to have exclaimed (as the New York Herald dispatches give him credit for) "By the eternal God, I will throw grape and canister into you," is something calculated to excite anything but praise of our commissioner.

Had the General gone to the levee as the duties of his office required, and compelled the contractors to pay wages due to the freedmen, there would have been no need of such an excitement as occurred at the time.

But the General loves to swear, and of course it would not do to let an occasion pass without letting out a regular Jacksonian.

To do him justice, however, we must publish the Herald's dispatch as we find it. It should not be read aloud where children could hear it, for we are anxious that the rising generation should not be tainted with the evil influence which it would be likely to impart:

GEN. MOWER'S SPEECH,--General Mower addressed the rioters yesterday, when two hundred passed his headquarters on their way to the New Basin, brandi-hing clubs and threatening to lynch the contractors there, as follows: "If you feel yourselves wronged you must apply to the proper authorities for redress, and you shall have it; but if you take this thing into your own hands, you may loose what rights you already possess. If you go on with this rioting, by the eternal God I will throw grape and canister into you. Now, disperse, and go to your homes or to your work." The mob immediately dispersed.

New Orleans Tribune, May 24, 1867.

45. THE CITY WORKINGMEN

We mean the discharging of a large number of workingmen, formerly employed by the department of streets and landings.

The number is now so much reduced that the service can hardly be performed. But there is something more. The workmen are not regularly paid. They must wait for their wage for months; and inasmuch as most of them cannot afford to live without their due, they feel compelled to discount their certificates, at a ruinous percentage. We are told that brokers take as high as twenty per cent. to discount said certificates, which moreover, are generally paid in part at least, with ten and twenty dollar city bills.

Under such circumstances, there is hardly a situation in the city, worse for a journeyman than to be employed by the Street Department. True work is scarce at this time of the year, when business is at a stand-still, the city deserted on account of a long and severe epidemic, and no traffic,

no commerce, carried on for the present. But this is no reason for the city
official to take advantage of these unfortunate circumstances, so as to oppress the men in the employ of the city. There is no humanity and no dignity in such a course. The government of a large and influential city as New
Orleans should be above such petty calculations. We are certainly and emphatically in favor of economy and order. But economie should be of dollars
not of cents; and they should not bear upon poor laborers, having but their
hands to earn their daily bread. The city should be punctual to pay the
monthly wages of these men. We are perfectly satisfied that this could be
done, through some care and exertion. Why should the laborers be kept waiting? The claim of labor is the most pressing and the most sacred of all.
The laborer has a privilege on the good and property of his employer. He is
the first to be paid and satisfied in case of bankruptcy, death and depar
ture. It behooves public administration to be conducted for sound principles, we set forth a just regard and a just consideration to labor.

New Orleans Daily Tribune, November 1, 1867.

46. THE BRITISH CONSUL IN BALTIMORE REPORTS ON
PROBLEMS CREATED OVER INTEGRATED SHIP CREWS

British Consulate
Baltimore November 11, 1867

My Lord

One result of recent elections in this and neighbouring States, by which
the Democrats have gained considerable influence, has already made itself apparent in connection with the employment of colored people in the merchant-
shipping service; and I deem it my duty respectfully to call your Lordship's
attention to facts that have come within my own cognizance, and which threat-
en to interfere with the interests of British Shipping--perhaps to a greater
extent at Baltimore than in any other Port in the United States--because political feelings run very high here, and because the conduct of the Negroes
in the more Southern States, on several recent occasions, has created towards
them a hostile feeling in Maryland.

Hitherto white and colored Seamen have been shipped indiscriminately on
board the same vessel,--whereas now the Shipping Masters and the Boarding-
house Keepers have--at a period when trade is extremely dull and seamen consequently plentiful, determined not to ship a white man on board the same
vessel with a colored man, and their combined power in the matter cannot be
counteracted by any means at my command--as through their medium alone can
Seamen be obtained.

In order to illustrate the practical result of such combination, I have
the honor to submit for your Lordship's consideration a case of recent date.

The British Ship "R. B. Mulhall" arrived here a short time ago with a
mixed crew of white and colored seamen, shipped at Liverpool, Nova Scotia,
for a term of twelve months. Soon after her arrival several of the men deserted (as is invariably the case here) but one colored man and two white men
have remained by her. When she was nearly ready for sea, the Captain told me
that the Shipping Masters positively refused to ship a white crew on board
the vessel so long as the colored man remained there.

This colored man, the Captain informed me, was an excellent Seamen,
whose services he was as anxious to retain as the man was desirous to remain
by the vessel until the expiration of his term of service.

I made inquiries and found the Master's statement correct and no doubt
rests on my mind that recent political events have been a means to create this
state of affairs.

My instructions give me no authority to compel a seaman to leave a ship without just cause, and yet I felt that--the case being without a precedent, as far as I am concerned,--I should not be justified in delaying the departure of the vessel for an indefinite period. I therefore determined--if necessary--to take some responsibility on myself by discharging the colored seaman and sending him home at the Ship's expense.

Fortunately, however, I was later able to persuade him to take his discharge on payment of additional wages; and the matter was so settled.

But,--as a considerable portion of the British ships trading to this Port, arrives from Demerasa, the West Indies, & with mixed crews engaged for six or twelve months, I fear that Societies and Individuals, belonging to the opposing political party,--so soon as they learn these difficulties, will oppose amicable settlements.

Under these circumstances I would solicit your Lordship's instructions, as to the means I may be permitted to adopt if cases of a similar nature present themselves again--but where the colored Seamen insist on remaining on board the vessel until their time of service shall have expired.

I have the honor to be, with the highest respect,

> My Lord
> Yours Lordship's
> Most Obedient
> humble Servant
> Harry Ranials

As reproduced in Herbert G. Gutman, "Documents on Negro Seamen During the Reconstruction Period," Labor History, 7 (Fall, 1966):308-09.

47. BLACK STEVEDORES STRIKE IN CHARLESTON, S. C.

A STRANGE PROCEEDING.--Yesterday morning a large number of colored stevedores, who have for many years, before and since emancipation, had a monopoly of loading and unloading ships at this port, stopped work on a demand for $2.50 and $3 per day. We regret this occurrence, because it can only end in loss and injury to the parties interested.

The merchants of Charleston controlling steamers and sailing vessels have always been known as liberal in their intercourse with the working people, and in spite of all the appeals that have been made to them, even under the pressure of political excitement, have refrained from giving preference against those colored men, and we are sure that a proper representation would have resulted in a satisfactory arrangement: but when a crowd of men with badges, insist upon fixing the compensation for service, and are not very particular, so long as the workman has a "badge," whether he is strong enough to handle a box of pickles or roll an empty-truck, there seems no redress but to make other arrangements.

We understand that Messrs. JAMES ADGER & CO. are loading the steam ship *Champion* with the help of a number willing of white citizens, who are anxious to work night or day, and that the steamer will be ready for sea at the appointed time.

There is a point beyond which forbearance ceases to be a virtue.

Charleston Daily Courier, October 4, 1869.

48.   STRIKE OF THE LONGSHOREMEN

Violence and Lawlessness on Adger's Wharf--The Negroes Endeavor to Throw a
White Man Overboard.

We have already alluded to the strike of the longshoremen, which commenced several days ago, and which still continues. No one will, of course,
deny the right of a body of laborers to demand higher wages from their employers, and to refuse to work if these demands are not complied with. These
men, composed of negroes, it seems have organized a protective union, and
have struck for higher wages. We learn that they demand $2.50 per day for
laborers, and $3 per day for foremen, and that the working days be comprised
between the hours of 7 A. M. and 5 P. M. They demand, also, forty cents per
hour additional for all work done after 5 P. M. With these demands the owners and agents of vessels in port have refused to comply, and were compelled
to rely upon their crews and such white labor as they could procure.

On Monday, (yesterday morning) the agent of the New York steamer at Adger's Wharf, had a conference with the strikers; and we are informed it was
agreed that twenty men should go to work at the price demanded, but that they
should work until six o'clock.

This having been agreed upon the twenty men proceeded to work, but had
scarcely begun when a messenger arrived, and they forthwith left, without
any explanation.

The strikers now had possession of the wharf, and drove off everybody,
white and black, whom they suspected of a desire to go to work. A gentleman who was engaged at work on the steamer was bidden by them to move off.
He refused to comply, when four of the stoutest of the ruffians seized him
for the purpose of pitching him overboard, and would have carried out their
intention had they not been prevented by a number of gentlemen who were
standing by. As usual, there was no policeman near by at the time, and one
was sent for, and requested to clear the wharf. This was done, and the work
proceeded. The conduct of these negroes is unbearable, and if the ringleaders can be identified they should be punished. To refuse to work is perfectly lawful, but they have no right to assault any man, white or colored, who
is willing to work, and they should be taught the lesson.

We trust that the agents of these vessels will send North, if white or
colored labor cannot be procured here, and obtain the necessary amount of
hands. Men who would be guilty of the lawlessness that characterized the
proceedings of yesterday are unfit to be trusted, and should not be employed.
We hope that there will be a sufficient police force stationed in the vicinity of the wharves to prevent the recurrence of these unlawful acts.

Since writing the above, we learn that the gentleman whose life was
threatened can identify the parties and will have them indicted.

Charleston Daily Courier, October 5, 1869.

49.   ANOTHER LONGSHOREMEN STRIKE

Yesterday the Longshoremen, who seem to be bent upon striking at every
opportunity, were on another strike. The cause, as near as we could learn,
was as follows: Mr. G. B. STODDARD was employed as Stevedore on board the
bark *A. B. Wyman,* now being loaded for Liverpool. The fact coming to the notice of some of the shippers by the vessel who had objections to Mr. STOD-
DARD, they intimated their objections to the Captain, who thereupon discharged Mr. STODDARD. Upon this becoming known the Longshoremen struck, refused to work, and adjourned to the Military Hall, where the following resolutions were adopted:

Whereas, the shippers per the Boston bark A. B. Wyman, bound for Liverpool, have refused to ship any cotton on board of said vessel unless Captain G. G. Stoddard, Stevedore, is dismissed from loading said vessel; and whereas the shippers have declared that they make this demand on the sole ground that Captain Stoddard is a Republican, therefore

1. *Resolved,* By the Longshoremen's Protective Union of Charleston, that no member of this Union will work on board the bark A. B. Wyman, unless their brother member, Capt. G. B. Stoddard, be first restored to duty as stevedore on board of said vessel; and further, no member of this Union will aid in loading any vessel with cotton until the shippers withdraw all discrimination against longshoremen on account of their political sentiments, whether such members be Republicans or Democrats.

2. *Resolved,* That copies of these resolutions be forwarded for publication to the Boston Shipping Journal, the Boston Post, the New York Herald and Tribune, the Bath (Me.) Journal, and the papers in this city.

The strike extends along the entire wharves.

Charleston Daily Courier, October 14, 1869.

50. "THE COLORED TAILORS ON THE RAMPAGE"

Imitating the example set by the Longshoremen, the colored tailors have gotten up a strike for their own special benefit. Hurrah! we say. Let the colored workers bring more white labor to this city by their exorbitant demands. The more white men come, the better for the prosperity of the community, and white men will come when they can get better wages and cheaper living here than in the North. There are always a number of such persons out of employment in all the Northern cities, who will be glad to get permanent employment at remunerative wages, while these colored men, led on by demagogues, are deluding themselves with the idea that they are a necessity to the community. No man is a necessity to any community. The greatest of all men die, and he is missed but for a moment; but of all men, the one who is least needed is a colored tailor. If he must strike for the purpose of asserting his independence, he can do so to his heart's content. The master tailors have only to publish the fact, and their places will be supplied by others, who do not feel that a strike is a necessary part of a freeman's or freedman's existence.

We are glad to know that the master tailors have taken the same view of the question. The prices which they now offer will pay an industrious and capable man from $25 to $30 a week--wages high enough to tempt the best Northern white labor. For these prices the colored tailors were unwilling to work up to a late hour last night. If they continue to refuse what is offered, the master tailors will send an agent North at once to engage and bring out thirty-five journeymen tailors, and the colored strikers, without any work at all, may then practice their antics elsewhere.

The strike of the tailors commenced on Monday morning, since which time not a stitch of work has been done in any of the shops in the city. Last night, at nine, the word was: "The Board is still in session," said Board being the worshipful assembly of colored striking tailors in session at the Military Hall. There are tailors here who would be glad to work for the wages offered, but the strikers (following the example of the longshoremen) will not permit them.

One man who was bold enough to disregard the threats of the strikers, and worked in a shop, was set upon while the boss was at dinner, and forcibly taken away.

There are about one hundred colored tailors in this strike, and three whites.

Charleston Daily Courier, October 14, 1869.

CONDITION OF BLACK WORKERS IN THE NORTH
DURING RECONSTRUCTION

51. HOME FOR "COLORED SAILORS"

A Home for Colored Sailors has become an indispensible institution.
The colored sailor cannot be elevated without it, no more than this earth
can exist without the sun that shines. As a general thing, a man "once a
sailor is always a sailor." Thousands of our seamen enter the mercantile
marine and naval service at an early age, uneducated and unskilled in the
mechanical arts or scientific knowledge, and, therefore, have no chance of
promotion on shipboard, and no encouragement to follow the industrial pursuits of landsmen. Under these circumstances, the sailor's manhood becomes
a mere tool in the hands of evil-disposed persons.

Sailor's Magazine (March 1867):245-46.

52. CONDITION OF THE COLORED POPULATION
OF NEW YORK

THE COLORED POPULATION.

The colored population of New-York which numbered, according to the census of 1860, 12,000 persons, increased during the first years of the war,
from the arrival of contrabands and other causes, to 15,000. After the riotous uprising of the Irish against the colored people at the time of the draft,
in July, 1863, many of them left the City for fear of future ill-treatment,
and a gradual emigration has been since going on which has reduced their
numbers at the present time, according to the calculation of those among them
who have the best opportunities of judging, to something near 12,000. This
is exclusive of a floating population of seamen, ships' cooks, habitual wan-
derers, &c., amounting to 2,000 or 3,000. They are thus distributed: In the
neighborhood of Mulberry, Crosby, Chrystie, Delancey and Baxter streets,
about 1,500; in the Five Points Mission district, about 250; in Twenty-
seventh, Twenty-eighth, Twenty-ninth and Thirtieth streets, extending from
Fifth avenue to the North River, nearly 4,500; in the neighborhood of Thompson, Laurens, York, Wooster and Sullivan streets, between Bleecker and Canal
streets and from Bleecker to Eighteenth street, about 4,500; and some 1,500
scattered indiscriminately over the City. They change their residence so
frequently that it is difficult to arrive at a precise estimate of their
numbers, but this is believed among their own people to be a fair approxi-
mation.

THEIR PURSUITS.

The men are principally occupied as coachmen in private families, waiters in hotels and dining saloons, barbers, whitewashers, bricklayers and
kalsominers; while many of them are teamsters and longshoremen, and a few
work privately as artisans in different trades. In the Spring, Summer and
Autumn great numbers of them go as cooks, stewards and waiters on the various
river steamers, many more are employed as waiters in the hotels at the different Summer resorts and watering-places; and such is the exodus produced by
these causes that it is computed that there are twice as many more colored men
in the City during the Winter months, when the hotels are all closed and the
steamers laid up, than there are in the Summer time. This latter class are
generally compelled during the Winter to subsist upon what they have been
able to save from their Summer earnings; and in cases where they have been

improvident, or have not had employment during the entire season, very great
distances is often experienced by them.

The principal occupations of the women are washing and ironing--for
which they seem to have much aptitude--dressmaking and hairdressing, and a
certain number teach in the colored schools. The washerwomen seem, as a
class, to be very industriously inclined, and are generally contented with
the weekly money they earn. They are compelled of necessity to keep themselves and their places clean, and get up the linen committed to their charge
in a style fully equal to their white competitors, and in strange contrast
with the dusky color of their skins.

THEIR CHURCHES AND INSTITUTIONS.

In matters of religion, the great bulk of the colored people may be divided into two sections--Methodists and Baptists. The Methodists comprise
nearly two-thirds, and the Baptists about one-third, of the whole population;
though there are some Episcopalians, Roman Catholics, and Presbyterians.
They have two Methodist Episcopalian Churches, each of which has a special
section in the cemetery at Cypress Hill for the burial of their people. Zion
Church, at the corner of Bleecker and West Tenth streets, of which Rev.
WILLIAM F. BUTLER is the pastor, is valued with the ground on which it
stands, at $100,000, and has also great real estate belonging to it, in dif-
ferent parts of the City, valued at $100,000 more. There are also two Union
Methodist Churches, two Baptist, one Episcopalian, one Presbyterian, and one
Methodist Mission. The Roman Catholics are so few in number that they have,
as yet, no church of their own, but attend the churches of the whites. The
total amount of Chruch property in this City belonging to the colored people,
is valued at $455,000.

Their distinctive institutions are alike various and numerous, and appear to be very well supported by their own people. They have six public
schools, an Industrial and Educational School at No. 185 Spring-street,
which was opened last Summer, and which is daily crowded with pupils of all
ages, from 5 to 30 years, only too anxious to learn something and everything;
an Orphan Asylum, capable of accommodating 173 boys and girls, the highest
number yet reached; and an asylum for aged people, called "The Old Folks'
Home," which contains nearly 200 inmates. They have, moreover, several societies whose objects are relieving the poor, visiting and nursing the sick,
burying the dead and reclaiming drunkards. The Society of the Good Samaritan has six lodges, and numbers nearly 600 members; the Society of Love and
Charity has 850 members. Then there is the Society of the Sons of Wesley,
120 members; the Saloons' Men Society, 200 members; the Coachmen's Benevolent Society, the Young Men's Christian Benevolent Society, and the Mutual
Relief Society. These are all of a benevolent character. But these charitable and benevolent associations are by no means confined to the men.
Among the women there are the societies of The Daughters of Esther, a very
wealthy institution; The Daughters of Wesley, The Female Perseverance, The
Ladies' Mutual Relief, The Ladies' Loyal League, The Daughters of Zion,
and Tappin's Assistant Society, numbering altogether 2,000 members. There
are fourteen lodges of colored Freemasons, with 750 members, but they have no
connection with similar associations in New-York. The New-York lodges refused
admission to all negroes on the ground of their color, but they succeeded in
obtaining a charter direct from the Grand Lodge of England, and are governed
by the rules of that Order in that country. The Grand United Order of Odd
Fellows, which has four lodges with 350 members, also derives its charter
direct from England--the white lodges in this cith having declined to acknowledge their colored brethren. They have carried their animosity to such a
pitch as to procur their connection with the English branch of the Order, in
consequence of their having given a charter to the colored men of this and
other cities. The Union League Council, which has 1,500 members, is a purely
political club, having for its especial object the obtaining of negro suffrage. There is also a Young Men's Christian Association, consisting of 140
members, which has a reading-room and a lending library. A Literary Society
is attached to this institution, under whose auspices courses of lectures on
various improving topics are from time to time given. The Freedman's Bank,
in Bleecker-street, has now been in operation nearly two years, and has

received during that period deposits to the amount of $130,000. At the same
time, very many others of the savings banks of the City have the names of
colored customers on their books.

The *Zion Standard & Weekly Review* is a newspaper edited, printed and
published entirely by colored men, for the use and benefit of their own people. It is devoted to religion, news, politics, literature, science and the
general interests of the African race in this country--religious but not sectarian. Rev. DR. JAMES N. GLOUCESTER is the chief editor. The paper, which
has correspondents in all parts of the United States, from New-England to C
California, seems to have a fair advertising business, is very well gotten
up, and is altogether very creditable to the enterprise of its promoters.

THE PREJUDICE AGAINST THEM.

Throughout the whole of the exploration which I recently made, accompanied by an experienced officer of the Police force, through the quarters of
this City occupied by colored people, I met, in every direction, the most
startling evidences of the powerful effects of prejudice. Of all the difficulties with which they have to contend, that of prejudice against them for
their color's sake throws all others into the shade, and would seem under
present circumstances to be almost insuperable. This is a feeling which is
bitterly and intensely fostered by the Irish element, and quietly acquiesced
in by a very large portion of native-born citizens. If a colored man applies
for work at a new job, he always has to wait till the contractor sees whether
he can get enough white laborers for his purpose before he is taken on, and
it more often happens that he is at once refused employment, simply on the
ground of his color, although the contractor who refuses to employ him, may
be at the very moment short of his requisite number of hands; and, when he
does succeed in getting work, he has to accept lower wages, and is always expected to work harder than a white man, while his fellow-workmen "put upon"
him whenever they get the opportunity, and ceaselessly jeer at him and make
him the butt of their jokes. To my inquiries, "Why do you not break up this
wretched colony and move into more comfortable quarters," one invariable
answer was returned: "We find it so difficult to persuade any one to rent
us a decent place on account of our color. Hundreds of us would gladly pay
twice the rent to live in some more respectable neighborhood; but the landlord's will not accept us as tenants on any terms, declaring that, should
they let a couple of rooms to a colored man, all their white lodgers would
immediately give them notice to leave." It has happened on many occasions
that men, who have succeeded in obtaining work at a long distance from their
homes in the negro quarters, and who were naturally anxious to remove themselves and their families to the immediate neighborhood of their work, have
actually offered to different landlords much more rent than they could possibly hope to get from white men, and have been curtly told: "I never let my
rooms to a nigger." The consequence is that the poor fellow often has to
walk three miles to and from his work; and three miles is a long distance after
a hard day's labor. Again, many members of the Trades Unions refuse to work
on a building job if colored men be employed; and the Irish, especially, have
often made combinations to compel the masters to discharge them. Neither will
they work for masters who take colored apprentices. I was informed by highly
respectable persons, who were by no means desirous of glossing over the faults
of their people, that they did not know a single workshop in this city where a
colored man could get employment as an artisan, however respectable or however
clever at his trade he might be, or where a colored lad would be taken as an
apprentice.

But this prejudice against the African people, on account of their color,
is by no means confined to the laboring classes. Respectable hotels almost
invariably refuse to admit colored people within their doors. The proprietors
of ice-cream, oyster and dining saloons, and the keepers of liquor stores,
even of a second or third rate class, refuse to furnish them with refreshments.
Rev. WILLIAM F. BUTLER, pastor of Zion Church, a man of gentlemanly manners
and appearance, and of some consideration education, assured me that one day
last Summer he entered, in company with Mrs. BUTLER, an ice-cream saloon, by
no means a fashionable one, and requested to be supplied with refreshments; in
answer to which request he was informed that they were not in the habit of

accommodating colored people, and must refuse to serve him. On another occasion, not long ago, Mr. BUTLER walked into a dining saloon on Sixth-avenue,
about 4 o'clock in the afternoon. The place was empty, and he was readily
served with dinner, which he partook of, paid for, and departed without a
single remark being made by the proprietor. A day or two afterward he repaired to the same saloon, but on this occasion at midday. The dining room
was nearly full of white people. The proprietor immediately walked across
the saloon to him, and informed him that he could not dine there at that
hour, but if he chose to come later in the afternoon, after all their white
customers had left, he would then allow him to be served with dinner, but
not before.

Again, some of the theatres refused to admit colored persons at all,
while those who did condescend to do so only allow them to sit in one part
of the house--the tier of seats immediately beneath the roof. But perhaps
one of the most astonishing instances of this prejudice occurred last Summer;
and that in a quarter from whence it might have been least anticipated. The
Christian Convention of ministers of all denominations, which was then assembled in this City, thought proper to set the bad example of Christian charity
and brotherly love to all the world of not inviting their colored brother
ministers to attend their sittings.

The only class in this City who appear to be really uninfluenced by this
intolerant spirit of prejudice against the color of the negro are the Germans. They seem, as a general thing, to have no objection to let lodgings to
them; they willingly employ them and pay them fair wages--quite as much as
they would pay a white man of equal skill and powers of work. Moreover, when
they do employ a colored man, they treat him properly, and not simply as *the
nigger*.

After making a searching and patient inquiry into the condition, ways
and habits of the colored population of New-York, I can come to but one con-
clusion--that, in spite of all their efforts to the contrary, they are kept
back by circumstances over which they themselves have no control; that if
they could get rid of this inveterate and all-powerful hostility of the Irish
to them, on account of their color, they would soon make rapid progress; but
that till that desirable consummation is brought about, they will go on much
in the same way as they have done for years past. . . .

CRIMINAL STATISTICS.

Much stress is laid by some unthinking persons on the unusually heavy
proportion of criminals among the colored population of this City. There is
no denying that crime does exist among them to a deplorable extent, but not
to anything like the amount that is generally supposed. A careful analysis
of the official statistics of crime published annually by the Board of Commissioners of Public Charities and Correction, accompanied by a fair and just
consideration of all the circumstances of the case, would, I think lead un-
biased persons to considerably modify their views on this head. I find that
during the year 1867 there were no less than 47,313 men and women committed
to prison from the different City Police Courts--16,144 whites, or about
5 1/5 per cent of the whole white population, taking it at 900,000, and
1,169 blacks, or 9 3/4 per cent of the whole colored population, with few
exceptions, are all poor, that numbers of them, however willing they may be
to work, find the greatest difficulty in obtaining employment, that there
is a terrible amount of ignorance among the lower classes of them, and that
they labor under social disadvantages to which no other race in the universe
is exposed; and, when we consider that those equally poor among the white
population are but a small proportion of its total, (there is, perhaps, no
metropolitan city in the world where there is so little real poverty as
there is in the City of New-York,) and the great bulk of which contributes
but a very small quota to the criminal classes, it must be conceded that the
proportion of colored criminals is not greater than, if even so great as,
that of the whites; certainly nothing like so great as the proportion of the
criminals among their great enemies, the Irish, who contributed 21,079 persons to the City prisons during the year 1867, against 15,871 native Americans, 7,336 Germans, 1,421 English, 363 French, 410 Scotch, 228 Italians,
and 280 Canadians. The criminal classes are, incontestably, recruited from
among the poor and uneducated. Of the 47,313 persons committed to the City

prisons in 1867, the degree of education of 255 was unknown; 625 were well-educated; 30,390 could only read and write; 12,604 could only read, and 3,439 could neither read nor write. It would then be a fairer mode of making a comparison between the white and colored criminal classes to take a ratio of proportion of the poor and uneducated in each race, and then to work out the percentage of criminals from that ratio. Moreover, the colored people assert that the offences committed among them are by no means of so serious a character as those committed among the whites; and that whereas many whites somehow or other manage to escape the punishment to which they have rendered themselves liable, no colored man is ever allowed to get off.

Another great disadvantage under which many of them labor, arises from the fact that this species of ostracism from respectable neighborhoods compels numbers of them to reside in the Eighth Ward. In that district they are all packed like sardines in a box, in ricketty old houses, whose walls, floors and staircases are begrimed with dirt and where a decent mode of living is almost impossible; some of the houses being actually unprovided with water-closets of any description. It is hardly to be expected where the common decencies of life cannot be observed, that demoralization and degradation can be avoided. Many of the people are so poor that they are compelled to resort to the pawnsh ps in the Winter time in order to provide food and fuel for their families; and thus, from want of work, their furniture and clothing go, bit by bit, till there is nothing left for them but the workhouse or a prison. However, this is not the case with all of them, and it is wonderful to see how clean and comfortable many of these poor people will make even the miserable rooms in which they live look. But in these instances I generally found that the man or his wife had employment of some kind or another. It is another example of the old saying that "misery makes men callous."

New York Times, March 2, 1869.

53. A WHITE VIEW OF THE BLACK WORKER

Negro Laborers.

As a rule the negro does not take kindly to steady labor. He can be made to work, it is true; but, left to his own guidance, he would be content with little pay provided he was liable to illegible work. Give him his choice between a shilling an hour and a dollar a day, he would accept the former, and with great industry earn the first three or four shillings. Then he would weary of his task, throw it up in disgust, and devote the balance of the day to lounging or to playing policy. To this statement there are, of course, exceptions. Not a few negroes labor zealously all day, doing a full white man's work, and we doubt not if more opportunity was afforded, the number of these negroes would be found to increase. But after all, our general rate applies.

Black Tradesmen, Mechanics, Etc.

Negroes sometimes make capital carpenters. Edward Latham, in Chrystie street, is said to be an illustration of this statement. Colored blacksmiths are also found to be good workmen oftimes. As tailors, the negroes are known to be comparatively skillful. . . . As barbers, negroes have few equals among the Caucasians. As whitewashers, they "defy competition," while as caterers they are inimitable. With equal chances, one half the male blacks in New-York would rival Delmonicos or Martinez. Almost all the rich negroes of the Metropolis have made their pile as caterers.

New York World, March 16, 1867.

54. ESTIMATED NUMBER OF NEGROES IN SELECTED OCCUPATIONS
IN NEW YORK CITY, 1867, BASED ON EIGHTH WARD,
NEW YORK CITY

Occupations	Number
Schoolteachers	
(Male and Female)	50
Thieves	
(Male and Female)	250
Cartdrivers	50
Shoemakers	20
Barbers	60
Longshoremen	20
Writers, Editors	10
Caterers	300
Saloon-keepers and	
Employees	
(Male and Female)	90
Mechanics	30
Professional	
Musicians	25
Merchants	2
Professional	
Orators	6
Tailors	30
Laundresses	500
Prostitutes	200
Nurses	100
Waiters and Cooks	
(Public and Private)	2,000
Whitewashers	400
Notary Publics	2
Ministers	20
Doctors and Druggists	20
Bootblacks and Chimney Sweeps	100
Coachmen	500
Fortune Tellers	20

New York World, March 16, 1867.

55. CHARACTERIZATION OF SELECTED OCCUPATIONS FOR
NEGROES IN NEW YORK CITY, 1867

"Many"

    Barbers
    Caterers
    Waiters, Public and Private
    Laundresses
    Cooks
    Private Coachmen

"A considerable percentage or number"

> Whitewashers
> Oyster-openers
> Fortune tellers
> Cartdrivers and porters
> Thieves
> Prostitutes

"A Certain Number"

> Dyers
> Bootblacks

"A Few"

> Nurses
> Chimney Sweeps
> Shoemakers
> Tailors
> Carpenters
> Blacksmiths
> Laborers
> Saloonkeepers
> Ministers
> School teachers
> Professional musicians

"Very Few"

> Longshoremen
> Mercantile agents
> Doctors
> Notary publics
> Druggists
> Writers and Editors
> Orators

"A Select and Envied Baker's Dozen"

> "Gentlemen of leisure"

New York World, March 16, 1867.

56. COACHMEN'S UNION LEAGUE SOCIETY, INC.

Just before the eventful Civil War had closed in 1864, while the spirit of the freeman of the South and the freeman of the North was high, a group of Negroes, chiefly coachmen, fired with ambition and hopes, looking toward a new day of justice, freedom and achievement, formed the Coachmen's Union League Society, Inc. of New York City. Note that in definite and succinct preamble, the foundation of the organization is set forth: "We, the subscribers, reflecting duly upon the various vicissitudes of life to which mankind is continually exposed and stimulated by the desire of improving our condition, do conclude that the most efficient method of securing ourselves from the extreme exigencies of life to which we are liable to be reduced is by uniting ourselves in a body for the purpose of raising a fund for the relief of our members."

That these pioneers of vision, courage and faith builded more wisely
than they knew for the advancement of the race is admirably attested by the
present strength, idealism and constructive policy of the society. Verily
it has become an institution of social and economic consequence and merit to
the Negro in New York in particular and the country in general.

But this enviable status of accomplishment and promise was not attained
without indescribable struggle and sacrifice. The tried and true membership
have been put to the acid test. They have been weighed in the balance and
happily, *not* found wanting. Persistently, resistlessly and ceaselessly, the
present administration led by the capable and dynamic personality. Theodore
H. Smith, the President, assisted by an able and loyal staff of officers and
Board of Trustees, has piloted the organization from the small membership of
137 in 1920 to the astonishing and remarkable membership of 1,200; and, in
assets from the humble sum of $8,000 to the laudable figure of $85,000 or
more. But this figure of membership, though significant, does not tell the
whole story of the growth and influence of the Coachmen's. Their's is a
quality membership. They are not alone content with securing a member.
They want men who have the will to pull together, to cooperate for the up-
building of the organization in particular and the race in general. This
spirit is contagious, it pervades their every meeting; their every officer.
This is, to say the least, a healthy antidote to divisive and disintegrating
tendencies that have too often constituted the rock upon which many worthy
institutions of the race have foundered. But the members of a group which
are not intelligently aware of the reasons for and the value of their unity
are seldom reliable and loyal in a crisis. Their unity is unstable, ephem-
eral and insecure. Hence, the present administration has inaugurated monthly educational meetings when some prominent person lectures on some vital
topic of the day. This is an admirable stroke of constructive vision and
foresight. It keeps the membership awakened, alert and abreast of the
changing world and the advancing strides of the world of color.

It is significant to note in this connection too that the Coachmen's,
unlike many organizations is not only benevolent to its members, but, according to its ability, ministers to the needs and spreads the sunshine
of cheer and happiness among the distressed who seek their aid.

As a result of the wise and progressive leadership of the existing administration, the interest of the organization is not limited to the work of
taking care of the sick and burying the dead, though it is unusually prompt,
efficient and generous in performing this eminently necessary and important
task, but it embraces also the social, civic, religious and educational life
of the race. Such worthy movements as the National Association for the Advancement of Colored People, the National Urban League, the Y. W. C. A., the
Y. M. C. A. have been beneficiaries of its philanthropy. As a part of its
educational program, it plans to contribute to a different Southern Negro
school every year. It has heretofore confined its benefactions by way of
helping schools to the Kawlaguia.

Such is a work of wide social usefulness. It is a program which will
immediately arrest the attention and command the approbation of the most
critical and skeptical. One might reasonably think that such was the far-
thest reaches of its scope. But not so. Realizing that charity, though imperative, is merely superficial, merely a palliative, that it must be ever
repeated, that it does not go to the roots of our racial and social malad-
justments, the Coachmen's plan the establishment of a free employment department for its membership, and to acquire real estate when feasable and advantageous, both of which policies are fundamental, basic and calculated to remove the cause of the conditions which necessitate charity. For obviously
when a man or woman is sure of a job, the ghost and fear of want will not
arise. Instead of being a burden he is an asset to society. And it is a
matter of common knowledge that when a group possesses property it, ipso
facto, possesses power. And power is the only thing the white race respects.
The possession of property too renders a race or person independent. With
property, it is no longer the object of pity. It no longer seeks alms. It
is capable of standing erect and of standing alone, "a consummation devoutly
to be wished" by any people.

Still the Coachmen's Society is not solely concerned about itself standing alone. This is manifest from the fact that its active President,

Theodore Smith, initiated a plan to form a confederation of all of the benevolent societies of New York, one of whose laudable objects was to build a big hall to house all of the benevolent and fraternal organizations, thereby keeping within the race financial resources that are now lavishly poured into the coffers of white property owners. It is to be regretted that this plan of far-reaching and incalculable consequences to the group died aborning as a result of the failure of some of the societies to appreciate its immense business and social significance.

Let us hope that this plan of confederation will be resurrected, prosecuted and effectuated at no distant date for it is a step in the right direction toward the emancipation of the negro from economic bondage in Harlem. Besides it will serve as a potent inspirational example for the Negro in other cities throughout the country.

But unbaffled and undismayed, the Coachmen's purchased a home of their own at 252 West 138th Street. It is a magnificent structure, beautifully appointed and elegantly equipped and furnished. It provides a group of splendidly arranged lodge rooms, commodious and comfortable, for the accommodation of various societies. Add to this a grill room efficiently conducted by Mr. Braxton and the Coachmen's Home is at once a distinct credit and tribute to the Negroes of Harlem.

The stalwart, loyal and progressive types of men which brought this triumph to pass are:

> Theodore Smith, President
> John D. Younger, Jr., Financial Secretary
>
> *Board of Trustees.*
>
> Jordan B. Robinson, Chairman.
> Nathaniel J. Lucas, Secretary
> Leon A. De Kalb.
> John H. Braxton.
> Thomas D. Barnum, Treasurer.

The Messenger (September, 1925):320

PART IX

EXCLUSION OF BLACKS FROM WHITE UNIONS DURING
EARLY RECONSTRUCTION

EXCLUSION OF BLACKS FROM WHITE UNIONS DURING
EARLY RECONSTRUCTION

The practice of barring blacks from membership in craft unions is an old one in America. The documents in Part IX reveal the early racial rationale for this pattern of discrimination, and vividly illustrate how it worked in practice against those people of color whose credentials were frequently flawless.

Writing in 1868, one white member of the New York coopers' union expressed sentiments which demonstrate that the bastardiza·'on of social-darwinism had already taken root, and provided the rationale for exclusion of blacks from craft unions. Using the ever-ready shibboleth that "birds of the feather flock together," this white worker believed that it was against "nature" for blacks and whites to live and work on close terms, and that the "inferior" races were destined to disappear. This unionist's rationale reflected the conception, so popular then and now, that the craft union is a closed fraternity rather than an instrument for the elevation of the working classes generally. Since control was based on exclusion, it was easy to take the next step toward refusing admission to Negroes. In brief, racial unity was preferred to working-class consciousness (Doc. 1). This point of view was challenged by the editor of the Workingman's Advocate, the organ of the National Labor Union, who favored class solidarity as an organizing principle (Doc. 2).

Few cases illustrate the results of racial exclusion from the crafts better than the rejection of Lewis H. Douglass from the Columbia Typographical Union in Washington, D. C. As the son of Frederick Douglass, Lewis had learned the craft of typesetting in his father's own shop at an early age. Possessing considerable skill and experience, it had been easy for Douglass to obtain a position at the Government Printing Office. On the job, Douglass earned the respect of his peers, who were represented by the typographical union. When Douglass applied for membership in the union, however, he was denied admission on the contrived grounds that he had previously worked in a printing office out west without being a member of the shop union. Douglass and his allies protested that he had not been permitted to join because of his race, and asserted that this was the motivation behind his rejection this time as well. Douglass's position reflected the dilemma of black craftsmen; even though he was barred from the union because of his color, the same union charged him with being anti-union (a "rat").

The rejection led to a serious struggle between the racist and non-racist factions in the Columbia Typographical Union, and the controversy drew considerable comment in the labor press, especially the New National Era, which vigorously protested the action taken by the union (Doc. 3-10). The conflict was duly noted by other craft organizations, and many rushed to shore up their restrictive mechanisms (Doc. 11-12).

RACE DISCRIMINATION IN THE COOPER'S UNION, 1868

1. "BIRDS OF THE FEATHER FLOCK TOGETHER"--A WHITE
COOPER'S VIEW OF RACE

New York, Dec. 6, 1868

To the Editor of the WORKINGMAN'S ADVOCATE

In your issue of the 23rd of Nov., I notice that a resolution adopted by
the United Coopers, No. 4, of New York, to the effect that a colored man
working in Mr. Brigg's shop, and complained of by his shopmates requesting
the union to take action in the matter, and the action taken by the union,
leaving it optional with the men most interested whether they would work with
the colored man or not, has furnished the text for the false side of your editorial entitled "False and True," and your text for True being furnished by
a section in the constitution of a homestead association. Now, Mr. Editor, I
shall ask you to be kind enough to give me space in your widely circulated
and useful paper, to set the action of the nation, of which I am a member,
right in the eyes of our fellow-workman throughout the country. Now sir, I
shall meet your arguments in rotation. In the first place you say it is
quite evident a strike or a discharge afforded the only remedy. Now sir, the
union knew previous to taking action, that neither one or the other was necessary, for the foreman of the shop in which the colored man was working had
signified his intention to discharge him if the men working in the shop wished it to be done; and it is my belief if the men working with the negro had
signified their intention to work with him, a permit to work without a card
would have been granted by the union. I agree with you as regards organizations, and believe they should be established on the broadest basis, so broad
as to embrace all who know what it is to sell their labor, but I disagree
with your mode of organizing. I believe organization should not be promiscu-
ous, and instead of saying wise indeed are those who organizes on a basis
without respect to race or sex, I should be inclined to say unwise indeed,
and not from any prejudice or respect to caste. I disrespect caste, and hold
and maintain that it is assumed; not inherited from nature; but I also hold
that caste is not race, and while legislation should meet all races alike,
ignore caste in the different races and place all alike on a sound democratic
basis, yet such a result as this does not argue for a moment that the barriers
of race should be torn down and all races be received into the social embrace,
no more than the Arab steed and jackass in the same field, enjoying all the
blessings of heaven alike, should fraternise and become social equals.

The next turn your editorial takes, I consider a groundless threat. We
all know that the negro is a free man, never again to be bought and sold, and
who does not feel thankful that the greatest stain on the fair issue of our
country is removed by the act of emancipation, now seeing they are free as
all of God's creatures are by nature, and should be by practices. Such being
the case, the question then arises, what are the duties of a free man in a
free country? It is an easy matter to solve by each person seeking himself
the question. Then what you claim for your self you should willingly grant
to others, and that is in this country a voice in making the laws we live under, and in whose eye all should be on an equality, all receive alike the same
protection. Now, sir, you will see by my sentiments that I consider that although that colored cooper is not as yet my political equal in this state he
should be. But you say political equality to the negro will be political enmity to labor, because the white laborer refuses to place himself on a social
platform with the negro laborer, and I must confess, honestly, that I have not
the slightest ambition to work with a negro, to meet him in our trade unions,
or do anything that would have a tendency to break down the demarcations of
race that God has seen fit to ordain, and for those reasons, I know that no
sensible negro will be my political opponent, and furthermore, no sensible
negro will demand such concessions, for it takes them out of their element. I
am sure that poor colored cooper, surrounded by thirty white men, just felt

as I would feel surrounded by a like number of blacks, and I am sure I have
not the least wish to realise the feeling. The old saying birds of a feather flock together, has always proved true in the past, and will. I feel
persuaded, in the future, and I think that the lines of demarkation between
races will be more closely drawn in the future than they were in the past.
My reasons for thinking so are these: First, freedom leaves the negro at
liberty to turn their faces in any direction they wish; secondly, a growth in
intelligence consequent upon their changed relations in life, will enable
them to see that they are contending against odds in competing with a superi-
or and more enterprising race; and thirdly, self-preservation will cause them
to draw from the unequal contest and colonize by themselves, and it is my
serious impression that if such a course should not be pursued they will the
sooner disappear before the coward march of the white race, which is destined,
I believe, at no very remote date to supplant all the races of the globe. As
regards their political action, in that I see nothing to fear. Some, like
the minority of our own race will have minds of their own, and act with us
and for us, while the mass like the many of our own race, will be the puppets
of political gamblers. I have now come to the pleasing contrast, and I must
say that I cannot see the parrellel between the societies.

     The society you have branded as false, is a protective society composed
of men of the same race who assemble at these meetings on a social, not a political equality, and only separate to co-mingle more closely.

     The true society is a speculating enterprises, where one person's money
is as good as another's, and when they separate they may not meet again until
the next meeting.

                              I remain, yours truly,
                                   John Hewitt, Member of United Coopers'
                                        No. 4, New York

Workingman's Advocate, December 12, 1868.

                          2.   CASTE VS. RACE

     In the ADVOCATE of Dec. 12th, there appeared a communication from a mem-
ber of the United Coopers' Union, No. 4, of New York, in which exception was
taken to an article which appeared in our issue of Nov. 28th, under the caption of "THE FALSE AND THE TRUE," wherein we commented on the reported action
of said union, in regard to the complaint of one of its members in refusing to
work with a colored cooper; and stated that such action was calculated to produce a conflict between the two races which would necessarily prove injurious
to the interests of both.

     We have carefully read the protest of our correspondent, and as before
stated, fail to see, wherein he meets a single point raised by our objection.
In reply to our statement that it was self-evident that a strike or discharge
afforded the only remedy, he says?

     Now sir, the union knew previous to taking action, that neither one or
the other was necessary, for the foreman of the shop in which the colored man
was working had signified his intention to discharge him if the men working
in the shop wished it to be done; and it is my belief if the men working with
the negro had signified their intention to work with him, a permit to work
without a card would have been granted by the union.

     Exactly so; which goes to prove that his *color* was the only objectionable
feature raised. In the article referred to we said nothing whatever of social
equality, never for a moment hinted at it, but viewed the question as one of
principle. We said:

     The dignity of labor must be practically recognized. Unpalatable as the
duty may be the issue must be met, and wise indeed is that organizations,
which instead of fighting the dead issues of the past, accepts the situation

in good faith, and uses its influence to enlighten and enroll the colored
element in the ORGANIZED ARMY OF LABOR. Certainly no one is so deeply interested in securing such a result as the man who earns his living by honest
toil.

In other words, that as trades unions had proved necessary to the white
mechanic, in resisting the unjust demands of capital, it was equally essential that the colored race, in their new relationship, should be taught their
advantages, else their influence would be exerted in the wrong direction. We
did not dictate or even suggest *how* these organizations should be formed. We
did know, however, that in every northern city colored organizations and
churches exist, though we have yet to learn of the first objection to such
societies, on the ground that their recognition would necessarily involve a
recognition of *social* equality.

Again, our crime, to illustrate more clearly his position, makes use of
the following language:

While legislation should meet all races alike, ignore caste in the different races and place all alike on a sound democratic basis, yet such a result as this does not argue for a moment that the barriers of race should be
torn down and all races are received into the social embrace, no more than
the Arab, steed and jackass in the same field, enjoying all the blessings of
heaven alike, should fraternize and become social equals.

So we say, but we can't allow our friend to dodge the issue in this manner. While we should utter no protest against the Arab steed refusing to
fraternize with his jackass-ship, we should most decidedly object to his refusing to allow him to eat grass enough to subsist on, which is substantially
the position assumed. But let us examine a little farther into this bugbear
of *social* equality. Let us suppose, for example, that Mr. Briggs should, in
an emergency, take off his coat for a day or two, and go to work among his
operatives, would be even for the time being, as his *social equals,* or *vice
versa*. Not at all, unless both employer and employes are exception to the
rule. Why then all this buncombe, about the social equality of the negro
when he insists upon the privilege of earning his living by the sweat of his
brow?

In view of what we have said, the congratulations of our correspondent on
the emancipation of the negro face, his willing concession of political privileges seems rather inconsistent. In fact we fail, to see the freedom. Political equality means that the negro race shall have an equal vote with the
Caucasian in shaping the destiny and future legislature of the country. Yet
strange to say the privileges of competing with them in the race of life.
[illegible   ] The claim that the character of the negro will ultimately compel him to abandon the field to the white mechanic is altogether
gratuitons. So long as he was a *chattel* no correct opinion could be formed
of his capacity; now that he is a freeman *independent on his own exertions*--
his relation is entirely changed, while the future alone can determine what
that capacity is.

But it is needless to pursue this question further. We cannot conclude,
however, without remarking that the conclusions of our correspondent seem to
be as defective as his premises. Referring to his belief that the line of
demarcation between the white and black race will be more closely drawn in the
future than in the past, he says:

My reasons for thinking so are these: First, Freedom leaves the negro
at liberty to turn their faces in any direction they wish; secondly, a growth
of intelligence consequent upon their changed relations of life, will enable
them to see that they are contending against odds in competing with a superi-
or and more enterprising race; and thirdly, self-preservation will cause them
to draw from the unequal contest and colonize by themselves, and it is my a
serious impression that if such a course should not be pursued they will the
sooner disappear before the onward march of the white race, which is destined,
I believe, at no very remote date, to supplant all the races of the globe.

With regard to the first proposition, we answer, the freedom referred to
reminds us of the freedom of the British pauper--freedom to starve. The second is a sword which cuts both ways: If the inferiority of the black race is
self-apparent, *why* not leave their destiny to the inexorable logic of events?

The third is an opinion directly at variance with the experience of the past,
and the testimony of the ablest thinkers of the age, many of whom agree that
color is the result of a climatic agency.

But we have done. That our readers may more readily understand, however
our true position; and wherein we differ from our New York friend, we reprint
the following from our November article, every word of which we now re-af-
firm:

The line of demarcation is between the robbed and the robbed, no matter
whether the wronged be the friendless widow, the skilled white mechanic or
the ignorant black. Capital is no respecter of persons, and it is the very
nature of things a sheer impossibility to degrade one class of laborers without degrading all. To make labor dignified, therefore, we must dignify the
laborer, no matter what his calling or social position.

Workingman's Advocate, January 2, 1869.

LEWIS H. DOUGLASS AND THE TYPOGRAPHICAL UNION

3. MR. DOUGLASS AND THE PRINTERS

MEETING OF THE WASHINGTON UNION--THE APPLICATION OF DOUGLASS REPORTED FAVOR-
ABLY--THEY ADJOURN WITHOUT ACTION.

Washington, June 20th.--Typographical Union No. 101, of this city, met
last night. The anticipation that the case of Lewis H. Douglass, for admission or rejection into the Union, would come up, had the effect of bringing
together one of the largest representations of the compositors of this city
ever congregated at one meeting. Two of the Committee on Nominations reported in favor of ten applicants, including Lewis H. Douglass. As to the
last named, they said he had served a sufficient length of time at the business; that he gives satisfaction as a compositor; that he has a good character; is not a "rat," and that there is no reason except his race and color
that should deprive him of becoming a member of the Typographical Union. Being, therefore, a fair man they recommended that he be admitted to membership
in Columbia Typographical Union. A minority report was submitted, signed by
the remaining member of the Committee. After stating the facts in the case,
he says the plain requirements of the law of this Union and of the National
Union are not to admit to membership a printer without card, who comes from a
place where a Union exists, unless he brings from such Union a certificate
satisfactorily explaining why he has none, and that the character Douglass
established for himself in Denver still attaches, and does not lift him above
the operation of the general law, outside of which Union No. 101 cannot safely travel. A motion was made to lay the latter or minority report on the
table. The vote was taken amid frequent interruptions and great confusion,
and resulted in Yeas 229, Nays 164. The announcement of the vote was received with applause mingled with hisses. On motion, the majority report was
adopted amid enthusiastic cheering and confusion. The Union proceeded to vote
seriatim upon the candidates proposed for admission, with the exception of
Lewis H. Douglass. Three names having been balloted for and the candidates
elected, the President was about to read the fourth, when a motion to adjourn
was made, and this prevailed amid great disorder and excitement.

National Anti-Slavery Standard, July 3, 1869.

4. THE TYPOGRAPHICAL UNION--PREJUDICE AGAINST COLOR.

Address of the Majority of Columbia
Typographical Union.

WASHINGTON, D. C., July 3d, 1869.

To the President of the International Typographical Union:

Sir--A minority of the members of Columbia Typographical Union, No. 101,
at a meeting held on Saturday, June 26th, adopted an address to be forwarded
to you as President of the International Typographical Union, in which they
set forth certain alleged grievances, and ask "that you will give a speedy
relief from the difficulties which environ and the evils which threaten, *even
though the revocation of the charter of No. 101 and the granting of a new
character be necessary to do so.*

The proceedings of the meeting of the *minority* of said Union, together
with this address, having received considerable publicity, we, the *majority*
deem it our duty to calmly and respectfully acquaint you with the *facts,* to
the end that you may act understandingly and with a view to the best interests of the craft.

For some time past an enmity has been manifested towards the members of
our Union employed at the Government Printing Office, by those employed elsewhere, which on more than one occasion has threatened the disruption of the
Union. This animosity arises in part, no doubt, from political differences.
Many of those embraced in the minority have either taken an active part
against the nation during the late rebellion, or strongly sympathized with
those engaged in endeavoring to destroy our country and its free institutions;
while the members comprising the majority, nearly if not quite all, heartily
sustained the government in its struggle for existence, many of whom imperil-
led their lives and some sacrified their limbs in its defense. Another cause
of difference, consequent in a great measure upon the above, that very many
of the employes of the Government Printing Office have been drawn from various cities and towns of the Northern and Western States, taking the places of
those who were reared in Washington and vicinity. Still another cause of
discontent may be found in the fact that certain ambitious demagogues, of the
rule-or-ruin order, having lost most of their former prestige in the Union,
in consequence of the above-mentioned changes, are struggling to regain their
leadership by desperate measures; hence they now ask for the revocation of
the charter of a Union that they can no longer control, and the granting to
them of a new charter that they may build up a Union which they can control.

The present cause of disaffection, or rather the excuse now offered for
disturbance, arising from the application of a colored man for membership, is
presented in the following brief

History of the Douglass Imbroglio.

A few days before the regular May meeting of the Union, Mr. Lewis H.
Douglass obtained employment at the Government Printing Office. He at the
same time made application for membership and obtained from the proper officer
of the Union a permit to work until his case could be acted upon. The news
spread rapidly; it created great excitement, and caused a great rally at the
May meeting of those opposed to this recognition of the right of colored men
to earn as honest livelihood on equal terms with whites. Deeming it impolite
to oppose the admission of Mr. Douglass on the ground of *color,* the minority
resorted to the subterfuge of denouncing him as a *rat.* As soon as his name
(with others) had been referred to the Committee on Nominations, (which committee is charged by the constitution with the duty of examining into all applications for membership,) and, before the committee had time to report, this
minority became clamorous for immediate action. Resolutions were introduced
which asserted that Mr. Douglass had been *rejected* by the Denver Union *as an
improper person,* censured the Financial Secretary for granting him a permit to
work and ordered a revocation of said permit.

The authors of this resolution, knowing its utter falsity, and fearful
of its contradiction, demanded and loudly insisted upon the previous question.
A scene of the wildest confusion followed. A point of order was now raised,

that after an application for membership had been referred to the committee
on nominations for investigation and report, and before the committee had
time to report, resolutions prejudging the case could not be entertained.
The chair sustained the point of order. The confusion now became so great
that it was found impossible to transact any other business, and the Union,
by a vote of 158 to 150, adjourned.

Before the time for our next regular meeting arrived, the National Typographical Union assembled at Albany. One of the delegates from this Union,
elected before this question came up or was foreseen, acting in the interest
of the minority, without any instructions from the Union--without the knowledge, advice, or consent of its membership--introduced a resolution, which
was adopted by that body, censuring the Congressional Printer for employing
L. H. Douglass, *"an avowed rat,"* calling upon Columbia Union to reject his
application, and pledging the support of the National Union in such action.

This action of the National Union was unjust, absurd, and unparalleled,
as will be seen by the following considerations:

1. The National Union had no jurisdiction of the matter, and consequently its action was extra-judicial and not binding. Each subordinate Union is
of necessity the judge of the qualifications of applicants for membership
subject to the requirements of the Constitution and the National Union. In
this instance no appeal had been taken, no constitutional requirement violated, and the case not properly brought before the National Union.

2. The National Union, by its action, attempted to prejudge and decide
a case while yet in the hands of the Committee on Nominations of this Union,
before said committee had an opportunity to report, and before any action in
the case by the Union had been possible.

3. This action of the Union was based upon the simple assertion of one
of Mr. Douglass' most violent enemies, without a particle of evidence being
produced on either side, and without giving the accused, or his friends, any
notice or opportunity of hearing or defense.

4. The decision was contrary to truth and evidence, as is clearly shown
by the reports of the committee, and documents in our possession.

5. The action of the National Union was contrary to law, custom, and
usage is in this or any other similar organization.

We deny most emphatically that Mr. Douglass is *an avowed rat,* or that
the term rat is in any manner applicable to his case. The National Union de-
fines a *rat* to be one who works for less than Union prices, and nothing else
constitutes ratting. Not a particle of evidence has yet been adduced to
show that he ever worked an hour for less than Union prices, or that he ever
knowingly worked in an unfair office, or that the charge of ratting was ever
preferred against him until after his application was made to this Union. On
the contrary, the proprietor of the office in which Mr. Douglass worked in
Denver, and in which it is charged he ratted, certifies that he paid him
Union prices, is willing to make oath to that effect, and offers his books
for inspction as verification. The Secretary of the Denver Union, under official seal, certifies that Mr. Douglass is not a rat.

Knowing that great injustice had been inflicted upon Mr. Douglass and
his friends by the minority of Columbia Union, and by the National Union, we
determined to use all Constitutional means in our power to defeat their
schemes and elect Mr. Douglass. At the regular June meeting of Columbia U-
nion there was an unusually large attendance of the members, the opponents of
Mr. Douglass coming in full force with black balls in their pockets. The majority of the Committee on Nominations reported favorably on the application
of Mr. Douglass. A minority (one member) of the committee reported adversely,
without, however, adducing any satisfactory reason for his rejection. A motion was made to lay the minority report on the table, which was carried--
ayes 229, nays 164. The majority report was then adopted *viva voce.* Before
a ballot in his case was taken, the Union upon motion adjourned, as it had a
constitutional right to do.

The motion to lay the minority report on the table was a test vote. The
result--229 against 164--showed that the friends of Mr. Douglass had a large
majority, but not a two-thirds majority, which is necessary to elect. If a
ballot had been taken at that meeting it would have resulted in the rejection
of Mr. Douglass. The consequence would have been, a compulsion of the members
of the Union employed at the Government Printing Office, numbering over 270,

to strike. Such a strike could have ended only in defeat, as it would have
been a strike not directed against the government as an employer, but a
strike in opposition to the principles of the government itself, in conflict
with the moral sentiment of the nation, and at war with the spirit of the
age. The majority, the friends of Douglass, who voted for adjournment, not
only voted thus because they had the constitutional right to do so, but because they were determined to preserve the Union in accordance with their
solemn obligations as members; while the minority, the opponents of Mr. Douglass, the men who now ask you to revoke our charter, voted against adjournment, because they would rather see the Union destroyed than be without the
control thereof.

After adjournment, the minority, in a high state of excitement, held an
informal meeting, at which divers threats were made by the leaders--among
others, that they would reject every candidate proposed hereafter by the majority, for the purpose of keeping down our numbers--forgetting their obligations to the principles of the Union; that they would form a Union of
themselves, and have our charter revoked, and that they would never *whitewash*
any one of the majority. Various charges were made, without any foundation
in fact, against the Congressional Printer, among others, that he always had
been and is now a rat in principle, and had combined with other employing
printers to break down the Union. Violent language, calculated to provoke
disturbance, was freely indulged in. Finding, however, that little attention was given to their blustering, they subsequently called the meeting of
the 26th and resolved upon the address to you heretofore named. The men who
made these threats and these charges are the men who are now controlling the
movement which is to result, as they hope, in the revocation of our charter.

We think it is proper, in this connection, to call your attention to
the attitude in which the minority have placed themselves by their action of
the 26th. When they became members of the Union they pledged themselves to
support the consitution, by-laws, etc., as required by article III, section
4, thereof. By their action of the 26th they have violated this pledge.
Article XIII. of the Constitution provides:

"This Union shall not be dissolved as long as fifteen members desire to
preserve its organization."

These members, (the minority), as long as fifteen members are opposed
to it--and the majority are opposed to it--have no right to ask for the revocation of our charter. The majority, which is over two hundred, are determined to preserve the Union. The minority have pledged themselves *as long as
fifteen members desire to preserve this Union,* to uphold it. In violation of
their pledge they now ask you to destroy it.

A review of the facts in the case of Mr. Douglass cannot fail to convince any unprejudiced mind that the entire ground of objection to him is on
account of his color. The less hypocritical of his opponents admit this,
and even the most violent and unfair leaders of the minority formally offered to compromise the difficulty by granting Mr. Douglass a permit from the
Union to work as long as he desired, provided we would withdraw his name from
the Union, thus virtually confessing that he was a fair printer, and they
were willing that he should work, but were determined to prevent the admission of colored men into the Union. This proposition, it is needless to say,
was promptly rejected by the advocate of Mr. Douglass on the ground that it
was in violation of the letter and spirit of the constitution of the Union
to license rats, (the minority claim that Mr. Douglass is a rat), or to work
with them, that if Mr. Douglass was a fair printer he should be admitted into the Union, and, not, he should not be allowed to work in a fair office;
that the printers of the Government Printing Office could not consent to work
with a fellow-craftsman who was deemed unworthy to become a member of the
Union.

We do not believe that *color* should be made a bar to the admission of
Mr. Douglass, because--

1. It is not made so by the constitution of our Union.

2. Because distinction on account of color is antagonistic to the spirit of the age and the laws of the land.

3. Such distinctions are detrimental to the best interests of labor
associations, by forcing those of a different color into competition with us,
which must eventually, if persisted in, insure the reduction of the prices

of labor and the ruin of labor associations.

4. Because it is unjust, and a relic of that barbarism which was en-
gendered by the system of slavery now happily abolished in our country.

Our convictions on this subject are lasting and sincere. There is a
principle underlying the question of the admission of Mr. Douglass, which we
are unwilling to sacrifice--a principle for which many of us have fought and
more have voted and labored--a principle involving the rights of human nature. The simple admission or rejection of one or a dozen applicants for
membership is a matter of small consequence compared with the sacrifice of
principle that a minority ask us to make.

Many of us have been, for years, identified with the labor movement.
We have among us men who have presided over Typographical Unions in other
cities, and participated in the deliberations of the National Union when it
was in its infancy, and have never faltered in their devotion to the principles of the organization. We have not forgotten the long hesitation and
final reluctance of the old Columbia Typographical Society to unite with the
National Union or the terms upon which they united. This union would not
then have been accomplished, but for the accession to that old Society of
members from distant Unions. Considering all these circumstances, it is far
from agreeable to see the National Union arrayed against its life-long
friends, to gratify the unwarranted prejudices of these new converts, who
now seek to break up the Union and bring untold evils upon the craft, simply
because the minority are not permitted to rule.

We do not propose to abandon the Union, or the principles upon which it
is founded, under any circumstances. We have as yet violated no constitutional requirement, nor do we intend to violate any, but shall use every
honorable and constitutional means to secure the recognition of equal rights
for all fair printers without distinction on account of color. We ask no
special favors of the National Union in this struggle for equal rights; but
we *demand and insist* that there shall be no interference with us by the National Union in the exercise of our constitutional rights and privileges.
Columbia Union is able to settle the present difficulty in its own time and
way in such a manner that it will remain settled for all time to come. If,
however, the officers of the National Union should so far outrage law, courtesy, and common usage, as to act upon the suggestion of the minority of our
membership, and declare our charter forfeited and grant a new charter to said
minority, we shall be driven to the necessity of appealing to our fellow-
craftsmen throughout the country to withdraw from the National Union and to
organize a new National Typographical Society, which shall be founded on the
principles of justice to all men, regardless of race or color.

We should very deeply regret to be compelled to resort to such a revolutionary measure as this would be, but self-preservation, the highest of all
laws, would leave us no other choice. In such a contest we would be sustained by the whole power of the government wherever its influence could be
brought to bear in our behalf, by the great majority of the press of the
country, by the pulpit unanimously, and by the public sentiment as overwhelming as that which emancipated the slave and gave him a common legal and political status. There can be no doubt upon whose standard victory would
eventually rest.

We appeal to you, therefore, with no common earnestness not to hurl into the midst of our organization so consuming a firebrand as the one to which
you are asked to give your official sanction, which would be without warrant
in the letter or spirit of the instrument from which you derive your power.

We hope you will not follow the counsels of a prejudiced, selfish, desperate minority, and thus commit the National Union, so far as you can, to a
course which must produce ill will, discord, and eventual disruption. May
you be endowed with that wisdom and prudence which is so much needed in this
crisis.

To grant the request of the minority would only more inflame the passions and prejudices already charged with too much mischief, and it would
surely read the national organization into two antagonistic bodies, each
claiming similar powers and jurisdiction. You may rest assured that there
are not less than three hundred printers within the jurisdiction of this
Union who never will yield their rights and privileges as members at the dictation of a factious minority.

Mr. President, a grave responsibility rests upon you. We hope you will not convulse, read, and finally destroy that union of our noble craft, which has been so happily and successfully established after years of toil, by causelessly and unlawfully interfering with what should have been a purely local question. Union and equal rights is our motto; may it be yours likewise.

National Anti-Slavery Standard, July 17, 1869.

5. FREDERICK DOUGLASS ON THE REJECTION OF HIS SON, LEWIS, FOR MEMBERSHIP IN THE INTERNATIONAL TYPOGRAPHICAL UNION

. . . Lewis is made a transgressor for working at a low rate of wages by the very men who prevented his getting a high rate. He is denounced for not being a member of a Printer's Union by the very men who would not permit him to join such a Union. He is not condemned because he is not a good printer, but because he did not become such in a regular way, the regular way being closed against him by the men now opposing him.

Suppose it were true that this young man had worked for lower wages than white printers receive, can any printer be fool enough to believe that he did so from choice? What mechanic will ever work for low wages when he can possibly obtain higher? Had he been a white young man, with his education and ability, he could easily have obtained employment, and could have found it on the terms demanded by the Printer's Union.

There is no disguising the fact—his crime was his color.

New York Times, August 8, 1969.

6. THE TYPOGRAPHICAL UNION'S JUSTIFICATION

That there are deep-seated prejudices against the colored race no one will deny; and these prejudices are so strong in many local unions that any attempt to disregard or override them will almost inevitably lead to anarchy and disintegration . . . and surely no one who has the welfare of the craft at heart will seriously contend that the union to thousands of white printers should be destroyed for the purpose of granting a barren honor of membership to a few Negroes.

Printers' Circular reprinted in Proceedings of the International Typographical Union of 1870 (Philadelphia, 1870), p. 140.

7. THE TYPOGRAPHICAL UNION DENOUNCED

The Columbia Typographical Union of this city met on Saturday night last. The application of LEWIS H. DOUGLASS, WILLIAM A. LAVELETTE, FREDERICK

DOUGLASS, Jr., and KEITH SMITH, colored compositors, for admission, having been evaded and postponed from several other meetings of this Union, was down on the calendar for action at this January meeting of the Union. In accordance with their most inwardly prejudice the Union adjourned without any action on these applications. This Union is composed largely of members who are working under a Republican administration, and who themselves profess to accept the policy of the administration of not proscribing men for reason of color, race, or previous condition.

New National Era, January 26, 1871.

8. "COLORED PRINTERS"

It seems to be, in the eyes of the Columbia Typographical Society of this city, a great misfortune, if not a crime, for a colored man to learn the art of printing, and then endeavor to earn his daily bread by plying that bocation. That combination of white printers, many, if not most, of whom are employed in the Government Printing Office, assume to say that a printer shall not be employed in this city who is not a member of some Typographical Union which is in fellowship with the Columbians. Under this rule Mr. Lewis H. Douglass, nearly two years ago, applied for work and was put to case in the Government Printing Office, by the present Congressional Printer. To avoid difficulty he also applied for membership in the Columbia Union. His case has been under consideration ever since, without coming to any termination. He is neither admitted to membership nor rejected, but is kept in the Union as a sort of foot-ball for the prejudices of men who have been educated to think that the colored man has no rights that the white man is bound to respect.

We briefly alluded to this case last week, and we now refer to it again, for the reasons that it interests every friend of freedom and human rights in the country. Since the application of Mr. Douglass for membership, three other colored printers--Messrs. William A. Lavalette, Keith Smith, and Frederick Douglass, Jr.--have filed applications for membership in the Union, and have been treated with the same unjust and unjustifiable line of conduct that has followed the case of their predecessor. This treatment is not only very unjust, but it is offensive and unmanly. Inasmuch as these applications have been entertained by the Union, the least that can be done, in justice to the applicants, is to put the question to a test-vote which shall decide it one way or the other. If these colored printers are not to be admitted to membership, then why keep them under years of suspense? If the Union must follow out its laws and resist the employment of colored men in the Government service, why not bring that issue to the front at once? We see no better time than now, while Congress is in session, for the trial of that issue. We have no authority for representing what the course of the Congressional Printer will be under such an issue, but we have confidence that he will stand firmly by the right of the colored man to earn his livelihood by a trade that he has learned at the expense of years of patient and unrewarded toil. We have no fear of his receding from the position he took on this question at the outset, and has held steadily ever since. We believe that if he should be menaced by a "strike," for the reason that he employes colored men who are kept out of the Union by narrow and bitter prejudice, he will say to those who thus confront his authority, "Strike! and let the worst be known."

We do not see how these colored printers can retain their self-respect and continue their applications for membership with an organization that studiously and continuously treats their cases with palpable neglect, if not with contempt and scorn. We see no way now but for these men to withdraw their applications for membership, and leave the Union, which presumes to dictate to the Congressional Printer who he shall and who he shall not employ in the Government Printing Office, to settle between themselves the question of jurisdiction and authority over the management of that establishment. In this way the end may be reached.

New National Era, February 2, 1871.

9. LAVALETTE'S DEFENSE

To the Columbia Typographical Union, No. 101:

Inasmuch as the Columbia Typographical Union, No. 101, has assumed to say that no printer, however qualified, shall work within their jurisdiction who is not a member either of their or some other Union subordinate to a concern known as the National Typographical Union, and made other regulations concerning prices, qualifications to membership, etc., which to it seemed good in the premises, the undersigned, having obtained the promise of employments in the Government Printing Office, by the Hon. A. M. Clapp, Congressional Printer, and desiring to comply with the usages, however ancient or recent at the time of his coming, made formal applications for membership to said Union.

The majority of the committee, to whom was referred said application for membership, saw no just cause why I should not be admitted to fellowship in said Union as a competent workman, and recommended an imitation.

However deficient in mental caliber some men are for great occasions, they occasioned its possess unbounded perspicacious talents for technicul- ties. After the report of the Committee on Nominations had been delivered to your conclave, in American embryo, far-seeing, future statesman (how un- grateful are republics! fifteen months have elapsed and the people of this great nation have not only not rewarded, but have not even recognized, his genius!) saw a technical informality, which caused the application to lie over for two months. During the interin of which, I was frequently told that *printers* had no mean prejudices; that if it had not been for them the history of six or more thousand years would be comparatively unknown; that the onward progress of science would be checkmated; that they are the indis- pensible gentleman who devote their lives to the salvation and preservation of all arts, and are content to die martyra to their singular avocation for the benefit of the world. How credulous I was!

The second time having arrived for the consideration of my application, brought with it that of Mr. Lewis H. Douglass, and together they were post- poned for one year. The applications of Messrs. Smith and Frederick Doug- lass, Jr., underwent the same fate.

As a gentleman possessing docile and lawabiding proclivities, I waited for the year to be fully complete and ended. On the day of the evening to which my "case" had been postponed I addressed a note to the Union, through its president, (Mr. Webb,) the gist of which was essentially as that given in the *Daily Patriot* of the 4th instant.

To effectuate the purposes for which your organization is formed, you require, in a measure, not only unity of interests, but a degree of moral responsibility, integrity of character, indefatigable devotion and vim in each individual member--all of which are essential in a crises, or else I utterly misunderstand the relation you hold to each other and the object of your formation. Entertaining these exalted notions of the character of your august assembly, with a firm purpose of embodying them in, and making them a part of, my individuality and the basis of a future conduct, I believed then, and do now, that I would not only lose my self-respect, compromise the con- duct of my former life, be unworthy the respect and confidence of your or- ganization in quiet employment or emergent times, but would lose the formal recognition of my employer and those who are temporarily placed over me, if I allowed the Union to again meet and daily with my case, when I could give

a broad but respectful suggestion of the probable consequences of such action in a letter addressed to the Union, as before mentioned.

I placed that letter in the hands of Mr. Coffin, to be read before the
adjournment of the state meeting in January, that the members of the Union
might take due notice thereof and govern themselves accordingly. I learned
the next day, by the morning papers and otherwise, that the letter was not
read, and the Union adjourned without reaching my case; that the new president arbitrarily adjourned the meeting, contrary to the expressed wishes of
a majority then present and voting. I intimated that I was dissatisfied with
such treatment, and that no man with common sense and self-respect would
stand it.

A few days later I proposed to Mr. Coffin, after a brief *resume* of the
field, that for me to retain my self-respect, and the Union to retrieve itself from the stigma of indifference to the just rights of a competent fellow-workman, a special meeting might be holden to adjust matters. Mr. Coffin fell in with my proposition, and through his personal friendship for me
and zeal for the absolute rights of all, the required number was obtained
requesting a special meeting.

It was hinted to me on the day of the meeting that a point of order
would be raised and sustained by the president, the meeting would be adjourned, and I would thereby receive a complete snub. I thought, and I said at
the time, that surely gentlemen would have a better care to their own interests than to precipitate me into acting that part I should have long ago.

I took it for granted that printers possessed all the intelligence the
world gave them credit for. The note above referred to, as addressed to the
Union, was couched in courteous, firm, and comprehensive English. The charge
that I only intimated a withdrawl is giving me credit for diplomatic talents
which those I am intimately acquainted with believe to be contrary wise.
Those who had any conversation with me will testify that I was unequivocal in
my expressions, and firm in my determination, to have a vote at all hazards
on the evening of the 3d instant.

When I make application for work I do it upon the consciousness of my
competency at a workman. When I made application for membership in your
Union, I did it with a disposition to comply with your regulations. Do not
console yourselves into the belief that you have a shrine to which I suppli-
cate to worship rules as I found them is all you can charge upon me. I never
asked admission as a colored printer. If you proposed to make war upon those
who favor my admission and me on the ground that I was born outside of your
orthodox complexion, however gallantly my friends and self might have fought
you, we could never succeed in removing that distinguished and indellible
landmark that makes us so conspicuous in all the avenues of life.

The pretended friends, who have a constitutional weakness, superinduced
by climatic, geographical, esthatical, or other cause to me unknown, (and for
which I know this region to be quite prolific; who could or would not be for
forced into voting outside a stated meeting, ("no coercionists," I mean,) do
not even merit a negro's contempt.

To my sincere friends, for the insults, vexation, and obloquy they have
undergone for the sake of having justice done a fellow-workmen, whose friendship to me requires a justification of my action in peremptorily withdrawing
my application, and for whom this letter was mainly written this is my defense.

At the time Mr. Douglass wrote a letter in answer to some inquires concerning his petition for membership, I did not then, and do not now, approve
of the course he pursued. I told him that I considered his compliance with
the curious as detracting from his personal dignity. An unsuccessful attempt
was made to inveigh me into writing a letter to the Union upon which to
build a fool's claim to sympathy or influence the action of the Union.

In filling up a blank petition I did all I could in the premises. By
your constitution no historical or biographical sketch, esthetical or ethno-
logical tests are required; hence I believed it would be presumption on my
part to inflict anything of that nature on your assembly. I made application
in the manner required of all who propose to affiliate with or work in your
jurisdiction, contenting myself to be bound by and conform to your regulations.

The technical informality, the propriety at his time, the absolute ignoring, and the direct snub, each occurring in the order in which they are named, as a subterfuge to dodge the issue, is more than I can, is more than I would, bear from you if the strength of your organization were multiplied by one hundred. I have already gone to the verge of that point, whereas one step further and honor goes beyond recall. May I forever fail to pronounce or write another word of the English language if I cross that point at this or any other time.

The cause of a strike cannot (should it occur) be charged to me. If the printers of Washington, or any other place, have no more manliness, no more humanity, no more fellowship toward each other than to persist in a bullheaded course of conduct, the result of which is to throw a majority of their comrades upon the benevolence of the public and their poor pittances, and perhaps reduce the price of their own labor one-third or one-half, I think you need go and quaff anew at the fountain of unadulterated common sense. The course of such conduct does not even merit the dignity of the name *prejudice*.

The thrust at my sensitive feelings was conscious and premeditated.

> "Fate never wounded more deep the generous heart,
> Than when a blockhead's *insult* points the dart."

feelings of a senstive man stung to the quick can experience, to a warfare upon your organization, until you shall have so far recovered common sense, as to cry, "Hold! we'll act the part of men."

I am alone responsible for my action. It is not for me to say that the other colored printers appreciate the circumstances as I do.

If there is one among you so vile who would not do, under the circumstances, as I have done, you fellowship a thing which is not worthy of the name man, but ought to be denounced by his own family and execrated by his comrades.

. Very respectfully, yours,
W. A. Lavalette.

New National Era, February 9, 1871.

10.   EDITORIAL RESPONSE TO LAVALETTE'S DEFENSE

In another column we publish a letter written by William A. Lavalette, a colored compositor, employed at the Government Printing Office, giving his reasons for withdrawing his application for membership to the Columbia Typographical Union, No. 101. We think that he is correct in withdrawing under the circumstances. In his characterization of Mr. Lewis H. Douglass's letter in answer to questions propounded to him by one who was urging his admission on the Union, he is in error. Mr. Douglass certainly did not depart with any dignity by answering questions such as are propounded to every applicant for membership to the Union. Nor did Mr. Lewis H. Douglass write the letter with any knowledge that it would be published, but simply to enable his friends to present his case to the Union correctly. At the time Mr. Douglass made application for membership his opponents thought to defeat his admission on technical grounds and to leave the question of color out. Mr. Douglass's friends proceeded to meet them on those grounds, and the letter of Mr. Douglass to D. W. Flynn (to which Mr. Lavalette has reference) was used for the purpose of showing that the changes brought against Douglass were erroneous.

New National Era, February 9, 1871.

EXCLUSION OF BLACKS FROM OTHER UNIONS

11.   THE BRICKLAYERS AND THE "COLORED QUESTION "

Expulsion of the Navy-yard Members from the Union--a Letter from one of the
    Expelled.

    Washington, Jun ` 19th.--On Thursday evening the Bricklayers Union held
a regular meeting, aι :*ich the subject of the employment of two colored men
in the Navy-Yard here was taken up. The committee to whom the matter had
been referred reported that two colored men were employed in the yard, upon
the same footing as the whites, and gave the names of six members of the U-
nion who were working with them, in defiance of the rules of the Union. A
resolution for the expulsion of the six men was offered, and adopted after
considerable debate. One of the expelled members sent the following letter
to the Union:

WASHINGTON, D. C., June 8, 1869.

    Bricklayers' Union No. 1., Washington, D. C.--
GENTLEMEN:--At a meeting of the Union, held June 3d, 1869, it was resolved,
by a large majority of the members that myself and other members of the
Union employed in the Navy-Yard should stop work or be expelled from the
Union. This demand is made us from the fact that colored bricklayers are
employed in the yard. We respectively are not allowed to vote without a property qualification; Massachusetts, which requires an educational qualification; and Pennsylvania, Maryland and other States where the ballot is withheld from the negro. The representation will be lessened in the North, East
and West, but it will not be affected in the South, as all those who are excluded from the ballot box for participation in the rebellion will be counted
in making up the basis of representation.

National Anti-Slavery Standard, July 3, 1869.

12.   EXCLUDING NEGROES FROM WORKINGMEN'S ASSOCIATIONS

    Some of the workingmen's associations here, warned by the troubles of
the Printers' Union, are taking measures to keep the negro out of their membership. The house carpenters held a meeting last evening, at which a constitution was adopted, wherein the word "white" was inserted in all places
where the character of the members of the association is described. Some objection was made that the word was unnecessary, because if the name of a negro was presented for membership he could be rejected by a vote of the association. A majority of the members, however, thought that it was better to
make assurance doubly sure, by providing that negroes would be ineligible to
membership, and this was finally agreed to. It is said that other workingmen's associations will take similar action.

New York Herald, July 9, 1869.

13.   RATIONALE FOR EXCLUSION STATED BY THE
CARPENTERS AND JOINERS

Resolved that we are ever willing to extend the hand of fellowship to every laboring man, more especially to those of our own craft; we believe that the prejudices of our members against the colored people are of such a nature that it is not expedient at present to admit them as members or to organize them under the National Union.

Proceedings of the Fifth Annual Session of the Carpenters and Joiners, Workingman's Advocate, October 2, 1869.

PART X

THE DEMAND FOR EQUALITY

Part X

THE DEMAND FOR EQUALITY

Lewis Douglass' embarrassing exclusion from the Columbia Typographical Union because of his race was an all too frequent occurrence for black craftsmen. More serious than the personal insult was the demoralizing effect such discrimination produced in the black community generally. Since the future seemed to offer no reward for the perseverance required to learn a skill, there was no incentive for Negroes to make the necessary sacrifices. Consequently the earning capacity of blacks as a group was certain to decline even further. Frederick Douglass articulated what most black workers felt intuitively when he denounced such a society which rendered free men slaves to poverty (Doc. 1). These deplorable conditions led one black newspaper editor to question whether the American trade unions ought to be ridiculed for their selfishness or their stupidity (Doc. 3), and probably explains why Afro-Americans sided with the Chinese exclusion issue (Doc. 2).

Even though most white unions practiced, and their organs advocated, racial exclusion, one labor newspaper was a remarkable exception to the rule. Most of the documents (4-20) in Part X are taken from the Boston Daily Evening Voice, the only labor paper of the period to champion solidarity and equality among the black and white working classes. Among the labor periodicals of the time, it was clearly exceptional, while in its social vision, it still stands above the vast majority of labor publications.

The Voice was a product of an offensive launched in 1863 by American employers to destroy the new unions which sprouted in every major city to fight for the workers' share in the wealth stimulated by the Civil War. In November 1864, the morning newspapers in Boston discharged the union printers, who in turn went on strike. The locked-out printers then began to publish the Voice, which quickly expanded until it claimed the largest circulation of any workingman's paper in New England.

One of the major issues the paper confronted was whether white workers could afford to ignore black workers. The issue was of crucial importance. By 1864 slavery was destroyed and several million blacks were added to the nation's labor supply. If they remained unorganized, blacks would be used as a ready supply of strikebreakers. Consequently, the Voice called for an end to racial exclusion, and advocated working-class solidarity, and racial equality through Radical Reconstruction. Motivated partially by their past association with the abolitionist movement, and partially by a practical desire to uplift American laborers generally, the editors undertook to educate the workers on the value of this twin policy. They relied on appeals to justice and self-interest. "Equality" and "injustice" were interrelated concepts with profound significance for the working classes. In order to succeed, the Voice argued, the labor movement had to appeal to the people's inherent sense of justice, and the movement needed the public's support. But the struggle to improve the economic status of the white working-class was dependent upon the destruction of slavery and poverty. How could the labor movement appeal to justice if it denied entry to ex-slaves and people of color? Moreover, how could the white workers improve their economic status if employers broke strikes with blacks who were excluded from the unions? Clearly whites could not afford to be indifferent to the plight of black people.

It soon became evident, however, that the Voice was waging a losing battle. So straight-forward a position on the issue of race was too progressive for the period and found little support in the labor movement. In 1867, therefore, the paper abandoned its campaign if not its convictions.

WHITE LABOR AND BLACK LABOR: THE BLACK VIEWPOINT

1.   FREDERICK DOUGLASS ON THE PROBLEMS OF BLACK LABOR

Everywhere we are excluded from lucrative employment. We have secured
our freedom from slavery to individuals, yet we are slaves to society. We
have neither the favor nor the friendship of the people around us. It cannot be denied that circumstances conspire against us. We are made to feel
the depression of a fearful prejudice. Our countrymen have not yet forgiven
the Almighty for making us black. We are discriminated against in a thousand ways. In some sections even our wages are kept back by fraud. Men refuse to lend, rent, or sell land to us. Printers unions and other mechanical associations, exclude us. Men are determined that our sons shall not
learn trades or work at trades where they have learned them, and yet we are
in a Christian country, where men who deny us the privilege of getting bread,
ask God every morning to give them their daily bread.

*Undated speech on Industrial Progress, Frederick Douglass Papers, Library
of Congress.*

2.   THE CHINESE IN CALIFORNIA

From the Pacific State, news comes of the most unchristian treatment to
the Chinese. Treatment that makes one ask, Can it be possible? Possible
that a man born in a Christian land would do it? Possible that a Christian
community would sanction it? Seared must be the conscience of that man or
that society. Yet is this state of the people's conscience a legitimate
fruit of slavery? Wrath can just as easily vent itself upon a yellow skin
as on a black. A poor helpless Chinese, is no more than a poor helpless Negro. The demon spirit that could maltreat and rob the one, will not spare
the other. We hope all the colored people of the Pacific Coast will keep
their garments clean from any act of oppression against these measurably
helpless strangers. "Remember that thou wast a servant in the land of
Egypt." Well do we remember the eloquent denunciations of Bishop Ward
against this worse than heathenish treatment. Dear Bishop keep up the fire.
Make California ring with your plea for the Chinese. Instruct all of our
ministers to speak in their behalf. Tell the people to take this kindred
colored race by the hand and help them up to civilization and to Christ. By
reason of mutual suffering and mutual prejudice we can reach them. They will
hear us. They will, may we not fervently hope, be willing to receive Christ
at our hands.[66]

The Christian Recorder, July 24, 1869.

3.   THE AMERICAN TRADES-UNIONS

Chas. Reade in his new story published in the *Galaxy*, "Put Yourself in
His Place," is holding up to the world's contempt the British Trades-Union.
Would that we had an American Chas. Reade to picture forth the ineffable

meanness of the American Trades-Unions. We know not which is made to appear
most, their selfishness or their stupidity. The printers of Washington City
lately showed the length of their ears, and now the telegram informs us that
the bricklayers of the Navy Yard are about to have the country judge of the
sweet braying of their voices.

How shall we speak of these Trades-Unions legislating in regard to col-
or? Who are these that look down upon the lowly Negro with contempt? They
are white men, who with the doors of every college in the land standing open
to them, with gratuitous scholarships on every hand, yet, had they not spirit
enough to enter, and become more than hewers of wood. They are white men,
surrounded with other white men by the scores, who were ready to take them
by the hand and lift them up to the higher walks of life, yet such was the
worthlessness of their souls, that they aspired not to be above the drawers
of water. They are white men, with every office in government open to them,
aye inviting them to enter and enjoy, yet were they destitute of a shadow of
honorable ambition, and were content to carry the load of life. These are
the men who say the Negro shall not work by their side--the Negro, who, with
almost every college door in the land closed against him, yet became well
read--the Negro who had few to help him up but many to push him down, yet
reached the top--the Negro who, with Miss Columbia, frowning if he even looked at a mail-bag, yet has he got it, and distributes its contents abroad.
the Negro shall not work by their side! Do they fear him? dread to come in
contact with him? True he has shown more zeal than they, more aspiration,
more ambition; for we verily think, judging from their past record, that had
they been bondmen, with all their boasted Saxon blood, they would have been
even more patient than the patient Negro. With all their liberty, they have
done no more than the Negro has in slavery. Both are laborers, both are mechanics.

In conclusion we have only to exhort all the American Trades-Unions to
action consistent with common sense, and the spirit of our American democracy.

The Christian Recorder, June 19, 1869.

A WHITE LABOR VOICE FOR BLACK EQUALITY

4. "JUSTICE"

Our readers have not failed to notice that statements respecting white
and colored laborers in the city of Baltimore. Whites refuse to work with
blacks. It is not very strange that such should be the case in a city so
long the capital of a slave State, and so late the hotbed of secession; we
know that the prejudice against the negro is not confined to the States where
he has been a slave. But things are not as they were--our country is entering upon a new experience, and new issues are coming before the people. We
must forget the things which are behind, and press forward to those which are
before. The workingmen's movement is a birth of the new conditions in which
the country is placed, and to succeed it must maintain its relation to those
conditions and not do violence to the spirit that called it forth.

On what is our movement based? On one idea--JUSTICE. We demand justice
--just wages and just treatment as citizens. We hold that the employer is no
more favored of God or the constitution of the country than the employee,--
that the former has no more right to wealth and its comforts and luxuries
than the latter. We point to the fact that labor produces all wealth, and we
claim our just share of the product. If we are ignorant, we say, let us have

our rights, that we may not be forced to continue in ignorance. We say that
no man, because he is stronger, has any right to tread us under foot. We
ask no favors, but our right--the right to work and the right to enjoy our
earnings.

Now it is obvious if we demand our own rights as men we must concede to
other men theirs. If we insist that employers are no better than we, we
must not pretend to be better than others. If we claim justice we must do
justice. We cannot succeed on any other ground. To attempt to do so is to
tear away the very foundation on which we essay to build. A child might understand that if we are not willing to do justice we can never hope to get
it.

The workingmen's success is simply impossible without united and harmonious action. If the machinist says to the wielder of the pick and shovel,
I will not associate with you,--if you want better wages you must get it on
your own hook; if the clerk says to the coal-heaver, between you and I there
is a gulf fixed; or if the white says to the black, I do not recognize you
as a fellow workman; and these feelings prevail, there is the end of hope for
the labor movement.

Look at it a moment. There are now four million of the negro race about
to enter the field of free labor. If we take them upon equal ground with
ourselves in the contest for the elevation of labor, they become an ally; but
if we reject them--say we will not work in the shop with them, what is the
result? The black man's interests and ours are severed. He that might have
been our co-operator becomes our enemy. This vast force of four million
workers is in the field against us. We refuse their alliance; the enemy sees
and seizes his opportunity, and the black man becomes our competitor. He
will underwork us to get employment, and we have no choice but to underwork
him in return, or at least to work as low as he, or starve. Shall we then
be so blind and suicidal as to refuse to work with the black man? Here he
is--a power to tell on one side or the other in the contest for the elevation of labor. Shall this power be used on our side, or on the side of our
opponents? It is first offered to us. Shall we reject it? We hope there
is more intelligence among workingmen than to persist in the indulgence of
an old prejudice when that indulgence is the ruin of their cause.

No, brother workingmen, side by side with every sone of toil we must win
our cause. To elevate a class only is to do nothing. We have to establish
a principle--the principle of justice--if we would have a secure foundation
for our work. When we fully comprehend and honor this principle we shall be
irresistible, and our rising will be as strong and sure as the rising of the
sun, and as beautiful and blessed.

Boston Daily Evening Voice, October 5, 1865.

5. NEGRO LABOR IN COMPETITION WITH WHITE LABOR

In a recent editorial we pointed out the vital importance to the great
cause of labor that the negro should be recognized as brother laborer; stating that if we did not extend a hand to him and help him up he would pull me
down; that there were four million of his race in the country who must live
by their work, and that capitalists would not scruple to hire them in preference to white workmen when they could get their services cheaper, the consequence of which, of course, would be to bring down the price of white labor. Here is a fact in point which may go further than anything we could
say:

"A railroad company in Michigan has lately made application to the
Freedmen's Bureau for four hundred negro laborers, to be employed in the
construction of a new line of road in that State. They offer to pay such
laborers eighty-seven and a half cents per day, and board them."

Boston Daily Evening Voice, October 14, 1865.

6. THE BOSTON HOD-CARRIERS' STRIKE, 1865

It is said that a party of hod-carriers, who have been receiving two
and a half dollars a day, have demanded an advance; that the employer refused
to accede and employed a party of negroes; that the police were ready to put
down any attempt on the part of the white hod-carriers to molest the negroes,
--which is not objected to, if the same police are ready to put down an attempt on the part of capitalists, sitting in their bank parlors and count-
ingrooms, and contractors sitting in the mechanics' exchange, concerting
plans to compel workingmen to work at the prices dictated by the nabobs who
have the control of money, and through this control can say to the laboring
man, work at our price or starve. Why is it more cruel for the hod-carrier
to fight against his competitor than for the capitalist to say to him, we
will starve your wife and children unless you conform to our demand? Both
are wrong, entirely wrong, and need reform. But is there not reason to fear
that some police officers perform with alacrity the duty (as they call it)
of mauling a hod-carrier, while they are little skittish when called upon to
protect the hod carrier from the oppression of capital? Now the question is
asked, why should the negro be willing to carry a hod cheaper than anybody
else? Why should he be induced to do so? Why should not the hod-carrier
be as well paid as the contractor? And why should not the contractor be as
well paid as the merchant, or moneylender? Indeed it might be asked, why
should the money-lender be paid at all, seeing that money is a creature of
the government, created for the common good at the common expense, and
should not be tampered with. At any rate, keep the moneylender at six per
cent. If this will not support him, let him go to work or retrench his expenses. Do not let him take advantage of the demand for money which himself
and the other bank directors have created, and say to the contractor, take
the extra interest out of the hod carriers' and other laborers' wages; and
say to the merchant, charge to the consumer. Why should not the hours of
the hod-carrier furnish him with as much money as the hours in any other indispensable vocation?

When will workingmen learn that competition among themselves to get employment of the capitalists is suicide? that this competition is just what
keeps the workingman under the thumb of capital? and this is the face of the
fact that all of what is called capital is the result of labor performed by
workingmen. The result of the hod-carrier strike proves that workingmen
should feel that the successful management of the boss and capitalist in this
case is a blow at all labor; and harder blows are yet to be delivered, unless
all workingmen are as willing and able to combine as the capitalists. One of
two things should be done--either repeal all the legislation in favor of capital and against labor, or else enact laws which shall protect labor as well
as capital.

If the negro hod-carrier will underbid the white hod-carrier because
the negro can live cheaper, soon the white will underbid the black, because
he has learned to live still cheaper, and then again the black the white, until the lowest rate obtains; and so it will be as long as it is necessary
that every laborer shall change his labor into money and a few banks or a
combination of banks can control the money.

Many capitalists and opponents of the eight-hour law and other labor
reforms, look upon the contest between black and white as a good joke. Pity
it is so, but so it is. Are we to have a "poor white trash?"

Boston Daily Evening Voice, November 15, 1865.

7. "MANHOOD SUFFRAGE THE ONLY SAFETY FOR FREEDOM"

The question of negro suffrage, now dividing the country, is one of
which it is important that the friends of the Labor Movement should entertain just views. Reformers of all men are necessitated to cast out prejudice and feeling, and base their action upon sound principle. Prejudice
contending with prejudice makes a fruitless fight; but truth is a power
which, though often resisted, nothing can overcome.

"The eternal years of God are here."

No principle has been made clearer by the facts and discussions of the
workingmen's movement than that of mutual relation and dependence among all
the ranks of labor. The whole united power of labor is necessary to the
successful resistance of the united power of capital. Otherwise, those left
out of the union are forced, in self-defense, to take a position antagonistic to their brethren or class, and become co-operation with the enemy. If
the Trades' Unions of white men exclude black men, black men are obliged to
underwork, and thus injure the cause of the white men. On the same principle, it is a damage to the cause of white labor that black labor should be
ignorant and degraded. Our Trades' Unions all recollect that one of the
first and most formidable difficulties they had to encounter was the no-ap-
prenticeship system, by which incompetent workmen were admitted to competition with skilled workmen; and they from the first saw the remedy-an efficient apprenticeship law, which should secure the thorough instruction of
every tradseman. It does not require much thought to discover that the four
millions of Southern negroes, now entering the field of free labor, stand in
precisely the same relation to labor in general as the unskilled workmen of
our Northern workshops to the skilled workmen. In self-defence this skilled
labor must elevate the unskilled.

Now the old aristocratic and slaveocratic spirit of the South is denying to the freedman the rights of citizenship, and determined to keep him
under a despotism worse if possible than slavery itself; and President Johnson, and we know not how large a party in the North, are in favor of leaving
to the negro-hating white population of the Southern States the whole question of what shall be the condition of the negro in those States. No workingman should be found with that party. An opportunity is afforded us, by
right action on this question, to strike a telling blow for the cause of labor; while the mistake of opposing negro suffrage may require the lapse of a
generation to rectify it. Our fathers foresaw that the only safe standing-
place outside of aristocratical and monarchical government was the platform
of freedom and equality; and in the recent war we have had a solemn warning
that we must carry out that principle or leave for history the sad task of
writing down democratic government a failure. The thinkers of the Revolution had the mission to plant among the nations this principle of government;
and to the workers--the workingmen--of this day is committed the important
task of bringing to maturity that which they planted.

Some prejudice exists against giving the vote into ignorant hands. But
we need not fear. The greater danger is in withholding it. One of Wendell
Phillip's pithy expressions is--"Universal suffrage means taking a bond from
the wealthy and learned to educate the poor." The moment the uneducated
holds in his hand the power of a ballot, it becomes the interest of every
man who owns property to see that he is rightly instructed in the use of it.
By giving the ballot we raise; by withholding it we degrade. The degradation
of the negro has nearly ruined the country; let us now learn wisdom by our
experience, and save ourselves by elevating him. [67]

There is no safety to free principles but in universal or manhood suffrage. If we limit it to class, we deny the very principle for which our
fathers sacrificed. We are already not without our practical warnings of
the danger of departing from this principle. As influential a paper as the
New York Herald strenuously advocates a property suffrage. It holds that it
is not fair that a poor man's vote should count as much as a rich man's; and
proposes that the amount of property a man owns shall determine how many
votes he shall be entitled to cast--making the property of the country to be
represented through the ballot-box instead of the men. This is not

democracy. And workingmen ought to know that capitalists generally sympathise with this view. Henry J. Raymond of the New York Times, and a member
of Congress, too, says in his paper that "universal suffrage is an unmiti-
gated curse." We are sorry to say that at least one paper that sometimes
professes sympathy with the workingmen echoes the same sentiment. We allude
to the Chicago Post.

Let the workingman beware. The South has been the battle-ground of the
rebellion, which undertook to establish the slavery of the negro; and it is
one the same battleground that capital will undertake to secure an advantage
by denying the right of suffrage to the freedman. Our most far-seeing
statesmen are already battling manfully for the principle, and the workingmen are wofully blind to the support of their champions. In opposing negro
suffrage, capital is playing a deeper game against labor than it has yet undertaken; and it can succeed only with the help of the laboring classes. If
we understand the groundwork of our freedom, and the hope of our cause of
Labor, we shall hold the right of suffrage sacred and dear, jealously guard-
ing it against the least infringement.

Boston Daily Evening Voice, December 28, 1865.

8. "OUR TRUE POSITION"

The Detroit Daily Union "protests in the name of the workingmen of Detroit," against our article on "Manhood Suffrage," in which we tried to show
to workingmen the true course to take in reference to the question of according suffrage to the negro. The Union thinks the position taken in that article inconsistent with our previous advice not to affiliate with any party;
because, in its opinion, "the question of manhood, or negro, suffrage is
purely a political question," and one on which the workingmen of the country
"hold and will hold their own opinions, pro and con." The Union also quotes
a paragraph from our article concerning the President's position on the question, and says there is no mistaking our intent "to array the workingmen
against the President upon the negro suffrage question," with whose "position
the workingmen, as such, have nothing to do." It regards it as "wicked to
thrust this negro question--this brand not cooled--into the councils of the
workingmen;" and can only see in our course "an over-zeal in the cause, or a
wicked betrayal of it to politicians." [68]

As the Union's sentiments are doubtless shared by many honest workingmen, our rejoinder must be somewhat extended. The editor of the Union calls
our arguments for negro suffrage "specious," but we submit to the judgment of
all intelligent friends of the movement that the following is sound reasoning.
The negroes, by emancipation, enter into the field of free labor, and become
competitors with white workingmen. They must therefore, on the principles of
the workingmen's movement, be elevated to the intelligence and rights which
white workingmen enjoy, so they can co-operate with them, or they will operate against them by underworking. To secure that elevation the right of suffrage is indispensable. Freedom is secured only by freedom. Tyrants fancy
their security--they certainly have no other--lies in enslaving the world;
but freemen are secure only when all are free. The terrible lesson which
this nation has had of the cankering effects of slavery upon the liberties of
the country, nearly accomplishing its destruction, should forever set at rest
the question whether freedom is safe in the midst of slavery. If the workingmen have learned anything, it is that there can be no hope of their success but in union--the union of all who labor; and that intelligence is the
first requisite to success. How mad and suicidal, then, to hold up one hand
for the degradation of the negro, while the other is raised for the elevation
of the white laborer. Capital knows no difference between white and black
laborers; and labor cannot make any, without undermining its own platform and
terring down the walls of its defence.

The Union says: "The question of manhood or negro suffrage is a purely
political question, and one which, at this time, is perhaps the principal if
not the only question that divides the people politically. Therefore, to
adopt it either way into the creed of the workingmen is practically to commit the workingmen to the controlling influences of the political party
whose fold they thus enter." The Union's objection arises from a misapprehension of our position; and owing to the same misapprehension we are charged by it with inconsistency. We hold now, as we did before the election,
that the workingmen must cease to act with the old parties entirely, and be
a party of themselves. We take this ground, because the workingmen have a
distinct issue to present, and because there is absolutely no hope for them
while they continue to act with the present political parties. The most
ruinous war upon the workingmen's interests has been carried on through the
enginery of the political parties, which are controlled by capital. The
workingmen must come out from those parties entirely, now and forever. But
it does not follow that they must forsake a principle because it happens to
be held by either of the parties. The conductors of this paper feel it
their duty to contend that the workingmen should urge upon Congress some
measures of relief to the people from the unjust burdens of the national
debt. This is a part of the platform of the Democratic party. Do we therefore go over to the Democrats? No. Neither do we go over to the Republicans by advocating negro suffrage.

But the Union doubtless thinks that the old prejudice against the negro, still existing in the minds of workingmen will cause enstrangement and
division in our ranks, if negro suffrage is agitated. We would certainly be
tender of people's prejudices; but, as we have shown, we are engaged in a
great work, in which the question of negro or manhood suffrage--of universal
freedom--of consistent democracy--is fundamental and vital. We must teach
truth--we must walk in the light, or we are sure to stumble and come short of
our aim.

These workingmen have profited very little by the lessons of the movement who have not learned that their views are likely to be modified by future experience. To all of us the workingmen's movement is a school, in
which the great subject of Man and his Relations is to be unfolded. In entering this school, we cut away from old authorities, and lay our ear close
to nature for instruction; and in seeking the new way, which leads through
the rubbish of old dogmas to labor's elevation--we can allow no old shackles
of prejudice to fetter us.

We should, indeed, present a figure nothing less than ridiculous, contending for great principles on pigmy party platforms,--demanding reform of
the nation, and not willing to reform ourselves--professing to teach, and
too stupid to learn--arising to depart out of Egypt, and carrying all its
idols with us!

The Union charges us with hostility to President Johnson, because we
said that he was "in favor of leaving to the negro-hating white population
of the Southern States the whole question of what shall be the condition of
the negro in those States," and, alluding to the party which opposed negro
suffrage, added emphatically, "no workingman should be found with that party."

We have to reply to this that we are not opposed to men, but to principles. In the course of President Johnson there is much to commend, and
we shall be as heartily glad as any one if it shall prove that we have mis-
judged him on this suffrage question. But believing as we do that the full
recognition of the rights of all men is essential to the success of the
cause of American labor, as a faithful and advocate of its cause we are
bound to condemn that policy which would degrade any class of men, whoever
endorses it. We hope the Union will take the same ground.

The Union says, "With the President's position on that question we believe the workingmen, as such, have nothing to do." The workingmen "as such"
are mere workingmen--machinists, bricklayers, shoemakers, &ct. They do not
take part in public questions "as such"--as workingmen--but as citizens; and
as citizens, they have as much to do with the question of suffrage and the
President's position upon it, as any other citizens.

Boston Daily Evening Voice, January 12, 1866.

9.   "THE BROTHERHOOD OF LABOR IS UNIVERSAL"

We call attention to our readers (and all workingmen) to the following report of the meeting of Carpenters and Joiners Local Union No. 4, Charlestown, Massachusetts.

Address of H. B. Roys, President of Local Union No. 4

"In our Boston Union, we have two colored gentlemen, as good workmen as stood in Boston. They both worked for one man, and when their boss learned that they were about to join the Carpenters' Union, he went to one of them and said, 'Billy, I hear you are going to join that Carpenters' Union.' 'Yes, sir.' 'Well, you had better keep away from there; and if you do join, I shall have no more work for you, although you have worked for me thirteen years.' 'Well,' said Billy, 'I guess I might as well pick up my tools now as at any other time, for I shall join the Union.' The boss wished him to keep to work, and he would think of the matter. He went to the other one, with the same result. Both gentlemen joined the Union, and the boss is thinking of the matter yet, they suppose, as they have heard nothing from him."

Would that all workingmen would memorize the following testimony of the distinguished labor reformer, Ira Steward of the Machinists' Union, before the Massachusetts Legislative Committee:

"The brotherhood of labor is universal, and embraces all classes of workingmen of every degree and color. The wages of one man must bear some relation to the wages of every other or the employer would hire the cheapest labor."

Boston Daily Evening Voice, March 21, 1866.

10.   EQUAL RIGHTS FOR ALL

By George E. Davenport

Who would the rights of manhood claim
    Should yield them unto others;
For in God's eyes we're all the same,
    One common band of brothers.

What signifies our birth, our race,
    Our pride, or lofty station?
Or e'en the color of our face,
    All men, of every nation,

Thro' heaven's justice at their birth
    Co-equal rights inherit
And none may claim superior worth,
    Save by superior merit.

All alike, or poor, or rich,
    Beneath the light of heaven,
One right possess in common which,
    By God to them was given.

The right to freedom, justice, too,
    To work out their salvation;
The right untrammeled to pursue
    Their highest aspiration.

> Let us yield unto others then
>   What we our ourselves desire,
> And aim to live our fellow-men
>   In manhood's scales still higher.
>
> No ban, or race, or creed, but free
>   As air is to mankind,
> Let all the rights of manhood be
>   As a just God designed.

Boston Daily Evening Voice, March 21, 1866.

11. A JUST CRITICISM

The New Orleans Tribune (edited by colored men) have an article on the Eight-Hour system in its issue of February 11, in which, while it cordially endorses the movement, it very modestly and dispassionately criticises the course of the Workingmen's Central Committee of New Orleans (representing eleven different trades), which excludes colored men from membership of the associations represented. With the irresistible force of truth the Tribune asks:

"How will you get justice, if you yourselves are unjust to your fellow-laborers? You address Congress in these words: "Gentlemen, we have been wronged up to this time; we have been made to labor like beasts of burden without any regard to the immortal part of our nature. Give us redress. Give us justice; we want justice for us alone. We don't care if you perpetuate the wrong upon others; do with them as you please. We think for ourselves only; we do not speak for the sake of justice, for in that case we would speak for all; but we only think of ourselves."

The Tribune points out--what should be apparent to every workingman-- that if Congress should pass an eight-hour law discriminating on account of color, white labor would be at a discount, because black labor would be opposed to it, being obliged in self-defense to underbid it.

We copy another paragraph:

"Not only there is something wrong to make so noble a move subservient to prejudice and to political purposes, but there is a perfect inconsistency in such a course. Why! let us take for instance, tailors. All, or nearly all, the important shops of this city belong to colored men. So that this Committee says to the public: "we are too good to associate WITH colored fellow laborers," when, at the same time, everybody knows that they do not find themselves too good to work UNDER colored employers! These colored employers control the tailor's trade in NEW ORLEANS. You accept colored men for bosses, and you would oppose them as fellow laborers! Be consistent before all."

Boston Daily Evening Voice, March 30, 1866.

12. MOVEMENT TO BRING BLACK LABOR NORTH

The Washington correspondent of the Post says of the Southern negroes: An immigration society is suggested here to transplant to the manufacturing localities of New England some two or three thousand of the more able-bodied and see if they cannot, in the land of schools, be taught to read and write.

The aim it is said, is to lower the price of labor. An influx of colored girls to Lowell is suggested for the inception of the scheme. They have the undoubted right to go where they please, and the means to be provided for locomotion, it is said, will not be wanting.

This is just what such papers as the Post would like to see; and it is just what we shall see if the negroes are not to have the rights of citizenship at the South. They will come North as competitors in the labor market with the Northern workingmen and workingwomen. It behooves the laboring classes to see to it that they defeat those who are about to act against the interests of all laborers, black and white,--by proscriptive legislation at the South. If they wish to come North, they have the right; but they prefer to live South, and they should not be compelled to exile themselves.

Boston Daily Evening Voice, April 3, 1866.

13. EIGHT-HOUR MEN IN NEW ORLEANS ENCOUNTER A STUBBORN FACT

Mr. Ira Steward, President of the Grand Eight-Hour League of Massachusetts, on seeing in our paper an extract from an editorial in the New Orleans Tribune (a paper edited by colored men), and being struck by its admirable sentiments, addressed to the editors a pithy letter which is published in the Tribune on the 22d ult., with introductory editorial remarks. Both the editorial introduction and the letter of Mr. Steward are well worthy to be transferred to these columns; but are too long for the space we have to spare. [69]

The remarks of the editor of the Tribune, however, embody some facts which we cannot dispense with. He says the Tribune is the only paper in New Orleans that has spoken in favor of the Eight-Hour System, yet the paper is repudiated by the eight-hour men of the Crescent City, because its editors will not bind themselves to limit the claim to the white workingmen. They therefore patronize only the Bee, the Times, and other papers that denounce them.

The Tribune continues:

"They (the white workingmen) want something right for themselves, but for themselves only, exclusively; and they imagine that a man can get justice when he says: "for justice's sake do justice to me; but, above all, do not do justice to my neighbor."

"Is not this a strange blindness? As the President of the Massachusetts Grand League says in his communication, the policy of the bosses in the Southern States is to put one class of workingmen against the other; and as long as they can do that they feel secure. Those among our laboring population who favor the "white eight hour movement" will soon learn it to their own cost.

We already hear that the bricklayers have some experience on that matter. The white bricklayers had a strike for higher wages--for "white wages" only. Very well. The colored bricklayers, who are excluded from the benevolent associations continue to work, and the white men saw that they were about to be entirely dispensed with. They call on this very day, a general meeting of bricklayers, without distinction, at Economy Hall, at noon. And we hope that the colored bricklayers, before entering into any movement with their white companions, will demand, as a preliminary measure, to be admitted into the benevolent and other societies which are in existence among white bricklayers. As peers, they may all come to an understanding and act in common.

But should the white bricklayers intend to use their colored comrades as tools, and simply to remove the stumbling block they now find in their way, without any guaranty for the future, we would say to our colored brethren: keep aloof, go back to your work, and insist upon being recognized as men and equals before you do anything.

Labor equalizes all men; the handcraft of the worker has no color and belongs to no race. The best worker--not the whitest--is the honor and pride of his trade.

Boston Daily Evening Voice, May 7, 1866.

14. "THE BOSTON VOICE AGAIN "

(The following was written several weeks ago, and has been crowded out:)
Under this head the Detroit Union takes us up on a charge of violating our "expressed determination not to allude again" to the subject of negro suffrage. The violation of which we are charged consisted in taking notice of an article of its own on toadyism to English nobility,--which it very justly considered "unbecoming in a people whose laws recognize no distinction of birth or blood,"--and just calling attention, as we did in five or six lines, to the inconsistency on its part of ignoring the human rights of the colored man.

Now we never meant to "express" any such "determination," are nearly sure we did not; but if we did we hasten to "take it back." We only meant to discontinue what we perceived to be a fruitless discussion with the Union, knowing that the more you argue against a man's prejudices the more prejudiced he becomes; and wishing to save to the labor cause what there was to save of one who seemed to be zealous and efficient, we forbore to overwhelm him with arguments, rather leaving him to his reflections. We thought, innocently enough, when, some time afterwards, we saw him blowing the aforesaid pretty bubble that if we just touched it with the point of our pen the instant evanishing of his bright creation might set him to reasoning on cause and effect.

But it didn't and the Union comes down upon us in the most pugnacious style. If we had space we would copy the whole of its effusion, which we think would be considered decidedly rich.

It charges us with advocating suffrage for the negro, but never "intimating the remotest desire that it should be extended to white females," or Indians, or foreign born residents. Well, as this is a serious charge, we will answer seriously, that it is because we were not called upon to do so-- the question not being up for discussion. If it will help the Union any, we will say that we are for equal and impartial freedom and right without distinction of sex or color. But one thing at a time. The work now before the country is the reconstruction of the States which were in the rebellion; and the success of the working men's cause depends upon the right settlement of the vital questions involved in that work. So we think.

The Union goes on:
"The iron molders of Troy may starve on their strike; the engineers of the Michigan Southern road may be crushed under the heels of that giant monopoly; little white children eight years of age may blister the tender skin upon their infantile hands in the cotton mills of Massachusetts, upon the pittance of $2.50 per week at eleven hours a day toil, under its very nose. All these things, as the columns of the DAILY VOICE prove, day by day, are secondary considerations to that paper. They occupy the obscure corners-- the back seats of the VOICE, just as the colored population of Massachusetts occupy the back seats, or no seats at all, in the churches where the cottonlords--the white child killers, assemble to *worship* God!"

We copy this just to show the absurdity of the charge. There is not a paper in the country which contains as much labor matter, or whose editorials on this subject have been so widely circulated by the labor press. Probably each daily issue of the VOICE contains more matter on the subject than a whole week's issue of the Union.

Here is a piece of logic which was not learned in the schools. The Union exclaims:

"Human rights, indeed! What are they? Life, liberty and the pursuit
of happiness. Temperance conduces to happiness. [We cannot quote the whole
paragraph. The writer goes on to say that] intemperance is a vice which
causes tenfold more misery and crime than would the eternal deprivation of
suffrage to the negro; and yet the Boston VOICE beholds with complacency
(a misstatement) the onward march of this grand wrong."
     The idea of making temperance one of the "inalienable rights" of the
Declaration will strike the reader, we think.
     After delivering itself of the above confused conception, we are pre-
pared to hear in the next sentence such a ridiculous utterance as this:
     "While we are bound to defend and maintain every right to which [any
man, white or black] is entitled as a workingman, we have nothing to do with
his political status or his social privileges."
     It might be interesting to read a statement from the Union of what it
considers "every right" of the workingman "as a workingman," without hinging
upon "political status or social privileges."
     But the reader will be hardly prepared to see the Union flatly contra-
dict itself a sentence or two further on, as follows:
     "We would elevate labor while we would level aristocracy. The extremes
of society should be discouraged by every true American."
     Yet the Union has "nothing to do" with the workingman's "political
status or social privileges!"
     It is due to the Union to say that it is not accustomed to get so far
astray from logic and common sense--an aberration which is sure to happen in
any man's case who undertakes to exalt democratic principles with one hand
and spurn the negro with the other. Colorphobia is indeed a terrible malady.

Boston Daily Evening Voice, May 14, 1866.

15. LABOR STRIKE AT WASHINGTON

     A telegraphic despatch to a morning paper says:
     "The white Irish workmen engaged in clearing out the canal which runs
through Washington, who have been working on the eight hour plan, and who
are expected to vote for the re-election of Mayor Wallack, stuck today for
higher pay. A gang of colored men promptly took their places, but the white
men refused to permit them to work and began to pelt them with stones. The
police came, arrested the ringleaders and locked them up, after which the
colored men shoveled away away unmolested."
     We don't like that,--the most of it, perhaps none of it. We believe
eight are enough hours per day for any man to work at clearing the filth
from a canal; and if the Workmen were getting insufficient wages they were
justified in striking. But we don't like the idea of other laborers, white
or colored, taking their places after they had struck, and we don't like the
pelting measure. The strike was badly managed. Henceforth let there be an
understanding between all laborers, white and black, that the employer cannot play off the one class against the other. This will be much more for
the interest of both classes than either underworking or pelting each other.
     The Eight Hour men of Washington have nominated H. N. Easby as their
candidate for Mayor. We wish every laboring man in the city could have the
privilege of voting for him.

Boston Daily Evening Voice, May 15, 1866.

16. CAN WHITE WORKINGMEN IGNORE COLORED ONES?

We long ago warned the workingmen of the country that this could not be, or that the attempt would be suicide to their cause. This is too obvious to require argument; and yet almost everywhere we find workingmen insane as to oppose the elevation of the colored laborers. In doing this they oppose their own.

The other day we recorded one fact calculated to open the eyes of this class of people. Here are two more. The first is, that

The laborers strike in St. Louis--which included both the white and colored laborers--has resulted in success.

The second is thus reported:

"The Eight-Hour League of the New Orleans workingmen rigidly excludes negroes from membership. The black laborers were equally in favor of short time, but were denied cooperation. The whites recently struck without notifying the colored men, and were much disgusted the next day at finding their places filled by Africans."

We notice that the Boston Herald copies this statement this morning, obviously for the purpose of exciting hatred of the negro in the mind of its thoughtless readers. We copy it for another purpose--that of teaching an important practical lesson to our thoughtful readers.

How many kicks like that which the workingmen of New Orleans have received will be required to give them the hint that they cannot ignore the stubborn fact that the colored labor of the country is henceforth in competition with the white; and if the white will not lift the colored up, the colored will drag the white down?

Boston Daily Evening Voice, May 21, 1866.

17. THE STRIKE AGAINST COLORED MEN IN CONGRESS STREET

We should judge by the appearance of the blacks now on the work that some of them were recently arrived from the South, and rather green at Northern work. The boss builder told us he paid them the same as he had paid the white men, and to our question whether they proved as capable hands he said he could not tell without further trial; but he should given them a pretty thorough trial before he hired Irishmen again. Irishmen should make a dispassionate note of this, and learn that when they strike against colored men, they do not hurt the colored men, but themselves only.

Boston Daily Evening Voice, August 17, 1866.

18. WORK FOR LABOR REFORMERS

Over eighty woolen and calico mills are at present being built in Georgia. They are to be run on the fourteen-hour rule, and are to compete with the factories of the North. We ask the operatives in our New England mills, will your hours of labor ever be reduced, while you are forced to compete with men, women and children who work fourteen hours a day? Nay, will you not be obliged to work more hours than you do even now? We pray you to see to it that those Southern mills be not worked by serfs and the children of

serfs. If they shall be, you have not yourselves so many political privileges but that you shall certainly work for serf's wages.
    What must be done?
    The answer is an obvious as the question--by maintaining the rights of
labor, South as well as North. The already degraded colored population of
the South may easily be subjected to the hardes exactions of capital, and
capital will not be slow to avail itself of its opportunity. Doubtless
cheap labor is one of the allurements to these enterprises. The fact here
given should flash upon every mind the truth of the universal brotherhood of
labor.

Boston Daily Evening Voice, August 22, 1866.

19. COLORPHOBIA

    This peculiar disease, confined entirely to the white race, is of quite
modern origin, nothing being recorded of it in history. About twenty-five
years since it assumed its most malignant type, and was then first named and
its symptoms described by that eminent practitioner, Nataniel P. Rogers.
His specific for it was liberal doses of "Herald of Freedom," taken once a
week,--this being as often as the patient could bear the remedy, which was
very powerful,--though the malady yielded, but slowly even to such treatment.
Other physicians treated the disease with equal judgment, using similar med-
icines, though under different names. A very eminent doctor persistently
prescribed "Liberator," another styled his searching preparations, Speeches;
another, Songs. The present manifestations of the disease requiring a modification of the treatment, some of the once favorite remedies have been dis-
continued. It is believed the disease is dying out, many portions of the
country being quite free from it; though we occasionally hear of very desperate cases. But these are in remote and out of the way places, where the
moral diet is gross, and the people have not been served by enlightened physicians. [70]
    These brief notes naturally slipped from our pen as we laid down the
Detroit Daily Union, after the perusal of two articles devoted to the VOICE
and the Republican party and the colored representatives; and concluding as
follows: "We put the question, therefore, to the Boston VOICE directly, and
shall respectfully request an answer,--Is John Morrissey as worthy of the
suffrages of the workingmen of New York as the negroes it extols are of the
workingmen of Massachusetts?" [71]
    If we had space we would let our readers see both the articles of the
Union. They reveal a clear case of color-phobia, and we are sorry; for the
Union would be a very useful paper if it could be cured. But we have already
tried our hand, and the poor sufferer refuses to take our medicine. He does
not get any better; rather worse, we fear. Alack-a-day!
    We mean no disrespect for the editor of the Union; he has got a bad dis-
order, and we could not help being amused at the antics it makes him perform,
even if he were our own father. We will, however, put a sober face and answer his question.
    First, it is necessary to the reader's understanding to explain that the
Union thinks the VOICE a Republican (!) paper (the Republicans here believe
anything but that); and in its article to which this question is appended it
quotes two passages;--one from the VOICE rejoicing over the election of the
colored men, and the other from the Cincinnati Times (a Republican journal),
relating to the election of John Morrissey, of whom, and whose election, and
the Democratic party, it spoke in terms which did not please the Union. The
Union,--strangely enough, we think,--speaks of John Morrissey's election as
"a triumph" of the workingmen of New York. "He was," says this paper, "a
poor, hard-working boy, an iron moulder by trade--and it is but a few years
since he was enabled to leave the shop and live upon his income." His

history is well known to be that of a pugilist and a gambler. "His income"
is the plunderings of the "faro-bank;" and because he was originally a
moulder, the Union thinks he may be regarded as a workingman and that his
election is a matter of rejoicing.

Now we would not do injustice to Mr. Morrissey. He says in a card published previous to the election that he wishes to reform, and we are willing
he should have a chance,--as well as the rest of the plunderers and pugilists
who go to Congress, but have been cunning or dishonest enough to pursue their
trade in a "respectable" way. And indeed we have more hope of Morrissey's
reformation than of theirs. He has always done his wickedness openly, and
proved that he has honor and generosity which are noble traits. These are
our sentiments of Mr. Morrissey.

With the colored gentlemen elected in Boston to the State Legislature we
are not acquainted; but they are highly spoken of by those who know them.
They are from the ranks of labor, and will hold up their hands for labor reform. There is no fear that they will do discredit to the white or the black
race, and therefore, being workingmen, they are certainly worthy of workingmen's support. The Union will see that the mere accident of color is of no
account with us. We believe

"A man's a man for a' that."

If the Union is not directly answered, we think the nut is cracked, and
we leave it to pick out the meat.

Boston Daily Evening Voice, November 17, 1866.

20. A WORKINGMAN'S REMINDER

Whoever spurns his fellow man
Because of his color, race, or creed
And places him beneath a ban,
Is guilty of a wrong indeed.

Boston Daily Evening Voice, September 2, 1867.

PART XI

THE BLACK RESPONSE TO COLORPHOBIA

THE BLACK RESPONSE TO COLORPHOBIA

    The National Labor Union grew out of the consciousness that the local ef-
forts of workers could never remedy the evils they suffered. It was evident
that only by "nationalizing" their struggle and by establishing working-class
solidarity could the workers hope to win a better life. In the first attempt
to set up a national labor federation after the Civil War, several leading
trade unionists issued a call for a national convention. The assembly which
founded the NLU met in Baltimore in August 1866, with sixty delegates representing 60,000 people. No mention of black workers emerged until the 1867
convention, when the committee on Negro labor requested that the question of
admitting black workers be delayed in order to avoid a split of the delegates.
The committee declared that since the constitution did not bar blacks, there
was no reason to debate the point. Two black delegates were admitted to their
seats, however (Doc. 1-3). The Boston Daily Evening Voice hailed the convention's recognition of blacks as brothers and "co-laborers" (Doc. 4), while the
white feminist, Elizabeth Cady Stanton, chided black workingmen for not being
more forceful in their efforts to unionize (Doc. 6).
    When the NLU met again in 1869, a delegation of black unionists was pre-
sent. The convention did not go on record as favoring integration, but did
adopt a resolution encouraging the organization of separate Negro trade unions
which would be affiliated with the NLU. Although segregation was still maintained, the 1869 convention marked the first occasion when a national gathering of white workers authorized the admission of black unionists to participate as affiliated union representatives, and advocated the organization of
black trade unions. The reform press hailed this as a major breakthrough,
and the Woman's Rights Convention, which was meeting in Cleveland at the time,
applauded the NLU for its progressive stance (Doc. 9-10).
    The 1869 NLU convention brought national attention to Isaac Myers of the
Baltimore Colored Caulkers' Trade Union Society, who spoke for the black delegation while the white members listened "with the most profound attention" .
(Doc. 7). Myers was a leading black spokesman in Baltimore when, in 1865, the
white caulkers and carpenters mobbed their black counterparts and drove them
from the shipyards. In response, Myers helped to organize the Chesapeake Marine Railway and Dry Dock Company, as well as the Caulkers' Union, which employed the 300 black workers driven off their jobs. With the timely assistance
of government contracts, the venture succeeded (Doc. 11-13).
    Although the white unionists listened to Myers with keen interest, fun-
damental political differences were to prevent the blacks from accepting affiliation. Along with many labor reformers of the period, the NLU advocated
repudiation of the war debt by paying those with government bonds in "green-
backs" rather than gold. Furthermore, the NLU consistently condemned the Republican party as an agent of Wall Street and President Grant as their spokesman. For blacks this represented heresy. After all, the Radical Republicans
were responsible for most of the political gains achieved by Negroes since the
Civil War, while the Democrats represented the forces of oppression. Rather
than divide black workers by accepting the NLU position, as it assuredly would
have, Myers and other black unionists issued a call for a Colored National Labor Union to meet in convention in January 1869. The first of its kind in
American history, the black union delegates met in Washington, D. C. (Doc. 14).
    The final selections in Part XI presage the call and proceedings of the
Colored National Labor Union, which introduce volume II of this series.

THE NATIONAL LABOR UNION AND BLACK LABOR, 1866-1869

1. THE "COLORED QUESTION" AT THE NATIONAL LABOR
UNION CONVENTION, 1867

Mr. Phelps, from the Committee on Negro Labor, reported that, having had the subject under consideration, and after having heard the suggestions and opinions of several members of this Convention--pro and con--have arrived at the following conclusions:

That, while we feel the importance of the subject, and realize the danger in the future of competition in mechanical negro labor, yet we find the subject involved in so much mystery, and upon it so wide diversity of opinion amongst our members, we believe that it is inexpedient to take action on the subject in this National Labor Congress.

RESOLVED, that the subject of negro labor be laid over till the next session of the National Labor Congress.

The report was extensively discussed, Mr. Trevellick taking strong ground against it on the ground that the negro will bear to be taught his duty, and has already stood his ground nobly when member of a trades union.

Mr. Harding opposed it because he did not like to confess to the world that there was a subject with which they were afraid to cope, and Mr. Green thought that the consideration of the subject had been too long deferred already. He well remembered that this very question was at the root of the rebellion, which was the war of the poor white men of the South, who forced the slaveholders into the war. (Interruption.)

Mr. Peabody was against the adoption of the report. He did not want to see a single labor organization misrepresented in that congress, black or white. The difficulty, if ever laid over, would be even greater than now.

Mr. Phelps said in New Haven there were a number of respectable colored mechanics, but they had not been able to induce the trades' unions to admit them. He asked was there any union in the states which would admit colored men.

Mr. Van Dorn was sorry that the word "black" or "colored" had been used in the convention. He believed in meeting the difficulty, however, as it had been raised, and would vote to take in the black worker as a duty to a common brotherhood. The colored man was industrious, and susceptible of improvement and advancement.

Mr. Kuykendall said that the negro or white man had not been mentioned in the constitution already adopted, and there was no need of entering on any discussion of the matter.

Mr. Mitchell had looked on the matter as being fully settled.

Mr. Cather understood the intention to be to legislate for the good of the entire laboring community of the United States. There was no necessity for the foisting of the subject of colored labor, or the appointment of a committee to report thereon. He had no doubt that the blacks would combine together of themselves and by themselves, without the assistance of the whites. God speed them; but let not the whites try to carry them on their shoulders.

Mr. Ellacott moved to recommit the report to the hands of the committee, and Mr. Lucker suggested that they would not be expected to report.

Several other gentlemen concurred in this view, claiming that these questions were settled when the constitution was adopted.

Mr. Gibson said it would be time enough to talk about admitting colored men to trades' unions and to the Congress when they applied for admission.

Mr. Sylvis said this question had been already introduced in the South, the whites striking against the blacks, and creating an antagonism which will kill off the trades' unions, unless the two be consolidated. There is no concealing the fact that the time will come when the "negro will take possession of the shops if we have not taken possession of the negro. If the workingmen of the white race do not conciliate the blacks, the black vote will be cast against them."

Mr. Peabody said that the capitalists of New England now employed foreign boys and girls in their mills, to the almost entire exclusion of the
native-born population. They would seek to supplant these by colored workers. He thought there was little danger of black men wanting to enter white
trades' unions any more than Germans would try to join the English societies
in America. . . .

[The report was recommitted, and the committee afterwards reported "that
after mature deliberation they had come to the conclusion that the constitution already adopted prevented the necessity of reporting on the subject of
negro labor." This report was adopted.]

Workingman's Advocate, August 24, 31, 1867.

2. THE LABOR CONGRESS

We have availed ourselves today of the reports of the Chicago Post and
Tribune for an account of the doings of the Labor Congress on Wednesday and
Thursday. We do not know how faithful these reports may be, but they are
the best at hand.
    It will be seen that Mr. Kuykendall and Mr. Schlaeger were admitted to
seats, which fact we are glad to set to the credit on the Congress: but the
fact that these gentlemen's two seats were questioned as they were is no credit to our representatives. [72]
    And while we are in the critical mood, we cannot forbear to say that the
debate on the question of negro labor was also very discreditable to a body
of American labor reformers. The question should not have come up at all,
any more than the question of redheaded labor, or blue-eyed labor. Of course
the negro has the same right to work and pursue his happiness that the white
man has; and of course, if the white man refuses to work with him, or to give
him an equal chance, he will be obliged, in self-defence, to underbid the
white, and it is a disgrace to the Labor Congress that several members of
that body were so much under the influence of the silliest and wickednest of
all prejudices as to hesitate to recognize the negro. When we need to get
rid of prejudices and learn to take catholic views, they have nailed their
prejudices into this platform. We shall never succeed till wiser counsels
prevail and these prejudices are ripped up and thrown to the wind. The labor
reform is labor rising into noble and dignified manhood, in the name of God
and humanity, or it is the weak and contemptible menace of slaves. We have
some good men in this Congress, but not enough of them, this is evident.

Boston Daily Evening Voice, August 27, 1867.

3. "SHALL WE MAKE THEM OUR FRIENDS, OR SHALL CAPITAL BE
ALLOWED TO TURN THEM AS AN ENGINE AGAINST US?"

The condition of the negro as a slave, and the moral and economical efforts of slavery, were discussed by the press, from the public rostrum, and
in the halls of Congress for years and years with great energy and zeal;
what shall be his status as a free man is at present a matter of no less national anxiety. But aside from this, his interest as a workingman, and especially the part he is to take in advancing the cause of labor have, as yet,
received no consideration. It is in this last respect exclusively that, the

question has an interest for the friends of the labor reform; an interest of
such vital importance that, delicate as the question may be, and notwithstanding the impossibility of expressing an opinion in reference to it,
which would meet with the universal approval of the workingmen of America,
the committee feel that it would be a sad dereliction to pass it by unno-
ticed.

The first thing to be accomplished before we can hope for any great results is the thorough organization of all the departments of labor. This
work, although its beginning is of such rec- it date, has progressed with
amazing rapidity. Leagues, societies and associations exist in all the large
towns and cities, and in many villages and country districts. There are
central organizations _n many of the states, and one national labor congress,
the result of whose deliberation on the future welfare of the country can
scarcely be overestimated. In this connection we cannot overlook the important position now assigned to the colored race in this contest. Unpalatable
as the truth may be to many, it is needless to disguise the fact that they
are destined to occupy a different position in the future, to what they have
in the past; that they must necessarily become in their new relationship an
element of strength or an element of weakness, and it is for the workingmen
of America to say which that shall be.

The systematic organization and consolidation of labor must henceforth
become the watchward of the true reformer. To accomplish this the co-operation of the African race in America must be secured. If those most directly
interested fail to perform this duty, others will avail themselves of it to
their injury. Indeed a practical illustration of this was afforded in the
recent importation of colored caulkers from Portsmouth, Va., to Boston,
Mass., during the struggle on the eight hour question. What is wanted then,
is for every union to help inculcate the grand, ennobling idea that the interests of labor are one; that there should be no distinction of race or nationality; no classification of Jew or Gentile, Christian or Infidel; that
there is but one dividing line--that which separates mankind into two great
classes, the class that labors and the class that lives by others' labor.
This, in our judgment, is the true course for us as workingmen. The interest
of all on our side of the line is the same, and should we be so far misled by
prejudice or passion as to refuse to aid the spread of union principles among
any of our fellow toilers, we would be untrue to them, untrue to ourselves
and to the great cause we profess to have at heart. If these general principles be correct, we must seek the co-operation of the African race in America.

But aside from all this, the workingmen of the United States have a
special interest in seeking their co-operation. This race is being rapidly
educated, and will soon be admitted to all the privileges and franchises of
citizenship. That it will neither die out nor be exterminated, is now regarded as a settled fact. They are there to live amongst us, and the question to be decided is, shall we make them our friends, or shall capital be
allowed to turn them as an engine against us? They number four millions
strong, and a greater proportion of them labor with their hands than can be
counted from among the same number of any other people on earth. Their moral
influence, and their strength at the ballot-box would be of incalculable
value to the cause of labor. Can we afford to reject their proffered co-operation and make them enemies? By committing such an act of folly we would
inflict greater injury upon the cause of Labor Reform than the combined efforts of capital could accomplish. Their cherished idea of an antagonism
between white and black labor would be realized, and as the Austrian despotism makes use of the hostility between the different races, which compose
the empire to maintain her existence and her balance, so capitalists, north
and south, would foment discord between the whites and blacks, and hurl the
one against the other, as interest and occasion might require, to maintain
their ascendancy and continue the reign of oppression. Lamentable spectacle!
Labor warring against labor, and capital smiling and reaping the fruits of
this mad contest.

Taking this view of the question, we are of the opinion that the interests of the labor cause demand that all workingmen be included within its
ranks, without regard to race or nationality; and that the interests of the
workingmen of America especially requires that the formation of trades'

unions, eight hour leagues, and other labor organizations, should be encouraged among the colored race; that they be instructed in the true principles of labor reform, and that they be invited to co-operate with us in the
general labor undertaking. The time when such co-operation should take effect we leave to the decision and wisdom of the next congress, believing
that such enlightened action will be there developed as to redound to the
best and most lasting interests of all concerned. . . .

*John R. Commons, Ulrich B. Phillips, Eugene A. Gilmore, Helen L. Sumner, and
John B. Andrews (eds.), A Documentary History of American Industry (New York:
Russell & Russell, 1958), vol. 9, pp. 157-60.*

4. ADDRESS TO THE WORKINGMEN OF THE
NATIONAL LABOR UNION

We are greatly pleased to see the high stand taken by the Address of the
two topics which are at the same time most important, and least understood,
--the relation of woman and the relation of the colored race in our movement.
The ignorance and prejudice which make the labor reform necessary are necessarily the great obstacles it has to encounter; and the VOICE having for
some time contended all alone, among the advocates of labor reform, for the
recognition of the truths here involved, we hail this emphatic endorsement
by the Labor Congress of this doctrine that woman must be paid the same for
the same work as man, and that the negro must be recognized as a brother and
co-laborer or there can be no elevation to labor, as one of the most encouraging signs of progress which are now cheering the thoughtful and observing
friends of reform.

Boston Daily Evening Voice, June 26, 1867.

5. THE PRESENT CONGRESS

The adjourned session of Congress has furnished another proof, if any
were wanting, of the utter incapacity of that body to provide the relief
which the people demand from those oppressive conditions which are the joint
results of an expensive war, legislative prodigality, if not corruption, and
a stupid incompetency to comprehend the only methods by which the nation may
issue from its embarrassments.
    If it be the atmosphere of Washington which dwarfs men who, before they
become members of Congress have, at least, ordinary intelligence, the sooner
the capital is removed the better. If the mere fact of being a congressman
necessarily stunts the human faculties, it becomes a philanthropic duty to
abolish Congress, if, indeed, the abolition of that body is not demanded by a
natural law which expels everything lifeless from the living organization.
The Congress which has just adjourned, imagines the nation to be in exactly
the condition which gave rise to the questions in the popular mind, at the
conclusion of the civil war, while in fact the nation, following in the direction of those forces which broke down the right of property in man has
passed out of the circumstances which made these questions pertinent. The
history of the United States but marks the steps of a grand revolution. In
1776 it was a question of colonial independence, born of the denial of the
right of representation. In 1860, the question changed its phase from national to individual independence. Jefferson's Declaration of Independence

which the facts of each day are writing down, not on parchment, but upon the
human soul, is individual. The one proposed to break down the power of a
foreign despotism, the other the tyranny of false principles. These principles underlying our social organization, which distributes society into
classes, dooms some to poverty and others to affluence; crown a tyrant, in
comparison with whose rule the sceptre of George the Third was mild.

Workingman's Advocate, August 3, 1867.

6. ELIZABETH CADY STANTON CHIDES BLACK UNIONISTS [73]

. . . If colored men had been as wide awake as women, instead of idly
waiting for republican abolitionists, now melted into one apostle, Wendell
Phillips (having announced his adhesion in last week's *Standard)*, they would
have had their Labor Unions, and their delegates to this "National Labor
Congress." Such representative men as John L. Langston, Robert Purvis, and
Frederick Douglass, would have been readily admitted, and would not only
have dignified their race, but by their learning, eloquence, and power have
added to the ability and interest of the union. We urge the colored men of
the nation to remember that "they who would be free themselves must strike
the blow;" hence, if they are not represented in the next National Labor Congress to be held in Pittsburgh, Penn., August, 1869, it is their own fault.
You see, friends, so soon as we women get a foothold among the "white males,"
instead of selfishly rejoicing in our own good fortune, forgetting all that
are behind, we turn to help our colored brother up to the same platform.
The world never hears us say, "this is the woman's hour," for in the world
of work, as in politics, we demand the equal recognition of the whole people.
    One thing was clearly understood in the Convention--that the workingmen
would no longer be led by the nose by politicians, as they proposed to have a
people's party in '72. They feel that it is a matter of no consequence which
party succeeds in the coming election, as their condition will be precisely
the same in the success of either Grant or Seymour. As to all the talk
about a country, with Grant we shall have peace, and with Seymour war, so
long as neither party proposes Universal Suffrage, or a Sound Monetary System, it makes no difference to the masses which succeeds; or, whether they
are made slaves by brute force or cunning legislation. [74]
                                                    E. C. S.

The Revolution, October 1, 1868.

1869 CONVENTION OF THE NATIONAL LABOR UNION

7. FIRST DELEGATION OF BLACK UNIONISTS ADMITTED TO A
WHITE LABOR CONVENTION

Address of the Colored Delegates
to the Convention

Philadelphia, Wednesday, Aug. 18, 1869.

The Convention was called to order at 9 A.M., President Lucker in the chair. . . .

Mr. ISAAC MYERS, (colored,) of Maryland, said that he had an address prepared by the colored delegates to this Congress which he wished to read. He would not take up the time of the Convention at this stage of the proceedings, however, but asked the privilege of reading the document during the last quarter of an hour of this morning's session. Leave to read was granted unanimously. . . . [75]

The following address prepared by the colored delegates for presentation to this Convention, and by a vote this morning, appointed to be heard at 11:00 A.M., was then read by Mr. ISAAC MYERS, (colored,) of Maryland. The whole Convention listened to the reader with the most profound attention and in perfect silence. Mr. MYERS, who is a light-colored mulatto, a ship carpenter from Baltimore, read the document in a full, round voice, with proper emphasis, and in a clear and distinct manner. The reading was at times interrupted with applause, and at the close, many delegates advanced and warmly congratulated him. The address was ordered to be printed, and the hour of 12 o'clock having arrived, the Convention adjourned till 2 P.M.

ADDRESS OF THE COLORED DELEGATE.

The following is the address of the Colored Delegates to the National Labor Congress:

Mr. President and Members of the National Labor Convention:

GENTLEMEN: It would be an act of great injustice to your Godlike charity should I allow the deliberations of this Convention to close without returning you the thanks of four millions of our race for your unanimous recognition of their right to representation in this Convention. We sympathize with you in the loss of your great leader and champion, the immortal WILLIAM H. SYLVIS. God in his wisdom has called him to "that bourne whence no traveler returns," and our prayers shall ever be that his immortal spirit shall ever hover around the Throne, and bathe its wings in the morning dews of Heaven. He labored incessantly for you and your prosperity. No distance was too far for him to travel. No hours of labor were too long for him to work while he advocated eight hours for you--eight hours for rest, eight hours for study, and eight hours for work. He gave all of his hours in laboring to bring about that glorious result. His heart, soul, mind and strength were absorbed in his labor of love, and to-day, by one stroke of the unerring pen of President U. S. GRANT, you are enjoying the first fruits of victory. Write his faults in the sand, and his virtues in the granite. Gentlemen, silent but powerful and far-reaching is the revolution inaugurated by your act of taking the colored laborer by the hand and telling him that his interest is common with yours, and that he should have an equal chance in the race for life. These declarations of yours are ominous, and will not only be felt throughout the length and breadth of this great Republic, but will become another great problem in American politics for the kings and dynasties of Europe to solve. It is America and it is only Americans that can work up and work out such great revolutions in a day. God grant that it may be as lasting as the eternal hills. I speak to-day for the colored men of the whole country, from the lakes to the Gulf--from the Atlantic to the Pacific--from every hill-top, valley and plan throughout our vast domain, when I tell you that all they ask for themselves is a fair chance; that you and they may make one steady and strong pull until the laboring man of this country shall receive such pay for time made as will secure them a comfortable living for their families, educate their children and leave a dollar for a rainy day and old age. Slavery, or slave labor, the main cause of the degradation of white labor, is no more. And it is the proud boast of my life that the slave himself had a large share in the work of striking off the fetters that bound him by the ankle, while the other end bound you by the neck.

The white laboring men of the country have nothing to fear from the colored laboring man. We desire to see labor elevated and made respectable; we desire to have the hours of labor regulated, as well to the interest of the laborer and the capitalist. And you, gentlemen, may rely on the support of the colored laborers of this country in bringing about this result. If

they have not strictly observed these principles in the past, it was because
the doors of the workshops of the North, East and West were firmly bolted
against them, and it was written over the doors: "No Negro admitted here."
Thus barred out, thus warned off, his only hope was to put his labor in the
market to be controlled by selfish and unscrupulous speculators, who will
dare do any deed to advance their own ends.

Mr. President and gentlemen, American citizenship with the black man is
a complete failure, if he is proscribed from the workshops of this country--
if any man cannot employ him who chooses, and if he cannot work for any man
whom he will. If citizenship means anything at all, it means the freedom of
labor, as broad and as universal as the freedom of the ballot. I cannot tell
how far your action in admitting colored delegates on this floor is going to
influence the minor organizations throughout the country. Shall they still
proscribe the colored labor, or will they feel bound to follow your noble
example of Monday? The question being today asked by the colored men of this
country is only to be answered by the white men of the country. We mean in
all sincerity a hearty cooperation. You cannot doubt it. Where we have had
the chance, we have always demonstrated it. We carry no prejudices. We are
willing to forget the wrongs of yesterday and let the dead past bury its
dead. An instance of this may be found in my own native Maryland. After we
had been driven from shipyard to shipyard, until at last we were kicked completely out and cast upon the cold charity of the world, we formed a cooperative union, got it incorporated, raised $40,000, bought a shipyard, gave
employment to all of our men and now pay them, outside of their wages, fifty
percent on their investment. And is that all? No. We give employment to
their political creed, and to the very men who once sought to do us injury.
So you see, gentlemen, we have no prejudice. We have issued a call for a
National Labor Convention, to meet in the City of Washington the first Monday in December next. Delegates will be admitted without regard to color,
and I hope you will be well represented in that convention. Questions of the
mightiest importance to the labor interest of the United States will be disposed of. We will be very glad to have your cooperation there, as you have
ours now. The resolutions of this convention will have an important bearing
on that convention. The more you do here, the less we will have to do there.

The colored men of this nation are entirely opposed to the repudiation
of the national debt. They go in for every honest dollar borrowed to be
honestly paid back, and on the terms stipulated in the original agreement.
Any other course is more ruinous to the laborer than to the capitalist. The
permanence, not of this administration nor of any other, but of the government itself, depends on the honest paying of its debts. A dishonest government, like a dishonest individual, will be arrested, tried, convicted and
punished.

The money borrowed was from individual pockets. The slaveholders of the
South and their sympathizers in the North forced us to borrow that money. It
was borrowed to put down the rebellion, not to put down slavery, for that was
not in the contract. Liberty to the slave was a bird hatched by the eggs of
the rebellion. And of all men in the United States, the laboring men of the
North, East and West are most benefited by the money borrowed. You know that
had you not whipped slavery, slavery would have whipped you. If the rebellion had succeeded, slavery would have soon spread over the entire country,
and you white laboring men of the country would have been forced to work for
what a man chose to give you, and that very often under the lash, as was the
case in South Carolina. What has stopped this? The money that our government
borrowed in good faith. Has the government paid too much for its use? We
think you will find it is no fault of the government, but of those who rebel-
led against it. These are questions that require your weightiest consideration. The workingmen of this country are a vast power, can take care of
themselves, and will not be hoodwinked by any political demagogue in or out
of power. What we want is low prices for the necessaries of life, and honest
administration of the government, reasonable hours of labor, and such a compensation for the time made as will afford us an independent living. We want
no land monopolies, any more than money monopolies or labor monopolies. We
want the same chance for the poor as is accorded to the rich--not to make the
rich man poorer, but the poor man richer. We do not propose to wage a war on
capital, and we do not intend to let capital wage a war on us. Capital and

labor must work in harmony; reforms, to be made successful, must be founded on the soundest principles of political economy. We feel that in the person of President Grant the workingmen have a strong friend. After the quibbling of the Attorney General, and others in authority, whether Congress meant you should have a day's wages for eight hours' labor, President Grant ordered, and it was declared, that eight hours was a day's labor, for which there should be no reduction of pay. His is a type of Americanism as handed down by the Fathers. He cannot be an aristocrat, he cannot feel himself above the common people, and any measure looking to the elevation of the working-men of this country, we believe, is sure to have his support. The colored men of the country, we believe, are sure to have his support. The colored men of the country thoroughly indorse him.

Gentlemen, again thanking you for what you have done, and hoping you may finish the good work of uniting the colored and white workingmen of the country by some positive declaration of this convention, I wish you a complete success.

New York Times, August 19, 1869.

8. PHILADELPHIA LABOR CONVENTION--ADDRESS
OF THE COLORED DELEGATES

The following is the main portion of the address of the Colored Delegates to the National Labor Congress-- It was read by Mr. Isaac Myers, (colored) of Maryland. The whole Convention listened to the reader with the most profound attention and in perfect silence. Mr. Myers is light colored, a ship carpenter, from Baltimore read the document in a full, round voice, with proper emphasis, and in a clear and distinct manner. The reading was at times interrupted with applause, and at the close many delegates advanced and warmly congratulated him. The address was ordered to be printed.

Silent but powerful
                    complete success.

National Anti-Slavery Standard, August 28, 1869.

9. "THEY GAINED THE RESPECT OF ALL"

To any one who has watched the deliberations of this congress of artisans and working-men, one peculiar fact stands out in bold relief, viz., that the barriers of class and caste have been broken down, so far as the laboring classes of the country are concerned, if we are to take the solemnly-avowed sentiments of this body as indicative of the feelings that exist among the constituencies therein represented. For the first time in the history of this nation a convention has been held in which working-men and working-women, white and black, loyalists and ex-rebels, have met together upon terms of perfect equality, for the purpose of taking deliberative action on vital questions affecting equally the interests of all. In this respect the convention was a novelty, and is deserving of more than a mere passing notice.

In elaborating this point, he notices that colored members were welcomed to the deliberations of an assembly, the majority of whose members are of a political organization which might well be regarded as hostile to any such affiliation; that a native Mississippian delegate, an ex-Confederate officer, in addressing the convention, refers to a colored delegate who had preceded

him as "the delegate from Georgia;" that a native Alabama delegate, who had
owned negroes as chattels, sat at the committee board with a black man, and
signed the report under this man's name; and that an ardent and avowed Democratic partisan from New York declared, with bold frankness, that he asked
for himself as a mechanic and a citizen no privilege that he was not willing
to concede to every other man, white or black.

He also notices that these colored men gained the respect of all, and
credits Mr. Peter C. Brown, of Philadelphia, a real ebony negro, with disen-
tangling a parlimentary snarl into which the assembly had got itself, by
giving a straightforward statement of the condition of the question, and following it up by a motion to reconsider, which was the very action needed to
solve the difficulty. He also credits Mr. Isaac Myers with an address which
drew forth universal praise; and Mr. R. H. Butler, "of the veriest sombre
hue," with a brief speech "replete with good sense and an excellent appreciation of the power of words" against the importation of coolies, and in recognition of the fellowship shown his friends and people. It was noticeable,
too, that whenever a colored delegate addressed the chair, all eyes were simultaneously turned in the direction of the speaker, and the courtesy of general attention to his remarks was invariably paid to him--a matter that the
white members were not, in every instance, able to command.

As a result, he argues that the great wall of caste and color, which has
hitherto divided the laboring classes, is no longer unsurmountable. Whether
the negro has overleaped the obstacle, or made a breach through it, is im-
material. The simple fact remains, that he has gone beyond it, reached the
other side, and is to be, hereafter, an equal in the great field of competi-
tive labor.

The American Workman (Boston), August 28, 1869.

10. RESOLUTION PASSED AT THE WOMEN'S RIGHTS CONVENTION IN
CLEVELAND, NOVEMBER 26, 1869

Giles B. Stebbins then made some interesting remarks, closing them by
offering the following resolution, which was adopted:
Resolved, That the National Labor Congress, representing five hundred
thousand of the working men of our country, at its late session in Philadelphia, by recognizing the equal membership of and rights of men and women, of
white and colored alike, showed a spirit of broad and impartial justice worthy of all commendation, and we hail its action as a proof of the power of
truth over prejudice and oppression which must be of signal benefit to its
members in helping that self-respect intelligence and moral culture by which
claims of labor are to be gained and the worker truly ennobled and elevated
. . . .

National Anti-Slavery Standard, December 4, 1869.

THE FIRST BLACK LABOR LEADER: ISAAC MYERS, THE
BALTIMORE CAULKERS, AND THE COLORED TRADES UNIONS OF MARYLAND

11. A BIOGRAPHICAL SKETCH OF ISAAC MYERS CAREER

Mr. Isaac Myers of Baltimore, Md. The founder and President of the Aged
Ministers Home of the AME Church is in every sense of the word a self-made
man. Born of poor parents in a slave state, that afforded no school privileges for colored youths, his success in life is a noble example of what push
and pluck can accomplish under the most adverse circumstances. He received
a common school education in the private day school of Rev. John Fortie and
at the age of 16 was apprenticed to James Jackson, a prominent colored man
in his day to learn the trade of ship caulking; how thoroughly he mastered
the business may be inferred from the fact that at the age of 20 he was superintending the caulking of some of the largest clipper ships that were
then being built in that once famous ship-building city.
In the year 1860 he entered the wholesale grocery of Woods, Bridges, and
Co., which became, during the war, the largest establishment of its kind
south of Mason and Dixon's line. He acted here in the double capacity of
chief porter and shipping clerk and acquired a knowledge of the grocery business in all its branches that subsequently served a good purpose.
Leaving the above establishment in 1864 he organized and successfully
conducted a company grocery store, which if left to the control of his judgment would have been today one of the great institutions of Baltimore.
In 1865 he resigned the management of the above institution, and returned to the shipyard. In this year the great strike against colored mechanics
and long-shoremen was inaugurated under the leadership of the notorious "Joe"
Edwards. The city was under the control of "Know Nothing" influence, and in
sympathy with the strikers, and notwithstanding the bold fight made under the
leadership of Mr. Myers, Wm. F. Taylor and Charles O. Fisher, every colored
mechanic in the shipyards and longshoreman, over 1,000 were driven from their
employment. It was at this juncture that the executive and great organizing
abilities of Mr. Myers were first demonstrated. In December of this year he
conceived the idea of the colored people buying a shipyard and marine railway. The proposition was submitted to a number of merchants who promised
their work. He called meetings in all the colored churches of Baltimore; organized a company, and within four months raised $10,000 cash in shares of
five dollars each, exclusively from colored people; purchased of James N.
Muller his yard and railway for $40,000, and 300 colored caulkers and carpen-
ters found immediate employment. For a while they enjoyed almost a monopoly
of the business of the city, also giving employment to a large number of
white mechanics. He secured a government contract of $50,000, against the
combined competition of ship builders of Wilmington, Philadelphia, Baltimore,
and Alexandria. The moral influence of this organization restored the longshoremen, but the stevedores, taking the advantage of the situation, and condition of the men, cut their pay. He organized the workmen, prepared a protest and submitted it to the merchants, who ordered the pay restored to $2.50
per day, upon the penalty of giving their work to Philadelphia stevedores.
The entire debt of the shipyard was paid off in five years from the profits
of the business, after which he left it to enter the political arena. The
same year he was appointed a messenger to the Hon. John L. Thomas, collector
of customs of Baltimore, being the second colored man appointed to a position
under the Federal Government in Maryland.
In January 1870, at the suggestion of George T. Downing of Rhode Island,
Fred G. Barbadoes and the late Rev. J. Sella Martin, a conference of the
leading Republicans of the country, white and colored, was held at the residence of U. S. Senator Pomeroy in Washington, D. C. and it was desired to
petition Hon. John A. J. Cresswell, Postmaster General, to appoint Mr. Myers
a special agent of the Postoffice Department. The application received the
endorsement of the Committees on Postoffice and Postroad of the U. S. Senate

and House of Representatives, the only endorsement of the kind on record, and on March 7, 1870, Mr. Myers received his commission, and was assigned to the supervision of the mail service in the Southern States with headquarters at Washington, D. C. About this time the Labor Question, under the leadership of the great champion of labor, Trevellick, was seriously agitating the mind of the country, it being their purpose to put in nomination a national ticket, and as a condition precedent, to divide the colored vote in the Southern States by the organization of labor clubs. Mr. Myers grasping the situation, and to offset Trevellick's scheme, issued a call for a National Labor Convention of Colored Men, which met in the City of Washington, January 10, 1871. It is a historical fact that this was the largest and best representative convention of colored men ever held in the United States. The convention remained in session five days, and formed a national plan for the educational and industrial organization of colored people and elected Mr. Myers president. Within six months a State organization was formed in nearly all of the Southern States, as well as in some of the Eastern and Western States. In August of the same year, Mr. Myers appointed Mr. Isiah C. Wears, of Philadelphia, and Peter H. Clark, of Ohio, as delegates representing the Colored National Union and the three met the great National Labor Congress at Cincinnati, August 14th, the largest gathering of white labor men ever assembled in this country, their purpose being the organization of the Labor Reform party. The position taken by Myers, Wear, and Clark was against the amalgamation of politics with labor. After a careful summing up of the plans and purposes of the congress, on the fifth day Myers made a very characteristic speech in defense of General Grant's administration, and in support of the Republican party as the friend of labor, the only speech of the kind made in the convention; it produced considerable excitement and threw the convention into a tumult. It was with the greatest difficulty that he was protected from personal assault on the floor of that convention. He was forced back over the railing into the space occupied by newspaper correspondent, by the pressure of the excited delegates. The speech was published in most of the leading newspapers of the country, August 18, 1871. In the state campaign of North Carolina, 1872, he rendered invaluable service, and the success of the National ticket, owes more to any of the political managers of that campaign, of which evidence in his possession will show. In the following year the Hon. Fred Douglass was elected president, since which time the National Labor Union has ceased to exist. . . .

In 1879 he retired from the service and opened a coal yard in Baltimore. He was in 1882 editor and proprietor of the Colored Citizen, a weekly campaign newspaper, published in Baltimore. In the same year he was appointed a United States gauger, and became one of the most proficient and popular men on the force. He resigned the position of United States gauger Feb. 2, 1887, the day the Democratic collector took charge of the office, and was the only man in the State who made a voluntary resignation. In the Presidential campaign of 1888 he was Secretary of the Republican Campaign Committee, of Maryland; also rendered valuable service on the stump. In 1888 he organized the Maryland Colored State Industrial Fair Association. Their first fair held in that year, eclipsed any similar one ever held by colored associations in the United States. He organized and is President of the Colored Business Men's Association, of Baltimore; he also organized the first Building and Loan Association of that city. He has been 15 years superintendent of Bethel A.M.E. School of Baltimore. It is generally regarded as the leading Sabbath School of that denomination, and is pronounced by Secretary Smith "the banner S.S. of the world." He is also a trustee of said church, and Secretary of the Board. He is past grand master of Masons of Maryland, and author of a Masons Digest, favorably commented on by Masonic writers, is also a prominent Odd Fellow and Good Samaritan.

He is the author of a drama in three acts, entitled "The Missionary."

The Freeman (Indianapolis), October 12, 1889.

12. THE COLORED MEN'S SHIP YARD

We alluded to this enterprise some months since, but not until last week
were we able to understand its magnitude and importance. For many years
past, in the city of Baltimore, the caulking of vessels had been done mainly
by colored men. Hundreds of them were engaged in this business, and had acquired a reputation for superior skill and efficiency, that was known wherever American vessels landed. In October 1865, the few white caulkers combined
with the ship carpenters and insisted that colored men should be discharged
from the yards. The employers would not accede to this: whereupon this
wicked combination had recourse to the most terrible violence, and by the use
of pistol, club and knife in the hands of superior numbers they succeeded in
driving them from all the shipyards.
Thrown suddenly out of an employment which had engaged a life-time,
these men, most of whom had dependent families to support, were indeed in a
distressed condition. They held a meeting for consultation and mutual solace.
At this meeting Mr. Isaac Myers, a young man of noble heart, keen penetration,
and determined energy, proposed that they form a compnay, purchase a ship yard
and carry on business themselves. This was readily agreed to, and they immediately commenced to negotiate with Mr. Jas. M. Muller, Jr., for the purchase of his extensive ship-yard and railway. He was astonished at their
proposition, and was loath to part with his business, but seeing the condition of the colored men, he agreed to sell out to them for forty thousand
dollars. The caulkers immediately began to hold a series of meetings to interest fellow citizens in the enterprise. Ten thousand dollars worth of
stock was soon taken. Among the stockholders are Rev. Bishop D. A. Payne,
D. D., and Frederick Douglass, Esq.
Having secured ten thousand dollars, they succeeded, through the influence of Samual Dougherty, a colored ship captain, in borrowing thirty thousand dollars from Capt. Wm. Applegarth, which was secured by a mortgage on
the ship-yard payable in six years. They took possession of the ship-yard
February 12th, 1866, Captain Samuel Dougherty superintending. . . .
Two hundred and fifty colored men, frequently a greater number, are employed in this yard as carpenters and caulkers, which is a greater number
than is employed by any five ship-yards in Baltimore. The average wages is
three dollars per day.
During the six months which this yard has been in operation, the books
show that twenty-eight thousand dollars worth of work has been done. Mr.
William Applegarth, who made the loan to the company, has had twelve thousand dollars worth of work done. Some of the ship owners who were the greatest opponents of this enterprise are now among its best patrons. One of the
once bitter enemies of the "nigger ship-yard" has now a large ship on its
railway undergoing repairs. . . .

The Christian Recorder, August 11, 1866.

13. CONDITION OF THE COLORED PEOPLE

Maryland, and especially Baltimore, contains a larger proportion of
skilled colored labor than any portion of the country, New Orleans not excepted. We may, therefore, hope to see its colored citizens, take and hold a
leading position in all that tends to make them useful. One of the best evidences of thrift and enterprise I have noticed, so far, are the building and
other self-help associations which exist here. The first-named societies
were inspired by the successful economy and activity of the Germans. There
are at least 25 colored societies in the city. There are several known as
"The National Relief Association No. 1," etc. The admission fee is $2.50 and

ten cents a week is required thereafter. . . .

Among the noteworthy efforts is an operative brickyard, owned in five-
dollar shares, and run by the share-holders themselves. It is doing very
well, but I have been unable to get its balance-sheets, and we cannot state
the amount and results of business done.

At various times, during the past four or five years, attempts have
been made to establish cooperative stores, but they have not succeeded,
chiefly because the parties engaged have not the knowledge or patience to
carry out such experiments. The most interesting movement I have found is
that known as the Cheseapeake Marine Railway and Dry Dock Company, which, as
it illustrates the tyranny of caste and the manner by which it can be defeated, when even energy, industry, skill, and determination (are) combined,
deserves some extended notice. The company, or rather its leading corpora-
tors, have already attained more than a local fame, from the fact that from
among them came the movement which resulted in the recognition last year at
the Philadelphia Labor Congress of colored labor delegates, and subsequently
of the organization at Washington in December following of the National Colored Labor union. Now for the origin of this enterprise. Baltimore, had
always been famous as a ship-building and repairing entrepot. In slave
times a large portion of the ship caulkers especially were colored men, as
were also many ship-carpenters. In all other trade connected with this interest, a considerable share of the skilled, and nearly all of the unskilled
labor, was colored. As a rule they were and are excellent mechanics. Frederick Douglass once worked in the very yard now owned by colored men. When
last in Baltimore, he visited the yard, and took the caulker's tool in hand
once again. The slave power was strong enough to protect these colored mechanics, many of them being slaves. When the war terminated, however, the
bitter hostility, hitherto, suppressed, against colored labor, manifested
itself in violent combinations. As Mr. Gaines, the present manager of the
company, informed me, extermination of colored mechanics was openly declared
to be the aim of their white rivals. The combination was against all labor,
but manifested mostly in the shipbuilding trades. The white mechanics all
struck, even refusing to work, where colored cartmen and stevedores were employed. There was no antagonism or complaint on account of wages, as the
colored men were as strenuous as the whites in demanding full pay. The
Trades Unions, to which, of course, colored men were not admitted, organized
the movement. In the yards on one side of the Patapsco River the colored
caulkers were driven off in 1865. In 1866 the general strike was organized.
The bosses did not sympathize with the white mechanics, and to the credit of
many, be it said, they stood out as long as possible. Very sson the strike
threatened to become general against all colored labor, mechanical or otherwise; the violence threatened to be extended even to hotel waiters of the
proscribed race. The atrocious movement was industriously fomented by the
active men in Andrew Johnson's reaction. [76]

At last the leading colored caulkers, carpenters, and mechanics, seeing
what the crusade meant, determined on a vigorous protective effort. Their
conclusion was reached in the organization of the Maryland Mutual Joint
Stock Railway Company, whose capital was to consist of 10,000 shares at $50.
About 2000 shares were taken within a few days, and $10,000 subscribed, 100
shares being the largest amount taken by any one person. Most of the shares
were taken in ones, twos, and threes, by mechanics, caulkers, laborers, even
the barbers and washerwomen being represented. The shipyard and marine railway they now own belonged to Jas. L. Mullen and Son, earnest Union men and
warm defenders of equal rights to their workmen. They offered to sell and
asked no more than the place was worth--$40,000. The bargain was closed;
another honorable gentleman, Capt. Sipplegarth, ship-owner, builder and nav-
igator, came forward and loaned them the remaining $30,000, on six years'
time, at moderate interest, with the privilege of paying at any time within
the six years, taking a mortgage on the property itself.

It is interesting to note their progress from this fair start. The plan
embraced only ordinary business rules, and their managers have never attempted the introduction of either the industrial partnership idea, or more distinctive cooperative principles. The value of the enterprise, whoever, is
in the lesson it teaches of what quiet energy and industry will do toward
conquering prejudices and combinations.

The Company was organized and got to work by Feb. 2, 1866, employing
at first 62 hands, nearly all skilled men, and some of them white. Business
was depressed, the outrageous strike having driven it away from the port,
and the work did not average for some months more than four days per week,
at the average wages of $3 per day. At the present time the Company are a-
ble to employ, fulltime, 75 hands. From Feb. 2, 1866, to Jan. 1, 1867, its
business amounted to about $60,000, on which the profits were nearly or
quite 25 percent or $15,000. The next year was better for them, though
business was generally very dull. In carrying out their work and paying
their men, they had to resort to borrowing as a rule. They never had a note
protested. Within four years from organization they completed the payment
for their yard and railway, lifting the mortgage in June last. In 1868 they
were incorporated by the title I have given, having done business previously
under the firm name of John H. Smith and Co. Most of their trade is with
Eastern ship-owners and masters. At the present time they do, and have done
for three years past, more repairing than any other company on the Patapsco
River. This success has not been achieved without serious trouble. Intimidation has been practiced on their patrons. In two instances, where profitable jobs were pending, they have been driven off by white mobs; in one case
a white man who took charge of their working force was shot dead. What added point to the act was the fact that he was ordinarily one of their bitterest antagonists. On another occasion, having hired the Canton Marine Railway to take up a large ship which they were caulking and repairing, the
whites threatened to strike, and so the Railway Company refused to allow its
use. Still they have perservered, and today are masters of the situation.
They have had some good contracts, in one case repairing Government dredges
and tugs.

The managers think the feeling against them decidedly subsiding. They
accredited this fact mainly to their ability to employ labor and pay for it
promptly. They think that men have been forced to a sense of shame by finding no resentments cherished on the part of the corporaters of the Chesapeake
Company. To some extent, more recently, they believe that the dread of Chinese labor induces the ultra-trades unionists to desire their (the colored
mechanics') favor. It is worth noting that they are not, and never have been
members of the trades unions. Their business rules, as stated to me by the
manager, are simple. Asking why they did more ship repair work than other
firms or companies possessing equal facilities, the reply was: 1st, because
our labor is of the best; the men we employ are thoroughly skilled, and 2nd,
we seek to retain custom as well as make money. We have never lost a patron
except by outside intimidation. We try to accommodate, work hard and over-
time to finish jobs, and always use the best materials. These are good
rules, and this is a good record. . . .

The ownership of their works, buildings, and machinery valued at $40,000
and a business valued at not less than $65,000, and a business of at least
$75,000 per annum is no bad result of a movement designed to resist caste and
race oppression. If, now, these stockholders would go further and recognize
labor as entitled to profits equally with capital, if only in the partial
principle of the famous Briggs Colliery (England), it would become still more
a shining mark, and have as the noblest laurels the generous fact that it
taught here the solution of the labor and capital problem. In one sense,
even now, the material projected by the builder has become the corner-stone;
but if this corporation of working men could be induced to do the larger
thing, and establish an industrial co-partnership, how much more truly would
the old Scriptural illustration be realized?

New York Tribune, September 1, 1870.

14. THE NATIONAL CONVENTION OF THE COLORED MEN OF THE REPUBLIC

By Isaac Myers

Should there be a convention of the colored men of the Republic at this time? is a question being asked and discussed by prominent white and colored men North and South. I answer, yes! we must have a National Convention of the colored men from every State in the Union, to be held in the city of Washington, January 13th, 1869, because 1st we are not citizens of the United States. Article IV, Sec. 2 of the Constitution of the United States says: "The citizens of each State *shall* be entitled to all privileges and immunities of citizens in the several States." If we are citizens of the United States, why cannot a colored man who is a voter in Massachusetts, and who removes to the State of Pennsylvania and lives there the same time it would take a white resident be a voter? Why cannot he vote? Either the State law is supreme, or Congress is powerless to enforce the Constitution of the United States. Then where do we stand in either case? Citizens of a particular state are at the will and pleasure of a majority, even if that majority is made up of "Repeaters," and Naturalization Frauds. The "But" in the Fourteenth Amendment to the Constitution provides for a disfranchisement of a portion of the citizens of any State. And may not any of the Reconstructed States at any future time as the laws of the United States now stand, disfranchise their colored citizens? Would they not be willing to lose one-half of their representation in Congress temporarily to accomplish this result? Certainly they would. So long as this temptation remains will it not inspire the enemies of our race to work with the hope of one day having possession of the government--declare the Reconstruction acts of Congress null and void? . . .

2. We want the franchise laws of each State to apply equally to every man irrespective of his race or color who may be a legal resident of the State in which he resides. And to do this we want a National Convention representing all the colored people of the United States to ask Congress to give us a Constitutional Amendment written in the plainest language, guaranteeing to all the male citizens of the United States, without regard to race or color, the right to vote at all elections, national or local, that may be held in any and each of the States and territories that compose the United States, also making it a high crime with a heavy penalty against any person or persons who shall interfere with said right, guaranteeing the whole power of the Government to execute said penalty. It must be evident to the best minds that this is the next great National problem to settle. . . .

3. We want the Public School laws of the different States to apply equally to white and colored pupils. . . . Therefore let our National Convention present this question to the country, asking that justice in this direction be given to the colored American.

The objection of providing ample schools and facilities for the education of colored children that now exists in some of the States, is a lack of common sense on the part of their law makers. It is a fatal blunder at statesmanship. If there were a possibility of annihilating or exterminating the "inevitable Negro" then some advantages might be pled for not educating him, but no such possibility exists, and never will exist, here he will stay and increase in numbers, until Gabriel shall blow his trumpet. Hence the great absurdity and shallow-mindedness of those who claim to be American statesmen. To educate the colored man, is to make him see his manhood and respect it. To educate him is to make him see the true value of citizenship and protect it.

To educate him is to make him a profitable laborer, mechanic or merchant that will add to the wealth and influence of the State. To educate him is to allow him to understand the true principles of Government, and make him loyal proof against domestic or foreign enemies. It is for the colored people of the country to press this question until we have all the doors of the public schools open to us. Don't let it be said of us, that we pay our taxes

to support public schools and never disturb our brains, and the brains of
our lawmakers, about the rights and privileges of our children, to be educated in them without restriction as to how much they shall learn.

4. We want the colored men of the country to know and be seriously impressed, that industry and enterprise will bring that long prayed for Mil-
lenium of prosperity, good will and happiness, which is essential to American citizenship.

We want every boy to have a trade, to be the master of some profession.
This is the nation's source of wealth.

It is unfortunate as it is unjust, that the colored boy is not permitted
to enter the workshops of the Northern cities to learn a trade. But parents
of Northern children can combine their capital and build shops of their own,
can set in motion a thousand spindle, anvils, axes and trowels, and can buy
the best white talent North or the best colored talent South, and not only
educate their sons in the various branches of manufacture and mechanics,
but become merchants themselves by bringing into the market a commodity, the
result of their own capital and enterprise.

The colored people of the South have free access to all and every
branch of trade and mechanics, it is with them to rise rapid and high and to
develop the capacity and worth of the colored man; from them we shall expect
much, when the Congress of the United States shall make them citizens in
fact as well as in name. When they shall have the right to vote without intimidation and when they shall not be kicked out of their Legislatures because they are not white.

We want and must have a National Convention to consider and present all
these and more questions to the American people, and to our people and make
that Convention respectful, let every hamlet, town, city, county and state
in the Union, at any cost, send their delegates to Washington on the 13th of
January, 1869 and present our claims calmly and dispassionately to the American Congress and to the American nation.

The Christian Recorder, November 28, 1868.

15.   COLORED TRADES' UNION IN BALTIMORE

Meeting of Colored Persons--A meeting of colored men, embracing members
of some of the trades, was held last evening at the Douglass Institute, for
the purpose of effecting an organization into trades unions and societies.
Isaac Myers was called to the chair, and on his motion James Morris was selected as temporary chairman, and Wesley Howard temporary secretary. Isaac
Myers, after prayer had been made, stated the object of the meeting to be
that of organizing the colored mechanics of the city and State. He said that
white mechanics have their trades unions, and refuse to allow colored men to
work with them, and he thought that colored men should be alive to their interests, and organize in the same manner.

The bestowing even of the franchise upon the colored men would benefit
them but little if they did not organize and protect themselves and their
families in this manner. He alluded to the plan now on foot to import Chinese laborers into the South to take the place of colored men. These Chinese could be procured for $50 and even $25 a year. The colored men were
respected, and more deference was shown them every day. As an instance, he
mentioned the case of the printer boy Douglass, who had made application for
permission to work in a printing office at Washington. The very fact of the
Washington Typographical Union postponing action in his case was evidence
that the rights of the colored man were being treated with consideration.
He continued at length, urging the importance of unity of action on the part
of the colored people.

The next speaker was George Myers, who remarked that the question under
consideration was of much more importance than any other to the colored race,

for without organization they could accomplish nothing, but with it everything. He read from a speech recently delivered by the Hon. Henry Wilson,
at Rochester, before the workingmen, during which he stated that "the sad-
dest spectacle every presented to the American people is the spectacle presented at the capital of the republic of a class of workmen laboring to prevent another workman from working for the government of the United States."
Organization, he remarked, was the only way in which the colored man could
influence State Legislatures to do away with class legislation. It was the
duty of colored men to look after their rights in the labor market. He then
spoke of the Labor Congress which is to assemble in a few days in the city
of Philadelphia, and gave it as his opinion that the influence of meetings
held in Baltimore would be felt in that body. The speaker concluded by urging unity of action in this matter on the part of the colored people as essential to their prosperity and happiness.

    Wm. L. James next addressed the meeting, and at the conclusion of his
remarks a motion of Isaac Myers, for the appointment of a committee of five
on permanent organization was adopted. J. C. Pindell, Geo. Myers, H. C.
Hawkins, Ignatius Gross and Reuben Gearing were appointed the committee, and
retired to another room. In the interim James Harris, of Canada East, a
bricklayer and plasterer, addressed those present, stating that he had heard
a good report of them in his far distant home. He was followed by Wm. Hare,
painter, whose remarks were well received by the meeting, after which the
committee returned and reported as permanent officers the following named:

    President, Isaac Myers; vice-presidents, Ignatius Gross and Wm. L.
James; recording secretary, J. C. Fortie; assistant secretary, J. P. Harris;
corresponding secretary, H. C. Hawkins, and treasurer, James Norris.

    On motion the report was accepted, and Isaac Myers was conducted to the
chair, and returned his thanks for the honor conferred on him.

    A motion by George Myers for the appointment of an executive committee
was adopted, one from each trade being selected by the respective branches.
The committee consists of the following-named: Reuben Gearing, tanner; Wm.
E. Wilkes, cooper; George Myers, caulker; Peter Nelson, blacksmith; James
Cornish, ship-carpenter; Moses Jennings, house carpenter; Daniel Davis, engineer and machinist; Thomas J. Harris, bricklayer; John W. Goldsborough,
cabinet-maker; Wm. Hare, painter; Daniel Harris, plasterer; Goerge Grason,
brickmaker; Henson Williams, tinner; Ignatius Gross, iron-moulder; Charles
Cornish, wheelwright; Samuel Hyer, block and pump maker; John H. Tabb, hat-
ter; Richard Griffin, cigarmaker; Saml. Caution, sailmaker; Wm. Tidings,
silversmith; Daniel Finley, coopersmith; James Jackson, stove-maker, and S.
S. Brown, shoemaker.

    The committee is to meet on Friday night, to prepare the rules, &c., to
govern the body hereafter. A finance committee was, on motion, appointed by
the president, and consists of Wesley Howard, Ignatius Gross, Frisby Ritch-
field, Jas. Harris and George R. Wilson. The meeting then adjourned to next
Monday evening.

Baltimore Sun, July 20, 1869.

16. CONVENTION OF COLORED MECHANICS

    An adjourned meeting was held last evening in the basement hall of the
Douglass Institute of the delegates to the Convention of Colored Mechanics
which assembled at the same place on the previous Monday. The object of the
Convention has been previously stated, which was called for the purpose of
organizing the colored mechanics and tradesmen of the city and State into
societies or trades-unions, such as are adopted by white mechanics throughout
the country. The hall was well filled, and the various branches of mechanism
represented.

Mr. Isaac Myers, President, called the Convention to order, when, by request, Mr. Alfred McLane opened the proceedings with prayer.

The Secretary, Mr. J. C. Fortie, then read the proceedings of the previous meeting, which were approved by the Convention.

Mr. George Myers, Chairman of the Executive Committee, then presented the following preamble and resolutions:--

Whereas, Divine Providence has ordained that man shall obtain his living by the sweat of his brow.

And whereas, An honorable living can only be obtained by honest, industrious and patient toil.

And whereas, An organized and unjust effort has been, and is now being put forth by our white fellow-citizen *mechanics* of the several States to prevent men of African descent from obtaining a living at any one of the trades.

And whereas, Said effort is unwise, unjust, unchristianlike and unrepublican, and its tendency is to degrade and render burdensome a large portion of our race; and who if allowed to work at any employment for which they are capacitated, would elevate the race of their identity, the better to prepare them to support their families, educate their children, and the more intelligently discharge the responsible duties of American citizenship. Therefore be it

Resolved, That we believe it to be expedient and right for the colored men of Maryland and of the several States to organize Trades or Labor Unions, with a view to accomplishing the following results: First, to ascertain the number of colored mechanics and their particular branch, second, to place that labor in the market as will be to the best interest of the laborer and capitalist.

And further be it resolved, That where colored labor cannot find a market because of the existence of organized superior force, that cooperative or joint stock associations be organized, that colored labor may find employment and be made productive.

And further be it resolved, That no person shall be proscribed from membership on account of his race, color or nationality.

And further be it resolved, That we recommend the use and study of Wayland's Political Economy in all the colored mechanical and labor associations in this State, believing that when the relationship between capital and labor is more generally understood, a better feeling will exist between the employer and the employed, and the vexed question of wages be adjusted without the resort to strikes.

And further be it resolved, That we shall encourage in all our associations the wisdom of each member being a regular depositor in some Savings Bank, a member of some Building Association, and hold a policy of Accidental or Life Insurance.

The resolution having been read a second time, Mr. Lemuel Griffin made a few remarks recommending that the Convention should act with caution in whatever they undertook; and while he did not oppose the report of the committee, it was his belief that the preamble should be amended somewhat, especially that portion which spoke of efforts put forth by the white mechanics to prevent colored men from obtaining a living.

Mr. George Myers replied to Mr. Griffin, and said that it was well known that the white mechanics had organized with the above object, and as the colored men would soon be *citizens,* they should assert their rights.

Mr. Isaac Myers, President, also advocated the adoption of the resolutions. The meeting, he said, which had been held in that hall the previous Monday evening had been echoed by the press throughout the length and breadth of the country. White men know that when the Fifteenth Amendment is adopted the colored men will be allowed to enter the workshops of the country. They had assembled for the purpose of laying down a great principle. By combining and organizing the colored men would be enabled to present a respectable front, and it was only in this way that their full strength could be ascertained.

The resolutions, after some further debate, were then adopted by the Convention.

The committee also submitted the following resolutions, looking to the organization of trades unions and labor societies, and calling a State

Convention, which were adopted:

Resolved, That the members of each particular trade and labor association convene at some convenient place on Friday evening, August 6th, 1869, for the purpose of organization and the election of officers.

And be it further resolved, That said organizations furnish the Executive Committee with the list of its members, and the place of their residence.

Resolved, That a State Labor Convention be held in the city of Baltimore on the 12th day of September in each and every year, to be composed of five delegates from each trades union or labor organization throughout the State.

And be it further resolved, That the President of each organization shall constitute an Executive Committee, together with the President and officers of the State Convention, who shall be members *ex-officio* of the Executive Committee.

And be it further resolved, That said Executive Committee shall have power to make such general laws and regulations as will best accomplish the object of the organization.

Also authorizing a call for a National Convention, for which Mr. Isaac Myers

Whereas, In the course of events it has pleased Divine Providence, through the agency of war, to change the relationship between capital and labor; and *whereas,* by said change a general disarrangement of labor of all kinds does exist; therefore,

Be it resolved, That this State Convention do call a National Labor Convention of the colored men of the several States, to meet in the city of Washington on the first Monday in December, in the year of our Lord 1869.

Resolved, That the Executive Committee prepare a call for said Convention, to be disposed of as soon as the committee may decide.

And be it further resolved, That no proscription be made in the admission of delegates to said Convention on account of race or color.

A motion was made by Mr. Hare to substitute Richmond, Va., in place of Washington as the place for holding the National Convention, but on being put to vote was negatived by a vote of yeas 12, nays about 20.

On motion it was resolved that five delegates be appointed to the National Labor Convention (white) that meets in the city of Philadelphia, August 16, 1869.

Delegates—Isaac Myers, James Hare, Ignatus Gross, Squire Fisher and Robert H. Butler.

On motion of J. C. Fortie it was resolved that Frederick Douglass, Esq., be invited to address the citizens of Baltimore on the subject of labor.

After some further business the Convention adjourned to meet on the 6th of August.

The Christian Recorder, August 14, 1869.

NOTES AND INDEX

1   The life of Leo Africanus was almost as fascinating as his well-known travel accounts of Africa. Born in Spain in 1494, he moved with his family to North Africa shortly thereafter and entered the Moroccan diplomatic service while still in his teens. Between 1513 and 1515, he went on a long caravan journey, led by his uncle, and gained a first-hand acquaintance with fifteen Negro kingdoms of the Western Sudan. In 1518 he was captured by Christian pirates, who were so impressed with his great learning and wide travel that they took him to Rome as a present for the Pope. The young Moor won the favor of Leo X, who freed him, gave him a pension, and conferred upon him his own name. When captured by the pirates, Leo Africanus (the name he is known by) had with him a rough draft of his travel experiences. In 1526 he completed the work, and it was published in Italian under the title *The History and Description of Africa and the Notable Things Therein Contained*. John Pory, a friend of the great geographer Richard Hakluyt, translated the volume into English in 1600.

2   Denmark Vesey (c. 1767-1822) was born in Telemarque, and for twenty years he sailed with his ship-captain master to the Caribbean. Vesey purchased his own freedom with money he won in a lottery, and successfully invested in several business ventures. Vesey was literate and acquired considerable knowledge from his master. He settled in Charleston, South Carolina, and became a Methodist minister. Determined to strike a blow for the freedom of slaves, Vesey devised an intricate conspiracy, the full extent of which was never divulged, for the slaves to take the city of Charleston in the summer of 1822. The plot failed, however, and Vesey and forty-six others were executed. Although the conspiracy was never implemented, it constituted the most extensive plot in the history of slavery in the United States.

Nat Turner (1800-1831) led the most serious of the slave revolts ever actually executed in the United States. Born a slave in Southampton County, Virginia, Turner was always a "mysterious" individual to blacks as well as whites. He was of obviously superior intelligence, skilled as a carpenter, and became an "exhorter." Turner believed himself to be a divine instrument, appointed by a vengeful god to exact retribution from whites and to free his people from bondage. He and about sixty fellow slaves launched their insurrection in the summer of 1831, killing fifty-seven whites before the revolt was quashed. An hysterical manhunt followed whereby over 100 innocent black victims were killed. Eventually, twenty blacks, including Turner himself, were hanged for their role in the uprising. News of the revolt spread through the South like a shock wave, creating fear and a demand for an intensification of protective security measures.

Richard Allen (1760-1831) was born a slave and grew up near Dover, Delaware. At seventeen he underwent a religious conversion, and then he converted his master. Allen hired himself out and in three years had saved enough to purchase his own freedom. He became a circuit preacher and eventually settled in Philadelphia, where large numbers of blacks came to hear him preach at St. George's Methodist Church. Before long, Allen withdrew his following because of discrimination and organized the African Methodist Episcopal Church. In 1816, after twenty-two years of litigation, the new church was officially chartered. That same year, a number of A. M. E. ministers met in Baltimore, organized into a conference, and elected Allen its first bishop. Along with other close associates of his race, such as James Forten and Absolom Jones, Allen was also a leading abolition and civil rights exponent in Philadelphia.

When Allen pulled out of St. George's Church, it was Absolom Jones who helped lead the flock. Together they organized the Free African Society of Philadelphia, a religious and mutual aid association. Jones preferred the Anglican traditions of liturgy, however, and split with his

friend to establish the African Protestant Episcopal Church. The two
religious leaders remained friends, nevertheless, and labored together
for improvements in the black community of Philadelphia.

3   A cooper was a skilled craftsman who made wooden barrels.

4   The Mid-Lothian Coal Mining Company operated several mines about ten
miles outside of Richmond, Virginia. It was one of the largest users
of slave labor in the southern coal industry.

5   During the 1840s, the James River and Kanawha Company built a canal
from Richmond to the headwaters of the Kanawha River on the western side
of the Blue Ridge Mountains.

6   The Tredegar Iron Company was the largest iron producer in the Ante-
Bellum South, and one of the largest users of slave labor. The owner,
Joseph Anderson, was determined to teach slaves even the most skilled
crafts of iron manufacture.

7   The *Enquirer* was published in Richmond, Virginia. This particular
article refers to the strike of 1847, when white ironworkers walked off
the job because the owner of the Tredegar Iron Company introduced black
slaves into their department. The whites lost the strike, and the black
bondsmen stayed.

8   Frederick Douglass (1817-1895), abolitionist, orator, journalist,
public servant, was born of a slave mother and a white father in Tuck-
ahoe, Maryland, in 1817. He never knew his mother well, but lived with
his grandparents until the age of eight, when he was raised by "Aunt
Katy," who was in charge of rearing slave children on the plantation of
Colonel Edward Lloyd. As a young man he experienced both cruelty and
indulgence, but never lost his human spirit. He turned on his cruelest
master and lived to understand that resistance could pay, even for slaves.
Douglass was sent to Baltimore where he learned the trade of ship caulking. By tracing the letters on the prows of ships he also learned how
to write. On September 3, 1838, armed with seamen's papers supplied by
a free Negro, Douglass boarded a train in Baltimore and escaped to New
Bedford, Massachusetts. Five months later he first came into contact
with William Lloyd Garrison's anti-slavery weekly, *The Liberator*, and in
1841 delivered his first speech at a convention of the Massachusetts
Anti-Slavery Society. He was immediately employed as an agent of the
Society, and rapidly became the most famous of all the black abolitionists as well as one of the greatest orators of his day.
      At first Douglass confined his speeches to personal experiences as a
slave, but soon began to denounce slavery, calling for its immediate abolition. The more polished his speech became, the fewer people believed
that he actually had been a slave. To dispel all such doubts, in 1845
Douglass published his *Narrative of the Life of Frederick Douglass*, even
at the risk of reenslavement. Douglass resolved to go abroad to England
and for two years he spoke against slavery throughout the British Isles.
In 1847, with his legal freedom purchased by British friends for 150
pounds, he left London to resume the battle against bondage in America.
After settling in Rochester, New York, he started his newspaper, *The
North Star*, later renamed *Frederick Douglass' Paper*.
      Differences soon developed between Douglass and his white abolition-
ist colleagues. Garrison did not believe another newspaper was necessary, and he also disagreed with the other reforms Douglass favored, such
as temperance and woman's rights.

When the Civil War came, Douglass fought for the enlistment of black men into the Union army, and assisted in recruiting the 54th and 55th Massachusetts colored regiments which later won distinction in battle. As the war progressed, Lincoln conferred with Douglass as a representative of his people. During his last years Douglass was successively Secretary of the Santo Domingo Commission, Marshal and Recorder of Deeds of the District of Columbia, and finally United States Minister to Haiti. Douglass remained an active reformer literally until the day he died, collapsing after attending a woman's suffrage meeting.

9   William Wells Brown (1815-1884) was born a slave in Kentucky. He escaped to the North and became an effective anti-slavery leader, novelist (author of *Clotel, or The President's Daughter*, the first novel published by an American Negro), playwright and historian. In 1854, years after he had escaped from slavery, his English friends, worried for his safety under the Fugitive Slave Act of 1850, purchased Brown's freedom for $300. Besides being one of the most active abolitionist lecturers, Brown was deeply involved in the temperance, woman's suffrage, prison-reform, and the peace movements.

10   Elijah P. Lovejoy (1802-1837) was a prominent white abolitionist and newspaper editor. After he closed his shop in St. Louis, he moved to Alton, Illinois. There, he published the Alton *Observer*, which was attacked four times because of its anti-slavery stance. Lovejoy died defending his press in 1837.

11   Dr. Benjamin T. Tanner (b. 1835) was born free in Pittsburgh. He attended Avery College, and Western Theological Seminary. In 1863 he became a pastor in the District of Columbia, and organized schools for the Freedmen's Society. In 1868 Tanner was elected chief secretary and editor of the African Methodist Episcopal Church organ, the *Christian Recorder*. Wilberforce University honored him with a D.D. degree, and in 1884 Dr. Tanner was promoted to the editorship of the *A. M. E. Review*.

12   As a young man, Frederick Douglass was sent to Edward Covey, a "slave breaker" who specialized in cracking the spirit of slaves who were difficult to handle. Whipped daily for the slightest infraction of impossibly strict rules, Douglass finally decided to fight back, and in a hand-to-hand struggle, forced Covey to quit beating him. Thus, at the age of seventeen, Douglass discovered that he was not afraid to die, and that the only way to halt a tyrant was to fight back.

13   A sometime pastor, Charles T. Torrey (1813-1846) gave up the ministry for anti-slavery agitation. Torrey became a leader of conservative abolitionists in Massachusetts who revolted against William Lloyd Garrison because of his heretical views regarding the Sabbath, government, and woman's rights. This group founded the *Massachusetts Abolitionist*, of which Torrey became editor. Shortly thereafter, he resigned and went to Washington, D. C. to work as a correspondent. At the 1842 "Convention of Slaveholders," held in Annapolis, Maryland, Torrey was arrested when the delegates discovered that he was an abolitionist. The case attracted national attention, but Torrey was released within five days. Two years later, however, Torrey was arrested again. After moving to Baltimore, he began helping slaves escape, and once again he created a national furor. This time Torrey was sentenced to six years at hard labor, but after serving only one year, he died from tuberculosis. Torrey became another martyr to the anti-slavery cause.

14   The Emancipation Proclamation, issued by President Lincoln to become
effective in January 1863, freed slaves only where the Federal troops
were not in control to enforce the order, that is, those slaves living
in areas still in rebellion against the government of the United States.
It specifically ruled out of the terms of emancipation all slave areas
where Federal troops were present, in Louisiana, Virginia, and the border states. Slavery was legally ended by the Thirteenth Amendment to the
Constitution. In April 1864 and January 1865, the Senate and House respectively voted for the adoption of an amendment to the Constitution
providing that neither slavery nor involuntary servitude, except as punishment for crime for which the party had been convicted, should exist
within the United States or any place under its jurisdiction. The Amendment was then sent to the various states for ratification, which occurred in December 1865.

15   Samuel Ringgold Ward (1817-c.1864) was brought to New York at the
age of three by his parents, who escaped from slavery in Maryland. Ward
received an education, taught school, and became a preacher. A leading
anti-slavery agent, he became famous as an orator. After the fugitive
slave bill became law in 1850, Ward spoke out so vehemently against it
that he was forced to flee to Canada. He never returned to the United
States, but continued to lecture in Canada and England. He died in
Jamaica.

16   David B. Ruggles (1810-1849) was born free in Norwich, Connecticut,
but moved to New York when he was seventeen. For a time he operated a
grocery business in the city, but abandoned the store to become a travelling agent for the *Emancipation*, an organ of the New York City Anti-
Slavery Society. At age twenty-four Ruggles opened a bookstore for
anti-slavery publications, which was burned in 1835. Ruggles also
published a *Slaveholder's Directory*, which listed the names of those
who were friendly to the slave interests, and printed the first Negro
weekly magazine, *The Mirror of Liberty*. During his years of helping
fugitive slaves, Ruggles estimated that he assisted at least 1,000 runaways. For his efforts local police frequently jailed him, but he was
unswerving in his efforts to help the victims of slavery.

17   James H. Hammond (1807-1864) graduated from South Carolina College
in 1825, read law in Columbia, and was admitted to the bar in 1828.
Hammond built a very lucrative practice at Columbia, entered politics,
and in 1830 established the *Southern Times* to support the nullification
cause. After marrying into a wealthy family. he retired from politics
and became a highly successful cotton planter. For the next twenty-five
years Hammond supported the withdrawal of the Southern states from the
Union, advocated the death penalty for abolitionists, and absolutely
opposed emancipation. Hammond was elected to the governorship in 1842
and served two terms. Elected to the United States Senate in 1857, he
served in that body until his resignation upon Lincoln's election in
1860. Hammond owned thousands of acres, over 300 slaves, and became an
expert on "scientific" planting.

18   Christopher G. Memminger (1803-1888) was a prominent South Carolina
lawyer and public servant. After graduation from South Carolina College
in 1819, Memminger practiced law in Charleston. In 1836 he was elected
to the state house of representatives where he gained a reputation as a
sound financier. Although he was convinced of the righteousness of slavery, Memminger opposed independent action against the anti-slavery
forces as both dangerous and fruitless. When secession finally seemed
inevitable, Memminger stepped to the forefront, and at the southern convention in Montgomery, he was chairman of the committee which drafted
the provisional constitution of the Confederate States. President of

the Confederacy Jefferson Davis, appointed Memminger Secretary of the
Treasury. Because of his handling of Confederate financial policy,
Memminger was subjected to severe criticism, which forced his resigna-
tion on June 15, 1864. After the war he practiced law in Charleston.

19   William P. Powell was born in New York, the exact date unknown. For
a short time he lived in New Bedford, Mass., probably between whaling
voyages. In 1837 he called a meeting of black abolitionists to meet
in New Bedford and draw up a list of acceptable candidates for public
office according to their interest in liberty and equal rights. By
1840, however, Powell moved back to New York to stay. In that year he
was already operating a "Boarding House for Seamen under the Direction
of the American Seamen's Friend Society." The Society which supported
the Colored Seamen's Home was a protestant missionary organization ded-
icated to saving the souls of seamen through sobriety. Its monthly
journal, the *Sailor's Magazine,* enjoyed a wide circulation among seamen.
As victims of the most sordid kinds of exploitation, black seamen were
in dire need of such a home.
        Powell wrote articles condemning the discrimination encountered by
defenseless black seamen and petitioned Congress to put a stop to the
most vile forms, especially the widespread southern practice of imprisoning colored sailors at their own expense while in port. The Colored
Seamen's Home offered the seaman at least one safe refuge.
        Powell was a founder of the Manhattan Anti-Slavery Society in 1840,
and served as its secretary. He and the Society became well-known in
New York for their opposition to the Fugitive Slave Law of 1850.
        Powell moved to England in 1851 so that his children could receive
an education. During the ten years he spent in England, Powell spoke to
many anti-slavery audiences about the black condition in the U.S. and
attempted to mobilize pressure on the British government to take firmer
steps against the imprisonment of black seamen in Southern ports.
        Feeling that the Civil War would bring major changes in the U.S.
for his people, in 1861 Powell returned to New York, where he quickly
resumed his old activities, advocating an organization of black seamen
which would protect their rights. This organization, the American Seamen's Protective Union Association, the first seamen's organization of
any color or kind in the U.S., was founded in 1862 by Powell and several black seamen, at Powell's Colored Seamen's Home. See Part VII.

20   "The late intended Insurrection" is an obvious reference to the attempted revolt of Denmark Vesey, of Charleston, in 1822. See note 2.

21   The *Ram's Horn* began publication in New York City on January 1,
1847. For eighteen months the anti-slavery paper was published by two
black activists, Willis A. Hodges and Thomas Van Rensselaer. Following
a disagreement between them, Hodges retired and left the paper entirely
in the hands of Van Rensselaer. The paper appeared only once more, in
June 1848. Frederick Douglass was affiliated with the *Ram's Horn* for a
brief time prior to the founding of his own newspaper, *The North Star.*
In August 1847 the *Ram's Horn* announced that Frederick Douglass would
be a regular contributor, but the following November Douglass was cited
as the assistant editor to Van Rensselaer. The exact nature of his relationship to the paper is unknown, for it is possible that he merely
lent his name to bring prestige to the paper. For a time Douglass ten-
tatively planned to merge the *Ram's Horn* and *The North Star.* By November 5, 1847, however, he had abandoned whatever ideas he had in that
direction for on that date Douglass announced his decision to publish
The North Star.

22   Harriet Beecher Stowe's *Uncle Tom's Cabin, or Life Among the Lowly*
was first published as a serial (June 5, 1851-April 1, 1852) in the

National Era, an antislavery paper of Washington, D.C., and as a book
in two volumes on March 20, 1852. The book depicted the cruelties of
slavery and caused an outburst of denunciation in the slave states.

23   Theodore Tilton (1835-1907) was a famous editor and reformer during
the turbulent Civil War era. He attended the Free Academy (later the
College of the City of New York) from 1850 to 1853, and gained some
experience reporting for the *New York Tribune.* An ardent evangelical
Christian and abolitionist, he joined the *New York Observer,* a weekly
Presbyterian publication, but resigned within one year because of its
lukewarm stand on the abolition of slavery. Tilton then became editor
of the *Independent,* a Congregationalist journal, and transformed it
into a publication of broad appeal. His promising career was disrupted
prematurely, however, by the well-known Beecher scandal. In the summer
of 1870 his wife confessed to adultery with the prominent pastor of
their church, Henry Ward Beecher. At first Tilton tried to shield his
wife, but gossip forced the affair into public view. The case smoldered
for several years, and Tilton lost his job with the *Independent.* The
final blow, on July 20, 1874, he publicly charged Beecher with adultery,
before the Plymouth Church congregation. Public opinion refused to accept the charge, however, and a trial in 1875 resulted in a hung jury.

24   The "Harper's Ferry affair" and the "Helper pamphlet" further intensified feelings between North and South over the slavery issue. In
1859 the radical abolitionist, John Brown, made his now-famous quixotic
raid on the arsenal located there. Hinton Rowan Helper, born into an
impoverished white family of North Carolina, spoke for poor southern
whites in his *The Impending Crisis,* published in 1857. Although Helper
despised blacks, his writing constituted a virulent attack on slavery,
which he believed brought economic ruin to the small free farmers. To
circulate his book in the South was a crime.

25   Martin Robinson Delany (1812-1885) was born in Charles Town, Virginia (now in West Virginia), the grandson of slaves and the sone of free
Negroes. His father's father was supposed to have been an African
chieftain of the Golah tribe, captured with his family in battle, sold
as a slave and brought to America. His mother's father was said to
have been an African prince of the Mandingo line in the Niger Valley,
who was captured in war, enslaved, sold and transported to America.
     Delany received his first instruction in reading from peddlers of
books, continued his studies under the Reverend Louis Woodson, in Pittsburgh, and went on to study medicine at Harvard, became a doctor, was
one of seventy-five black officers in the Union Army, wrote a novel,
ran for the office of lieutenant governor of South Carolina, and named
his daughter Ethiopia. His little book *The Condition, Elevation, Emigration, and Destiny of the Colored People of the United States, Politically Considered,* published in Philadelphia in 1852 at his own expense,
is a remarkable source of information about the free black population of
the antebellum North, and contains important suggestions for improvement
of their conditions. One sentence in the Appendix of his book is the
most quoted in the work: "We are a nation within a nation, as the Poles
in Russia, the Hungarians in Austria, the Welsh, Irish and Scotch in the
British dominions." The acknowledged "Father of Black Nationalism,"
Delany advocated founding a new Negro nation on the eastern coast of
Africa "for the settlement of colored adventurers from the United States
and elsewhere." In 1859 Delany travelled in Africa for about a year
seeking places to which black Americans might emigrate. He signed
treaties with eight kings of Abeokuta for grants of land to establish
American Negro colonies in the Yoruba area. From Africa, Delany went
on to London, and after stirring up an international incident at the
International Statistical Congress in London with his assertion that "I
am a Man"--a remark which caused all but one member of the American

delegation to walk out of the Congress in protest--he continued to lecture on Africa in England and Scotland for almost seven months. He returned to the United States in 1861, six weeks after the Civil War had
broken out.

In February 1865 Martin R. Delany was commissioned a major in infantry and ordered to recruit an "armee d'Afrique" in South Carolina.
But the end of the war cut short the project. Delany, however, continued to work in the South, served for three years in the Freedmen's
Bureau, and became active in South Carolina politics. In 1874 the
state Republican Party split over the issue of reform, and Delany became the nominee for lieutenant governor for the reform faction, shar-
ing the ticket with the gubernatorial candidate, Judge John T. Green.
The attempt was lost, and Delany also made several blunders which ensured his ultimate failure in South Carolina politics. The worst was
his support of Wade Hampton who won the 1876 gubernatorial race, and
opened the door for a return to white supremacy in South Carolina.

26   See notes 6 and 7.

27   The Millerites were followers of William Miller (1782-1849), a farmer from New York who declared that the world would end in 1843 with the
second coming of Christ. When the appointed time passed without incident, a new date was set for 1844. When that date also passed quietly, the Millerites finally set the date for Christ's coming sometime
in the indefinite future. During a period of intense evangelical fer-
vor, camp-meetings, and revivals, the message of William Miller caused
a considerable stir among some elements of society and he was roundly
denounced by traditional religious leaders.

28   Benjamin Banneker (1731-1806) was born in Ellicot, Maryland, to a
free mother and a slave father. As a youth he attended an integrated
school, and later became a highly regarded astronomer, inventor, and
mathematician. In 1861 Banneker constructed the first wooden clock
made in America, and in 1789 he predicted the solar eclipse. In 1791
he began the publication of a series of almanacs which won him considerable acclaim in Europe as well as America. When Thomas Jefferson
questioned that a black man could possess such intelligence, Banneker
composed a reply which has become a classic denial of intellectual inferiority based on race.

29   William Whipper (1805-1895) was a leading figure in the national and
state conventions of colored people during the 1830s. He was a founder,
in 1835, of the short-lived American Moral Reform Society, which emerged
from the convention movement, and edited the *National Reformer,* the
Society's organ. In Columbia, Pennsylvania, where he was engaged in
the lumber business, Whipper was a conductor on the Underground Railroad.

30   David Walker was born in North Carolina in 1785, to a free Negro
mother and a slave father. Little is known about his early life except that he was apparently well-travelled and achieved some degree of
education. Unable to endure life in the South, Walker moved to Boston
sometime during the 1820s. By 1827 he operated a shop near the wharves
which sold reconditioned clothing. Walker also became the Boston agent
for *Freedom's Journal,* an anti-slavery paper published in New York and
the first black newspaper in America. He also delivered numerous lectures against slavery throughout the city. In an effort to reach the
slaves, in 1829 he published *An Appeal to the Coloured Citizens of the
World,* in which he called upon the slaves to revolt. Walker hoped to
smuggle his pamphlets into southern ports by sewing them in the linings

of the clothing he sold to sailors bound for southern ports. The
South went to extraordinary lengths to suppress the document, and rumors circulated that a $1,000 reward had been placed on Walker's life
by irate southerners. One morning in 1830, Walker was murdered.

31   The New York African Free School was established in New York City in
1787 by the Society for Promoting the Manumission of Slaves and Protecting such of them as have been or may be Liberated. The initial en-
rollment of forty-seven increased dramatically, and between 1787 and
1815 the average number of black students in attendance was eighty-
seven. Most of these students received their education free of charge.
A number of future black leaders attended the African Free School.

32   The New York black who applied for a carman's license was Henry
Graves whose case is presented in Part III. The effort of the Ohio
Legislature "to consign the negroes to starvation" is a reference to the
hated Black Laws passed in Ohio which were highly discriminatory against
Negroes. See item 6., Part IV.

33   Lane Theological Seminary of Cincinnati provided the scene for one
of the most dramatic events in the war against slavery in the West.
Under its first president, Lyman Beecher (from 1832-1850), numerous
young abolitionists enrolled for study at Lane. One of the more energetic of these students was Theodore Dwight Weld, who had been converted
by Charles Finney, and became an ardent reformer like his teacher. Weld
and about forty of Finney's other converts were highly active in Cincinnati's black community. But their ideas about social equality, and
their activities on behalf of blacks, created problems with the towns-
people and the Lane administration. Fearing a loss of public support
for the institution, Beecher banned the lectures and lyceums for Negroes
which the students had been conducting. Most of the Lane student body
then withdrew, and with funds provided by the Tappan brothers of New
York, established a new theological school in connection with Oberlin
College, near Cleveland, Ohio.

34   Moyamensing was a district in Philadelphia where many blacks lived
and worked. It was the scene of numerous race riots during the three
decades prior to the Civil War. "Hunkerism" refers to the "hunkers," a
conservative faction of the Democratic Party in New York during the
1840s. The name stems from their desire to retain the entire "hunk" of
patronage and traditional policy, especially regarding slavery.

35   William Lloyd Garrison (1805-1879) was the most vehement of the white
abolitionists in New England. From 1829 to 1830 he and Benjamin Lundy,
another prominent Baltimore abolitionist, co-edited the *Genius of Universal Emancipation,* until the anti-slavery paper was forced to close.
Following a prison sentence for libel, Garrison returned to his native
city of Boston. In 1831 he was among those who organized the New England Anti-Slavery Society. Garrison drafted part of the constitution,
and in 1832 became Corresponding Secretary of the new organization. The
following year he and fifty other abolitionists met in Philadelphia and,
on December 4, 1833, formed the American Anti-Slavery Society. For
many years (1831-1865) Garrison edited *The Liberator,* one of the most
outspoken of the anti-slavery papers. Although he favored the "moral
suasion" approach, and rejected violence as a tactic, Garrison's out-
spokenness, and sometimes eccentric behavior, earned him notoriety in
some quarters. Southerners threatened him with bodily harm, and the
Georgia legislature went so far as to place a $5,000 reward upon his
head.

36   Robert Purvis was born on November 4, 1810, in Charleston, South
        Carolina, the son of William Purvis, an English merchant, and a Jewish-
        Moorish mother, Harriet Judah. In 1819 William Purvis sent the entire
        family to Philadelphia, where his three sons could be educated. He
        died in 1825 leaving an inheritance of $125,000. Robert Purvis was ed-
        ucated in private schools in Philadelphia spent some time at Pitts-
        field Academy and finished his education at Amherst College. He
        left college to devote himself to the antislavery movement and at the
        age of seventeen made his first public speech against slavery. Purvis,
        a wealthy Negro who lived in a fine home in a suburb of Philadelphia,
        was one of a group of black Americans who gave Garrison money to help
        him launch *The Liberator* in 1831. Two years later Purvis became a
        charter member of the American Anti-Slavery Society. He was also a
        founder of the Pennsylvania Anti-Slavery Society, "president" of the
        Pennsylvania Underground Railroad, and a vigorous fighter against dis-
        crimination against Negroes until his death in 1898.

37   Fanneuil Hall, a public meeting place in Boston, was founded in 1742
        as a gift from the wealthy merchant, Peter Fanneuil. During the
        colonial period it became the traditional site for public protests
        against unpopular British measures, and during the Ante-Bellum Era it
        was a favorite place for anti-slavery meetings.

38   There were several such societies in both northern and southern
        cities. For an example of a southern association see Doc. 35, Part II.

39   "Considerable excitement" was an understatement for the reactions
        produced by kidnappings of blacks in Harrisburg. At least two riots
        were ignited by such incidents, one in 1825 and another in 1850. See
        Mary D. Houts, "Black Harrisburg's Resistance to Slavery," *Pennsylvania
        Heritage* 4 (December, 1977):9-13.

40   Emeric De Vattel (1714-1767), a Swiss-born jurist who published ex-
        tensively, is known primarily for his legal studies, especially *Droit
        des gens* (1758). He became privy councillor in the cabinet of Dresden,
        but his health broke under a heavy workload, and he died in 1767. His
        fame during the period cited in the text rested on his making the legal
        ideas of Woelff accessible to political and diplomatic circles.

41   Zachary Taylor, twelfth President of the United States (1849-1850),
        had become a national hero during the Mexican War (1846-1848) and was
        the victorious Whig candidate for the presidency in 1848. After only
        six months in office, Taylor died from acute gastroenteritis. The most
        distinguished member of his cabinet was Secretary of State John M.
        Clayton, previously a Senator from Delaware. When pressured to act
        against South Carolina for imprisoning a free black seaman who was a
        British subject, Clayton's only response was that he had no power to
        force states to comply with the treaties which prohibited such actions.
        Lord Palmerston was the British Prime Minister at the time of the in-
        cident.

42   Matthew Galbraith Perry (USN) was entrusted with the mission of open-
        ing trade with Japan. In 1853 he anchored his fleet near Tokyo, and so
        impressed the Japanese with its power that a commercial treaty was
        signed between the U.S. and Japan in 1854. The suggestion is that if a
        powerful squadron were sent to Charleston, the problems black seamen
        encountered there would cease.

43   James McCune Smith (1813-1865), a leading black physician, writer, and abolitionist, was born in New York City, the "son of a slave, owing his liberty to the Emancipation Act of the State of New York and of a self-emancipated bondswoman." He was educated in the African Free School and entered the University of Glasgow in 1832, receiving the degrees of B.A. in 1835, M.A. in 1836, and M.D. in 1837. Following a short period in the clinics of Paris, he returned to New York City and for twenty-five years was a noted doctor and surgeon. But his fame rested largely on his activities in the struggle of the black community of New York for equality and on his battle against slavery. Smith was a frequent lecturer and spoke often in support of the physical and moral equality of the black race. His most famous lecture was his discourse in 1859 on Thomas Jefferson's widely quoted claim that "the blacks, whether originally a distinct race, or made distinct by time and circumstances, are inferior to the whites in the endowments of both body and mind."

44   Alexander Crummell (1819-1898), a graduate of Oxford University, England, was a leading clergyman in the North before the Civil War. Between 1853 and 1873 he was active in Africa as an agent of the American Colonization Society. After his return from Africa, he continued to play a prominent role in the United States as a clergyman, political leader, and lecturer. Here are portions of an address Crummell delivered before the Freedman's Aid Society, Methodist Episcopal Church, Ocean Grove, New Jersey, August 15, 1883.

45   On December 28, 1816, the American Society for Colonizing the Free People of Colour of the United States (popularly known as the American Colonization Society) was organized. The Society, supported by influential groups, aimed to colonize free Negroes in Africa and thus rid the United States of a "troublesome presence." Although some leading free Negroes supported colonization, believing that black people could never achieve freedom and dignity in the United States, most free Negroes opposed the scheme from its inception. They were convinced that the promoters of the Society wished to get rid of the free Negro in order to make slavery secure, and they were repelled by the racist arguments directed by the Society against free Negroes as an inferior, degraded class who should be removed from the United States. They charged, furthermore, that the Society, by encouraging anti-Negro prejudice, was responsible for the deprivation of rights already enjoyed by free Negroes.

46   Charles L. Reason (1818-1898) was born in New York and attended the African Free School. In 1844 he became professor of belles lettres at New York Central College in McGrawville, New York. He resigned in 1852 and became director of the Institute for Colored Youths in Philadelphia. George B. Vashon, a graduate of Oberlin College, lawyer and poet, also held a professorship of belles lettres at New York Central College. Charles H. Langston (1817-1892), brother of the more famous John Mercer Langston (see note 61), was a vocal black leader in Ohio. He was particularly active in resisting the Fugitive Slave Law passed in 1850.

47   James W. C. Pennington (1809-1870) was born in slavery on the Eastern Shore of Maryland, and was trained as a blacksmith, a trade he followed until he was about twenty-one, when he decided to run away. Befriended by a Pennsylvania Quaker, he stayed with him for six months and began what was to be an extensive education under his direction. After attending evening school in Long Island, he taught in colored schools and, at the same time, studied theology. Pennington became a pastor in the African Congregational Church, held pastorates in Hartfort, Connecticut, and represented that state at the World's Anti-

Slavery Convention in London in 1843. He was also a delegate to the
World's Peace Society meeting in London that same year. He bought his
freedom in 1851 for $150. Pennington was the author of *A Text Book of
the Origin and History, &c., &c., of the Colored People,* published in
1841, and *The Fugitive Blacksmith,* the story of his early life, published in London in 1849. In 1855, together with Dr. James McCune
Smith and the Reverend Henry Highland Garnet, the Reverend Pennington
organized the Legal Rights Association for the purpose of establishing
the rights of Negroes to use public conveyances in the city. The Association fought the cases for Negroes kept off the streetcars.

48   George T. Downing (1819-1903) of New York attended Mulberry Street
School, and while there formed friendships with a number of adolescents
who eventually became race leaders, such as Alexander Crummell, James
McCune Smith, and Henry Highland Garnet. Still in his teens, Downing
was arrested for smuggling a fugitive slave out of jail, and later he
became an active anti-slavery advocate. During the Civil War he organized several black regiments. While in Washington looking after the
interests of black soldiers, he accepted an offer to run the House of
Representatives restaurant. Several years later, he moved to Rhode
Island, opposed separate schools for the races, and was instrumental in
eliminating the dual educational system. He was a close friend of
Charles Sumner, the civil rights senator from Massachusetts.

49   Charles Lenox Remond (1810-1873) was an active Abolitionist and
served for many years as an agent of the American Anti-Slavery Society.
Remond was the first black Abolitionist speaker to address large audiences. In 1840 he attended the World Anti-Slavery Convention in London.
After spending two years lecturing in Great Britain and Ireland, he returned to the United States in 1842 and became involved in the campaign
to end segregation on the railroads of Massachusetts. Segregation was
finally abolished in April 1843.

50   William Cooper Nell (1816-1874) was an untiring black abolitionist
from Boston. Connected with Garrison's *Liberator* for many years, Nell
won fame as an orator and also as one of the first black historians in
the United States. He began collecting Negro historical data and produced in 1852 the study, *Services of Colored Americans in the Wars of
1776 and 1812,* followed four years later by the *Colored Patriots of
the American Revolution.* But it was his leadership in the desegrega-
tion campaign in Boston's schools which won Nell his greatest fame.
Under his direction, Negroes in Boston deluged the Massachusetts legislature with petitions demanding the abolition of separate schools and
had them taught privately until in 1855 a law was enacted requiring public schools in the state to admit students without regard to color.

51   Schoolteacher, dentist, physician, lawyer, graduate of the American
Medical College in Philadelphia, member of the Massachusetts Bar, proficient in Greek and Latin, Dr. John S. Rock was one of the leaders of
the movement for equal rights for black Americans in the North. Dr.
Rock used the lecture platform effectively to challenge the racist concept that Negroes were inferior to whites.
        John S. Rock was born in Salem, New Jersey, in 1825. He was a teach-
er in the public schools during 1844-48, and in the following year he
finished studying dentistry under Dr. Harbert Hubbard. In 1850 he began
practicing dentistry in Philadelphia, and in 1851 he received a silver
medal for the creation of artificial teeth and another silver medal for
a prize essay on temperance. In 1852 he graduated from the American
Medical College in Philadelphia, and the following year began the practice of medicine and dentistry in Boston. He was admitted to practice
law in Massachusetts in 1861 and on September 21 of that year received

a commission from the governor as justice of peace for seven years for the city of Boston and the County of Suffolk.

In February, 1865, presented by Charles Sumner as a candidate to argue cases before the Supreme Court, Rock was sworn in by Chief Justice Salmon P. Chase as the first Negro to be accredited as a Supreme Court lawyer. He died in Boston on December 3, 1866.

"August Celebration" refers to the West Indiana Emancipation celebration.

52   The cry "America for Americans" was raised during the 1850s by nativists of the Know-Nothing Party, which opposed the further admission of foreign immigrants. The *Pilot* was a newspaper which voiced the concerns of Irish immigrants, and therefore opposed nativism. The paper did not, however, extend a liberal view toward blacks.

53   Jefferson Davis (1808-1889), graduated from West Point in 1828. Resigning his commission after the Black Hawk War, he settled on his Mississippi plantation, "Brierfield," and became a successful planter. In 1845, Davis was elected as a Democrat to Congress, but he resigned when the Mexican War began in 1846, and accepted command of the "Mississippi Rifles." Because his unit played a crucial role in the victory at Monterey, General Taylor appointed Davis to the peace commission to negotiate the surrender. In 1847 he once again resigned from the Army and Mississippi elected him to the United States Senate. In 1853, he became secretary of war in the cabinet of Franklin Pierce, where he served until 1857, when Davis reentered the Senate. Davis resigned in 1861 when Mississippi seceded from the Union. In 1862 he was inaugurated president of the Confederate States of America, and attempted the impossible task of leading the South to separate nationhood. When the Confederacy fell in 1865, he was captured in Georgia and imprisoned in Fortress Monroe for two years. The ex-president was never brought to trial, but neither did he ask for a federal pardon. This barred him from further public office and the last two decades of his life were spent in relative poverty.

54   Henry Highland Garnet (1815-1881) was born a slave in Maryland, the son of an African chief who had been kidnapped and sold into slavery. He escaped with his parents in 1824 and settled in New York City. Garnet was educated in the African Free School No. 1 and at Oneida Institute. A brief stay at the Canaan Academy in Canaan, New Hampshire, in 1835 was interrupted when the academy was destroyed by an infuriated mob opposed to the education of negroes. Garnet prepared for the ministry, and in 1842 was licensed to preach. He became pastor of the Liberty Street Presbyterian Church in Troy, New York, and later of the Shiloh Presbyterian Church in New York City, a pastorate he held for more than forty years, during which time he became the foremost Negro clergyman in the city.

In August 1843 Garnet attended the National Convention of Negro Citizens at Buffalo, New York, and delivered a militant speech calling for slave rebellions as the surest way to end slavery. It was the most radical speech by a black American during the antebellum period. The proposal stirred the delegates and failed by one vote of being adopted. After he had read the speech, John Brown, the martyr of Harper's Ferry, had it published at his own expense.

Garnet travelled widely, and prior to the Civil War favored the emigration of blacks to Africa. During the 1850s he was president of the African Civilization Society, an organization which encouraged that policy. Following the war, he served as Recorder of Deeds in Washington, D.C., and in 1881 he was appointed Minister to Liberia. Garnet died only a few months after his arrival in Monrovia.

55   Born in Delaware in 1815, Rev. J. P. Campbell served as an African
Methodist Episcopal clergyman in Pennsylvania. In 1856 he became editor of the A.M.E. newspaper, *The Christian Recorder,* one of the most
widely circulated black newspapers of that century. Campbell became a
bishop in 1864, and in 1876 Wilberforce University conferred the D.D.
degree upon him.

56   Carl Schurz (1829-1906) was born in Germany. An exceptional student,
he became a doctoral candidate in history in 1847 at the University of
Bonn. The 1848 revolution intervened, however, and Schurz, an active
student leader and follower of Professor Gottfried Kinkel of Bonn, an
exponent of democratic institutions, became an army officer with the
revolutionary forces. When the abortive revolution failed, Schurz freed
his mentor from prison in a daring escape, and the two made their way to
England. In 1852 Schurz sailed for the United States where he quickly
mastered the English language and entered Republican politics in Wiscon-
sin, where he settled in 1855. Soon a successful lawyer, during the
1860 presidential campaign Schurz exercised his considerable oratorical
powers on behalf of Lincoln. Once in office, President Lincoln appointed Schurz minister to Spain. Schurz resigned in 1862, however, to become a brigadier-general in the Union Army. Schurz resigned after Lee's
surrender. From July through September 1865, he travelled throughout
the South as an agent of President Johnson to report on the conditions
he found there. The report Schurz submitted is still of considerable
historical value. Then Schurz entered a journalistic career, serving
as editor or correspondent for several major newspapers, including
Horace Greeley's *New York Tribune.* Schurz moved to St. Louis, Missouri,
in 1867, and a year later was elected to the United States Senate at the
age of forty. In the Senate, he became noted for his anti-Grant, anti-
corruption position, and was prominent in the Liberal Republican wing of
the party. In 1877 Schurz became Secretary of the Interior in Ruther-
ford B. Hayes' cabinet.

57   Whitelaw Reid (1837-1912) was born near Xenia, Ohio. After graduation from Miami University (Oxford, Ohio) in 1856, he began a career as
a journalist. He first served as a legislative correspondent in Columbus for the Cincinnati *Times* and other Ohio papers, until he became city
editor for the Cincinnati *Gazette.* Almost immediately, however, he became a war correspondent, and achieved wide recognition and acclaim for
his reporting from the front. Immediately following the war, Reid travelled throughout the South. In 1866, his observations were published
under the title *After the War,* which is still of historical interest.
In 1868, he joined the *New York Tribune,* became its managing editor,
and turned the paper into an effective organ for Horace Greeley's presidential bid in 1872. Greeley, who edited the *Tribune,* lost the race
and shortly thereafter died. Reid then took charge of the nation's most
powerful newspaper at age thirty-five. An ardent Republican, Reid was
appointed ambassador to France by Benjamin Harrison in 1888. In 1892
Reid shared the ticket with Harrison as the vice-presidential candidate,
but lost the election. Reid strongly favored America's imperialist ventures in the Caribbean and the Pacific, and McKinley appointed him a member of the American commission to negotiate peace with Spain in 1898.
In 1905, Theodore Roosevelt appointed Reid ambassador to Great Britain
where he died.

58   The "eight-hour system" refers to the number of hours in a single work
day proposed by those who favored a reduction from the traditional twelve
hours. For an explanation of the eight-hour movement and its rationale,
see note 69.

59   The *Workingman's Advocate* was the official organ of the National Labor
Union, published simultaneously in Philadelphia by John H. Sylvis, and

in Chicago by Andrew C. Cameron.

60   Henry Clay Warmoth, a carpetbagger governor of Louisiana, rode into
office in 1868 with the black vote. Hence the appellation "negro worshipper." His lt. governor was P. B. S. Pinchback, a mulatto Republican
who engineered the impeachment of Warmoth for corruption. J. C. Taliaferro, a scalawag associate justice of the Louisiana Supreme Court, swore
in Pinchback as governor in place of Warmoth. Taliaferro was also a leader of the Independent Radical faction which was trounced in the general
election of 1868, and won by the Warmoth machine.

61   John Mercer Langston (1829-1897) was born in Virginia to a slave mother and a white plantation master. Langston's father sent him to Cincinnati, Ohio, to be educated. Later he graduated from Oberlin College
in 1849. In addition to a degree in theology, which he earned in 1853,
Langston studied law and became a member of the Ohio Bar in 1854. After
the war, he was elected president of the National Equal Rights League,
and was appointed as inspector-general of the Freedmen's Bureau. From
1869 to 1876, he served as dean and vice-president of Howard University.
Langston was appointed United States Minister to Haiti in 1877, and remained in the diplomatic service until 1885 when he became president of
the Virginia Normal and Collegiate Institute. In 1888 he was elected to
Congress from Virginia and served one term.

62   Horatio Seymour, a former governor of New York, became the Democratic
nominee for President at the 1868 convention. His running-mate was Francis P. Blair, Jr., son of the famous founder of the Washington *Globe*.
Like his father, Blair split from the Democrats to support Lincoln, but
could not support Radical Reconstruction, and returned to the Democratic
fold after the war.

63   A monumental figure in the American labor movement, William H. Sylvis
(1828-1869) was born in poverty, but had learned the trade of iron mould-
ing by 1852 when he finally settled in Philadelphia. Sylvis became an
officer in the local moulders union, and at his behest, the first Iron
Moulders International Union convention met in Philadelphia in 1859.
Active in the organization, Sylvis was elected treasurer of the national
union in 1860, and three years later the membership elected him president.
A staunch advocate of labor solidarity, Sylvis was instrumental in founding the National Labor Union, the first trades union federation in Amer-
ica, and became its president in 1868. That same year, he and Richard
Trevellick, another leader in the NLU, launched an organizational drive
in the South.
        Favoring a Labor Reform Party, Greenbackism, and the eight-hour day,
Sylvis also urged affiliation with the First International. In addition
to his union activities, he edited the *Iron-Moulders International Journal*.
Probably in 1869, Sylvis also became joint proprietor of the *Workingman's
Advocate*, the official organ of the NLU. Although Sylvis was a progressive for his time, and favored black and white unity in the labor struggle, he nevertheless believed that blacks were social inferiors to whites.
This underlying racism, and his strong ties to the Democratic Party, influenced Sylvis to sneer at Radical Republican governments in the South
and to express his repugnance to the social intermingling he found there.
        His letters and speeches were published posthumously by his brother,
James G. Sylvis.

64   William Craft and his wife Ellen escaped from slavery in Georgia.
Because she was light-complexioned, Ellen disguised herself as a wealthy
white woman travelling with her "servant" William. They became staunch
abolitionists, and after the Civil War returned to Georgia and established an industrial school for black youths near Savannah.

65   An 1842 graduate of the Military Academy, for the next twenty years
John Pope (1822-1892) served in various engineering posts throughout the
West. In 1862 he took command of the Army of the Mississippi, under
General Halleck's command, and won distinction in several campaigns. By
June 1862, Pope was given command of the Army of Virginia which was expected to protect Washington, D. C. He proved inadequate to the task,
and was decisively defeated at the Second Battle of Manassas (August 27-
30, 1862). Subsequently Pope was relieved of command, never to be employed in field operations again. He was then sent to the West where he
remained until his retirement at the rank of Major-General.

66   The *Christian Recorder*, official organ of the African Methodist Episcopal Church, took a consistently liberal view on Chinese exclusion.

67   A radical abolitionist and universal reformer, Wendell Phillips' fame
resulted primarily from his exceptional powers as an orator. People
flocked to hear him speak even though they generally disagreed with his
notions of racial brotherhood. After the Civil War, Phillips continued
to advocate unpopular causes, especially on behalf of workingmen.

68   The *Detroit Union* was a vehemently anti-Negro newspaper.

69   Ira Steward (1831-1883) was the father of the eight-hour work day.
In 1863 Steward served as a delegate to the convention of the International Union of Machinists and Blacksmiths in Boston, where he fought for
the passage of a resolution which for the first time demanded that the
eight-hour day be required by law. As president of the National Eight-
Hour League, Steward labored indefatigably for that measure through the
existing political parties. Following the Civil War, various eight-hour
laws were passed by state legislatures, but the multiple restrictions
written into the laws rendered many of them dead letters. Steward opposed Greenbackism as well as a separate labor party. He did, however, believe in the solidarity of labor and the inevitable evolution of a social-
ist state. Thus, in 1878 he and several American Marxists formed the
International Labor Union, the first significant attempt in America to
organize the unskilled workers.
        The eight-hour system advanced by Steward was novel for the time. He
believed that the shorter hours would provide increased leisure-time desires, and consequently, a demand for higher wages. This upward pressure
on wages would then stimulate the introduction of labor-saving machinery,
which in turn facilitated mass production, and hence an increase in the
purchasing power of the masses. In order to insulate mass purchasing
power from the depressing effects of unemployment, the work day must be
reduced to eight hours. Steward believed that ultimately the working
class would accumulate enough capital to control the economy, and thereby
usher in socialism. Steward's considerable influence declined precipi-
tously when organized labor opted to ignore politics to agitate economic
issues alone.

70   Nathaniel P. Rogers, an abolitionist and poet from New Hampshire, was
a close associate of William Lloyd Garrison. Rogers edited the pioneer
anti-slavery newspaper, the *Herald of Freedom*, founded in 1838 in Concord, New Hampshire. Rogers also wrote for the New York *Tribune* under
the pseudonym "Old Man of the Mountain." Although an abolitionist,
Rogers' views on race were something less than egalitarian.

71   As a youth, John Morrissey (1831-1878) worked at an iron foundry, and
various other laboring jobs in Troy, New York, before moving to New York
City. There his penchant for brawling led him into a career of prize-

fighting. In 1853 he defeated Yankee Sullivan, which gave Morrissey
some claim to the heavyweight championship. He rose rapidly as a gambler, saloon-keeper, labor leader among the Irish, and politician in the
city. A confidant of Commodore Vanderbilt, Morrissey won and lost several fortunes on Wall Street. Mostly to annoy his more sedate neighbors,
he ran for Congress in 1866, and to the surprise and consternation of
many New Yorkers, he won. Morrissey served two terms in Congress (1867-
1871) before he moved to Saratoga. In 1875 and 1877 Morrissey was elected to two terms in the state senate. Although sober citizens were appall-
ed by his antics, Morrissey enjoyed great popularity among the working
classes. When he died in 1878, 15,000 friends followed his coffin to
the cemetery.

72   Mr. Kuykendall and Mr. Schlaeger were white delegates.

73   Elizabeth Cady Stanton (1815-1902) pioneered the woman's rights movement in America. Born in Johnstown, New York, she attended the famous
seminary of Emma Willard at Troy, New York, and graduated in 1832. For
a time Stanton studied law with her father. She became a leading exponent of the woman-suffrage cause, and with Lucretia Mott, officially
launched the movement at Seneca Falls, New York, in 1848. This was the
first woman's right convention in United States history. She later assisted Susan B. Anthony in editing the militant feminist magazine, *Revolution* (1868-1870). An able orator and writer, she devoted her life to
liberal causes, and was one of the authors of the multi-volume *History
of Woman Suffrage*.

74   Ulysses S. Grant was the successful Republican candidate for the
presidency in 1868, and Horatio Seymour the losing Democratic candidate.

75   At the third national convention of the National Labor Union, held in
Philadelphia, August 1869, nine of the 142 delegates were Negroes. One
of these delegates was Isaac Myers, representing the Colored Caulkers'
Trades Union Society of Baltimore and the first important black labor
leader in the United States. During the convention, Myers was commissioned by the black delegates to voice their thanks for the "unanimous
recognition" of the Negro worker's right to representation in the gathering. The speech was delivered on August 18, 1869, is an historic appeal
for unity of black and white workers, and probably the first published
labor speech of a black union leader. The reporter of the New York
Times wrote that "the whole Convention listened . . . with the most
profound attention . . . and at its close delegates advanced and warmly
congratulated him."

76   "Andrew Johnson's reaction" referred to President Johnson's conservative, and racist, resistance to Radical Republican attempts to insur-
ing political equality for ex-slaves.